CliffsNotes®

CSET® Multiple Subjects with CD-ROM

3RD EDITION

by
Jerry Bobrow, Ph.D., and Stephen Fisher, M.A.

Contributing Authors

Joy Mondragon-Gilmore, M.S.

Andrea Markowitz, Ph.D.

Harold D. Nathan, Ph.D.

Jeri Jones, M.A.

Ed Kohn, M.S.

Johanna Hays, M.A.

Bob DiPietro, M.A.

Jan Christinson, M.A.

Barbara Swovelin, M.A.

George Crowder, M.A.

Michele Spence, B.A.

Pitt Gilmore, B.A.

Houghton Mifflin Harcourt
Boston New York

About the Authors

Stephen Fisher, M.A. is the author of numerous test preparation books, including CliffsNotes NTE, MSAT and CSET preparation guides. Mr. Fisher is a recognized authority in the field of test preparation and has developed materials and taught CSET preparation classes at colleges and universities throughout California. Mr. Fisher was an award winning teacher and administrator in the Beverly Hills Unified School District and retired as principal of El Rodeo School, a California Distinguished School.

Jerry Bobrow, Ph.D., was the founder of Bobrow Test Preparation Services, administering test preparation programs at over 25 California institutions for over 30 years. Dr. Bobrow authored over 30 national best-selling test preparation books, and his books and programs have assisted over two million test-takers. Each year BTPS offers lectures to thousands of students preparing for graduate, college, and teacher credentialing exams.

Authors' Acknowledgments

Bobrow Test Preparation Services would like to thank Suzanne Snyder, Ph.D., project editor, and Christina Stambaugh, editorial manager, for John Wiley & Sons, Inc., for their careful review of the manuscript; Linnea Fredrickson and Melinda Masson, our editors; Cindy Hadash and Ann Rothstein for their assistance; and Maya Hadash for her graphic contributions.

Editorial

Acquisition Editor: Greg Tubach

Project Editors: Suzanne Snyder and Christina Stambaugh

Copy Editors: Marylouise Wiack and Emily Hinkel

Technical Editors: Scott McDougall, Jane Burstein, Carol Klages, Tom Page

Composition

Proofreader: Shannon Ramsey

John Wiley & Sons, Inc., Composition Services

CliffsNotes® CSET® Multiple Subjects with CD-ROM, 3rd Edition

Copyright © 2012 Houghton Mifflin Harcourt

Library of Congress Control Number: 2011945011
ISBN: 978-1-118-17653-5 (pbk)
ISBN: 978-1-118-21543-2; 978-1-118-21018-5; 978-1-118-21007-9 (ebk)

Printed in the United States of America

DOO 10 9 8 7 6 5   4500480608

For information about permission to reproduce selections from this book, write to Permissions, Houghton Mifflin Harcourt Publishing Company, 215 Park Avenue South New York, New York 10003.

www.hmhco.com

CliffsNotes®

CSET® Multiple Subjects
with CD-ROM

Dedication

This book is dedicated to the memory of Dr. Jerry Bobrow, award-winning author and educator who assisted thousands of prospective teachers to reach their career goals. Dr. Bobrow died prior to the publication of this book after a two-year battle with cancer. His lifelong commitment to helping others seek advancement through higher education continues with CliffsNotes® CSET: Multiple Subjects with CD-ROM, 3rd Edition. Dr. Bobrow recognized that all people have unique abilities and believed that one's highest potential is achieved through learning. Born in Rome, Italy, he is survived by his wife of 33 years, Susan, his children, Jennifer, Adam, and Jonathan, and his parents, Abram and Julia Bobrow, both Holocaust survivors.

Table of Contents

Chapter 6: Subtest III: Human Development 334

Chapter 7: Subtest III: Visual and Performing Arts 366

PART II: TWO FULL-LENGTH PRACTICE TESTS

PART III: APPENDICES

Preface

Congratulations on your decision to become a teacher. The CSET: Multiple Subjects examination evaluates your knowledge and application of seven primary subjects that are reflected in classroom instruction and the Multiple Subjects Teaching Credential. The test includes Reading, Language, and Literature; History and Social Science; Mathematics and Science; and Physical Education, Human Development, and Visual and Performing Arts.

CliffsNotes CSET Multiple Subjects with CD-ROM will help you to achieve your instructional goals and improve your competence in subject-matter areas. Thousands of potential elementary school teachers have found that this comprehensive study guide presents the necessary skills and content to be successful on the CSET. This book is not meant to be a substitute for formal college courses, but can help you analyze your strengths and provide you with instructional strategies to overcome your weaknesses. The proven test-taking strategies are designed to complement your understanding of the exam areas, test format, and question types.

In keeping with the fine tradition of CliffsNotes, this guide was developed by leading educators in the field of test preparation to give you the best preparation possible. For over 30 years, the authors of this study guide have been successfully assisting thousands of potential teachers to prepare for the CSET. The strategies, techniques, and materials presented in this guide have been researched, tested, and evaluated in CSET preparation classes offered at many leading California universities, county offices of education, and school districts. BTPS Testing is a leader in the field of teacher credential exam preparation, and continues to offer CSET preparation classes at the request of many California state universities.

Navigating This Book

This study guide is designed to provide you with important information and provide the tools necessary for successful preparation. As you work through this book, try to follow the recommended sequence of topics within each chapter and take detailed notes on the pages of the book to highlight important facts and concepts. Each chapter presents subject matter material in a structured format to enhance your learning. Many of the sample problems are arranged with built-in sequential learning strategies in mind. Read the material in the order that it is presented. After reading the introductory material in the "Analysis of Exam Areas" section that begins each chapter, focus on specific areas in the chapter reviews to develop your skills and awareness of CSET test questions.

Three full-length model practice tests (two in the book and one additional on the accompanying CD-ROM) will give you the opportunity to practice what you have learned in the chapter reviews. The CD-ROM provides you with computer-based practice to help develop your computer skills. All three practice tests include answers with thorough explanations. Finally, the last part of this book includes a checklist on page 574 to serve as a reminder of "things to do" before you take the exam.

- **Introduction: An Overview of the CSET:** This is a general description of the CSET exam—test format, scoring, general strategies, and frequently asked questions, as well as information about the computer-based test format.
- **Part I—Subject Analyses and Reviews:** Each review chapter focuses on three parts:
  1. **Analysis of exam areas** with a focus on introducing and analyzing content specifications.
  2. **Sample question types** with an emphasis on suggested approaches and examples.
  3. **Comprehensive review of subject domains** provides glossaries, outlines, strategies, descriptions, summaries, and diagnostic tests in some areas. Subject domains include:

        Reading, Language, and Literature

        History and Social Science

        Mathematics

        Science

        Physical Education

        Human Development

        Visual and Performing Arts

- **Part II—Two Full-Length Practice Tests (in-book)**: The practice tests include answers and in-depth explanations, and sample constructed-response essays. The practice tests are followed by analysis worksheets to assist you in evaluating your progress.
- **Part III—Appendices:** The "Charts, Graphs, Maps, Cartoons, and Diagrams" appendix provides various sample questions that contain charts, tables and graphs, along with strategies for approaching such questions. "The Final Touches" contains some final tips and reminders to help you do your best on the day of the exam.
- **CD-ROM:** The CD-ROM contains the two full-length practice tests from the book, plus one additional full-length practice test with answers and in-depth explanations. PDFs of the Introduction, review chapters, and appendices are also included on the CD.

Creating Your Customized Study Plan

There are many "best" ways to study for the CSET. Understanding your unique learning abilities and applying this understanding to a customized study plan will aid in your success on the CSET. Simply, the goal of preparation is to increase your overall score as much as possible to pass the CSET in all domains. Before you can begin your preparation, start by exploring subject areas that may require additional time and review. Start your preparation for the CSET with an *action plan* that recognizes your test-taking strengths and weaknesses that you can personally develop and execute. There are many pathways to learning, and as many different learning styles. This is why we have included hundreds of sample and practice problems with step-by-step explanations that are designed to enhance your learning style. While creating your customized study plan, it is recommended that you:

- Assess your strengths and weaknesses.
- Start with a general plan and move to a specific plan.
- Be time-wise.

Assess Your Strengths and Weaknesses

The universal first step in assessing your strengths and weaknesses is to discover your individual baseline. Assess where you are at right now. By starting with the "Analysis of Exam Areas" section at the beginning of each chapter, you will be able to evaluate the areas in which you need to improve. If time is of the essence, at least consider working through a range of sample questions to get a sense of your starting point. Then compare your results with the scores you would like to have. Note that you will be expected to get approximately 70% of the questions correct in order to pass each subtest. You'll want to focus the majority of your limited study time on the areas that require the most growth. Starting with a look at the growth you need is also a good way to estimate how much overall time you will need to devote to studying. Then set goals for your study time and be willing to frequently adapt and revise your goals as you evaluate your progress.

Start General and Move to a Specific Plan

Even after you've defined the areas that need work, increasing your scores might not be as easy as simply studying for a set time each day (though that's a good start!). Again, you know yourself best. Use outside resources for remedial research and instruction, such as university teacher libraries to study state-approved classroom textbooks, subject-focused material, and internet resources. Most people find it useful to start by learning general principles and skills of one specific domain at a time, and then progressing to memorizing important facts and concepts within that domain. For example, you should start your *general* math review with basic arithmetic (fractions, percents, decimals, and so on), and then move to a *specific* plan to tackle certain types of basic arithmetic problems (mixed fractions, converting percents to decimals, and so on). Again, start general and move to more specific problems and concepts within each domain. As you progress in your preparation, moving from a general plan to a specific plan, you will notice that you may frequently revise and modify your plan to adapt to newly learned concepts.

Be Time-Wise

Your study plan depends on the total amount of time left until the test date. If the test is tomorrow, focus on understanding procedure and instructions (and gathering the necessary identification and a map to the test site). If the test is four months from now, you can start with training skills and expect that an understanding of test procedures will materialize as you work your way methodically through this guide. If you have the time, don't forget to check your progress along the way and be sure to practice using computer-based material! Every time you take a practice test, you might need to revise how you prioritize your study time.

Study Guide Checklist

❏ 1. Read the CSET: Multiple Subjects information materials (registration bulletin) available online at www.cset.nesinc.com.

❏ 2. Review the information and online computer-simulated sample problems available online at www.cset.nesinc.com.

❏ 3. Become familiar with the test format (pages 1–2).

❏ 4. Read "Frequently Asked Questions," starting on page 3. Learn about the computer-based CSET, starting on page 4.

❏ 5. Review general strategies for multiple-choice and constructed-response essay questions, starting on page 5.

❏ 6. Carefully read "Analysis of Exam Areas" in each chapter.

❏ 7. Review Reading, Language, and Literature domain in Part I, starting on page 13.

❏ 8. Review History and Social Science domain in Part I, starting on page 57.

❏ 9. Review Mathematics domain in Part I, starting on page 122.

❏ 10. Review Science domain in Part I, starting on page 228.

❏ 11. Review Physical Education domain in Part I, starting on page 306.

❏ 12. Review Human Development domain in Part I, starting on page 334.

❏ 13. Review Visual and Performing Arts domain in Part I, starting on page 366.

❏ 14. Review Charts, Graphs, Maps, Cartoons, and Diagrams, starting on page 559, as needed for approaches to questions with diagrams.

❏ 15. Take Practice Test I, starting on page 411.

❏ 16. Check your answers (page 448), fill in the analysis sheets (pages 449–450), and review the answer explanations, starting on page 451. For constructed-response questions, read the sample responses, starting on page 458, and use the evaluation form (page 10) to evaluate your responses.

❏ 17. Review weak areas as necessary. Remember to review by subtest areas.

❏ 18. Take Practice Test II, starting on page 489.

❏ 19. Check your answers (page 524), fill in the analysis sheets (pages 525–526), and review the answer explanations, starting on page 527. For constructed-response questions, read the sample responses, starting on page 534, and use the evaluation form (page 10) to evaluate your responses.

❏ 20. Review weak areas as necessary. Now focus your review.

❏ 21. Carefully read "The Final Touches," page 574.

❏ 22. For additional practice, take Practice Test III on the CD-ROM.

Introduction: An Overview of the CSET

The California Subject Examination for Teachers (CSET) is a computer-based teacher exam for prospective elementary school teachers. The test was developed by the California Commission on Teacher Credentialing (CTC) with the understanding that future teachers should be able to apply the same skills on the CSET as taught to students in their classroom. The test focuses on knowledge and critical thinking skills that are considered fundamental to educators.

Effective preparation for the CSET begins with strategic planning and preparation. This is why you should contact your local school district, university credential preparation office, or state department of education for more information about credential and employment prerequisites.

Format and Scoring

The format of the CSET consists of multiple-choice and constructed-response essay questions that are divided into three subtests and seven different subject areas.

Scoring

Seventy percent of the overall questions are multiple choice and thirty percent of the questions are short constructed-response essay questions. **To pass the CSET, you must attain a minimum scaled score of 220 on each subtest and answer approximately 70 percent of the questions correctly.** Your final score is based on the number of questions you answer correctly. There is no penalty for guessing on a question so try to answer every question to achieve your best possible results. Carefully review the table below for specific scoring guidelines and for more information about the number of questions you will need to answer in order to pass each subtest.

Many test-takers ask about the differences between raw scores and scaled scores. *Raw scores* are simply the number of questions you answer correctly. For example, if you answer 41 multiple-choice questions correctly out of 52 possible on Subtest I, your raw score will be 41 plus the score of your constructed-response questions. *Scaled scores*, on the other hand, are computed by converting the total number of questions answered correctly into a "scale" that best represents the level of difficulty. Each subtest's scaled scores range from 100 to 300. This means that each question will not have the exact value of one point per question. This conversion is important to help to ensure the fairness of the test. For example, if your raw score is 41, but your copy of the CSET is slightly more difficult than other versions, your score of 41 will be converted into a scaled score that best represents this level of difficulty.

The scoring and passing standards are subject to change. Visit www.cset.nesinc.com for updated exam information.

CSET Format and Scoring			
Subtest Subjects	**Number of Questions**		**Approximate Percentage of Overall Exam**
	Multiple-Choice Questions	**Constructed-Response Essays**	
Subtest I			
Reading, Language, and Literature	26	2	18%
History and Social Science	26	2	18%
Subtest I Total Questions	**52**	**4**	**36%**
Minimum Passing Score: 220 **To pass Subtest I, you will need to answer approximately 35 multiple-choice questions correctly, and receive an average score of 2 on each constructed-response essay.**			
Subtest II			
Science	26	2	18%
Math	26	2	18%
Subtest II Total Questions	**52**	**4**	**36%**
Minimum Passing Score: 220 **To pass Subtest II, you will need to answer approximately 35 multiple-choice questions correctly, and receive an average score of 2 on each constructed-response essay.**			
Subtest III			
Physical Education	13	1	9%
Human Development	13	1	9%
Visual and Performing Arts	13	1	9%
Subtest III Total Questions	**39**	**3**	**27%**
Minimum Passing Score: 220 **To pass Subtest III, you will need to answer approximately 26 multiple-choice questions correctly, and receive an average score of 2 on each constructed-response essay.**			
Total Questions 143 multiple-choice questions 11 Constructed-Response essays			
Total time: 5 hours • If taking each Subtest separately, you will be allowed 180 minutes (3 hours) for Subtests I and II, and 135 minutes (2 hours and 15 minutes) for Subtest III. • In addition to the testing time, 15 minutes is provided to complete a nondisclosure agreement and a computer tutorial.			

Getting Started: Five Steps to Success on the CSET

Step 1 – Awareness

Become familiar with the test—the test format, test directions, test material, and scoring—by reading this study guide. You should also visit the CSET website at www.cset.nesinc.com.

Step 2 – Assess Your Strengths and Weaknesses

Know what to expect on the CSET to assess your strengths and weaknesses by reviewing the "Analysis of Exam Areas" section at the beginning of each review chapter. As you assess any areas that may require increased study time, you will be able to develop a study plan that is unique to your personal goals. If you would like to focus your attention on one or two subject areas, rather than the entire seven subjects, keep in mind that you are allowed to register for one subtest at a time.

Step 3 – Question Types

Become familiar with the two types of questions: multiple-choice and constructed-response essay questions. The "Analysis of Exam Areas" section at the beginning of each review chapter provides exercises and sample questions for each domain and each question type.

Step 4 – Strategies and Techniques

Study the computer-based strategies outlined in the next section. Remember that if it takes you longer to recall a strategy than to solve the problem, it's probably not a good strategy for you to adopt. The goal in offering strategies is for you to answer questions in a straightforward manner. Try not to get stuck on any one question. Taking time to answer the most difficult question on the test correctly, but losing valuable test time, won't get you the score you deserve. Most importantly, remember to answer every question, even if you answer with only an educated guess since there is no penalty for guessing. It is to your advantage to answer all questions.

Step 5 – Practice, Practice, Practice

Practice is the key to your success on the CSET. Our study guide includes sample practice exercises in each review chapter and three full-length practice tests with answers and explanations. Two practice tests are in the book and one additional practice test is on the accompanying CD-ROM to provide you with a simulated "computer-based practice experience." Additional practice problems are available on the CSET website (www.cset.nesinc.com).

Frequently Asked Questions

Q. Which teacher exam should I take?

A. The California Subject Examination for Teachers (CSET): Multiple Subjects is the examination adopted by the Commission on Teacher Credentialing (CTC) for evaluating subject-matter competence of applicants for the Multiple Subject Teaching Credential. If you have questions about which exam to take, contact the California Commission on Teacher Credentialing Information Services, www.ctc.ca.gov, 1900 Capitol Avenue, Sacramento, CA 95811-4213, (916) 445-7254 or (888) 921-2682, or credentials@ctc.ca.gov.

Q. Who administers the CSET?

A. The CSET: Multiple Subjects is a part of the CSET Program, which is administered by Evaluation Systems, Pearson Education, www.cset.nesinc.com, (916) 928-4003 or (800) 205-3334, P.O. Box 340880, Sacramento, CA 95834-0880.

Q. How do I register?

A. Online registration for the computer-based exam is available on the CSET website at www.cset.nesinc.com. The CSET Registration Bulletin is also available online and will provide you with up-to-date registration information. The CSET is scheduled by appointment only on a first-come, first-served basis. Schedule your exam as early as possible to get your desired appointment date. To confirm your registration or to change the test date, time, or location, go to www.pearsonvue.com/cset/ or call (800) 989-8532. You must register at least four calendar days before you plan to take the test.

Q. Where is the CSET given?

A. The CSET: Multiple Subjects test is administered statewide by computer at Pearson Professional Centers. Visit the Pearson VUE website for updated locations (www.pearsonvue.com/cset). You must report at least 30 minutes before your scheduled testing time, and you cannot be more than 15 minutes late or you will be considered a "no show."

Q. What materials should I take to the test?

A. Take your current government-issued photo and signature identification (driver's license or passport). Be sure the name on your I.D. matches the name on your CSET registration. Student identification is not acceptable. For identity verification, a digital signature and/or palm scan will be taken. No scratch paper, cell phones (or other electronic devices), calculators, backpacks, hats, food/drinks, books, or other aids will be permitted in the test center. All personal items must be stored outside the testing room in the lockers provided. Go to the CSET website for updated information.

Q. How much time do I have to complete each subtest?

A. Five hours are given for the entire testing session. You can choose to take any one or all three subtests within a single testing session. If taking each subtest separately on different dates, you will be allowed 180 minutes (3 hours) each for Subtests I and II, and 135 minutes (2 hours and 15 minutes) for Subtest III.

Q. How long are my subtest scores good?

A. Passing scores on any subtest must be applied toward a credential within five years of the test date on which the scores were earned.

Q. What is a passing score?

A. A score of 220 on each subtest is necessary to pass the exam. The score range on each subtest is 100 to 300.

Q. When will I get my score report?

A. Unofficial test results are available at the end of your computer-based session. Your official test score will be mailed to you about two to four weeks after you take the test and will also be available on the CSET website (www.cset.nesinc.com) at that time.

Q. Can I take the CSET: Multiple Subjects more than once?

A. Yes. But you must wait 45 calendar days before you can retake the test.

Q. Should I guess on the test?

A. Yes! Since there is no penalty for guessing, make an educated guess when necessary. In the multiple-choice section, first try to eliminate some of the choices to increase your chances of choosing the right answer. Don't leave any questions unanswered. In the short constructed-response essay section, be sure to give a response to each essay question.

Q. Will I be given scratch paper?

A. Yes. Scratch paper (or a writing board) will be provided. Use the scratch paper to plan your essay, take notes, and to use the elimination and plus-minus strategies outlined in the next section.

Taking the Computer-Based CSET

All of the material covered in this book—subject matter reviews, practice multiple-choice test questions and explanations, and practice constructed-response essays—will help to prepare you for the computer-administered test. Because the CSET is computer-based, once you have reviewed the material presented in this book, it is important that you practice questions that simulate computer skills. This is why we have provided you with **three practice tests on the accompanying CD-ROM** (the two tests from the book, plus one additional practice test).

Advantages of taking the CSET by computer are detailed here:

- Numerous test dates are available because appointments can be scheduled throughout the year. Be sure to call early to make your appointment because time slots fill up quickly.

- You are allowed time on the computer-administered exam to review a computer tutorial program.

- Computer-friendly functions help you to navigate freely on the test. The computer will allow you to "flag a question" for later review, and will allow you to view a list of incomplete, complete, or unseen questions.

- The on-screen calculator will help calculate your math problems. Calculators can be viewed in "standard" or "scientific" format. When you review the problems in this study guide, practice using a similar calculator. A word of caution: only use the on-screen calculator for time-consuming problems (square roots, long division, etc.); you will lose valuable test time if you use the calculator for every problem.
- Writing tools for the constructed-response essays include: cut, paste, undo, redo, copy, and a word counter.
- Your unofficial multiple-choice scores are available immediately after the test.
- Your answers are recorded electronically, which can reduce the chance of human error.

Computer-Administered Tutorial

Immediately before taking the computerized test, you will be led through a tutorial that will show you how to read and answer the questions for each section on the CSET. In addition, Pearson offers a video (go to www.pearsonvue.com/ppc/) to view the layout of the test center to help you feel at ease. You do not need advanced computer skills to take the computer-based exam. Basic computer skills are sufficient to operate the mouse, keyboard, and word processor. Remember that you are allowed enough time to work through a tutorial, so take advantage of this excellent opportunity to learn more about what you will encounter on the test.

Computer Screen Layout

The following example shows the complete, incomplete, or unseen questions screen. This example is for informational purposes only and does not reflect an exact reproduction of the official CSET computer screen.

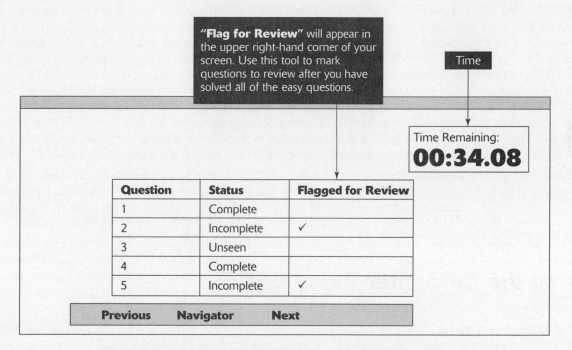

"**Flag for Review**" will appear in the upper right-hand corner of your screen. Use this tool to mark questions to review after you have solved all of the easy questions.

Time

Time Remaining:
00:34.08

Question	Status	Flagged for Review
1	Complete	
2	Incomplete	✓
3	Unseen	
4	Complete	
5	Incomplete	✓

Previous   Navigator   Next

General Strategies for Multiple-Choice Questions

There is no right or wrong method to answer questions on the computer-based CSET, but these proven test-taking strategies will help you approach the CSET with greater ease and confidence. These strategies will also help you to narrow down your choices, which will statistically increase your chances of improving your final score.

The multiple-choice questions cover a broad range of topics while considering two different question types. To be successful on the exam, you need to recall basic facts and major concepts that are important in seven different subject areas. The facts and concepts on the CSET are often presented in subtle variations of selected answer choices that make it difficult for test-takers to narrow down the answer choices. Subtle variations in answer choices can also distract you from choosing the right answer.

Consider the following guidelines to help you do your best on the CSET:

- **Manage your time wisely.** When you begin the exam, make a mental note of the time you start and keep track of the time that appears in the upper right hand corner of your computer screen. If you are taking all three subtests in one day, you should try not to spend more than 1 to 1½ minutes on any one multiple-choice question and no more than 8 minutes on any one short-constructed response question.

  Note: If you take less than three subtests (on different days), time will not be a critical factor since you will have more time to complete individual subtests (3 hours to complete Subtest I or Subtest II; and 2 hours and 15 minutes to complete Subtest III). See the CSET website for up-to-date-information at www.cset.nesinc.com.

  With sufficient practice, you will almost automatically know when a problem is taking you too long to answer. If you consider spending the same amount of time on each question, and leave at least 5 minutes to recheck each subtest (15 minutes total), the approximate time you should spend on each subtest is:

  - **Subtest I** – 1 hour and 10 minutes to answer 52 multiple-choice questions (or 35 minutes for each domain of 26 questions); and 32 minutes to answer four essay questions (or 8 minutes per essay).
  - **Subtest II** – 1 hour and 10 minutes to answer 52 multiple-choice questions (or 35 minutes for each domain of 26 questions); and 32 minutes to answer four essay questions (or 8 minutes per essay).
  - **Subtest III** – 51 minutes to answer 39 questions (or 17 minutes per domain of 13 questions each); and 24 minutes to answer three essay questions (or 8 minutes per essay).

- **Complete one subject at a time.** If you are taking the entire CSET in one day, you will be able to move throughout the entire exam by clicking the "previous," "next," and "navigator," icons. Although you may wish to first complete the subject areas where you are best prepared (i.e. history/social science before you complete math), you should always complete one section (domain) at a time. *Do not be tempted to skip around from subject to subject during the exam.* Finish one section (domain) before you move to the next section. Your brain is like a computer that runs at its best efficiency when the "input information" is systematic and organized. In other words, each thought you have is connected to the next thought by connecting neuro pathways. In order to "think" efficiently you must be systematic in your approach. Tackle the problems one section at a time and one thought at a time. For example, Subtest I has two main domains (subjects), reading/language/literature and history/social science. Answer all of the reading/language/literature questions *before* you tackle history/social science.

- **Read each question carefully.** Do not make a hasty assumption that you know the correct answer without reading the whole question and all the possible answers. It is common to jump to conclusions and select the wrong answer choice after reading only one or two of the answer choices. Note that some of the answer choices only show a "part" of the correct answer. You must look at the entire list of answer choices.

- **Watch for negative words.** Another common mistake is misreading a question that includes the words *except* or *not*. These types of questions reverse the meaning of the questions and ask for the opposite to be true in order to select the correct answer. It is helpful to write down brief notes on your scratch paper to avoid misreading a question (and therefore answering it incorrectly). Simply write down "not" or "except" on your scratch paper as a reminder to reverse your thinking.

- **Fill-in the correct answer.** Be very careful that your response matches your intended response. When answering questions quickly, it is common to click on the wrong answer choice by mistake.

Two general computer-based strategies will help you on the CSET: the elimination strategy and the plus-minus strategy.

The Elimination Strategy

When making your answer selection, try to eliminate as many of the answer choices as possible. Using this method will help you make an educated guess among the remaining choices. For example, if you know that answer choice C is incorrect, simply write down the letter C on your scratch paper (or writing board) and cross it out with a diagonal line. It will just take a few seconds to use this strategy, but will help to keep you from reconsidering impossible answer choices.

When you can eliminate one or more choices, the statistical odds of answering the question correctly will significantly increase. For example, if you can eliminate one answer choice, you have a 25% greater chance of answering the problem correctly. If you can eliminate two answer choices, you will have a 50% chance of answering correctly. And if you can eliminate three answer choices, you will have determined the correct answer at 100% accuracy. Your scratch paper should look something like this:

5. ?A
   B̸
   C̸
   D

The Plus-Minus Strategy

Many people who take the CSET do not get their best possible score because they spend too much time on difficult questions, leaving insufficient time to answer the easy questions. Do not let this happen to you. The plus-minus approach will help you categorize problems so that you can focus your attention on problems that you are able to answer quickly. Since every question is worth the same point value, making use of this approach will help you to quickly identify problems that are *easy, solvable* (+), and *difficult* (–) and be able to move quickly through the test.

Start by drawing two columns on the scratch paper (or writing board) provided at the test center. Label the top of the first column with a plus symbol (+) and the top of the second column with a minus symbol (–). Follow these steps:

1. Answer the easy questions immediately.
2. Write down the question number (and possible choices) in the plus "+"column for any question that seems *solvable* but seems to be too time-consuming.
3. Write down the question number (and possible choices) in the minus "–"column for any problem that seems too *difficult* to solve.

	Guidelines to Identifying Problems	
	Easy	Answer easy questions immediately. This type of question is answered with little or no difficulty, and requires little or minimal thought.
+	**Solvable**	Some questions require additional time. For example, passage poems and multiple-multiple questions are designed to take longer. You will recognize this type of question because it appears to be solvable but is overly time-consuming. This type of question leaves you feeling, "I can answer this question, but I need more time." A time-consuming question is a question that you estimate will take you more than 1½ minutes to answer, but you decide to answer it later. When you face this type of question, write down the problem number (with possible choices and any other notes), click on the icon "flag for review," then make an educated guess and quickly move on to the next question. When you review the list of incomplete, complete, unseen, and flagged questions (using the navigator button), you can easily refer back to your notes to know which answer choice has been eliminated. Go back to this type of question after you have solved all of the easy problems. Remember that you should only work on one section at a time, but you should take advantage of moving around within a section. Do not proceed to the next section without answering all possible questions within that section. Remember, you are not penalized for wrong answers so guess before moving on; never leave a question unanswered. If you run out of time, you will at least have an answer recorded.
–	**Difficult**	The difficult question appears "impossible to solve." When you come to a question that seems impossible to answer, write down the question number, with any notes, on your scratch paper. Don't bother with the difficult-type question unless you have checked all of your work and have answered all of the "easy" and "solvable" ones first. Your time may be better spent reviewing your work to be sure you didn't make any careless mistakes on the questions you thought were easy to answer. You may want to pick one of the letter answer choices (A, B, C, or D) and use that letter on all difficult questions. Remember, there is no penalty for wrong answers, and statistically your chances are better if you pick one letter and use it on all unanswered questions.

The computerized test allows you to go forward and backward, and navigate from question to question. For those questions that could not be answered immediately within a domain, quickly write down the question number in the most appropriate of the two columns, including any notes to help trigger your memory when you go back to the question. Do not proceed to the next subtest or domain without answering all questions within your section.

Your scratch paper should look like this:

History and Social Science

+	−
3. B or C	1. A or B, not C
11. A, not B	6. not D
15. C	14. A

TIP: Don't waste time deciding whether a question is solvable. Since you just have over 1 to 1½ minutes to answer each question, you must act quickly.

General Strategies for Constructed-Response Questions

At the end of each multiple-choice subtest, there are short constructed-response questions. As you approach the constructed-response essay questions at the end of each domain (subject area), use the "next" and "navigation" tool on your computer to briefly scan (read quickly) the group of questions allotted to the subject area. Do not attempt to answer an individual question at this point. Simply scan for general content to decide which question you will work on first. Select the question that you feel the most comfortable with to give you your best possible score. Answer that essay question first.

If you are taking all three subtests in one sitting, allow yourself approximately 8 minutes to pre-write and respond to each essay question and follow these guidelines.

- **Write notes on the scratch paper provided.** You only have about 8 minutes to plan and write your response. Use the scratch paper (or writing board) provided for writing notes to help you organize your thoughts and pertinent facts and information needed to answer the question. You can take a minute to organize your thoughts by using word clusters, lists, phrases, or simply individual words. Do *not* attempt to make a complete outline of your answer. Time constraints limit the effectiveness of detailed outlines.

- **Stay focused on the main point of the assignment.** Write down key words and phrases from the question to help you stay focused. One of the primary reasons that test-takers do not perform well on the constructed-response essay section is that they do not stay focused on the topic and do not respond to the *complete assigned task*. Answer all parts of an individual question. Do *not* spend an inordinate amount of time on any individual factor in a question that asks for multiple factors. Your overall score will be based on your ability to answer all parts of the question, not simply *one* part. It's easy to skip part of the question due to the time pressure. For example, you may list two causes *but* forget to list the two results. Many questions call for an answer associated with causes, effects, and consequences. Other common types of questions will ask you to draw an inference or provide a conclusion. Still others will ask you to compare or contrast two concepts, theories, time periods, or styles. In addition, watch for key words such as *identify, list, compare, discuss, determine,* and *describe* as you read the question.

- **Paraphrase the question.** Paraphrase silently to yourself before attempting to answer the question. It is essential that you clearly understand what the question is asking. However, do not restate the question in your introductory sentence; it is redundant and unnecessary.

- **Answer each question.** Before skipping a question, read it a few times to see if you can gain insight concerning the question. The questions are generally designed so that you can receive at least partial credit if you have some knowledge of the subject. Partial answers will get partial credit. Even an answer that receives one point will be added to your total points. One point may not seem like much now, but earning one point is better than zero, especially if you're one point away from passing.

- **Abbreviate the writing process.** The essay is a short-constructed response, *not* a formal three-, four-, or five-paragraph essay. It does not need to be a polished essay because you are trying to convey to the CSET readers what you know about the subject area. Spend a couple of minutes organizing your response to make sure that you cover important points. You may show steps, use bullet points, make drawings, etc. Unless specifically asked, do *not* write a conclusion or summary for any question. The question format does not normally require this type of response.

- **Be specific, clear, and concise.** The CSET readers are looking for specific, factual details and for concrete evidence of some kind to support your points. When you write your short answer, be very specific if you can and use one or two specific examples. Your answers will be more convincing and easier for you to write. For example, if you are asked to write about the short story, it may be much easier to base your answer on a story you know than try to discuss the short story in general.

- **Be aware of time management.** Pace yourself. Do *not* write an extended, definitive answer to any individual question that will take substantially longer than 8 minutes or that requires more than a page. The maximum score you can receive on any one question is three points. If you spend too much time on one question, you may not have time to adequately complete your other responses.

- **Math problems.** Explain math questions conceptually; that is, describe how the answer is arrived at first, and then explain the computations in written form. Or you may wish to compute the answer on scratch paper first and then describe the steps you followed to reach the solution. Sometimes, computing the answer on scratch paper first will reinforce the process or give insight into the problem.

Rubric for Understanding Your Scores

Constructed-response essays are evaluated by at least two readers who understand the constraints on the writer taking this examination. Essays are evaluated and based on the degree you understand and respond to the assigned topic using the following scale.

Score	Response Criteria
3	Responses assigned a "3" thoroughly understand the topic, and the purpose of the assignment is fully achieved. These responses: ❑ Deal with all parts of the assignment. ❑ Explain clearly and, when appropriate, support their conclusions. There is specific relevant supporting evidence. ❑ Reveal a good understanding of the subject matter and show accurate application of relevant content specifications. ❑ Show a command of relevant knowledge and skills.
2	Responses assigned a "2" understand the topic adequately, and the purpose of the assignment is largely achieved. These responses: ❑ Employ acceptable relevant supporting evidence when required. ❑ Deal with most of the requirements of the topics. ❑ Reveal adequate understanding of the subject matter and show accurate application of the relevant content specifications. ❑ Show a general command of relevant knowledge and skills.
1	Responses assigned a "1" only partially achieve the task at hand. These responses: ❑ Fail to explain or support important points or parts of the topic. ❑ Give little or no relevant supporting evidence. ❑ Show an inadequate understanding of the subject matter related to the topic. ❑ Show limited or no application of relevant content specifications. ❑ Show little or no command of relevant knowledge and skills.
U	Responses assigned a "U" (for Unscorable) present little or no understanding of the assigned question. Essays may be illegible, may be primarily in a language other than English, or may have insufficient length to score.
B	Blank responses are assigned a "B."

Evaluating Your Short Constructed Responses

Answer the questions below as you evaluate your constructed-response practice essays in this study guide.

1. To what extent does the response reflect an understanding of the relevant content and academic knowledge from the applicable CSET: Multiple Subjects domain?

2. To what extent does the essay respond to the given task(s)?

3. How accurate is the response?

4. Does the response demonstrate an effective application of the relevant content and academic knowledge from the applicable CSET: Multiple Subjects domain?

5. To what extent does the response provide specific supporting examples, evidence, and rationale based on the relevant content and academic knowledge from the applicable CSET: Multiple Subjects domain?

PART I

SUBJECT ANALYSES AND REVIEWS

Subtest I: Reading, Language, and Literature; History and Social Science

Subtest II: Mathematics; Science

Subtest III: Physical Education; Human Development; Visual and Performing Arts

Content

The Reading, Language, and Literature section concentrates on the components of reading literacy, language and linguistics, nonwritten and written communication, and the elements, concepts, conventions, and interpretations of literature. Reading and language studies include the operations of language development and its use in oral and written expression. Literature studies include both narrative and expository texts and written materials of all disciplines. The scope of questions allows CSET candidates to demonstrate their understanding and knowledge of reading, literature, and language. This section also tests their ability to use higher-order thinking skills in analyzing problems relevant to the topics and to apply the principles of the language arts in a variety of contexts.

The multiple-choice section contains 26 questions, which are grouped together, and two short constructed-response questions. The two essay questions are chosen from the three domain areas. The questions cover the following major content areas and focus on the topics listed under each.

Analysis of Exam Areas: Content Specifications* in Reading, Language, and Literature

*These are the actual California state content specification standards, available online.

Domain 1: Language and Linguistics

1.1 <u>Language Structure and Linguistics</u>

❑ Candidates are able to identify and demonstrate an understanding of the fundamental components of human language, including phonology, morphology, syntax, and semantics, as well as the role of pragmatics in using language to communicate.

❑ In the context of these components, candidates reflect on both the potential for differences among languages and the universality of linguistic structures.

❑ Candidates must demonstrate knowledge of phonemic awareness (e.g., the processes of rhyming, segmenting, and blending).

❑ Candidates apply knowledge of similarities and differences among groups of phonemes (e.g., consonants and vowels) that vary in their placement and manner of articulation.

❑ Candidates must recognize the differences between phoneme awareness and phonics.

❑ Candidates must know the predictable patterns of sound-symbol and symbol-sound relationships in English (the Alphabetic Principle).

❑ Candidates identify examples of parts of speech and their functions, as well as the morphology contributing to their classification.

❑ Candidates recognize and use syntactic components (such as phrases and clauses, including verbals) to understand and develop a variety of sentence types (e.g., simple, compound, and complex sentences).

1.2 Language Development and Acquisition

❑ Candidates apply knowledge of both the development of a first language and the acquisition of subsequent ones.

❑ Candidates describe the principal observable milestones in each domain and identify the major theories that attempt to explain the processes of development and acquisition.

❑ Candidates demonstrate that they understand the range of issues related to the interaction of first languages and other languages.

❑ Candidates are able to recognize special features that may identify a pupil's language development as exceptional, distinguishing such features from interlanguage effects.

1.3 Literacy

❑ Candidates understand and use the major descriptions of developing literacy.

❑ In both English speakers and English learners, candidates identify the progressive development of phonemic awareness, decoding, comprehension, word recognition, and spelling (including its complexities related to the interaction of phonology, the Alphabetic Principle, morphology, and etymology).

❑ Candidates understand how these processes interact with the development of concepts, of vocabulary (including relationships among etymologies and both denotative and connotative word meanings), and of contextual analysis.

1.4 Assessment

❑ In assessing developing literacy, candidates apply knowledge of the implications that language development and differences have for the processes of learning to read and reading to learn.

❑ Candidates know and apply a range of assessment methods and instruments to the respective and interrelated developing abilities in listening (for aural/oral languages), speaking, reading (decoding and comprehension), vocabulary, and spelling conventions.

Domain 2: Nonwritten and Written Communication

2.1 Conventions of Language

❑ Applying their knowledge of linguistic structure, candidates identify and use the conventions associated with what is called standard English.

❑ Candidates recognize, understand, and use a range of conventions in both spoken and written English, including varieties of sentence structure, preferred usage, and conventional forms of spelling, capitalization, and punctuation in written English.

2.2 Writing Strategies

❑ Candidates describe the stages of the writing process. They understand the purpose and techniques of various prewriting strategies (e.g., outlining, webbing, and note taking).

❑ Candidates revise and edit writing, drawing upon their understanding of principles of organization, transitions, point of view, word choices, and conventions.

2.3 <u>Writing Applications</u>

❑ Candidates demonstrate their knowledge of principles of composition, such as paragraphing, transitional phrases, appropriate vocabulary, and context.

❑ Candidates compose and/or analyze writing according to conventions in different genres, including narrative, interpretive, descriptive, persuasive, and expository writing, as well as summaries, letters, and research reports.

❑ Candidates understand and are able to use bibliographic citations in a standard format.

2.4 <u>Nonwritten Communication</u>

❑ Candidates demonstrate knowledge of nonwritten genres and traditions, and their characteristics (e.g., organization), including narratives, persuasive pieces, research presentations, poetry recitations, and responses to literature.

❑ Candidates apply understandings of language development stages, from preproduction (beginning) to intermediate fluency, to children's developing abilities in such areas.

❑ Candidates analyze speech in terms of presentation components (e.g., volume and pace) and pronunciation fluency, and identify the integration of nonverbal components (e.g., gesture) with verbal elements (e.g., volume).

❑ Candidates demonstrate knowledge of dialects, idiolects, and changes in what is considered standard oral English usage and their effects on perceptions of speaker performance, with attention to the dangers of stereotyping and bias.

❑ Candidates demonstrate an understanding of the potential impact on nonwritten presentations of images, sound, and other features from electronic media.

2.5 <u>Research Strategies</u>

❑ Candidates demonstrate their ability to use a variety of research sources, both print and electronic.

❑ Candidates interpret such research, putting to use their findings and interpretations to construct their own reports and narratives.

❑ Candidates understand the importance of citing research sources, using recognizable and accepted conventions for doing so.

Domain 3: Texts

3.1 <u>Concepts and Conventions</u>

❑ Candidates analyze narrative and expository texts, with special attention to children's literature, from a range of cultures, for both literary elements and structural features.

❑ Candidates identify themes derived from cultural patterns and symbols found in rituals, mythologies, and traditions.

❑ Candidates identify and analyze evidence of an author's or narrator's perspective in both fiction and nonfiction.

❑ Candidates identify and evaluate structural devices in prose and poetry (such as rhyme, metaphor, and alliteration), and they examine the connections among organizational structures, the writer's viewpoint, and the goals of reading.

3.2 <u>Genres</u>

❑ Candidates analyze texts in different literary genres (novels, short stories, folk and fairy tales, and poetry of various types, for example), as they are represented in different cultures, according to their structure, organization, and purpose.

❏ Candidates demonstrate an understanding of structural features and their applications in various types of expository and narrative materials, including popular media such as magazines and newspapers.

❏ Candidates understand and evaluate the use of elements of persuasive argument in print, speech, videos, and in other media.

3.3 Interpretation of Texts

❏ Candidates analyze both implicit and explicit themes and interpret both literal and figurative meanings in texts, from a range of cultures and genres, using textual support for inferences, conclusions, and generalizations they draw from any work.

❏ Candidates evaluate the structure, purpose, and potential uses of visual text features, such as graphics, illustrations, and maps.

❏ Candidates recognize and analyze instances of bias and stereotyping in a text.

Sample Questions and Explanations for the Multiple-Choice Section

Each of the following examples represents an area tested on the Reading, Language, and Literature multiple-choice segment. An analysis follows each question.

Domain 1: Language and Linguistics

1.1 Language Structure and Linguistics

1. Which of the following vowel patterns is most inconsistent in its pronunciation?

   A. ai
   B. ee
   C. ea
   D. oa

The correct answer is C. First, identify the information you are looking for. In this case, the vowel patterns . . . most inconsistent in its pronunciation. Next, you may wish to try using these vowel patterns in some words. You will notice that in Choice C, *ea* is commonly associated with more than one pronunciation, such as dream (long *e* sound) or dread (short *e* sound).

2. A second grader is unable to blend phonemes into a word that is said aloud by the teacher. For example, after hearing /c/ /a/ /t/, the child says "kitten."

   Using the information above, what does this suggest to the teacher for instruction?

   A. The student would benefit from manipulating magnetic letters while working within a small group to match sounds with letters.
   B. The student would benefit from practice in blending skills with a volunteer or teacher's aide.
   C. The student is unaware of syllables and needs explicit instruction in this area.
   D. The student needs more instruction in phonemic awareness including formal and explicit reading instruction.

The correct answer is D. Remember to determine the important words in the question: <u>suggest to the teacher for instruction</u>. Phonemic blending is a skill a student should possess by age six, or first grade. The teacher needs to assess the student's phonemic awareness to determine areas of weakness and remediate as needed. Even though the student has completed kindergarten and first grade, this skill has not been mastered by the student. Choice A, matching sounds to letters, is not a phonemic awareness task. Choice B would help the student practice the skills, but the student needs more instruction before practice can begin. Blending and segmenting are important prerequisites to reading, and students need practice and explicit instruction in this skill.

3. In a multiple-choice exercise, a student, who speaks a second language at home, is asked to identify the word that matches a picture of a throne. The choices are:

    A. thrown
    B. throne
    C. throwne

    The student chooses answer A but doesn't understand why it is marked as incorrect. What could this error suggest to the teacher for further instruction?

    A. This student's difficulty is with correct spelling, and the teacher should recognize that the student would benefit from adding this word to his or her weekly spelling list.
    B. This student is confusing homophones, and the teacher can provide individualized instruction to help the student differentiate between words that sound the same.
    C. The teacher needs to provide an environment that promotes independent reading to help this student with vocabulary.
    D. This student's reading and vocabulary development can be furthered by extra classroom lessons provided by a teacher's aide or parent volunteer.

The correct answer is B. Focus on the information that is provided with the question. The information states that the student speaks a second language at home and makes an error on a multiple-choice question. Confusing *throne* and *thrown* is a common error for students who hear another language at home. Additionally, students might be more familiar with the word *thrown,* and possibly would have seen it in print before. The teacher should recognize that this student needs additional individualized instruction to clarify these words. Choice A is incorrect because this student is not experiencing a "spelling problem." While independent reading promotes increased vocabulary, as suggested in Choice C, this is not the best solution for this student's difficulty. Choice D contains correct statements but does not specifically address the question.

1.2 Language Development and Acquisition

4. While teaching an art lesson in a Project Head Start classroom, the teacher walks around the room to observe the children's paintings. Raymond holds up his painting and exclaims, "This tree was made by me!" Next Melanie holds up her painting, saying, "I make it!" Nicole eagerly displays her painting and says, "I paint my hands," and David shows his painting and says, "Me paint."

    Based on language development and the understanding of syntax, which response most closely exhibits the speech pattern of a five-year-old?

    A. "This tree was made by me!"
    B. "I make it!"
    C. "I paint my hands."
    D. "Me paint."

The correct answer is A. Choice B, "I make it," is not a possible answer, since a five-year-old, unlike a preschooler, knows how to speak with correct syntax (rules for organizing words into sentences) and pragmatics (rules for conversation). In language development, a child must master a complex system of rules to learn language. In Choice D, "Me paint," David's language indicates he's about two years old. A two-year-old uses just enough words to get their meaning across (telegraphic speech), such as this two-word sentence, while a five-year-old has the ability to combine words into phrases and sentences. Children begin rehearsing language long before they ever attend school. However, the correct use of syntax and verbal constructions, such as in Choice A, "This tree was made by me," will not occur until the child is about four to five years old.

5. A two-year-old child points to his favorite book and says, "book." Which of the following responses by a mother represents the best method to help this child develop linguistically correct speech patterns?

 A. Speaking naturally, "Yes, this is your favorite book, called *Goodnight Moon*."
 B. Speaking with infant-directed speech, "Yes, book."
 C. After careful thought, "Yes, this is your favorite book, called *Goodnight Moon*."
 D. Speaking with infant-directed speech, "Yes, this is your favorite book, called *Goodnight Moon*."

The correct answer is A. Answers B and D refer to infant-directed speech, which is also known as *motherese* or *parentese*. Adults use this type of language and a higher-pitched voice to respond to infants. It is sometimes referred to as "baby talk." Strategies that help to improve a child's natural ability to speak linguistically correct English include: (1) recasting—rephrasing what the child has said in a different way, (2) expanding—restating in a linguistically correct form, (3) labeling—identifying what is said, and (4) echoing—repeating the one- or two-word sentences the child has said. These strategies help to improve language patterns and must be a natural extension of how parents respond to children. The response to the child should not be planned or rehearsed, so Choice C is incorrect.

1.3 Literacy

6. A first-grade teacher plans a mid-year reading lesson for a class with many English learners from diverse sociocultural backgrounds. Which of the following should the teacher consider first before preparing her lesson?

 A. Preparing visual tools (e.g., pictures, illustrations, diagrams)
 B. Preparing a portfolio for each child with strategies for individual instructional needs
 C. Preparing strategies for teaching reading lessons written in their native language(s) to meet individual needs
 D. Including read-aloud reading material that is culturally sensitive

The correct answer is B. In a balanced, comprehensive reading program, the teacher must provide reading materials to meet the reading level of all students in the class. To develop materials that help children become skilled readers, the teacher must first develop and prepare individual student portfolios that diagnose and meet individual needs. Answers A and D are important instructional tools that can be included in reading lessons, but they should be introduced after initial assessments and possible intervention strategies are conducted.

7. A fourth-grade teacher is working with a student who is trying to decode the word *upsetting*. Read the passage printed below and use it to answer the following question about their conversation.

Teacher: Can you read this word?

Student: Yes. It's *upsing*.

Teacher: Does *upsing* make sense?

Student: No. I guess not.

Teacher: You've read part of the word. Try again.

Student: Oh! It's *upping*.

Teacher: You've read the first syllable and the last syllable. Now I want you to focus on the middle part of the word. Can you try the word again?

Student: *Up-set-ting*.

Teacher: You just read all of the syllables in the word. Try to put them together quickly to read the word.

Student: *Upsetting, upsetting*. I got it. The word is *upsetting*!

Teacher: Great job! You figured out the word *upsetting*.

Based on the above conversation, this student would most clearly benefit from:

A. participating in an organized, effective phonics program.
B. paying attention to structure and syntactic cues.
C. explicit instruction and guided practice decoding multisyllabic words.
D. instruction in decoding prefixes and suffixes.

The correct answer is C. At first glance, Choice D may seem correct. However, the student is having difficulty reading the whole word, not just the beginning and ending. The student actually read the prefix and suffix correctly. While choices A and B are important for word identification, they may not remediate the student's specific decoding problem. Explicit and systematic instruction is particularly beneficial for children who are having difficulty learning to read because it teaches the student a logical and sequential relationship of letters and sounds.

8. The part of the word *synchronous* that means *time* is:

A. chron
B. syn
C. sync
D. ronous

The correct answer is A. *Chron* comes from the word *chronos*, which means *time*. The word *synchronous* is an adjective describing events that happen, or states that exist, at the same time.

1.4 <u>Assessment</u>

9. During a history lesson, a fourth-grade classroom teacher requests that students submit a writing sample about what it must be like to be a child of immigrants coming to the United States. One student submits the following writing sample:

   > When my dad came, he did not *speek* English because he was born in a *diffirent* country, called Guatemala. No one could understand him because of his *axcent*. He was a good *electrichen*. I think my dad is *amazzing*.

   In analyzing the student's spelling errors, how should the teacher begin to interpret the student's spelling development, and how might the teacher plan for further spelling instruction?

   A. First, the teacher must identify the spelling errors in this student's paper. The teacher should return the paper to the student for corrections so the student can add the misspelled words to his weekly spelling list.

   B. After identifying the student's spelling errors, the teacher should add these words to her weekly class spelling list to enable her students to achieve mastery of these words. In future spelling lessons, the teacher should group her students according to the words they are having difficulty spelling and then provide activities to help them with these words.

   C. The teacher should identify the misspelled words in this student's writing sample and should add this sample to other samples of this student's work. For further information about this student's spelling development, the teacher should administer a spelling inventory and analyze the results. This would provide her with more information on which to base word-study lessons for her class.

   D. The teacher notices on this sample that this student has made some errors in words that have doubled consonants, but she needs more information to determine this student's spelling development. Future lessons should include class activities with the misspelled words from each student.

The correct answer is C. Before answering this question, ask yourself, "Is this student making appropriate errors for a fourth grader?" In this case, the answer is yes. The teacher can gain more information about the student's spelling stages if she collects samples of the student's writing, from both formal inventories and daily writing. This allows the teacher to compare the student's spelling abilities. Remember that while all students will pass through the same stages of development, they will pass through at different time periods. The inventory can provide the teacher with valuable information about each student's spelling development and subsequently help her in planning spelling instruction.

10. A first-grade teacher notices that a student is struggling with reading. He is in the lowest-achieving reading group, and although the teacher has tried some strategies to improve his reading, he is making minimal progress. What are the next steps the teacher should take in working with this student?

    A. Assess his reading and target instruction to meet identified skill needs. In addition, keep anecdotal records of reading behavior and communicate with parents to gain assistance.

    B. Request the help of specialists, such as the reading specialist, resource specialist, or counselor at the school, to make a joint decision on how to best help the student.

    C. Send home more homework for the child to practice reading skills at home with his parents.

    D. Read more often with the child to provide encouragement and increase his confidence level; have the child model volunteers or peer tutors who provide the student with increased reading time.

The correct answer is A. The first step of effective classroom intervention is to diagnose and assess the student's reading ability, while maintaining records of the student's reading behavior. This will help the teacher identify skill needs and develop explicit strategies for intervention (i.e., communication with the parents, increasing instruction time, dividing skills into smaller steps, etc.). Choice B is an excellent option once the teacher has attempted classroom intervention strategies, but the classroom is always the first level of intervention before the student is referred to a specialist. Choice D presents excellent strategies for reading skill development, but the teacher must first realize the importance of early and continual assessment of reading as a tool for targeting instruction and planning intervention.

Domain 2: Nonwritten and Written Communication

2.1 Conventions of Language

> 11. Which of the following sentences is incorrect?
>
>   A.   Neither of the women paid her bills.
>   B.   Susan and Alice are in the play.
>   C.   The committee gave awards to my sister and I.
>   D.   The vote was split among the three candidates.

The correct answer is C. The pronouns *I* and *me* are often misused. When the pronoun is the subject of a verb (called **subjective** or **nominative**), you should use *I*. When the pronoun is the object of a preposition, as in this case, you should use *me*. To test your answer, simply read the sentence with the pronoun object silently. For example, "The committee gave awards to I." After reading this to yourself, you should quickly understand that the pronoun *me* sounds better than *I*. The incorrect sentence, Choice C, is an example of the improper use of a pronoun.

> 12. Which of the following sentences contains an error in diction?
>
>   A.   In the beginning, Sam seemed confident.
>   B.   Considering the complexity of the situation, Phil and me were not overly concerned.
>   C.   Talia's speeches usually have a persuasive affect on her audience.
>   D.   Ben and Jon worked hard but were paid very little for their efforts.

The correct answer is C. You should first notice a key phrase, <u>error in diction</u>. Next, consider what is a diction error? A **diction error** refers to improper word usage—when to use *between* or *among*, *allusion* or *illusion*, *invoke* or *evoke*, etc. In Choice C, *persuasive affect* should be *persuasive effect*. *Affect* is usually used as a verb, while *effect* is a noun. Choice B contains an error but not a diction error.

2.2 Writing Strategies

> 13. Which one of the following paired writing techniques best describes the discovery process in writing an effective essay?
>
>   A.   content and body.
>   B.   deduction and induction.
>   C.   invention and prewriting.
>   D.   rhetoric and arrangement.

The correct answer is C. Here, you are being asked to determine a process that a writer uses to gather and discover ideas. Therefore, you must look for an initial step in the writing process. The older term for the idea-discovering process is **invention.** The term more often used today is **prewriting.** Prewriting is the initial brainstorming step in which a writer gathers ideas and examples.

> 14. Philip is a seventh-grade student taking a forty-minute, in-class essay exam. If Philip has managed his time wisely, with three or four minutes left, he should:
>
>   A.   try to quickly write a summary or conclusion.
>   B.   proofread his essay, making only minor changes.
>   C.   make major revisions in the introduction.
>   D.   erase any extraneous marks on his paper.

The correct answer is B. Notice that this question is asking what Philip should do with his last three or four minutes of a timed essay. If Philip managed his time wisely throughout, he should have spent about four or five minutes prewriting, about thirty minutes of actual writing, and the last three or four minutes reviewing and proofreading his essay. At this time, he should make only minor changes and correct errors.

2.3 <u>Writing Applications</u>

---

15. Read the following paragraph carefully and arrange the four sentences in the most coherent order.

    [1]The effect of the pill will not change. [2]Otherwise you might take the wrong pill or take a pill at the wrong time. [3]If you are taking several pills, be sure to pay close attention to the change in shape or color. [4]Changing from a brand-name medicine to a generic, you may find that the pill is a different shape or a different color.

    A. 4-2-3-1
    B. 2-3-1-4
    C. 3-4-1-2
    D. 4-1-3-2

The correct answer is D. Sentence 1 logically follows sentence 4 because sentence 4 speaks of a change, and sentence 1 begins with comments on something that will remain unchanged. Sentence 2, which begins with *Otherwise*, logically follows sentence 3, which begins with *If*. And the sentence pair 3 and 2 logically follows the pair 4 and 1.

Read the passage below and answer the two questions that follow.

[1]The fund-raising practices of the political parties in this country are clearly out of control. [2]A previously undisclosed transcript has revealed that Richard Nixon's secret White House slush fund, which was used to silence the Watergate burglars, came from illegally donated campaign money. [3]After Nixon resigned, his successor, Gerald Ford, pardoned him. [4]Gerald Ford has joined Presidents Carter and Bush in urging campaign funding reforms. [5]Recent hearings have shown all too clearly that both parties have been guilty of highly questionable fund-raising practices. [6]Unless laws are changed, the shoddy practices of the last 30 years will undoubtedly continue.

16. Which of the following numbered sentences is the *least* relevant to the main idea of this paragraph?

    A. Sentence 1
    B. Sentence 2
    C. Sentence 3
    D. Sentence 4

The best answer is C. The paragraph is about campaign financing and the need for reform. All the other references to former presidents are relevant to this issue, but Ford's pardon of Nixon is not.

---

17. Which one of the following numbered sentences expresses a matter of opinion rather than fact?

    A. Sentence 1
    B. Sentence 2
    C. Sentence 3
    D. Sentence 4

The best answer is A. The assertion that fund-raising practices are *out of control* is the opinion of the author. There is some evidence to support this opinion, but it clearly reflects the author's point of view and is not based on fact. The other sentences are merely stating facts.

2.4 Nonwritten Communication

18. In most dictionaries, the explanation of the meaning of pronunciation symbols is usually found:

   A. in the beginning of the spelling section of the dictionary.
   B. in an appendix of the dictionary.
   C. at the bottom of each page.
   D. with each word, before the definition of the word.

The correct answer is C. Most American dictionaries repeat the explanation of the pronunciation symbols at the bottom of every page so the reader can look from the word to the bottom of the page without having to look elsewhere in the book.

19. Identify the correct type of publication for the bibliographical notation below:

   Vivian Gornick, *Women in Science* (New York: Simon and Schuster, 1984), pp. 70–71.

   A. An anthology
   B. A magazine
   C. A book
   D. A newspaper

The correct answer is C. To answer this question you must be familiar with citation styles such as: Modern Language Association (MLA), Chicago Manual (CM), and American Psychological Association (APA) styles. Using Chicago style, as illustrated above, the bibliographical notation refers to a book, Choice C. An anthology, Choice A, lists the author (first and last name), title of the work (in quotes), name of the anthology (underlined or italicized), editor's name (first and last), city (colon), publisher, year (in parenthesis), and page number. A magazine article, Choice B, would list the author (first and last name), article title (in quotes), magazine name, date (day-month-year), and page number. A newspaper, Choice D, lists the title of news article (in quotes), name of the newspaper (underlined), newspaper name, date (day-month-year), section, and page number. .

2.5 Research Strategies

20. A seventh-grade English teacher asks her class to do a report on a current famous actor. The report is due the next day. Which of the following would be most helpful in getting useful information quickly?

Line	Source	Information
1	tabloid	to get the latest gossip
2	Internet search engine	to get background information and a list of movies
3	encyclopedia	to find information about the actor
4	screen actor's directory	to find the actor's agent

   A. Line 1
   B. Line 2
   C. Line 3
   D. Line 4

The correct answer is B. Although the tabloid may give interesting gossip, the student needs useful information for a report, so eliminate Choice A. In this case, the Internet search engine would be most helpful because the student could acquire a great deal of information quickly. Choice B looks like a good choice so far. Although an encyclopedia could give information about a current actor, it probably wouldn't be as up-to-date information as that which could be found with the Internet search engine; eliminate Choice C. Finding an actor's agent would be helpful if you could actually speak to the agent or interview the actor. Unfortunately, since the report is due the next day and making contact could take a great deal of time, Choice D is not feasible.

21. Use the information below to answer the question that follows.

    Einstein, Albert, *Meaning of Relativity.* 5th Edition, 1956, Princeton University Press, pp. 26–29

    The reference above is probably an example taken from the bibliography of a(n):

    A. literary periodical.
    B. anthology of essays.
    C. student's term paper.
    D. newspaper editorial.

The correct answer is C. The *Meaning of Relativity* would probably not be in a literary periodical because it is not considered a literary work; eliminate Choice A. A newspaper editorial would probably not be about the meaning of relativity, but even if it was, the information taken would not be four pages, and a standard bibliographic notation would not be given. The writer would probably mention the source in the context of his or her editorial. Choice D can be eliminated. An anthology is a compilation of works or small pieces of works. You can see by the notation that the *Meaning of Relativity* is not an essay. Eliminate Choice B. This work is being listed in a fairly standard bibliographic form that may be used on a bibliography page. Because of the nature of the work, the format of the notation, and the fact that page references are given, this is probably from a student's term paper.

Domain 3: Texts

3.1 Concepts and Conventions

22. Read the poem below; then answer the question that follows.

    Gather ye rosebuds while ye may:
    Old time is still a-flying
    And this same flower that smiles today
    Tomorrow will be dying.

    The figure used in the third line of the poem is an example of:

    A. personification.
    B. simile.
    C. metaphor.
    D. irony.

The correct answer is A. Many literature questions test the ability to recognize the correct use of literary terminology. For example, knowing that a **simile** (Choice B) is a comparison using *like* or *as* and that **irony** (Choice D) is a technique in which a writer conveys a meaning opposite from the words actually used would allow you to eliminate both of these choices. **Personification** (Choice A) gives human qualities to an inanimate object. Here, the flower is given the human ability to smile.

23. All of the following words or phrases could be used to define the word "persona" *except*:

    A. protagonist.
    B. mask.
    C. second voice.
    D. alter ego.

The correct answer is A. The **protagonist** (hero or heroine) is one of the main characters of a literary work and is usually in conflict with the **antagonist** (villain). The other three choices are definitions of *persona*. The easiest way to answer this question, if you are not familiar with the word *persona*, is to realize that choices B, C, and D are synonyms and can therefore be eliminated.

---

24. The point in a plot that is called the climax refers to the:

    A. development of the setting.
    B. turning point of the story.
    C. falling action.
    D. ending of the story.

The correct answer is B. The point in a plot where there is a rising action and in which a conflict takes a decisive turn is its **climax**. This is typically followed by falling action. Other terms associated with the development of a narrative include setting, characterization, and **denouement**, which refers to the solution of a problem or the final outcome of the conflict in a literary work.

3.2 Genres

---

25. A ballad is best described as a:

    A. short story that was later adapted to music.
    B. narrative poem that tells a story and was written to be sung.
    C. conversation or dialogue written to music.
    D. musical short story that uses sophisticated language.

The correct answer is B. Here, try to remember the ballads you know and recall the names or techniques associated with them. For example, you might remember "Tom Dooley," and that a **ballad** is a poem that tells a story and originally was written to be sung. The language of a ballad is simple. It is a folk poem, not the product of sophisticated writers.

---

26. Read the passage below; then answer the question that follows.

Once I passed through a populous city imprinting my brain for future use with its shows, architecture, customs, traditions,
Yet now of all that city I remember only a woman I casually met there who detained me for love of me.
Day by day and night by night we were together—all else has long been forgotten by me.

The passage above is an example of:

    A. prose.
    B. free verse.
    C. a sonnet.
    D. metered poetry.

The correct answer is B. This question deals with the techniques of poetry. This passage is an example of free verse, which is not rhymed and which does not have a regular metrical pattern. Although these lines lack regular meter, they are more rhythmic than most prose. If the passage were prose, there would be no capital letter in *Yet*, which does not begin a sentence, and there would be no break in the continuity of the printing. Choice C, a sonnet, is a poem having fourteen lines, usually in iambic pentameter, and a formal arrangement of rhymes. This poem is obviously not in a formal arrangement of lines.

3.3 <u>Interpretation of Texts</u>

---

27. In literary criticism, which of the following best describes an omniscient point of view?

    A. The main theme of a story

    B. Developing characterization with a view to correcting the inherent flaws in the main characters in the story

    C. The author's ability to comment on the thoughts of the characters and the meaning of the action in a story

    D. The use of allegory in describing events

The correct answer is C. An **omniscient point of view** is a way of telling a story that allows the author to enter the minds of his or her characters. It is a vantage point from which the narrator can see, know, and report whatever he or she chooses. An omniscient point of view can use either the first or third person. The author is free to comment on the inner thoughts of characters while developing external details. Charles Dickens often employed the omniscient point of view.

Read the passage below; then answer the two questions that follow.

The quiet child is one of our concerns today. Our philosophy about children and speaking in the classroom has flip-flopped. Today we are interested in what Ruth Strickland implies when she refers to the idea of "freeing the child to talk."

28. Which of the following is implied by this passage?

    A. Teachers in the past have preferred quiet and reticent students.

    B. The behavior of children in the classroom is a trivial concern that can change abruptly.

    C. Whether or not a child is quiet determines the quality of his or her education.

    D. There are fewer quiet children today than in the past.

The correct answer is A. The final sentence in the passage expresses an interest in and appreciation for talking children, thus implying that the "flip-flop" is a change from the past preference for quiet children.

---

29. What is the tone of the passage?

    A. uncertain

    B. despairing

    C. apprehensive

    D. informational

The correct answer is D. Authors frequently make use of **tone** to communicate in writing what is often conveyed through facial expressions and voice inflections in verbal communication. It's not *what* is written, but rather *how* it is written that sets the tone. Although the passage starts out by mentioning concerns, there is no worry or apprehension in the passage. Since the passage provides information, the best description of the tone of the passage is informational.

30. Use the passage below from "The Notorious Jumping Frog of Calaveras County" by Mark Twain to answer the question that follows.

"Maybe you don't," Smiley says. "Maybe you understand frogs and maybe you don't understand 'em; maybe you've had experience, and maybe you ain't only a amature, as it were. Anyways, I've got my opinion, and I'll resk forty dollars that he can outjump any frog in Calaveras County."

The slang and spelling errors in the preceding passage indicate which of the following?

A. The author is nearly illiterate.

B. The reader is made to feel comfortable.

C. The rustic setting is emphasized.

D. The story is centuries old.

The correct answer is C. Twain used colloquial language to enhance the rustic setting essential to the battle of wits between sharper and bumpkin.

31. Use the excerpt from *Alice's Adventures in Wonderland* by Lewis Carroll to answer the question that follows.

The executioner's argument was that you couldn't cut off a head unless there was a body to cut if off from . . .

The King's argument was that anything that had a head could be beheaded, and that you weren't to talk nonsense.

The Queen's argument was that, if something wasn't done about it in less than no time, she'd have everybody executed, all around.

The discussion above about the Cheshire Cat shows the author's delight in:

A. compassion.

B. logic.

C. plot.

D. terror.

The correct answer is B. Lewis Carroll was an English mathematician whose delight in logic led him to write humorous poems and novels, which carry every point to a logical and very funny extreme. In the passage, the three arguments make a sort of ridiculous sense.

Sample Questions and Strategies for the Short Constructed-Response Section

The following are representative Reading, Language, and Literature short constructed-response questions for each area covered. Strategies are included, as well as a sample response for each exercise.

Domain 1: Language and Linguistics

> 1. Use the information below to complete the exercise that follows.
>
> After reading a big book to her students, who are gathered on the rug at the front of the room, the teacher asks one of her kindergarten students to find a "word" on the page of text and to "frame" that word with her hands. Then the teacher requests that the student frame any word on the page before her. The student comes to the front of the room where the big book is displayed and uses her hands to frame a whole line of text instead of just one word. After the teacher ascertains that the student has understood the task, she plans an intervention. Using your knowledge of reading instruction, discuss a classroom intervention that the teacher might plan for this student.

Strategy

Focus on the key words and the task to be completed. In this case, you are to discuss a classroom intervention. Note that this question describes a classroom scenario in which students are gathered to listen to the teacher read a big book. This is a common activity in early primary classrooms. The task that the teacher is asking the student to perform is described. Additionally, it is noted that the student understands the task.

Sample Response

Children in kindergarten are learning early conceptual skills to help prepare them to read. Teachers can help these beginning readers gain mastery of these skills by engaging them in activities that focus on *print concepts*. The mastery of print concepts is a reliable predictor of reading success. A good classroom intervention for a struggling student would include activities that promote print concepts, such as the understanding of "word." Some activities that the teacher could use are having the students track print as the teacher reads, counting words, and explaining that there are empty spaces between words. Some benchmarks in print concepts include identifying the front and back of the book, discriminating between a letter and a word, knowing uppercase and lowercase letters, recognizing word and sentence boundaries, knowing where to begin reading on a page, and understanding that print goes from top to bottom and left to right.

> 2. Complete the exercise that follows. Identify and discuss three factors that inhibit language acquisition during early to middle childhood.

Strategy

Notice the key phrases and the key words in the question. Notice that you need to identify and discuss three factors. Next, focus on factors that inhibit language acquisition. If some factors don't immediately come to mind, think of factors that would *help* in language acquisition. Then write about how the absence of those factors would inhibit language acquisition.

Sample Response

Three factors that inhibit language acquisition are insufficient mental, emotional, and social growth:

- **Mental growth**—As children grow mentally, they expand their ability to retain information. If this mental growth is slowed, words could be more difficult to learn and memorize.
- **Emotional growth**—As children come in touch with expressing their feelings, their language base usually expands. If a child has inhibitions or emotional problems, this could slow his or her need or will to acquire language.

- **Social growth**—As children learn to interact with other children, additional language becomes necessary. If this social growth is slowed, and there is less interest or exchange, language growth may be inhibited.

---

3. Use the information below to complete the exercise that follows.

   When evaluating a student's reading, a first-grade teacher notes that when reading orally, the student continually omits the silent "e." Shown below are the actual words as written and the mispronunciation by the student.

written word	student pronunciation
hate	hat
tape	tap
cope	cop

   Write a response in which you include explicit instruction and/or activities that would be helpful to the student. Make sure to cite specific examples to support your recommendations.

Strategy

Since you are given an in-class situation, carefully read the information to make sure that you understand the situation. Next, focus on the tasks to be completed and determine the key words—include explicit instruction and/or activities that would be helpful to the student. Make sure to cite specific examples to support your recommendations. Do some prewriting to list and organize your ideas.

Sample Response

The teacher needs to call the student's attention to whether what he or she is reading makes sense and do more explicit instruction in vowel recognition.

The student also needs explicit instruction in recognizing word patterns, especially those with the ending silent "e." The student would benefit from focused feedback and effective instruction in the role of the silent "e" in words.

Activities could include focused attention to the final "e," word sorting, and exposure to print that includes words of this type. This student needs to also focus on the similarities and differences of words. Word instruction using word-sorting games and simple word games would also be beneficial.

Domain 2: Nonwritten and Written Communication

---

4. Complete the exercise that follows.

   Standard American English is a dynamic language that is constantly changing. Write a response in which you

   - identify three reasons for these changes;
   - discuss these changes; and
   - give examples of these changes.

Strategy

Note the task given. In this case, you are asked for three reasons. Next, note the information given in the prompt. Read this carefully. Focus on key words in the prompt—*identify three, discuss, give examples*. When writing your answer, be sure to address each bullet. Also, use "buzzwords" when you can, that is, words that are used in the field and show knowledge of the subject.

Sample Response

Standard American English is constantly changing due to modern technology, infusion of foreign languages, and inclusion of slang expressions.

One reason that our language is changing is the necessity for new words that relate to modern technology. As we invent or discover new items or processes, new names must be created to describe the items or processes accurately. For example, the word *taser* refers to a new electronic self-defense mechanism.

A second reason for the change is the infusion of words from foreign languages. As foreign words are used more frequently, they become part of our vocabulary. For example, the word *valet* is of French origin,

A third reason for the change is the inclusion of words that were once considered slang expressions. These slang expressions give new meanings to words. For example, the expression *chill out* doesn't mean to become cold but rather to become calm.

---

5. Complete the exercise that follows.

   There are many techniques that an author may use to make a short story more interesting. Using your knowledge of writing, prepare a response in which you:

   - identify two techniques that an author can use to make a short story more interesting; and
   - describe how these techniques work.

Strategy

Read the question twice, noting key points, before attempting to answer it. You might write out <u>identify two techniques</u>, <u>short story</u>, <u>interesting</u>, <u>describe how</u>, and <u>work</u>. Ask yourself what techniques might make *any* prose more interesting. For example, you might consider figurative language, multiple points of view, flashback, or foreshadowing and then decide on the the two that seem most appropriate for the short story.

Sample Response

Two techniques that would make a short story more interesting are the use of flashback and foreshadowing:

- The use of **flashback**, a technique in which the narrative moves to a time prior to that of the main story, can make a short story more interesting by giving it depth. By using this technique, the author can reveal why characters are what they are and behave as they do, by showing the reader details of their earlier lives.
- **Foreshadowing** is a technique that uses clues to suggest events that have not yet occurred. It is often used to create suspense and thus make the story more interesting. Foreshadowing allows the author to link seemingly minor details to important events developed later in the story.

Domain 3: Texts

---

6. Read the following poem; then complete the exercise that follows.

   A slumber did my spirit seal
   I had no human fears:
   She seemed a thing that could not feel
   The touch of earthly years.
   (5) No motion has she now, no force,
   She neither hears nor sees;
   Rolled round in earth's diurnal course,
   With rocks, and stones, and trees.

   Write a response in which you explain the circumstance of this poem, that is, what has happened. Discuss the use of contrast in the poem.

Strategy

Read and note both of the tasks you are asked to perform: explain the circumstance of this poem (identify the speaker and what has happened), and discuss the contrast employed in the poem. As you read and focus on the poem, ask questions about the meaning and use of words. If some words do not make sense to you, try to interpret them in a metaphorical sense. Consider the rhyme scheme and whether the poem tells a story.

Focus on the use of specific words and their function in the meaning of the poem. For example, consider the word *slumber* in line 1 and the separation from the human condition in lines 3 and 4 (*could not feel / The touch of earthly years*). In lines 5 and 6, *no motion*, *no force*, and *neither hears nor sees* may be images associated with death. Note the negative words *no*, *neither*, and *nor*, which may suggest a contrast.

Sample Response

The first stanza describes the speaker's realization that "she" is dead and can no longer feel in a human way. The tense is the past. The second stanza, in the present tense, suggests a new reality for the woman. She has returned to the earth and has become a part of nature, just as much as the "rocks," "stones," and "trees."

The two stanzas contrast not only in the use of past and present tense, but also in that, in the first stanza, the speaker sees only the fact that the woman is dead, but by the end of the second stanza, he or she has realized that even though she, herself, has "no motion" and "no force," she shares in the movement of the "earth's diurnal course."

---

7. Read the poem below by Samuel Daniel (1595); then complete the exercise that follows.

> When men shall find thy flower, thy glory pass,
> And thou, with careful brow sitting alone,
> Received hast this message from thy glass,
> That tells thee truth, and says that all is gone,
> (5) Fresh shalt thou see in me the wounds thou madest,
> Though spent thy flame, in me the heat remaining,
> I that have loved thee thus before thou fadest;
> My faith shall wax, when thou art in thy waning.
> The world shall find this miracle in me,
> (10) That fire can burn when all the matter's spent;
> Then what my faith hath been thyself shall see,
> And that thou wast unkind thou mayst repent.
> Thou mayest repent that thou hast scorned my tears,
> When winter snows upon thy golden hairs.

Write a response in which you:

- Describe the situation of this poem. Who is the speaker and the person addressed and what are their circumstances?
- Discuss the images the speaker uses to describe the woman and to describe his feelings.

Strategy

You may wish to try the approach of assessing the tasks first and then reading the poem. In this way, you'll know what to look for as you read. As you read the tasks, write out the words describe the situation. You should also write out speaker, person addressed, and circumstances. Next, write out discuss the images the speaker uses. Now that you are focused in on what to look for, carefully read the poem. Remember, you are asking the following questions: "Who is the speaker?" "Who is the speaker talking to?" "What are the circumstances?" "What images is the speaker using to describe the woman and the author's feelings?"

Sample Response

The speaker of this poem is a man addressing a beautiful young woman with whom he is in love. The young woman does not return the man's love, but he nevertheless vows to be faithful to her, even when she has grown old and is no longer beautiful. The lady's youth is indicated by the verb tenses (the future tense of "shall find" and "shall see") and by the phrase "before thou fadest." At the time of the poem, the lady's golden hair has not yet turned white.

The poem compares the lady's beauty to a flower, to a flame, and to the fuel that feeds the flame of the man's love. The man's love is compared to wounds, to heat, to faith, and to a miracle. The most important source of imagary is religious, and the speaker's love is presented as a religious veneration of the lady. His love is miraculous because like a fire that burns without fuel, it will continue even after the beauty, which inspired his love, has faded away.

Review of Domains

> "Reading is at the heart of education. The knowledge of almost every subject in school flows from reading."
> —Jim Trelease (2001)

Domain 1: Language and Linguistics

Teaching children to read effectively may be the single most significant contribution toward the educational achievement of the developing child. The acquisition of solid reading skills opens the doorway to all other academic disciplines as it provides children with unlimited access to new information while strengthening cognitive brain structures. The path toward literacy begins during early childhood and continues through adolescence and into adulthood. Children do not have to be highly intelligent to become successful readers, but it is important for children to develop early reading skills in order to gain opportunities for future learning possibilities. The CSET: Multiple Subjects identifies the need for potential teachers to demonstrate their competency at providing children with skilled literature and language instruction.

Stages of Reading Development		
THE EMERGENT READER		
Age	**Developmental Expectation**	**Reading Instruction**
Early Childhood to Pre-K Pre-alphabetic	Beginning of awareness that text progresses from left to right. Children scribble and recognize distinctive visual clues in environmental print, such as letters in their names.	Begin phonemic awareness ■ Help to recognize print in environment ■ Help to make predictions in stories ■ Observe pretending to read ■ Help to recognize letter shapes
THE BEGINNING READER		
K to Second (Third) Grade Alphabetic	Letters are associated with sounds. Children begin to read simple CVC words (such as mat, sun, pin). They usually represent such words with a single sound, and later spell with the first and last consonant: for example, CT for cat. When writing later, vowels are included in each syllable. Children now rhyme and blend words. When reading later, they begin to recognize "chunks," or phonograms.	Systematic and explicit instruction, including: ■ Phonics, phonemic awareness, blending, decoding ■ Vocabulary word-attack skills, spelling ■ Text comprehension ■ Listening and writing
THE FLUENT READER		
Fourth to Eighth Grade Orthographic	Students read larger units of print and use analogy to decode larger words. Decoding becomes fluent. Reading, accuracy, and speed are stressed.	Systematic and explicit instruction, including: ■ Word-attack skills (multisyllabic words) ■ Decoding ■ Spelling and vocabulary ■ Fluency ■ Text comprehension (context skills) ■ Utilizing metacognition
THE REMEDIAL READER		
Third to Eighth Grade Students who do not demonstrate competency	The key approach to successful reading programs is preventive rather than remedial while understanding that there is a full range of learners in the classroom. Therefore, students who are struggling to read are taught from the same systematic framework taught in the early grades of successful readers.	Reading instruction includes re-teaching all of the modalities taught as a "beginning reader" listed above and emphasizing: ■ Assessment of identified reading weakness ■ Teaching explicit strategies based on diagnosis ■ Linking instruction to prior knowledge ■ Increasing instruction time ■ Dividing skills into smaller steps while providing reinforcement and positive feedback

READING TERMS AND DEFINITIONS	
Phoneme	A phoneme is the smallest part of spoken language that makes a difference in the meaning of words. English has about 41 phonemes. A few words, such as *a* or *oh*, have only one phoneme. Most words, however, have more than one phoneme: The word *if* has two phonemes (/i/ /f/); *check* has three phonemes (/ch/ /e/ /k/), and *stop* has four phonemes (/s/ /t/ /o/ /p/). Sometimes one phoneme is represented by more than one letter.
Phoneme Manipulation	When children work with phonemes in words, they are manipulating the phonemes. Types of phoneme manipulation include blending phonemes to make words, segmenting words into phonemes, deleting phonemes from words, adding phonemes to words, or substituting one phoneme for another to make a new word.
Grapheme	A grapheme is the smallest part of written language that represents a phoneme in the spelling of a word. A grapheme may be just one letter (such as b, d, f, p, s) or several letters (such as ch, sh, th, -ck, ea, -igh).
Phonics	Phonics is the understanding that there is a predictable relationship between phonemes (the sounds of spoken language) and graphemes (the letters and spellings that represent those sounds in written language). Good phonics instruction is systematic and explicit. **Systematic** is a plan of instruction which includes a carefully selected set of letter-sound relationships that are organized into a logical sequence. **Explicit** programs provide teachers with precise directions for the teaching of these relationships. Phonics instruction is most effective when it begins in kindergarten or first grade, and approximately two years of phonics instruction is sufficient for most students.
Phonemic Awareness	Phonemic awareness is the ability to hear, identify, and manipulate the individual sounds—phonemes—in spoken words. It is the understanding that sounds work together to make words, and it is the most important determinant toward becoming a successful reader.
Phonological Awareness	Phonological awareness is a broad term that includes phonemic awareness. In addition to phonemes, phonological awareness activities can involve work with rhymes, words, syllables, and onsets and rimes.
Syllable	A syllable is a word part that contains a vowel or, in spoken language, a vowel sound (e-vent; news-pa-per; ver-y).
Decoding	Decoding is the analysis of spoken or written symbols in order to understand their meaning. This primarily refers to word identification.
Segmenting (Segmentation)	When children break words into their individual phonemes, they are segmenting the words. They are also segmenting when they break words into syllables and syllables into onsets and rimes.
Onset and Rime	Onsets and rimes are parts of spoken language that are smaller than syllables but larger than phonemes. An onset is the initial consonant(s) sound of a syllable (the onset of bag is b-; of swim, sw-). A rime is the part of a syllable that contains the vowel and all that follows it (the rime of bag is -ag; of swim, -im).
Blending	When children combine individual phonemes to form words, they are blending the phonemes. They also are blending when they combine onsets and rimes to make syllables and combine syllables to make words.
Morpheme	A morpheme is a unit of meaning that cannot be divided into smaller elements, such as the word "book."
Semantics	Semantics is the analysis and study of meanings of words, phrases, and sentences. This is useful as a strategy in decoding to analyze the word that "sounds" correct in a sentence.
Syntax	Syntax is the examination of various ways that words combine to create meaning, the study of how sentences are formed, and the pattern or structure of word order in sentences.

Language Key Terms and Concepts

Child-directed speech (CDS) or motherese: Adults modify their speech to make it easier for children to learn language, including modifying sentence structure, repeating key words, and focusing on present objects. First words are spoken by 12 months and are usually familiar objects or persons. First sentences are spoken by 18 to 24 months and are usually two-word sentences (telegraphic speech).

Fast mapping: A process whereby young children are able to use context to arrive at a quick guess of a word's meaning. Nouns (objects) are easier to fast map than verbs (actions).

Habituation: Infants and children repeat sounds that are reinforced. Children can distinguish abstract rules for sentence structure. For example, in an experiment, a 7-month-old listened to nonsense sounds (wo fe wo). When changed to (ga ti ti), the infant was able to discriminate based upon the patterns of repetition.

Holophrase: A single word that expresses a complete thought. These include *symbolic gestures*, where the child shows an understanding that symbols (words) represent a specific object, desire, or event (e.g., blowing on food to mean *hot*), or *representational gestures*, which involve gesturing to show what the infant desires (e.g., holding up a bottle to show an infant wants more to drink).

Overregularizations: In early childhood, children begin to use past tenses and plurals in speech. About this time, they also begin to add regular forms on irregular nouns, saying "foots" instead of "feet."

Private speech: Talking out loud to oneself with no intention to communicate with others. This helps children to integrate language and thought.

Telegraphic speech: Simplified speech or an early form of speech. This is usually a two-word sentence spoken by a 2-year-old. First sentences consist of just enough words to get the meaning across (e.g., I cold).

Reading Assessments

Formal and informal reading assessments are used with students in grades K through 8 to target areas of strength and weakness, to monitor student reading development, and to aid the teacher in planning reading instruction.

Alphabet knowledge: Identify and form letters.

Concepts about print: Tests important concepts about books, including the front and back of a book; that print tells the story; the concept of letters, words, and sentences; and that spaces have a purpose.

Phonemic awareness: Estimates the level of phonemic awareness in students.

Phonics test: Tests phonics skills that are needed in reading.

High frequency word recognition: Measures word recognition out of context. In general, proficient readers can read words in and out of context, and poor readers over-rely on context for decoding. This also assists the teacher in determining a level to start testing in oral reading inventories.

Oral reading inventory: Graded passages that give an indication of the fluency with which a student is able to read. Also evaluated are accuracy, reading rate, reading level, and comprehension level.

Spelling inventory: Through examination of words spelled correctly and incorrectly, a student's skills can be classified into developmental spelling stages. In this way, skills are examined that directly tie to reading. This assists in planning appropriate spelling and reading instruction.

Phonemic Awareness

Phonemic awareness is the ability to notice, think about, and work with the individual sounds in spoken words. This awareness is strongly related to reading achievement. To become proficient readers, children must be able to perceive and produce specific sounds of the English language and understand how the sound system works. Before children learn to read print, they need to become aware of how the sounds in words work. They must understand that words are made up of speech sounds, or phonemes. **Phonemes** are the smallest parts of sound in a spoken word that make a difference in the word's meaning.

Although phonemic awareness is a widely-used term in reading, phonemic awareness is *not* phonics. Phonemic awareness is the understanding that the sounds of *spoken* language work together to make words. Phonics is the understanding that there is a predictable relationship between phonemes and graphemes, the letters that represent those sounds in *written* language. If children are to benefit from phonics instruction, they need phonemic awareness. The reason is that children who cannot hear and work with the phonemes of spoken words will have a difficult time learning how to relate these phonemes to the graphemes when they see them in written words.

Implications of Teaching Phonemic Awareness in the Classroom

1. Teachers help children recognize which words in a set of words begin with the same sound. ("*Bell, bike,* and *boy* all have /b/ at the beginning.")
2. Teachers help children isolate and say the first or last sound in a word. ("The beginning sound of *dog* is /d/." "The ending sound of *sit* is /t/.")
3. Teachers help children combine or blend separate sounds in a word to say the word ("/m/, /a/, /p/—**map**").
4. Teachers help children break or segment a word into its separate sounds ("up—/u/, /p/").

Classroom Expectations: How to Teach Phonemic Awareness

Effective phonemic awareness instruction teaches children to notice, think about, and work with (manipulate) sounds in spoken language. This helps children become aware of English sound systems, consonants, and vowels. Teachers can use a variety of instructional methods; however, teaching one or two types of phoneme manipulation—specifically, blending and segmenting phonemes in words—is likely to produce greater benefits. Instruction should also be explicit about the connection between phonemic awareness and reading.

An Example of Teaching Phoneme Manipulation—Blending and Segmenting		
Step One		Teacher: Listen: I'm going to say the sounds in the word **jam**—/j/ /a/ /m/. What is the word?
Step Two	Say the word out loud	Teacher: You say the sounds in the word **jam**.
Step Three	Write the word down	Teacher: Now let's write the sounds in **jam**: /j/, write **j**; /a/, write **a**; /m/, write **m**.
Step Four	Read the word together	Teacher: (Writes "jam" on the board). Now we're going to read the word **jam**.

Phonological Awareness

A common misunderstanding about phonemic awareness is that it means the same as phonological awareness. The two names are *not* interchangeable. Phonemic awareness is a subcategory of phonological awareness. The focus of phonemic awareness is narrow—identifying and manipulating the individual sounds in words. The focus of **phonological awareness** is much broader. It includes identifying and manipulating larger parts of spoken language, such as words, syllables, and onsets and rimes—as well as phonemes. It also encompasses awareness of other aspects of sound, such as rhyming, alliteration, and intonation.

Implications of Teaching Phonological Awareness in the Classroom

1. Teachers help children identify and make oral rhymes. *"The pig has a (wig)."*
   "Pat the (cat)."
   "The sun is (fun)."
2. Teachers help children identify and work with syllables in spoken words: *"I can clap the parts in my name: An-drew."*
3. Teachers help children identify and work with onsets and rimes in spoken syllables or one-syllable words. *"The first part of sip is s-."* *"The last part of win is -in."*

Phonics

Phonics instruction teaches children the relationships between the letters (graphemes) of written language and the individual sounds (phonemes) of spoken language. It teaches children to use these relationships to read and write words. Teachers of reading programs sometimes use different labels to describe these relationships, including the following:

- graphophonemic relationships
- letter-sound associations
- letter-sound correspondences
- sound-symbol correspondences
- sound-spellings

Regardless of the label, the goal of phonics instruction is to help children learn and use the Alphabetic Principle—the understanding that there are systematic and predictable relationships between written letters and spoken sounds. Knowing these relationships will help children recognize familiar words accurately and automatically and "decode" new words. In short, knowledge of the Alphabetic Principle contributes greatly to children's ability to read words both in isolation and in connected text.

Criticisms of Phonics Instruction

Critics of phonics instruction argue that English spellings are too irregular for phonics instruction to really help children learn to read words. The point is, however, that phonics instruction teaches children a system for remembering how to read words. Once children learn, for example, that *phone* is spelled this way rather than *foan*, their memory helps them to read, spell, and recognize the word instantly and more accurately than they could read *foan*. The same process is true for all irregularly spelled words. Most of these words contain some regular letter-sound relationships that can help children remember how to read them. In summary, the alphabetic system is a mnemonic device that supports our memory for specific words.

Implications of Teaching Phonics in the Classroom

1. **Assess** phonics and other word identification strategies. Select and use formal and informal tools such as decoding tests, fluency tests, and sight word checks to collect data, and analyze to plan instruction.
2. **Plan** instruction that is systematic, explicit, and sequenced according to the increased complexity of linguistic units including sounds, phonemes, onsets and rimes, letters, letter combination syllables, and morphemes.
3. **Explicitly** teach and model phonics, decoding, and other word identification strategies in reading for meaning. Positive explicit feedback for word identification errors is an essential strategy in this process.
4. **Select** and design resource material and strategies for assessment and instruction. Resources include materials for teaching decoding, word identification strategies, and sign word mastery in multiple and varied reading and writing experiences.
5. **Provide fluency practice** in a variety of ways:
   - Practice **decoding** and word-attack skills so that they become **automatic** in reading text.
   - Provide **application** and practice decoding skills to fluency in decodable (controlled vocabulary) text and word recognition skills taught out of context.
   - Continue to **develop fluency** through the use of decodable texts and other texts written at the student's instructional level.
6. **Provide ongoing assessment** to demonstrate the student's progress toward the mastery of State Standards.

Systematic and Explicit Instruction

Programs of systematic phonics instruction clearly identify a carefully selected and useful set of letter-sound relationships and then organize the introduction of these relationships into a logical instructional sequence. Children learn to use these relationships to decode words that contain them. Systematic instruction is *particularly beneficial for children who are having difficulty learning to read* and who are at risk for developing future reading problems.

Effective programs offer phonics instruction that:

- helps teachers explicitly and systematically instruct students in how to relate letters and sounds, how to break spoken words into sounds, and how to blend sounds to form words.
- helps students understand why they are learning the relationships between letters and sounds.
- helps students apply their knowledge of phonics as they read words, sentences, and text.
- helps students apply what they learn about sounds and letters to their own writing.
- can be adapted to the needs of individual students, based on assessment.
- includes alphabetic knowledge, phonemic awareness, vocabulary development, and the reading of text, as well as systematic phonics instruction.

Non-Systematic Instruction

Programs of phonics instruction that are not systematic do not teach consonant and vowel letter-sound relationships in a prescribed sequence. Rather, they encourage informal phonics instruction based on the teacher's perceptions of what students need to learn and when they need to learn it. Non-systematic instruction often neglects vowels, even though knowing vowel letter-sound relationships is a crucial part of knowing the alphabetic system. Non-systematic programs do not provide practice materials that offer children the opportunity to apply what they are learning about letter-sound relationships.

Non-systematic programs often include:

- literature-based programs that emphasize reading and writing activities. Phonics instruction is embedded in these activities, but letter-sound relationships are taught incidentally, usually based on key letters that appear in student reading materials.
- basal reading programs that focus on whole-word or meaning-based activities. These programs pay only limited attention to letter-sound relationships and provide little or no instruction in how to blend letters to pronounce words.
- sight-word programs that begin by teaching children a sight-word reading vocabulary of from 50 to 100 words. Only after they learn to read these words do children receive instruction in the Alphabetic Principle.

Fluency

Fluent readers read aloud effortlessly and with expression. Their reading sounds natural, as if they are speaking.

Fluency is the ability to read a text accurately and quickly. When fluent readers read silently, they recognize words automatically. They group words quickly to help them gain meaning from what they read. Fluent readers read aloud effortlessly and with expression. Their reading sounds natural, as if they are speaking. Readers who have not yet developed fluency read slowly, word by word. Their oral reading is choppy and plodding.

Fluency is important because it provides a bridge between word recognition and comprehension. Because fluent readers do not have to concentrate on decoding the words, they can focus their attention on what the text means. They can make connections among the ideas in the text and between the text and their background knowledge. Fluent readers recognize words and comprehend at the same time and focus their attention on making connections among the ideas in a text and between these ideas and their background knowledge. Less fluent readers focus their attention on figuring out the words and tend to have little attention left for comprehending the text.

Fluency develops gradually over considerable time and through substantial practice. At the earliest stage of reading development, students' oral reading is slow and labored because students are just learning to "break the code"—to attach sounds to letters and to blend letter sounds into recognizable words. Even very skilled readers may read in a slow, labored manner when reading texts with many unfamiliar words or topics.

Even when students recognize many words automatically, their oral reading still may be expressionless, not fluent. To read with expression, readers *must be able to divide the text into meaningful chunks*. These chunks include phrases and clauses. Readers must know to pause appropriately within and at the ends of sentences and when to change emphasis and tone.

Implications of Teaching Fluency Instruction in the Classroom

1. Teachers are good models of fluent reading. By listening, students learn how a reader's voice can help written text make sense.
2. Teachers should read aloud to students daily.
3. Teachers should help students practice orally rereading text that is reasonably easy for them—that is, text containing mostly words that they know or can decode easily. In other words, the texts should be at the students' independent reading level and relatively short (probably 50 to 200 words) depending upon the age.
4. Teachers should assess to see if the text is at the students' independent reading level. The student should be able to read with about 95 percent accuracy, or misread only about 1 of every 20 words. If the text is more difficult, students will focus so much on word recognition that they will not have an opportunity to develop fluency.
5. Teachers use a variety of reading materials, including stories, nonfiction, and poetry. Poetry is especially well suited to fluency practice because poems for children are often short and they contain rhythm, rhyme, and meaning, making practice easy, fun, and rewarding.

Reading Difficulty Assessment

Easy Text: Readers show that no more than 1 in 20 words are difficult (95 percent success).

Challenging Text: Readers show that no more than 1 in 10 words are difficult (90 percent success).

Difficult Text: Readers show that more than 1 in 10 words are difficult (less than 90 percent success).

Instructional Strategy: How to Calculate Fluency

Total words read – errors = words correct per minute

1. Select two or three brief passages from appropriate grade-level material (regardless of students' instructional levels).
2. Have individual students read each passage aloud for exactly one minute.
3. Count the total number of words the student read for each passage. Compute the average number of words read per minute.
4. Count the number of errors the student made on each passage. Compute the average number of errors per minute.
5. Subtract the average number of errors read per minute from the average total number of words read per minute. The result is the average number of words correct per minute (WCPM).
6. Repeat the procedure several times during the year. Graphing students' WCPM throughout the year easily captures their reading growth.
7. Compare the results with published norms or standards to determine whether students are making suitable progress in their fluency. For example, according to one published norm, students should be reading approximately 60 words per minute correctly by the end of first grade, 90 to 100 words per minute correctly by the end of second grade, and approximately 114 words per minute correctly by the end of third grade.

Reading Aloud Exercises				
Student-Adult Reading	**Choral Reading**	**Tape-Assisted Reading**	**Partner Reading**	**Readers' Theatre**
In student-adult reading, the student reads one-on-one with an adult. The adult can be you, a parent, a classroom aide, or a tutor. The adult reads the text first, providing the students with a model of fluent reading. Then the student reads the same passage to the adult with the adult providing assistance and encouragement. The student rereads the passage until the reading is quite fluent. This should take approximately three to four rereadings.	In choral, or unison, reading, students read along as a group with you (or another fluent adult reader). They might follow along as you read from a big book, or they might read from their own copy of the book you are reading. Predictable books are particularly useful for choral reading, because their repetitious style invites students to join in. Begin by reading the book aloud as you model fluent reading. Students should read the book with you three to five times total (though not necessarily on the same day). At this time, students should be able to read the text independently.	In tape-assisted reading, students read along in their books as they hear a fluent reader read the book on an audiotape. For tape-assisted reading, you need a book at a student's independent reading level and a tape recording of the book read by a fluent reader at about 80 to 100 words per minute. The tape should not have sound effects or music. For the first reading, the student should follow along with the tape, pointing to each word in her or his book as the reader reads it. Next, the student should try to read aloud along with the tape. Reading along with the tape should continue until the student is able to read the book independently, without the support of the tape.	In partner reading, paired students take turns reading aloud to each other. More fluent readers can be paired with less fluent readers. The stronger reader reads a paragraph or page first, providing a model of fluent reading. Then the less fluent reader reads the same text aloud. The stronger student gives help with word recognition and provides feedback and encouragement to the less fluent partner. The less fluent partner rereads the passage until he or she can read it independently. Partner reading need not be done with a more and less fluent reader. Two readers of equal ability can practice rereading after hearing the teacher read the passage.	In readers' theatre, students rehearse and perform a play for peers or others. They read from scripts that have been derived from books that are rich in dialogue. Students play characters who speak lines or a narrator who shares necessary background information. Readers' theatre provides readers with a legitimate reason to reread text and to practice fluency. Readers' theatre also promotes cooperative interaction with peers and makes the reading task appealing.

Vocabulary

Vocabulary refers to the words we must know to communicate effectively. In general, vocabulary can be described as oral vocabulary or reading vocabulary. **Oral vocabulary** refers to words that we use in speaking or recognize in listening. **Reading vocabulary** refers to words we recognize or use in print.

Implications of Teaching Vocabulary Instruction in the Classroom

Implement Strategies for Teaching Specific Words

A teacher plans to have his third-grade class read the novel *Stone Fox* by John Reynolds Gardiner. In this novel, a young boy enters a dogsled race in hopes of winning prize money to pay the taxes on his grandfather's farm. The teacher knows that understanding the concept of taxes is important to understanding the novel's plot. Therefore, before his students begin reading the novel, the teacher may do several things to make sure they understand what the concept means and why it is important to the story. For example, the teacher may:

- engage students in a discussion of the concept of taxes.
- read a sentence from the book that contains the word *taxes* and ask students to use context and their prior knowledge to try to figure out what it means.
- ask students to use *taxes* in their own sentence.

Provide Repeated Exposure to Words

A second-grade class is reading a biography of Benjamin Franklin. The biography discusses Franklin's important role as a scientist. The teacher wants to make sure that her students understand the meaning of the words *science* and *scientist*, both because the words are important to understanding the biography and because they are obviously very useful words to know in school and in everyday life.

Use Word Parts

Knowing some common prefixes and suffixes (affixes), base words, and root words can help students learn the meanings of many new words. For example, if students learn just the four most common prefixes in English (un-, re-, in-, dis-), they will have important clues about the meaning of about two-thirds of all English words that have prefixes. Prefixes are relatively easy to learn because they have clear meanings (for example, *un-* means *not* and *re-* means *again*); they are usually spelled the same way from word to word; and, of course, they always occur at the beginnings of words.

Use Context Clues

Context clues are hints about the meaning of an unknown word that are provided in the words, phrases, and sentences that surround the word. Context clues include definitions, restatements, examples, or descriptions. Because students learn most word meanings indirectly, or from context, it is important that they learn to use context clues effectively.

Use Dictionaries and Other Reference Aids

When students use reference aids, they can easily eliminate inappropriate definitions based upon context of the defined word. For example, in searching for the definition of the word *board* in a dictionary, students can eliminate the wrong definitions of *board* by looking at the word in the context of the sentence. In this example, one definition of *board* is, "to get on a train, an airplane, a bus, or a ship." The teacher next has students substitute the most likely definition for *board* in the original sentence to verify that the sentence makes sense. "The children were waiting to *get on* the buses."

Text Comprehension

Even teachers in the primary grades can begin to build the foundation for reading comprehension. Reading is a complex process that develops over time. Although the basics of reading—word recognition and fluency—can be learned in a few years, reading to learn subject matter does not occur automatically. Teachers should emphasize text comprehension from the beginning, rather than waiting until students have mastered "the basics" of reading. Instruction at all grade levels can benefit from showing students how reading is a process of making sense out of text, or constructing meaning. Beginning readers, as well as more advanced readers, must understand that the ultimate goal of reading is comprehension.

Metacognition

Metacognition can be defined as "thinking about thinking." Good readers use metacognitive strategies to think about and have control over their reading. Before reading, they might clarify their purpose for reading and preview the text. During reading, they might monitor their understanding, adjusting their reading speed to fit the difficulty of the text and "fixing up" any comprehension problems they have. After reading, they check their understanding of what they read.

Implications of Teaching Comprehension Instruction in the Classroom

Multiple strategies are available to help students gain reading comprehension competency. Teachers can help students improve reading comprehension skills by practicing the following multiple strategies:

- ask questions about the text they are reading.
- ask students to summarize parts of the text.
- help students clarify words and sentences they don't understand.
- ask students to predict what might occur next in the text.
- talk about the content.
- model, or "think aloud," about their own thinking and understanding.
- lead students in a discussion about text meaning.
- help students relate the content of their reading to their life experiences and to other texts they have read.

The first four of the above are the primary strategies.

TEXT COMPREHENSION CLASSROOM ACTIVITIES	
Monitoring Comprehension	Students who are good at monitoring their comprehension know when they understand what they read and when they do not. They have strategies to "fix" problems in their understanding as the problems arise. - Identify **where** the difficulty occurs. ("I don't understand the second paragraph on page 76.") - Identify **what** the difficulty is. ("I don't get what the author means when she says, 'Arriving in America was a milestone in my grandmother's life.'") - **Restate** the difficult sentence or passage in their own words. ("Oh, so the author means that coming to America was a very important event in her grandmother's life.") - **Look back** through the text. ("The author talked about Mr. McBride in Chapter 2, but I don't remember much about him. Maybe if I reread that chapter, I can figure out why he's acting this way now.") - **Look forward** in the text for information that might help them to resolve the difficulty. ("The text says, 'The groundwater may form a stream or pond or create a wetland. People can also bring groundwater to the surface.' Hmm, I don't understand how people can do that . . . Oh, the next section is called 'Wells.' I'll read this section to see if it tells how they do it.")
Using Graphic and Semantic Organizers	**Graphic organizers** illustrate concepts and interrelationships among concepts in a text, using diagrams or other pictorial devices. Graphic organizers are known by different names, such as maps, webs, graphs, charts, frames, or clusters. **Semantic organizers** (also called *semantic maps* or *semantic webs*) are graphic organizers that look somewhat like a spider web. In a semantic organizer, lines connect a central concept to a variety of related ideas and events.
Answering Questions	Question-answering instruction encourages students to learn to answer questions better and, therefore, to learn more as they read. One type of question-answering instruction simply teaches students to look back in the text to find answers to questions that they cannot answer after the initial reading. Another type helps students understand question-answer relationships—the relationships between questions and where the answers to those questions are found. In this instruction, readers learn to answer questions that require an understanding of information.
Generating Questions	Teaching students to ask their own questions improves their active processing of text and their comprehension. By generating questions, students become aware of whether they can answer the questions and whether they understand what they are reading. Students learn to ask themselves questions that require them to integrate information from different segments of text.

Recognizing Story Structure	**Story structure** refers to the way the content and events of a story are organized into a plot. Students who can recognize story structure have greater appreciation, understanding, and memory of stories. In story structure instruction, students learn to identify the categories of content (setting, initiating events, internal reactions, goals, attempts, and outcomes) and how this content is organized into a plot. Often, students learn to recognize story structure through the use of story maps. Story maps, a type of graphic organizer, show the sequence of events in simple stories. Instruction in the content and organization of stories improves students' comprehension and memory of stories.
Summarizing	A **summary** is a synthesis of the important ideas in a text. Summarizing requires students to determine what is important in what they are reading, to condense this information, and to put it into their own words. Instruction in summarizing helps students identify or generate main ideas, connect the main or central ideas, eliminate redundant and unnecessary information, and remember what they read.
Making Use of Prior Knowledge	Good readers draw on prior knowledge and experience to help them understand what they are reading. You can help your students make use of their prior knowledge to improve their comprehension. Before your students read, preview the text with them. As part of previewing, ask the students what they already know about the content of the selection (for example, the topic, the concept, or the time period). Ask them what they know about the author and what text structure he or she is likely to use. Discuss the important vocabulary used in the text. Show students some pictures or diagrams to prepare them for what they are about to read.
Using Mental Imagery	Good readers often form mental pictures, or images, as they read. Readers (especially younger readers) who visualize during reading understand and remember what they read better than readers who do not visualize. Help your students learn to form visual images of what they are reading. For example, urge them to picture a setting, character, or event described in the text.

Domain 2: Nonwritten and Written Communication

2.1 Conventions of Language

Selective Review of Grammar and Usage

CSET candidates should focus on understanding the basic knowledge of grammar, word choice (usage), sentence structure, punctuation, and spelling of standard written English. This selected review of grammar and usage is intended to familiarize you with common grammatical rules and conventions.

Subject-Verb Agreement

First focus on the verb or verbs. A plural subject goes with a plural verb; a singular subject goes with a singular verb. Following is an example of an error in subject-verb agreement:

> *Here on the table is an apple and three pears.*

Focus on the verb (*is*) and ask yourself what the subject is. In this sentence, the subject (*an apple and three pears*) follows the verb. Since the subject is plural, the verb must be plural — *are* instead of *is*. The correct sentence should read:

> *Here on the table are an apple and three pears.*

Verb Tenses

Another verb error occurs when the verb tenses (past, present, future) are inconsistent. Most verbs are regular. For example:

Past: I walked yesterday.

Present: I walk today.

Future: I will walk tomorrow.

If there are two verbs in the sentence, make sure that the verb tense of each is appropriate. Here's an example of an incorrect verb tense:

He _walked_ for miles and finally _sees_ a sign of civilization.

Walked describes the past; sees describes the present. Sees must be changed to <u>saw</u> so that the whole sentence describes the past. The correct sentence should read: _He walked for miles and finally saw a sign of civilization._

Some verbs are irregular and require special constructions to express the past and past participle. Here are some of the most troublesome irregular verbs.

Some Troublesome Irregular Verbs		
Present	**Past**	**Past Participle**
begin	began	begun
do	did	done
go	went	gone
hang (to execute)	hanged	hanged
hang (to suspend)	hung	hung
lay (to put in place)	laid	laid
lie (to rest)	lay	lain
sit (to be seated)	sat	sat
raise (to lift up)	raised	raised
rise (to get up)	rose	risen
swim	swam	swum

Adjectives and Adverbs

A common error is using an adjective when an adverb is required or vice versa. Adjectives describe things (nouns and pronouns), and adverbs describe actions (verbs). Here's an example of an error:

The mechanic _repaired_ my engine and _installed_ a new clutch _very quick_.

In this case, actions are being described (_repaired_ and _installed_ are verbs), so the word that describes those actions should be an adverb, _quickly_ instead of _quick_. As you might notice, adverbs often end with _–ly_. The correct use of the adjective _quick_ in a sentence occurs in this example: "The quick work of the mechanic pleased me very much." In this case, a thing is being described (_work_), so an adjective is appropriate.

Pronouns

A pronoun takes the place of a noun. Watch for correct pronoun references, and note whether the pronoun should be in the subjective or objective case. Following is an example of a pronoun error:

We rewarded the workers _whom_, according to the manager, _had done_ the most imaginative job.

To test between _who_ and _whom_, try replacing _whom_ with either _him_ or _them:_ "them…had done the most imaginative job." To test whether _who_ is correct instead, try substituting _he_ or _they:_ "they…had done the most imaginative job." Remember, if _him_ or _them_ fits when substituted, _whom_ is correct. If _he_ or _they_ fits when substituted, _who_ is correct. The correct sentence should read: _We rewarded the workers who, according to the manager, had done the most imaginative job._

Parallelism

Phrases in a sentence are parallel when they have the same grammatical structure. Here is an example of an error in faulty parallelism:

He liked swimming, weight lifting, and to run.

To run is incorrect. It should be an *–ing* word like the other items. The correct sentence should read:

He liked swimming, weight lifting, and running.

Idioms

To native English speakers, certain expressions "sound right" because they are so commonly used. Such expressions are "idiomatic" and are correct simply because they are so widely accepted. Following is an example of an error in idiom expression:

The young man had been <u>addicted of</u> drugs ever since his thirteenth birthday.

The correct idiom is *addicted to*, not addicted of.

Dangling or Misplaced Modifiers

A dangling modifier is an introductory phrase that does not refer clearly or logically to a subsequent modifier (usually the subject) in a sentence. A misplaced modifier is one that is placed too close to a word that it could but should not modify. Here's an example of a dangling modifier:

Strolling along the beach, a wave suddenly drenched us.

This sentence seems to say that the *wave* is doing the *strolling.* A correct sentence clarifies the modifier as follows:

While we were strolling along the beach, a wave suddenly drenched us.

Following is an example of a misplaced modifier:

Ann prepared a roast for the family that was served burned.

In this case, because *that was served burned* is so close to *family,* the sentence seems to say that the *family* was *burned.* Here is a corrected version.

Ann served a burned roast to the family.

Note that this correction also eliminates excessive words.

Punctuation: The Comma and the Semicolon

The Comma

Certain parts of sentences are separated from one another by using a comma.

Use a comma before a coordinating conjunction in a compound sentence. Example:

I felt happy about my new job, <u>but</u> the pay was not quite enough.

Use a comma to set off interrupting or introductory words or phrases. Example:

<u>*Safe in the house*</u>*, we watched the rain fall outside.*

Use a comma to separate a series of words or word groups. Example:

<u>*Diet*</u>*,* <u>*exercise*</u>*, and* <u>*rest*</u> *all contribute to good health.*

Use a comma to set off nonessential clauses and phrases that are descriptive but not needed to get across the basic meaning of the sentence. Such phrases are termed nonrestrictive. Example:

Harold, <u>who dislikes school</u>, is failing English.

Use a comma to set off appositives (second noun or noun equivalents that give additional information about a preceding noun). Example:

Mr. Johnson, <u>a teacher</u>, ran for chairman of the school board.

The Semicolon

The semicolon is like a balance. It always separates elements of equal power of meaning: two or more words, phrases, or sentences. *It should never separate a main clause from a subordinate clause or a word or phrase from a clause.*

Use a semicolon to separate main clauses when the separation is not done by a coordinating conjunction (and, but, or, nor, for). Example:

Ask Joe for the book; he still has it.

Use a semicolon to separate items in a series when there are commas within the items. Example:

Nora's dress was red, blue, and green; Lucy's was lilac and white; and Helen's was black, turquoise, and white.

Punctuation: The Colon

The colon is a formal introducer. It usually translated to mean *as follows*. The colon should be employed sparingly and never after *is, are, was,* or *were* when presenting a series. The major use of the colon is to introduce a formal appositive, list, summary, quotation, example, or other explanatory material whether or not the words as follows or the following are used. Example:

The following attended (or, Those who attended are as follows): Bob, Mary, Jack, and Sue.

Patrick Henry's words were the rallying cry of the revolt: "Give me liberty or give me death!"

2.2 <u>Writing Strategies</u>

CSET candidates need to understand the steps of the writing process and the purpose of each step.

Step 1: Prewriting

Prewriting is the initial brainstorming step in which the writer gathers ideas and examples. The purpose of the prewriting process is to organize one's thoughts and plan the order to present points, examples, arguments, and so on. The most popular methods of prewriting include clustering, webbing, outlining, and note taking.

- **Clustering,** or **webbing,** is a popular method for initial brainstorming and organizing of thoughts. Take a few moments to think about all of the elements of the topic and connect them to the central topic. The writer starts with the main idea in the center of the page inside a circle. Then, related ideas are written in groups, and their circles are connected to the main idea with lines. A sample cluster might look like this.

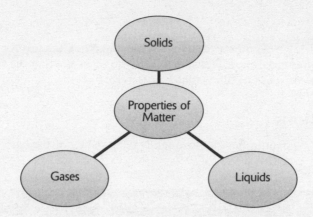

- **Outlining** is the most formal and traditional form of organizing. The main advantage of outlining is that it clearly organizes each main idea, which examples or ideas will be discussed, and the order in which they will all be presented. Outlining visually displays the difference between main ideas (identified by roman numerals), supporting ideas (identified by capital letters), and minor points (identified by numbers).

A sample outline for information about the theatre in ancient Greece might look like this:

I. Dionysia

  A. Took place in spring

  B. Centered on theatre performances

    1. Four days long

    2. Business suspended

    3. Prisoners let out on bail

II. Physical aspects of the theatre

  A. Immense in size; seated 14,000 to 15,000

  B. Outdoor performances

- **Note taking** is a versatile prewriting method that can take many forms, such as listing, free-writing, mapping, charting, bulleting, and so forth.

Step 2: Drafting

The drafting step logically follows prewriting. At this stage, you develop the initial draft of actual sentences and paragraphs. You should not worry about correctness or editing; rather, you should follow the organizational plan set up in the prewriting stage and incorporate all ideas into the essay. The purpose of drafting is simply to get all of the prewriting ideas into print.

Step 3: Revising

At the revising stage, writers begin fine-tuning the wording of the draft and/or rearranging the ideas or paragraphs. This is the time to think about changes that will make the writing more logical and forceful. For instance, you may decide to move a paragraph to a different location, rewrite a topic sentence, add a new example, or improve the essay through addition or deletion. The goal of revising is to ensure that the ideas flow logically and that the writer's points are presented with clarity.

Step 4: Editing

During the editing step, writers clean up diction and syntax. You may decide to combine some sentences for effect or reword others for clarity. Of course, you may choose to move entire paragraphs around or combine them during editing, but the more you practice planning in the prewriting phase, the less you should need to make such major changes during the editing step. The purpose of editing is to check the flow of ideas and precision of presentation.

Step 5: Proofreading

This final proofreading step of the writing process allows writers to check the text for mechanical and diction errors (spelling, punctuation, grammar, etc.). This step allows you to ensure that the final draft is as accurate and error-free as possible using the conventions of standard written English.

2.3 Writing Applications

Candidates preparing for the CSET must have a thorough understanding of the basic principles of composition and genres in writing.

PRINCIPLES OF COMPOSITION	
Paragraphing	Paragraphing is the visual clue that holds ideas together for both readers and writers. Traditionally a paragraph has a topic sentence that focuses the paragraph's purpose. Well-developed paragraphs also provide examples while exhibiting clear reasoning and logical analysis of ideas. In a multiparagraph essay, each paragraph is usually classified into one of three areas: introduction, body paragraphs, or conclusion. *Sometimes on the CSET exam you will be presented with a short paragraph (ranging from approximately five to nine sentences), and you will be asked to choose which sentence should be moved to another location in the paragraph.* Be sure to examine the logical development of ideas in this case, understanding how paragraphs build concepts coherently, without gaps in understanding.
Transitional Phrases	Transitional phrases are the words and phrases that move the reader on to new ideas. Sometimes subtle, sometimes obvious, transitions help the reader understand not only ideas but also their relationship to one another. Some traditional transitions to introduce ideas include *for example, additionally, for instance, furthermore,* and so on. Transitions that show a change in direction include *however, on the other hand, conversely,* and so on. Transitions are also used between paragraph units, such as the *not only … but also …* formula that reminds the reader of the important point in a previous paragraph and how it relates to the thrust of the current one.
Context	Context gives the reader and writer a sense of appropriateness for different writing situations. For example, one clearly follows different writing conventions when writing a letter to the editor, an essay, a diary entry, a descriptive piece, or a letter of complaint. The writing context often dictates the appropriate tone, as well as vocabulary, organization, and so on.

GENRES IN WRITING	
Narrative	Narrative writing is a work that tells a story, usually in roughly chronological order. Whether fiction or nonfiction, the events in a narrative work are presented in a story-like fashion that builds to a scene of climactic action. Examples of narrative writing include stories, poems, plays, fables, myths, and biographies.
Interpretive	Interpretive writing is evident in a written work that explains, explores, or considers the significance of an event, a work of art, and so on. Interpretive writing requires the writer to think critically and then present the results of his or her thinking. Examples of interpretive essays include research papers, critiques, summaries, and analyses.
Descriptive	Descriptive writing typically describes a person, place, or thing in such a way that the reader has a vivid impression of the written work. The written work has a basic purpose of describing something such as an emotion, event, or location. The use of evocative imagery and phrasing that engages all of the senses plays a dominant role in descriptive writing.

Persuasive	Persuasive writing is designed to take a stand on an issue and convince the reader of the plausibility or correctness of that stand. Persuasive writing often employs an appeal to the reader's logic or ethics and uses strong and credible logic. The persuasive essay asks you to defend a position or issue. Techniques often found in persuasive writing include emphasizing benefits while ignoring drawbacks; creating a list of "for and against" points; using transitions such as *furthermore, moreover,* and *therefore;* making opposing viewpoints seem like minor problems; asking rhetorical questions; and ending with a positive and thought-provoking statement. *Examples of persuasive essays are arguments, biases, opinions, studies, counterclaims, and reasoning.*
Expository	Expository writing is a mode of writing in which the purpose is to inform, explain, clarify, describe, or define a subject to the reader. Expository writing is meant to "expose" information. The expository essay topic usually asks you to write about real people, events, things, and places. Well-written exposition maintains focus on its topic and provides facts in order to inform its reader. It should be unbiased and accurate and use a scholarly third-person tone. *Examples of expository writing can be found in magazine and newspaper articles, nonfiction books, travel brochures, business reports, memorandums, professional journals, oral presentations, encyclopedia articles, research essays, business letters, and many other types of informative writing.*
Other Genres	Other genres include such varied types as personal journals and diaries, letters, summaries, and research papers.

2.4 <u>Nonwritten Communication</u>

Speech

CSET candidates should be familiar with conventions of effective speech presentation. Some key points to consider when evaluating a speech include the following issues.

Concepts That May Influence Bias and Stereotyping in Oral English Usage
Dialect usually refers to the distinctive variety of vocabulary, grammar, and pronunciation spoken by members of an identifiable regional group, nation, or social class.
Idiolect is the particular variety of a language used by an individual speaker or writer, which may be marked by peculiarities of vocabulary, grammar, and pronunciation.

- **Eye contact:** A good speaker establishes eye contact with the audience in a manner that is engaging and appropriate. A good speaker avoids looking down, looking over the heads of the audience, or addressing just one member or one section of the audience.

- **Volume and tone of voice:** An effective speaker's tone varies naturally and appropriately according to the content. His or her volume is clear and suitable for the audience and venue. A good speaker modulates his or her volume at appropriate points in the delivery to engage the audience in the content.

- **Pacing and clarity:** Effective speakers enunciate clearly and properly, using a natural pace that is governed by the syntax and content. Words are never slurred or run together. Good speakers do not use fillers such as um, ah, and like.

- **Hand gestures:** Effective speakers also know when to use hand gestures and how to employ them appropriately to enhance their presentation. Poor speakers keep their hands in their pockets, play with their hair, or fidget inappropriately.

- **Posture:** Good speakers face the audience squarely with a natural stance; they do not shift their weight or stand askew; they do not lean informally to one side or the other, nor do they lean on a lectern or podium.

2.5 Research Strategies

CSET candidates should understand a wide variety of research sources, both in print and electronic forms, and how to use them effectively in reports and narratives.

Print Resources	Common print resources include books, encyclopedias, professional journals, newspapers, magazines, and other periodicals.
Electronic and Internet Resources	Electronic resources include all aspects of the Internet; naturally, candidates should be familiar with the difference between a general-use Internet search site, such as Wikipedia — which may be useful to a certain extent but inappropriate for serious research — and highly reputable sites that are considered appropriate for serious research. Other electronic sources could include films and broadcast media.
Citing Sources	Understanding proper documentation and bibliographic citation is essential. Using a standardized style manual, such as *The Chicago Manual of Style* or that of the Modern Language Association (MLA), is most helpful.

Domain 3: Texts

The text section of the CSET encompasses the overall study of literature and emphasizes children's literature. This section includes its genres, themes, structures, purposes, and so forth. CSET candidates may be asked to analyze or identify items such as themes, structural features, and author's perspective; they may be asked to understand a piece's organization and/or purpose; or they may be asked to draw inferences and make conclusions while evaluating a work. The test questions in Domain 3 are largely drawn from both fiction and nonfiction, so a basic understanding of the structure of different types of genres is an essential starting point.

3.1 Concepts and Conventions

The CSET emphasizes the literary and structural elements of children's literature, including patterns and symbols found in rituals, mythologies, and traditions. Children's literature consists of novels, short stories, folk tales, fairy tales, and poetry as represented from a range of cultures. Developing an appreciation for literature evolves in time as a result of environmental experiences including a classroom rich in literature instruction. The purpose of teaching children's literature is to provide students with an appreciation of a lifetime of reading enjoyment. Children begin with reading literature through illustrated texts and gradually advance to become young adult-readers of text. As students gain appreciation for literature, they are more prepared for advanced reading of narrative and expository texts of literature.

3.2 Genres

Novels use the same basic literary conventions as do short stories, but they expand them by presenting more complicated plots, adding subplots, creating more nuanced characters, and deepening the development of ideas. After children have mastered the mechanics of reading, between the ages of nine and twelve, they are prepared to sustain the more difficult challenge of reading a novel. The novel genre encompasses a wide range of types and styles, including picaresque, epistolary, gothic, romantic, realist, and historical novels.

Short stories are popular forms of literature in the elementary school classroom. The short story is a condensed story, usually ranging in length from 2,000 to 10,000 words, most often with a purpose that is singular or limited. They are made up of elements such as plot, character, setting, point of view, and theme. They are often based on a common dramatic structure that introduces the terminology one uses to analyze fiction of all types. These dramatic elements include:

- **Exposition:** the introduction of setting, main characters, and conflict.
- **Rising action:** the event or events that allow the protagonist to make his or her commitment to a course of action as the conflict intensifies.
- **Climax:** the point of highest interest in terms of the conflict, the point with the most action, or the turning point for the protagonist.
- **Falling action:** the events that follow from the protagonist's action in the climax.
- **Denouement (resolution):** the point when the conflict is resolved, remaining loose ends are tied up, and a moralis intimated or stated directly.

Folk tales are as old as language. They adapt from culture to culture and enrich our world with customs and beliefs. They are generally defined as prose narratives that follow traditional storylines that arise from oral traditions in histories. The original author of the folk tale is never known. This genre includes fairy tales, legends of all types, fables, tall tales, and humorous anecdotes. Most folk tales have arisen through a similar process: recombining traditional elements ("motifs") and/or transferring an established plot ("tale-type") from one hero, one location, or one era to another. CSET candidates should keep in mind that telling tales is culturally universal and shares a commonality with primitive and advanced societies alike. Folk tales may be classified into the following categories:

- **Legends** are narratives that often include creation stories and explain tribal beginnings. These tales may incorporate supernatural beings or quasi-historical figures (e.g., King Arthur, Lady Godiva). These legends are told and retold as if they are based on facts, and they are always set in a specific time and place.
- **Fairy tales** are presented as entirely fictional pieces, and they often begin with a formulaic opening line, such as "Once upon a time..." or "In a certain country there once lived..." Recurring plots recount the supernatural adventures and mishaps of youngest daughters, the misadventures of transformed princes, and encounters with mermaids, wood fairies, and elves (e.g., Cinderella, Rumplestiltskin, Snow White, Sleeping Beauty, Hansel and Gretel).
- **Animal folk tales** abound in every culture; in most cases, the animal characters are clearly anthropomorphic and display human personalities.

Myths are the most difficult of the genres to precisely define. Myths always evoke events of a time long past, and they generally concern the adventures and misadventures of gods, giants, heroes, nymphs, satyrs, and larger-than-life villains, all entities that reside outside of ordinary human existence yet are entwined in our collective consciousness. Myths are set in a time altogether different from our human, historical timeline, and often occur at the beginning of creation or in some timeless past age. A culture's myths are usually closely related to its religious beliefs and rituals. A myth is a sacred narrative in the sense that it holds religious or spiritual significance for those who tell it, and it contributes to and expresses their system of core thoughts and values.

Poetry begins with the rhythm of a child's first heartbeat and is an excellent instructional tool for students to gain enthusiasm for literature. Children bring vivid images to life as they listen to the rhythmic patterns of poetry in the classroom. Poetry encompasses works written in verse, perhaps with a meter and rhyme scheme, and uses written language in a pattern that is sung, chanted, or spoken to emphasize the relationships between words and ideas on the basis of sound as well as meaning. This pattern is frequently associated with a rhythm or meter, and may be supplemented by rhyme or alliteration or both. Poetry is a more condensed and refined medium than is prose or everyday speech; it often includes variations in syntax and more frequent and elaborate use of figures of speech, principally metaphor and simile. All human cultures have their own poetry, although it is used for a wide variety of purposes. Generally, poetry is employed in statements and writings that call for heightened intensity of emotion, for dignity of expression, or for subtlety of contemplation. Poetry is valued for combining the aural pleasures of sound with the tempting freshness of ideas, whether these ideas are solemn or comical.

While poetry has many divisions and classifications, the three major categories of poetry are narrative, dramatic, and lyric.

The Use of Figurative Language in Poetry and Prose		
	Definition	**Example**
Alliteration	The repetition of usually initial consonant sounds in two or more words or syllables.	Alliteration is found in a poem entitled "The Searchers" by Kenyan poet, John Roberts. *I remember a dog ran out from an alley, sniffed my trousers, scented rags...* The /s/ sounds in the words *sniffed* and *scented* mimic the sounds of smelling, and thereby create an image for the reader of the act of smelling.
Analogy	A comparison of similar traits between dissimilar things in order to highlight a point of similarity.	We scored a touchdown on the educational assistance plan.
Figurative Language	A word or phrase that departs from literal language. The most common examples are metaphor and simile.	*Winter's end* implies the end of a person's life.
Hyperbole	Deliberate exaggeration for effect.	The whole world's problems are on my shoulders.
Imagery	Words or phrases that appeal to the senses (sound, smell, taste, and feel).	The siren in the night played a haunting tone.
Irony	The use of words to suggest the opposite of their intended meaning.	A parent tells a teenager, "Oh, your room is really clean."
Literal Language	The actual definition of the word.	*Winter's end* is the end of winter.
Metaphor	A figure of speech in which something is described as though it were something else.	In Robert Frost's "The Road Not Taken," the diverging roads are a metaphor for the choices people must make in their lives.
Personification	The assignment of a human trait to a nonhuman item or characteristic.	The angry sea crashed against the wall.
Simile	A figure of speech that has a direct comparison between unlike things using *like* or *as*.	You are as quiet as a mouse.
Symbol	Usually concrete objects or images that represent abstract ideas.	The eagle is often used as a symbol of freedom.

3.3 Interpretation of Texts

Some students have trouble with sight-reading poetry because they don't know where to start. They see the word "death" in the first line and "tomb" in the third and jump to the conclusion that this poem (which, in fact, is a sentimental lover's pitch to a woman who has turned him down) must be about mortality and spend the next ten minutes trying to make the poem fit these gloomy expectations. To avoid premature conclusions, and to prepare yourself for the kind of questions that may be asked, try going through each poem asking the following questions in an order similar to the table below.

Analyzing Poetry	
What is the dramatic situation?	Who is the speaker? Or who are the speakers? Is the speaker male or female? Where is he or she? When does this poem take place? What are the circumstances? Sometimes you'll be able to answer all of these questions and sometimes you'll be able to answer only a few questions and sometimes only vaguely. No matter. Already you've begun to understand the poem.

What is the structure of the poem?	What are the parts of the poem and how are they related to each other? What gives the poem its coherence? What are the structural divisions of the poem? In analyzing structure, your best aid is the punctuation. Look first for complete sentences indicated by periods, semicolons, question marks, or exclamation points. Then ask how the poem gets from the first sentence to the second and from the second to the third. Are there repetitions such as parallel syntax or the use of a simile in each sentence? Answer these questions in accordance with the sense of the poem, not by where a line ends or a rhyme falls. Think about the logic of the poem. Does it ask questions and then answer them? Or develop an argument? Or use a series of analogies to prove a point? Understanding the structure isn't just a matter of mechanics. It will help you understand the meaning of the poem as a whole and to perceive some of the art—the formal skills—that the poet has used.
What is the theme of the poem?	You should now be able to see the point of the poem. Sometimes a poem simply says, "I love you"; sometimes the theme or the meaning is much more complex. If possible, define what the poem says and why. A love poem usually praises the loved one in the hope that the speaker's love will be returned. But many poems have meanings too complex to be reduced to single sentences.
Is the meaning clear?	Make sure you understand the meaning of all the words in the poem, especially words you think you know but which don't seem to fit in the context of the poem. Also make sure you understand the grammar of the poem. The word order of poetry is often skewed, and in a poem, a direct object may come before the subject and the verb. ("His sounding lyre the poet struck" can mean a poet was hit by a musical instrument, but as a line of poetry, it probably means the poet played his harp.)
What is the tone of the poem?	Tone is a slippery word, and almost everyone has trouble with it. It's sometimes used to mean the mood or atmosphere of a work, although purists are offended by this definition. It can also mean a manner of speaking, a tone of voice, as in "The disappointed coach's tone was sardonic." But its most common use as a term of literary analysis is to denote the inferred attitude of an author. When the author's attitude is different from that of the speaker, as is usually the case in ironic works, the tone of voice of the speaker, which may be calm, businesslike, or even gracious, may be very different from the satiric tone of the work, which reflects the author's disapproval of the speaker. Because it is often hard to define tone in one or two words, questions on tone do not appear frequently on multiple-choice exams, but an essay topic may well ask for a discussion of the tone of a poem or a passage of prose.
What are the important images and figures of speech?	What are the important literal sensory objects—the images—such as a field of poppies or a stench of corruption? What are the similes and metaphors of the poem? In each, exactly what is compared to what? Is there a pattern in the images, such as a series of comparisons, all using men compared to wild animals? The most difficult challenge of reading poetry is discriminating between the figurative ("I love a rose"—that is, my love is like a rose, beautiful, sweet, fragile) and the literal ("I love a rose"—that is, roses are my favorite flower).

Common Themes in Literature

CSET candidates also need to be familiar with common themes, patterns, and symbols found in the literature, mythologies, and traditions of different cultures.

- One reoccurring truth of mythology is that whatever happens among the gods and other mythical beings is in some way a reflection of human events on earth.
- Many themes and motifs recur in the myths of various cultures and ages.
- A common theme in many cultures explains the creation of the world; these range from a god fashioning the earth from abstract chaos to a specific animal creating it from a handful of mud.
- Other myths of cyclical destruction and creation are paralleled by myths of seasonal death and rebirth.
- Another common theme is the idea of a long-lost golden age of seeming perfection from which humanity has degenerated (e.g., Hesiod's Golden Age and the Garden of Eden in Jewish and Christian thought).

- The motif of a gigantic flood is extremely widespread; it is one element of a group of myths that concern the destruction and re-creation of the world or a particular society.

- Other recurring myths explain the origin of fire or its retrieval from some being that refuses to share it, the expectation of transcendent changes in the millennium to come, or the complex relationships between the living and the dead.

Literature Key Terms and Concepts

Allegory: A story in which people, things, and events have another meaning. An example of allegory is Orwell's *Animal Farm*.

Allusion: A reference in a work of literature to something outside the work, especially to a well-known historical or literary event, person, or work. Lorraine Hansberry's title *A Raisin in the Sun* is an allusion to a phrase in a poem by Langston Hughes. In *Hamlet*, when Horatio says, "ere the mightiest Julius fell," the allusion is to the death of Julius Caesar.

Attitude: A speaker's, author's, or character's disposition toward or opinion of a subject. For example, Hamlet's attitude toward Gertrude is a mixture of affection and revulsion, changing from one to the other within a single scene.

Autobiography: An author's account of his or her own life.

Biography: An accurate history of a single person.

Climax: Normally the point of highest interest in a novel, short story, or play. As a technical term of dramatic composition, the climax is the place where the action reaches a turning point, where the rising action (the complication of the plot) ends, and the following action (the resolution of the plot) begins.

Connotation: The implications of a word or phrase, as opposed to its exact meaning (denotation). Both *China* and *Cathay* denote a region in Asia, but to a modern reader, the association of the two words is different.

Convention: A device of style or subject matter so often used that it becomes a recognized means of expression. For example, a lover observing the literary love conventions cannot eat or sleep and grows pale and lean.

Denotation: The dictionary meaning of a word, as opposed to connotation.

Diction: Word choice. Essay questions on a passage of prose or a poem could ask you to talk about diction or about "techniques" that include diction. Any word that is important to the meaning and the effect of a passage can be used in your essay. These words are also details.

Euphemism: A figure of speech using indirection to avoid offensive bluntness, such as deceased for dead or remains for corpse.

Figurative language: Writing that uses figures of speech (as opposed to literal language or that which is actual or specifically denoted), such as metaphors, similes, and irony. Figurative language uses words to mean something other than their literal meaning. "The black bat night has flown" is figurative, with the metaphor comparing night and a bat. "Night is over" says the same thing without figurative language. No real bat is or has been on the scene, but night is like a bat because it is dark.

Genre: A literary form, such as an essay, novel, or poem. Within genres like the poem, there are also more specific genres based upon content (love poem, nature poem) or form (sonnet, ode).

Hyperbole: Deliberate exaggeration, overstatement. As a rule, hyperbole is self-conscious, without the intention of being accepted literally. "The strongest man in the world" and "a diamond as big as the Ritz" are hyperbolic.

Imagery: The images of a literary work; the sensory details of a work; the figurative language of a work. Imagery has several definitions, but the two that are paramount are the visual, auditory, or tactile images evoked by the words of a literary work and the images that figurative language evokes.

Irony: A figure of speech in which intent and actual meaning differ, characteristically praise for blame or blame for praise; a pattern of words that turns away from direct statement of its own obvious meaning. The term irony implies a discrepancy. In verbal irony (saying the opposite of what one means), the discrepancy is between statement and meaning. Sometimes, irony may simply understate, as in "Men have died from time to time..."

Jargon: The special language of a profession or group. The term *jargon* usually has pejorative associations, with the implication that jargon is evasive, tedious, and unintelligible to outsiders.

Literal: Not figurative; accurate to the letter; matter of fact or concrete.

Lyrical: Songlike; characterized by emotion, subjectivity, and imagination.

Metaphor: A figurative use of language in which a comparison is expressed without the use of a comparative term like *as*, *like*, or *than*. A simile would say, "Night is like a black bat"; a metaphor would say, "The black bat night." When Romeo says, "It is the east, and Juliet is the sun," his metaphors compare her window to the east and Juliet to the sun.

Narrative techniques: The methods involved in telling a story; the procedures used by a writer of stories or accounts. *Narrative techniques* is a general term that asks you to discuss the procedures used in the telling of a story. Examples of the techniques you might use are point of view, manipulation of time, dialogue, or interior monologue.

Novel: A fictional narrative in prose of considerable length. Shorter works are called novellas, and even shorter ones are called short stories.

Omniscient point of view: The vantage point of a story in which the narrator can know, see, and report whatever he or she chooses. The narrator is free to describe the thoughts of any of the characters, to skip about in time or place to speak directly to the reader.

Oxymoron: A combination of opposites; the union of contradictory terms. Romeo's line "feather of lead, bright smoke, cold fire, sick health" contains four examples of the device.

Parable: A story designed to suggest a principle, illustrate a moral, or answer a question. Parables are allegorical stories.

Paradox: A statement that seems to be self-contradicting but, in fact, is true. The figure in a Donne sonnet that concludes "I never shall be chaste except you ravish me" is a good example of the device.

Parody: A composition that imitates the style of another composition, normally for comic effect. A contest for parodies of Hemingway draws hundreds of entries each year.

Personification: A figurative use of language that endows nonhumans (ideas, inanimate objects, animals, abstractions) with human characteristics.

Plot: The interrelated actions of a play or a novel that move to a climax and a final resolution.

Point of view: Any of several possible vantage points from which a story is told. The point of view may be omniscient, limited to that of a single character, or limited to that of several characters, as well as other possibilities. The teller may use the first person and/or the third person.

Rhetorical question: A question asked for effect, not in expectation of a reply. No reply is expected because the question presupposes only one possible answer.

Rhetorical techniques: The devices used in effective or persuasive language. The most common examples include devices like contrast, repetitions, paradox, understatement, sarcasm, and rhetorical question.

Satire: Writing that seeks to arouse a reader's disapproval of an object by ridicule. Satire is usually comedy that exposes errors with an eye to correcting vice and folly. Examples of satire can be found in the novels of Charles Dickens, Mark Twain, and Joseph Heller.

Setting: The background to a story; the physical location of a play, story, or novel. The setting of a narrative will normally involve both time and place.

Simile: A directly expressed comparison; a figure of speech comparing two objects usually with *like*, *as*, or *than*. It is easier to recognize a simile than a metaphor because the comparison is explicit—for example, "My love is like a fever," "My love is deeper than a well," "My love is as dead as a doornail."

Soliloquy: A speech in which a character who is alone speaks his or her thoughts aloud. A monologue also has a single speaker, but the monologuist speaks to others who do not interrupt. Hamlet's "To be, or not to be" and "O! what a rogue and peasant slave am I" are soliloquies.

Strategy (or **rhetorical strategy**): The management of language for a specific effect. The strategy or rhetorical strategy of a poem is the planned placing of elements to achieve an effect. The rhetorical strategy of most love poems, for example, is deployed to convince the loved one to return the speaker's love. By appealing to the loved one's sympathy ("If you don't return my love, my heart will break."), or by flattery ("How could I not love someone as beautiful as you?"), or by threat ("When you're old, you'll be sorry you refused me."), the lover attempts to persuade the loved one to love in return.

Structure: The arrangement of materials within a work; the relationship of the parts of a work to the whole; the logical divisions of a work. The most common principles of structure are series (A, B, C, D, E), contrast (A versus B, C versus D, E versus A), and repetition (AA, BB, AB). The most common units of structure are play (scene, act), novel (chapter), and poem (line, stanza).

Style: The mode of expression in language; the characteristic manner of expression of an author. Many elements contribute to style, and if a question calls for a discussion of style or of "stylistic techniques," you can discuss diction, syntax, figurative language, imagery, selection of detail, sound effects, and tone, using those that are appropriate.

Syllogism: A form of reasoning in which two statements are made and a conclusion is drawn from them. A syllogism begins with a major premise ("All tragedies end unhappily") followed by a minor premise ("*Hamlet* is a tragedy") and a conclusion ("Therefore, *Hamlet* ends unhappily").

Symbol: Something that is simultaneously itself and a sign of something else. For example, winter, darkness, and cold are real things, but in literature they are also likely to be used as symbols of death. Yorick's skull is a symbol of human mortality, and Melville's white whale is certainly a symbol, but exactly what it symbolizes has yet to be agreed upon.

Theme: The main thought expressed by a work.

Thesis: The theme, meaning, or position that a writer undertakes to prove or support.

Tone: The manner in which an author expresses his or her attitude; the intonation of the voice that expresses meaning. Tone is described by adjectives, and the possibilities are nearly endless. Often a single adjective will not be enough, and tone may change from chapter to chapter or even line to line. Tone may be the result of allusion, diction, figurative language, imagery, irony, symbol, syntax, or style.

Tragedy: Now defined as a play with a serious content and an unhappy ending. Shakespeare's *Hamlet* and Miller's *Death of a Salesman* are examples.

Content

The History and Social Science section concentrates on significant historical events, issues, and basic social science concepts. Because of the multidisciplinary approach of this section, almost all multiple-choice and constructed-response questions require knowledge of both history and the social sciences. Also, using higher-level/critical-thinking skills is essential in answering the majority of questions in this area. A number of questions will require exercising critical-thinking skills in demonstrating an understanding of charts, graphs, tables, maps, political cartoons, original documents, and short quotations.

The multiple-choice section, which contains 26 questions grouped together, and 2 short constructed-response questions cover the following major content areas and focus on the topics listed under each.

Analysis of Exam Areas: Content Specifications* in History and Social Science

*These are the actual California state content specification standards, available online.

Domain 1: World History

1.1 Ancient Civilizations

❑ Candidates trace the impact of physical geography on the development of ancient civilizations (i.e., Mesopotamian, Egyptian, Kush, Hebrew, Greek, Indian, Chinese, and Roman civilizations).

❑ They identify the intellectual contributions, artistic forms, and traditions (including the religious beliefs) of these civilizations.

❑ They recognize patterns of trade and commerce that influenced these civilizations.

1.2 Medieval and Early Modern Times

❑ Candidates describe the influence of physical geography on the development of medieval and early modern civilizations (i.e., Chinese, Japanese, African, Arabian, Mesoamerican, Andean Highland, and European civilizations).

❑ They trace the decline of the Western Roman Empire and the development of feudalism as a social and economic system in Europe and Japan.

❏ They identify the art, architecture, and science of Pre-Columbian America. Candidates describe the role of Christianity in medieval and early modern Europe, its expansion beyond Europe, and the role of Islam and its impact on Arabia, Africa, Europe, and Asia.

❏ They trace the development of the Renaissance and Scientific Revolution in Europe.

❏ They define the development of early modern capitalism and its global consequences.

❏ They describe the evolution of the idea of representative democracy from the Magna Carta through the Enlightenment.

Domain 2: United States History

2.1 Early Exploration, Colonial Era, and the War for Independence

❏ Candidates identify and describe European exploration and settlement, and the struggle for control of North America during the Colonial Era, including cooperation and conflict among American Indians and new settlers.

❏ They identify the founders and discuss their religious, economic, and political reasons for colonization of North America.

❏ They describe European colonial rule and its relationship with American Indian societies.

❏ Candidates describe the development and institutionalization of African slavery in the western hemisphere and its consequences in Sub-Saharan Africa.

❏ They describe the causes of the War for Independence, elements of political and military leadership, the impact of the war on Americans, the role of France, and the key ideas embodied within the Declaration of Independence.

2.2 The Development of the Constitution and the Early Republic

❏ Candidates describe the political system of the United States and the ways that citizens participate in it through executive, legislative, and judicial processes.

❏ They define the Articles of Confederation and the factors leading to the development of the U.S. Constitution, including the Bill of Rights.

❏ They explain the major principles of government and political philosophy contained within the Constitution, especially separation of powers and federalism.

❏ Candidates trace the evolution of political parties, describe their differing visions for the country, and analyze their impact on economic development policies.

❏ They identify historical, cultural, economic, and geographic factors that led to the formation of distinct regional identities.

❏ They describe the westward movement, expansion of U.S. borders, and government policies toward American Indians and foreign nations during the Early Republic.

❏ They identify the roles of Blacks (both slave and free), American Indians, the Irish and other immigrants, women, and children in the political, cultural, and economic life of the new country.

2.3 Civil War and Reconstruction

❏ Candidates recognize the origin and the evolution of the antislavery movement, including the roles of free Blacks and women, and the response of those who defended slavery.

❏ They describe evidence for the economic, social, and political causes of the Civil War, including the constitutional debates over the doctrine of nullification and secession.

❑ They identify the major battles of the Civil War and the comparative strengths and weaknesses of the Union and the Confederacy.

❑ They describe the character of Reconstruction, factors leading to its abandonment, and the rise of Jim Crow practices.

2.4 The Rise of Industrial America

❑ Candidates recognize the pattern of urban growth in the United States, the impact of successive waves of immigration in the nineteenth century, and the response of renewed nativism.

❑ They understand the impact of major inventions on the Industrial Revolution and the quality of life.

Domain 3: California History

3.1 The Pre-Columbian Period Through the Gold Rush

❑ Candidates identify the impact of California's physical geography on its history.

❑ They describe the geography, economic activities, folklore, and religion of California's American Indian peoples.

❑ They discuss the impact of Spanish exploration and colonization, including the mission system and its influence on the development of the agricultural economy of early California.

❑ They describe Mexican rule in California.

❑ They state the causes of the war between Mexico and the United States and its consequences for California.

❑ They describe the discovery of gold and its cultural, social, political, and economic effects in California, including its impact on American Indians and Mexican nationals.

3.2 Economic, Political, and Cultural Development Since the 1850s

❑ Candidates identify key principles of the California Constitution, including the Progressive-era reforms of initiative, referendum, and recall, and they recognize similarities and differences between it and the U. S. Constitution.

❑ They identify patterns of immigration to California, including the Dust Bowl migration, and discuss their impact on the cultural, economic, social, and political development of the state.

❑ They identify the effects of federal and state law on the legal status of immigrants.

❑ They describe historical and contemporary perspectives on cultural diversity in the United States and in California.

❑ Candidates understand the development and identify the locations of California's major economic activities: mining, large-scale agriculture, entertainment, recreation, aerospace, electronics, and international trade.

❑ They identify factors leading to the development of California's water-delivery system, and describe its relationship to California geography.

Sample Questions and Explanations for the Multiple-Choice Section

Each of the following examples represents an area tested on the History and Social Science multiple-choice segment.

Domain 1: World History

1.1 Ancient Civilizations

---

1. Ancient Egypt and Mesopotamia are essentially different in all of the following *except*:

    A. the predictability of their river systems.

    B. natural protection against foreign invaders.

    C. a bureaucratically administered state.

    D. length of dynastic rule.

The correct answer is C. This question calls for understanding the similarities and differences between two ancient civilizations and knowledge of the geography of each. You can arrive at the correct answer through a *process of elimination*. Choice A is incorrect because in Egypt the Nile's *annual* floods were predictable, while in Mesopotamia (modern-day Iraq), floods were often unpredictable and destructive. Choice B is incorrect because Egypt's natural barriers (desert and sea), as well as its isolation from other civilizations, greatly hindered foreign invaders, while the flat plains of Mesopotamia invited invasion. Consider the succession of political power in the region (Sumeria, Babylonia, Assyria, Persia, and so on) as opposed to Egypt, which remained a distinct political entity. The *only* common characteristic listed is bureaucratic government. The pharaoh of Egypt and the kings of Mesopotamia ruled through the privileged class of nobles and priests.

---

2. Historically, which of the following best describes the Hindu caste system?

    A. This flexible system allowed for upward social mobility.

    B. Social status depended solely on wealth.

    C. People could marry above their caste.

    D. No amount of success would allow a person to move from one caste to another.

The correct answer is D. The concept of the caste system originated in India (1500 B.C.) as part of the teachings of Hinduism. The caste system divided people into four distinct and inflexible groups: Priests and teachers; rulers and warriors; merchants and artisans; and the lowest caste, peasants and servants. People who did not belong to any group were the *untouchables*. Members of one caste could not marry or even eat with members of another caste. The caste system was outlawed in India in 1950.

---

3. The sea influenced the growth and development of many cultures. This was especially evident in the civilizations of the Aegean. Which of the following Aegean civilizations developed a flourishing culture as a direct result of trade and commerce on the Aegean Sea?

    A. Sumerians

    B. Phoenicians

    C. Assyrians

    D. Mycenaeans

The correct answer is D. To answer this question, you need to identify Aegean civilizations. Of the choices given, only the Mycenaeans were centers of Aegean civilization and depended on the Aegean Sea to develop and extend their culture. This was also true of Aegean civilizations such as Crete and Troy. The Phoenicians (B) were the greatest seafaring civilization in the ancient world, developed extensive trade networks throughout the Mediterranean, and set up distant trade networks and trading colonies such as Tyre and Sidon. The Sumerians (A) were the first civilization in Mesopotamia and would have used the Tigris and Euphrates rivers for trade and commerce, as well as areas surrounding the Persian Gulf. The Assyrian empire (C) originated in the highland region of the upper Tigris River but grew to encompass the entire area of the Fertile Crescent. The Assyrians were a warrior nation who terrorized conquered people.

4. India, China, Egypt, and Mesopotamia share the importance of a great river system in their earliest development as a civilization. Which of the following rivers is *not* directly linked to the development of the civilization with which it is paired?

   A. India—Ganges River
   B. China—Yellow River
   C. Egypt—Nile River
   D. Mesopotamia—Tigris and Euphrates rivers

The correct answer is A. The question calls for understanding how the natural environment influenced the development of the first civilizations. The Ganges in eastern India is "sacred" to Indians but was not the geographical river area that led to the development of Indian civilization. The Ganges was associated with the rise of the Mauryan Empire in 322 B.C. The earliest Indian civilization, the Harappa culture, developed around the Indus River Valley in 2500 B.C. Other river valley civilizations of the ancient world included the Tigris and Euphrates (Mesopotamia), the Nile (Egypt), and the Yellow River (China).

5. The Hellenistic Age began with the death of Alexander the Great. Which of the following is *not* considered a characteristic of the Hellenistic Age?

   A. The fusion of Greek and Eastern cultures
   B. Economic centralization in Athens
   C. An increase in international trade and commerce
   D. An end to the Greek city-state system as a major political entity

The correct answer is B. The Hellenistic Age (323 B.C. to c. 30 B.C.) was a time of great economic growth and expansion. Rhodes, Alexandria, and Antioch replaced Athens in commercial importance. Dynasties were established in Macedonia, Egypt, and Persia following Alexander's death. The new "Hellenistic" world saw the expansion of Greek culture, the rise of cities, and the virtual disappearance of the Greek city-state, or polis, as an administrative center.

1.2 Medieval and Early Modern Times

6. The principal objective of Russia's desire to expand in the direction of the Ottoman Empire was to:

   A. gain permanent access to the Mediterranean Sea.
   B. gain control over the Caspian Sea.
   C. prevent the formation of an Austro-Prussian military alliance.
   D. limit the influence of Islam and reestablish Christian rule.

The correct answer is A. This question requires understanding of the role of geography in political decision making. Russia was landlocked and did not have a geographical outlet to the Mediterranean. You must also recognize that the Ottoman Empire was centered in Turkey, whose borders include the Black Sea (north) and the Mediterranean Sea (south). Historically, a characteristic of Russian foreign policy from the seventeenth century onward was to obtain permanent access to the Mediterranean. A port on the Black Sea would allow Russia to better control its own destiny. Britain and other European countries, however, prevented the territorial expansion of Russia in the direction of Turkey. The European objective was to maintain the current balance of power. The most notable attempt by Russia to upset the balance resulted in Russian defeat during the Crimean War (1853–56). Historically, the Ottomans played a significant role in European politics. By the middle of the sixteenth century, the Ottomans controlled not only Turkey but most of southeastern Europe, the Crimea, Iran, and a majority of the Middle East. However, by the nineteenth century, the Ottoman Empire was contemptuously referred to as the "Sick Man of Europe" and depended on English intervention (especially directed against Russia) for its political survival. You could eliminate Choice B by recognizing that the Caspian Sea was part of Russia's traditional borders.

7. Feudalism became the way of life in Europe following the collapse of the Roman Empire. Which best describes feudalism in the early Middle Ages?

   A. The church declined but still had a significant impact on society.
   B. There were no formal countries, but the fiefdom held economic and political power.
   C. Knights became the soldiers of the king.
   D. Peasant uprisings were common during this period.

The correct answer is B. Feudalism was the government system of the Middle Ages. The system was based on land ownership called fiefs. The person who was allowed by a lord to use his land was called a vassal and the land was called a fief. In return for protection against invaders, people who used the land were expected to be loyal to the landowner. Feudal society was divided into three classes: the nobles, the clergy, and the peasants.

8. Why was Europe referred to as Christendom during the Middle Ages?

   A. The majority of the ruling class were Christians.
   B. The Church became the preserver of civilization in both political and religious life.
   C. Medieval society had fixed classes: nobility, clergy, and peasants.
   D. Kings and nobles deeded gifts of land to the Church in return for a promise of eternal salvation.

The correct answer is B. The Church became the preserver of civilization in the early Middle Ages and was its unifying force. As the Western Roman Empire was under relentless attack from barbarian tribes, people looked to the Church for salvation. Choice C is a true statement but does not address the question. Choice D is partially correct. The Church did enter into feudal contracts and became an extensive landholder. At one point in the Middle Ages, the Church owned approximately a third of the land. However, the land, or fief, was not obtained with a promise of eternal salvation attached.

9. The Scientific Revolution transformed society and changed the way people looked at the natural world. In doing so, science came in direct conflict with the teachings of the Church. Which scientist was tried by the Inquisition in the seventeenth century for supporting the heliocentric (sun-centered) theory of the solar system?

   A. Nicholas Copernicus
   B. Isaac Newton
   C. Galileo Galilei
   D. Rene Descartes

The correct answer is C. The Inquisition's primary purpose was to eradicate heresy and strengthen the Catholic Church. The Scientific Revolution began in earnest in the sixteenth century. Scientists worked out new theories about the universe. For more than a thousand years, the prevailing thought accepted Ptolemy's geocentric theory that the earth was the center of the universe. Copernicus believed the sun was the center of the solar system, and the earth moved around it. Copernicus' theories were rejected by the Catholic Church. With the development of the telescope, Galileo was able to prove that Copernicus was correct. Galileo was questioned before the Inquisition. In 1633, fearing execution, Galileo recanted the heliocentric view of the solar system. Isaac Newton was the most influential scientist of the Enlightenment and is credited with discovering the theory of gravity as well as the Three Laws of Motion. He philosophized about the "natural order" of the universe and that the laws of nature maintained order.

---

10. All of the following were necessary for the Industrial Revolution to begin in England *except* the:

    A. existence of large quantities of coal and iron.
    B. rapid increase in the English middle class.
    C. large supply of cheap labor.
    D. growth of the canal system.

The correct answer is D. The Industrial Revolution began in England largely due to favorable geographic and social conditions. England had abundant reserves of coal and iron. Rivers provided the necessary waterpower to run machinery. The necessary labor force was in place following the enclosure movement that forced thousands of people from rural land to cities. Also, investment capital supplied by a burgeoning middle class provided money to purchase equipment for the emergent factories. Choice D was a result of the Industrial Revolution. The water and rail system greatly expanded to meet the demands of the new industrial system. Other results of the Industrial Revolution included a tremendous increase in productivity, the rapid rise in industrial cites, and a division of society into distinct classes of capital and labor.

---

11. John Locke's political ideas had a dramatic impact on the development of democratic political thought in the late eighteenth century. Locke's basic assumption about natural laws stood in direct contrast to which of the prevailing doctrines of the time?

    A. Absolutism
    B. Capitalism
    C. Individualism
    D. Mercantilism

The correct answer is A. The leading thinkers of the eighteenth-century Enlightenment supported liberal, humanitarian, and scientific trends of thought. The Scientific Revolution of the seventeenth and eighteenth centuries allowed for inquiring, reasoning, and the scientific method of determining truth. John Locke, an English philosopher, believed that people made a contract with their government to protect natural rights. Locke wrote about the inalienable rights to life, liberty, and the pursuit of happiness. Locke's ideas influenced both the United States *Declaration of Independence* (1776) and the French *Declaration of the Rights of Man and Citizen* (1789) and stood in direct contrast to the theory of absolute monarchs and the divine right of kings (rule by God's will). Absolutism refers to the absolute rule of monarchs with unlimited power. Absolutism evolved from the limited power of the ruling class during the Middle Ages to the Age of Absolutism in the sixteenth through the eighteenth century.

---

12. Which of the following economic systems would best facilitate the theories of social Darwinism?

    A. Capitalism
    B. Socialism
    C. Communism
    D. Fascism

The correct answer is A. Proponents of social Darwinism expanded Darwin's theory of evolution to include society as a whole. Darwin, in *On the Origin of Species* (1859), theorized that evolution is a continuous process in which successful species adapt to their environment in order to survive. The social Darwinists viewed society as a "struggle for existence." Only the "fittest" members of society would survive. The accumulation of wealth was considered a visible sign of a successful adaptation, and virtue and wealth became synonymous. However, for social Darwinism to succeed, it was thought that a free and open economic system was needed. Capitalism (with the private ownership of land, freedom of choice, a competitive free-market system, and limited government restraints) was regarded as the "natural environment" in which "survival of the fittest" could be tested. The social Darwinists also believed that some races were superior to others, that poverty indicated unfitness, and that a class-structured society was desirable.

Domain 2: U.S. History

2.1 Early Exploration, Colonial Era, and the War for Independence

---

13. Which line in the table below correctly pairs the European colonial power with its original geographical area of control in North America?

Line	Colonial Power	Area of Initial Control
1	Spain	Southwest of North America and Florida
2	England	Canada through the Great Lakes
3	France	Oregon Territory and Alaska
4	Netherlands	Southeast of North America

    A. Line 1
    B. Line 2
    C. Line 3
    D. Line 4

The correct answer is A. Remember that the question calls for knowing colonization patterns in North America. European colonization also took place in central and South America and was largely controlled by Spain and to a lesser extent, Portugal. Of the choices given, only Spain is correctly associated with its corresponding area of control in North America. England claimed the Atlantic coast of North America below Canada and set up the thirteen colonies. The English colonies were divided into New England, Middle, and Southern colonies with distinct geographical, cultural, and economic differences. England also had colonies in the Caribbean. France controlled the Mississippi River region, the Louisiana Territory, the Great Lakes, and Canada. The Netherlands controlled a small area in the Hudson River Valley.

---

14. Which of the following English colonies was *not* founded as a result of religious persecution?

    A. Maryland
    B. Rhode Island
    C. Pennsylvania
    D. Georgia

The correct answer is D. Georgia, founded by James Oglethorpe, became the last of the original thirteen colonies. Oglethorpe brought debtors and former prisoners to Georgia to provide a population base to protect Georgia from Spanish territorial expansion. The other choices were all established with religious freedom as a cornerstone of the colony. Maryland (Catholic), Rhode Island (extensive freedom for all religions), and Pennsylvania (Quakers) were established to provide for religious freedom. Other colonies founded on the premise of religious freedom included Massachusetts (Puritans) and Delaware (Quakers). It is important to note that with the exception of Rhode Island, religious freedom only extended to the dominant religion of the colony.

---

15. Which of the following is the *least* likely reason the French aided the English colonies during the American Revolution?

    A. France agreed with the ideals as set forth in the Declaration of Independence.
    B. France viewed the revolution as a means to gain territory at the expense of Britain.
    C. France wanted to limit the economic growth of England.
    D. France and England were already at war on the European continent.

The correct answer is A. It is extremely unlikely that France, with an absolute monarch in King Louis XIV, would have embraced the ideals of the Declaration of Independence (1776). The declaration declared that the people had inalienable rights and that governments were set up to serve the people. Unjust governments that usurped the power of the people should be overthrown. France saw the American Revolution as a means to weaken the military and political power of the English. A weaker England would in turn result in a stronger France. France still resented the loss of Canada to the English as a result of the Seven Years' War (1756–63). Following the French and Indian War, England became the greatest colonial, commercial, and naval power in the world. By 1779, both France and Spain had recognized the American colonies as an independent country.

---

16. The following are dates and events leading to the American Revolution. Which of the following dates and events are correctly matched?

    A. 1765: Britain defeats France in the French and Indian War.
    B. 1770: Colonists stage the Boston Tea Party.
    C. 1774: The First Continental Congress meets to consider action against the British.
    D. 1776: Britain passes the Intolerable Acts to punish the colonies for resisting British rule.

The correct answer is C. The First Continental Congress met in 1774 to protest the Intolerable Acts. As a result of the Boston Tea Party (1773), Britain passed a series of acts designed to punish the colonists: closing the port of Boston, trying colonists for high crimes in England, and quartering British troops in colonial homes. The colonists referred to these acts as "intolerable" and demanded their repeal. The year 1770 marked the date of the Boston Massacre, and 1765 was the date of the Stamp Act. Both these events were background causes of the American Revolution.

---

17. The initial ideals of a social contract as set forth in the Declaration of Independence borrowed heavily from:

    A. John Locke
    B. Adam Smith
    C. Thomas Jefferson
    D. Francois Voltaire

The correct answer is A. The *Declaration of Independence* (1776) was based on the ideas of the English Enlightenment philosopher John Locke. Locke, in his *Second Treatise of Civil Government* (1690), set forth basic ideas embodied in the *Declaration of Independence.* He believed that people had certain natural rights including life, liberty, and the pursuit of happiness; that government was set by the consent of the governed; and that it was the right of the people to overthrow unjust governments. Thomas Jefferson (C), the author of the *Declaration of Independence,* relied heavily on Locke's theories. Adam Smith (B), the author of the *Wealth of Nations,* is considered the father of modern economics. He theorized that the laws of the market place and not government regulations dictate national economies. Voltaire (D), an eighteenth-century French Enlightenment philosopher, wrote brilliantly about injustice. His ideas found expression in the French *Declaration of the Rights of Man and Citizen* (1789).

2.2 The Development of the Constitution and the Early Republic

18. A power *not* written into the Constitution but exercised by the Supreme Court as early as 1803 is:

    A. implied power.
    B. judicial review.
    C. the power to determine the number of justices on the Supreme Court.
    D. the power to decide cases involving disputes between states.

The correct answer is B. Here, you need to understand the evolution of political power among the three branches of government. Judicial review was not provided for in the Constitution but was exercised by the Supreme Court in the famous *Marbury v. Madison* case (1803). Judicial review refers to the power of the federal courts to interpret the Constitution and to declare acts of Congress unconstitutional. Judicial review allows the courts to exercise "checks and balances" over the legislative and executive branches. In *McCulloch v. Maryland* (1819), the Supreme Court affirmed the right of Congress to use implied powers (A) and exercise the "necessary and proper" clause of Article I. The power to determine the number of Supreme Court justices (C) is given to Congress.

---

19. Hamilton's Financial Plan favored all of the following *except*:

    A. passing an excise tax on whiskey.
    B. protecting the agricultural interests of the South.
    C. favoring the industrial sector of the economy.
    D. establishing a national currency.

The correct answer is B. Alexander Hamilton proposed a series of laws designed to protect the emerging industrial economy of the new nation. His plan called for using the power of the federal government to strengthen the manufacturing interests of the country. His plan came in direct conflict with the agricultural interests of the South. The southern states were against expanding the power of the federal government at the expense of the rights of the states. His plan for a protective tariff designed to protect emergent domestic industries against foreign competition especially angered the South. The industrial sector of the country was primarily in the North and Hamilton's plan to protect the American manufacturer seemed to offer little in the way of direct benefit to the South. Hamilton's financial plan directly led to the rise of political parties in the new nation. The Federalists (Hamilton and Adams) favored a strong central government and the Anti-Federalists (Jefferson and Madison) favored strong state governments.

---

20. Which of the following statements is the best example of Federalism as practiced in the early Republic?

    A. Local governments are sovereign in matters of local concern.
    B. Democracy must be limited to prevent a foreign takeover.
    C. The Constitution allows for a simple amendment process as evidenced by the Bill of Rights.
    D. The federal government is divided into three branches of government: executive, legislative, and judicial.

The correct answer is A. Federalism is a system based on a written constitution in which state and federal governments have distinct functions. The national government is sovereign (independent) in such matters as interstate commerce, declaring war, and making treaties. Unless there is a constitutional conflict, state governments are generally sovereign in matters of local control such as passing local and state laws. The Tenth Amendment to the Constitution states that powers not granted to the federal government by the Constitution exclusively, or denied to the states, are "reserved" to the states. Choice D deals with checks and balances and separation of powers. In practice, it has been difficult to determine the dividing line between national and state power.

---

21. Based on the vote in Congress, the War of 1812 was unpopular in the Northeast. Why was the northeast section of the United States opposed to this war?

    A. The impressment of U.S. sailors by England did not affect the Northeast.
    B. The Northeast had strong Loyalist ties with the former mother country.
    C. The war was being fought because of the expansionist goals of the West.
    D. The Federalist Party disliked a strong central government.

The correct answer is C. The impressment of American sailors by the British and continued British violations of U.S. neutrality were the leading factors in declaring war against England in 1812. However, the Northeast viewed the war as a land grab by western war hawks (those who favored war) who wanted to obtain Canada for the United States. The War of 1812 intensified the sectional interests developing in the country following the Revolutionary War. The Federalist opposition to the War of 1812 harmed its credibility as a political party and led to its demise. One important result of the War of 1812 was that the new nation gained international respect as a country.

22. The Magna Carta was a significant influence on the American Constitution. Which of the following was *not* a fundamental concept of the Magna Carta in American law?

    A. The importance of a written Constitution
    B. The concept of religious freedom
    C. The right to due process of law
    D. The protection against excessive bail

The correct answer is B. This difficult question calls for understanding which of the major points of the Magna Carta were included in the Constitution. In 1215, King John was forced by the nobles to sign the Magna Carta. The Magna Carta limited the power of the king and increased the power of the nobles. Certain rights were established by law. The concepts of representative government, taxation with representation, trial by jury, and due process of the law were inherent in the document. However, freedom of religion was inconsistent with feudal rule in the Middle Ages.

2.3 Civil War and Reconstruction

23. The development of abolitionist thought was a result of many factors. Which of the following had the most profound effect on the national antislavery movement prior to the Civil War?

    A. *The Red Badge of Courage*
    B. The Dred Scott Decision
    C. *Uncle Tom's Cabin*
    D. "John Brown's Body"

The correct answer is C. *Uncle Tom's Cabin*, written by Harriet Beecher Stowe in 1852, intensified both the antislavery debate and abolitionist attitudes in the United States. The book portrayed vivid tales of the injustices and inhumanity of slavery. By the eve of the Civil War (1860), the book had a profound impact on turning public opinion against slavery and had sold over two million copies. A popular legend has it that President Lincoln, on meeting Mrs. Stowe, proclaimed, "So you are the little lady who wrote the book that started the Civil War." The South condemned the book as an unfair portrayal of southern life. Choice B, The Dred Scott Decision (in 1857), was a Supreme Court case that prohibited slaves from suing the Federal government on the grounds that slaves were not citizens. This injustice was overturned by passage of the Fourteenth Amendment.

24. John C. Calhoun proposed the Doctrine of Nullification in opposition to the high protective tariffs passed by Congress in 1832. The doctrine threatened the stability of the new nation. According to the Doctrine of Nullification, the power to declare an act of Congress unconstitutional rested with the:

    A. state legislature.
    B. president.
    C. Supreme Court.
    D. Congress.

The correct answer is A. The tariff of 1832 led to the Nullification Crisis of that year. John C. Calhoun, who was vice president of the United States, supported South Carolina's nullification legislation that allowed a state to nullify an act of Congress. South Carolina said that the federal government could not collect the tariff. A crisis was averted with the Compromise of 1833. Although the tariff was lowered, President Jackson threatened to send in Federal troops to stop nullification. Subsequently, South Carolina repealed the Ordinance of Nullification and a constitutional crisis was averted. This issue intensified the sectional issue that would lead to the Civil War.

25. During the Civil War, geographical considerations often determined military strategy. One of the major military strategies of the North was based on geographically dividing the South at the:

    A. Appalachian Mountains.
    B. Mississippi River.
    C. Gulf of Mexico.
    D. Ohio River Valley.

The correct answer is B. Northern control of the Mississippi River would effectively isolate five southern states from the Confederacy (Louisiana, Mississippi, Arkansas, Tennessee, and Texas). Controlling the Mississippi River would geographically split the Confederacy and limit the supply avenues open to the South. Choices A and D should have been eliminated since both areas were already under Union control at the start of the Civil War. The military strategy of the North was based on the inevitability of the South having to fight a defensive war. This same approach led to the blockade of the southern coast. With the fall of Vicksburg in 1863, the Mississippi came under Union control.

26. Which of the following is true regarding Andrew Johnson's presidency during Reconstruction?

    A. President Johnson favored a non-conciliatory approach to the defeated South.
    B. President Johnson vetoed numerous Radical Republican congressional acts.
    C. President Johnson was impeached by the Senate of the United States.
    D. President Johnson campaigned in favor of the Fourteenth Amendment's provision to extend citizenship to former slaves.

The correct answer is B. President Andrew Johnson's Reconstruction policy (1866–67) of leniency to the defeated South angered and frustrated the Radical Republicans in control of Congress. Johnson vetoed a number of bills designed to protect the freedom of the former slaves. Among the acts vetoed were the acts creating the Freedmen's Bureau and several civil rights acts. Over the opposition of Johnson, the Radicals in Congress passed Reconstruction acts that divided the South into five military districts, disenfranchised white southern males, and forced states to ratify the Fourteenth Amendment, which extended citizenship to former slaves. A constitutional crisis resulted when Johnson removed a government official in violation of the Tenure of Office Act. The House impeached Johnson, but he was acquitted by one vote in the Senate (1867).

27. Which of the following represents the proper chronological order (from earliest to most recent) based on the emergence of each as a national party in the United States?

    A. Whig, Republican, Democratic, Federalist
    B. Federalist, Whig, Democratic, Republican
    C. Federalist, Democratic, Whig, Republican
    D. Democratic, Federalist, Republican, Whig

The correct answer is C. The correct chronological order is Federalist Party (1789), Democratic Party (1824), Whig Party (1832), and Republican Party (1854). Simply by knowing which of the parties listed developed first (the Federalists) or which last (the Republicans) would allow you to eliminate two choices.

2.4 The Rise of Industrial America

28. Which of the following had the most revolutionary impact on the economic development of the American West during the nineteenth century?

    A. The long drive
    B. The invention of barbed wire
    C. The refrigerated railroad car
    D. The steamboat

The correct answer is B. To analyze this difficult question, you must recognize that the term *revolutionary* implies a substantial and far-reaching impact. Also, you must take into consideration the concept of the economic development of the West (a geographic area) and the time frame (all of the 1800s). You can eliminate (A), moving cattle from one area to another (for example, from Texas to Wyoming), and (C), the refrigerated railroad car (invented in the late nineteenth century), because neither was revolutionary in the economic development of the West. The steamboat (D) affected the economic development of the Mississippi basin but is too limited an answer to be correct. But barbed wire was revolutionary in its economic impact on the West because it doomed the open cattle range, making it possible for thousands of homesteaders to fence off land to prevent roaming cattle from destroying crops. The commercial practicality of barbed wire, made possible by the machine invented by J. F. Glidden in 1874, resulted in much open-range land being privately owned by 1890, encouraging the development of stock farming, centralization, and town building. Some historians compare the importance of barbed wire in the West to that of the cotton gin in the South.

---

29. The vast majority of immigrants to the United Sates in the period from 1840 to 1880 primarily came from:

    A. Eastern and southern Europe.
    B. Northern and western Europe.
    C. Central and southern Europe.
    D. Northern and central Africa.

The correct answer is B. From 1840 to 1880, approximately 10 million people immigrated to the United States, largely from northern and western Europe. This wave of immigration was referred to as the "old" immigration. The year 1882 marked the high point of the old immigration. Eighty-seven percent of all immigrants up to this date were from northern and western Europe. In contrast, the "new" immigrants came from eastern, central, and southern Europe. By 1890, the new immigrants totaled over 50 percent of the total immigrant population. This percentage rose to 80 percent by 1914. The new wave of immigration had a profound effect on American society—socially, politically, and economically.

---

30. In the decades immediately preceding the Civil War, approximately 65 percent of the industrial expansion in the United States was in the Northeast. All of the following are reasons for this growth *except:*

    A. availability of abundant natural resources.
    B. completion of the transcontinental railroad.
    C. access to the Great Lakes and ports for foreign shipments.
    D. availability of cheap labor.

The correct answer is B. The transcontinental railroad was completed in 1869, after the Civil War. While rail travel aided the industrialization of the Northeast, the transcontinental railroad did not affect this growth. When President Lincoln signed the Pacific Railroad Act (1862), it called for building a railroad from Omaha, Nebraska, to Sacramento, California. The reasons for the Northeast's dominance were directly related to available resources, efficient transportation, abundant supplies of power, and an excellent access to markets.

Domain 3: California History

3.1 The Pre-Columbian Period Through the Gold Rush

31. Which of the following accurately describes California Indians prior to European contact?
    A. California had the greatest concentration of Indians in North America.
    B. Economies were based on agriculture.
    C. Desert and mountain barriers did not isolate tribes.
    D. Men and women used sweathouses for purification.

The correct answer is A. California Indians at the time of European contact numbered approximately 300,000. At this same time, the entire Indian population in the continental United States numbered fewer than 1 million. The majority of California Indians were hunter/gatherers, which eliminates (B). Choice C should have been quickly eliminated based on the geographical features of California, which isolated many tribes (for example, the Pomo in northern California, the Miwok in the Sierra Nevada, the Chumash in coastal California, and the Mojave in the desert). While sweathouses were used for purification, they were for the exclusive use of males (D).

32. The legal basis on which the United States obtained California from Mexico in 1848 was:

    A. annexation.
    B. purchase.
    C. treaty.
    D. revolt.

The correct answer is C. The Treaty of Guadalupe Hidalgo (1848), which ended the Mexican War, handed over all lands between Texas and the Pacific to the United States, including California. Acquisition of California fulfilled the vision of an American empire stretching from the Atlantic to the Pacific, the Manifest Destiny of the United States. Texas was acquired through annexation (A) in 1845. Purchase (B) enabled the United States to obtain Louisiana from France in 1803, a small strip of land south of the Gila River from Mexico (the Gadsden Purchase) in 1853, and Alaska from Russia in 1867.

33. Which of the following was the most important food of the Indians occupying the foothill regions of California prior to historic contact?

    A. Yucca plants
    B. Fish and large game
    C. Seeds and berries
    D. Acorn nuts

The correct answer is D. In analyzing this question, you must recognize the limiting factors in the question (food, foothill regions, and historic contact), which allows you to eliminate obviously wrong answers. The most important and only reliable food for the majority of California Indians, including Indians of the foothills, was acorn nuts. You can eliminate B because coastal and river Indians, not foothill Indians, would have eaten fish, and few Indians included large game animals as a regular part of their diet. While seeds and berries (C) were a part of the Indians' diet, because grasses and wild oats covered many hills and valleys, and while yucca plants were used as both a food and a basket source, prior to European contact (1500s), it was the acorn (the nut of the oak tree) that was the Indians' staple food source. Almost all California Indians depended on acorn meal because oaks grew in most parts of California. After pounding the acorn kernel into a powder, Indians used water to leach the acorn's bitter tannic acid. The resulting meal could be boiled into a mush, baked into cakes, or stored.

34. The discovery of gold in California in 1848 and resulting statehood in 1850 changed the political landscape of the United States primarily because:

    A. territorial clashes with Mexico resulted in the Mexican War.
    B. there was a temporary resolution to the free state/slave state controversy.
    C. the South lost control of the House of Representatives.
    D. immigrants to California favored constitutional protection for slavery.

The correct answer is B. The discovery of gold in California changed the political landscape. California went from a territory with approximately 15,000 settlers in 1847 to statehood with 92,000 in 1850. The question of whether California would be a slave or free state had a profound effect on national politics. Prior to 1850, the balance of slave and free states in the Senate was 15/15. When California became a free state, the balance shifted to the North. In effect, antislavery legislation could pass through Congress. The Compromise of 1850 averted a constitutional crisis when the South accepted California statehood in return for the Fugitive Slave Law. The Mexican War ended in 1848 (A). The South lost control of the House (based on population) in the 1830s (C).

35. Many native California tribes were regionally located. However, the majority of native Californians lived in or near the:

    A. northern coastal region and the Klamath River.
    B. southern coastal region and the Channel Islands.
    C. Central Valley and the western slopes of the Sierra Nevada.
    D. Mojave Desert and the Colorado River.

The correct answer is C. Today, the coastal areas are heavily populated. However, hundreds of years ago, native populations were concentrated in the Central Valley and the slopes of the Sierra Nevada Mountains. The Maidus of the Sacramento Basin and the Miwoks of the Sierras were the main tribes of this region.

3.2 Economic, Political, and Cultural Development Since the 1850s

36. Cesar Chavez is most closely associated with political reforms in which of the following areas?

    A. Unionization of migrant farm workers
    B. Bilingual education for Hispanic students
    C. Medical treatment for the indigent and homeless
    D. Voter registration for undocumented aliens

The correct answer is A. In answering the question, first attempt to place Cesar Chavez in a historical time period, which is often sufficient to give you a historical perspective. Cesar Chavez attempted to unionize migrant (seasonal) farm workers in the early 1960s. He was able to accomplish many of his political objectives through a nationwide boycott of the California lettuce and grape industries to force growers to compromise at the bargaining table. You could quickly eliminate Choice D because only citizens of the United States can register to vote. Undocumented aliens or documented aliens (workers possessing a green card legally permitting them to work in the United States) are not American citizens. Choices B and C concerned Chavez, but the focus of his work was always the migrant farm worker. The question asks for the area most associated with Chavez. By establishing the United Farm Workers (UFW) union, Chavez provided a political forum and powerful collective-bargaining agency for migrant workers. Those who joined the UFW were not only Hispanics; many Filipino and Anglo workers also readily joined. Prior to Chavez's efforts, migrant workers were intimidated by the power of agribusiness. Chavez's belief in nonviolence, coupled with his brilliant political acumen and popular support, resulted in better pay and working conditions for migrant workers.

37. With the election of Hiram Johnson as governor of California, the Progressive Movement *failed* to achieve reforms in which of the following areas?

    A. Adding amendments to the California Constitution to protect workers' rights
    B. Passage of the initiative, referendum, and recall
    C. Passage of civil rights legislation
    D. Establishing a railroad commission

The correct answer is C. The Progressive Movement in California attempted to protect the working class from the monopolistic control of big business, especially the railroad industry. Hiram Johnson was elected governor of California (1910) on a Progressive platform. The aim of the Progressives was to bring government closer to the people. The crown jewel of the California Progressive Movement was passage of the initiative, referendum, and recall (B). The Progressive Party in California, however, was nativist and strongly anti-Asian. The California legislature passed the Alien Land Act (1913), which prohibited the Asian immigrants from both citizenship and land ownership.

38. California has produced many national leaders, including three presidents. Which of the following California national political leaders was a native Californian who became President of the United States?

    A. Ronald Reagan
    B. Richard Nixon
    C. Herbert Hoover
    D. Earl Warren

The correct answer is B. Richard Nixon was born in Yorba Linda, California, and was the 36th President of the United States. Although Ronald Reagan (A) lived in California for many years, he was born in Illinois and was the 40th President. Herbert Hoover (C) also lived in California for many years but was born in Iowa. Earl Warren (D) was never President; he was a famous Chief Justice of the Supreme Court.

39. Which line in the table below incorrectly associates the California insignia with the item?

Line	Insignia	Item
1	State flower	California golden poppy
2	State bird	California condor
3	State tree	California redwood
4	State freshwater fish	California golden trout

    A. Line 1
    B. Line 2
    C. Line 3
    D. Line 4

The correct answer is B. The California valley quail in 1931 became the official state bird. The valley quail was selected because it is considered an indigenous game bird. The California condor is an endangered species and until recently was on the verge of extinction. The giant California redwood is almost entirely confined to forests of California. The profusion of the California golden poppy and its lore in California history resulted in the poppy being named the state flower in 1903. The California golden trout is one of the four native trout species of the rugged Kern River system.

40. Which of the following decades saw the greatest percentage increase in migration to California?

    A. 1830–1840
    B. 1870–1880
    C. 1940–1950
    D. 1990–2000

The correct answer is C. The question calls for the greatest percentage increase. Of the decades given, the 1940–1950 period saw the greatest percentage population increase. The economic impact of the post-WWII years is comparable to the impact of the Gold Rush in 1849. Like the Gold Rush era, the war years were a period of extraordinary population growth. In 1940, California ranked fifth among the states in population with approximately 7 million people. In 1950, the California population reached 10.5 million (approximately a 50 percent increase) and became the second-largest state in population. By the early 1960s, California surpassed New York as the most populous state.

41. *The Octopus: A California Story* (1901), by Frank Norris, vividly describes the negative impact of monopolies on the lives of many California citizens. Which one of the following industries was the focus of *The Octopus*?

- **A.** The meatpacking industry
- **B.** The fishing and canning industry
- **C.** The railroad industry
- **D.** The oil industry

The correct answer is C. Frank Norris described in *The Octopus* (1901) the far-reaching and destructive practices of the California railroad monopolies. The story chronicles the domination of the railroad industries by the robber barons, who systematically destroyed small agricultural businesses with unfair practices. *The Octopus* had a direct effect on the California reform movement, which led to legislation that prohibited rebates and other unfair business practices.

Sample Questions and Strategies for the Short Constructed-Response Section

Following are representative History and Social Science short constructed-response questions from each area covered. Strategies and a sample response are included with each question.

Domain 1: World History

1. Complete the exercise that follows.

   In A.D. 476, the Roman Empire, which had lasted for over five centuries, collapsed. Using your knowledge of world history, prepare a response in which you:

   - identify three significant causes that led to the fall of the Roman Empire;
   - select two of the causes you have identified; and
   - explain why those causes were decisive factors in bringing about the collapse of the Roman Empire.

Strategy

The question calls for identifying three factors that led to the collapse of Rome. Before attempting to answer the question, consider factors that would lead to the collapse of any empire (war, famine, economics, climatic changes, civil unrest, and so forth). Ask yourself why after five centuries Rome would fall. Note that this information was stated in the question. Decide how many of the general factors you listed might apply to the fall of Rome. As you think about the question, you might recall that barbarians were responsible for sacking Rome, or that the army had gone through far-reaching changes, or that Christianity was a factor.

Sample Response

The first major cause to explain the fall of Rome was an ineffective political system. The second major cause was an economic decline, and the third major cause was military invasion from Germanic and Asiatic tribes.

The political problems confronting Rome led directly to Rome's downfall. There wasn't a formal system in place to choose Roman emperors. Some were chosen directly by the emperor, others were heirs to the throne, while still others were even able to buy the throne. This informal and often corrupt process of succession resulted in weak and ineffective rulers and many political assassinations. By the end of the fifth century, the emperors were so weak that they were the puppets of the military, often bribing the army to stay in power. The political problems contributed to the second and third significant reasons for the fall of Rome.

The economy of Rome was in decline. To support the ever-increasing needs of the army, the emperors repeatedly raised taxes. This created tremendous burdens on the population, with the common people being most affected. The continual economic crises resulted in a rise in poverty and unemployment. Trade and commerce, keystones in stabilizing the Roman economy, declined. The government reduced the value of the coins in circulation, which caused runaway inflation. With money worthless, business was hurt, crime increased, and political instability worsened.

2. Complete the exercise that follows.

   Hinduism is considered one of the world's major religions and has influenced religious, political, and social thought for over four thousand years.

   Using your knowledge of world history, prepare a response in which you:

   - Identify the geographic area associated with the origin of the Hindu religion and the areas where it spread;
   - List four key beliefs of the Hindu religion; and
   - Explain how two of those beliefs separate Hinduism from other major religions of the world.

Strategy

This question calls for recognizing geographic areas associated with Hinduism, as well as understanding key aspects of the Hindu belief system. If you are not sure of the answer, identify other major religions of the world (Christianity, Islam, Judaism, and so on). What geographic area is associated with the birth of these religions? Does this help in locating the origin of the Hindu religion? If India comes to mind, what religious beliefs or customs are associated with India? Are there any sacred animals? Does the sacred cow come to mind? Is the Hindu religion polytheistic (belief in many gods) or monotheistic (belief in one god)? Does this help in contrasting Hindu beliefs with the belief system of other major religions?

Sample Response

The Hindu religion originated in the Indus River Valley of India and primarily spread to and throughout Southeast Asia. Four key beliefs of the Hindu religion include the following: (1) that each person is born into a caste or social group; (2) a belief in reincarnation; (3) that the cow is considered sacred; and (4) a belief in polytheism (multiple deities).

Hinduism is a polytheistic religion believing in thousands of gods and goddesses. The three main gods are Brahma, the Creator; Vishnu, the Preserver; and Shiva, the Destroyer. Christianity, Islam, and Judaism are monotheistic religions. The Hindu religion believes in reincarnation. The Hindus believe that after death all people will be reborn in either human or animal form. To Hindus, nothing truly dies and the spirit in death passes from one living thing to another. The belief in reincarnation is closely tied to the Hindus' belief in the caste system. While other major world religions may believe in life after death or the concept of heaven, they do not believe in reincarnation or the rebirth of the soul into a new body, a soul that will continue to live before reaching a state of perfection.

---

3. Complete the exercise that follows.

   Sparta and Athens were the most important city-states in ancient Greece. Both city-states developed a unique culture and distinct political structure.

   Using your knowledge of world history, prepare a response in which you:

   - identify two characteristics specific to Athenian culture and two characteristics specific to Spartan culture;
   - select one of the characteristics you have identified; and
   - explain how the characteristic you have chosen defined the historical development of the city-state.

Strategy

The intellectual contributions of Ancient Greece shaped the modern world. Ask yourself if you can identify the geography of Greece. Would this help to explain differences in the development of the two city-states? From a general knowledge of Ancient Greece, one should be aware that Athens and Sparta were quite different in their development. Partial credit on the response could be obtained by simply detailing that Sparta was a military state and Athens developed democracy. Spend a few moments trying to make connections in answering the question. Are there recent movies on Sparta that would provide information pertinent to the question? Has the role of Iran (ancient Persia) been in the news in relationship to Greece? Can you identify any intellectual contributions of Ancient Greece, such as architecture, government, philosophy, theatre, and medicine, that might help in answering the question?

Sample Response

Athens was the leading city of Ancient Greece. Athens is credited with establishing the world's first democracy and developing democratic institutions. Athens is also credited with the development of philosophy as represented by Sophocles and Socrates. The Socratic method of teaching developed during this period. Sparta was unique in establishing a state based almost entirely on military preparedness. It was believed that only through a strong military would the Spartan way of life survive. Death in battle was considered an honor; cowardice was considered a disgrace.

Sparta was essentially a warrior state, dependent on a superior military. It was essential for Spartans to be subservient to the interests of the state in order to maintain power. The purpose of government was to keep up the military strength of the state. The rigid structure of Spartan society allowed the Spartans to rule even though Spartan citizens were outnumbered by noncitizens by about ten to one. It was the constant threat of rebellion that resulted in Sparta being set up as a military state. The state owned most of the land. Large families were discouraged. At birth, all Spartan males belonged to the state, and by the age of seven, boys enrolled in military-style camps. The Spartan way of life even extended to mothers examining newborn children to determine if they were healthy. Those that were not were left to die.

Domain 2: U.S. History

> 4. Complete the exercise that follows.
>
> In the decades following ratification of the Constitution, the issue of the scope and authority of the federal judiciary needed resolution. Court decisions during the era of Chief Justice John Marshall (1801–35) shaped the role of the Supreme Court in the national government.
>
> Using your knowledge of U.S. history, prepare a response in which you:
>
> - identify two important cases during Marshall's tenure as chief justice;
> - select one of the cases you have identified; and
> - explain the facts before the Supreme Court, the questions before the court, and the importance of the court's decision.

Strategy

You should be familiar with John Marshall and his impact on U.S. constitutional law. Marshall served for 34 years as chief justice (1801–35) and his decisions shaped the role of the Supreme Court. What questions did the Marshall court have to decide? Start by attempting to recall any landmark or significant Supreme Court cases of the period. Probably two cases would come to mind, *Marbury v. Madison* and *McCulloch v. Maryland*. If you cannot recall specific cases, attempt to recall issues that might confront the court in determining the extent of federal power. For example, the right to review legislation, the extent of states' rights, the scope of federal authority, or who controls commerce.

Sample Response

Two court cases resolved by the Marshall court were *Marbury v. Madison* in 1803 and *McCulloch v. Maryland* in 1819.

In the *McCulloch v. Maryland* case, Congress had chartered a national bank. The state of Maryland opposed the concept of a national bank and placed high taxes on the bank. The bank's officer refused to pay the tax and Maryland sued the national government for payment.

There were two main questions before the court: the first, did Congress have the authority to establish a national bank; and the second, if Congress had such authority, did a state have the authority to tax a federal institution?

The court's decision established the concept of implied powers or powers not directly stated in the Constitution. The court stated that Congress has the authority to make all laws that are necessary and proper and therefore a national bank is constitutional. The court also stated that a state does not have the authority to tax a federal institution. The significance of this decision is that it strengthened the national government and limited the powers of the states.

> 5. Complete the exercise that follows.
>
> One of the central features of the U.S. Constitution is the principle of separation of powers. Using your knowledge of U.S. history, prepare a response in which you:
>
> - identify each branch of government;
> - explain the principle of separation of powers; and
> - explain the functions of each branch of government and one power associated with that branch.

Strategy

There are basic principles inherent in the U.S. Constitution. Always read the question for hints in answering what is asked. For example, the question already tells the candidate that there are *branches* of government. (How many?) How is power *separated* or divided among those branches? If you are unsure of the answer, identify what you already know about the Constitution. What terms come to mind in defining constitutional power? Possibly terms such as president, congress, the courts, checks and balances, the Bill of Rights, judicial review, national supremacy, and so on. What about how bills become laws?

Sample Response

The three branches of government are the legislative, executive, and judicial branches.

The Constitution distributes power so that it is shared and that no one branch of government can become all powerful. By having three distinct branches of government with specific powers, the possibility of abuse of power is reduced. The structure also encourages broad deliberation before legislation is passed.

The legislative branch, or Congress, is responsible for making laws; the executive branch, or president, is responsible for enforcing laws; and the judicial branch, or courts, is responsible for interpreting laws. The legislative branch has the power to declare war; the executive branch can veto acts of Congress; the judicial branch can declare acts of Congress unconstitutional.

> 6. Complete the exercise that follows.
>
> At the beginning of the Civil War, the North defined a number of military strategies designed to force the South to surrender.
>
> Using your knowledge of U.S. history, prepare a response in which you:
>
> - identify three military objectives of the North at the start of the Civil War;
> - select one of the objectives; and
> - explain the rationale for the objective and how successful the North was in accomplishing the objective.

Strategy

In preparing to answer the question, ask yourself what a military strategy is. Remember that the question does not call for political strategies. At the beginning of the Civil War, the North had many substantive advantages, such as an established army, substantially more miles of railroad, a stronger industrial base, and stronger financial institutions. As you start to assess the question, focus on the geography of the North and South. This might help in determining potential northern military objectives. Would blockading the southern coast be a military objective? Again, look at the geography of the south. Why would controlling the Mississippi River be a military objective? Ask yourself questions as you focus on possible military strategies. Where were the capitals of the North and South located? Did the closeness of these two cities dictate military strategy?

Sample Response

The military strategy of the North at the start of the Civil War was based on geographical considerations. The primary objective was to capture the Southern capital at Richmond, Virginia. A further strategy was to blockade the South's Atlantic seaports, cut off trade, and economically strangle the South. Also, the North wanted to split the Confederacy at the Mississippi River. By doing so, Southern forces would be divided east and west and the South would have to fight a two-front war.

The capital at Richmond was the political symbol of the South. The South was relying on recognition from France and England to further its objective of secession. If the Southern capital fell, the North was certain the foreign countries would see the South as an unsustainable political entity. The North also hoped that capturing Richmond would force the South to capitulate quickly, thus ending the war.

Although Richmond was less than one hundred miles from Washington, D.C., it actually took four years (until 1865) to accomplish this objective. The first attempt to capture Richmond ended in failure at Bull Run in 1861. After being repulsed in the Peninsular Campaign in 1862, the North abandoned its plan to immediately capture Richmond.

Domain 3: California History

7. Complete the exercise that follows.

   In 1848, the California Gold Rush began after James Marshall discovered gold in the American River near present-day Sacramento. The impact of this discovery was far-reaching.

   Using your knowledge of U.S. and California history, prepare a response in which you:

   - identify the immediate consequences of this discovery; and
   - explain how one of the consequences had a direct impact on the issue of slavery in the United States.

Strategy

You are expected to be familiar with major events that shaped California history and in this case also had an impact on U.S. history. The California Gold Rush was such an event. What occurred as a result (consequences) of this discovery? What are you already familiar with? Have you visited historical sites associated with this discovery (Sutter's Mill or gold mining towns along historic Highway 49)? Can you recall events, museum exhibits, or terms associated with the discovery—or even nicknames, such as "the Golden State" or "the 49ers." Slavery was a national issue. What effect did the discovery of gold have on the slavery issue? Was it political? What was happening in the United States during this period?

Sample Response

The immediate consequences of the discovery of gold in 1848 included a dramatic increase in the population of California. In less than two years, California went from a territory to statehood. Trade and commerce expanded, especially in the San Francisco and Sacramento areas. Transportation systems developed to accommodate the mining and cattle frontiers, and the mistreatment of non-European peoples, including the Chinese and Indians, was commonplace.

The population explosion resulting from the Gold Rush transformed California politically, socially, and economically. In less than two years, California had enough citizens to apply for statehood. The national question was whether California would be a slave or free state. At the time, the Senate was equally divided between slave and free states at 15 each. As long as this balance remained, the South could block any antislavery legislation from passing Congress. California became a free state and the balance was upset. Fearing a loss of political power, the South threatened to leave the Union. The Compromise of 1850 admitted California as a free state but also provided for the Fugitive Slave Law. This law made it illegal to harbor runaway slaves. The Compromise of 1850 was only a temporary fix. The issue of slavery would continue to dominate national politics.

8. Complete the following exercise.

Father Junípero Serra is credited with establishing the California mission system. The mission system was instrumental in the development of California's culture and economy.

Using your knowledge of California history, prepare a response in which you:

- list three reasons for establishing the mission system;
- explain two negative aspects of the mission system; and
- explain one reason why the mission system collapsed.

Strategy

It is helpful to recall general information about the mission system before attempting to answer the questions. You have most likely visited various California missions (San Juan Capistrano, San Luis Obispo, Santa Barbara, etc.). What was the role of the Catholic Church in establishing the mission system? What features did missions have in common (surrounding walls, central churches, workshops, farmland, etc.)? Would surrounding walls indicate safety concerns? What about indigenous peoples (Indians) and the actual building of the missions? Would treatment of the Indians help in determining negative aspects of the mission system? Most institutions collapse when the purpose in establishing them is no longer relevant. When the last mission was established in Sonoma in 1823, the move to secularize the missions was in full swing.

Sample Response

The missions were religious settlements run by the Catholic Church. The primary goal was to convert the Native Americans to Christianity and to teach them the Spanish way of life. This was true for the 21 missions established in Alta California from 1769 to 1823. Besides their religious purpose, the missions had other important goals. The missions were established to provide agricultural land and food staples for the emerging Spanish population. Another purpose was to establish permanent Spanish settlements in Alta California. It was hoped that the establishment of the missions would attract Spanish settlers to California and at the same time discourage both English and Russian colonization of Alta California.

The most glaring negative aspect of the mission system was associated with the mistreatment of the Indian population. Local Indian populations provided the forced labor to build the missions, often under brutalizing conditions. European diseases such as typhus and smallpox decimated the mission Indians. There was a high infant mortality rate among the mission Indians and, as a result of the mission system, Native American culture was virtually eliminated.

The Mexican Revolution of 1821 ended centuries of Spanish domination over Alta California. During the Mexican period, there was a dramatic decline in the importance of the missions. Converting the Indians to Christianity was no longer relevant and the development of farming communities, or pueblos, eliminated the agricultural purpose for maintaining the mission system. By 1834, the secularization or privatization of the missions was complete.

Subject Matter Skills and Abilities Applicable to the Content Domains in History and Social Science

Candidates for Multiple Subject Teaching Credentials utilize chronological and spatial thinking. They construct and interpret timelines, tables, graphs, maps, and charts. They describe the cultural, historical, economic, and political characteristics of world regions, including human features of the regions such as population, land use patterns, and settlement patterns. They interpret primary and secondary sources, including written documents, narratives, photographs, art, and artifacts revealed through archeology. They recognize the differing ramifications of historical and current events for people of varying ethnic, racial, socioeconomic, cultural, and gender backgrounds. Candidates draw on and apply concepts from history and other social studies, including political science and government, geography, economics, anthropology, and sociology. They draw on and apply basic economic concepts. Candidates explain major concepts of philosophy (including concepts of religion and other belief systems) and their impact on history and society. They explain basic concepts of demography, including factors associated with human migration.

Review of Domains

The following outlines cover the major areas of world history, U.S. history, California history, and geography. Each outline is an intensive review of the key points, facts, terms, and major concepts associated with each discipline.

Domain 1: World History

I. EARLY CIVILIZATIONS

With the advent of the domestication and cultivation of crops, for the first time, humans were able to abandon nomadic hunting and gathering and settle in one place. From this singular development in human history, great civilizations took root and flourished. The first of these centered on four major river systems in the Near East, Africa, and Asia. While other smaller civilizations developed in these regions, the first four provided the foundation from which all others emerged.

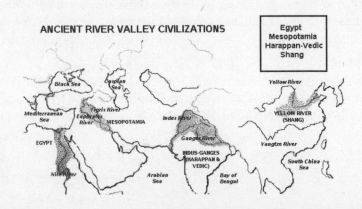

Four River Valley Civilizations		
Geography	Civilization	Development
Southwest Asia Tigris and Euphrates rivers	Mesopotamia	Writing (cuneiform) Organized government Written law code (Hammurabi's Code) Systematized religion (Zoroastrianism) Astronomy; Astrology

Northeastern Africa Banks of Nile River Mediterranean and Red seas	Egypt	Complex religion of gods, rituals, and governance (pharaoh) Writing (hieroglyphics) Engineering and building (pyramids) Mathematics
Southern Asia Indus and Ganges rivers Arabian Sea	India	Urban culture Planned cities (i.e., citywide sanitation systems) Metallurgy (gold, copper, bronze, tin) Measurement (weight, time, length, mass)
East Asia Yellow River	China	Writing Commerce Government

A. The Near East.

  1. The ancient Near East comprised the Tigris and Euphrates Valley, the Fertile Crescent, and the Nile Valley.

  2. Cultural contributions associated with the ancient Near East:

   a. The first system of independent states.

   b. The first system of writing (cuneiform and hieroglyphics).

   c. The first massive architectural achievements (ziggurat and pyramid).

   d. The first lasting monotheism.

   e. The beginning of science, mathematics, and astronomy.

   f. The first codification of law.

B. Selected achievements of Mesopotamian civilizations.

  1. The Sumerians were the creators of Mesopotamian civilization (3500–3000 B.C.).

   a. Material progress included large-scale irrigation projects, an advanced system of mathematics, and the invention of the wheel.

   b. The ziggurat was the center of community life and served as a temple, storehouse, and treasury.

   c. Sargon established the first empire (c. 2371 B.C.).

  2. The Babylonians conquered Sumeria and established a new empire (2300–1750 B.C.).

   a. The code of Hammurabi was the first universal written codification of laws in recorded history (c. 1750 B.C.).

   b. Babylonian achievements included a centralized government and advancements in algebra and geometry.

  3. The Hittites (2000–1200 B.C.) conquered much of Asia Minor and northern Mesopotamia; a major contribution included the invention of iron smelting, which revolutionized warfare.

  4. The Assyrians created an empire based on military superiority, conquest, and terrorism (911–550 B.C.).

   a. Military techniques included siege warfare, intimidation, and the use of iron weapons.

   b. Assyria created a centralized government, a postal service, an extensive library, and a system of highways.

  5. The Chaldeans established the New Babylonian Empire under Nebuchadnezzar (605–538 B.C.).

   a. They conquered Mesopotamia, Syria, and Palestine.

   b. They developed astrology, astronomy, advanced government bureaucracy, and architectural achievements such as the Hanging Gardens of Babylon.

  6. The Persians attempted to unify the entire Near East under one rule (500s B.C.).

   a. Persia established an international government.

   b. Zoroastrianism was an ethical religion based on concepts of good and evil.

   c. Persia failed to conquer the Greeks; Persia was eventually conquered by Alexander the Great (334–331 B.C.).

C. Unique contributions of smaller civilizations of the Near East.

  1. The Phoenicians became the first explorers, traders, and colonizers of the ancient world; their civilization reached its peak in 1000 B.C.

  a. They invented the first true alphabet.

  b. They dominated Mediterranean commerce and exported manufactured glass and purple dye (royal purple).

  2. The Lydians occupied western Asia Minor (500s B.C.).

  a. Their culture reached its zenith under King Croesus (Golden King).

  b. They were responsible for the first coinage of money.

  3. The Israelites established the first lasting monotheism.

  a. Saul established the first kingdom in Palestine (c. 1030–1010 B.C.).

  b. After the death of Solomon (922 B.C.), the Hebrews were divided into two kingdoms (Israel and Judah).

  c. Disunity and conquest resulted in the destruction of Israel (722 B.C.) and Judah (586 B.C.).

  d. The revolt of the Israelites against Rome resulted in the destruction of Jerusalem (A.D. 70) and the forced dispersal of the Jews from Palestine (Jewish Diaspora, c. A.D. 132–135).

D. Egypt established a civilization in the Nile Valley (3000 B.C.).

  1. Defensible borders generally spared Egypt from the repeated political disruptions characteristic of Mesopotamia.

  2. Egyptian history can be broadly outlined in specific time periods that reflect the changes taking place in Egypt over a 3,000-year period.

  3. Significant aspects of Egyptian civilization include the following:

  a. Egyptian life was dominated by concerns for the afterlife, religion, and the pharaoh.

  b. Medical advances and specialized surgery were major contributions.

  c. The Egyptians invented a hieroglyphic writing system.

  d. Commerce flourished throughout Arabia, India, and part of Africa.

  e. Agriculture was the basis of the economy.

  f. Monumental architecture reflected remarkable building and engineering feats, as well as mathematical precision.

  g. Annual flooding in the Nile was the basis for the sustained economy; the Nile had an impact on all of Egyptian society.

II. THE GREEK WORLD

The Ancient Greek world included the islands and lands surrounding the Aegean Sea. Its rugged landscape of mountains and valleys, as well as the scattered islands of the sea, led to the development of independent city-states rather than one unified empire. The Minoan, Mycenaean, Hellenic, and Hellenistic civilizations of this world introduced innovations in the arts, architecture, literature, philosophy, and government that continue their foundational role in Western civilization up to the present day.

Greek Contributions: 4000–323 B.C.	
Organized warfare	Mycenae; Sparta
	Phalanx
Literature	Epic poetry (Iliad; Odyssey)
	Plays (drama, tragedy, comedy)
History	Herodotus (The Persian Wars)
	Thucydides (The Peloponnesian War)

Architecture	Columns and Colonnades
	Parthenon
Arts	Theatre
	Sculpture
	Decorative pottery
Government	Democracy (Athens)
	Oligarchy (Sparta)
	Bureaucracy (Alexander the Great)

A. Greece is a land of mountains separated by deep valleys.

   1. Scarcity of good agricultural land encouraged seafaring in eastern Greece.

   2. The southern mainland, with adequate agricultural resources, relied on farming.

B. The Aegean background includes the Minoan and Mycenaean civilizations.

   1. The Minoan civilization of Crete (c. 4000–1400 B.C.) based its prosperity on extensive commerce.

   2. The Mycenaean civilization (c. 2000–1150 B.C.) developed heavily fortified cities and based prosperity on trade and warfare.

      a. Dorians conquered the Peloponnesus (peninsula of southern Greece) and ushered in a "dark age" characterized by violence and instability (c. 1150–800 B.C.).

      b. Ionia became the birthplace for the Hellenic civilization.

C. Greek civilization was dominated by Athens and Sparta.

   1. Direct democracy was established in Athens (c. 507 B.C.).

   2. The Age of Pericles (460–429 B.C.) represented the zenith of Athenian society and the height of its democracy.

   3. Athens became a world commercial center and cosmopolitan city.

   4. Sparta developed a totalitarian and militaristic state dependent on slave labor to sustain its agricultural system.

   5. After defeating the Persians, conflict between Athens and Sparta dominated Greek politics.

D. The Peloponnesian War (431–404 B.C.) devastated both Sparta and Athens (and their Greek city-state allies).

   1. Sparta was victorious but unable to unite the Greek city-states.

   2. Greek individualism was a catalyst in the collapse of the Greek city-state alliances.

E. Alexander the Great (356–323 B.C.) of Macedonia established the Hellenic Age (the fusion of Greek culture with the East).

   1. Alexander conquered Persia, Asia Minor, and Egypt and established a world empire.

   2. Bureaucracy replaced the *polis* (city-state) as the form of government.

F. Contributions of the Greek world.

   1. Greeks founded most of the major philosophical schools, established the systematic basis for the scientific method, and perfected advances in shipbuilding and commerce.

   2. Greek civilization established democracy and a system of law to improve society.

   3. In architecture, sculpture, art, literature, and the performing arts, the Greeks were dominant.

III. THE ROMAN WORLD

The Latin tribe of Rome rose to conquer and consolidate a great Republic on the Italian peninsula, and from there, a great Mediterranean empire was created. From Republic to Empire, Roman civilization lasted for nearly a thousand years, bringing their talent for practical organization of society and their extension of Greek culture to western Europe, the Near East, and North Africa.

Roman Contributions	
Roman law	Rule of law/Equality before the law
	Civil and contract law codes
Engineering and architecture	Concrete
	Arch
	Roman roads
	Aqueducts and cisterns
	Monumental buildings
Culture	History
	Literature: Virgil (*Aeneid*) Ovid (*Metamorphoses*)
	Rhetoric

A. The Roman Republic (509–27 B.C.) started after Etruscan control was overthrown.

    1. Roman society was divided into the patricians (propertied class), plebeians (main body of Roman citizens), and slaves.

    2. Roman government was based on consuls, the Senate, and the Centurial Assembly.

    3. The Roman army became the most powerful military organization in the world.

    4. After the Punic Wars with Carthage (146 B.C.), Rome emerged as the dominant power in the Mediterranean.

        a. Rome incorporated Greek culture into its empire.

        b. Roman expansion resulted in a world republic.

    5. Economic and political decline and repeated civil wars ravaged the Roman Republic.

        a. Caesar was assassinated in 44 B.C.

        b. Augustus became the first emperor of the Roman Empire (27 B.C.).

B. The Roman Empire lasted for five centuries.

    1. The Pax Romana (Roman peace) was two centuries without a major war (27 B.C.–c. A.D. 180).

    2. By the end of the second century A.D., Rome was in economic and political decline, which weakened the empire.

    3. Constantine attempted to stem the tide.

        a. The empire split into the Western and Eastern Roman Empires.

        b. Barbarian invasions by the Goths, Vandals, and Huns devastated Rome, and it fell in A.D. 476.

        c. The Eastern Roman Empire at Constantinople remained intact; Byzantium survived until 1453.

    4. Causes for the fall of Rome.

        a. The immediate cause was continuous barbaric invasion.

        b. Internal factors included political instability, decreasing farm production, inflation, excessive taxation, and the decline of the military, including the use of mercenaries.

        c. The rise of Christianity divided the empire.

C. Roman contributions to the western world.

    1. Its greatest contribution was in the field of law.

    2. Romans revolutionized building construction, engineering, and road construction (200,000 miles of roads).

    3. Roman civilization passed on monumental architecture (the Colosseum, aqueducts, and so on).

    4. The Romans continued the Greek tradition in literature, art, sculpture, and the humanities.

IV. THE RISE OF CHRISTIANITY

Around 6 B.C. in the Roman province of Judea, Jesus was born, becoming an influential rabbi. His death by crucifixion, and his resurrection as the Christ (Greek for messiah) were writings in the Gospels. The work of an early Jewish convert to Christianity, Paul of Tarsus, brought the teachings of Jesus to non-Jews throughout the Mediterranean world. Firmly rooted in the collapsing world of Roman rule, Christianity met resistance from Roman emperors. Despite this official opposition, the Christian promise of a better world to come continued to win converts just as Rome was fending off invaders and economic ruin. Eventually adopted as the official religion of Rome's divided empire by Constantine in A.D. 313, Christian teachings and doctrines developed by "Church Fathers" such as Augustine were granted a foothold in both the western and the eastern worlds.

A. Basic doctrines.

   1. Christianity began with the teachings of Jesus of Nazareth (compassion for the poor and downtrodden).

   2. It emphasized the *Holy Bible* as the word of God, the sacraments as the instruments of God's grace, and the importance of a moral life for salvation.

   3. Paul the Apostle was responsible for the spread of Christian theology and the resulting response from the Roman Empire.

   4. St. Augustine (A.D. 354–430) became the first great Christian philosopher; he wrote *Confessions* and *City of God.*

B. Reasons for the spread of Christianity (the Roman period).

   1. Individual conviction in one's beliefs (solidarity) had grown during the Roman persecution period.

   2. The efficiency and organization of the early church administration.

   3. Doctrines that stressed equality and immortality.

   4. The conversion of Constantine to Christianity (A.D. 313).

   5. The establishment of Christianity as the official Roman religion (A.D. 380).

   6. The establishment of the supremacy of the pope at the time imperial Rome was disintegrating.

V. THE EARLY BYZANTINE CIVILIZATION

Emperor Constantine provided the foundation of the Byzantine Empire by establishing Constantinople as a "New Rome" in the East on the ruins of ancient Byzantium. Set strategically where Europe and Asia meet, it became the heart of the Roman imperial system in A.D. 476 with the collapse of the western empire. Under the Byzantine rulers, a great civilization based on trade and Roman law lasted until A.D. 1453.

Byzantine Accomplishments

- Greek language and cultural accomplishments preserved
- Center for world trade and exchange of culture
- Codification of Roman law ("Justinian Code")
- Eastern Church ("Greek Orthodox") converted Slavic people to Christianity
- New focus for art; glorification of Christianity

A. Constantine established a "New Rome" at Constantinople in A.D. 330.

   1. Constantinople was strategically located, had excellent defensible borders, and was a crossroads of world trade.

   2. With the fall of Rome (A.D. 476), the Eastern Roman Empire became known as the Byzantine Empire.

B. Reasons for the Byzantine Empire's success. (The empire lasted for 1,000 years.)

   1. Economic prosperity was based on domination of the commercial trade routes controlled by Constantinople and a monopoly of the silk trade.

   2. The Byzantines made excellent use of diplomacy to avoid invasions and they were geographically distant from the tribes who sacked Rome.

    3. Codification of Roman law by Justinian (A.D. 528–565) strengthened the bureaucracy.

    4. Constantinople was a fortress city with excellent defensible borders.

C. Reasons for the decline of the Byzantine Empire.

    1. Its geographic proximity to the Arabs, Slavs, and Seljuk Turks, all of whom were becoming more powerful.

    2. The loss of commercial dominance over the Italians.

    3. Religious controversy with the West and a subsequent split with the Roman Catholic Church.

    4. The sack of Constantinople during the fourth Crusade.

    5. The fall of Constantinople (A.D. 1453) marked the end of the Byzantine Empire.

D. Achievements of the Byzantine Empire.

    1. It preserved the heritage of Greco-Roman civilization while the West was culturally stagnant.

    2. It spread civilization to all of eastern Europe.

    3. It preserved the Eastern Orthodox Church.

    4. Its economic strength was based on the stability of its money economy.

VI. THE RISE OF ISLAM

Emerging from the deserts of Arabia, Mohammed appeared as a messenger of God (*Allah*) and a prophet of Allah's monotheistic faith. According to Islamic traditions, Mohammed was last in a line of prophets that traced back to Abraham and included Jesus. Working to unite the disparate tribes of Arabia under the articles of a single faith, Mohammed managed to conquer and bring most of the Arabian Peninsula under his control by the time of his death in A.D. 632. Under his successors, the conquest of surrounding regions in the name of Islam brought the lands of Mesopotamia, Persia, and all of North Africa and southwestern Asia into the Muslim fold, creating a vast Islamic empire. Through flourishing trade, Muslims would bring their advances in government, commerce, science, and the arts to the rest of the world.

Muslim Contributions	
Institutions	**Globalization**
Hospitals	Exploration
Medical schools	Work of scholars
Libraries	Trade (Atlantic, Mediterranean, Indian Ocean, China Sea)
Universities	
Agriculture	**Science**
Cash crops	Methodology; theory and experimentation
Crop rotation	Astrolabe
Irrigation	Alchemy
Mathematics	**Arts**
Algebra	Calligraphy
Algorithms	Illuminated manuscripts
Arabic numerals	Glazed pottery
Decimal point	Persian and Arabian mythology

Medicine	Technology
Forceps	Mechanical clocks
Bone saw	Pointed arch
Scalpel	Stained glass
Surgical needle	Windmill

A. The Muslim Empire and the rise of Islam.

   1. Islam is based on the teachings of Mohammed (A.D. 570–632).

      a. The spread of Islam started in the seventh century A.D.

      b. The *Koran* became the center for Islamic moral and ethical conduct.

      c. Mohammed established a theocracy based on Islamic law.

   2. The Muslim empire was ruled by Arab caliphs.

      a. Arabs conquered much of the Byzantine and Persian empires, including North Africa, and Spain.

         (1) The Battle of Tours (A.D. 732) resulted in Franks halting Muslim expansion in Europe.

         (2) Muslim Spain lasted from A.D. 711 to 1031.

      b. The Umayyad dynasty increased Arab lands (A.D. 661–750).

   3. The Muslim Empire divided.

      a. The Abbasids overthrew the Umayyads—the capital moved to Baghdad.

      b. Iberian and North African Muslims broke with Baghdad's control.

   4. Turks assumed leadership of the Muslim world.

      a. The Seljuks fought the crusaders and regained lost land.

      b. Mongols invaded the eastern Muslim Empire.

      c. The Ottoman Empire expanded territory and lasted for many centuries.

      d. Constantinople was the center of the Ottoman Empire.

B. Islamic civilization.

   1. Government and religion developed the framework for prosperity.

      a. Arabs preserved the cultures of the peoples they conquered.

      b. Religious pilgrimages led to the spread of new ideas.

      c. The caliphs improved farming methods and crop yields.

      d. Trade and commerce led to a high standard of living in cities.

      e. Military expansion also served as a vehicle for cultural exchange between the Arab and western worlds.

   2. Trade helped to spread Islamic culture.

      a. Many factors helped trade expand, including no taxation and strong banking practices.

      b. Muslim trade spread Islamic culture to foreign lands.

      c. Ibn Battuta (A.D. 1305–1368) spread Islamic culture by traveling widely.

   3. Science and the arts flourished under Muslim rule.

      a. Muslim works on medicine, astronomy, and mathematics were highly advanced.

      b. Architecture and literature flourished in Muslim culture.

      c. Poetry and philosophy were common themes in Islamic books.

VII. THE EARLY MIDDLE AGES (c. A.D. 500–1000)

With the collapse of Rome and sweeping advances of Germanic and Viking raiders, Europe entered a time of chaotic political, economic, and urban decline. The story of the Early Middle Ages is one of a struggle back toward stability. Both the Christian Church and local nobles exercised their authority to form a new kind of society, creating the foundation for a politically reorganized Europe of competing nation-states.

Feudalism	
Political	Hierarchical and interdependent
	Church
	Lords/nobles
	Vassals/lesser lords
	Knights
	Peasants
	Grants of land given by lords in exchange for oaths of loyalty
	Private armies of vassals and their knights protected lords and their lands
	Peasants owed labor and obedience
	All owed loyalty and obedience to the Church
Economic	Manor estates
	Owned by lords
	Peasant serfs given land to work in exchange for percentage of crop
	Free peasants worked as skilled laborers
	Dues and fees charged for tenancy, use of roads, bridges, etc.
Outcomes	Political
	Stability
	Leading lords emerged as kings
	Foundation for nation-states
	Economic
	Self-sufficiency
	Foundation for urbanization
	Productive surpluses and specialization of skills would lead to trade
	Trade would lead to growth of towns and cities
	Christian value system institutionalized by the Church

A. The destruction of Rome resulted in a period of decline (A.D. 500–800, the Dark Ages).

B. The Franks became the dominant Germanic tribe.

    1. Clovis (A.D. 481–511) was converted to Christianity.

    2. Domestic feuds and civil war broke out among the Merovingians (A.D. 561).

        a. Political power shifted away from the monarchy.

        b. Charles Martel halted the Muslim advance into Europe at the Battle of Tours (A.D. 732). Martel's victory helped preserve western civilization.

C. The Carolingians replaced the Franks as legitimate rulers.

    1. Pepin the Short (A.D. 747–768), appointed by the pope as king, and established the Papal States on former Byzantine lands.

    2. Charlemagne (A.D. 768–814) dominated the political structure of the early Middle Ages.

        a. He was crowned "Emperor of the Romans" by Pope Leo in A.D. 800 and had a major impact on the history of Europe.

        b. He revived the concept of the Holy Roman Empire and established authority over secular rulers.

     c. His empire included most of the former Roman Empire and additional Germanic lands between the Rhine and Elbe rivers.

     d. The Carolingian Renaissance resulted in the establishment of a palace academy with a prescribed academic curriculum.

   3. The Frankish system of inheritance hastened the dissolution of the Frankish Empire.

     a. The Treaty of Verdun (A.D. 843) divided Charlemagne's empire among his three grandsons.

     b. Carolingian rule ended in the tenth century because of the decline in central authority and the invasions of the Scandinavian tribes.

D. The Viking (Norse) invaders pillaged the coasts of Europe in the eighth century.

   1. The Danes were responsible for the major invasions of England.

   2. Alfred the Great (A.D. 871–99) established the English kingdom after stemming the Danish invasions.

   3. In France, the Carolingian king was forced to cede Normandy to the Vikings.

E. Society in the Middle Ages was based on the feudal system.

   1. Under feudalism, political authority was dominated by the landed nobility.

   2. Manorialism was the agricultural organization and economic foundation of feudalism.

VIII. THE LATER MIDDLE AGES (c. 1000–1500)

The Middle Ages were a time of transition in Europe. Out of feudal customs and traditions that included Greek and Roman classical culture, influences from the Arab world and the East, and tenets of Judeo-Christian belief, evolved a modern Europe and the foundations of Western civilization emerged.

A. The rise of feudal monarchs resulted in the development of the nation-states of France.

   1. By the early thirteenth century, royal authority had expanded and France had become a European power.

   2. Conflicts with the pope over the extent of religious rule resulted in an increase in the authority of the monarch.

   3. The Hundred Years War (1337–1453) between England and France resulted in the English being driven out of most of France.

B. The Norman Conquest had a profound impact on the development of the culture, language, and judicial system of England.

   1. The Battle of Hastings (1066) ended Anglo-Saxon rule in England.

   2. By the twelfth century, English common law was firmly established.

   3. The Magna Carta (1215) limited the power of the king. It is the most important document in English constitutional law.

   4. By the fourteenth century, the English Parliament was firmly established.

     a. Parliament gained power at the expense of the king.

     b. The House of Lords (titled nobility) and the House of Commons (gentry and middle classes) composed Parliament.

C. Spain and Portugal during the later Middle Ages.

   The Reconquista reestablished Christian control over Muslim Spain in 1492.

     a. The Spanish state was marked by strong, absolutist rule.

     b. The monarch instituted inquisitions and also expelled the Jews.

D. The Holy Roman Empire during the late Middle Ages.

   1. The pope was dominant in religious matters and the monarch in secular matters.

   2. A continuing power struggle evolved between the papacy and the secular ruler during the late Middle Ages.

E. Characteristics of medieval civilization during the late Middle Ages.

   1. Society was based on a strict class division: clergy and nobility were the privileged class, peasants and artisans were the work force, and serfs were tied to the land.

2. The decline of feudalism and manorialism was evident by the twelfth century and complete by the sixteenth century.

3. The commercial revival led to the rise of towns.

   a. A true middle class emerged.

   b. Economic activities in the towns were supervised by the guild system (merchant and craft guilds).

   c. The Crusades led to the revival of international trade.

4. Education stressed the liberal arts.

   a. Theology influenced both religion and politics.

   b. Universities were created in Paris, Oxford, and Cambridge during the eleventh and twelfth centuries.

   c. Latin was the language of intellectual Europe; vernacular was used by the twelfth century.

5. Philosophy (Scholasticism) dealt with the consistency of faith and reason.

6. Architecture was dominated by the Romanesque (eleventh to twelfth century) and Gothic (thirteenth to fifteenth century) styles.

F. Historical interpretations of the Middle Ages.

   1. The Middle Ages were a period of transition between ancient and modern Europe.

   2. The Middle Ages were unique with a distinctive culture.

England's Magna Carta (1215)	
Key provisions	King's authority limited by law
	Rights of the king's subjects declared (i.e., habeas corpus)
	Respect for legal procedures
Modern influence	Constitutionalism
	Individual rights
	Due process of the law

IX. THE RENAISSANCE (c. 1350–1600)

Initiated in the trade-enriched, independent city-states of Italy, the revival of intellectualism, literature, philosophy, and artistic achievement known as the Renaissance spread westward and into northern Europe. The Renaissance continued the road started in the Middle Ages that would lead to modern Europe.

A. The Renaissance began in Italy during the fourteenth century.

   1. Conflicts between the papacy and the Holy Roman Empire in the thirteenth and fourteenth centuries resulted in regional autonomy for the Italian city-states.

   2. The heritage of the Greek and Roman civilizations contributed to the development of the Italian Renaissance.

   3. The Crusades focused attention eastward (on Greece and the Near East).

   4. By the fourteenth century, the move toward secularization was predominant.

B. Literature and philosophy reflected the new secular trends.

   1. Humanism stressed the importance of the individual.

   2. Machiavelli's *The Prince* stressed that "the ends justify the means" as a political philosophy.

   3. The influence of the "classical" arts was strong, and a new emphasis was placed on science.

C. The Renaissance spread throughout Europe.

   1. The Renaissance of northern Europe emphasized the teachings of Christianity and placed less reliance on humanism.

   2. The French Renaissance reflected a democratic realism.

   3. The English Renaissance did not flower until the Elizabethan Age.

D. General characteristics of the Renaissance.

   1. The emphasis was on man rather than God.

   2. There was a reawakening or rebirth of classical models.

   3. The ideal of the "universal man" was widely held.

Renaissance—Rebirth of Classical Greek and Roman Culture

- Works of Greeks and Romans reconnected Europeans with their ancient heritage
- Emphasis on "humanism"
    - Progress through rational thought
    - Universal nature of the human condition
- Secularism
    - Writings of the Greek and Roman philosophers and commentaries on their works
    - Free politics and governance from Church control
- Realism and formalism
    - Art that emphasized the lives of everyday people; realistic rather than idealized depictions
    - Architecture based on Greek and Roman forms

X. THE REFORMATION

Renaissance secularism created tension between princely kingdoms and the authority of the Church. There also emerged within the Church questions about its worldly rather than spiritual interest in acquiring power and wealth. This internal struggle led to a rift in the Church, the rise of Protestant faiths, and more than a century of religious warfare.

A. The Protestant Reformation and the development of western civilization.

   1. Reasons for the Reformation.

      a. Dissatisfaction with church ritual and Latin overtones.

      b. Humanism emphasized man's needs and concerns.

      c. The printing press allowed mass communication.

   2. Martin Luther (1483–1546) questioning the right of the pope to grant indulgences was a primary cause.

      a. Luther's *Ninety-five Theses* served as a catalyst in starting the Reformation.

      b. Lutheranism allowed for a state church system controlled by individual German princes.

   3. Calvinism made Protestantism an international movement.

      a. The doctrine of predestination was central to Calvinistic belief.

      b. Calvinism became a revolutionary anti-Catholic movement.

   4. The Act of Supremacy (1534) marked the beginning of the English Reformation.

      a. The king of England became the head of the church.

      b. The pope's refusal to annul the marriage of Henry VIII to Catherine of Aragon initiated the break.

      c. Elizabeth I (1558–1603) firmly established Protestantism in England and established the Anglican Church.

B. The Counter Reformation (Catholic Reformation) attempted to halt the spread of Protestantism.

   1. The Jesuits (Society of Jesus) became the official Catholic response to the Reformation; Jesuits also initiated missionary and educational endeavors.

   2. The Council of Trent (1545–63) defined the doctrines of Catholicism and reinforced papal authority.

C. Effects of the Reformation.

   1. The medieval political unity of Europe was replaced by the spirit of modern nationalism.

   2. The authority of the state was strengthened.

   3. The middle class was strengthened.

4. Calvinism gave capitalism its psychological base.
5. Religious wars reflected the fervor of the times.

Reformation		
Location	**Leaders**	**Foundation and Impact**
Northern Germany	Martin Luther	Salvation through faith rather than sacraments
		Rejection of hierarchical priesthood and papal authority
		Luther's excommunication initiated the Reformation; "Lutheranism" developed its own following.
		Decentralized religious authority in favor of local German princes
Geneva (Switzerland)	John Calvin	Doctrine of Predestination
		Rejection of all forms of worship and practice not traced to Biblical tradition
		Basis of "Reformed Churches," which spread throughout Europe
England	King Henry VIII	Political rather than religious break with the Church
		Act of Supremacy removed authority of the pope
		Created the Anglican Church of England

XI. THE AGE OF ENLIGHTENMENT (1700–1789)

The disintegration of traditional feudal loyalties, the rise of powerful monarchies, and the collapse of a single religious doctrine caused European intellectuals to think about new ways of unifying and governing nation-states. Their exploration of new ideas in the "Age of Reason" was encouraged by the exciting processes and discoveries of the scientific revolution.

A. Philosophy influenced by the Age of Reason.
1. Christianity and church dogma were questioned.
2. The proper function of government was defined by Voltaire, Montesquieu, Locke, and Rousseau. Their ideas led to the philosophical bases for the American and French Revolutions.
3. In economics, the doctrine of "laissez faire" stood in opposition to regulated trade.
4. Adam Smith wrote the *Wealth of Nations* (1776) and advocated manufacturing as the true source of a nation's wealth.

B. Enlightened despotism grew out of the earlier absolutism of Louis XIV and Peter the Great; it advocated limited responsibility to God and church.

C. The culture of the eighteenth century was dominated by Neoclassicism.
1. There was an attempt to revive the classic style and form of ancient Greece and Rome.
2. In literature, the novel was the outcome; in architecture, the Rococo style was dominant.
3. In music, Haydn and Mozart emphasized the Classical era's formal symmetrical structures, simple rhythms, and tuneful melodies. Beethoven influenced both the Classical and the Romantic periods.

The Scientific Revolution and the Universe Reconsidered	
Nicolaus Copernicus (Astronomer)	Challenged the Church doctrine of a geocentric (earth-centered) theory of the universe
	Proposed and published his heliocentric (sun-centered) theory
Galileo Galilei (Mathematician, physicist, astronomer)	With a telescope, provided the first observational evidence in support of Copernicus
	Phases of Venus; four moons of Jupiter

Johannes Kepler (Mathematician, astronomer)	Man could understand God's intelligible plan through application of reason
	"Three Laws of Planetary Motion"—mathematical calculations regarding planetary orbits that supported heliocentric theory
Isaac Newton (Mathematician, physicist, astronomer)	Laws of motion and universal gravitation
	Laws of gravity proved the force of Earth's gravity on the orbit of the moon
	Applied to all planets; provided final proof of heliocentric theory

XII. THE FRENCH REVOLUTION

The French Revolution began as an attempt by the leaders of the industrial and commercial classes to end the injustices of the French monarchy. The rallying cry of the French Revolution, echoed in the words "Liberty, Equality and Fraternity," led to a Reign of Terror against the aristocracy. The fall of the Bastille on July 14 marks France's Fourth of July. Napoleon Bonaparte rose to power at a time of renewed social unrest in France.

A. Background to the French Revolution.

    1. An inequitable class structure was the basic cause of the revolution.

    2. A disorganized legal system and no representative assembly added to the problems of the government.

    3. Enlightenment philosophy influenced the middle class.

    4. The bankruptcy of the French treasury was the immediate cause of the revolution.

    5. The *Declaration of the Rights of Man and Citizen* defined enlightenment concepts of national law and the sovereignty of the people.

B. Napoleon and the First Empire (1804–15).

    1. Domestic reforms resulted in a more efficient government.

        a. No tax exemptions were allowed for lineage, and government promotion was based on ability.

        b. The Code of Napoleon modernized French law (equality before the law).

    2. International relations placed France against Europe.

        a. Napoleon won territory from the Holy Roman Empire and forced Spain to cede the Louisiana territory to France.

        b. The "continental system" was a failed French attempt to close the continent to British trade in hopes of destroying the British economy.

        c. The Battle of Waterloo (1815) ended in defeat for Napoleon and ended the French Empire. Napoleon was permanently exiled to St. Helena.

XIII. IMPACT OF THE INDUSTRIAL REVOLUTION ON EUROPE

Mechanization and inventions were the practical consequences of the scientific revolution. With a variety of factors favoring a new direction in economic development, these inventions were the engine that drove a revolution in manufacturing, industrial productivity, and transportation. In turn, the competing interests of industrial owners and the working class gave rise to an intellectual debate over economic systems and the distribution of their benefits.

A. The causes of the Industrial Revolution.

    1. The scientific revolution brought about new mechanical inventions.

    2. The availability of investment capital and the rise of the middle class provided an economic base.

    3. Conditions in England favored industrialization.

        a. The cotton textile industry was well established.

        b. Britain was a colonial and maritime power and was able to easily ship products.

        c. Coal, iron, and a plentiful supply of cheap labor were available.

B. The results of the Industrial Revolution.

1. A dramatic increase in productivity and the rise of the factory system.

2. Demographic changes (from rural to urban centers).

3. The division of society into defined classes (propertied and nonpropertied).

4. The development of modern capitalism (profits linked to the manufacturing of products).

C. The intellectual response to the Industrial Revolution.

1. The classical economists advanced the theory of *laissez faire* (limited government intervention in business affairs).

2. Thomas Malthus (1766–1834) theorized that population growth would far outstrip food production.

3. The revolutionary socialism of Karl Marx advocated a violent overthrow of the present economic system.

   a. History was seen as a class struggle between the exploiters (bourgeoisie) and the exploited (proletariat).

   b. *The Communist Manifesto* (1848), written by Marx and Friedrich Engels, advanced the theories of modern scientific socialism.

A Revolution in Production and Transportation	
Manufacturing **Birth of the factory system**	1733: **Flying shuttle** increased the speed of weavers
	1764: **Spinning jenny** increased the speed and output of yarn spinners
	1764: **Water frame** introduced the first power-driven machine to manufacture cloth
	1779: **Spinning mule**, a power-driven machine that produced fine, strong yarn
	1785: **Watt steam engine** meant that factories were no longer dependent on water sources for power
	1785: **Power loom** led to faster production of cloth
	1792: **Cotton gin** made it possible to meet increased demand for cotton by mechanizing the process for separating seeds from cotton fiber
Iron-making	1760: **Coke smelting** improved production of iron
	1783: **Grooved rollers** allowed iron-makers to roll out iron into different shapes
Transportation	1804: Steam engine used to develop the first **steam locomotive** (used initially to haul freight at coal mines and ironworks)
	1807: Steam engine used by American inventor Robert Fulton to build a **steamboat**

XIV. THE LANDS AND PEOPLES OF AFRICA

Africa is a vast continent of enormous geographical and cultural diversity. Traditionally, Africa is divided into the Saharan or desert cultures of the north, and sub-Saharan cultures of the rain forests, savannas, and interior. Relying on the continent's four substantial river systems, great trading empires grew and thrived. Their dominance of African history and economic development ended with the arrival of Europeans.

A. The topography of Africa is mainly composed of three regions: desert, savanna, and tropical rain forest.

1. The African continent is divided into many ecological regions, with the Sahara Desert dominating the continent.

2. Trade and commerce were connected to the geographical potential of the area.

3. Large populations flourished in the savanna and were primarily agrarian.

B. Africa is a land of geographical diversity.

1. Four rivers (Nile, Congo, Niger, and Zambezi) were important to Africa's economic history.

2. Egyptian civilization developed in the Nile Valley.

3. Africa above the Sahara is often associated with Arab influence.

4. The irregular coast line (no natural harbors) of the African continent restricted European exploration.

C. Ancient Africans made advances in their societies and cultures.

1. Lineage was the basis of tribal organization.

2. Religion, politics, and law became the focus of African culture.

3. Art and sculpture were emphasized.

D. African civilizations south of the Sahara.

    1. Famous empires grew in the West African savanna: Ghana, Mali, and Songhai.

    2. The East African Coast saw the development of city-states.

        a. East African civilization was based on international trade and seaport cities.

        b. Swahili culture developed its own language and thrived in the city-states.

        c. The Portuguese destroyed much of the East African trade after 1500.

    3. The Kingdom of Zimbabwe developed in the interior.

        a. Zimbabwe grew from an iron-working settlement.

        b. Huge stone structures were constructed.

        c. Zimbabwe's economy was based on the gold trade.

    4. Islam stimulated new states of West Africa and spread Islamic culture and religion.

    5. The forest states developed strong governments.

        a. Benin grew wealthy and powerful until European contact threatened society.

        b. Slave trade produced wealth for the cities and the expansion of the slave trade extended into Africa's interior.

        c. Trade, taxes, and a powerful government resulted in Asante becoming a strong state.

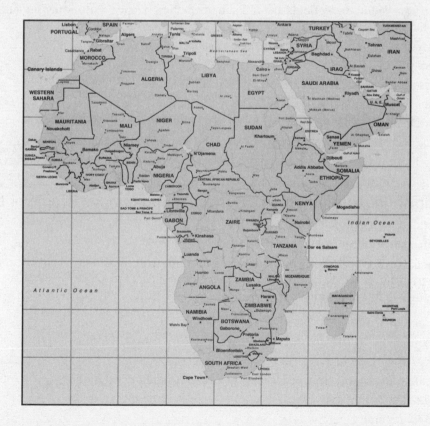

XV. NATIVE AMERICANS AND EARLY CULTURES IN AMERICA

Some 20,000 to 30,000 years ago, during the last Ice Age, the first humans crossed over the Bering Sea land bridge into the Americas. As they migrated southward, they inhabited the hemisphere from Alaska to Tierra del Fuego. Their widespread dispersion led to a diversity of languages and cultures, the most advanced of which were located in Mesoamerica and South America.

A. Early cultures in North America.

   1. American Indian culture developed over many centuries.

   a. The first American Indians originated from Asia.

   b. Agriculture changed some Indian culture from a nomadic existence to farming communities.

   2. North American Indians were quite skilled in many areas.

   a. The Hopewell people were skilled farmers and flourished in the Ohio and Mississippi valleys (200 B.C. to A.D. 400)

   b. Mississippian culture developed in A.D. 800 and built large religious mound structures.

   c. The Anasazi culture (A.D. 800–1300) developed in the Southwest, and the Anasazi were skilled builders (example, Mesa Verde cliff houses) and sophisticated farmers.

   d. The Pueblo Indians inhabited the Southwest after the Anasazi and built extensive adobe cities.

B. Early cultures in Mesoamerica.

   1. The Olmec (1200–400 B.C.) developed one of the first civilizations in Mesoamerica (the region that is now Mexico, Central America, and the western coast of South America).

   a. The Olmec developed an agricultural community.

   b. The Olmec developed the first calendar in America.

   2. The Mayas (A.D. 250–900) achieved a complex civilization.

   a. Mayan cities were trade and religious centers.

   b. The Mayas excelled in many fields including mathematics, science, astronomy, and engineering (pyramid building).

   3. The Aztecs (A.D. 1325–1521) conquered much of central Mexico.

   a. The Toltecs preceded the Aztecs.

   b. The Aztecs built a great city (Tenochtitlan) and ruled an empire.

   c. Religion and war dominated Aztec life.

   4. The Incas (A.D. 1200 – A.D. 1533) controlled a vast empire in South America.

   a. The Tiahuanaco culture developed in the Andes Mountains and the Incas unified an extensive empire.

   b. The Incas developed a sophisticated record-keeping system and were highly skilled craftsmen.

Impact of Spanish Exploration and Conquest on Indigenous People of the Americas

- Disease devastated native populations

  Smallpox, measles, typhus

  From Mexico, spread into American southwest and southward toward the Andes

  From 1520 to 1620, 20 million dead

  Conquest aided by weakening of native forces

- Aztecs conquered by Cortes in 1521
- Inca Empire conquered by Pizarro in 1533
- Mass transfer of wealth (gold and silver) from the Americas to Spain
- End of political and economic independence—organized for labor within the Spanish economic system
- Loss of native culture
- Conversion to Christianity

Advanced Native Cultures of the Americas

MESOAMERICA

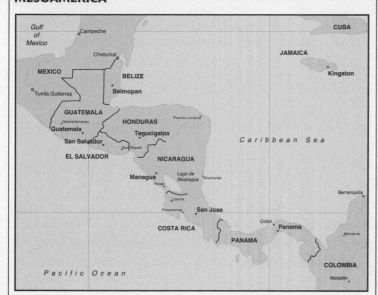

Olmec
- 1200–400 B.C.
- South-central Mexico
- Noted artwork in many media (jade, clay, basalt, and greenstone); monumental sculpture (colossal heads)

Maya
- A.D. 250–900
- Yucatan peninsula
- Only known written language of pre-Columbian Americas
- Sophisticated art
- Monumental architecture
    - ❏ Tikal
    - ❏ Palenque
- Mathematical and astronomical systems

Aztec
- 1325 A.D.–1521 A.D.
- Central Mexico
- Rich mythological and religious traditions
- Architecturally accomplished
    - ❏ City planning
    - ❏ Great Pyramid of Tenochtitlan
    - ❏ Temples and palaces
- Artistically advanced

SOUTH AMERICA

Inca
- A.D. 1200–1533
- Northwest coastal and inland region of South America (Peru)
- Engineering/architecture
    - ❏ Machu Picchu
    - ❏ Stone construction without mortar
    - ❏ Extensive road system linking empire together
- Art
    - ❏ Gold and silver working
    - ❏ Ceramics
    - ❏ Textiles

XVI. EARLY HISTORY OF INDIA, CHINA, AND JAPAN

Both India and China suffered invasion and outside rule over the course of their early histories. In India, this forced the native Hindus to exist side by side with their Muslim conquerors, creating a rich and diverse culture. China's history is dominated by a succession of ruling dynasties, all of whom left distinguishing marks on Chinese cultural and political history. In contrast, protected from invasion by their geography, feudal Japan developed a language, writing system, and artistic style distinctly its own.

A. India under Muslim rule.

    1. Muslims controlled India for centuries.

        a. Muslim invaders came into India in the eleventh and twelfth centuries and created kingdoms in the north.

        b. The Delhi Sultanate was the most powerful (1206–1526), and developed art and architecture.

    2. Hindus lived and worked under Muslim rule.

        a. Most Hindus were self-sufficient farmers.

        b. The caste system dominated Hindu life.

        c. Hindu religion believed in the supreme being (Brahman) and also in reincarnation.

    3. The Mughuls united and ruled most of India.

        a. After Babur invaded India, Akbar became the greatest Mughul ruler.

        b. The Mughuls were great builders (example, the Taj Mahal).

        c. The Mughul Empire declined quickly, and by 1750 the empire had fallen apart.

B. China from the Sungs through the Manchus.

    1. Chinese civilization continued under the Sungs (A.D. 960–1279).

        a. The Chinese Empire lost much territory after the fall of the Tang rulers.

        b. Advances in education, art, and science contributed to an improved way of life.

    2. The importance of city life in the Sung Empire.

        a. Foreign trade enabled populations to grow in cities, and to become sophisticated.

        b. The family was the focus of Chinese life.

        c. Women had lower status than men.

    3. The Mongols ruled in China.

        a. Genghis Khan united nomadic peoples and conquered China.

        b. Kublai Khan became emperor of China.

        c. Marco Polo, the Italian explorer, opened the door to trade with China and described the Mongol Empire.

    4. Chinese culture was maintained by the Ming and Manchu Dynasties.

        a. The Ming (native Chinese) ousted the Mongols.

        b. Ming (1368–1644) rulers limited contact with the West.

        c. The Manchus (1664–1911) overran China and followed a policy of isolationism, weakening China.

    5. The teachings of Confucius influenced Chinese culture.

        a. Confucius wanted to improve society.

        b. Confucius taught that certain virtues are guidelines to happy life.

C. The emergence of Japan.

    1. Japan's geography influenced its history.

        a. Japanese culture reflects a reverence for nature.

        b. Mountains, forests, and coastal areas determined cultural growth.

    2. Early Japanese civilization borrowed from China.

        a. Archeology has revealed Japan's ancient past.

        b. Japanese culture developed during the Heian Era (794–1156).

        c. Poetic form such as the Haiku developed and literature spread.

3. Feudalism and a samurai warrior-class developed.

 a. There were three periods of feudal government—Kamakura, Ashikaga, and Tokugawa.

 b. The Shogun was the actual ruler; the emperors were figureheads.

 c. Nobles struggled for power during the Ashikaga Shogunate (1394–1573).

 d. The arts flourished.

 e. Central government grew strong during the Tokugawa Era (1603–1868).

 f. The old Samurai class and feudal way of life declined, resulting in major political and social changes.

4. The accomplishments of the early Japanese.

 a. The Japanese developed their own language and sophisticated system of writing.

 b. They developed literature and poetry.

 c. They developed the Shinto religion.

 d. They placed great emphasis on a love of nature, beauty, and good manners.

Domain 2: U.S. History

U.S. Geography: An Overview

A. The Gulf Stream, an Atlantic warm-water current, warms the East Coast in winter and is responsible for excellent fishing.

B. The southeastern Coastal Plain extends along the coast from New Jersey to Texas and is generally low land.

C. The Piedmont (the foothills at the base of the Appalachian Mountains), the Appalachian Mountains, and the Cumberland and Allegheny plateaus are in the eastern region of the United States.

D. In the Northeast, the Appalachians meet the ocean, forming a rough, rocky coast.

E. West of the Appalachians, the wind (prevailing westerlies) is an important influence on climate.

 1. In the winter, cold air from the northwest produces freezing temperatures.

 2. In the summer, warm, moist southwesterly winds cause hot, humid weather.

F. Most of the interior is generally flat land.

 1. The eastern half is called the interior lowlands.

 2. The western half is called the Great Plains.

G. The Mississippi River drains the interior of the United States.

H. The crest of the Rocky Mountains is called the Continental Divide.

 1. Rivers that begin east of the Continental Divide flow toward the Atlantic Ocean.

 2. Western rivers flow toward the Pacific Ocean.

I. The land between the Rockies and the Sierra Nevada is called the Great Basin.

J. The Sierra Nevada and the Cascade Range form the western mountain ranges.

 1. The western slope of the Sierra Nevada borders the Central Valley of California.

 2. The Coast Ranges form the western wall of the Central Valley.

I. EXPLORATION AND COLONIZATION (1450–1763)

Intense interest in exploiting a lucrative trade in spices from Asia drove a period of exploration in search of trade routes to the Far East. The discovery of the vast continents of the Western Hemisphere was a direct result of exploratory voyages launched by Spain. Joining Spain in a chance to exploit these new lands were rivals Portugal, France, the Netherlands, and England. It was England that would emerge to dominate settlement of North America through the founding and expansion of its thirteen permanent colonies. In short order, the colonies developed regional characteristics defined by geography that were critical to their economic development.

Europeans in the New World				
Spain	1492	Columbus	West Indies; Bahamas
	1513	Balboa	Panama
	1519	Cortes	Mexico
	1532	Pizarro	Peru
Portugal	1500	Cabral	Brazil
Britain	1607	Virginia Co.	Jamestown (Virginia)
France	1608	de Champlain	Canada (Quebec)
	1682	La Salle	Louisiana
Netherlands	1609	Hudson	New Netherlands (New York)

While distinct geographically, economically, and in many ways socially, all of England's colonies based their governing systems, to one degree or another, on concepts of limited government, representation, and the rights of Englishmen guaranteed in a Bill of Rights. These long-standing traditions of England's government were transplanted in America by its new settlers, with the first important steps taken by the earliest colonies of Plymouth (Massachusetts) and Virginia. Amidst inviting economic and political conditions, the colonies flourished and their populations grew steadily. A stream of immigrants from England and other countries of Western Europe, a burgeoning birth rate, and the forced arrival of approximately one-half million slaves from Africa swelled the colonial population.

As the colonies grew and prospered, they created a society in many ways different from those in the homelands they left behind. A tradition of free public education was started in the villages of New England, religious tolerance supplanted an early religious dogmatism first established by the Puritans in Massachusetts, and a conscious choice was made to leave the idea of hereditary aristocracy behind in Europe. A society of mobile rather than fixed social classes existed with movement through the ranks neither legally guaranteed nor barred to anyone, with the exception of slaves.

A. The opening of new worlds was associated with the Age of Discovery.

    1. European explorers in search of Asia discovered a new continent.

    2. The Age of Discovery resulted in renewed European rivalry.

    3. Spain, France, England, Portugal, and the Netherlands competed for land.

B. England developed permanent colonies in North America.

    1. Geographic diversity helped to create distinct economic regions.

        a. The New England colonies were associated with shipbuilding and commerce.

        b. The middle colonies were associated with farming and commerce.

        c. The southern colonies were associated with tobacco, cotton, and slavery.

    2. The English colonies began to develop self-government.

        a. The House of Burgesses (1619) was an early colonial attempt at representative self-government.

        b. The Mayflower Compact (1620) was the basis for government by the consent of the governed.

        c. The colonists demanded their rights as Englishmen.

    3. The population of the colonies steadily increased.

        a. Large families of ten or more were common.

        b. Steady immigration from abroad increased the overall population.

        c. Europeans and Africans were the major population groups.

    4. The idea of free public education started in the colonies.

    5. Class distinctions were less rigid than in England, and a strong middle class emerged.

6. The most prevalent religion in the colonies was Protestant.

    a. A single, established church was not practical in America.

    b. The decline of Puritanism led to greater religious tolerance.

Region	Geography	Economy
New England	Mountainous	Shipbuilding
Massachusetts	Rolling hills	Fisheries
New Hampshire	Rocky soil	Commerce
Rhode Island	Cold to harsh winters	Lumbering
Connecticut	Short summer	Small-scale manufacturing
	Ports on the Atlantic	
Middle Colonies	Open fertile plains	Large-scale corn and grain production
Pennsylvania	Mild to cold winters	Commerce
New York	Long summers	Small-scale manufacturing
Delaware	Ports on the Atlantic	
New Jersey		
Southern Colonies	Broad, fertile coastal plains	Cash crop farming
Maryland	Warm winters	Tobacco
Virginia	Long, hot summers	Indigo
North Carolina		Rice
South Carolina		No measurable manufacturing
Georgia		

II. THE FORMATION OF THE NEW NATION (1763–1789)

The relationship between the British and their American colonies soured after victory in the French and Indian War. The British had rid themselves of French competition in North America, but they faced an enormous war debt. To force the colonies to help with the debt, the British enforced mercantile policies and levied taxes, actions that forced a showdown over political and economic freedom.

Against a great empire with all of its military advantages, the colonies fought a war for independence. Behind the leadership of George Washington and with help from the French, freedom was finally achieved. However, a new nation governing under the Articles of Confederation soon stumbled. Out of an attempt to fix weaknesses in the articles emerged a new, stronger government under the Constitution.

A. The French and Indian War (1756–63) was a key turning point in England's domination over North America.

   1. The English victory ended the French threat in America.

   2. The English victory encouraged colonial America to seek a more active voice in its own affairs.

B. Background to the American Revolution (1763–76).

   1. The English mercantile policy discouraged colonial economic independence.

   2. Colonial concepts of political and economic freedom were key factors leading to the American Revolution.

   3. Colonial opposition to British actions steadily increased during this period.

   4. The colonies used a variety of methods to change British actions; petitions, boycotts, and other measures were used.

   5. The Declaration of Independence stated the purposes for the colonies' break with England.

AMERICA'S DETERIORATING RELATIONSHIP WITH BRITAIN		
Action	**Date**	**Colonial Reaction**
Proclamation Act Banned settlement beyond the Appalachian Mountains to the colonists.	1763	Viewed as an attempt by the British to deny colonists the right to own land where they pleased. Most colonists ignored the act.
Sugar Act Import duties on sugar and other items were imposed.	1764	Colonists raised the issue of "taxation without representation." Boston merchants started a boycott of British luxury goods.
Stamp Act Imposed the first direct tax on the American colonies, requiring a tax on all printed materials.	1765	(1) "Sons of Liberty" used violence and intimidation against British stamp agents; (2) The "Stamp Act Congress" sent a petition to King George III. (3) The boycott extended to include all British goods.
Stamp Act Repealed; Declaratory Act Passed. The British government declared total power to legislate any laws governing the American colonies.		Colonists celebrated the repeal of the Stamp Act; they relaxed the boycott, but ignored the Declaratory Act.
Quartering Act Required colonists to house British troops and supply them with food.		Colonists in New York violently refused to comply.
Townshend Revenue Acts A new series of taxes imposed on paper, tea, glass, lead, and paint.	1767	Boycott against British luxury items; Sam Adams of Boston issued the "Circular Letter" to denounce taxation and coordinate reaction among the colonies.
Boston Massacre A Boston mob harassed British soldiers, who then fired point-blank into the crowd.	1770	Townshend Acts repealed, and all duties on imports into the colonies were eliminated except for tea.
Tea Act Maintained import tax on tea and gave the British East India Company a tea monopoly, allowing it to undersell American merchants.	1773	Colonial activists in Boston disguised themselves as Indians and dumped their cargo of tea into the harbor ("Boston Tea Party").
Coercive Acts ("Intolerable Acts") Shut down the port of Boston, ended self-rule in Massachusetts, and created the New Quartering Act for all colonies.	1774	"First Continental Congress" met and called for (1) noncompliance with Coercive Acts; (2) formation of militias; and (3) a boycott of and embargo on exports to Britain.
Lexington and Concord British troops searched out militia weapons depots to destroy them.	1775	Armed "minutemen" faced the British on Lexington Green; eight Americans died, and ten were wounded; at Concord, the "Continental Congress" met and called for volunteers; George Washington was appointed commander of the colonial army.

C. The American Revolution (1776–81) was fought to obtain independence.

    1. Problems of military effectiveness hindered the early colonial effort.

        a. Colonial armies were underequipped.

        b. There was widespread opposition to fixed military terms.

    2. Washington's leadership turned the tide of battle.

        a. The French Alliance (1778) brought needed men, equipment, and money to the American cause.

        b. The defeat of Cornwallis at Yorktown (1781) brought victory to the colonies.

D. The Articles of Confederation (1781–89) proved inadequate as a central government.

    1. The Articles held the nation together during the critical period.

    2. The Articles were limited by major weaknesses.

IMPORTANT BATTLES OF THE REVOLUTION

Battle	Commanders		Outcomes
Fort Ticonderoga May 10, 1775	American Ethan Allen Benedict Arnold	British William de la Place	American victory Americans seized the fort's one hundred cannons, which were badly needed by colonial forces.
Bunker Hill June 17, 1775	American Israel Putnam William Prescott	British William Howe	British victory British took the hill but suffered huge losses compared to the Americans. Americans proved that they could stand up to the British army but war would not be won easily.
Long Island August 27, 1776	American George Washington Charles Lee	British William Howe	British victory Despite defeat, Washington calmly and confidently managed a surprise evacuation of troops across the East River to Manhattan.
Trenton December 26, 1776	American George Washington Nathanael Greene	British Johann Rall	American victory Victorious surprise attack on Hessian forces rallied American spirit and confidence in Washington's leadership.
Princeton January 3, 1777	American George Washington	British Charles Cornwallis Charles Mawhood	American victory Encouraged the French government to send supplies to the Americans. In England, support for the war declined.
Saratoga October 17, 1777	American Horatio Gates	British John Burgoyne	American victory France and Spain declared war on Britain. Further weakened the British government under Lord North.
Yorktown October 19, 1781	American George Washington Comte de Rochambeau Comte de Grasse	British Lord Cornwallis Banastre Tarleton	American victory Tarleton's surrender brought war to an end. Britain recognized the independence of the United States of America.

Government under "The Articles of Confederation" Ratified March, 1781

- Established the first government for the United States of America.
- Successfully negotiated the Treaty of Paris to end the revolutionary war.
- Passed the **Land Ordinance of 1785,** creating a system for western land surveys and provisions for land sales.
- Passed the **Northwest Ordinance of 1787,** which established a process for western frontier regions to organize into territories and become new states.

Problems with Articles Become Clear during the "Critical Period" after the Revolutionary War (1781-1789)

- Had to rely on requesting funds from the states.
- Did not bind the states together in a true union.
- No centralized control over trade.
    - Uniform tariffs could not be imposed.
    - States could impose their own trade restrictions against other states.
- Thirteen different currencies continued to exist.
- No authority to borrow money inside or outside the United States.
- Lacked balance in Congress between large and small states.
    - All states given one vote, even though large states were expected to provide more financial support than small states.
- Changes or amendments needed for unanimous approval.
- No executive authority to balance the power of Congress or ensure that laws of Congress were carried out.

E. The need for a strong central government led to the framing of the Constitution (1789).

F. The government under the Constitution solved many major problems.

   1. A federal system was created that divided federal and state power.

   2. Separation of powers and checks and balances were included to limit the power of the central government.

New Government—"The Constitution"

Ratified June 21, 1788

- **Separation of Powers:** Executive along with Legislative and Judicial branches.

- **Checks and Balances:**

   Executive: veto power over legislation; appointment of federal judges, ambassadors, and other government officials.

   Legislative: override presidential vetoes; approve presidential appointments; impeachment of president and federal judges.

   Judicial: legislative oversight; independence guaranteed through lifetime appointments.

- **Federal System:** shared between the central government and the states.

- **Powers of Congress:** The power to tax, declare war, make treaties, etc.

   Regulate trade, mint, and distribute a single currency; declare war.

   Impose tariffs, and establish immigration laws.

   The power to tax, borrow money, and maintain the military forces of the nation.

- **The Great Compromise:** Created a bicameral, or two-house, Congress to balance the interests and influence of large and small states.

   House of Representatives: representatives apportioned based on the size of their population.

   Senate: all states granted two senators.

- **Bill of Rights:** Added to protect the rights of individuals and safeguard the sovereignty of the states over their own affairs (Tenth Amendment)

- **Amendments:** Established processes for amendment that required three-fourths approval of the states and two-thirds of each house of Congress.

III. THE NEW NATION (1787–1823)

The struggles of the new Constitutional government of the United States were numerous. The unstable financial foundations of the nation lacked a central vision and structures to guide the economic future; circumstances arose that challenged the Constitutional limits placed on the authority of the government, and America's relations with its nemesis Great Britain remained hostile and explosive.

Alexander Hamilton's response to the financial troubles of the nation gave rise to two political parties with vastly different views regarding the use of government's power and the overall direction of the nation. Foreign policy challenges further hardened the lines between Alexander Hamilton and his Federalist Party, and the anti-Federalists lined up behind Thomas Jefferson and his Democratic-Republican Party.

A. The early national period tested the new federal government.

   1. Hamilton's financial plan placed the national government on a sound financial basis.

      a. The national government paid back the state, national, and foreign debts to demonstrate the credibility of the new government.

      b. The national government encouraged American business expansion by passing excise taxes and a tariff.

      c. The national government raised revenue by initiating a tax on domestic whiskey.

    d. The national government authorized the use of coins and paper money to encourage the growth of commerce.

    e. The national government encouraged the development of a national bank to facilitate the expansion of business.

2. Hamilton's financial plan led to the development of political parties.

    a. The Federalist Party believed in the concept of a strong central government ruled by the manufacturing interests of the country. (Hamilton)

    b. The Anti-Federalist Party believed in the concept of limited federal power based on the farming interests of the country. (Jefferson)

    c. The Federalist Party favored the rich and the wealthy.

    d. The Anti-Federalists developed a political philosophy that believed in the worth of the individual.

Early National Period: Political Parties		
Issue	**Federalists** **(Hamilton)**	**Democratic-Republicans** **(Jefferson)**
Constitutional Powers	"Loose Construction" Authority to do whatever is "necessary and proper" according to the Conswtitution Centralized authority in the national government	"Strict Construction" Avoid tyranny by exercising only those powers expressly stated in the Constitution Decentralized authority to the states
Foundations of the Nation	Expansion and growth Banking Investment in business Manufacturing	Focus on yeoman farmers as the foundation of republicanism (sovereignty of the people)
Foreign Policy	Pro-England Conservative Constitutional monarchy	Pro-France Revolutionary Republicanism

3. Foreign policy during the early national period was weak and ineffectual.

4. The Louisiana Purchase (1803) became the greatest real estate purchase in U.S. history.

B. The War of 1812 (1812–15) was fought between the United States and Great Britain.

1. Among the causes of the War of 1812 were violations of U.S. neutrality and impressment of U.S. sailors.

2. The U.S. victory resulted in national pride, self-sufficiency, and foreign credibility.

C. The new nationalism (1816–23) followed the War of 1812.

1. The scope and authority of the Supreme Court were established during this period.

2. The Era of Good Feelings characterized the political successes of the Anti-Federalist Party.

3. The Monroe Doctrine defined American interests in the Northern Hemisphere.

4. The new nationalism led to the development of a new American culture.

5. The removal of the British from the northwestern frontier encouraged westward expansion.

The War of 1812 (1812–1815) The United States versus Great Britain	
Causes	Neutrality (Britain and France at war).
	British seizure of American merchant vessels.
	British practice of "impressment" (stopping U.S. merchant ships and forcing American sailors into service for the British navy).
	Conflict over frontier land.
	British agitation of Native Americans against American settlement on the frontier.
	"War Hawks" in Congress advocated pushing the British out of the frontier and even expelling them from Canada.
Battles	Battle of Lake Erie (1813): Naval battles led by Capt. Oliver Perry claimed Lake Erie for the United States.
	Battle of Baltimore (1814): British forces advanced through Washington, D.C. and burned the Capital. Britain failed to capture Fort McHenry, later immortalized in the Star Spangled Banner.
	Battle of New Orleans (1815): The final major battle of the war; it was fought after the war was already ended by the Treaty of Ghent. Andrew Jackson became an American Hero.

IV. THE RISE OF DEMOCRACY AND THE WESTERN MOVEMENT

In the decades after the War of 1812 and prior to the Civil War, two new parties emerged on the political landscape. The Whigs, born from the ashes of the Federalist Party, fought for their national vision against the Democratic Party, an updated version of Jefferson's Democratic-Republicans. Dominating this era was the monumental figure of Tennessean Andrew Jackson, "the hero of New Orleans." Opposing the old Hamiltonian view of an America dominated by financial elites, the Democratic Jackson championed the cause of the "common man" and the expansionist frontier western spirit—what journalist John O'Sullivan called the nation's "Manifest Destiny."

A. Jacksonian democracy (1826–36) symbolized the rise of the "common man."

   1. Jackson's war against the bank and the tariff were key issues for the new Democratic Party.

   2. Jackson initiated the spoils system in which political enemies are replaced by political friends.

   3. Jackson pursued nationalistic policies.

B. The Whig Party opposed the Democratic Party's belief in states' rights and instead favored a strong national government.

C. The territorial expansion of the United States reached from the Mississippi River to the Pacific Ocean.

   1. The rise of the new West created opportunities in transportation, education, politics, mining, and agriculture.

   2. The Trail of Tears (1838-1839) was the result of the forced relocation of Native Americans from tribal areas in the south to the Oklahoma territory.

   3. Manifest Destiny encouraged U.S. expansion to the Pacific.

   a. Texas was annexed to the United States in 1837.

   b. The Oregon Territory was added to the United States in 1846 and encouraged settlement of the Far West.

   c. The Mexican War (1848) added California and parts of the Southwest to the United States.

Westward Expansion 1812–1850		
Date	**Region**	**Expansion**
1812–1820	Louisiana Territory	Louisiana, Missouri added to the Union
	Old Northwest	Indiana, Illinois added to the Union
	Mississippi Territory	Mississippi, Alabama added to the Union
1821	Florida	Purchased from Spain
1830s	Old Southwest	Cleared of all remaining Native American resistance; "Trail of Tears" marked the removal of the Cherokee, Creek, Choctaw, Chickasaw, and Seminole to the Oklahoma Territory
1848	Mexican Cession	Mexican-American War ended in victory for United States; Treaty of Guadalupe Hidalgo ceded Utah, Nevada, California, Arizona, and New Mexico to the United States
	Pacific Northwest	Northwest boundary dispute with Britain settled; Oregon Territory organized
1850	Michigan Territory	Michigan added to the Union
	Louisiana Territory	Arkansas, Iowa, and Wisconsin added to the Union
	Republic of Texas	Texas annexed, and added to the Union
	Pacific Coast	California added to the Union

V. THE BACKGROUND OF THE CIVIL WAR AND RECONSTRUCTION (1800–1876)

As the nation expanded westward, the unresolved issue of slavery could no longer be ignored. As long as slavery was an institution limited to a handful of Southern states, many in the nation seemed willing to wait out its eventual demise. With growth and the opportunity for an expanded slave economy, the struggle over the vision of America's future brought the Union to the brink of destruction.

Despite attempts to avoid it, a four-year war was fought that tore the nation apart. An immensely costly victory by the forces for the Union and the assassination of a president, beloved by many, left some in the nation in no mood for reconciliation. Failed attempts to fully embrace freed slaves into the promise of democracy—and to reconstruct an unrepentant and devastated South—left the nation scarred for another century and beyond.

A. Geographic and economic factors contributed to the growth of slavery.
  1. The dependence on slavery and cotton created a unique Southern economy.
  2. The development of the "Cotton South" led to sectionalism.
B. The expansion of slavery was a political issue prior to the 1850s.
  1. The Missouri Compromise of 1820 limited the spread of slavery.
  2. The annexation of Texas (1837) added potential slave territory to the United States.
  3. The Mexican War (1848) was criticized as a proslavery, expansionist war.
C. The failure of the politics of compromise led to war.
  1. The Compromise of 1850 failed to hold the nation together. California was admitted as a free state and a fugitive slave law was passed.
  2. In the 1850s, slavery and sectionalism continued to threaten the Union.
  3. The failure of the Kansas-Nebraska Act (1854) led to bloodshed over the expansion of slavery and raised the issue of popular sovereignty.
  4. The Dred Scott decision failed to solve the slavery question. Slaves were not citizens and could not sue.
  5. The election in 1860 of Lincoln, a sectional candidate, made secession inevitable.
  6. The Confederate states of America were formed (thirteen southern states).

Causes of the Civil War		
Cause	**South**	**North**
Social-Economic Differences between North and South	Economy dependent on King Cotton and slave labor	Economy more industrial than agricultural; based on free labor
	Northern criticism viewed as an attack on Southerners' entire way of life	Modernity and progress; no future for feudal Southern society
States' Rights versus Federal Authority	Doctrine of nullification; states could nullify federal laws	Rejected nullification; Constitution made federal government supreme
Expansion of Slavery	Cotton exhausted soil of the "Old South;" expansion key to the South's survival	Expansion of slavery westward—would United States ever rid itself of slavery?
	New slave states admitted (Missouri, Kansas, and Texas)	No more slave states in the Union; California admitted as a free state in 1850.

D. The Civil War threatened the Union (1861–65).

    1. The North and South prepared for war.

        a. The North had an overall superiority in manpower, firepower, and economic resources.

        b. The South had advantages in leadership and territory.

    2. The Union strategy of isolating the South proved successful.

        a. The Union blockade economically strangled the South.

        b. The defeat at Gettysburg (1863) ended the Southern chances for foreign recognition.

        c. Economic and military weaknesses, along with a devastated South, led to Lee's surrender at Appomattox (1865).

Major Battles of the Civil War	
1861	**Fort Sumter**
	■ Union: Maj. Robert Anderson; Confederate: Gen. P. G. T. Beauregard
	■ Fort bombarded; surrendered by Anderson; opening battle of the war
	First Battle of Bull Run
	■ Union: Gen. Irvin McDowell; Confederate: Gen. Joseph Johnston
	■ Union forces expected a quick victory and a short war overall; routed by Confederates; the war would go on.
1862	**Antietam**
	■ Union: Gen. George McClellan; Confederate: Gen. Robert E. Lee
	■ The first battle fought on Northern soil; McClellan beat back Lee's invasion on the bloodiest single day in the war; Lincoln announced the Emancipation Proclamation.
1863	**Gettysburg**
	■ Union: Gen. George Meade; Confederate: Gen. Robert E. Lee
	■ Lee launched a second invasion of the North; Meade refused to pursue Lee, and the war continued; Lincoln delivered his Gettysburg Address; victory at Gettysburg made Northern victory inevitable.
	Vicksburg
	■ Union: Gen. Ulysses S. Grant; Confederate: Lt. Gen. John C. Pemberton
	■ Union victory cut off the western theatre from the South and split the confederacy at the Mississippi River.

1864	**Sherman's March to the Sea**
	■ Union: Maj. Gen. William Tecumseh Sherman; Confederate: Lt. Gen. John Bell Hood
	■ Sherman's troops captured Atlanta and pushed ahead to capture Savannah. The brutality of these battles and the burning of Atlanta left a legacy of bitterness toward the North.
1865	**Battle of Appomattox Courthouse**
	■ Union: Gen. Ulysses S. Grant; Confederate: Gen. Robert E. Lee
	■ Final engagement of the war; ended with Lee's surrender to Grant

E. Reconstruction attempts to reunite the nation (1865–66).

   1. Following the Civil War, the economic, political, social, and military reconstruction of the South was necessary.

   2. The president and Congress differed on how to reconstruct the South.

   a. The presidential plan emphasized tolerance for the defeated South.

   b. The congressional (Radical) plan emphasized the use of military force in treating the South like a conquered territory.

   3. Reconstruction was under Radical control from 1868 to 1876.

   a. The Fourteenth and Fifteenth Amendments were passed.

   b. Civil rights bills were passed.

   c. Military rule supported Radical Reconstruction.

   d. President Johnson was impeached for opposing Radical Reconstruction.

Presidential Reconstruction	**Congressional Reconstruction**
ABRAHAM LINCOLN/ANDREW JOHNSON	THADDEUS STEVENS/CHARLES SUMNER
"With malice toward none"	Punish the South
Amnesty plan—Southerners pardoned	South divided into five military districts
Confederate states must ratify Thirteenth Amendment, nullify state secession ordinances	States must ratify the Fourteenth Amendment—equal rights to freedmen
South must repudiate all debts owed by the Union to the Confederate states	State constitutions include a guarantee of full suffrage to freedmen
Provisional governors to protect rights of freedmen	Fifteenth Amendment—right to vote for freedmen

   4. The disputed election of 1876 ended Radical Reconstruction with the election of Hayes.

   a. Social justice for blacks received a setback.

   b. The national commitment to equal opportunity was delayed 100 years.

   c. Jim Crow Laws and Black Codes further restricted Black rights.

VI. A NEW ECONOMY (1876–1900)

With the Civil War behind them and an expanding nation in front of them, Americans enthusiastically pursued industrial growth. Industry contributed to new innovations in transportation, further settlement of the nation, the growth of cities, increased productivity, and new leisure activities.

A. The industrial development of the United States was encouraged by western expansion.

   1. The settlement of the West was aided by the Homestead Act (1862) and the transcontinental railroad (1869).

   2. Western industries were based on mining, cattle, and grain.

   3. Farmers and ranchers settled the Great Plains.

B. The industrial growth of the United States was greatly expanded.

   1. Inventions promoted industrial growth.

   2. Raw materials and geographic factors contributed to regional economic diversity.

   3. The development of communication and transportation aided the industrial growth of America.

   4. New methods of production such as division of labor, standardized parts, the assembly line, and mass production fostered the expansion of industry.

   5. Expanding markets at home and abroad encouraged industrial expansion.

   6. The development of the steel, mining, electric, petroleum, textile, and food-processing industries characterized the period.

C. Industrialization reflected changing attitudes and conditions.

   1. Mechanization and the factory system were introduced.

   2. The growth of labor unions resulted from problems caused by industrialization.

   3. Social, economic, and political changes became evident.

   4. The rise of cities paralleled the industrial growth of America.

   5. The need for government intervention increased.

      a. The Sherman (1890) and Clayton (1914) Antitrust Acts restricted the power of giant corporations.

      b. Workmen's compensation laws, child labor laws, and regulations on working conditions and minimum wages were part of the congressional reform movement to improve the plight of the working man.

   6. The need for the conservation of natural resources was a result of the continued industrial growth of America.

Domain 3: California History

I. PREHISTORIC PERIOD

California's earliest peoples descended from those who first left Asia by crossing the Bering Sea land bridge, arriving in North America about 20,000 to 30,000 years ago. It would take another 10,000 years for various groups to reach California and beyond. The migrating groups that arrived in California found a land of rugged mountains, extensive coastline, mild climate, and rich soil lying between the Pacific coastal ranges and the Sierra Nevada. The rugged topography of mountains and deserts isolated California's indigenous peoples from the cultures that developed on the Great Plains to the east and in Mexico to the south. The landscape made extended travel on foot within the region extremely difficult as well; thus, regional relations between tribal groups were limited, creating a diverse patchwork of isolated and distinct tribal groupings.

A. The first humans to enter North America crossed the Bering Strait land bridge at the end of the Pleistocene Period, or the last Ice Age, approximately 20,000 to 30,000 years ago.

   1. They migrated southward from Alaska and populated North and South America.

   2. They entered California approximately 15,000 years ago; evidence from the early-man archaeological site at Calico could push the date back to 50,000 years ago.

B. Native Americans of California.

1. General characteristics of California Indians prior to European contact.

   a. They spoke a great diversity of dialects.

   b. They represented the largest concentration of Indians in North America (estimated at 150,000 to 300,000).

   c. Dwellings reflected the groups' climatic and geographic locations: frame and plank houses in the north, brush shelters in the southern deserts, and earth houses along the coastal areas.

   d. The groups were not generally warlike, and weapons were not sophisticated (in comparison to those of the Plains Indians).

   e. Acorns were extensively used as a food source where oak trees were plentiful. This involved drying, storing, cracking, and leaching.

   f. The transportation reflected geographic factors: Balsa and raft-type boats were used in the south, and plank canoes were used in the north.

2. The shared heritage of the various tribes.

   a. Lineage was traced on the paternal side.

   b. Native tobacco and jimsonweed were widely used in ceremonial activities.

   c. Sweathouses were used (by men only).

   d. The groups' religions were similar in myths, creation stories, shamanism, and the influence of nature.

   e. Ceremonies dealt with birth, death, puberty, marriage, hunting, and so on.

   f. Fables dealt with animals and other natural phenomena of the region (coyote, raven, bear, snake, thunder, and so on).

   g. Roles were sex differentiated: The men hunted and fished, and the women gathered food and materials and killed small game.

   h. The oral story tradition was used by all California Indians.

3. Geographic factors isolated many tribes. Desert and mountain barriers restricted contact.

   a. Northern California tribes included the Yurok, Hupa, Modoc, and Pomo.

   b. Central California tribes included the Maidu and Miwok.

   c. Coastal tribes included the coastal Miwok, Esselen, and Chumash.

   d. Desert tribes included the Mojave and Serrano.

   e. Sierra Nevada tribes included the Miwok and Mono.

4. Their material belongings were similar.

   a. Subsistence agricultural implements: mortar and pestle, metate, grinding slab, and digging sticks.

   b. Receptacles: baskets (most famous), pottery, wood, and stone bowls.

   c. Musical instruments: drum, rattle, flute, rasp, and bow.

   d. Money: clam disks and olivella shells.

II. SPANISH CONQUEST

The Spanish first became aware of California in the 1500s after Cortés's conquest of Mexico in 1519. Cortés and others explored farther north but failed to find any fabled cities of gold or to imagine any great promise for future settlement. Focusing on the richer parts of its empire in Mexico, Peru, and the Philippines, Spain presumed possession of California but paid it little attention. Not until the mid-1700s did outside interest in the region finally prompt the Spanish to make their presence in California a permanent one. As a result, a string of 21 missions were built, linked by California's first transportation route, the *El Camino Real*.

A. The search for the Seven Cities of Cibola by Cortes in the 1530s resulted in Spanish exploration of the Baja peninsula.

1. Spain was interested in conquest and wealth.

2. Exploration centered on a search for an island inhabited by Amazon-like women who used golden weapons.

San Francisco de Solano (1823)
San Rafael Arcángel (1817)
San Francisco de Asís (1776)
El Presidio de San Francisco
San José (1797)
Santa Clara de Asís (1777)
El Pueblo de San Jose de Guadalupe
Santa Cruz (1791)
San Juan Bautista (1797)
El Presidio de Monterey
San Carlos Borromeo de Carmelo (1770)
Nuestra Señora de la Soledad (1791)
San Antonio de Padua (1771)
San Miguel Arcangel (1797)
San Luis Obispo de Tolosa (1772)
La Purísima Concepción (1787)
Santa Inés (1804)
Santa Bárbara (1786)
El Presidio de Santa Bárbara
San Fernando Rey de España (1797)
San Buenaventura (1782)
El Pueblo de Nuestra Senora la Reina de Los Angeles
San Gabriel Arcángel (1771)
San Juan Capistrano (1776)
San Luis Rey de Francia (1798)
El Presidio de San Diego San Diego (1769)
El Camino Real
PACIFIC OCEAN

Spanish Missions in California.

B. Cabrillo discovered San Diego Bay, the Santa Barbara Islands, Point Conception, and Point Reyes (1542–43).

   1. He searched for a water passage between the Pacific and Atlantic oceans.

   2. Future voyages traveled the entire coast of California.

C. Drake, an English explorer, sailed up the California coast in 1579 and claimed the area for England.

   1. The threat from England compelled Spain to colonize California.

   2. Spanish explorations discovered safe harbors at Monterey and San Francisco.

   3. For the next 100 years, Spanish colonization of California was minimal.

D. Russian excursions along the northern American coast (1800s) resulted in renewed Spanish efforts to colonize California.

   1. Russian fur interests in Alaska pushed southward.

   2. Russians established Fort Ross 80 miles north of San Francisco Bay in 1812 as a trading post.

   3. The American government also viewed Russian exploration of the California coast as a threat.

      a. The Monroe Doctrine (1823) restricted European colonization of the Americas.

      b. The Spanish reacted to potential Russian, British, and American presences by establishing presidios (military forts) and pueblos (small settlements) in valleys around San Francisco Bay.

E. The Spanish established the California missions.

   1. Jesuits established five permanent settlements in Baja California in the early 1700s.

   2. Franciscan friars established 21 Spanish missions along the California coast from San Diego to Sonoma (one day's journey apart at completion in 1823).

      a. The purpose was to convert the Indians to Christianity, establish cultural and agricultural centers, and populate Alta California for Spain.

      b. Both the "sword" and the "cross" were used to subdue the Indians.

   3. Father Serra is credited with the development of the mission system; his lasting contributions are controversial.

   4. Around 1830, the mission system began a secularization process. By 1836, most mission property was privately owned.

California Missions	
Purpose	■ Create permanent and self-sufficient Spanish settlements in California ■ Defend Spanish empire to the south in Mexico ■ Win Catholic converts among indigenous people
Organization	■ Built in areas with high concentration of native population ■ Church, workshops, kitchens, living quarters, and storerooms constructed from materials on hand ■ Cultivation of cereal grains, grapes, fruit trees, and olives; raising of livestock

Positive Outcomes	■ Provided presidios (Spanish garrisons) with food and goods ■ In some cases enjoyed great economic success ■ Gave Spanish a foothold in California
Negative Outcomes	■ Fatally exposed the Indians to European diseases ■ Destroyed native culture ■ Exploited indigenous labor force

III. MEXICAN RULE IN CALIFORNIA (1821–1846)

Mexico gained its independence from Spain in 1822 but put no greater imperative on the development and political control of California than had Spain. Within the region now known as *Alta California,* a system of feudal estates enlarged by the sale of Spanish mission lands made local landowners the real power in California. Seeing a future of independence unlikely with the Russians, British, French, and Americans all poised to seize their vulnerable territory, some *Californios* looked to Europeans to free them from Mexico's rule. Others rejected the Old World authority of monarchs and favored annexation by the United States instead.

Spain	Mexico
Alta California was a colony of Spain. California not viewed as a reliable source of revenue	Territory of the Republic of Mexico
Spanish colonization did not start until the late eighteenth century. Spanish presence never strong enough to enforce restrictions on trading with non-Spanish merchants.	Mexican authority never strong. Mexico allowed trade with foreigners and issued land grants to individual Mexican citizens.
Spanish colonization was built on three strategies: Missions: Self supporting religious centers. Twenty one missions built between 1769–1823. Presidios (garrisons): Established to provide costal defense and protection to the pueblos and missions. Pueblos (towns): Developed to provide agriculture for the presidios and as population centers.	Missions secularized and lands sold to powerful local families (Californios) Ranchos owned by Californios—the dominant institutions Mexican rule marked by feuds among the ranchos and with Mexican government. Encroachment of non-Mexicans into California increased.

A. After Mexican independence from Spain in 1822, California residents exerted increased control in local political matters.

B. The land-grant system and the ranchos fueled independent action.

C. By 1845, the Californios (provincial Californians) expelled the last of the Mexican governors.

D. American trappers (including Jedediah Smith), explorers (including Kit Carson and Joseph Walker), and a variety of wagon masters opened California to American settlement.

IV. CALIFORNIA'S INDEPENDENCE FROM MEXICO (1846–1848)

A. Migrations of American pioneer families in the 1840s swelled the American population in California.

1. American pioneers settled in the San Joaquin and Sacramento valleys.

2. They increased the demand that California become part of the United States.

B. President Polk indirectly supported the annexation of California.

1. John C. Frémont, possibly acting on presidential orders, raised the U.S. flag near Monterey, and then retreated from the area.

2. War was declared on Mexico in 1846 (the Mexican-American War).

a. The Bear Flag Revolt prematurely captured California (1846).

b. Commander Sloat captured Monterey Bay and claimed the area for the United States.

    c. General Stockton captured Los Angeles; Governor Pico and General Castro retook the area for Mexico.

    d. Stockton and Kearney defeated Pico and raised the American flag over Los Angeles in 1847.

  3. The Treaty of Guadalupe Hidalgo (1848) transferred California from Mexican to American control.

California 1848–1850

- California ceded by Mexico to the United States (Treaty of Guadalupe Hidalgo)
- Military government established
- Discovery of gold at Sutter's Mill in 1848
    - "Rush" of 100,000 new immigrants
- Deadlock in Washington over organizing California as a territory due to slavery debate
- Californians held constitutional convention of their own
    - Created an unofficial state government
    - Slavery prohibited
- California admitted to the Union as a free state via Compromise of 1850

V. GOLD DISCOVERED IN CALIFORNIA

During Mexican rule, Americans moving to California were few and far between—trappers crossing the Sierra Nevada and traders traveling the rugged trail connecting Santa Fe, New Mexico, with the outpost of Los Angeles. By the 1840s, however, white settlers began to move from Missouri westward. It was a group of these settlers who, worried that the Mexican government was about to make a move against them, marched into Sonoma in 1846 and raised their grizzly bear flag, proclaiming California an independent republic. When word finally reached them that the United States was already at war with Mexico, the "Bear Flag Revolt" was abandoned, and the rebels joined John C. Frémont in the "California Battalion" fighting to make California a part of the United States.

A. The discovery of gold by James W. Marshall in 1848 changed the political, social, and economic history of the state.

  1. "Gold fever" became a national phenomenon; the California settler population increased tremendously from 15,000 in 1847 to 92,000 in 1850, and 380,000 in 1860.

  2. This population growth led to statehood. (California was the thirty-first state.)

B. The Compromise of 1850 allowed California to be a free state.

  1. Slavery was prohibited, which upset the balance of free and slave states.

  2. California statehood became a background issue to the Civil War.

VI. CALIFORNIA FROM THE CIVIL WAR TO THE TURN OF THE CENTURY

Powerful business interests controlled California politics and the Republican Party, ensuring support for both President Lincoln and the Union cause. California's distance kept it out of the war, but the state sent gold and recruits eastward. In the meantime, both a railroad grant and authorization to build the Central Pacific link to the transcontinental railroad were secured. In 1862, the Homestead Act allowed citizens to claim free land if they would live on it and improve it for five years. Thus, throughout post–Civil War California, mining, the railroad, and farming combined to promote waves of immigration from the eastern United States, China, and Ireland. Ensuing periods of economic boom and bust then fueled California's long history of troubled relations with immigrants, regarded as unwanted competition during economic downturns.

A. The completion of the transcontinental railroad in 1869 completed Manifest Destiny.

  1. The Central Pacific met the Union Pacific at Promontory, Utah. Immigrant labor was used: Chinese on the Central Pacific and Irish on the Union Pacific.

  2. The Big Four (Hopkins, Crocker, Huntington, and Stanford) controlled the railroad industry and most of the California political scene.

B. Economic depression hit California in the 1870s; a cycle of boom and bust was begun.

1. The depression was characterized by low wages, high unemployment, railroad abuses (unfair pricing and rebates), and the restriction of water rights by land monopolies.

2. The collapse of the Bank of California in 1875 (and other financial institutions) further weakened the California economy.

C. Open hostility toward the Chinese erupted.

1. They were blamed for most of the economic problems (backlash from the mining and railroad frontier).

2. The Chinese Exclusion Act was passed by Congress in 1882.

3. By 1877, politicians, newspapers, and citizens urged open agitation against the Chinese in California.

4. The Workingmen's Party was established. It was nativist, anti-Chinese, and anti-big business (1877).

    a. It demanded a constitutional convention and populist-type reforms.

    b. The California Constitution (1879) codified anti-Chinese legislation.

D. The California land boom of the 1880s swelled the population again.

1. The ensuing bank collapse in 1887 devastated the economy.

2. Hard times and economic retrenchment followed.

California and Immigrant Relations (1850–1880s)	
1850	Foreign Miners' Tax imposed by California legislature; $20 monthly tax on foreign miners
1854	California Supreme Court excluded all nonwhite races from testifying against a white person (case involved Chinese witness testifying in a murder trial)
1879	California constitution denied voting rights to any "native of China" (repealed 1926)
1882	Chinese Exclusion Act passed by Congress
1884	San Francisco school board adopted "separate but equal doctrine" and segregated Chinese schoolchildren from all others

VII. EARLY TWENTIETH-CENTURY CALIFORNIA

By the turn of the century, immigration continued to swell with newcomers pouring in from the Midwest and from Japan. Economic competition in agriculture between the Japanese and transplanted Midwestern farmers revived earlier discriminatory efforts that had once targeted the Chinese. Along with immigrants, populism and the Progressive Era made their way to California, bringing reform to municipal and state governments long corrupted by the powerful railroad interests and machine politics.

A. New immigration (mainly from the Midwest) led to a dramatic population increase.

B. Fears of the "yellow peril" were raised again.

1. Japanese were imported in large numbers to work in agriculture. They displaced Anglo workers and resentment grew.

2. Asians were restricted from naturalization at the turn of the century.

3. The San Francisco Board of Education segregated Caucasians and Asians in 1905.

4. The resentment led to an international "Gentlemen's Agreement" (1907).

    a. Japanese immigration to the United States was voluntarily restricted (but the measure was ineffective in reducing tension).

    b. Integrated schools were permitted.

    c. Agitation against Asians continued.

C. Populist reforms aimed to bring government closer to the people.

1. Hiram Johnson (a progressive) was elected governor, and a reform program was initiated.

    a. Twenty-three amendments were added to the California Constitution (1911).

    b. The provisions included women's suffrage; initiative, referendum, and recall; workmen's compensation; a new railroad commission; and others.

California's Progressive Reforms	
1902	Los Angeles introduced the initiative, referendum, and recall to city charter
1909	State legislature approved the Direct Primary, taking choice of nominees from office out of hands of political machines
1910	Progressive governor Hiram Johnson election along with a progressive legislature
1911	Initiative, referendum, and recall added to state's constitution
	Railroad regulation
	Regulation of all public utilities
	Women granted the vote
	Workers' compensation law
	Alien Land Law prohibited aliens not eligible for citizenship (Japanese) from purchasing or leasing land in California

2. Anti-Japanese agitation continued.

   a. The Japanese were ineligible for citizenship (national law), they could not own land (the California Alien Land Act), and more restrictive federal legislation was passed against them in 1913 and 1924.

   b. The U.S. Supreme Court upheld anti-Japanese legislation.

3. The labor movement lost political power after an anarchist bombing in Los Angeles (1910).

VIII. CALIFORNIA FROM WORLD WAR I TO 1930

Oil, moviemaking, and agriculture drove California's economy and fueled its growth. After the discovery of oil in Los Angeles County and throughout the Los Angeles basin in the 1920s, oil became the most profitable economic venture in Southern California. With the advent of film as a popular form of entertainment, major studios bought property on the outskirts of Los Angeles, creating the legendary studio town of Hollywood. With cheap land available and a river of immigrants flooding the state, agriculture also boomed. By 1919, California's fruit, nut, and olive growers were outproducing all other similar farm interests in the rest of the nation. Much of this economic growth focused on Southern California, driving a wedge between established political elites in the northern half of the state and new power brokers in the southern half.

A. World War I produced a new economic boom.

   1. Wages, production, manufacturing, and commerce expanded rapidly.

   2. The Panama Canal was opened in 1914, which extended international links.

   3. An influx of immigrants arrived in the 1920s.

      a. Economic advances were tied to movie, oil, and agricultural production.

      b. A real-estate boom fueled the housing industry.

      c. By 1930, the California population had grown to six million, an increase of 65 percent during one decade. It was now the sixth most populous state.

B. California politics were characterized as a power struggle between the north and south and between rural and urban areas.

IX. CALIFORNIA FROM 1930 TO 1960

The Great Depression hit California as it did all other states. However, isolated from the environmental disaster of the Dust Bowl, California agriculture continued to be productive, attracting displaced farmers and other workers from the rest of the country. World War II revived the nation's economy but nowhere more than in California. The great economic boom lasted well beyond the war, resulting in what some would call "the second gold rush."

A. The economic collapse of 1930 resulted in large-scale unemployment, bank failures, and foreclosures.

B. The economic downturn renewed the call for political reform.

    1. Upton Sinclair (a reform candidate) ran unsuccessfully for governor on a platform for political change.

    2. The Utopian Society promoted economic and social reform.

    3. The Townsend Plan favored pensions for the aged and a graduated income tax.

C. Depression-era California.

    1. Dust Bowl migrants added more than 350,000 to the population.

    2. Economic and social problems, including homelessness, confronted the state.

D. Impact of the Depression in California.

Impact of the Great Depression

- 375,000 "Okies" and "Arkies" migrated out of the Dust Bowl Midwest to California

    142 agricultural workers for every 100 jobs by 1934

    Wages fell to $0.15 per hour in Imperial and San Joaquin fields

- Mexican repatriation

    Competition for agricultural jobs made Mexican workers a target

    Mexican nationals and Mexican Americans deported or forcibly repatriated

- Film industry providing a relatively inexpensive ($0.15 per ticket) escape from reality, *increasing* the popularity of Hollywood films

- Falling prices and rising surpluses forced production cuts in oil industry

---

E. The U.S. entry into World War II brought economic revitalization to California.

    1. California's manufacturing base was greatly increased (airplanes, ships, and other war products).

    2. California became the "defense center" of the nation.

F. Japanese-Americans were relocated from coastal areas to inland detention camps (1942).

    1. Constitutional and moral questions were raised.

    2. The Japanese were forced to sell their homes and businesses on short notice at huge losses.

    3. Manzanar, a World War II Relocation Center, became a national historic site in 1992.

G. Huge defense contracts following the war fueled economic prosperity.

    1. Hundreds of thousands of armed-forces personnel migrated to California.

    2. The need for public services increased.

    3. Pollution and water became political issues.

Impact of World War II on California	
Economic	Aircraft and shipbuilding industries boomed with defense work
	■ 11.9 percent of all U.S. government war contracts
	■ 17 percent of all war supplies made in California
	■ Defense boom lasted through next three decades
	More military bases and installations than any other state
	Oil and mineral resource production at maximum levels
	New industries supported defense efforts throughout the state
	Film industry increased production (entertainment and war propaganda movies)

continued

Impact of World War II on California, continued	
Social	Tensions of war and rising immigration affected race relations ■ 1942: forced detention of thousands of Japanese and Japanese Americans ■ 1943: Zoot Suit Riots; Mexicans primary targets; African Americans and Filipinos also victimized
Demographic	Industrial growth prompted new wave of migration and population boom ■ 1940 population 6,907,387 1942: Bracero Program initiated in California farm fields, started new wave of Mexican immigration (program lasted until 1964) ■ 1950 population 10,586,223 ■ 1960 population 15,717,204

X. RECENT DEVELOPMENTS IN CALIFORNIA HISTORY

California's strong economy has been supported by its mild climate, its resources, and an abundant workforce. The state continues to draw newcomers, forcing officials and citizens to face multiple challenges of sustaining economic growth; providing adequate public services and education to a huge population; urban issues of poverty and violence; rising numbers of immigrants, both legal and illegal; and how to access and efficiently use its shrinking resources, particularly water.

A. Economic advantages of California.

1. The gross domestic product (GDP) ranks California number one in the nation.
2. The California GDP ranks it among the top 10 *countries* in the world.
3. Vast natural resources (oil, timber, minerals, and so on) and abundant fertile land allow for future growth.
4. California leads the nation in manufacturing and agricultural production.
5. The higher education system (junior colleges, state colleges, and universities) is among the finest in the nation.

B. Five primary economic regions.

1. Hollywood (entertainment)
2. Southern California (aerospace)
3. Central Valley (agriculture)
4. Silicon Valley (computers/high technology)
5. Napa Valley, Sonoma Valley, Santa Barbara, and Paso Robles (wine)

C. Five primary sectors for employment.

1. Trade, transportation, and utilities
2. Government
3. Professional and business services
4. Education and health services
5. Leisure and hospitality

D. California water delivery system.

In a state of more than 36 million people, with 23 million of those living in the dry southern part of the state and 6.5 million living in the "fruit basket" of the Central Valley, fresh water is a precious resource and its availability a pressing issue. While about 75 percent of the state's water resources originate north of Sacramento, 80 percent of the demand lies in the southern two-thirds of the state.

Engineering has proven to be the controversial solution to California's water problems, with the creation of the Hetch Hetchy Aqueduct to provide water to the Bay Area of San Francisco and the California, Los Angeles, and Colorado aqueducts that meet the water needs of Los Angeles and San Diego counties. With population and demand continuing to grow, California must consider new solutions to this centuries-old problem.

1. Central Valley Project brought water from Northern to Southern California.

    a. Series of dams and reservoirs first started during the Depression.

    b. Shasta Dam is the largest water reclamation project in the state.

2. Los Angeles Aqueduct brought water from Owens River to Los Angeles.

    a. William Mulholland spearheaded the controversial project .

    b. Negative impact on Owens Valley and Mono Lake.

3. Salton Sea helps irrigate the Imperial Valley

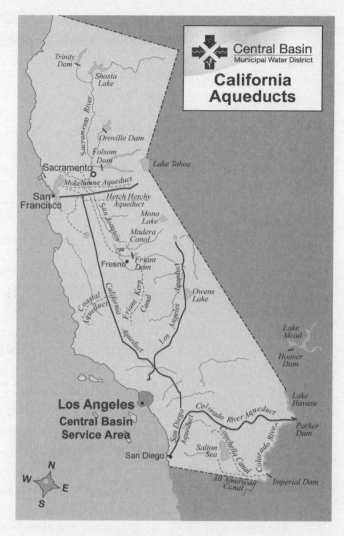

California Aquaducts.
Courtesy of Central Basin Municipal Water District.

California Geography

I. THE PHYSICAL GEOGRAPHY AND TOPOGRAPHY OF CALIFORNIA REPRESENTS GREAT DIVERSITY

California is a land of varied climate, topography, critical resources, and great natural beauty. The third-largest state in land size, California covers an extensive area of 163,693 square miles. While its coastal climate is mild and even cool along the central and northern coast, the southeastern part of the state is hot and dry. Across much of this region stretch the parched and hostile landscapes of the Mojave and Colorado deserts.

The profile of the northern part of the state contrasts with that of the southern. Rainfall varies throughout the north from 15 inches to 50 inches per year. At the extreme end of the scale, the redwood forests of the northern coast can receive more than 100 inches of rain. California's high mountain ranges, including the Sierra Nevada, the Cascades, and the Trinity Alps, receive snow during the winter months. Here resorts like Lake Tahoe and Mount Shasta can receive more than 10 feet of snow per year—and often more in a given winter season.

This precipitation feeds California's most significant rivers, including the Trinity River in the far northern part of the state, the Colorado River, and the Sacramento and San Joaquin rivers, which converge into a geographically rare inverted delta in the northern Central Valley. Also notable is the largest alpine lake in the United States, Lake Tahoe, shared by California and Nevada.

A. California extends approximately 800 miles from north to south and ranges from 150 to 350 miles east to west.

B. California borders Oregon, Nevada, Arizona, and Mexico.

C. Mount Whitney, at 14,495 feet, is the highest peak in the continental United States. Death Valley is the lowest point, at 282 feet below sea level.

D. California shows dramatic changes in topography across the state: rugged mountain peaks, fertile valleys, dense forests, ocean boundaries, and extensive deserts.

E. California geology evidences faulting, folding, alluvial and sedimentary deposition, and volcanic activity.

F. California is a region of frequent seismic activity. The San Andreas Fault system extends for 500 miles. Its movement is largely horizontal, with the west side of the fault moving northward and the east side moving southward.

G. Growing seasons extend throughout the year. In many areas of the state, there are just two distinct seasons: a mild, wet winter and a relatively long, dry summer.

H. Southern California's climate is characterized as Mediterranean and is unique in the United States. The state has many diverse microclimates, though generally the coastal climate is mild and the interior is much more extreme. The interior basins have the most extreme temperatures.

I. Few California rivers are navigable. Notable rivers are the San Joaquin and the Sacramento (and their tributaries), and the Colorado.

II. CALIFORNIA ENCOMPASSES SEVEN DISTINCT REGIONS

A. The Coast Ranges.

1. There are mountains along the western coast of California, extending from the Klamath Mountains in the north (Oregon border region) to the southwestern section of the Sierra Nevada (Southern California).

2. The San Andreas Fault system divides this region along a north/south axis.

3. The range is approximately 550 miles long.

4. The plant diversity ranges from giant redwoods in the north to chaparral in the south.

5. The mountains are a series of parallel ranges formed by sedimentary deposition uplifted by faulting and folding.

6. The climate of the Coast Ranges varies from low-pressure areas that produce fog and rain in the northern sections to a Mediterranean-type condition in the south.

B. The Klamath Mountains.

1. The Klamath Mountains are located in the northwestern corner of the state.

2. They are an extension of the Coast Ranges.

3. The mountains are rugged, steep, and in the 6,000- to 8,000-foot range.

4. The area receives heavy precipitation, and dense forests cover the mountains.

C. The Sierra Nevada (the Snowy Range).

1. The Sierra Nevada range is about 400 miles long and follows the eastern border of the state, forming the eastern wall of the Central Valley.

2. The mountains were formed through extensive uplifting and subsidence and are characterized as fault-block mountains. The backbone of the range is igneous rock.

3. They are the highest mountains in California, with many serrated peaks around 13,000 feet. Mount Whitney is located at the southern end.

4. The peaks have sharp drop-offs on the eastern side and have been a barrier to east/west transportation. The mountains have gentle slopes on the western side, which has trapped water to the benefit of Central Valley agriculture.

5. Sierra Nevada streams cut deep valleys. Gold was discovered in these streams where it was eroded from veins in the rocks.

6. The Sierra Nevada causes a rain-shadow effect: Clouds rise against the high mountain peaks, causing them to drop their moisture. This has created fertile valleys on the west side and a dry landscape on the east side.

7. Ice Age glaciers have created the current mountain profiles. Yosemite National Park's U-shaped valleys were carved by glacial action.

8. Southern California is dependent upon the average, annual 70 inches of rain and snow that fall on the Sierra Nevada for its water supply.

D. The Central Valley.

1. The Central Valley separates the Sierra Nevada and the Coast Range.

2. The valley extends from the northwest to the southeast for 400 miles and is an average of 50 miles wide.

3. The valley is a flat, sedimentary plain. The soil is fertile and makes the valley the major agricultural region of the state.

4. Sixty percent of California's farmland is located in the Central Valley.

5. A majority of the state's water supply is caught in the Central Valley as runoff from the Sierra Nevada.

6. The Sacramento Delta, encompassing 1,200 square miles of waterways, is located where the Sacramento (south-flowing) and San Joaquin (north-flowing) rivers meet.

E. The Basin and Range.

1. This extreme landscape of short, parallel mountain ranges and desert basins extends along the eastern border of California.

   a. The northern section is part of a lava plateau.

   b. The southern section is generally dry. The Mojave Desert is the major geographical feature in the south.

2. The Northwest and Southwest Great Basin, the Northwestern Sonoran Desert, and the Salton Sea Trough are significant areas in this region.

3. Death Valley (in the Mojave Desert), the lowest point in the United States, was formed by faulting (not erosion).

4. The system extends into Nevada and Utah.

5. Irrigation with water from the Colorado River has allowed large-scale farming in the Imperial and Coachella valleys.

F. The Cascade Range and Modoc Plateau.

1. The southern extreme of the Cascade Range is located in the northeastern corner of California. It extends 550 miles northward into Canada.

2. The area is separate from the Sierra Nevada and is about 25 miles wide.

3. The Cascade Range mountains were formed exclusively by volcanic activity. Many, like Mt. Shasta (14,162 feet), are dormant or extinct volcanoes.

4. Lassen Peak is the largest plug-dome (filled with magma) volcano in the world.

5. The Modoc Plateau is a level tableland of volcanic origin.

G. The Transverse and Peninsular ranges.

1. This area extends from Santa Barbara to San Diego.

2. The Transverse/Los Angeles ranges extend in an easterly (transverse) direction from the coast. (All other California ranges extend north and south.)

3. These ranges include the Santa Ynez, Santa Monica, San Gabriel, and San Bernardino mountains.

4. The Los Angeles Basin is the state's largest coastal basin and was formed by the alluvial deposition of soil from the surrounding mountain ranges.

5. The Peninsular ranges extend south from the San Bernardino Mountains in Baja California and from the Pacific Ocean east to the Salton Sea Trough.

6. The faulted eastern sections of the Peninsular ranges are characterized by sharp drop-offs. It is a complex region of active fault zones. Significant faults include the San Jacinto (near Palm Springs) and the Elsinore.

Content

The Mathematics section of the CSET focuses on the fundamentals of mathematics in elementary school. This includes the ability to communicate an understanding of math while logically solving problems. Because this section assesses reasoning and problem solving, only a minimal amount of computation is required. Non-programmable calculators are supplied for this part of the exam.

No knowledge of advanced-level mathematics is required for this exam, but real-life situations requiring a knowledge of several content areas will be used. Test takers should be familiar with commonly encountered terms in mathematics: prime numbers, factors, integers, ratio, area, perimeter, volume, parallel, perpendicular, polygon, etc.

All scratch work is to be done in the test booklet. You should get used to this procedure because no scratch paper is allowed into the testing area.

The multiple-choice section contains 26 questions grouped together and 2 short constructed-response questions. The following major content areas are covered with focus on the topics listed under each.

Analysis of Exam Areas: Content Specifications* in Mathematics

*These are the actual California state content specification standards, available online.

Domain 1: Number Sense

1.1 Numbers, Relationships Among Numbers, and Number Systems

- ❑ Candidates understand base ten place value, number theory concepts (e.g., greatest common factor), and the structure of the whole, integer, rational, and real number systems.
- ❑ They order integers, mixed numbers, rational numbers (including fractions, decimals, and percents), and real numbers.
- ❑ They represent numbers in exponential and scientific notation.
- ❑ They describe the relationships between the algorithms for addition, subtraction, multiplication, and division.

❑ They understand properties of number systems and their relationship to the algorithms [e.g., 1 is the multiplicative identity; $27 + 34 = 2 \times 10 + 7 + 3 \times 10 + 4 = (2 + 3) \times 10 + (7 + 4)$].

❑ Candidates perform operations with positive, negative, and fractional exponents, as they apply to whole numbers and fractions.

1.2 Computational Tools, Procedures, and Strategies

❑ Candidates demonstrate fluency in standard algorithms for computation and evaluate the correctness of non-standard algorithms.

❑ They demonstrate an understanding of the order of operations.

❑ They round numbers, estimate the results of calculations, and place numbers accurately on a number line.

❑ They demonstrate the ability to use technology, such as calculators or software, for complex calculations.

Domain 2: Algebra and Functions

2.1 Patterns and Functional Relationships

❑ Candidates represent patterns, including relations and functions, through tables, graphs, verbal rules, or symbolic rules.

❑ They use proportional reasoning such as ratios, equivalent fractions, and similar triangles to solve numerical, algebraic, and geometric problems.

2.2 Linear and Quadratic Equations and Inequalities

❑ Candidates are able to find equivalent expressions for equalities and inequalities, explain the meaning of symbolic expressions (e.g., relating an expression to a situation and vice versa), find the solutions, and represent them on graphs.

❑ They recognize and create equivalent algebraic expressions [e.g., $2(a + 3) = 2a + 6$], and represent geometric problems algebraically (e.g., the area of a triangle).

❑ Candidates have a basic understanding of linear equations and their properties (e.g., slope, perpendicularity); the multiplication, division, and factoring of polynomials; and graphing and solving quadratic equations through factoring and completing the square.

❑ They interpret graphs of linear and quadratic equations and inequalities, including solutions to systems of equations.

Domain 3: Measurement and Geometry

3.1 Two- and Three-dimensional Geometric Objects

❑ Candidates understand characteristics of common two- and three-dimensional figures, such as triangles (e.g., isosceles and right triangles), quadrilaterals, and spheres.

❑ They are able to draw conclusions based on the congruence, similarity, or lack thereof, of two figures.

❑ They identify different forms of symmetry, translations, rotations, and reflections.

❑ They understand the Pythagorean theorem and its converse.

❑ They are able to work with properties of parallel lines.

3.2 Representational Systems, Including Concrete Models, Drawings, and Coordinate Geometry

❑ Candidates use concrete representations, such as manipulatives, drawings, and coordinate geometry, to represent geometric objects.

❑ They construct basic geometric figures using a compass and straightedge, and represent three-dimensional objects through two-dimensional drawings.

❑ They combine and dissect two- and three-dimensional figures into familiar shapes, such as dissecting a parallelogram and rearranging the pieces to form a rectangle of equal area.

3.3 Techniques, Tools, and Formulas for Determining Measurements

❑ Candidates estimate and measure time, length, angles, perimeter, area, surface area, volume, weight/mass, and temperature through appropriate units and scales.

❑ They identify relationships between different measures within the metric or customary systems of measurements and estimate an equivalent measurement across the two systems.

❑ They calculate perimeters and areas of two-dimensional objects, and surface areas and volumes of three-dimensional objects.

❑ They relate proportional reasoning to the construction of scale drawings or models.

❑ They use measures such as miles per hour to analyze and solve problems.

Domain 4: Statistics, Data Analysis, and Probability

4.1 Collection, Organization, and Representation of Data

❑ Candidates represent a collection of data through graphs, tables, or charts.

❑ They understand the mean, median, mode, and range of a collection of data.

❑ They have a basic understanding of the design of surveys, such as the role of a random sample.

4.2 Inferences, Predictions, and Arguments Based on Data

❑ Candidates interpret a graph, table, or chart representing a data set.

❑ They draw conclusions about a population from a random sample, and identify potential sources and effects of bias.

4.3 Basic Notions of Chance and Probability

❑ Candidates can define the concept of probability in terms of a sample space of equally likely outcomes.

❑ They use their understanding of complementary, mutually exclusive, dependent, and independent events to calculate probabilities of simple events.

❑ They can express probabilities in a variety of ways, including ratios, proportions, decimals, and percents.

Using the Calculator

The CSET: Multiple Subjects exam allows the use of calculators, and you will be given one to use on the computer screen (see page 5). Even though no question will require the use of a calculator—that is, each question can be answered without a calculator—in some instances, using a calculator will save you valuable time.

You should:

❏ Check for a shortcut to any problem that seems to involve much computation. But use your calculator if it will be time effective. If there appears to be too much computation or the problem seems impossible without the calculator, you're probably doing something wrong.

❏ Before doing an operation, check the number that you keyed in on the display to make sure that you keyed in the right number. You may want to check each number as you key it in.

❏ Before using your calculator, set up the problem and/or steps on scratch paper. Write the numbers on paper as you perform each step on the calculator.

❏ Be sure to carefully clear the calculator before beginning new calculations.

Take advantage of being allowed to use a calculator on the test. Learn to use a calculator efficiently by practicing with a similar handheld calculator before your test day. First focus on how to solve the problem, and then decide if the calculator will be helpful. Remember, a calculator can save you time on some problems, but also remember that each problem can be solved without a calculator. A calculator will not solve a problem for you by itself. You must understand the problem first.

Sample Questions and Explanations for the Multiple-Choice Section

Each of the following examples represents an area tested on the Mathematics multiple-choice section. Note that although the following questions are listed under their major content area, many questions may test more than one area. An analysis follows each question.

Domain 1: Number Sense

1.1 Numbers, Relationships Among Numbers, and Number Systems

1. In the expression 2.34×10^{-3}, what does the 4 represent?

   A. $\dfrac{4}{100,000}$

   B. $\dfrac{4}{100}$

   C. 4

   D. 40

By underlining or circling what you are looking for, you will be sure that you are answering the right question. Here the emphasis is on the "$\underline{4}$". The first thing that needs to be done is to transform this number from scientific notation into decimal notation. Since the exponent on the number 10 is *negative* 3, the decimal point will be moved to the left three places from the current position. That produces the decimal number 0.00234. Next, you locate the "4" and read the position it is in.

0	0	2	3	4
tenths	hundredths	thousandths	ten-thousandths	one-hundred-thousandths

The correct answer is Choice A; however, had the original expression been 2.34×10^3, the decimal point would have been moved three places to the right from the current position. That would have produced the decimal value 2,340. In that case, the "4" would represent the value forty, and the correct answer would be Choice D.

---

2. Which of the following best places the given values on a number line?

$A = \dfrac{5}{6}, B - \dfrac{3}{2}, C = \dfrac{4}{9}$

A.
```
        A B                           C
 ───────●─●───────────────────────────●───────
```

B.
```
        C A                           B
 ───────●─●───────────────────────────●───────
```

C.
```
        A C                           B
 ───────●─●───────────────────────────●───────
```

D.
```
        B A                           C
 ───────●─●───────────────────────────●───────
```

The correct answer is B. Spotlight the words <u>number line</u> in the question to highlight what the question is asking. On a number line, number values increase as you read from left to right. Therefore, the number with the least value would be on the far left, and the number with the greatest value would be on the far right.

In Choice B, it is recognized that $\dfrac{4}{9}$ is less than one-half, $\dfrac{5}{6}$ is more than one-half but less than one, and $\dfrac{3}{2}$ is more than 1, so the correct sequence should be C-A-B.

This problem can also be done by converting the fractions into equivalent fractions with a common denominator. The least common denominator is 18.

$$\frac{5}{6} = \frac{15}{18}$$

$$\frac{3}{2} = \frac{27}{18}$$

$$\frac{4}{9} = \frac{8}{18}$$

From this, the order from smallest to largest becomes $\dfrac{4}{9}, \dfrac{5}{6}, \dfrac{3}{2}$

This problem could also be done using decimal equivalents.

$$\frac{5}{6} = 0.8333\ldots$$

$$\frac{3}{2} = 1.5$$

$$\frac{4}{9} = 0.444\ldots$$

From this, the order from smallest to largest becomes $\dfrac{4}{9}, \dfrac{5}{6}, \dfrac{3}{2}$.

Suppose each of the values given were negative?

$$A = -\frac{5}{6}, B = -\frac{3}{2}, C = -\frac{4}{9}.$$

Now which best places these values on a number line?

A.

B.

C.

D.

The value that is *most negative* has the *least value* and would be located farthest to the left on the number line. In this case, the correct answer is D.

---

3. Tom attempts to multiply $23,000 \times 45,000$ using scientific notation. Which of the following is the correct answer in scientific notation?

   A. 10.35×10^8
   B. 9.35×10^8
   C. 1.035×10^8
   D. 1.035×10^9

The correct answer is D. First, change each number to scientific notation:

$$23,000 = 2.3 \times 10^4$$
$$45,000 = 4.5 \times 10^4$$

Now multiply the numbers together $(2.3 \times 4.5) = 10.35$

Then multiply the tens together $(10^4 \times 10^4) = 10^8$

Finally, change 10.35×10^8 to scientific notation, which is 1.035×10^9.

Remember, scientific notation is written as a number from 1 through 9 times 10 to some power.

---

4. The number 480 written in prime-factored form is $2^a \times 3^b \times 5^c$.

   What is the value of $a(b + c)$?

   A. 5
   B. 6
   C. 7
   D. 10

The correct answer is D. Underline the words <u>prime-factored form</u>. Below are two of several ways to factor the number 480 until all you have are prime numbers.

480

$(48) \times (10)$

$(6 \times 8) \times (2 \times 5)$

$(2 \times 3 \times 2 \times 4) \times (2 \times 5)$

$(2 \times 3 \times 2 \times 2 \times 2) \times (2 \times 5)$

$(2 \times 2 \times 2 \times 2 \times 2 \times 3 \times 5)$

$2^5 \times 3^1 \times 5^1$

480

$(80) \times (6)$

$(40 \times 2) \times (2 \times 3)$

$(20 \times 2 \times 2) \times (2 \times 3)$

$(10 \times 2 \times 2 \times 2) \times (2 \times 3)$

$(5 \times 2 \times 2 \times 2 \times 2) \times (2 \times 3)$

$(2 \times 2 \times 2 \times 2 \times 2 \times 3 \times 5)$

$2^5 \times 3^1 \times 5^1$

Now $a = 5$, $b = 1$ and $c = 1$. The value of $a(b + c) = 5(1 + 1)$
$$= 5(2)$$
$$= 10$$

1.2 <u>Computational Tools, Procedures, and Strategies</u>

5. Which of the following is the best approximation of $\dfrac{(.889)(55)}{9.97}$ to the nearest tenth?

   A. 49.1

   B. 7.7

   C. 4.9

   D. .5

When you are asked to approximate, first check to see how far apart the answer choices are as a guide to how freely you can approximate. Notice here that the answers are not close. Now, making some quick approximations, $.889 \approx 1$ and $9.97 \approx 10$, which leaves the problem in this form:

$$\frac{1 \times 55}{10} = \frac{55}{10} = 5.5$$

The closest answer is C, and it is therefore the correct answer. Notice that choices A and D are not reasonable. You could also use your calculator for this question to obtain an exact answer and then round to the nearest tenth.

6. What is the final cost of a watch that sells for $49.00 if the sales tax is 7%?

   A. $49.07

   B. $49.70

   C. $52.00

   D. $52.43

The correct answer is D. Some questions, such as this one, need to be completely worked out. If you don't see a fast method but you do know that you could compute the answer, use your calculator. In this case, since the sales tax is 7% of $49.00,

$$7\% \text{ of } \$49.00 = (.07)(\$49.00) = \$3.43$$

The total cost of the watch is therefore

$$\$49.00 + \$3.43 = \$52.43$$

7. If a mixture is $\frac{3}{7}$ alcohol by volume and $\frac{4}{7}$ water by volume, what is the ratio of the volume of alcohol to the volume of water in this mixture?

   A. $\frac{3}{7}$

   B. $\frac{4}{7}$

   C. $\frac{3}{4}$

   D. $\frac{4}{3}$

The correct answer is C. "Pulling" information out of the word problem structure can often give you a better look at what you're working with, giving you additional insight into the problem. When pulling out information, actually write out the numbers and/or letters to the side of the problem, putting them into some helpful form and eliminating some of the wording. Here, the first bit of information that should be pulled out is what you're looking for—*ratio of the volume of alcohol to the volume of water*.

Rewrite it as $A:W$ and then into its working form, $\frac{A}{W}$. Next, you should pull out the volumes of each: $A = \frac{3}{7}$ and $W = \frac{4}{7}$.

Now, the answer can be easily determined by inspection or substitution. Using $\frac{\frac{3}{7}}{\frac{4}{7}}$, invert the bottom fraction and multiply to get $=\frac{3}{7_1} \times \frac{{}^1 7}{4} = \frac{3}{4}$. The ratio of the volume of alcohol to the volume of water is 3 to 4.

8. The problem below shows the addition of three two-digit numbers.

$$\begin{array}{r} 3z \\ 75 \\ +x4 \\ \hline 2y2 \end{array}$$

   If x, y, and z each represent a different digit from 0 to 9, what is the value of $(x)(y)(z)$?

   A. 0
   B. 3
   C. 6
   D. 12

The correct answer is A. Before you start to answer this question, you should underline or circle what you are looking for: $(x)(y)(z)$.

To solve this problem, first start in the ones column: $z + 5 + 4 = 2$, so z must be 3, and you'll have to carry the 1.

Now work out the tens column $1 + 3 + 7 + x = \Box y$. Simplifying gives $11 + x = \Box y$, but the hundreds column is 2, so x must be 9 because that is the only way you can carry a 2 for the hundreds column. If x is 9, then $11 + 9 = \Box y$, so y is 0. Therefore, $z = 3$, $y = 0$, and $x = 9$.

Remember that you are solving for $(x)(y)(z)$. $(9)(0)(3) = 0$.

9. 51×6 could best be **_calculated mentally_** by:

  A. $49 \times 6 + 2 \times 6$
  B. $30 \times 6 + 21 \times 6$
  C. $23 \times 6 + 28 \times 6$
  D. $50 \times 6 + 1 \times 6$

The correct answer is D. Some problems, such as this example and the next example, may not ask you to solve for a numerical answer. Rather, you may be asked to set up an equation or expression related to the problem. You might also be asked to recognize which problem wording would use a particular expression in order to be solved. A quick glance at the answer choices will help you know what is expected.

In example 5, even though all answer choices produce the result of 51×6, only Choice D is the best way to quickly calculate the result mentally. You can now see that

$$51 \times 6 = 50 \times 6 + 1 \times 6$$
$$= 300 + 6$$
$$= 306$$

10. For which of the following problems would the calculation of $1.5 \div 0.25$ be appropriate?

  A. John has $1\frac{1}{2}$ feet of wire that he wants to cut into 3-inch pieces. How many pieces can he make?

  B. Mary's drive to work usually takes her 1 hour and 30 minutes. Due to a delay today, it will take her 15 minutes longer for her drive. How long will her drive be today?

  C. There are $\frac{3}{2}$ pounds of chocolate to put into 4 containers. How many pounds of chocolate will go in each container?

  D. A $\frac{1}{4}$-mile road is to be paved in $1\frac{1}{2}$ days. On the average, how much will be paved per day?

The correct answer is A. To find the problem most appropriate, you must figure out the arithmetic that could be used to solve the problem and see which translates into the given expression. Choice A requires you to take a length of $1\frac{1}{2}$ feet and see how many 3-inch pieces go into it. This could be done by converting each measure into inches. There are 18 inches in $1\frac{1}{2}$ feet. Therefore, you could have used the form $18 \div 3$. You could also have converted each measurement into feet. Then $1\frac{1}{2}$ feet could be expressed in decimal form as 1.5 feet, and 3 inches would become $\frac{3}{12}$ or $\frac{1}{4}$ foot, or 0.25 feet in decimal form. So the arithmetic could be expressed as $1.5 \div 0.25$. Choice B requires you to add the 15 minutes to the 1 hour and 30 minutes. Since there are 60 minutes in an hour, 1 hour and 30 minutes becomes $1\frac{1}{2}$ hours and 15 minutes becomes $\frac{15}{60}$ or $\frac{1}{4}$ hour. So the arithmetic is $1\frac{1}{2}$ added to $\frac{1}{4}$. In decimal form, this is $1.5 + 0.25$.

Choice C requires you to divide $\frac{3}{2}$ by 4. In fraction form, this would look like $\frac{3}{2} \div \frac{4}{1}$. In decimal form, this becomes $1.5 \div 4$. Notice that $\frac{4}{1}$ is not the same as $\frac{1}{4}$. Therefore, $\frac{3}{2} \div \frac{4}{1}$ is not the same as $\frac{3}{2} \div \frac{1}{4}$.

Choice D requires you to take $\frac{1}{4}$ and divide it by $1\frac{1}{2}$. In decimal form, this becomes $0.25 \div 1.5$. Since division is not reversible, this is not the same as $1.5 \div 0.25$.

Domain 2: Algebra and Functions

2.1 Patterns and Functional Relationships

---

11. 1, 3, 6, 10, 15 . . .

Which of the following is the next number in the sequence given above?

A. 20
B. 21
C. 25
D. 26

The correct answer is B. Notice that the pattern here is based on the difference between the numbers.

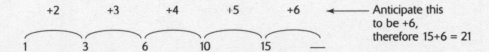

Therefore, the answer is 21.

---

12. If $x > 1$, which of the following decreases as x increases?

A. $x + x^2$
B. $2x^2 - x$
C. $2x - x^2$
D. $x^3 - 3x$

The correct answer is C. This problem is most easily solved by taking each expression and substituting simple numbers for x. Notice that x is restricted in value. We are told that $x > 1$. So use simple replacements for x that are greater than 1.

x	$x + x^2$	$2x^2 - x$	$2x - x^2$	$x^3 - 3x$
2	$2 + (2)^2 = 6$	$2(2)^2 - 2 = 6$	$2(2) - (2)^2 = 0$	$(2)^3 - 3(2) = 2$
3	$3 + (3)^2 = 12$	$2(3)^2 - 3 = 15$	$2(3) - (3)^2 = -3$	$(3)^3 - 3(3) = 18$
4	$4 + (4)^2 = 20$	$2(4)^2 - 4 = 28$	$2(4) - (4)^2 = -8$	$(4)^3 - 3(4) = 52$

From this table, we observe that only for the expression $2x - x^2$ does its value decrease as the value of x increases.

Note: if there were no restrictions given on the x, be sure to include a negative number, zero, and a positive number to get the full picture.

13. Use the table below to answer the question that follows.

x	y
1	1
2	4
3	9
4	16

Which of the following graphs best represents the data in the table above?

A.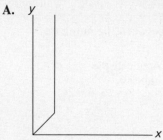

B.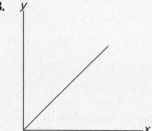

C.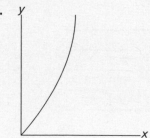

D.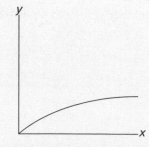

The correct answer is C. A careful analysis of this chart reveals that $x^2 = y$. When x is 1, y is 1; when x is 2, y is 4; when x is 3, y is 9, etc. The graph in C best represents the plotting of these points.

2.2 <u>Linear and Quadratic Equations and Inequalities</u>

---

14. If $x + 6 = 9$, then $3x + 1 =$

    A.   3
    B.   9
    C.   10
    D.   34

The correct answer is C. You should start by concentrating on $\underline{3x + 1}$ because this is what you are solving for. Solving for x leaves $x = 3$. Then substituting into $3x + 1$ gives $3(3) + 1$, or 10. The most common mistake made in solving this problem is to solve for x, which is 3, *and mistakenly choose A as the answer.* But remember, you are solving for $3x + 1$, not just x. You should also notice that most of the other choices would all be possible answers if you made common or simple mistakes. *Make sure that you are answering the right question.*

---

15. If $\left(\dfrac{x}{4}\right) + 2 = 22$, what is the value of x?

    A.   40
    B.   80
    C.   100
    D.   120

The correct answer is B. If you cannot solve this algebraically, you could use the *"work up from the choices"* strategy. Start with Choice C, 100. What if $x = 100$?

$$\left(\frac{x}{4}\right) + 2 = 22$$

$$\left(\frac{100}{4}\right) + 2 \overset{?}{=} 22$$

$$25 + 2 \overset{?}{=} 22$$

$$27 \neq 22$$

Note that since 27 is too large, Choice D will also be too large. Therefore, try Choice A. If Choice A is too small, then you know the answer is Choice B. If Choice A works, the answer is Choice A.

$$\left(\frac{x}{4}\right) + 2 \overset{?}{=} 22$$

$$\left(\frac{40}{4}\right) + 2 \overset{?}{=} 22$$

$$10 + 2 \overset{?}{=} 22$$

$$12 \neq 22$$

Since Choice A is too small, the answer must be Choice B.

---

16. Which of the following will always give the same value as $a(b + c) + b(a + c)$?

    A. $2ab + 2c$
    B. $2ab + a + b$
    C. $2ab + ac + bc$
    D. $2ab + ac + c$

The correct answer is C. Substituting numbers for variables can often be an aid to understanding a problem. Remember to substitute simple numbers because *you* have to do the work. The above problem can be solved this way. Let $a = 1$, $b = 2$, and $c = 3$. Then:

$$a(b + c) + b(a + c) = 1(2+3) + 2(1+3)$$
$$= 5 + 8$$
$$= 13$$

A. $2ab + 2c$	**B.** $2ab + a + b$	**C.** $2ab + ac + bc$	**D.** $2ab + ac + c$
$2(1)(2) + 2(3) = 10$	$2(1)(2) + 1 + 2 = 7$	$2(1)(2) + 1(3) + 2(3) = 13$	$2(1)(2) + 1(3) + 3 = 10$

Only Choice C has the same result.

The problem could also have been solved by using the distributive property.

$$a(b + c) + b(a + c) = ab + ac + ab + bc$$
$$= 2ab + ac + bc$$

---

17. Barney can mow the lawn in 5 hours, and Fred can mow the lawn in 4 hours. How long will it take them to mow the lawn together?

 A.   5 hours

 B. $4\frac{1}{2}$ hours

 C.   4 hours

 D. $2\frac{2}{9}$ hours

The correct answer is Choice D. Suppose that you are unfamiliar with the type of equation for this problem. Try the "reasonable" method. Since Fred can mow the lawn in 4 hours by himself, it will take less than 4 hours if Barney helps him. Therefore, choices A, B, and C are unreasonable and only Choice D is possible.

Using the equation for this problem gives the following calculations.

$$\frac{1}{5} + \frac{1}{4} = \frac{1}{x}$$

In one hour, Barney could do $\frac{1}{5}$ of the job, and in 1 hour, Fred could do $\frac{1}{4}$ of the job. Unknown $\frac{1}{x}$ is that part of the job they could do together in one hour. Now, solving, you calculate as follows.

$$\frac{4}{20} + \frac{5}{20} = \frac{1}{x}$$
$$\frac{9}{20} = \frac{1}{x}$$

Cross multiplying gives $\qquad 9x = 20$

Therefore, $\qquad x = \frac{20}{9}$ or $2\frac{2}{9}$

18. Which of the following are the possible values for x in the quadratic equation $x^2 + 3x + 2 = 0$?

    A.   1, 2

    B.   2, 3

    C.   –1, –3

    D.   –1, –2

The correct answer is D. You could solve the quadratic equation by first factoring $x^2 + 3x + 2 = 0$ into $(x + 2)(x + 1) = 0$. Next, set each factor equal to 0 and solve.

$$x + 2 = 0, \text{ so } x = -2$$
$$x + 1 = 0, \text{ so } x = -1$$

So –1 and –2 are the possible values.

Another method would be to simply plug in the choices to see which ones worked.

Domain 3: Measurement and Geometry

3.1 Two- and Three-Dimensional Geometric Objects

19. *Use the diagram below to answer the question that follows.*

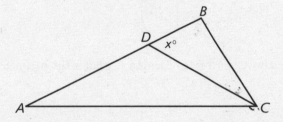

    In the triangle above, $\overline{CD}$ is an angle bisector, angle ACD is 30°, and angle ABC is a right angle. What is the measurement of angle x in degrees?

    A.   30°

    B.   45°

    C.   60°

    D.   75°

The correct answer is C. When you are given a diagram to work with, quickly drawing a diagram as you read the question can save you valuable time. It can also give you insight into how to solve the problem because you will have the complete picture clearly in front of you.

Here, you should read the problem and note as follows.

In the triangle, $\overline{CD}$ is an angle bisector *(stop and mark in the drawing)*, angle ACD is 30° *(stop and mark the drawing)*, and angle ABC is a right angle *(stop and mark the drawing)*. What is the measurement of angle x in degrees? *(Stop and mark in or circle what you are looking for in the drawing.)*

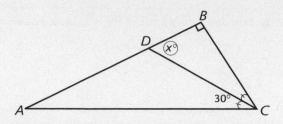

Now, with the drawing marked in, it is evident that, since angle *ACD* is 30°, angle *BCD* is also 30° because they are formed by an angle bisector (divides an angle into two equal parts). Since angle *ABC* is 90° (right angle) and angle *BCD* is 30°, angle *x* is 60° because there are 180° in a triangle.

$$180 - (90 + 30) = 60$$

Always draw diagrams as you read descriptions and information about them. This includes what you are looking for.

---

20. *Use the diagram below to answer the question that follows.*

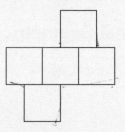

If each square in the figure above has a side of length 1, what is the perimeter of the figure?

A.   8
B.   12
C.   14
D.   16

The correct answer is B. This is also a case in which drawing a simple diagram with the facts is helpful. Mark the known facts.

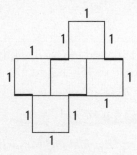

You now have a calculation for the perimeter: 10 *plus* the darkened parts. Now, look carefully at the top two darkened parts. They will add up to 1. (Notice how the top square may slide over to illustrate that fact.) The same is true for the bottom darkened parts. They will add up to 1. Thus, the total perimeter is 10 + 2, or 12.

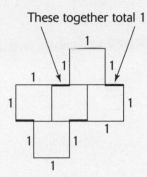

These together total 1

Another method is to slightly alter the figure without changing outcomes. For example, the perimeter of the figure will not change if the top and bottom squares are moved to be directly over the center square. The new figure would then look like this:

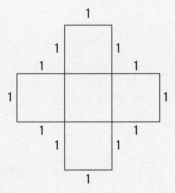

The perimeter is now more easily seen as being 12.

---

21. *Use the diagram below to answer the question that follows.*

△ ABC is isosceles
AB = AC

The perimeter of the isosceles triangle shown above is 42". The two equal sides are each three times as long as the third side. What are the lengths of each side?

A. 15, 15, 12
B. 18, 18, 6
C. 13, 14, 15
D. 12, 12, 20

The correct answer is B. Once again, draw a diagram of the given information.

Mark the equal sides.

AB and AC are each three times as long as BC.

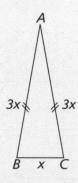

The equation for perimeter is

$$3x + 3x + x = 42$$
$$7x = 42$$
$$x = 6$$

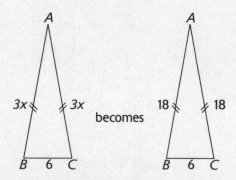

becomes

Note that this problem can also be solved working from the answers. Choice C is eliminated since a triangle with side measurements of 13, 14, and 15 is not an isosceles triangle. Choice D is eliminated since a triangle with side measurements of 12, 12, and 20 does not have a perimeter of 42. Choice A is eliminated since the value 15, the long side, is 3 more than 12, NOT 3 times as long as 12.

22. As pictured below, camp counselor Craig builds a footbridge from the summer camp to the lake so the campers will not have to crawl down a perpendicular 6-foot cliff and then trudge through 8 feet of swamp.

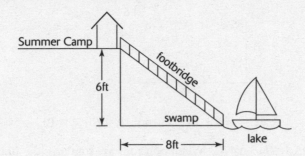

How long (in feet) is the footbridge?

A. 14
B. 12
C. 11
D. 10

To solve this, you need to find the hypotenuse (the footbridge) of the right triangle by using the Pythagorean theorem:

$$a^2 + b^2 = c^2$$
$$(6)^2 + (8)^2 = c^2$$
$$36 + 64 = c^2$$
$$100 = c^2$$
$$10 = c$$

The correct answer is D.

You may have noticed that the sides of this right triangle were multiples of the 3–4–5 triangle, 6–8–10. This would have saved you time.

23. In triangle ACD below, $\overline{BE}$ is parallel to $\overline{CD}$. $AB = 6$. $BC = 4$. $BE = 4$.

How long is $\overline{CD}$?

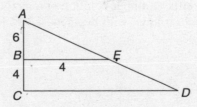

A. $\dfrac{8}{3}$

B. 4

C. 6

D. $\dfrac{20}{3}$

The correct answer is D. This problem can be more easily seen if you separately draw the two triangles.

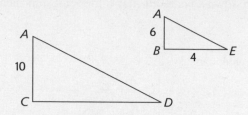

$$AC = AB + BC, \text{ and so } AC = 6 + 4 = 10.$$

Now see two similar triangles, $\triangle ACD \sim \triangle ABE$. When polygons are similar, sides in the same positions are proportional in length. Create a proportion:

$$\frac{\text{small triangle}}{\text{large triangle}} \quad \frac{AB}{AC} = \frac{BE}{CD}$$

Replace the lengths with their respective values, and let $CD = x$.

$$\frac{6}{10} = \frac{4}{x}$$
$$6x = 40$$
$$x = \frac{40}{6}$$

which reduces to $\frac{20}{3}$.

3.2 Representational Systems, Including Concrete Models, Drawings, and Coordinate Geometry

24. If point $P\,(1, 1)$ and point $Q\,(1, 0)$ lie on the same coordinate graph, which of the following must be true?

   A. P and Q are equidistant from the origin.
   B. P is farther from the origin than P is from Q.
   C. Q is farther from the origin than Q is from P.
   D. Q is one-half the distance of P from the origin.

The correct answer is B. In some problems, such as this one, sketching diagrams or simple pictures can be very helpful because the diagram may tip off either a simple solution or a method for solving the problem. In this case, connecting points P, Q, and O form a right triangle with hypotenuse OP. Hence, OP is longer than PQ. P is farther from the origin than P is from Q.

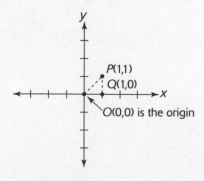

25. Use the diagram below to answer the question that follows.

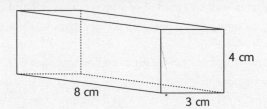

The figure above is a rectangular solid with its longest edges 8 cm long and the shorter edges 3 cm and 4 cm long, as shown.

Which of the following must be true about the figure above?

A.   The volume is 28 cm³.
B.   The surface area is 136 cm².
C.   The area of each face is equal.
D.   The area of the largest face is equal to twice the area of the smallest face.

The correct answer is B. To find the surface area, first find the area of the bottom, front, and right side. Since opposite faces have equal areas, double each area found, and add the results together.

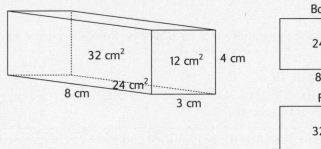

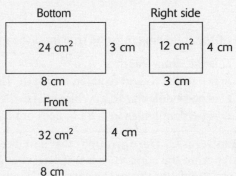

Top and bottom: $8 \times 3 = 24 \times 2 = 48$ cm²
Front and back: $8 \times 4 = 32 \times 2 = 64$ cm²
Right and left: $3 \times 4 = 12 \times 2 = \underline{24}$ cm²
                              136 cm²

Even though one of the faces has an area of 24 cm², and the smallest face has an area of 12 cm², and 24 is twice 12, the face with an area of 24 cm² was not the largest face.

26. *Use the information given below to answer the question that follows.*

- The point of a compass was placed on point *A* of line segment *AB* and an arc was drawn.
- Next, without changing the compass, the point of the compass was placed on point *B* of line segment *AB*, and another arc was drawn.
- The intersections of the arcs were connected, forming line segment *CD*.
- The final drawing is shown below.

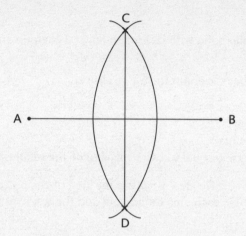

Which of the following must be true from the operations that have been performed on line segment *AB*?

A. $\overline{CD}$ is the same length as $\overline{AB}$.
B. $\overline{CD}$ is parallel to and equal in length to $\overline{AB}$.
C. $\overline{CD}$ is perpendicular to and bisects $\overline{AB}$.
D. $\overline{CD}$ is perpendicular to $\overline{AB}$ but does not bisect $\overline{AB}$.

The correct answer is C. The operations that have been performed bisect $\overline{AB}$ and make $\overline{CD}$ perpendicular to $\overline{AB}$. Since the distance on the compass has not been changed, when the arcs drawn from each endpoint intersect at *C* and *D*, they are equidistant from the endpoints. Connecting *C* and *D* gives a line segment that bisects $\overline{AB}$ and is perpendicular to it (also called a perpendicular bisector).

27. Use the graph below to answer the question that follows.

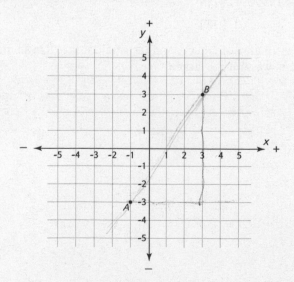

What is the slope of the line passing through points A and B?

A. $-\dfrac{3}{2}$

B. $-\dfrac{2}{3}$

C. $\dfrac{2}{3}$

D. $\dfrac{3}{2}$

The correct answer is D. To find the slope of the line joining points A and B, you could notice that the line joining points A and B goes up as it goes to the right. This means the line will have a positive slope. (A line that goes down as it goes to the right has a negative slope. A line that is horizontal has a zero slope. A line that is vertical has an undefined slope or no slope.) This eliminates choices A and B as possible answers. Slope is defined as the vertical change over the horizontal change as you go from one point to another on the line. (This is sometimes referred to as *rise over run*).

Notice that going from point A to point B requires a "rise" of 6 units and a "run" of 4 units. The fraction $\dfrac{6}{4}$ reduces to $\dfrac{3}{2}$.

To find the slope of the line, you could also have used the slope formula.

Given two points with coordinates (x_1, y_1) and (x_2, y_2),

$$\text{Slope} = \frac{y_2 - y_1}{x_2 - x_1}$$

Using the coordinates of $A(-1, -3)$ and $B(3, 3)$, simply plug into the formula:

$$\frac{y_2 - y_1}{x_2 - x_1} = \frac{(3) - (-3)}{(3) - (-1)} = \frac{3 + 3}{3 + 1} = \frac{6}{4} = \frac{3}{2}$$

3.3 Techniques, Tools, and Formulas for Determining Measurements

28. If all sides of a square are doubled, the area of that square:

    A. is doubled.
    B. is tripled.
    C. is multiplied by 4.
    D. remains the same.

The correct answer is C. One way to solve this problem is to draw a square and then double all its sides. Then compare the two areas. Another way to solve this problem is to draw a square and select a value to represent the length of one side. Then find the area of this square. Next, draw a new square and select as the length of one its sides double the length selected for the first square. Find the new area and compare that with the original area.

Original square
(suppose you select 5 as a length of one side)

New square
(each side is doubled, and so now each side is 10)

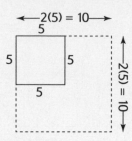

The area of this square is $5 \times 5 = 25$

The area of the new square is $10 \times 10 = 100$

Now look over the answer choices. The new area is multiplied by 4.

---

29. What is the maximum number of milk cartons, each 2" wide by 3" long by 4" tall, that can fit into a cardboard box with inside dimensions of 16" wide by 9" long by 8" tall?

    A.   18
    B.   20
    C.   24
    D.   48

The correct answer is D. Drawing a diagram, as shown below, may be helpful in envisioning the process of fitting the cartons into the box. Notice that 8 cartons will fit across the box, 3 cartons deep and 2 "stacks" high.

$8 \times 3 \times 2 = 48$ cartons

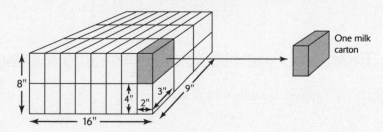

Another approach to this problem would be to find the volume of the cardboard box and the volume of the milk carton. Then find how many of the milk cartons "go into" the cardboard box. The expression "go into" is an indication of division. Note: The solution only works if the milk cartons fit exactly without leaving any open spaces.

$$V_{\text{cardboard box}} = 16" \times 9" \times 8" = 1{,}152\text{in.}^3$$
$$V_{\text{milk carton}} = 2" \times 3" \times 4" = 24\text{in.}^3$$
$$1{,}152 \div 24 = 48$$

---

30. Which equation can be used to find the perimeter, P, of a rectangle that has a length of 18 feet and a width of 15 feet?

    A. $P = (18)(15)$
    B. $P = 2(15)(18)$
    C. $P = (2)15 + 18$
    D. $P = 2(15 + 18)$

The correct answer is D. Notice that it is not necessary to calculate the answer. You need only identify the correct formula for doing so. The perimeter of the rectangle can be found by adding the length to the width and doubling this sum.

$$P = 2(15 + 18)$$

Choice C, (2)15 + 18, is incorrect because by the rule of order of operations, only the 15 is multiplied by 2, not the sum of 15 and 18.

Domain 4: Statistics, Data Analysis, and Probability

4.1 Collection, Organization, and Representation of Data

31. If 20 carpenters work a total of 880 hours, what is the average number of hours each carpenter worked?

   A.   20
   B.   40
   C.   44
   D.   80

The correct answer is C. You should first determine what you are looking for, <u>the average number of hours worked</u>. Next, simply divide 880 by 20 and you get 44.

32. The following table shows Teresa's scores on her first-semester Economics exams.

Date	Score
September 27	90%
October 6	80%
October 12	90%
November 2	87%
November 14	83%
November 21	91%
December 4	88%
December 13	96%

What is her median score on the Economics exams?

   A. $87\frac{1}{2}$
   B.   88
   C.   89
   D.   90

The correct answer is C. To find the median, first put the scores in order from least to greatest.

$$80, 83, 87, 88, 90, 90, 91, 96$$

Next, find the score in the middle. But, since there is an even number of scores, you must take the average of the two middle scores. The average of 88 and 90 is 89.

33. A scientist collected the following data for the weight of different mice:

Mouse number	Weight
1	5 oz.
2	7 oz.
3	6 oz.
4	12 oz.
5	5 oz.
6	8 oz.

The scientist discovered that his scale was off by 0.5 oz. and each mouse weighed 0.5 oz. more than what he recorded. Which of the following statistical values would not be affected by this change?

A. Mean
B. Median
C. Mode
D. Range

The correct answer is D. You should first focus on <u>would not change</u>. To find the mean of a set of scores, you would add the scores and divide by the number of scores. Since each score will increase by 0.5, the total will increase by 6(0.5) or a total of 3.0. The new total will still be divided by 6, and so the mean will increase by a total of 0.5. To find the median, you would list the values from smallest to largest and find the score in the center. Since there is an even number of scores, the median will be the mean of the two middle scores. Since each score has gone up by 0.5, the new median will be 0.5 more than the old median.

To find the mode, you would find the score repeated most often. Since each score has been increased by 0.5, the new mode will be 0.5 more than the old mode. To find the range of a set of data, you take the difference of the maximum and minimum scores. Since each has been increased by 0.5, the difference between them has remained the same.

4.2 <u>Inferences, Predictions, and Arguments Based on Data</u>

34. Use the graph below to answer the question that follows.

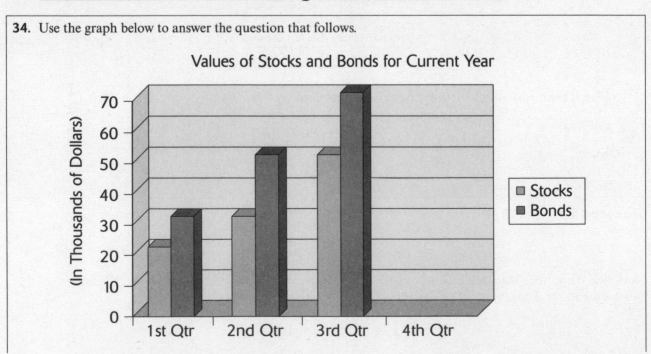

Values of Stocks and Bonds for Current Year

Of the following, which is the best prediction of the possible value of stocks in the fourth quarter?

A. $50,000
B. $60,000
C. $70,000
D. $80,000

The correct answer is D. Notice that the question is asking about the value of stocks, so make sure to write out prediction, value, stocks, and fourth quarter. Focus on stocks. Now take a careful look at the value of stocks in each quarter—the first quarter is $20,000, the second quarter is $30,000, and the third quarter is $50,000. The increase is $10,000 from the first quarter to the second quarter, and $20,000 from the second quarter to the third quarter. It would be reasonable to predict that the increase would be $30,000 from the third quarter to the fourth quarter (increases of $10,000, $20,000, $30,000), so the value of stocks in the fourth quarter could be $30,000 more than the third quarter (50,000 + 30,000), or $80,000. Since there is not a lot of data given (only three quarters), other predictions are possible, but D is the best choice of the ones given.

35. Use the graph below to answer the question that follows.

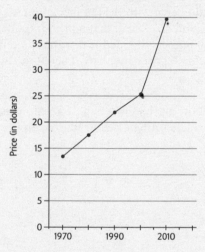

Average Lamp Prices (and Projection)

Which of the following is the best estimation of the percent increase of average lamp prices from the year 2000 to the year 2010?

A. 13%
B. 24%
C. 39%
D. 50%

The correct answer is D.

To find the percent increase, use the following formula:

$$\frac{\text{difference}}{\text{starting point}} \times 100 = \text{percent increase}$$

Now plug in the values,

$$\frac{\text{year } 2010 - \text{year } 2000}{\text{year } 2000}$$

$$\frac{39 - 26}{26} = \frac{13}{26} = \frac{1}{2} \times 100 = 50\%$$

4.3 Basic Notions of Chance and Probability

---

36. Each of the numbers 7 through 27 are placed on separate index cards and placed in a bowl. One of the index cards is selected at random. What is the probability the number selected was *not* a prime number?

A. $\dfrac{2}{7}$

B. $\dfrac{3}{10}$

C. $\dfrac{5}{7}$

D. $\dfrac{3}{4}$

The correct answer is C. You should first focus on <u>not a prime number</u>. To find the probability of an event, you make a fraction that puts the number of favorable outcomes possible on top and the total number of total possible outcomes on the bottom of the fraction. The most common error made in this problem is in calculating the total number of outcomes possible. Most people take $27 - 7 = 20$ as that total. The correct subtraction is $27 - 6 = 21$. You are subtracting the numbers 1 through 6 that are not being used from the numbers 1 through 27. Therefore, the probability fraction should begin with the number 21 on the bottom. Next, find out how many of the numbers from 7 to 27 are prime numbers. Recall that a prime number is a counting number greater than 1 that only has 1 and itself as counting numbers that divide it without a remainder. The prime numbers from 7 to 27 are 7, 11, 13, 17, 19, and 23. This makes 6 prime numbers. Therefore, there are $21 - 6 = 15$ numbers that are not prime. The probability becomes $\dfrac{15}{21} = \dfrac{5}{7}$.

---

37. There are 3 green, 4 red, and 7 yellow marbles in a bag. If a yellow marble is selected first and not replaced in the bag, what is the probability of selecting a yellow marble on the second draw?

A. $\dfrac{3}{7}$

B. $\dfrac{4}{7}$

C. $\dfrac{1}{2}$

D. $\dfrac{6}{13}$

The correct answer is D. First determine what you are looking for, <u>probability of yellow marble on second draw</u>. Since there is a total of 14 marbles and 7 are yellow, the probability of selecting a yellow marble on the first draw is $\dfrac{7}{14}$. If a yellow marble is selected on the first draw, then 6 yellow marbles are left out of 13 total marbles. Therefore, the probability is $\dfrac{6}{13}$.

---

38. What is the probability of tossing a penny twice so that both times it lands heads up?

A. $\dfrac{1}{8}$

B. $\dfrac{1}{4}$

C. $\dfrac{1}{3}$

D. $\dfrac{1}{2}$

The correct answer is B. The probability of throwing a head in one throw is

$$\frac{\text{chances of a head}}{\text{total chances (1 head} + \text{1 tail)}} = \frac{1}{2}$$

Since you are trying to throw a head *twice*, multiply the probability for the first toss $\frac{1}{2}$ by the probability for the second toss (again $\frac{1}{2}$). Thus, $\frac{1}{2} \times \frac{1}{2} = \frac{1}{4}$, and $\frac{1}{4}$ is the probability of throwing heads twice in two tosses. Another way of approaching this problem is to look at the total number of possible outcomes:

	First Toss	Second Toss
1.	H	H
2.	H	T
3.	T	H
4.	T	T

Thus, there are four different possible outcomes. There is only one way to throw two heads in two tosses. Thus, the probability of tossing two heads in two tosses is 1 out of 4 total outcomes, or $\frac{1}{4}$.

---

39. How many different combinations of sports jackets, shirt, and slacks are possible if a person has 4 sports jackets, 5 shirts, and 3 pairs of slacks?

    A. 4
    B. 5
    C. 12
    D. 60

The correct answer is D. Since each of the 4 sports jackets may be worn with 5 different shirts, there are 20 possible combinations. These may be worn with each of the 3 pairs of slacks for a total of 60 possible combinations. Stated simply, $5 \times 4 \times 3 = 60$ possible combinations.

Sample Questions and Strategies for the Short Constructed-Response Section

Following are representative mathematics short constructed-response questions from the areas covered. Strategies and a sample response are included with each question.

Note: Drawings presented in the following sample responses are intended for instructional purposes only. They are meant to provide visual illustrations of selected problems. On the actual computer-based CSET, you will not be able to draw your responses.

Number Sense

1. One way to mentally multiply 15×103 without simply calculating is to multiply 15×100 and then 15×3 and add the results.

Using your knowledge of mathematics and mathematical properties:

- identify the method or mathematical property used;
- explain how this method works; and
- check your method by calculating the results.

Strategy

Note the key words in the tasks given. In this problem, you are given three tasks: <u>identify the method or mathematical property</u>, <u>explain this method</u>, and <u>check by calculating</u>. Notice that the problem says, "without calculating," so some insight into the method is necessary. If you do not spot the method without calculating, or do not immediately know the property, calculate the answer and work backward. Often, you will understand the method or the insight involved after calculating an answer.

Sample Response

The method used here is really the distributive property of multiplication over addition. This can be shown generally as $a(b + c) = ab + ac$. Notice that a is distributed to b and c.

Since 15×103 is really $15(100 + 3)$, you could simply distribute as follows.

$$(15 \times 100) + (15 \times 3)$$

Now it is simple to mentally compute that 15×100 is 1500, and 15×3 is 45. Next, add $1500 + 45$, which totals 1545.

To check the answer, simply multiply 15×103, which gives 1545. Since both answers are the same, the method has been checked.

---

2. Use the diagram and the information below to complete the exercise that follows:

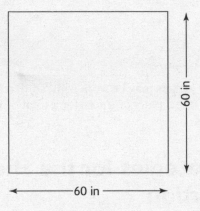

60 in

←——— 60 in ———→

☐ Rectangular tile that is twice as long as it is wide

You are asked to create a square wall design from rectangular tiles that must be twice as long as they are wide. The wall is to be 60 inches square and all the rectangular tiles must have measurements that are in a whole number of inches. The tiles must completely fill the square with no overlapping tiles, no empty spaces, and no tiles going beyond the borders of the square.

Using your knowledge of number theory and geometry:

■ find three different sizes of these rectangular tiles and determine how many of each size could be used to fill the square wall; and

■ determine the fewest number of the specified rectangular tiles that could fill the square wall.

Strategy

Always attempt to identify what you are being asked to do. In this case, you are being asked to <u>find three different sizes AND how many of each size,</u> and <u>determine the least number</u> of tiles needed to fill the square.

Sample Response

In order for the rectangular tiles to fill the square, both the width and length measurements of the rectangle must be factors of 60, the length of each side of the square. The problem states that the length of the rectangle must be twice the width. Here are the three smallest possible rectangles and how many of each would be needed to fill the square. (Remember that you will not be able to draw your response when you take the actual exam.)

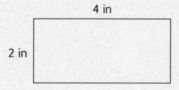

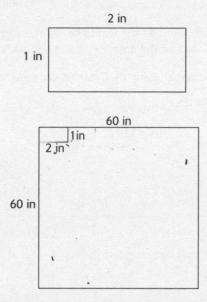

Since the square is 60 inches on each side, $60 \div 2 = 30$ would be the number of tiles that can be put next to each other across the top, and $60 \div 1 = 60$ would be the number of rows of such tiles.

Therefore, there would be $30 \times 60 = 1800$ tiles that measure 1 inch by 2 inches that fill the square.

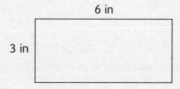

Since the square is 60 inches on each side, $60 \div 4 = 15$ would be the number of tiles that can be put next to each other across the top, and $60 \div 2 = 30$ would be the number of rows of such tiles.

Therefore, there would be $15 \times 30 = 450$ tiles that measure 2 inches by 4 inches that fill the square.

Since the square is 60 inches on each side, $60 \div 6 = 10$ would be the number of tiles that can be put next to each other across the top, and $60 \div 3 = 20$ would be the number of rows of such tiles.

Therefore, there would be $10 \times 20 = 200$ tiles that measure 3 inches by 6 inches that fill the square.

To determine the least number of rectangular tiles that can fill the square, you must use the largest possible rectangle with sides that are factors of 60 and whose length is twice the width. To do this, begin with even factors of 60 to represent the length; half of that would be the width.

Below is a chart of possible rectangles with the length twice the width.

Length	2	4	6	10	12	20	30	60
Width	1	2	3	5	6	10	15	30

From this, it can be seen that the largest possible rectangle would be 30 inches wide by 60 inches long.

Since the square is 60 inches on each side, $60 \div 60 = 1$ would be the number of tiles that can be put next to each other across the top, and $60 \div 30 = 2$ would be the number of rows of such tiles.

Therefore, $1 \times 2 = 2$ would be the fewest rectangular tiles that fill the square.

Algebra and Functions

> **3.** Complete the exercise that follows.
>
> The expression $4x + 3y + 2y + 4x$ is not in simplest form.
>
> Using your knowledge of algebra:
>
> - simplify the expression; and
> - explain your method.

Strategy

Always identify the information you are being asked to do. In this case, you are being asked to <u>simplify the expression</u> and <u>explain your method</u>. Note the variables given and focus on the procedure. List the steps as you go through the process.

Sample Response

The expression $4x + 3y + 2y + 4x$ can be simplified to $8x + 5y$. Since you can combine only like terms, that is, x's with x's and y's with y's, you should rearrange and regroup the terms as follows: $(4x + 4x) + (3y + 2y)$. Now, combining like terms produces $4x + 4x$ is $8x$ and $3y + 2y$ is $5y$. So the simplified version is $8x + 5y$.

> **4.** Complete the exercise that follows.
>
> Find the product of $(x + 5)$ and $(x + 3)$.
>
> - Demonstrate and explain the product using an algebraic method.
> - Demonstrate and explain the product using a geometric method.

Strategy

Always focus on the key words and phrases in the question. In this case, you are being asked to <u>demonstrate and explain the product using an algebraic method and a geometric method</u>.

Sample Response

Finding the product of $(x + 5)$ and $(x + 3)$ means to multiply the expressions together: $(x + 5)(x + 3)$. This requires the use of the distributive property. First, the "x" in the first parentheses is distributed over the $(x + 3)$. Second, the "5" in the first parentheses is distributed over the $(x + 3)$. Third, you simplify the result by combining like terms.

$$(x + 5)(x + 3) = x(x + 3) + 5(x + 3)$$
$$= x^2 + 3x + 5x + 15$$
$$= x^2 + 8x + 15$$

A geometric model that requires multiplication of two values is finding the area of a rectangle.

Visualize a rectangle with sides that have a length of $x + 5$ and a width of $x + 3$, and then find the area of the rectangle. (Note: The drawing below is for informational purposes only.)

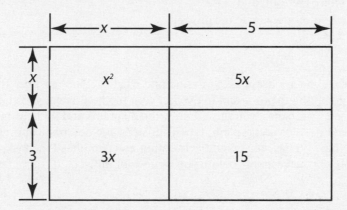

Inside each of the smaller rectangles is a value that represents its area.

The area of the large rectangle is expressed as the result of $(x + 5)(x + 3)$ [length times width].

The area of the large rectangle can also be expressed as the sum of the smaller rectangles inside it.

$$\text{Therefore, } (x + 5)(x + 3) = x^2 + 3x + 5x + 15$$
$$= x^2 + 8x + 15$$

Measurement and Geometry

5. Use the diagram and information given below to complete the exercise that follows.

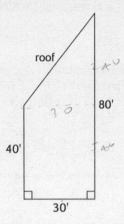

The cross-sectional diagram of a downtown office building shown above has the dimensions given.

Using your knowledge of algebra and geometry:

- find the length along the roof; and
- explain your method of arriving at the answer.

Strategy

First, attempt to identify what you are being asked to find and what else you must do. In this problem, you are being asked to find the <u>length along the roof</u> and to <u>explain your method</u>. Next, you should carefully read the information given. In geometry problems, you should draw the diagrams and fill in as many dimensions as possible. Since you are being asked to solve and explain, type your steps and describe your method in finding the answer. Finally, make sure that you have answered the question and completed the tasks given. It may help you to sketch the diagram to visualize your response before you write your answer.

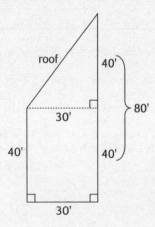

Sample Response

By drawing a line that divides the diagram into two parts—a rectangle and a right triangle—the length of the roof can be determined. The upper triangular section has a base of 30 feet and a height of 40 feet. Using the Pythagorean theorem for right triangles,

$$30^2 + 40^2 = (\text{length along the roof})^2$$
$$900 + 1{,}600 = (\text{length along the roof})^2$$
$$2{,}500 = (\text{length along the roof})^2$$

Taking the square roots of both sides gives

$$50 = \text{length along the roof}$$

You could also recognize that the sides of the right triangle are in a 3-4-5 ratio, which is commonly found in right triangles.

---

6. Use the diagram and the information below to complete the exercise that follows.

The perimeter of the square that is circumscribed around the circle with center at O is 40 inches.

Using the information given and your knowledge of algebra and geometry:

- determine the area of the shaded region; and
- explain how you arrived at your answer.

Strategy

First, identify the task at hand. You are being asked to <u>find the area of the shaded region</u> and <u>explain your procedure</u>. Next, sketch the diagram and fill in the given information. Since the outside figure is a square, you should mark each of the sides as equal. Solve the problem, paying special attention to the steps you use. Explaining these steps will complete your task.

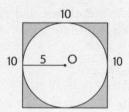

Sample Response

To find the area of the shaded region, subtract the area of the circle from the area of the square.

To find the area of the square, you need the length of one side of the square. Since the perimeter of the square is 40 inches, and all the sides of a square are of equal length, the length of each side can be found by dividing 40 inches by 4. Therefore, each side of the square is 10 inches. The area of a square is found by multiplying one side by itself, and so the area of the square is 10 inches × 10 inches = 100 square inches.

To find the area of the circle, you need the length of the radius. Since one side of the square is 10 inches, the distance from the center of the circle to the circle, or the radius, would be half that, or 5 inches. To find the area of a circle, you use the formula $A = \pi r^2$. Therefore, the area of the circle is $\pi(5)^2 = 25\pi$.

The shaded region has an exact area of $(100 - 25\pi)$ square inches. If a two-place decimal approximation is wanted, π can be replaced with 3.14 and then the approximate area is 21.5 square inches.

7. Use the diagram and the information below to complete the exercise that follows.

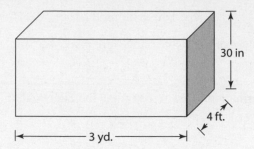

A large fish tank, shown in the diagram, is in the shape of a rectangular prism. Its length is 3 yards, its width is 4 feet, and its height is 30 inches. The fish tank starts out empty and is filled at the rate of 15 cubic inches per second.

Using your knowledge of geometry and measurement:

- determine how many hours it would take to fill the tank two-thirds full; and
- write an expression to explain your steps.

Strategy

First, identify the task at hand. You are to find <u>how many **hours**</u> it would take to fill the tank **two-thirds** <u>full</u>, <u>show your work</u>, and <u>explain your steps.</u> Next, remember in geometry and measurement problems, you need to do the problem one piece at a time, not all at once. So decide which piece you are going to start with and then go from there.

Sample Response

First, you notice that the dimensions are given in inches, feet, and yards. To determine which to convert to, look for a clue in the question. Since the tank is filled at the rate of 15 cubic inches per second, use inches as the common measure.

Height: 30 in. = 30 in.

Width: 4 ft. = 4(12 in.) = 48 in.

Length: 3 yd. = 3(36 in.) = 108 in.

The task is to fill the tank two-thirds full. To do this, first find the capacity of the tank (the volume, when it is full), and then multiply that by $\frac{2}{3}$. The volume of a rectangular prism is found by multiplying length by width by height.

Volume (full) = (108 in.)(48 in.)(30 in.) = 155,520 cu. in.

Volume ($\frac{2}{3}$ full) = ($\frac{2}{3}$)(155,520 cu. in.) = 103,680 cu. in.

Since the tank is filled at the rate of 15 cubic inches per second, taking the 103,680 cubic inches and dividing by 15 cubic inches per second would give how many seconds it takes to fill the tank two-thirds full.

103,680 cu. in. ÷ (15 cu. in./sec.) = 6,912 sec. It will take 6,912 seconds to fill the tank two-thirds full.

But the question asked how many hours it will take. In order to convert seconds to hours, first convert seconds to minutes, and then convert minutes to hours.

$$6{,}912 \text{ sec.} \div (60 \text{ sec./min.}) = 115.2 \text{ min.}$$
$$115.2 \text{ min.} \div (60 \text{ min./hr.}) = 1.92 \text{ hrs.}$$

It will take 1.92 hours to fill the tank two-thirds full.

Statistics, Data Analysis, and Probability

> **8.** Use the information below to complete the exercise that follows.
>
> **Total: 20 days of vacation**
> 10 days of sightseeing
> 5 days of shopping
> 4 days of relaxing and swimming
> 1 day of travel
>
> Using your knowledge of data analysis, charts, and mathematics:
>
> - describe the construction of a pie chart showing percentages to reflect the breakdown of vacation days; and
> - explain the reason for the size of each of the sections.

Strategy

First, attempt to identify what you are being asked to do. In this problem, you are being asked to <u>describe a pie chart</u> and to <u>explain the reason for the size of each of the sections</u>. Next, carefully review the information given, keeping in mind that the total in a pie chart is 100%. When constructing a pie chart, always start by keeping in mind that 50% is half of the circle and 25% is a quarter of the circle. Sketch a simple pie graph on scratch paper showing the largest amount or section first. Keep in mind that you can use scratch paper as a "straight edge" and the corner as a right angle. This can be helpful when constructing your visual samples.

Sample Response

When constructing a pie chart, the following information and calculations can be used to fill in the chart and explain why each section is a certain size. The last number indicates the percentage of the circle designated for each task.

10 days of sightseeing out of 20 total is $\frac{10}{20} = \frac{1}{2} = 50\%$.

5 days of shopping out of 20 total is $\frac{5}{20} = \frac{1}{4} = 25\%$.

4 days of relaxing and swimming out of 20 total is $\frac{4}{20} = \frac{1}{5} = 20\%$.

1 day of travel out of 20 total is $\frac{1}{20} = 5\%$.

The total number of days is 20, which is 100%.

9. Complete the exercise that follows.

   Sara flips a two-sided coin three times.

   Using the information given and your knowledge of probability:

   - determine the probability of getting three heads in a row;
   - determine the probability of getting exactly two tails; and
   - explain how you arrived at your answers.

Strategy

First, attempt to identify what you are being asked to do. In this problem, you are being asked to find the <u>probability</u> for certain events and to <u>explain</u> how you arrived at your answers. Next, solve the problem, showing your work. Note the steps that you used to get the answer. Explaining your procedure—the steps—will complete your work.

Sample Response

In order to calculate a probability, you need to know how many total outcomes are possible and how many of those are favorable. Probability is the comparison of favorable outcomes to total outcomes. Although you will not be able to draw lines, you can use the space bar or tab key to set up columns. A tree diagram helps in illustrating the total possible outcomes and recognizing which of them are favorable. The diagram shows the possibilities if a head or tail was tossed first.

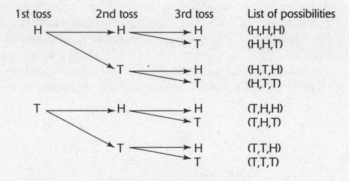

From the diagram, you can see that there are a total of 8 possibilities.

Of these 8, only one shows three heads in a row, (H,H,H). Therefore, the probability of getting three heads in a row is $\frac{1}{8}$.

Of the 8 total possibilities, 3 have exactly two tails, (H,T,T), (T,H,T), and (T,T,H). Therefore, the probability of getting exactly two tails is $\frac{3}{8}$.

10. Use the table below to complete the exercise that follows.

Annual Rainfall	
Year	Inches
1985	300
1990	302
1995	304
2000	306
2005	308

Using your knowledge of data analysis, graphs, and mathematics:

- construct a line graph that represents the information given;
- using the graph, predict what the annual rainfall was in 1980 and 2015; and
- explain your procedure in graphing and predicting.

Strategy

First, try to identify what you are being asked to do. In this case, you are asked to <u>describe a line graph</u>, <u>predict</u> a past and future value using the graph, and <u>explain your procedures</u>.

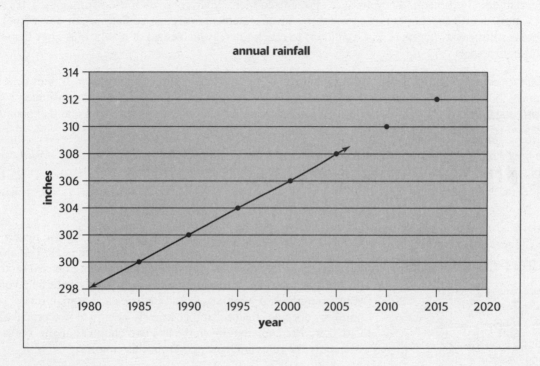

Sample Response

The numbers along the left, the vertical side, of the line graph represent the annual rainfall. Since the rainfall increases only by 2s, and the problem asks for a prediction before 1985, I began the scale 2 below the lowest value and increased by 2s. The numbers along the bottom, the horizontal numbers, indicate the years starting with 1980 and increasing in 5-year increments.

Since the annual rainfall in 1985 was 300 inches, the graph would be appropriately marked where the vertical line through 1985 meets the horizontal line through 300. This would be done for each pair of data values. A line segment would be drawn from each data point to the next one. These segments would appear to be part of a single line. The pattern on the graph to be shown is that for every 5-year increment, there was an increase of 2 inches of annual rainfall over the previous 5-year increment. Based on this, the annual rainfall in 1980 should be 2 inches less than in 1985, and so in 1980 the rainfall was 298 inches. Extending the line until it crosses the vertical line for 2015, it would appear to correspond to an annual rainfall of 312 inches. This goes along with the idea that for every 5-year increment, the rainfall increases by 2 inches over the previous 5-year increment.

Subject Matter Skills and Abilities Applicable to the Content Domains in Mathematics

Candidates for Multiple Subject Teaching Credentials identify and prioritize relevant and missing information in mathematical problems. They analyze complex problems to identify similar simple problems that might suggest solution strategies. They represent a problem in alternate ways, such as words, symbols, concrete models, and diagrams, to gain greater insight. They consider examples and patterns as means to formulating a conjecture.

Candidates apply logical reasoning and techniques from arithmetic, algebra, geometry, and probability/statistics to solve mathematical problems. They analyze problems to identify alternative solution strategies. They evaluate the truth of mathematical statements (i.e., whether a given statement is always, sometimes, or never true). They apply different solution strategies (e.g., estimation) to check the reasonableness of a solution. They demonstrate that a solution is correct.

Candidates explain their mathematical reasoning through a variety of methods, such as words, numbers, symbols, charts, graphs, tables, diagrams, and concrete models. They use appropriate mathematical notation with clear and accurate language. They explain how to derive a result based on previously developed ideas, and explain how a result is related to other ideas.

Subtest II: Mathematics Review

MATH REVIEW SECTION OVERVIEW

Domains 1 and 4*: Math Diagnostic Test

Domain 1: Number Sense

Domain 4*: Statistics, Data Analysis, and Probability

Domain 2: Algebra Diagnostic Test

Domain 2: Algebra

Domain 3: Geometry Diagnostic Test

Domain 3: Geometry

*Because Domain 1 and Domain 4 primarily involve arithmetic skills, they have a combined diagnostic test; furthermore, the review of Domain 4 precedes the Domain 2 review.

The following pages are designed to give you an intensive review of the skills and concepts necessary to be successful on the CSET Multiple Subjects math section. The material will be presented based on the domains tested. This section contains diagnostic tests to help you assess your strengths and weaknesses, and includes a thorough review of basic number concepts, algebra, and geometry. There are two practice tests with complete explanations in the last two chapters of this book to help you apply the rules and concepts from this chapter.

The computer-based CSET Multiple Subjects exam allows the use of a calculator. The calculator will appear on your computer screen. Even though no question will require the use of a calculator—that is, each question can be answered without a calculator—in some instances, using a calculator will save you valuable time.

Domains 1 and 4 Overview: Math Concepts	
Domain 1: Number Sense Numbers Relationships Among Numbers Number Systems	• Base ten place value, number theory concepts (e.g., greatest common factor), and the structure of the whole, integer, rational, and real number systems. • Integers, mixed numbers, rational numbers (including fractions, decimals, and percents), and real numbers. • Numbers in exponential and scientific notation. • Relationships between the algorithms for addition, subtraction, multiplication, and division. • Properties of number systems and their relationship to the algorithms, [e.g., 1 is the multiplicative identity; $27 + 34 = 2 \times 10 + 7 + 3 \times 10 + 4 = (2 + 3) \times 10 + (7 + 4)$]. • Perform operations with positive, negative, and fractional exponents, as they apply to whole numbers and fractions.
Domain 1: Number Sense Computational Tools, Procedures and Strategies	• Demonstrate fluency in standard algorithms for computation and evaluate the correctness of non-standard algorithms. • Demonstrate an understanding of the order of operations. • Round numbers, estimate the results of calculations, and place numbers accurately on a number line. • Demonstrate the ability to use technology, such as calculators or software, for complex calculations.
Domain 4: Statistics, Data Analysis, and Probability Collection, Organization, and Representation of Data	• Understand graphs, tables, and charts. • Understand mean, median, mode, and range of a collection of data. • Basic understanding of the design of surveys, such as the role of a random sample. • Understand inferences, predictions, and arguments. • Understand basic notions of chance and probability.

Domains 1 and 4: Math Diagnostic Test

Questions

1. Which of the following numbers are integers? $\frac{1}{2}$, –2, 0, 4, 3.2

2. Which of the following are rational numbers? 5.8, 6, $\frac{1}{4}$, π, $\sqrt{4}$, $\sqrt{7}$

3. List the prime numbers between 30 and 40.

4. List the composite numbers between 17 and 29.

5. List the first 4 positive perfect squares.

6. List the first 4 positive perfect cubes.

7. Find the greatest common factor for 36 and 48.

8. Find the least common multiple for 36 and 48.

9. List the properties that are represented by each of the following:

   (a) $3 + 0 = 3$

   (b) $4 \times 1 = 4$

   (c) $3 + 6 = 6 + 3$

   (d) $4 \times (6 \times 2) = (4 \times 6) \times 2$

   (e) $3 + (-3) = 0$

   (f) $4(3 + 5) = 4(3) + 4(5)$

   (g) $\left(1\frac{1}{2}\right) \times \left(\frac{2}{3}\right) = 1$

10. Write the value 360,000 in scientific notation.

11. Write the value 0.0032 in scientific notation.

12. Simplify $3[3^2 + 2(4 + 1)]$.

13. Round 23,467.0684 to the nearest thousand.

14. Round 23,467.0586 to the nearest thousandth.

15. $-8 + 5 =$

16. $8 - 17 =$

17. $-20 - (-14) =$

18. $-3 - 2(12 - 15) =$

19. $-12 \div 3 =$

20. $-30 \div (-6) =$

21. $0 \div 12 =$

22. $10 \div 0 =$

23. $6 = \frac{?}{4}$

24. Change $5\frac{3}{4}$ to an improper fraction.

25. Change $\frac{32}{6}$ to a whole number or a mixed number in lowest terms.

26. $\frac{2}{5} + \frac{3}{5} =$

27. $\frac{1}{3} + \frac{1}{4} + \frac{1}{2} =$

28. $1\frac{3}{8} + 2\frac{5}{6} =$

29. $\frac{7}{9} - \frac{5}{9} =$

30. $11 - \frac{2}{3}$

31. $6\frac{1}{4} - 3\frac{3}{4} =$

32. $\frac{1}{6} \times \frac{1}{6} =$

33. $2\frac{3}{8} \times 1\frac{5}{6} =$

34. $\frac{1}{4} \div \frac{3}{2} =$

35. $2\frac{3}{7} \div 1\frac{1}{4} =$

36. $0.07 + 1.2 + 0.471 =$

37. $0.45 - 0.003 =$

38. $\$78.24 - \$31.68 =$

39. $0.5 \times 0.5 =$

40. $8.001 \times 2.3 =$

41. $0.7 \overline{)0.147}$

42. $0.002 \overline{)12}$

43. $\frac{1}{3}$ of $\$720 =$

44. Change 0.5% to a decimal.

45. Change 0.3 to a percent.

46. Change $\frac{5}{8}$ to a percent.

47. Change $12\frac{1}{2}\%$ to a fraction in lowest terms.

48. Put the following values in order from least to greatest: $\sqrt{17}, 6\frac{1}{2}, 225\%, \frac{29}{5}, 3.4$

49. What is 46% of 58?

50. 15% of what is 30?

51. What percent of 60 is 45?

52. Find the percent-increase from 25 to 40.

53. Find the percent-decrease from 40 to 25.

54. Use the given set of data to answer each of the following: $\{1, 2, 6, 4; 6, 3, 6, 1, 16\}$

    (a) The mode for the set of data is ___.

    (b) The mean for the set of data is ___.

    (c) The median for the set of data is ___.

    (d) The range for the set of data is ___.

55. Between what two integers on a number line will you find $\sqrt{45}$?

56. Simplify the radical expression $\sqrt{45}$.

57. How many centimeters are there in 2 meters?

58. How many kilograms are there in 30,000 grams?

59. 3 liters = _____ deciliters

60. How many quarts are there in 3 gallons?

61. 12 ounces is what part of a pound?

62. 54 inches = _____ yards

63. What is the probability of tossing two standard dice so that their sum is 8?

Answers

1. $-2, 0, 4$

2. $5.8, 6, \frac{1}{4}, \sqrt{4}$

3. $31, 37$

4. $18, 20, 21, 22, 24, 25, 26, 27, 28$

5. $1, 4, 9, 16$

6. $1, 8, 27, 64$

7. 12

8. 144

9. **(a)** additive identity

   (b) multiplicative identity

   (c) commutative property for addition

   (d) associative property for multiplication

   (e) additive inverse

   (f) distributive property

   (g) multiplicative inverse

10. 3.6×10^5

11. 3.2×10^{-3}

12. 57

13. $23,000$

14. $23,467.059$

15. -3

16. -9

17. -6

18. 3

19. -4

20. 5

21. 0

22. Undefined (does not exist)

23. $? = 24$

24. $\frac{23}{4}$

25. $5\frac{2}{6} = 5\frac{1}{3}$

26. $\frac{5}{5} = 1$

27. $\frac{13}{12} = 1\frac{1}{12}$

28. $4\frac{5}{24}$ or $\frac{101}{24}$

29. $\frac{2}{9}$

30. $10\frac{1}{3}$ or $\frac{31}{3}$

31. $2\frac{2}{4} = 2\frac{1}{2}$ or $\frac{5}{2}$

32. $\frac{1}{36}$

33. $4\frac{17}{48}$ or $\frac{209}{48}$

34. $\frac{2}{12} = \frac{1}{6}$

35. $\frac{68}{35}$ or $1\frac{33}{35}$

36. 1.741

37. 0.447

38. $\$46.56$

39. 0.25

40. 18.4023

41. 0.21

42. $6,000$

43. $\$240$

44. 0.005

45. 30%

46. 62.5% or $62\frac{1}{2}\%$

47. $\frac{1}{8}$

48. $225\%, 3.4, \sqrt{17}, \frac{29}{5}, 6\frac{1}{2}$

49. 26.68

50. 200

51. 75%

52. 60%

53. 37.5% or $37\frac{1}{2}\%$

54. (a) 6

(b) 5

(c) 4

(d) 15

55. 6 and 7

56. $3\sqrt{5}$

57. 200

58. 30

59. 30

60. 12

61. $\frac{12}{16} = \frac{3}{4}$

62. $\frac{3}{2}$ *or* $1\frac{1}{2}$ *or* 1.5

63. $\frac{5}{36}$

Domain 1: Number Sense

Symbols, Terminology, and General Mathematical Information

Common Math Symbols

Symbol References	
=	is equal to
≠	is not equal to
>	is greater than
<	is less than
≥	is greater than or equal to
≤	is less than or equal to
‖	is parallel to
⊥	is perpendicular to
≈	is approximately equal to

Important Equivalents

$\frac{1}{100} = .01 = 1\%$

$\frac{1}{10} = .1 = .10 = 10\%$

$\frac{1}{5} = \frac{2}{10} = .2 = .20 = 20\%$

$\frac{3}{10} = .3 = .30 = 30\%$

$\frac{2}{5} = \frac{4}{10} = .4 = .40 = 40\%$

$\frac{1}{2} = \frac{5}{10} = .5 = .50 = 50\%$

$\frac{3}{5} = \frac{6}{10} = .6 = .60 = 60\%$

$\frac{7}{10} = .7 = .70 = 70\%$

$\frac{4}{5} = \frac{8}{10} = .8 = .80 = 80\%$

$\frac{9}{10} = .9 = .90 = 90\%$

$\frac{1}{4} = \frac{25}{100} = .25 = 25\%$

$\frac{3}{4} = \frac{75}{100} = .75 = 75\%$

$\frac{1}{3} = .33\frac{1}{3} = 33\frac{1}{3}\%$

$\frac{2}{3} = .66\frac{2}{3} = 66\frac{2}{3}\%$

$\frac{1}{8} = .125 = .12\frac{1}{2} = 12\frac{1}{2}\%$

$\frac{3}{8} = .375 = .37\frac{1}{2} = 37\frac{1}{2}\%$

$\frac{5}{8} = .625 = .62\frac{1}{2} = 62\frac{1}{2}\%$

$\frac{7}{8} = .875 = .87\frac{1}{2} = 87\frac{1}{2}\%$

$\frac{1}{6} = .16\frac{2}{3} = 16\frac{2}{3}\%$

$\frac{5}{6} = .83\frac{1}{3} = 83\frac{1}{3}\%$

$1 = 1.00 = 100\%$

$2 = 2.00 = 200\%$

$3\frac{1}{2} = 3.5 = 3.50 = 350\%$

Groups of Numbers

Natural Numbers (counting numbers): 1, 2, 3, 4,... (the numbers you would **_naturally_** count by). The number 0 is not a natural number.

Whole Numbers: 0, 1, 2, 3, 4,... (the natural numbers together with 0).

Integers: ... –3, –2, –1, 0, 1, 2, 3,... (all the whole numbers together with their opposites).

Rational Numbers: All values that can be expressed in the form $\frac{a}{b}$, where a and b are integers and $b \neq 0$,

or

when expressed in decimal form, the expression either terminates or has a repeating pattern.

> Examples:
>
> $4\frac{1}{2} = \frac{9}{2}$; therefore, $4\frac{1}{2}$ is a rational number.
>
> 0.3 is a terminating decimal; therefore, 0.3 is a rational number.
>
> 0.134343434... is a repeating decimal; therefore, 0.134343434... is a rational number.

Irrational Numbers: Any value that exists but is not rational.

> Examples:
>
> π The decimal name for pi starts out 3.14159265... The decimal name for pi does not terminate nor does it have a repeating pattern.
>
> $\sqrt{2}$ The decimal name for the square root of 2 starts out 1.41421356... The decimal name for the square root of 2 does not terminate nor does it have a repeating pattern.

Real Numbers: All the rational and irrational numbers.

Prime Number: A natural number greater than 1, and that only has 1 and itself as divisors. (An alternate definition is a natural number that has exactly two different divisors.) The first seven prime numbers are 2, 3, 5, 7, 11, 13, 17.

Composite Number: A natural number greater than 1 that is not a prime number. (An alternate definition is a natural number that has at least three different divisors.) The first seven composite numbers are 4, 6, 8, 9, 10, 12, 14.

Square Numbers: The results of taking integers and raising them to the 2nd power (squaring them). An alternate definition is the result when numbers are multiplied by themselves. The first seven positive square numbers are 1, 4, 9, 16, 25, 36, 49.

> Examples:
>
> $(-3)^2 = 9$; therefore, 9 is a square number.
>
> $(0)^2 = 0$; therefore, 0 is a square number, but is not a positive square number.

Cube Numbers: The results of taking integers and raising them to the 3rd power (cubing them). The first seven positive cube numbers are 1, 8, 27, 64, 125, 216, 343.

> Examples:
>
> $(-3)^3 = -27$; therefore, –27 is a cube number.
>
> $(0)^3 = 0$; therefore, 0 is a cube number.

Measures

Customary System, or English System

Length

> 12 inches (in.) = 1 foot (ft.)
> 3 feet = 1 yard (yd.)
> 36 inches = 1 yard
> 1,760 yards = 1 mile (mi.)
> 5,280 feet = 1 mile

Area

> 144 square inches (sq. in.) = 1 square foot (sq. ft.)
> 9 square feet = 1 square yard (sq. yd.)

Weight

> 16 ounces (oz.) = 1 pound (lb.)
> 2,000 pounds = 1 ton (T)

Capacity

> 2 cups = 1 pint (pt.)
> 2 pints = 1 quart (qt.)
> 4 quarts = 1 gallon (gal.)
> 4 pecks = 1 bushel

Time

> 365 days = 1 year
> 52 weeks = 1 year
> 10 years = 1 decade
> 100 years = 1 century

Metric System, or The International System of Units

The following prefixes are used in the metric system:

> milli $= \frac{1}{1000}$
>
> centi $= \frac{1}{100}$
>
> deci $= \frac{1}{10}$

Basic unit (meter, liter, gram):

> deca = 10
> hecto = 100
> kilo = 1000

Weight (gram)	
kilogram (kg)	1,000 grams
hectogram (hg)	100 grams
decagram (dag)	10 grams
Gram (g)	**1 gram**
decigram (dg)	0.1 gram
centigram (cg)	0.01 gram
milligram (mg)	0.001 gram

Volume (liter)	
kiloliter (kl or kL)	1,000 liters
hectoliter (hl or hL)	100 liters
decaliter (dal or daL)	10 liters
liter (l or L)	**1 liter**
deciliter (dl or dL)	0.1 liter
centiliter (cl or cL)	0.01 liter
milliliter (ml or mL)	0.001 liter

Length (meter)	
kilometer (km)	1,000 meters
hectometer (hm)	100 meters
decameter (dam)	10 meters
meter (m)	**1 meter**
decimeter (dm)	0.1 meter
centimeter (cm)	0.01 meter
millimeter (mm)	0.001 meter

Some approximations:

One meter is a little more than one yard.

One kilogram is about 2.2 pounds.

1000 kilograms is a metric ton.

One liter is a little more than one quart.

One kilometer is about 0.6 mile.

Math Words and Phrases

Words that signal an operation			
Addition	**Subtraction**	**Multiplication**	**Division**
Sum	Difference	Product	Quotient
Plus	Minus	Times	Ratio
Is increased by	Is decreased by	Of (Example: $\frac{2}{3}$ of 15 is what?)	Is a part of (Example: 3 is what part of 15?)
More than (Example: 3 more than 7 is what?)	Less than (Example: 3 less than 7 is what?)	At (Example: 3 at 5 cents cost how much?)	Goes into (Example: 4 goes into 28 how many times?)

Mathematical Properties

Some Properties (Axioms) of Addition and Multiplication

Commutative property – the order in which addition or multiplication is done does not affect the answer.

Commutative property for addition

$$2 + 3 = 3 + 2$$
$$5 = 5$$

Commutative property for multiplication

$$(2)(3) = (3)(2)$$
$$6 = 6$$

In general

$$a + b = b + a$$

$$ab = ba$$

Note: Subtraction does not have the commutative property.

Notice that $3 - 2 \neq 2 - 3$, ($3 - 2 = 1$ *but* $2 - 3 = -1$)

Note: Division does not have the commutative property.

Notice that $10 \div 2 \neq 2 \div 10$, ($10 \div 2 = 5$ *but* $2 \div 10 = \frac{2}{10}$ or $\frac{1}{5}$)

Associative property – the grouping, without changing the order, does not affect the answer.

Associative property for addition

$$8 + (4 + 2) = (8 + 4) + 2$$
$$8 + 6 = 12 + 2$$
$$14 = 14$$

Associative property for multiplication

$$8 \times (4 \times 2) = (8 \times 4) \times 2$$
$$8 \times (8) = 32 \times 2$$
$$64 = 64$$

In general,

$$a + (b + c) = (a + b) + c$$

$$a(bc) = (ab)c$$

Note: Subtraction does not have the associative property.

Notice $8 - (4 - 2) \neq (8 - 4) - 2$

$$8 - 2 \neq 4 - 2$$
$$6 \neq 2$$

171

Note: Division does not have the associative property.

Notice $8 \div (4 \div 2) \neq (8 \div 4) \div 2$

$$8 \div 2 \neq 2 \div 2$$
$$4 \neq 1$$

***Distributive property* — multiplication outside parentheses distributing over either addition or subtraction inside parentheses does not affect the answer.**

$$7(3 + 9) = 7(3) + 7(9)$$
$$7(12) = 21 + 63$$
$$84 = 84$$

In general, $a(b + c) = ab + ac$

$$5(12 - 3) = 5(12) - 5(3)$$
$$5(9) = 60 - 15$$
$$45 = 45$$

In general, $a(b - c) = ab - ac$

Note: You *cannot* use the distributive property with only one operation.

$$3(4 \times 5) \neq 3(4) \times 3(5)$$
$$3(20) \neq 12 \times 15$$
$$60 \neq 180$$

Special properties of 0 and 1

An *identity number* is a value that, when added to another number or multiplied with another number, does not change the value of that number.

***The identity number for addition is 0.* Any number added to 0 gives that number.**

$$0 + 3 = 3 + 0 = 3$$
$$0 + a = a + 0 = a$$

$0 + 3 = 3$ is an example of using the additive identity.

***The identity number for multiplication is 1.* Any number multiplied by 1 gives that number.**

$$1(3) = 3(1) = 3$$
$$1(a) = a(1) = a$$

$1(3) = 3$ is an example of using the multiplicative identity.

Inverses

***The additive inverse of a number (also known as the opposite of the number)* is a value that, when added to any number, equals 0. Any number added to its additive inverse equals zero.**

Since $7 + (-7) = 0$, 7 is the additive inverse of -7 and -7 is the additive inverse of 7.

The additive inverse of $a = -a$.

For any number a, $a + (-a) = 0$

$7 + (-7) = 0$ is an example of using additive inverses.

The *multiplicative inverse of a number (also known as the reciprocal of the number)* is a value that when multiplied with any non-zero number equals 1. Any non-zero number multiplied with its multiplicative inverse equals one.

Because $\frac{4}{5} \times \frac{5}{4} = 1$, we would say that $\frac{4}{5}$ is the multiplicative inverse of $\frac{5}{4}$, and $\frac{5}{4}$ is the multiplicative inverse of $\frac{4}{5}$.

The multiplicative inverse of a $(a \neq 0)$ is $\frac{1}{a}$ for any a $(a \neq 0)$, $a \times \frac{1}{a} = 1$

$\frac{4}{5} \times \frac{5}{4} = 1$ is an example of using multiplicative inverses.

Fractions

Fractions consist of two numbers separated by a bar which indicates division: the *numerator* is above the bar and the *denominator* is below the bar.

In the fraction $\frac{3}{5}$, the 3 is the numerator and the 5 is the denominator.

Generally, the denominator of a fraction tells you into how many equal parts something has been divided. The numerator tells you how many of these parts are being considered. In the example above, the fraction indicates that something has been divided into 5 equal parts and that 3 of those 5 are being used.

Proper Fractions and Improper Fractions

A fraction whose numerator is smaller than its denominator is called a *proper fraction*. All proper fractions have a value that is less than one. The fraction $\frac{3}{5}$ is an example of a proper fraction. A fraction whose numerator is the same or more than the denominator is called an *improper fraction*. All improper fractions have values equal to one or more than one. The fraction $\frac{6}{6}$ and the fraction $\frac{5}{4}$ are examples of improper fractions. $\frac{6}{6} = 1$ and $\frac{5}{4} = 1\frac{1}{4}$.

Mixed Numbers

When a value is expressed using a whole number together with a proper fraction, it is called a *mixed number*. The numbers $2\frac{3}{4}$ and $8\frac{5}{6}$ are both mixed numbers.

To change an improper fraction to either a whole number or a mixed number, you divide the denominator into the numerator. For example:

$$\frac{24}{3} = 8 \qquad\qquad \frac{19}{5} = 3\frac{4}{5}$$

$$3\overline{)24}^{8} \qquad\qquad 5\overline{)19}^{3}$$

$$\qquad\qquad\qquad \frac{-15}{4} = 3\frac{4}{5}$$

To change a mixed number back to an improper fraction, multiply the whole number by the denominator, add the numerator, and then place that value over the denominator. For example:

Change $6\frac{2}{5}$ into an improper fraction: $(5 \times 6) + 2 = 32$, therefore $6\frac{2}{5} = \frac{32}{5}$.

Reducing Fractions

A fraction must be reduced to *lowest terms*. This is done by finding the *greatest common factor* (GCF) for both the numerator and denominator and then dividing both the numerator and denominator by that value. For example:

Reduce $\frac{24}{36}$

Factors of 24 are 1, 2, 3, 4, 6, 8, 12, and 24. Factors of 36 are 1, 2, 3, 4, 6, 9, 12, 18, and 36.

The common factors of 24 and 36 are 1, 2, 3, 4, 6, and 12. The greatest common factor for 24 and 36 is 12. Dividing the numerator and denominator by 12, you get $\frac{2}{3}$.

This process could also have been done by finding some common factor and reducing by that factor. You would then repeat the process until the only common factor is 1. For example:

Reduce $\frac{24}{36}$

Both 24 and 36 have a common factor of 2, and so $\frac{24}{36} = \frac{12}{18}$.

Both 12 and 18 have a common factor of 2, and so $\frac{12}{18} = \frac{6}{9}$.

Both 6 and 9 have a common factor of 3, and so $\frac{6}{9} = \frac{2}{3}$.

Since 2 and 3 only have the common factor of 1, the fraction is now reduced to lowest terms.

Adding Fractions

To add fractions, you must first change all the denominators to their _least common multiple_ (LCM), which in fractions is known as the _least common denominator_ (LCD). This value is the least positive value that all the denominators will divide into without a remainder. One way to find this value is to make a list of the multiples for the values involved and then find the least common one. For example:

Find the LCM for 24 and 36.

Multiples of 24	Multiples of 36
24	36
48	72
72	108
96	144
120	180
144	216

Notice that 72 and 144 are both common multiples, but that 72 is the least common multiple.

Now apply this to the adding of fractions. For example:

$\frac{5}{24} + \frac{7}{36} = ?$ As we saw above, the LCD for 24 and 36 is 72.

$\frac{5}{24} = \frac{15}{72}$ Since 24 is multiplied by 3 to get 72, the 5 is also multiplied by 3.

$+\ \frac{7}{36} = \frac{14}{72}$ Since 36 is multiplied by 2 to get 72, the 7 is also multiplied by 2.

$\frac{29}{72}$ Now that the denominators are the same, add the numerators and keep the denominator.

Of course, if the denominators are already the same, keep that denominator, and simply add the numerators.

For example: $\frac{6}{11} + \frac{3}{11} = \frac{9}{11}$

Adding Mixed Numbers

To add mixed numbers, the same rule (find the LCD) applies, but make sure that you always add the whole number to get your final answer. For example:

$$2\tfrac{1}{2} = 2\tfrac{2}{4} \longleftarrow \begin{cases} \text{change one-half} \\ \text{to two-fourths} \end{cases}$$

$$+ 3\tfrac{1}{4} = 3\tfrac{1}{4}$$

$$5\tfrac{3}{4}$$

$$\longleftarrow \begin{cases} \text{remember to add} \\ \text{the whole numbers} \end{cases}$$

Subtracting Fractions

To subtract fractions, the same rule (find the LCD) applies, except that you subtract the numerators. For example:

$$\frac{7}{8} = \frac{7}{8}$$
$$-\frac{1}{4} = \frac{2}{8}$$
$$\frac{5}{8}$$

$$\frac{3}{4} = \frac{9}{12}$$
$$-\frac{1}{3} = \frac{4}{12}$$
$$\frac{5}{12}$$

Subtracting Mixed Numbers

When you subtract mixed numbers, sometimes you may have to "borrow" from the whole number, just like you sometimes borrow from the next column when subtracting ordinary numbers. For example:

$$\overset{4,\,11}{6\cancel{5}1}$$
$$- 129$$
$$522$$

$$\overset{3\tfrac{7}{6}}{4\tfrac{1}{6}}$$
$$- 2\tfrac{5}{6}$$
$$1\tfrac{2}{6} = 1\tfrac{1}{3}$$

you borrowed 1 from the 10's column

you borrowed one in the form $\tfrac{6}{6}$ from the 1's column

To subtract a mixed number from a whole number, you have to "borrow" from the whole number. For example:

$$6 \quad = 5\tfrac{5}{5} \longleftarrow \begin{cases} \text{borrow one in the form of} \\ \tfrac{5}{5} \text{ from the 6} \end{cases}$$

$$-3\tfrac{1}{5} = 3\tfrac{1}{5}$$

$$2\tfrac{4}{5}$$

$$\longleftarrow \begin{cases} \text{remember to subtract the} \\ \text{remaining whole numbers} \end{cases}$$

Multiplying Fractions

To multiply fractions, simply multiply the numerators; then multiply the denominators. If possible, reduce your answer to lowest terms. For example:

$$\frac{2}{3} \times \frac{5}{12} = \frac{10}{36}. \text{ Reduce } \frac{10}{36} \text{ to } \frac{5}{18}$$

Reducing when multiplying fractions: You could have reduced earlier in the process of multiplying these fractions. That would have allowed you to get to the reduced form sooner. To reduce, find a number that divides evenly into one numerator and one denominator. In this case, 2 will divide evenly into 2 in the numerator (it goes in one time) and 12 in the denominator (it goes six times). Thus

$$\frac{\overset{1}{\cancel{2}}}{3} \times \frac{5}{\underset{6}{\cancel{12}}} =$$

Now that you've reduced, you can multiply out as you did before.

$$\frac{\overset{1}{\cancel{2}}}{3} \times \frac{5}{\underset{6}{\cancel{12}}} = \frac{5}{18}$$

> **Remember, you may reduce early only when _multiplying_ fractions. This process does not apply to adding or subtracting of fractions.**

Multiplying Mixed Numbers

To multiply mixed numbers, first change any mixed number to an improper fraction. Then multiply as previously shown. To change mixed numbers to improper fractions:

1. Multiply the whole number by the denominator of the fraction.
2. Add this to the numerator of the fraction.
3. This is now your numerator.
4. The denominator remains the same.

Then change the answer, if in improper form, back to a mixed number and reduce if necessary. For example:

$$3\frac{1}{3} \times 2\frac{1}{4} = \frac{10}{3} \times \frac{9}{4} = \frac{90}{12} = 7\frac{6}{12} = 7\frac{1}{2}$$

Dividing Fractions

To divide fractions, invert (turn upside down) the second fraction and multiply. Then reduce if necessary. For example:

$$\frac{1}{6} \div \frac{1}{5} = \frac{1}{6} \times \frac{5}{1} = \frac{5}{6} \qquad\qquad \frac{1}{6} \div \frac{1}{3} = \frac{1}{6} \times \frac{3}{1} = \frac{3}{6} = \frac{1}{2}$$

Simplifying Fractions

If either numerator or denominator consists of several numbers, these numbers must be combined into one number. Then reduce if necessary. For example:

$$\frac{28+14}{26+17} = \frac{42}{43} \quad \text{or}$$

$$\frac{\frac{1}{4}+\frac{1}{2}}{\frac{1}{3}+\frac{1}{4}} = \frac{\frac{1}{4}+\frac{2}{4}}{\frac{4}{12}+\frac{3}{12}} = \frac{\frac{3}{4}}{\frac{7}{12}} = \frac{3}{4} \times \frac{12}{7} = \frac{36}{28} = \frac{9}{7} = 1\frac{2}{7}$$

Place Value

Each position in any number written in decimal form has *place value*. For instance, consider the number 109,876,543,210.12345 written in the chart below.

Place Value Chart

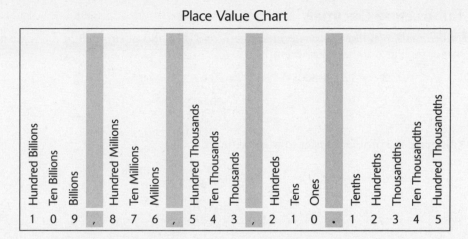

The 1 on the far left is in the hundred billions place, and the 1 written just to the right of the decimal point is in the tenths place. When the place value name ends with a "ths," it is an indication of being a fraction. The value 0.3 is read as "three tenths" and can be expressed in fraction form as $\frac{3}{10}$.

The value 5.23 is read as "5 and 23 hundredths" and can be expressed as the mixed number $5\frac{23}{100}$.

Rounding Off

To round off any number:

1. Underline the place value to which you're rounding off.
2. Look to the immediate right (one place) of your underlined place value.
3. Identify the number (the one to the right). If it is 5 or higher, round your underlined place value up 1. If the number (the one to the right) is 4 or less, leave your underlined place value as it is and change all the other numbers to its right to zeros. For example:

Round to the nearest thousands:

34<u>5</u>,678 becomes 346,000

92<u>8</u>,499 becomes 928,000

This works with decimals as well. Round to the nearest hundredth:

3.4<u>6</u>78 becomes 3.47

298,435.0<u>8</u>3 becomes 298,435.08

Decimals

Fractions may also be written in decimal form by using a symbol called a decimal point. All numbers to the left of the decimal point are whole numbers. All numbers to the right of the decimal point are fractions with denominators of only 10, 100, 1,000, 10,000, and so on, as follows:

$$0.6 = \frac{6}{10} = \frac{3}{5} \qquad\qquad 0.007 = \frac{7}{1000}$$

$$0.7 = \frac{7}{10} \qquad\qquad 0.0007 = \frac{7}{10,000}$$

$$0.07 = \frac{7}{100} \qquad\qquad 0.25 = \frac{25}{100} = \frac{1}{4}$$

Adding and Subtracting Decimals

To add or subtract decimals, just line up the decimal points and then add or subtract in the same manner you would add or subtract regular numbers. For example:

$$23.6 + 1.75 + 300.002 \qquad \begin{array}{r} = 23.6 \\ 1.75 \\ \underline{300.002} \\ 325.352 \end{array}$$

Adding in zeros can make the problem easier to work with:

$$\begin{array}{r} 23.600 \\ 1.750 \\ \underline{300.002} \\ 325.352 \end{array}$$

$$and \qquad 54.26 - 1.1 = \qquad \begin{array}{r} 54.26 \\ \underline{-1.10} \\ 53.16 \end{array}$$

$$and \qquad 78.9 - 37.43 = \qquad \begin{array}{r} 78.\overset{8}{9}\overset{1}{0} \\ \underline{-37.43} \\ 41.47 \end{array}$$

Whole numbers can have decimal points to their right. For example:

$$17 - 8.43 = \begin{array}{r} 1\overset{6}{7}.\overset{9}{0}\overset{1}{0} \\ \underline{-8.43} \\ 8.57 \end{array}$$

Multiplying Decimals

To multiply decimals, just multiply as usual. Then count the total number of digits above the line which are to the right of all decimal points. Place your decimal point in your answer so there is the same number of digits to the right of it as there was above the line. For example:

$$\begin{array}{r} 40.012 \quad \longleftarrow 3 \text{ digits} \\ \times \quad 3.1 \quad \longleftarrow 1 \text{ digit} \\ \hline 40012 \\ \underline{120036} \\ 124.0372 \quad \longleftarrow 4 \text{ digits} \end{array}$$

$\left\{\begin{array}{l}\text{total of 4 digits above the line that} \\ \text{are to the right of the decimal point}\end{array}\right.$

$\left\{\begin{array}{l}\text{decimal point placed so there is} \\ \text{same number of digits to the right} \\ \text{of the decimal point}\end{array}\right.$

Dividing Decimals

Dividing decimals is the same as dividing other numbers, except that if the divisor (the number you're dividing by) has a decimal, move it to the right as many places as necessary until it is a whole number. Then move the decimal point in the dividend (the number being divided into) the same number of places. Sometimes you may have to add zeros to the dividend (the number inside the division sign).

$$1.25 \overline{)5.} = 125 \overline{)500.}^{\;4.}$$

or

$$0.002 \overline{)26.} = 2 \overline{)26000.}^{\;13000.}$$

Conversions

Changing Decimals to Percents

To change decimals to percents:

1. Move the decimal point two places to the right.
2. Insert a percent sign.

    .75 = 75%   .05 = 5%

Changing Percents to Decimals

To change percents to decimals:

1. Eliminate the percent sign.
2. Move the decimal point two places to the left. (Sometimes adding zeros will be necessary.)

    75% = .75   5% = .05

    23% = .23   .2% = .002

Changing Fractions to Percents

To change a fraction to a percent:

1. Multiply by 100.
2. Insert a percent sign.

$$\frac{1}{2} = \left(\frac{1}{2}\right) \times 100 = \frac{100}{2} = 50\%$$

$$\frac{2}{5} = \left(\frac{2}{5}\right) \times 100 = \frac{200}{5} = 40\%$$

Changing Percents to Fractions

To change percents to fractions:

1. Divide the percent by 100.
2. Eliminate the percent sign.
3. Reduce if necessary.

$$60\% = \frac{60}{100} = \frac{3}{5}$$

$$13\% = \frac{13}{100}$$

Changing Fractions to Decimals

To change a fraction to a decimal, simply do what the operation says. In other words, $\frac{13}{20}$ means 13 divided by 20. So do just that (insert decimal points and zeros accordingly):

$$\frac{13}{20} = 20\overline{)13.00}^{\;.65} = .65 \qquad\qquad \frac{5}{8} = 8\overline{)5.000}^{\;.625} = 0.625$$

Changing Decimals to Fractions

1. Read it: 0.8 (eight-tenths)

2. Write it: $\frac{8}{10}$ or

3. Reduce it: $\frac{4}{5}$

1. Read it: 0.028 (twenty-eight thousandths)

2. Write it: $\frac{28}{1000}$

3. Reduce it: $\frac{7}{250}$

Using Percents

Finding Percent of a Number

To determine percent of a number, change the percent to a fraction or decimal (whichever is easier for you) and multiply. Remember, the word "of" means multiply.

What is 20% of 80?

$$\left(\frac{20}{100}\right) \times 80 = \frac{1600}{100} = 16 \ or \ .20 \times 80 = 16.00 = 16$$

What is 12% of 50?

$$\left(\frac{12}{100}\right) \times 50 = \frac{600}{100} = 6 \ or \ .12 \times 50 = 6.00 = 6$$

What is $\frac{1}{2}$% of 18?

$$\frac{\frac{1}{2}}{100} \times 18 = \left(\frac{1}{200}\right) \times 18 = \frac{18}{200} = \frac{9}{100} \ or \ .005 \times 18 = .09$$

Other Applications of Percent

Turn the question word-for-word into an equation. For "what," substitute the letter x; for "is," substitute an *equal sign*; for "of," substitute a *multiplication sign*. Change percents to decimals or fractions, whichever you find easier. Then solve the equation.

18 is what percent of 90?

$$18 = x(90)$$
$$\frac{18}{90} = x$$
$$\frac{1}{5} = x$$
$$20\% = x$$

10 is 50% of what number?

$$10 = .50(x)$$
$$\frac{10}{.50} = x$$
$$20 = x$$

What is 15% of 60?

$$x = \left(\frac{15}{100}\right) \times 60 = \frac{90}{10} = 9$$

or

$$.15(60) = 9$$

Percentage Increase or Decrease

To find the *percentage change* (increase or decrease), use this formula:

$$\frac{\text{change}}{\text{starting point}} \times 100 = \text{percentage change}$$

For example:

What is the percentage decrease of a $500 item on sale for $400?

Change: 500 – 400 = 100

$$\frac{\text{change}}{\text{starting point}} \times 100 = \frac{100}{500} \times 100 = \frac{1}{5} \times 100 = 20\% \text{ decrease}$$

What is the percentage increase of Jon's salary if it went from $150 per day to $200 per day?

Change: 200 – 150 = 50

$$\frac{\text{change}}{\text{starting point}} \times 100 = \frac{50}{150} \times 100 = \frac{1}{3} \times 100 = 33\,\tfrac{1}{3}\% \text{ increase}$$

Squares and Square Roots

To *square* a number, just multiply it by itself. For example, 6 squared (written 6^2) is 6×6 or 36. The value 36 is called a perfect square (the square of a whole number). Any exponent means to multiply by itself that many times. For example:

$$5^3 = 5 \times 5 \times 5 = 125$$
$$8^2 = 8 \times 8 = 64$$

Remember, $x^1 = x$ and $x^0 = 1$ when x is any number (other than 0).

Following is a list of some perfect squares:

$1^2 = 1$	$7^2 = 49$
$2^2 = 4$	$8^2 = 64$
$3^2 = 9$	$9^2 = 81$
$4^2 = 16$	$10^2 = 100$
$5^2 = 25$	$11^2 = 121$
$6^2 = 36$	$12^2 = 144$, etc

Square roots of nonperfect squares can be approximated. Two approximations you may want to remember are:

$$\sqrt{2} \approx 1.4$$

$$\sqrt{3} \approx 1.7$$

To find the *square root* of a number, you want to find some number that when multiplied by itself gives you the original number. In other words, to find the square root of 25, you want to find the number that when multiplied by itself gives you 25. The square root of 25, then, is 5. The symbol for square root is $\sqrt{}$. Following is a list of perfect (whole number) square roots:

$$\sqrt{1} = 1 \qquad\qquad \sqrt{36} = 6$$

$$\sqrt{4} = 2 \qquad\qquad \sqrt{49} = 7$$

$$\sqrt{9} = 3 \qquad\qquad \sqrt{64} = 8$$

$$\sqrt{16} = 4 \qquad\qquad \sqrt{81} = 9$$

$$\sqrt{25} = 5 \qquad\qquad \sqrt{100} = 10$$

Square Root Rules

Two numbers multiplied under a radical (square root) sign equal the product of the two square roots. For example:

$$\sqrt{(4)(25)} = \sqrt{4} \times \sqrt{25} = 2 \times 5 = 10 \; or \; \sqrt{100} = 10$$

and likewise with division:

$$\sqrt{\frac{64}{4}} = \frac{\sqrt{64}}{\sqrt{4}} = \frac{8}{2} = 4 \; or \; \sqrt{16} = 4$$

Addition and subtraction, however, are different. The numbers must be combined under the radical before any computation of square roots may be done. For example:

$$\sqrt{10+6} = \sqrt{16} = 4 \qquad\qquad \sqrt{10+6} \neq \sqrt{10} + \sqrt{6}$$
$$\sqrt{93-12} = \sqrt{81} = 9$$

Approximating Square Roots

To find a square root which will not be a whole number, you should approximate. For example:

Approximate $\sqrt{57}$

Since $\sqrt{57}$ is between $\sqrt{49}$ and $\sqrt{64}$, it will fall somewhere between 7 and 8. And because 57 is just about halfway between 49 and 64, $\sqrt{57}$ is therefore approximately $7\frac{1}{2}$.

Approximate $\sqrt{83}$

$$\sqrt{81} < \sqrt{83} < \sqrt{100}$$
$$9 < \sqrt{83} < 10$$

Since $\sqrt{83}$ is closer to the $\sqrt{81}$ than it is to the $\sqrt{100}$, the $\sqrt{83}$ will be closer to 9 than it is to 10. The decimal value of the $\sqrt{83}$ will then be between 9 and 9.5.

Therefore, $\sqrt{83} \approx 9.1$

Simplifying Square Roots

To simplify numbers under a radical (square root sign):

1. Factor the number into two numbers, one (or more) of which is a perfect square.
2. Take the square root of the perfect square(s).
3. Leave the others under the $\sqrt{\ }$.

Simplify $\sqrt{75}$

$$\sqrt{75} = \sqrt{25 \times 3} = \sqrt{25} \times \sqrt{3} = 5\sqrt{3}$$

Simplify $\sqrt{200}$

$$\sqrt{200} = \sqrt{100 \times 2} = \sqrt{100} \times \sqrt{2} = 10\sqrt{2}$$

Simplify $\sqrt{900}$

$$\sqrt{900} = \sqrt{100 \times 9} = \sqrt{100} \times \sqrt{9} = 10 \times 3 = 30$$

Scientific Notation

Very large or very small numbers are sometimes written in *scientific notation*. A number in scientific notation is written as a natural number from 1 to 9, and then multiplied by a power of 10. For original values larger than 1, the exponent on the 10 will be positive. For original values between 0 and 1, the exponent on the 10 will be negative.

For example:

2,100,000 written in scientific notation becomes 2.1×10^6.

Simply place the decimal point to the right of the first non-zero digit reading from left to right and then count how many places it was moved to get there.

$$\underset{6\ \ 5\ \ 4\ \ 3\ \ 2\ \ 1}{2{,}1\ 0\ 0\ 0\ 0\ 0.}$$

The decimal point was moved 6 places. The original value was more than 1, and so the exponent on the 10 will be positive.

0.000042 written in scientific notation becomes 4.2×10^{-5}.

The first non-zero digit from left to right is the "4." Place the decimal point to the right of the 4 and count how many places the decimal point moved.

$$\underset{1\ \ 2\ \ 3\ \ 4\ \ 5}{0.0\ 0\ 0\ 0\ 4{,}2}$$

The decimal point was moved 5 places. The original value was less than 1, and so the exponent on the 10 will be negative.

Change 3.72×10^4 out of scientific notation into decimal form. Since the exponent on the 10 is positive, the original number must be more than 1. Therefore, the decimal point must be moved to the right 4 places.

$$\underset{1\ \ 2\ \ 3\ \ 4}{3.7\ 2\ 0\ 0,}$$

Notice that in order to move the decimal point 4 places to the right, additional zeros must be inserted on the right. The final answer is 37,200.

Change 6.2×10^{-4} out of scientific notation into decimal form. In this case, the exponent on the 10 is negative, and so the original number must be between 0 and 1. Therefore, the decimal point must be moved to the left 4 places.

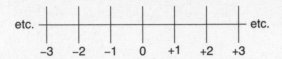

Notice that in order to move the decimal point 4 places to the left, additional zeros must be inserted to the left. The final answer is 0.00062.

Signed Numbers (Positive Numbers and Negative Numbers)

On a number line, numbers to the right of 0 are positive. Numbers to the left of 0 are negative, as follows:

etc. —|———|———|———|———|———|———|— etc.
  −3   −2   −1   0   +1   +2   +3

Given any two numbers on a number line, the one on the right is always larger, regardless of its sign (positive or negative).

Adding Signed Numbers

When adding two numbers with the same sign (either both positive or both negative), add the pure number portions (also known as *absolute values*) and keep the same sign that is on the numbers. Remember, when a number is written without a sign, it is assumed to be positive. For example:

$7 + 5 = 12$ $(-8) + (-3) = -11$ (the absolute value of −8 is 8 and the absolute value of −3 is 3)

$$\begin{array}{r} 7 \\ +5 \\ \hline 12 \end{array} \qquad\qquad \begin{array}{r} -8 \\ +(-3) \\ \hline -11 \end{array}$$

When adding two numbers with different signs (one positive and the other negative), subtract the pure number values and keep the sign on the number with the larger pure number value (keep the sign on the number with the larger absolute value). For example:

$5 + (-12) = -7$ (The −12 has the larger absolute value, so keep the negative sign: $12 - 5 = 7$)

$$\begin{array}{r} 5 \\ +(-12) \\ \hline -7 \end{array}$$

$-59 + (72) = 13$ (The 72 has the larger absolute value, so keep the positive sign: $72 - 59 = 13$)

$$\begin{array}{r} -59 \\ +72 \\ \hline 13 \end{array}$$

Subtracting Signed Numbers

To subtract is the same as to *add the opposite*. Change the sign of the number being subtracted, and then proceed as an addition problem. For example:

$12 - (-4) = 12 + (+4) = 16$

$$\begin{array}{c} 12 \\ \underline{-(-4)} \\ 16 \end{array} \quad \text{becomes} \quad \begin{array}{c} 12 \\ \underline{+(+4)} \\ 16 \end{array}$$

$-19 - 8 = -19 + (-8) = -27$

$$\begin{array}{c} -19 \\ \underline{-\ (8)} \\ -27 \end{array} \quad \text{becomes} \quad \begin{array}{c} -19 \\ \underline{+(-8)} \\ -27 \end{array}$$

$-23 - (-13) = -23 + (+13) = -10$

$$\begin{array}{c} -23 \\ \underline{-(-13)} \\ -10 \end{array} \quad \text{becomes} \quad \begin{array}{c} -23 \\ \underline{+(+13)} \\ -10 \end{array}$$

$18 - 33 = 18 + (-33) = -15$

$$\begin{array}{c} 18 \\ \underline{-33} \\ -15 \end{array} \quad \text{becomes} \quad \begin{array}{c} 18 \\ \underline{+(-33)} \\ -15 \end{array}$$

Multiplying or Dividing Signed Numbers

Multiply or divide the numbers as you normally would with the following rules regarding the sign on the answer:

The product or quotient of *two* numbers with the same sign will produce a positive answer.

The product or quotient of *two* numbers with opposite signs will produce a negative answer.

For example:

$(-3)(8)(-5)(-1)(-2) = 240$

The (-3) times (8) is a negative answer.
That negative answer times (-5) is a positive answer.
That positive answer times (-1) is a negative answer.
That negative answer times (-2) is a positive answer.

$$(-3)^3 = (-3)(-3)(-3) = -27$$
$$(-2)^4 = (-2)(-2)(-2)(-2) = 16$$
$$(-33) \div (3) = -11$$
$$\frac{-45}{-9} = 5$$
$$\frac{-3}{5} \times \frac{4}{7} = \frac{-12}{35}$$

Parentheses

Parentheses are used as grouping symbols. *When possible*, everything inside parentheses should be evaluated first before doing any other operations.

For example:

$$50(6 + 2) = 50(8)$$
$$= 400$$

(You could have applied the distributive property first, but you get the result faster by doing what was in the parentheses first.)

$$50(6 + 2) = 50(6) + 50(2) \text{ (applying the distributive property)}$$
$$= 300 + 100$$
$$= 400$$

What if the problem was $50(x + 6)$? Since you cannot evaluate $x + 6$ until you know what x is, you would apply the distributive property.

$$50(x + 6) = 50x + 50(6)$$
$$= 50x + 300$$

If there are parentheses inside other parentheses, you start with the most inside parentheses first and work your way out.

For example: $(4 - (11 - 15)) =$

You would begin with the $(11 - 15)$ since it is the innermost parentheses $(11 - 15 = -4)$.

$$(4 - (11 - 15)) = 4 - (-4)$$
$$= 4 + (4)$$
$$= 8$$

Order of Operations

There is an order in which the operations on numbers must be done so that everyone doing a problem involving several operations and parentheses would get the same results. The order of operations is:

1. **Parentheses:** Simplify (if possible) all expressions in parentheses.
2. **Exponents:** Apply exponents to their appropriate bases.
3. **Multiplication or Division:** Do the multiplication or division in the order it appears as you read the problem left to right.
4. **Addition or Subtraction:** Do the addition or subtraction in the order it appears as you read the problem left to right.

For example:

$$10 - 3 \times 6 + 10^2 + (6 + 12) \div (4 - 7)$$ parentheses first
$$10 - 3 \times 6 + \underline{10^2} + (18) \div (-3)$$ exponents next
$$10 - \underline{3 \times 6} + 100 + (18) \div (-3)$$ multiplication or division in order from left to right
$$10 - 18 + 100 + \underline{(18) \div (-3)}$$ multiplication or division in order from left to right
$$\underline{10 - 18} + 100 + (-6)$$ addition or subtraction in order from left to right
$$\underline{-8 + 100} + (-6)$$ addition or subtraction in order from left to right
$$\underline{92 + (-6)}$$ addition or subtraction in order from left to right
$$86$$

Here is an easy way to remember the order of operations: *Please Excuse My/Dear Aunt/Sally* (parentheses, exponents, multiply or divide, add or subtract)—**PEMDAS**.

Domain 4: Statistics, Data Analysis, and Probability

Some Basic Terms in Statistics

Measures of Central Tendency

The *mean (also known as the arithmetic mean)* of a set of data is the sum of the data values divided by the number of data values.

Example: Use this set of data to find the mean: 2, 2, 3, 5, 2, 6, 2, 6, 7, 9, 11.

$$\text{Mean} = \frac{2+2+3+5+2+6+2+6+7+9+11}{11} = \frac{55}{11} = 5$$

The *median* of a set of data is the value in the middle so that there are an equal number of data values to either side of it.

To find the median, arrange the data values from smallest to largest, including any repeats, and then find the middle value. If there is an odd number of data values, one of the data values will be in the middle. If there is an even number of data values, take the mean of the two middle values.

Example: Use this set of data to find the median: 2, 2, 3, 5, 2, 6, 2, 6, 7, 9, 11.

First, list the values in order from smallest to largest, including repeats: 2, 2, 2, 2, 3, 5, 6, 6, 7, 9, 11.
Second, find the middle value so that there is the same number of values on either side.

$$2, 2, 2, 2, 3, \underline{5}, 6, 6, 7, 9, 11$$

The median value is 5. Notice that there is the same number of scores on either side of the 5.
Suppose the data values did not have the 11.

$$2, 2, 2, 2, \underline{3, 5}, 6, 6, 7, 9$$

Now the 3 and 5 are the middle values. To find the median, find the mean of these two values.

The median now is $\frac{3+5}{2} = 4$

The *mode* of a set of data is the value repeated most often. In order to have a mode, some score had to be repeated.

Example: Use this set of data to find the mode: 2, 2, 3, 5, 2, 6, 2, 6, 7, 9, 11.

Since the value 2 was repeated most often, 2 is the mode.

The *range* of a set of data values is the difference between the maximum and minimum scores.

Example: Use this set of data to find the range: 2, 2, 3, 5, 2, 6, 2, 6, 7, 9, 11.

The maximum score is 11 and the minimum score is 2; therefore, the range is 11 – 2 = 9.

Probability

The probability of an event is the comparison of the total number of favorable outcomes to the total number of possible outcomes.

A probability is usually expressed in fraction form:

$$\frac{\text{total favorable outcomes}}{\text{total possible outcomes}}$$

Probability answers can also be expressed as percents or decimal values.

For example:

Suppose the natural numbers 4 through 20 were individually written on index cards and placed in a box. What is the probability that a prime number would be on the index card randomly chosen from the box?

First, consider the total number of possibilities. The natural numbers from 4 to 20 are used. If you subtract 20 – 4 and get 16, then you have found the number of natural numbers bigger than 4 but less than or equal to 20. If you were to count the natural numbers from 4 to 20, you would see that there are 17 of them. You could have subtracted 20 – 3 (since only the natural numbers 1, 2, and 3 are not used). Therefore, 17 represents the *total possible outcomes*. Now list the prime numbers from 4 to 20. The prime numbers are 5, 7, 11, 13, 17, 19. There are six of them. Therefore, 6 represents the *total favorable outcomes*.

So the probability of randomly selecting a prime number in this case is $\frac{6}{17}$.

What is the probability of tossing two standard dice and getting a sum of 5?

Standard dice are cubes with pips on the faces representing the values 1 through 6.

We can represent the outcomes in a table form. To distinguish the dice, call one of them "1st die" and the other "2nd die." In the table, we can show all the possibilities.

	1 (1st die)	2 (1st die)	3 (1st die)	4 (1st die)	5 (1st die)	6 (1st die)
1 (2nd die)						
2 (2nd die)			*			
3 (2nd die)						
4 (2nd die)						
5 (2nd die)						
6 (2nd die)						

The * is in the position representing the outcome that had a 3 on the 1st die and a 2 on the 2nd die.

From this table, you can see that there will be *36 total outcomes.*

Now mark on the table the locations representing the favorable outcomes. Recall that we are looking for the sum to be 5.

	1 (1st die)	2 (1st die)	3 (1st die)	4 (1st die)	5 (1st die)	6 (1st die)
1 (2nd die)				#		
2 (2nd die)			#			
3 (2nd die)		#				
4 (2nd die)	#					
5 (2nd die)						
6 (2nd die)						

The # was placed in the only locations where the sum of the numbers on the dice was 5. Notice now that there will be *4 favorable outcomes.*

So the probability in this case is $\frac{4}{36} = \frac{1}{9}$

Domain 2: Algebra Diagnostic Test

Questions

1. Solve for x: $x + 5 = 17$

2. Solve for x: $4x + 9 = 21$

3. Solve for x: $5x + 7 = 3x - 9$

4. Solve for x: $mx - n = y$

5. Solve for x: $\dfrac{r}{x} = \dfrac{s}{t}$

6. Solve for y: $\dfrac{3}{7} = \dfrac{y}{8}$

7. Evaluate: $3x^2 + 5y + 7$ if $x = -2$ and $y = 3$

8. Simplify: $8xy^2 + 3xy + 4xy^2 - 2xy =$

9. Simplify: $6x^2(4x^3y) =$

10. Simplify: $(5x + 2z) + (3x - 4z) =$

11. Simplify: $(4x - 7z) - (3x - 4z) =$

12. Factor: $ab + ac$

13. Factor: $x^2 - 5x - 14$

14. Solve for x: $x^2 + 7x = -10$

15. Solve for x: $2x + 3 \le 11$

16. Solve for x: $3x + 4 \ge 5x - 8$

17. Solve this system for x and y:

    $8x + 2y = 7$
    $3x - 4y = 5$

18. Use the following similar triangles to find the missing length.

 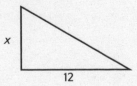

19. Use the following table to write an equation in the form "$y =$" that relates the y-values to the x-values.

x	y
2	5
4	9
6	13
8	17

Use the following information to answer questions 20 to 22.

A line passes through the points (3,10) and (0,4).

20. What is the slope of this line?

21. Write the equation of this line in slope-intercept form.

22. Any line that is perpendicular to this line will have what slope value?

23. A plumber charges $60 per hour to do work plus the cost of materials. Write an expression that represents his total charge (T) for a job requiring d dollars of materials and working n hours.

24. A triangle has a base of length ($x + 2$) and a height of length ($x - 5$). If x has a value of 10, find the area of this triangle.

Answers

1. $x = 12$

2. $x = 3$

3. $x = -8$

4. $x = \dfrac{(y+n)}{m}$

5. $x = \dfrac{rt}{s}$

6. $y = \dfrac{24}{7}$ or $3\dfrac{3}{7}$

7. 34

8. $12xy^2 + xy$

9. $24x^5 y$

10. $8x - 2z$

11. $x - 3z$

12. $a(b + c)$

13. $(x - 7)(x + 2)$

14. $x = -2$ or $x = -5$

15. $x \le 4$

16. $x \le 6$

17. $x = 1, y = -\dfrac{1}{2}$

18. $x = 9$

19. $y = 2x + 1$

20. slope = 2

21. $y = 2x + 4$

22. slope = $-\dfrac{1}{2}$

23. $T = 60n + d$

24. area = 30

Domain 2: Algebra

Domain 2 Overview: Algebra	
Patterns and Functional Relationships	❏ Represent patterns, including relations and functions, through tables, graphs, verbal rules, or symbolic rules. ❏ Ability to use proportional reasoning such as ratios, equivalent fractions, and similar triangles, to solve numerical, algebraic, and geometric problems.
Linear and Quadratic Equations and Inequalities	❏ Ability to find equivalent expressions for equalities and inequalities, explain the meaning of symbolic expressions (e.g., relating an expression to a situation, and vice versa), find the solutions, and represent them on graphs. ❏ Ability to recognize and create equivalent algebraic expressions [e.g., $2(a + 3) = 2a + 6$], and represent geometric problems algebraically (e.g., the area of a triangle). ❏ Have a basic understanding of linear equations and their properties (e.g., slope, perpendicularity); the multiplication, division, and factoring of polynomials; and graphing and solving quadratic equations through factoring and completing the square. ❏ Interpret graphs of linear and quadratic equations and inequalities, including solutions to systems of equations.

Part of the Domain 2 required information involves knowing certain math formulas for geometric objects. You should become familiar with the following charts.

Shape	Illustration	Perimeter	Area
Square	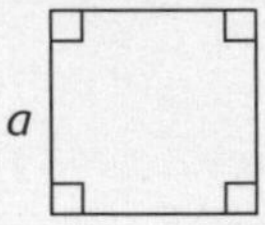	$P = 4a$	$A = a^2$
Rectangle	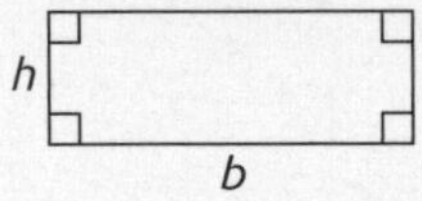	$P = 2b + 2h$ or $P = 2(b + h)$	$A = bh$
Parallelogram	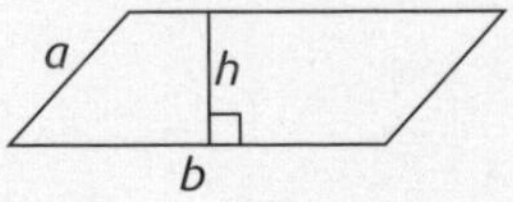	$P = 2a + 2b$ or $P = 2(a + b)$	$A = bh$
Triangle	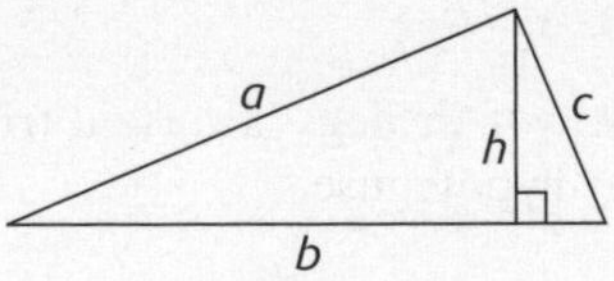	$P = a + b + c$	$A = \dfrac{bh}{2}$
Rhombus	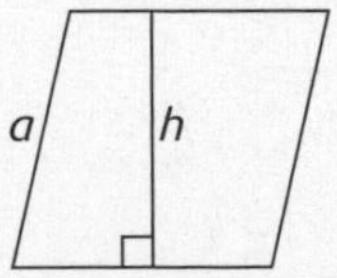	$P = 4a$	$A = ah$
Trapezoid	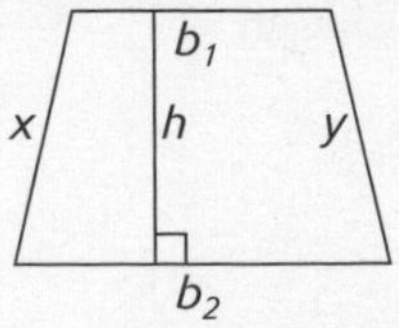	$P = b_1 + b_2 + x + y$	$A = \dfrac{h(b_1 + b_2)}{2}$
Circle	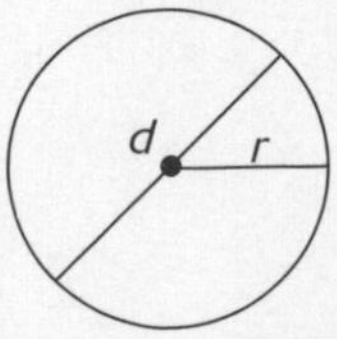	Circumference $C = \pi d$ or $C = 2\pi r$	$A = \pi r^2$

Shape	Illustration	Surface Area	Volume
Cube		$SA = 6a^2$	$V = a^3$
Rectangular Prism	Base	$SA = 2(lw + lh + wh)$ or $SA = (\text{Base-per})h + 2(\text{Base-area})$ Base-per means perimeter of the base. Base-area means area of the base.	$V = lwh$ or $V = (\text{Base-area})h$
Prisms in general	Base	$SA = (\text{Base-per})h + 2(\text{Base-area})$	$V = (\text{Base-area})h$
Cylinder	Base	$SA = (\text{Base-per})h + 2(\text{Base-area})$ or $SA = 2\pi rh + 2\pi r^2$ or $SA = 2\pi r(h + r)$	$V = (\text{Base-area})h$ or $V = \pi r^2 h$
Sphere		$SA = 4\pi r^2$	$V = \dfrac{4}{3}\pi r^3$

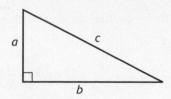

Pythagorean Theorem: $a^2 + b^2 = c^2$. The sum of the squares of the legs of a right triangle equals the square of the hypotenuse.

Evaluating Expressions

To *evaluate* an expression, just insert the value(s) given for the unknown(s) and do the arithmetic, making sure to follow the rules for the order of operations.

Examples:

1. Evaluate $2x^2 - 4y + 11$ if $x = 3$ and $y = -5$.

$$2x^2 - 4y + 11$$
$$2(3)^2 - 4(-5) + 11$$
$$2(9) - (-20) + 11$$
$$18 + 20 + 11$$
$$38 + 11$$
$$49$$

2. Evaluate $3(x - y)^2 - 3(x + y) - 7$ if $x = -2$ and $y = -6$.

$$3(x - y)^2 - 3(x + y) - 7$$
$$3[-2 - (-6)]^2 - 3[-2 + (-6)] - 7$$
$$3(-2 + 6)^2 - 3(-8) - 7$$
$$3(4)^2 - 3(-8) - 7$$
$$3(16) - 3(-8) - 7$$
$$48 - (-24) - 7$$
$$48 + 24 - 7$$
$$72 - 7$$
$$65$$

Applying some of the geometric formulas

Examples:

1. A triangle has a base of $(2x - 3)$ feet and a height of $(x + 2)$ feet. If $x = 10$, find the area of this triangle.

The formula for the area of a triangle is $A = \dfrac{bh}{2}$.

Replace the b with $(2x - 3)$ and the h with $(x + 2)$, and get $A = \dfrac{(2x-3)(x+2)}{2}$.

Now replace the x with 10 and evaluate.

$$A = \frac{2(10) - 3\,[10 + 2]}{2} = \frac{(20 - 3)(12)}{2} = 102 \text{ square feet}$$

2. A rectangular prism has a length of 5 inches, a width of 3 inches, and a height of 4 inches. Find the surface area of this prism.

The formula for the surface area of a rectangular prism is $SA = 2(lw + lh + wh)$

Replace l with 5, w with 3, and h with 4 and evaluate.

$$SA = 2(lw + lh + wh)$$
$$= 2[(5)(3) + (5)(4) + (3)(4)]$$
$$= 2[15 + 20 + 12]$$
$$= 94 \text{ square inches}$$

This last problem could also have been done using the generic formula for the surface area of a prism.

$$SA = (\text{Base-per.})h + 2(\text{Base-area})$$
$$= [2(l + w)](h) + 2(lw)$$
$$= [2(5 + 3)](4) + 2[(5)(3)]$$
$$= (16)(4) + 2(15)$$
$$= 64 + 30$$
$$= 94 \text{ square inches}$$

Equations

An *equation* is a relationship between numbers and/or symbols that says two expressions have the same value. Solving an equation for a variable requires that you find a value or an expression that has the desired variable on one side of the equation and everything else on the other side of the equation. By doing the same arithmetic to each side of the equation, you eventually can isolate the desired variable.

Examples:

1. $x - 5 = 23$. Solve for x.

Add 5 to each side of the equation.

$$\begin{array}{r} x - 5 = 23 \\ \underline{+5 \quad +5} \\ x \quad\;\; = 28 \end{array}$$

(Replace the original x with 28 and check to see if the resulting sentence is true.)

$$28 - 5 = 23$$
$$23 = 23$$

Therefore, $x = 28$ is a correct solution.

When two or more letters, or a number and a letter, are written next to each other, it is understood that these values are being multiplied together. Thus, $8x$ means 8 times x, and ab means the a-value times the b-value.

2. $3x + 4 = 19$. Solve for x.

Subtract 4 from each side of the equation.

$$\begin{array}{r} 3x + 4 = 19 \\ \underline{-4 \quad -4} \\ 3x \quad\;\; = 15 \end{array}$$

Divide each side of the equation by 3.

$$\frac{3x}{3} = \frac{15}{3}$$
$$x = 5$$

Replace the original x with 5 and check to see if the resulting sentence is true.

$$3(5) + 4 = 19$$
$$15 + 4 = 19$$
$$19 = 19$$

Therefore, $x = 5$ is a correct solution.

3. $4x + y = z$. Solve for x.

Subtract y from each side of the equation.

$$4x + y = z$$
$$\underline{\quad -y \qquad -y \quad}$$
$$4x \qquad = z - y$$

Divide each side of the equation by 4.

$$\frac{4x}{4} = \frac{z - y}{4}$$
$$x = \frac{z - y}{4}$$

4. $5x - 7 = 3x + 11$. Solve for x.

Subtract $3x$ from each side of the equation in order to get all of the variables on one side of the equation.

$$5x - 7 = 3x + 11$$
$$\underline{-3x \qquad -3x \qquad}$$
$$2x - 7 = \qquad 11$$

Add 7 to each side of the equation.

$$2x - 7 = 11$$
$$\underline{\quad +7 \quad +7 \quad}$$
$$2x \qquad = 18$$

Divide each side of the equation by 2.

$$\frac{2x}{2} = \frac{18}{2}$$
$$x = 9$$

Proportions

A *proportion* is a statement that says that two expressions written in fraction form are equal to one another. Proportions are quickly solved using a *cross multiplying* technique.

Examples:

1. Solve for x:

$$\frac{3}{x} = \frac{5}{7}$$

Using the cross multiplying technique, you get

$$5x = 21$$

Dividing each side of the equation by 5, you get

$$x = \frac{21}{5} \text{ or } 4\frac{1}{5}$$

This problem could also have been presented in written form as "3 is to x as 5 is to 7, find the value of x."

2. Solve for x:

$$\frac{2x+3}{x-4} = \frac{5}{6}$$

Using the cross multiplying technique, you get

$$6(2x + 3) = 5(x - 4)$$

Distributing on each side of the equation, you get

$$12x + 18 = 5x - 20$$

Subtracting $5x$ from each side of the equation in order to get all the unknowns on one side of the equation, you get

$$7x + 18 = -20$$

Subtracting 18 from each side of the equation in order to get all the knowns on one side of the equation, you get

$$7x = -38$$

Dividing each side of the equation by 7, you get

$$x = \frac{-38}{7} \text{ or } -5\frac{3}{7}$$

3. Solve for x:

$$\frac{p}{q} = \frac{x}{y}$$

Using the cross multiplying technique, you get $xq = py$

Dividing each side of the equation by q, you get

$$x = \frac{py}{q}$$

4. Triangle *ABC* is similar to triangle *DEF* with $AB = 6$, $BC = 9$, $AC = 12$, and $DE = 8$. Find the length of *DF*.

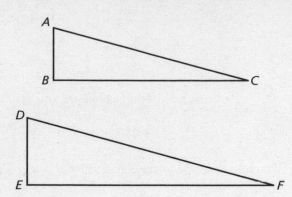

Similar triangles have corresponding sides forming proportions. That is, since triangle *ABC* is similar to triangle *DEF*, $\frac{AB}{DE} = \frac{BC}{EF} = \frac{AC}{DF}$; therefore, $\frac{6}{8} = \frac{9}{EF} = \frac{12}{DF}$.

$$\text{Now use } \frac{6}{8} = \frac{12}{DF}$$
$$6(DF) = 96$$
$$DF = 16$$

Inequalities

An inequality is a statement in which the relationships are not equal. Instead of using an equal sign (=) as in an equation, we use > (greater than) and < (less than), or ≥ (greater than or equal to) and ≤ (less than or equal to).

When working with inequalities, treat them exactly like equations, EXCEPT: If you multiply or divide both sides by a negative number, you must reverse the direction of the sign.

For example:

1. Solve for x: $2x + 4 > 6$

$$2x + 4 > 6$$
$$\underline{-4 \quad -4}$$
$$2x \quad\ > 2$$
$$\frac{2x}{2} > \frac{2}{2}$$
$$x > 1$$

2. Solve for x: $-7x > 14$ (divide by -7 and reverse the sign)

$$\frac{-7x}{-7} < \frac{14}{-7}$$
$$x < -2$$

3. Solve for x: $3x + 2 \geq 5x - 10$

$$3x + 2 \geq 5x - 10$$
$$\underline{\quad -2 \qquad\qquad -2}$$
$$3x \quad \geq 5x - 12$$
$$\underline{-5x \qquad\quad -5x}$$
$$-2x \quad \geq \quad -12$$

Divide both sides by -2 and reverse the sign.

$$\frac{-2x}{-2} \leq \frac{-12}{-2}$$
$$x \leq 6$$

Monomials and Polynomials

A *monomial* is an algebraic expression that consists of only one term. For instance, $9x$, $4a^2$, and $3mpxz^2$ are all monomials.

A *polynomial* is an algebraic expression that consists of two or more terms separated with either addition or subtraction. For example, $x + y$ is a polynomial with two terms, and $x^2 + 3x - 4$ is a polynomial with three terms.

Adding and Subtracting Monomials

To add or subtract monomials, they must be *like terms*. Like terms have exactly the same variables with exactly the same exponents on them. For example, $5x$ and $7x$ are like terms, but $5x$ and $7x^2$ are not like terms.

Examples:

1. Simplify the following: $15x^2yz - 18x^2yz$

   Since the variables on the two monomials are exactly the same with exactly the same exponents, you can add these monomials.

   $$15x^2yz - 18x^2yz = (15 - 18)x^2yz$$
   $$= -3x^2yz$$

2. Simplify the following: $17a + 7b - 12a - 10b$

   $$17a + 7b - 12a - 10b$$
   Rewrite with like terms near each other.
   $$17a - 12a + 7b - 10b$$
   $$(17 - 12)a + (7 - 10)b$$
   $$5a + (-3)b \text{ or } 5a - 3b$$

Adding and Subtracting Polynomials

To add or subtract polynomials, add or subtract the like terms in the polynomials together.

Examples:

1. $(3x^2 - 7x + 12) + (5x^2 + 9x - 19) = ?$

   $$(3x^2 - 7x + 12) + (5x^2 + 9x - 19)$$
   $$3x^2 - 7x + 12 + 5x^2 + 9x - 19$$
   $$3x^2 + 5x^2 - 7x + 9x + 12 - 19$$
   $$(3 + 5)x^2 + (-7 + 9)x + (12 - 19)$$
   $$8x^2 + 2x - 7$$

2. $(3x^2 - 7x + 12) - (5x^2 + 9x - 19) = ?$

$$(3x^2 - 7x + 12) - (5x^2 + 9x - 19)$$
(distribute the negative through the parentheses)
$$3x^2 - 7x + 12 - 5x^2 - 9x + 19$$
$$(3 - 5)x^2 + (-7 - 9)x + (12 + 19)$$
$$-2x^2 - 16x + 31$$

Multiplying Monomials

When an expression has a positive integer exponent, it indicates repeated multiplication. For example, x^3 indicates that x is used as a factor three times. That is, $x^3 = x \cdot x \cdot x$ and $x \cdot x \cdot x = x^3$

Now consider the following two examples:

$$(x^4)(x^3) = ?$$
$$(x^4)(x^3) \text{ means } (x \cdot x \cdot x \cdot x)(x \cdot x \cdot x) = (x \cdot x \cdot x \cdot x \cdot x \cdot x \cdot x) = x^7$$
$$(x^4)^3 = ?$$
$$(x^4)^3 \text{ means } (x^4) \cdot (x^4) \cdot (x^4) = (x \cdot x \cdot x \cdot x) \cdot (x \cdot x \cdot x \cdot x) \cdot (x \cdot x \cdot x \cdot x) = x^{12}$$

Examples:

1. $(7x^2)(-5x^3) = ?$

$$(7x^2)(-5x^3)$$
$$(7 \cdot -5)(x^2 \cdot x^3)$$
$$-35x^5$$

2. $(3xy^2)(-2x^4y^3) = ?$

$$(3xy^2)(-2x^4y^3)$$
$$(3 \cdot -2)(x \cdot x^4)(y^2 \cdot y^3)$$
$$-6x^5y^5$$

Multiplying Monomials with Polynomials and Polynomials with Polynomials

Examples:

1. $(-3x^2)(5x + 3) = ?$

$$(-3x^2)(5x + 3)$$
Use the distributive property.
$$(-3x^2)(5x) + (-3x^2)(3)$$
$$-15x^3 - 9x^2$$

2. $(3x + 5)(2x - 7) = ?$

$$(3x + 5)(2x - 7)$$
First distribute the $3x$ over the $(2x - 7)$, and then distribute the $+5$ over the $(2x - 7)$
$$3x(2x - 7) + 5(2x - 7)$$
$$6x^2 - 21x + 10x - 35$$
$$6x^2 - 11x - 35$$
This also means that $6x^2 - 11x - 35 = (3x + 5)(2x - 7)$

3. $(7x - 5)(7x + 5) = ?$

$$(7x - 5)(7x + 5)$$
$$7x(7x + 5) - 5(7x + 5)$$
$$49x^2 + 35x - 35x - 25$$
$$49x^2 - 25$$
This also means that $49x^2 - 25 = (7x - 5)(7x + 5)$

Factoring

To *factor* means to find two or more quantities whose product equals the original quantity.

Factoring out a Common Factor

Factor completely: $2y^3 - 6y$

1. Find the largest common monomial factor of each term.
2. Divide the original polynomial by this factor to obtain the second factor. (The second factor will be a polynomial.)

For example:

$$2y^3 - 6y = 2y(y^2 - 3)$$
$$x^5 - 4x^3 + x^2 = x^2(x^3 - 4x + 1)$$

Factoring the Difference between Two Squares

Factor: $x^2 - 144$

1. Find the square root of the first term and the square root of the second term.
2. Express your answer as the product of the sum of the quantities from step 1 times the difference of those quantities.

For example:

$$x^2 - 144 = (x + 12)(x - 12)$$
$$a^2 - b^2 = (a + b)(a - b)$$

Note: $x^2 + 144$ is not factorable.

Factoring Polynomials That Have Three Terms: $Ax^2 + Bx + C$

To factor polynomials that have three terms, of the form $Ax^2 + Bx + C$,

1. Check to see if you can monomial factor (factor out common terms). Then, if $A = 1$ (that is, the first term is simply x^2), use double parentheses and factor the first term. Place these factors in the left sides of the parentheses. For example, $(x \quad)(x \quad)$.
2. Factor the last term, and place the factors in the right sides of the parentheses.

To decide on the signs of the numbers, do the following:

If the sign of the last term is negative

1. Find two numbers whose product is the last term and whose difference is the coefficient (number in front) of the middle term.
2. Give the larger of these two numbers the sign of the middle term, and give the opposite sign to the other factor.

If the sign of the last term is positive

1. Find two numbers whose product is the last term and whose sum is the coefficient of the middle term.
2. Give both factors the sign of the middle term.

For example:

1. Factor: $x^2 - 3x - 10$

   First check to see if you can *monomial factor* (factor out common terms). Because this is not possible, use double parentheses and factor the first terms as follows: $(x \quad)(x \quad)$.

   Next, factor the last term (10) into 2 times 5. (Using the information above, 5 must take the negative sign and 2 must take the positive sign because they will then total the coefficient of the middle term, which is -3). Add the proper signs, leaving

$$(x - 5)(x + 2)$$

   Multiply the *means* (inner terms) and *extremes* (outer terms) to check your work.

$$(x - 5)\ (x + 2)$$
$$- 5x$$
$$+ 2x$$
$$- 3x \text{ (which is the middle term)}$$

   To completely check, multiply the factors together.

$$
\begin{array}{r}
(x - 5) \\
\times\ (x + 2) \\
\hline
+\ 2x - 10 \\
x^2 - 5x \\
\hline
x^2 - 3x - 10
\end{array}
$$

2. Factor: $x^2 + 8x + 15$

   $(x + 3)(x + 5)$

Notice that $3 \times 5 = 15$ and $3 + 5 = 8$, the coefficient of the middle term. Also note that the signs of both factors are +, the sign of the middle term. To check your work:

$$(x + 3)\,(x + 5)$$
$$+ 3x$$
$$+ 5x$$
$$+ 8x \text{ (the middle term)}$$

If, however, $A \neq 1$ (that is, the first term has a coefficient different than 1—for example, $4x^2 + 5x + 1$), then additional trial and error will be necessary.

3. Factor: $4x^2 + 5x + 1$

$(2x + \;\;)(2x + \;\;)$ might work for the first term. But when 1s are used as factors to get the last term— $(2x + 1)(2x + 1)$—the middle term comes out as $\underline{4x}$ instead of $5x$.

$$(2x + 1)\,(2x + 1)$$
$$+ 2x$$
$$+ 2x$$
$$+ 4x$$

Therefore, try $(4x + \;\;)(x + \;\;)$. This time, using 1's as factors to get the last terms gives $(4x + 1)(x + 1)$. Checking for the middle term,

$$(4x + 1)\,(x + 1)$$
$$+ 1x$$
$$+ 4x$$
$$+ 5x$$

Therefore, $4x^2 + 5x + 1 = (4x + 1)(x + 1)$.

4. Factor completely: $5x^3 + 6x^2 + x$

Factoring out an x leaves $x(5x^2 + 6x + 1)$

Now, factor as usual, giving $x(5x + 1)(x + 1)$

To check your work,

$$(5x + 1)\,(x + 1)$$
$$+ 1x \qquad \text{(the middle term}$$
$$\text{after } x \text{ was}$$
$$+ 5x \qquad \text{factored out)}$$
$$+ 6x$$

Solving Quadratic Equations

A quadratic equation is an equation that could be written as $Ax^2 + Bx + C = 0$. To solve a quadratic equation,

1. Put all terms on one side of the equal sign, leaving zero on the other side.
2. Factor.

3. Set each factor equal to zero.
4. Solve each of these equations.
5. Check by inserting your answer in the original equation.

For example:

1. Solve for x: $x^2 - 6x = 16$

Following the steps, $x^2 - 6x = 16$ becomes $x^2 - 6x - 16 = 0$.

Factoring, $(x - 8)(x + 2) = 0$

$x - 8 = 0$	*or*	$x + 2 = 0$
$x = 8$		$x = -2$
To check, $8^2 - 6(8) = 16$	*or*	$(-2)^2 - 6(-2) = 16$
$64 - 48 = 16$		$4 + 12 = 16$
$16 = 16$		$16 = 16$

Both values 8 and –2 are solutions to the original equation.

2. Solve for y: $y^2 = -6y - 5$

Setting all terms equal to zero, $y^2 + 6y + 5 = 0$

Factoring, $(y + 5)(y + 1) = 0$

Setting each factor to 0,

$y + 5 = 0$	*or*	$y + 1 = 0$
$y = -5$		$y = -1$
To check, $(-5)^2 = -6(-5) - 5$	*or*	$(-1)^2 = -6(-1) - 5$
$25 = 30 - 5$		$1 = 6 - 5$
$25 = 25$		$1 = 1$

A quadratic with a term missing is called an *incomplete quadratic*.

3. Solve for x: $x^2 - 16 = 0$

Factoring, $(x + 4)(x - 4) = 0$

$x + 4 = 0$	*or*	$x - 4 = 0$
$x = -4$		$x = 4$
To check, $(-4)^2 - 16 = 0$	*or*	$(4)^2 - 16 = 0$
$16 - 16 = 0$		$16 - 16 = 0$
$0 = 0$		$0 = 0$

4. Solve for x: $x^2 + 6x = 0$

Factoring, $x(x + 6) = 0$

$x = 0$	*or*	$x + 6 = 0$
$x = 0$		$x = -6$
To check, $(0)^2 + 6(0) = 0$	*or*	$(-6)^2 + 6(-6) = 0$
$0 + 0 = 0$		$36 + (-36) = 0$
$0 = 0$		$0 = 0$

Since Domain 2 includes linear equations, a review of coordinate geometry is now included.

Basic Coordinate Geometry Review

Coordinate Graphs (*x-y* Graphs)

A *coordinate graph* is formed by two perpendicular number lines. These lines are called coordinate axes. The horizontal line is called the *x-axis* or the *abscissa*. The vertical line is called the *y-axis* or the *ordinate*. The point at which the two lines intersect is called the *origin* and is represented by the coordinates (0, 0), often marked simply 0.

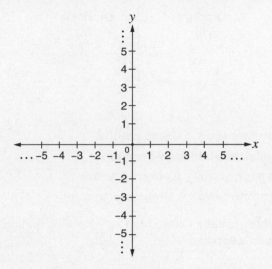

Each point on a coordinate graph is located by an ordered pair of numbers called *coordinates*. Notice the placement of points on the graph below and the coordinates, or ordered pairs, that show their location. Numbers are not usually written on the *x*- and *y*-axes.

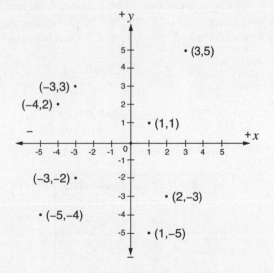

Also notice that on the *x*-axis, the numbers to the right of 0 are positive and to the left of 0 are negative. On the *y*-axis, numbers above 0 are positive and numbers below 0 are negative. The first number in the ordered pair is called the *x-coordinate* and shows how far to the right or left of 0 the point is. The second number is called the *y-coordinate* and shows how far up or down the point is from 0. The coordinates, or ordered pairs, are shown as (*x*, *y*). The order of these numbers is very important, as the point (3, 2) is different from the point (2, 3). Also, don't combine the ordered pair of numbers, because they refer to different directions.

The coordinate graph is divided into four quarters called *quadrants*. These quadrants are labeled as follows.

205

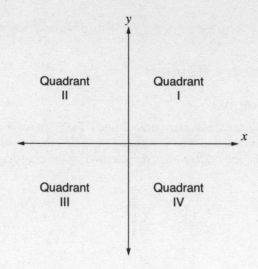

You can see that

- In quadrant I, x is always positive and y is always positive.
- In quadrant II, x is always negative and y is always positive.
- In quadrant III, x is always negative and y is always negative.
- In quadrant IV, x is always positive and y is always negative.

Graphs of equations in two variables (usually x and y) can be formed by finding ordered pairs that make the equation true, and then connecting these points.

Example:

1. Make the graph of the equation $2x + y = 6$.

   One way to do this is to set up a table of values with the x-values first, and then the y-values. You then replace one of the variables with values and find what the other variable would have to be for each replacement. If the x's were replaced with –2, –1, 0, 1, and 2, then find the corresponding y-values.

   $$\text{If } x = -2, \text{ then } 2(-2) + y = 6,$$
   $$\text{then } -4 + y = 6,$$
   $$\text{then } y = 10.$$

   The table below shows the x and y relationships in the previous question.

X	Y	(x,y) points
–2	10	(–2,10)
–1	8	(–1,8)
0	6	(0,6)
1	4	(1,4)
2	2	(2,2)

   Now plot these points.

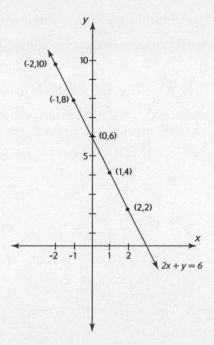

Notice that the points, if connected, form a line. An equation whose points, when connected, form a line is called a *linear equation*. All linear equations can be written in the form, "$y = mx + b$."

Rewriting $2x + y = 6$ in the "$y = mx + b$" form, you get $y = -2x + 6$. Notice in the graph, that the line passes through the y-axis at $y = 6$. This is known as the *y-intercept* of the graph. Also notice in the "$y = mx + b$" form that the b equals 6. The b in the $y = mx + b$ form becomes the y-intercept of the line.

Lines also have what is known as a *slope value*. The slope of a line gives a number value that describes its steepness and the direction in which it slants. If a line rises as it goes to the right, it has a *positive slope*. If a line falls as it goes to the right, it has a *negative slope*. If a line is horizontal, it has a *zero slope*. If a line is vertical, it does not have a slope value. In that case, we say the slope is *undefined* or that the line has *no slope*. The slope of a line is calculated by comparing the *rise* (the difference of the y-values), to the *run* (the difference of the x-values), when going from one point to another.

Using the points $(-2,10)$ and $(-1,8)$ we can calculate the slope the following way:

$$\text{Slope} = \frac{\text{rise}}{\text{run}} = \frac{10 - 8}{-2 - (-1)} = \frac{2}{-1} = -2$$

Regardless of which two points were chosen, the slope value would be the same. Notice that the line falls as it goes to the right, indicating that the slope is negative. Notice in the "$y = mx + b$" form of this line, that $m = -2$. When the equation of a line is written in the "$y = mx + b$" form, the m represents the slope of the line and the b represents the y-intercept.

When two lines are parallel, they will have the same slope values. When two lines are perpendicular, their slope values will be opposite reciprocals.

Examples:

1. A line passes through $(0,5)$ and $(2,11)$. Find the slope and y-intercept of this line.

   Since the line passes through $(0,5)$ and this is on the y-axis, the y-intercept is 5.

   Using $\frac{\text{rise}}{\text{run}}$, slope $= \frac{5 - 11}{0 - 2} = \frac{-6}{-2} = 3$ therefore, the slope of the line is 3.

2. A line passes through (0,5) and (2,11). Find the equation of this line in slope-intercept form.

    From the example above, the slope = 3 and the y-intercept is 5; therefore, the equation in slope intercept form is $y = 3x + 5$.

3. A line passes through (0,5) and (2,11). Any line perpendicular to this line will have what slope value?

    From the example above, this line has a slope of 3. Any line perpendicular to it will have the opposite reciprocal as its slope. Therefore, any line perpendicular to the line passing through (0,5) and (2,11) will have a slope of $-\frac{1}{3}$.

Domain 3: Geometry Diagnostic Test

Questions

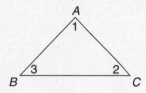

1. Name any angle of this triangle three different ways.

2. A(n) _____ angle measures less than 90 degrees.

3. A(n) _____ angle measures 90 degrees.

4. A(n) _____ angle measures more than 90 degrees.

5. A(n) _____ angle measures 180 degrees.

6. Two angles are complementary when their sum is _____.

7. Two angles are supplementary when their sum is _____.

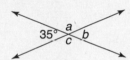

8. In the diagram above, find the measures of $\angle a$, $\angle b$, and $\angle c$.

9. Lines that stay the same distance apart and never meet are called _____ lines.

10. Lines that meet to form 90-degree angles are called _____ lines.

11. A(n) _____ triangle has three equal sides. Therefore, each interior angle measures _____.

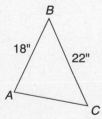

12. In the triangle above, AC must be smaller than _____ inches.

13. In the triangle above, which angle is smaller, $\angle A$ or $\angle C$?

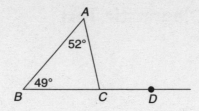

14. What is the measure of ∠*ACD* above?

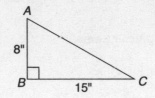

15. What is the length of $\overline{AC}$ above?

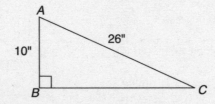

16. What is the length of $\overline{BC}$ above?

17. Name each of the following polygons:

A.

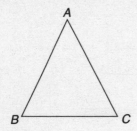

$AB = BC = AC$
$\angle A = \angle B = \angle C = 60°$

B.

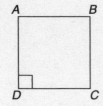

$AB = BC = CD = AD$
$\angle A = \angle B = \angle C = \angle D = 90°$

C.

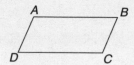

$\overline{AB} \parallel \overline{DC}$
$AB = DC$
$\overline{AD} \parallel \overline{BC}$
$AD = BC$
$\angle A = \angle C$

D.

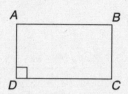

$AB = DC$
$AD = BC$
$\angle A = \angle B = \angle C = \angle D = 90°$

E.

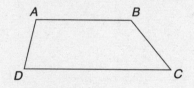

$\overline{AB} \parallel \overline{DC}$

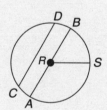

18. Fill in the blanks for circle R above:

A. $\overline{RS}$ is called the _____.
B. $\overline{AB}$ is called the _____.
C. $\overline{CD}$ is called a _____.

19. Find the area and circumference for the circle above $\left(\pi \approx \frac{22}{7}\right)$:

A. area =
B. circumference =

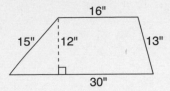

20. Find the area and perimeter of the trapezoid above:

    A.   area =

    B.   perimeter =

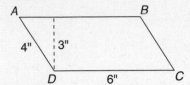

21. Find the area and perimeter of the figure above (*ABCD* is a parallelogram):

    A.   area =

    B.   perimeter =

22. Find the volume of the figure above if $V = (\pi r^2)h$. (Use 3.14 for π.)

23. What is the surface area and volume of the above cube?

    A.   surface area =

    B.   volume =

24. Triangle *QRS* is isosceles with a vertex angle that measures 40 degrees. Find the measures of the other two angles.

25. A 25-foot ladder leans against the wall of a building. The base of the ladder is 7 feet from the wall. How high up the wall will the ladder reach?

26. On a map, 2 inches represents a distance of 36 miles. On this map, points *A* and *B*, representing the cities of Alpha and Beta, are 15 inches apart. How long would it take someone to drive from Alpha to Beta at an average speed of 45 miles per hour?

27. *Use the following diagram to answer the question that follows.*

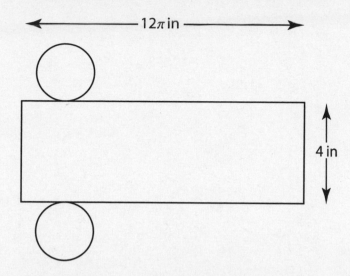

The figure above is a map of a cylinder. Find the volume of the cylinder.

28. *Use the diagram below to answer the question that follows.*

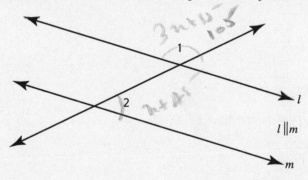

$l \parallel m$

Angle 1 has a measure of $3x + 15$ and angle 2 has a measure of $x + 45$. Angle 1 has how many degrees.

Answers

1. $\angle 3, \angle CBA, \angle ABC, \angle B$

    $\angle 1, \angle BAC, \angle CAB, \angle A$

    $\angle 2, \angle ACB, \angle BCA, \angle C$

2. acute

3. right

4. obtuse

5. straight

6. 90°

7. 180°

8. $a = 145°$

    $b = 35°$

    $c = 145°$

    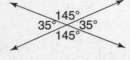

9. parallel

10. perpendicular

11. equilateral, 60°

12. 40 inches. Since $AB + BC = 40$ inches,

    $AC < AB + BC$, and

    $AC < 40$ inches

13. $\angle C$ must be the smaller angle, because it is opposite the shorter side AB.

14. $\angle ACD = 101°$

15. $AC = 17$ inches

16. Since $\triangle ABC$ is a right triangle, use the Pythagorean theorem:

$$a^2 + b^2 = c^2$$
$$10^2 + b^2 = 26^2$$
$$100 + b^2 = 676$$
$$b^2 = 576$$
$$b = 24"$$

17. **A.** equilateral triangle

    B. square

    C. parallelogram

    D. rectangle

    E. trapezoid

18. **A.** radius

    B. diameter

    C. chord

19. **A.** area $= \pi r^2$

    $\quad = \pi\,(7^2)$

    $\quad = \dfrac{22}{7}\,(7)(7)$

    $\quad = 154$ square inches

    B. circumference $= \pi d$

    $\quad = \pi(14)$ ($d = 14"$, because $r = 7"$)

    $\quad = \dfrac{22}{7}\,(14)$

    $\quad = 22(2)$

    $\quad = 44$ inches

20. **A.** area $= \dfrac{1}{2}(a+b)h$

    $\quad = \dfrac{1}{2}(16+30)12$

    $\quad = \dfrac{1}{2}(46)12$

    $\quad = 23(12)$

    $\quad = 276$ square inches

    B. perimeter $= 16 + 13 + 30 + 15 = 74$ inches

21. **A.** area $= bh$

    $\quad = 6(3)$

    $\quad = 18$ square inches

    B. perimeter $= 6 + 4 + 6 + 4 = 20$ inches

22. volume $= (\pi r^2)h$

    $\quad = (\pi \cdot 10^2)(12)$

    $\quad = 3.14(100)(12)$

    $\quad = 314(12)$

    $\quad = 3{,}768$ cubic inches

23. **A.** All six surfaces have an area of 4×4, or 16 square inches, because each surface is a square. Therefore, $16(6) = 96$ square inches in the surface area.

    B. Volume $=$ side $\times$ side $\times$ side, or $4^3 = 64$ cubic inches.

24. An isosceles triangle has two sides of equal length and the angles opposite those sides have equal measures. The vertex angle is the angle that is different from the other two angles. The sum of the angles of any triangle is always 180 degrees. If x represents each of the two equal angles, then

$$x + x + 40 = 180$$
$$2x = 140$$
$$x = 70$$

Each of the remaining angles has a measure of 70 degrees.

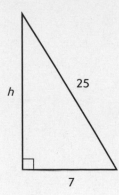

25. A model of this situation would be a right triangle with a hypotenuse of 25 and one leg of 7. Let h = how high the ladder will reach; then, using the Pythagorean theorem,

$$h^2 + 7^2 = 25^2$$
$$h^2 + 49 = 625$$
$$h^2 = 576$$
$$h = \sqrt{576} = 24$$

The ladder will reach a height of 24 feet.

26. First use proportions to find the distance that will be traveled.

$$\frac{\text{map distance (in.)}}{\text{actual distance (mi.)}}$$

$$\frac{2}{36} = \frac{15}{x}$$
$$2x = 540$$
$$x = 270 \text{ miles}$$

$$\text{Now use Rate} \times \text{Time} = \text{Distance}$$
$$(45 \text{ mi./hr.}) \times T = 270 \text{ miles}$$
$$T = 6 \text{ hours}$$

It will take 6 hours to travel from Alpha to Beta.

27. Use the formula for the volume of a cylinder.

$$V = (\text{Base-area}) \times \text{height where the Base is a circle.}$$

In this diagram, the length of the rectangular portion of the cylinder also represents the circumference of each circular base, and the width of the rectangular portion represents the height of the cylinder. Use the circumference formula for a circle,

$$C = 2\pi r.$$
$$12\pi \text{ (inches)} = 2\pi r \text{ (inches), divide each side of the equation by } 2\pi$$
$$6 \text{ inches} = r$$

Use the area formula for a circle,

$$A = \pi r^2$$
$$A = \pi(6^2)$$
$$A = 36\pi \text{ sq. in.}$$

Use the volume formula for a cylinder,

$$V = (\text{Base-area}) \times \text{height}$$
$$V = (36\pi \text{ sq. in.}) \times (4 \text{ in.})$$
$$V = 144\pi \text{ cu. in.}$$

The volume of the cylinder is 144π cubic inches.

28. When parallel lines are cut by a transversal, every pair of angles is either equal in measure or supplementary. Since angle 1 is obtuse and angle 2 is acute, they cannot be equal in measure. Therefore, the two angles are supplementary. Remember, you are asked to find the measure of angle 1.

$$\text{Angle 1} + \text{Angle 2} = 180$$
$$(3x + 15) + (x + 45) = 180$$
$$4x + 60 = 180$$
$$4x = 120$$
$$x = 30$$

the question was to find the measure of angle 1.

$$\text{Angle 1} = 3x + 15$$
$$= 3(30) + 15$$
$$= 105$$

Angle 1 has a measure of 105 degrees.

Domain 3: Geometry

Domain 3: Overview Geometry	
Two- and Three-Dimensional Geometric Objects	❏ Understand characteristics of common two- and three-dimensional figures, such as triangles (e.g., isosceles and right triangles), quadrilaterals, and spheres. ❏ Able to draw conclusions based on the congruence, similarity, or lack thereof, of two figures. ❏ Identify different forms of symmetry, translations, rotations, and reflections. ❏ Understand the Pythagorean theorem and its converse. ❏ Able to work with properties of parallel lines.
Representational Systems, Including Concrete Models, Drawings, and Coordinate Geometry	❏ Use concrete representations, such as manipulatives, drawings, and coordinate geometry, to represent geometric objects. ❏ Construct basic geometric figures using a compass and straightedge, and represent three-dimensional objects through two-dimensional drawings. ❏ Combine and dissect two- and three-dimensional figures into familiar shapes, such as dissecting a parallelogram and rearranging the pieces to form a rectangle of equal area.
Techniques, Tools, and Formulas for Determining Measurements	❏ Estimate and measure time, length, angles, perimeter, area, surface area, volume, weight/mass, and temperature through appropriate units and scales. ❏ Identify relationships between different measures within the metric or customary systems of measurements and estimate an equivalent measurement across the two systems. ❏ Calculate perimeters and areas of two-dimensional objects, and surface areas and volumes of three-dimensional objects. ❏ Relate proportional reasoning to the construction of scale drawings or models. ❏ Use measures such as miles per hour to analyze and solve problems.

Part of Domain 3 required information involves knowing certain math formulas for geometric objects. Refer back to the Domain 2 Review section to see charts that give formulas for area, perimeter, surface area, and volume of certain shapes.

Plane geometry is the study of shapes and figures in two dimensions (the plane).

Solid geometry is the study of shapes and figures in three dimensions.

A *point* is the most fundamental idea in geometry. It is represented by a dot and named by a capital letter.

Lines

A straight *line* is the shortest path connecting two points. It continues forever in opposite directions. A line consists of an infinite number of points. It is named by any two points on the line. The symbol ⟷ written on top of the two letters is used to denote that line.

This is line *AB*:

It is written: $\overleftrightarrow{AB}$

A line may also be named by one small letter. The symbol would not be used.

This is line *l*:

$l \longleftrightarrow$

A *line segment* is a piece of a line. A line segment has two endpoints, and is named by these two endpoints. The symbol ‾ written on top of two letters is used to denote that line segment.

This is line segment *CD*:

$$\overset{\longleftrightarrow}{\underset{\overline{CD}}{A \quad C \quad D \quad B}}$$

It is written: $\overline{CD}$

Note that it is a piece of $\overleftrightarrow{AB}$

A *ray* has only one endpoint and continues forever in one direction. A ray could be thought of as a half-line. It is named by the letter of its endpoint and any other point on the ray. The symbol —→ written on top of the two letters is used to denote that ray.

This is ray *AB*:

$$A \xrightarrow{\hspace{2cm}} B \longrightarrow$$

It is written: $\overrightarrow{AB}$

This is ray *BC*:

$$\longleftarrow C \qquad B$$

It is written: $\overleftarrow{BC}$

Note the order of the letters naming the ray. The endpoint is always mentioned first.

Angles

An angle is formed by two rays that start from the same point. That point is called the *vertex;* the rays are called the *sides* of the angle. An angle is measured in degrees. The degrees indicate the size of the angle, from one side to the other.

In the diagram, the angle is formed by rays *AB* and *AC*. *A* is the vertex.

$\overrightarrow{AB}$ and $\overrightarrow{AC}$ are the sides of the angle.

The symbol ∠ is used to denote an angle.

An angle can be named in various ways:

1. By the letter of the vertex—therefore, the angle above could be named ∠ *A*.

2. By the number (or small letter) in its interior—therefore, the angle above could be named ∠ 1.

3. By the letters of the three points that formed it—therefore, the angle above could be named ∠ *BAC*, or ∠ *CAB*. The center letter is always the letter of the vertex.

Types of Angles

- *Adjacent angles* are any angles that share a common side and a common vertex.

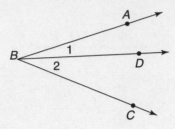

In the diagram, ∠ 1 and ∠ 2 are adjacent angles.

- A *right angle* has a measure of 90°. The symbol in the interior of an angle designates the fact that a right angle is formed.

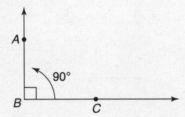

In the diagram, ∠ *ABC* is a right angle.

- Any angle whose measure is less than 90° is called an *acute angle*.

In the diagram, ∠ *b* is acute.

- Any angle whose measure is larger than 90° but smaller than 180° is called an *obtuse angle*.

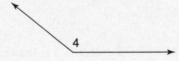

In the diagram, ∠ 4 is an obtuse angle.

- A *straight angle* has a measure of 180°.

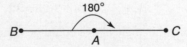

In the diagram, ∠ *BAC* is a straight angle (also called a line).

- Two angles whose sum is 90° are called *complementary angles*.

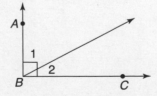

In the diagram, since $\angle ABC$ is a right angle, $\angle 1 + \angle 2 = 90°$.

Therefore, $\angle 1$ and $\angle 2$ are complementary angles. If $\angle 1 = 55°$, its complement, $\angle 2$, would be: $90° - 55° = 35°$.

- Two angles whose sum is 180° are called *supplementary angles*. Two adjacent angles that form a straight line are supplementary.

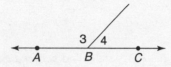

In the diagram, since $\angle ABC$ is a straight angle, $\angle 3 + \angle 4 = 180°$.

Therefore, $\angle 3$ and $\angle 4$ are supplementary angles. If $\angle 3 = 122°$, its supplement, $\angle 4$, would be: $180° - 122° = 58°$.

- A ray from the vertex of an angle that divides the angle into two equal pieces is called an *angle bisector*.

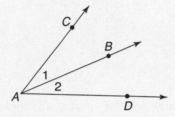

In the diagram, $\overrightarrow{AB}$ is the angle bisector of $\angle CAD$.

Therefore, $\angle 1 = \angle 2$.

- If two straight lines intersect, they do so at a point. Four angles are formed. Those angles opposite each other are called *vertical angles*. Those angles sharing a common side and a common vertex are, again, *adjacent angles*. Vertical angles are always equal.

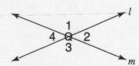

In the diagram, line l and line m intersect at point Q. $\angle 1$, $\angle 2$, $\angle 3$, and $\angle 4$ are formed.

$\angle 1$ and $\angle 3$ $\Big\}$ are vertical
$\angle 2$ and $\angle 4$ angles

$\angle 1$ and $\angle 2$
$\angle 2$ and $\angle 3$ $\Big\}$ are adjacent
$\angle 3$ and $\angle 4$ angles
$\angle 1$ and $\angle 4$

Therefore, $\angle 1 = \angle 3$
$\angle 2 = \angle 4$

Types of Lines

- Two or more lines that cross each other at a point are called *intersecting lines*. That point would be on each of those lines.

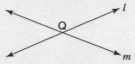

- Two lines that meet to form right angles (90°) are called *perpendicular lines*. The symbol ⊥ is used to denote perpendicular lines.

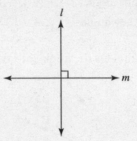

In the diagram, $l \perp m$.

- Two or more lines that remain the same distance apart at all times are called *parallel lines*. Parallel lines never meet. The symbol ∥ is used to denote parallel lines.

In the diagram, $l \parallel m$.

When two parallel lines are cut by a third line (called a transversal), the two sets of four angles formed (1, 2, 3, 4 and 5, 6, 7, 8) have the following relationship:

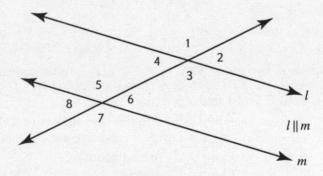

Angles in the same relative positions have the same measures. That means:

angle 1 = angle 5
angle 2 = angle 6
angle 3 = angle 7
angle 4 = angle 8

But since vertical angles are equal,

angle 1 = angle 3
angle 2 = angle 4

angle 5 = angle 7

angle 6 = angle 8

From this, we can see

angle 1 = angle 3 = angle 5 = angle 7

angle 2 = angle 4 = angle 6 = angle 8

From this, we can also see that for any two angles you select, if they are not equal to one another, they will be supplementary to one another.

Polygons

A *polygon* is a closed figure formed with line segments which are called the sides. (*Poly* means "many" and *gon* means "sides"; thus, *polygon* means "a many-sided figure.")

Triangles

A *triangle* is a three-sided polygon. It has three angles, or angular rotations, in its interior. The sum of the angles (or angular rotations) is always 180° (180 degrees). The symbol for triangle is △. A triangle is named by naming its vertices or corners. This is △*ABC*.

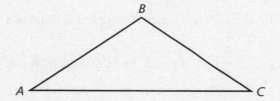

Triangles are classified by either their sides or their angles.

Classifying triangles by their sides:

- An *equilateral triangle* has all three of its sides of equal length, which in turn makes each of the three angles equal in measure. Therefore, each angle in an equilateral triangle has a measure of 60° since the sum of the angles in any triangle is 180°.

- An *isosceles triangle* has at least two of its sides equal in length. The angles opposite the equal sides in an isosceles triangle have equal measure.

- A *scalene triangle* has all three of its sides of different lengths. The angles in a scalene triangle will all have different measures, the largest angle will be opposite the longest side, and the smallest angle will be opposite the shortest side.

Classifying triangles by their angles:

- An *equiangular triangle* has all of its angles of equal measure; thus, each angle has a measure of 60°. An equiangular triangle is also equilateral.

- An *acute triangle* has each of its angles with measures less than 90°.

- An *obtuse triangle* has one of its angles with a measure greater than 90°.

- A *right triangle* has one of its angles with a measure equal to 90°.

From each vertex of a triangle, three segments can be drawn that have significance:

- An *altitude* (or *height*) is a segment that goes from a vertex of the triangle and makes a 90° angle with the opposite side, known as the *base*. Sometimes, the opposite side needs to be extended in order to accomplish this.

- A *median* is a segment that goes from one vertex of a triangle to the midpoint of the opposite side.
- An *angle bisector* is a segment that goes from one vertex of a triangle and divides the angle at that vertex into two smaller but equal angles.

In $\triangle ABC$ below, segment AD is the altitude from vertex A. In this case, the base, segment BC, needs to be extended in order for the segment AD to be able to make a 90° angle with the opposite side.

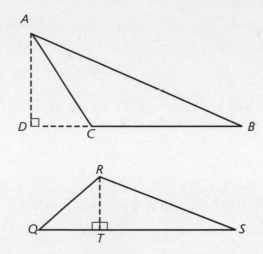

In $\triangle QRS$ above, segment RT is the altitude from vertex R. Segment RT makes a 90° angle with the base, segment QS.

In $\triangle ABC$ below, segment BD is a median from vertex B. Point D is the midpoint of segment AC, and so $AD = CD$.

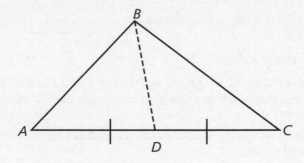

In $\triangle GHI$ below, segment HJ is an angle bisector from vertex H.

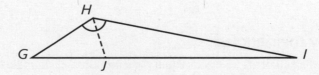

The measure of angle GHJ = the measure of angle IHJ.

- The sum of the lengths of any two sides of a triangle must be larger than the length of the third side.

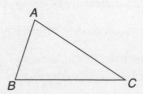

In the diagram of $\triangle ABC$:

$$AB + BC > AC$$
$$AB + AC > BC$$
$$AC + BC > AB$$

- If one side of a triangle is extended, the exterior angle formed by that extension is equal to the sum of the other two interior angles.

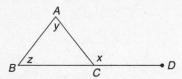

In the diagram of $\triangle ABC$, side BC is extended to D. The exterior angle formed is $\angle ACD$.

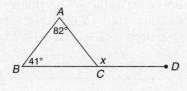

$$\angle x = \angle y + \angle z$$
$$x = 82° + 41°$$
$$x = 123°$$

Pythagorean Theorem

In any right triangle, there is a relationship between the lengths of the three sides. This relationship is referred to as the Pythagorean theorem. If the sides of a right triangle are labeled a, b, and c with c representing the longest of the three sides (the one opposite the right angle), then $a^2 + b^2 = c^2$

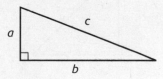

Example 1: Find the missing side in this right triangle.

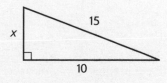

$$a^2 + b^2 = c^2$$
$$x^2 + 10^2 = 15^2$$
$$x^2 + 100 = 225$$
$$x^2 = 125$$
$$x = \sqrt{125}$$
$$x = \sqrt{25} \times \sqrt{5}$$
$$x = 5\sqrt{5}$$

Example 2: Find the missing side in this right triangle.

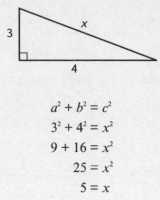

$$a^2 + b^2 = c^2$$
$$3^2 + 4^2 = x^2$$
$$9 + 16 = x^2$$
$$25 = x^2$$
$$5 = x$$

Any three sides of a right triangle are called *Pythagorean triples*. There are many Pythagorean triples with sides that are natural numbers. The above example is called the 3-4-5 Pythagorean triple. Some other common Pythagorean triples with natural numbers as sides are 5-12-13, 7-24-25, and 8-15-17. Any multiple of one of these will also form a Pythagorean triple. For example, if each side of a 3-4-5 triangle were doubled, it would form a 6-8-10 Pythagorean triple.

Other Right Triangles

There are two other special right triangles with which you need to be familiar. They are the 45-45-90 right triangle and the 30-60-90 right triangle.

The 45-45-90 Right Triangle

This right triangle is an isosceles right triangle. If each of the sides that form the right angle has a measure of 1, then using the Pythagorean theorem, you find that the hypotenuse has the value $\sqrt{2}$.

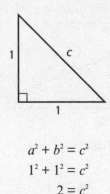

$$a^2 + b^2 = c^2$$
$$1^2 + 1^2 = c^2$$
$$2 = c^2$$
$$\sqrt{2} = c$$

If an isosceles right triangle had each of the equal sides with a measure of 5, then the hypotenuse would have a measure of $5\sqrt{2}$.

The 30-60-90 Right Triangle

This special right triangle is formed by cutting an equilateral triangle in half. If each of the short segments on segment AC has a length of 1, then segment AC has a length of 2, hence

$$AB = 2 \text{ and } BC = 2$$

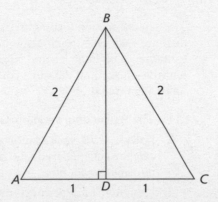

Now consider only $\triangle ABD$. Angle ABD has a measure of 30°, angle A has a measure of 60°, and angle ADB has a measure of 90°. This special right triangle has a hypotenuse twice as long as the short side, the side opposite the 30° angle. Using the Pythagorean theorem, we can find the measure of the side opposite the 60° angle.

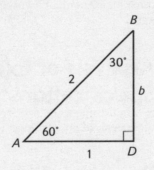

$$a^2 + b^2 = c^2$$
$$1^2 + b^2 = 2^2$$
$$1 + b^2 = 4$$
$$b^2 = 3$$
$$b = \sqrt{3}$$

If the short side of the 30-60-90 right triangle, the one opposite the 30° angle, had a measure of 5, the hypotenuse would have a measure of 10, and the side opposite the 60° angle would have a measure of $5\sqrt{3}$.

Chapter 4

Subtest II: Science

Content

The Science section focuses on primary scientific concepts, principles, and interrelationships in the context of real-life problems and significant science phenomena and issues. The Science questions in both the multiple-choice and the short constructed-response sections test the following three skills:

1. The explanation and application of concepts;

2. Process skills, such as interpreting a stimulus, ordering and categorizing material, and relating, inferring, or applying information found in various stimuli; and

3. Designing an experiment or investigating information necessary to explain an experiment.

The multiple-choice section contains 26 questions grouped together and 2 short constructed-response questions that cover the following three major content areas and focus on the topics listed under each area.

Analysis of Exam Areas: Content Specifications* in Science

*These are the actual California state content specification standards, available online.

Domain 1: Physical Science

1.1 <u>Structure and Properties of Matter</u>

❑ Candidates for Multiple Subject Teaching Credentials understand the physical properties of solids, liquids, and gases, such as color, mass, density, hardness, and electrical and thermal conductivity.

❑ They know that matter can undergo physical changes (e.g., changes in state such as the evaporation and freezing of water) and chemical changes (i.e., atoms in reactants rearrange to form products with new physical and chemical properties).

❑ They know that matter consists of atoms and molecules in various arrangements, and can give the location and motions of the parts of an atom (protons, neutrons, and electrons).

❑ They can describe the constituents of molecules and compounds, naming common elements (e.g., hydrogen, oxygen, and iron), and explain how elements are organized in the periodic table on the basis of their atomic and chemical properties.

❑ They can describe characteristics of solutions (such as acidic, basic, and neutral solutions), and they can refer to examples with different pH levels such as soft drinks, liquid detergents, and water.

❑ They know that mixtures may often be separated based on physical or chemical properties.

1.2 Principles of Motion and Energy

❑ Candidates for Multiple Subject Teaching Credentials can describe an object's motion based on position, displacement, speed, velocity, and acceleration.

❑ They know that forces (pushes and pulls), such as gravity, magnetism, and friction, act on objects and may change their motion if these forces are not in balance.

❑ They know that "like" electrical charges or magnetic poles produce repulsive forces, and "unlike" charges or poles produce attractive forces.

❑ They can describe simple machines in which small forces are exerted over long distances to accomplish difficult tasks (e.g., using levers or pulleys to move or lift heavy objects).

❑ Candidates can identify forms of energy, including solar, chemical, electrical, magnetic, nuclear, sound, light, and electromagnetic.

❑ They know that total energy in a system is conserved but may be changed from one form to another, as in an electrical motor or generator.

❑ They understand the difference between heat (thermal energy) and temperature, and understand temperature measurement systems.

❑ Candidates know how heat may be transferred by conduction, convection, and radiation (e.g., involving a stove, the earth's mantle, or the sun).

❑ They can describe sources of light, including the sun, light bulbs, or excited atoms (e.g., neon in neon lights) and interactions of light with matter (e.g., vision and photosynthesis).

❑ They know and can apply the optical properties of waves, especially light and sound, including reflection (e.g., by a mirror) or refraction (e.g., bending light through a prism).

❑ They can explain conservation of energy resources in terms of renewable and nonrenewable natural resources and their use in society.

Domain 2: Life Science

2.1 Structure of Living Organisms and Their Function (Physiology and Cell Biology)

❑ Candidates for Multiple Subject Teaching Credentials can describe levels of organization and related functions in plants and animals, including organ systems (e.g., the digestive system), organs, tissues (e.g., ovules in plants and heart chambers in humans), cells, and subcellular organelles (e.g., nucleus, chloroplast, and mitochondrion).

❑ They know structures and related functions of systems in plants and animals, such as reproductive, respiratory, circulatory, and digestive.

❑ They understand principles of chemistry underlying the functioning of biological systems (e.g., carbon's central role in living organisms; water and salt; DNA; and the energetics of photosynthesis).

2.2 Living and Nonliving Components in Environments (Ecology)

❑ Candidates for Multiple Subject Teaching Credentials know the characteristics of many living organisms (e.g., growth, reproduction, and stimulus response).

❑ They understand the basic needs of all living organisms (e.g., food, water, and space), and can distinguish between environmental adaptations and accommodations.

❑ They can describe the relationship between the number and types of organisms an ecosystem can support and relationships among members of a species and across species.

❑ They can illustrate the flow of energy and matter through an ecosystem from sunlight to food chains and food webs (including primary producers, consumers, and decomposers).

❑ They can identify the resources available in an ecosystem, and can describe the environmental factors that support the ecosystem, such as temperature, water, and soil composition.

2.3 Life Cycle, Reproduction, and Evolution (Genetics and Evolution)

❑ Candidates for Multiple Subject Teaching Credentials can diagram life cycles of familiar organisms (e.g., butterfly, frog, and mouse).

❑ They can explain the factors that affect the growth and development of plants, such as light, gravity, and stress.

❑ They can distinguish between sexual and asexual reproduction, and understand the process of cell division (mitosis), the types of cells and their functions, and the replication of plants and animals.

❑ They can distinguish between environmental and genetic sources of variation, and understand the principles of natural and artificial selection.

❑ They know how evidence from the fossil record, comparative anatomy, and DNA sequences can be used to support the theory that life gradually evolved on earth over billions of years.

❑ They understand the basis of Darwin's theory, that species evolved by a process of natural selection.

Domain 3: Earth and Space Science

3.1 The Solar System and the Universe (Astronomy)

❑ Candidates for Multiple Subject Teaching Credentials can identify and describe the planets, their motion, and that of other planetary bodies (e.g., comets and asteroids) around the sun.

❑ They can explain time zones in terms of longitude and the rotation of the earth, and understand the reasons for changes in the observed position of the sun and moon in the sky during the course of the day and from season to season.

❑ They can name and describe bodies in the universe, including the sun, stars, and galaxies.

3.2 The Structure and Composition of the Earth (Geology)

❑ Candidates for Multiple Subject Teaching Credentials can describe the formation and observable physical characteristics of minerals (e.g., quartz, calcite, hornblende, mica, and common ore minerals) and can differ types of rocks (e.g., sedimentary, igneous, and metamorphic).

❑ They can identify characteristics of landforms, such as mountains, rivers, deserts, and oceans.

❑ They can explain chemical and physical weathering, erosion, deposition, and other rock-forming and soil-changing processes, and the formation and properties of different types of soils and rocks.

❑ They can describe layers of the earth (crust, lithosphere, mantle, and core) and plate tectonics, including its convective source.

❑ They can explain how mountains are created and why volcanoes and earthquakes occur, and can describe their mechanisms and effects. They know the commonly cited evidence supporting the theory of plate tectonics.

❑ They can identify factors influencing the location and intensity of earthquakes.

❑ They can describe the effects of plate tectonic motion over time on climate, geography, and distribution of organisms, as well as more general changes on the earth over geologic time as evidenced in landforms and the rock and fossil records, including plant and animal extinction.

3.3 The Earth's Atmosphere (Meteorology)

❑ Candidates for Multiple Subject Teaching Credentials can explain the influence and role of the sun and oceans in weather and climate and the role of the water cycle.

❑ They can describe causes and effects of air movements and ocean currents (based on convection of air and water) on daily and seasonal weather, as well as on climate.

3.4 The Earth's Water (Oceanography)

❑ Candidates for Multiple Subject Teaching Credentials can compare the characteristics of bodies of water, such as rivers, lakes, oceans, and estuaries.

❑ They can describe tides and explain the mechanisms causing and modifying them, such as the gravitational attraction of the moon, sun, and coastal topography.

Sample Questions and Explanations for the Multiple-Choice Section

Each of the following examples represents an area tested in the Science multiple-choice section. An analysis follows each question.

Domain 1: Physical Science

1.1 Structure and Properties of Matter

---

1. Balance the following chemical equation by determining X.

$$2H_2 + X \rightarrow 2H_2O$$

    A. H_2O_2
    B. O_2
    C. $2H_2O$
    D. O_4

The correct answer is B. In balancing a chemical equation, atoms are not gained or lost but instead they change places. A chemical reaction can be written as a chemical equation, where the reactants are always on the left side of the equation and the products are always on the right side. The arrow points to the substances being formed. In a balanced equation, the number of atoms on one side of the equation always equals the number of atoms on the other side. The number in front of a molecule determines how many entire molecules there are. In balancing the chemical equation in the example above, 4 hydrogen atoms are in the reactants and 4 hydrogen atoms are in the product. Two oxygen atoms are in the product, and so 2 oxygen atoms need to be in the reactants. There are a total of 6 atoms in the reactants, and a total of 6 atoms in the product.

2. Which of the following best demonstrates the theory that molecules are always in motion?

    A. A spoonful of sugar is added to a cup of cocoa, and the cocoa becomes sweet in all parts of the cup.
    B. A small stone is dropped into a glass of water and falls straight to the bottom.
    C. An ice cube is placed in a cold container and melts very slowly.
    D. A drop of oil is added to a pan of water, and the oil floats to the top.

The correct answer is A. Recognizing that Choice B represents the effect of gravity and that Choice C represents a change in the state of matter would help you eliminate both because neither would best be explained by molecular motion. Understanding the properties of mixtures would eliminate Choice D. The correct answer addresses the movement of molecules in distributing the sugar to all parts of the cup. Similar distribution would result if a gas were released in a corner of a room. The gas would soon diffuse throughout the room as its molecules were evenly distributed.

3. Which of the following solutions would make litmus paper turn red?

    A. Liquid drain opener
    B. Salt water
    C. Vinegar
    D. Lye

The correct answer is C. Litmus paper changes color to red when dipped in an acid, and to blue when dipped in a base. The acid or alkaline strength of a solution is measured by the pH scale. On a pH scale, H represents hydrogen, as acids and alkalis have different hydrogen concentrations. The pH scale measures from 1 to 14, with 1 being the most acidic, 7 neutral, and 14 the most alkaline. Recognizing this would allow you to eliminate any non-acids as possible answers. Drain opener (A) usually contains lye (D), which is strongly alkaline; salt water (B) is also alkaline. Of the choices given, only vinegar is acidic.

4. Use the diagram and information below to answer the question that follows.

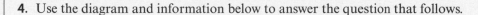

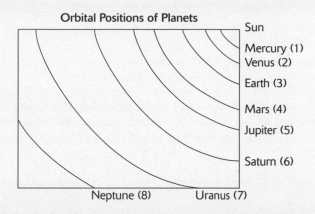

Orbital Positions of Planets

Sun
Mercury (1)
Venus (2)
Earth (3)
Mars (4)
Jupiter (5)
Saturn (6)
Neptune (8)   Uranus (7)

Planetary Data			
	Average Density (grams/cubic centimeter)	**Surface Temperature (degrees C)**	**Diameter at Equator (kilometers)**
(1)	5.3	345 to −175	5,000
(2)	5.2	500	12,100
(3)	5.6	10	12,800
(4)	4.0	−30 to −90	6,787
(5)	1.34	−150	142,800
(6)	0.70	−180	120,000
(7)	1.3	−190	51,800
(8)	1.7	−215	49,000

Objects float in water if they are lighter than an equal volume of water. An object with a density of 1.0 g/cm³ has a volume equal to that of the water it displaces.

Which planet or planets would be able to float if there were a water source large enough to hold it or them?

A.   Mercury
B.   Venus
C.   Saturn
D.   Jupiter and Uranus

The correct answer is C. You need only the data presented in the diagram, table, and the given information to correctly answer this question. You need no outside knowledge. The information given indicates that an object with a density of less than 1.0 g/cm³ floats in water. Therefore, the surface temperature and diameter sections of the table are irrelevant in answering this question. Saturn is the only planet listed with a density of less than 1.0 g/cm³ (0.70) and could theoretically float.

> **5.** Pure nitrogen is obtained commercially by first liquefying air, which is 78 percent nitrogen. Which of the following is the best method to condense air to a liquid?
>
> **A.** Lowering the temperature very quickly
> **B.** Lowering the pressure very quickly
> **C.** Lowering the temperature while raising the pressure
> **D.** Lowering the pressure while leaving the temperature constant

The correct answer is C. The liquefaction of air can be accomplished by changing temperature or pressure, or both. Lowering the temperature can change a gas into a liquid. Raising the pressure has the same result, since increased pressure forces molecules closer together. The most efficient procedure is to lower the air temperature while the pressure is increased.

Use the Abridged Periodic Table of the Chemical Elements below to answer questions 6, 7, and 8 that follow.

1							2
hydrogen							helium
H							He
3	4	5	6	7	8	9	10
lithium	beryllium	boron	carbon	nitrogen	oxygen	flourine	neon
Li	Be	B	C	N	O	F	Ne
11	12	13	14	15	16	17	18
sodium	magnesium	aluminum	silicon	phosphorous	sulfur	chlorine	argon
Na	Mg	Al	Si	P	S	Cl	Ar
19	20						
potassium	calcium						
K	Ca						
+1	+2	+3	+4, −4	+5, −3	−2	−1	0

valence for each column

> **6.** In the periodic table of the elements shown above, an element's atomic number indicates the number of:
>
> **A.** neutrons.
> **B.** electrons.
> **C.** protons.
> **D.** nuclei.

The correct answer is C. The periodic table of the elements is an important classification tool for chemists. Each horizontal row of elements is called a *period*. Properties of elements change greatly across any one row. There are seven periods of elements in the complete table. Important information is given about an element in each square of the periodic table. The chemical symbol of the element is in the middle of the square; the atomic weight of the element is usually directly below the symbol for each element (not shown in this abridged table); and the atomic number is usually shown at the top of the square. The *atomic number* of an element is the *number of protons of that element.* No two elements have the same atomic number. Elements in the periodic table are arranged in order of increasing atomic number.

7. Most of the elements in the periodic table are

   A. metals.
   B. gases.
   C. non-metals.
   D. compounds.

The correct answer is A. The vast majority of the elements in the periodic table are metals. Metals show a wide range of chemical and physical properties. Most metals are good conductors of heat and electricity and some, like iron and cobalt, are magnetic. Many metals in the periodic table are alkali metals, such as sodium and potassium. These metals are very reactive. The seventeen elements that are non-metals lack the properties of metals but are very common. Non-metals include oxygen, nitrogen, and carbon. Non-metals are poor conductors of electricity. Other elements in the periodic table include the seven metalloid elements and the seven gases. There are eighty metals in the periodic table.

8. Which of the following elements have the most similar chemical properties?

   A. Boron and carbon
   B. Sodium and chlorine
   C. Lithium and potassium
   D. Carbon and oxygen

The correct answer is C. Elements in the same group or column are likely to have the same chemical properties, based largely on the number of electrons in their outermost shell. For example, all the elements in column 1, starting with lithium, have one electron in their outermost shell. The metals in this group react violently with water.

1.2 Principles of Motion and Energy

9. The sun converts nuclear energy to electromagnetic energy and thermal energy. Which of the following is the best example of a change from thermal energy to chemical energy when solar energy reaches the earth?

   A. Evaporation of ocean water from solar energy
   B. Icebergs shrinking in size at extreme northern latitudes
   C. Sugars in the leaves of plants
   D. Compressed springs in a toy car

The correct answer is C. Plants convert solar energy into chemical energy through photosynthesis. Thermal energy or heat energy is the energy in substances. Chemical energy is stored in the bonds of atoms and molecules. Because plants manufacture carbohydrates, plants are examples of stored chemical energy. Choices A and B are examples of radiant energy. Choice D is an example of stored mechanical energy.

10. Use the picture below to answer the question that follows.

Which of the following would be an energy transformation pictured above?

   A. Mechanical energy is converted to heat energy.
   B. Chemical energy is converted to electrical energy.
   C. Electromagnetic energy is converted to light energy
   D. Electromagnetic energy is converted to heat energy

The correct answer is B. Energy transformations result when a change of form takes place. All forms of energy can be converted into other forms. The battery converts stored (potential) chemical energy to electrical energy. To be correct, the other examples could show the following: nuclear energy from the sun changing to electromagnetic energy; mechanical energy (machines in motion) turning a windmill; and chemical energy stored in food converting to mechanical energy when an individual moves.

---

11. Which statement best explains the following example? As a car is driven at high speeds for a long duration, the size of the tires temporarily increases.

    A.   Gases can be compressed to small volumes by pressure.
    B.   As the temperature of a gas increases, the volume increases.
    C.   When the pressure exerted on a gas is greatest, the volume is greatest.
    D.   A compressed gas pushes out equally in all directions.

The correct answer is B. The size, or volume, of the tires increases because the friction between the tires and the road causes heat. The increase in temperature increases the volume of the air in the tires, expanding them. Charles's law states that as temperature increases (at a fixed pressure), so does volume. Choices A and D are correct statements, but do not answer the question. Gases can be compressed, but the opposite happens in the tire example. Choice C is a misstatement.

---

12. A nuclear reactor that powers an electric generating plant relies on:

    A.   cold fusion.
    B.   fission.
    C.   fusion.
    D.   fission and fusion.

The correct answer is B. All nuclear reactors in use today obtain their energy through nuclear fission, which releases energy when a heavy nucleus splits into smaller fragments. You should eliminate cold fusion (A) because this process is only in the experimental stages as an alternative source of energy. (Cold fusion does not rely on thermonuclear heat energy input to generate nuclear energy; the hydrogen isotopes necessary for cold fusion are obtainable from ocean water.) In nuclear fusion (C), tremendous energy is released when very light nuclei unite to form a heavier nucleus. Stars, including the sun, derive their energy from nuclear fusion, as do hydrogen bombs.

---

13. A spacecraft uses its engines to escape the earth's gravitational pull. Once in space, the spacecraft does not need its engines to stay in orbit. Which of the following best explains why an astronaut in orbit is weightless?

    A.   The spacesuit creates an air-free environment.
    B.   The gravitational attraction of the moon balances that of the earth.
    C.   The earth's gravity pulls the spacecraft and the astronaut equally, but no force pulls the astronaut to the spacecraft.
    D.   Mass is decreased due to the weaker gravitational pull.

The correct answer is C. This question can be answered through a process of elimination. For example, eliminate Choice A because an individual in an air-free environment would suffocate and Choice D because mass remains constant even though location changes. (Note, however, that weight can change from the earth to the moon because weight is a function of gravity.) Although the question is introduced with information on gravity, its real focus is on weightlessness. In a spacecraft, an astronaut becomes weightless when centrifugal force (created by orbiting the earth) precisely counterbalances the gravitational pull of the earth.

14. Use the diagram below to answer the question that follows.

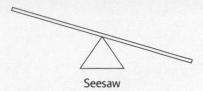

Seesaw

The diagram above illustrates a seesaw. A seesaw is an example of a(n):

A. lever.
B. inclined plane.
C. wedge.
D. pulley.

The correct answer is A. There are six simple machines: the wedge, the inclined plane, the screw, the lever, the wheel and axle, and the pulley. Simple machines allow an individual to do work by changing the direction of the force, multiplying the distance, or multiplying the force. Simple machines allow the individual to obtain a mechanical advantage. A ramp is an example of an inclined plane. An example of a wedge is an ax or even a zipper. Instead of an object moving across an inclined plane, the inclined plane moves. A pulley is a grooved wheel with a rope or other item wrapped around it. Raising and lowering window blinds is an example of a pulley system. A pulley can change the direction of a force or the amount of force.

A lever is a rigid object that rotates around a fixed point. To determine the mechanical advantage of a lever, the distance from the fulcrum to the input force is divided by the distance from the fulcrum to the output force. The force you exert on a machine is called the input force. The force exerted by the machine is called the output force. In the diagram of a seesaw, the fixed point is called the fulcrum. The fulcrum allows the rigid bar to rotate or pivot. A screwdriver is also an example of a lever.

15. Which characteristic of a wave must change in order to affect the pitch of a sound?

A. Amplitude
B. Wavelength
C. Frequency
D. Crest

The correct answer is C. A wave's crest is the top of its "hill." A wave's amplitude is its height, the distance between its resting position and its crest. Wavelength is defined as the distance between two consecutive points on a wave (crest to crest). The pitch of a sound depends on how fast the particles of a medium vibrate. The number of waves produced in a given time is the wave's frequency.

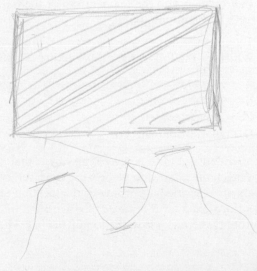

16. Use the diagram below to answer the question that follows.

Dispersion of Sunlight

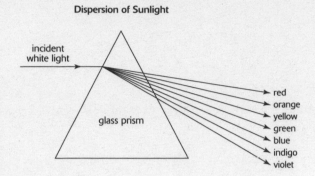

The above diagram shows the dispersion of sunlight through a prism.

Which of the following is *not* demonstrated by the diagram shown above?

A. Light is a photon particle and can act like a wave as seen by the variety of wavelengths.
B. Visible light comes in a rainbow of colors and sunlight is the combination of those colors.
C. A beam of sunlight will split into its constituent colors when it moves through a prism.
D. Violet is the longest wavelength represented by the prism.

The correct answer is D. The diagram shows the production of the color spectrum by shining sunlight through a glass prism. When light enters a prism, it is bent, or refracted, because the speed of light changes as it passes from one transparent medium to another (from water to air, from air to glass). While white light enters the prism, several colors of light leave the prism. The prism has separated white light into its basic colors, showing that white light is a mixture. The colors of the spectrum are visible in a rainbow because after a rainstorm, the air is full of tiny drops of water; each drop acts as a prism, splitting the light into the colors of the spectrum. Violet (D) is the shortest wavelength; red is the longest. The diagram does not indicate the wavelengths of the various colors.

17. As a covered kettle of vegetable soup continues to boil gently on the stove, what happens to the temperature of the soup?

A. It falls very slowly.
B. It remains the same.
C. It rises very slowly.
D. It rises rapidly.

The correct answer is B. The temperature of the soup remains the same. While the soup is boiling, both liquid and vapor are present in the covered kettle. The temperature of the liquid cannot be higher than its boiling point (212° Fahrenheit), and the temperature of the water vapor cannot be less than the boiling point. Therefore, the soup stays at the boiling point.

18. Which of the following is an example of a third-class lever?

A. A seesaw
B. A baby stroller
C. A baseball bat
D. A wheelbarrow

The correct answer is C. A lever is an object that is free to move around a fixed point, or fulcrum. A lever provides a mechanical advantage because the lever multiplies the force applied to an object. The three different types of levers are classified according to the location of the fulcrum relative to the input and output forces. A baseball bat is a third-class lever because the fulcrum is on the end of the bat, the input force (effort) is in the middle, and the output (resistance) is at the top of the bat. The effort comes from the person swinging the bat at the end of the handle; the heavier part of the bat (toward the far end) is the resistance. Such levers multiply distance but do not change the direction of the input force. Other examples of third-class levers include fishing poles and shovels. In a second-class lever, the fulcrum is at the end of the object, the output force is in the middle, and the input force is at the other end. These levers multiply force but do not change the direction of the input force. Examples of second-class levers include wheelbarrows, baby strollers, and bottle openers. In a first-class lever, the fulcrum is in the middle of the object, the output force is at one end of the object, and the input force is at the other end. Depending on the location of the fulcrum, these levers can multiply force or distance. Examples of first-class levers include seesaws, scissors, and pliers.

19. A commercial glass thermometer is partially filled with mercury. What physical principle best explains the use of mercury in thermometers?

   A. The change in air pressure when air is heated moves the mercury.
   B. Liquid mercury expands at regular intervals upon heating.
   C. The liquid mercury expands more than the glass.
   D. Gases expand more than liquids.

The correct answer is B. The scale marks on the thermometer are evenly spaced. Such a simple scale is possible only because liquid mercury expands regularly when heated, expanding upward. Choice C, although an accurate statement, does not identify the principle behind the use of mercury in a thermometer.

Domain 2: Life Science

2.1 Structure of Living Organisms and Their Function (Physiology and Cell Biology)

20. Enzymes are proteins that are essential during metabolism. Which of the following best summarizes the importance of enzymes in the metabolic process?

   A. They are secreted by the endocrine glands and regulate many bodily functions.
   B. They permit certain chemical reactions to proceed at significant speeds.
   C. They transfer energy from one complex molecule to another complex molecule.
   D. They release stored energy to all parts of the body.

The correct answer is B. In this question, you might note the terms *enzymes* and *metabolic process* and attempt to recall relevant information about them. Metabolism is the sum of the chemical and physical processes in living organisms and provides the basis for energy transfer, cell maintenance, and growth. Enzymes act as catalysts during the metabolic process. Without enzymes, many of the body's chemical reactions would not occur fast enough. The body uses enzymes to control its many thousands of chemical reactions, including the burning of food; lipase, for example, is an enzyme that helps in the digestion of fats.

21. Which of the following subcellular organelles is the control center of the cell?

   A. Chloroplast
   B. Nucleus
   C. Ribosome
   D. Mitochondrion

The correct answer is B. The cell is the smallest amount of living matter. The cell is divided into the cell membrane, the cell nucleus, and the cytoplasm. The main material within a cell, the cytoplasm, varies in consistency from a fluid to a semisolid. Embedded in the cytoplasm are functional bodies: the ribosome for constructing proteins and the chloroplast in plant cells necessary for photosynthesis. The nucleus is considered the control center of the cell because it has all the genetic instructions for the cell. The mitochondrion is the power house of the cell and is responsible for respiration.

22. Photosynthesis is essential for all life forms. Which of the following compounds constitutes the raw materials of photosynthesis?

    A.   Nitrogen and oxygen
    B.   Oxygen and glucose
    C.   Carbon dioxide and water
    D.   Carbon dioxide and oxygen

The correct answer is C. Plants use carbon dioxide gas and water as the raw materials for photosynthesis in the presence of the energy in sunlight to produce the products of sugar and oxygen. The sunlight strikes the chlorophyll in the chloroplasts of the plant's cells, initiating complex chemical reactions. The chlorophyll in green leaves absorbs blue and red light and reflects green light (the color of the leaves).

2.2 Living and Nonliving Components in Environments (Ecology)

23. Which of the following organisms are most truly independent in obtaining nourishment?

    A.   Bighorn sheep
    B.   Palm trees
    C.   Humans
    D.   Salamanders

The correct answer is B. In answering this question, you should particularly note, writing on the paper supplied, the words *most truly independent* and *nourishment.* True independence suggests not being subject to control by others or not requiring or relying on something else. Nourishment is food. Obtaining food independently is most associated with green plants because they are the only organisms that can manufacture food through photosynthesis (obtaining energy from sunlight and storing that energy as sugar). Since palm trees are the only green plants listed, that is the correct answer. All organisms depend on a food chain to obtain nourishment. All food chains start with the sun and transfer energy to green plants (the producers). Animals are either primary or secondary consumers and must get their energy from eating plants or other animals.

24. A student conducts an experiment to demonstrate changes that would possibly take place in the air in a sealed greenhouse containing many plants. Which of the following statements is the most likely result of this experiment?

    A.   The air becomes poorer in carbon dioxide.
    B.   The air becomes poorer in oxygen.
    C.   The air becomes richer in carbon dioxide.
    D.   The air becomes richer in carbon monoxide.

The correct answer is A. Before answering this question, visualize the situation given. Ask yourself questions such as these: What constitutes a sealed greenhouse? What is its environment? How does a greenhouse influence plant growth? It should be apparent that carbon monoxide (D), a poison, would not be characteristic of a greenhouse environment. You should also recognize that in a greenhouse (sealed or unsealed), photosynthesis takes place. Green plants combine carbon dioxide and water from the atmosphere (in the presence of sunlight) and release glucose (sugar), oxygen, and water as by-products. Because plants use carbon dioxide and water, the air would be poorer in these compounds but richer in oxygen. You can eliminate both B and C. The quickest way to answer this particular question, however, is to determine which statement is correct. Only Choice A is a true statement.

25. Ozone depletion is a serious environmental danger. Which of the following is *not* a true statement regarding ozone depletion?

    A. It was detected over the Antarctic region.
    B. It has the potential to change the genetic structure of phytoplankton.
    C. It is directly linked to a rise in the average temperature of the earth.
    D. It could lead to an increase in skin cancer.

The correct answer is C. Here, you are looking for *incorrect* information regarding ozone depletion; the choices include three true statements and one false statement. In this format, when you recognize a choice as a true statement, eliminate it. The breakdown of the ozone layer is primarily the result of an increase in chlorofluorocarbons (CFCs) in the atmosphere. CFCs are found in products used for refrigeration, air conditioning, insulation, or any products that use Freon. Eliminate Choice A because ozone depletion *was* detected over Antarctica. Eliminate Choice B because an increase in ultraviolet (UV) radiation, which the ozone layer blocks, *could* alter the genetic makeup of the tiny organisms at the beginning of the food chain. Eliminate Choice D because that same increase in UV *could* lead to an increase in skin cancer. Choice C is *not* true and is thus the correct answer. Ozone depletion is *not* directly related to the greenhouse effect (a warming trend caused by an increase in atmospheric carbon dioxide).

26. Look at the following table and select the answer that is a correct association between the plant group and the plant's characteristics.

Line	Plant Group	Chlorophyll	Leaves	Seeds	Flowers
1	Fungi	Yes	No	Yes	Yes
2	Algae	Yes	Yes	No	No
3	Ferns	Yes	Yes	No	No
4	Gymnosperms	No	Yes	Yes	Yes

    A. Line 1
    B. Line 2
    C. Line 3
    D. Line 4

The correct answer is C. Four of the five plant groups are given above. The more primitive groups are algae and fungi. These plants lack true roots, stems, and leaves. Fungi lack chlorophyll. The more advanced plants possess roots, stems, and leaves. Ferns are green plants that lack seeds and reproduce by means of spores. This allows ferns to reproduce without fertilization. The gymnosperms are cone-bearing plants (angiosperms—flowering plants—are omitted) that possess chlorophyll.

27. What is the chronological order of the evolutionary appearance of the following plants?

    A. Moss, pine, rose, fern
    B. Fern, moss, rose, pine
    C. Moss, fern, pine, rose
    D. Fern, rose, moss, pine

The correct answer is C. The moss and the fern are the two most primitive plants given. Neither reproduces by seeds, so you can assume that the chronological order had to begin with one of the two. Of the two plants with seeds (the pine and the rose), the plant with flowers is the most advanced. The pine tree is referred to as a *gymnosperm* and a flowering plant is referred to as an *angiosperm*.

28. The process by which an organism's internal environment is kept stable in spite of changes in the external environment is best described as:

    A. respiration.
    B. homeostasis.
    C. an organ system.
    D. the nervous system.

The correct answer is B. Homeostasis allows an individual to maintain a stable internal environment, regardless of changes in the external environment. For example, a person's body temperature remains at 37 degrees Celsius (98.6 degrees Fahrenheit) even if the air outside is much cooler. Perspiration on a hot day is another example of your body maintaining homeostasis. Stress is a key factor in triggering body changes that protect the individual; for example, blood to the brain increases; heart rate increases; sweating increases; and the digestive system slows. After the stressful situation subsides, the body returns to a normal metabolic state.

29. All of the following must necessarily exist for all known forms of life, except:

    A. air.
    B. carbon atoms.
    C. nucleic acids.
    D. water.

The correct answer is A. Some organisms (including many yeasts and bacteria) are *anaerobic*—that is, existing without free oxygen. For these organisms, in the process of fermentation, glucose is changed into ethanol and carbon dioxide anaerobically. All forms of life require water for biochemical reactions, reproduce by means of nucleic acid (DNA), and contain carbon atoms.

2.3 Life Cycle, Reproduction, and Evolution (Genetics and Evolution)

30. Use the diagram below to answer the question that follows.

    Based on a response to an external stimulus, which of the following terms most accurately describes the pictures above?

    A. Phototropism
    B. Geotropism
    C. Photosynthesis
    D. Respiration

The correct answer is A. *Phototropism* is the movement of a plant in a reaction to a stimulus (a light source). In phototropism, due to complex chemical changes, the plant bends towards the light source. *Geotropism* refers to the roots of a plant growing toward the center of the earth due to gravity. Photosynthesis is not the best answer, based on the evidence in the pictures that show a distinct change from day 1 to day 20.

31. In the following classification levels, which level has the most members?

A. Phylum
B. Species
C. Kingdom
D. Order

The correct answer is C. The kingdom is the broadest category and has the largest numbers. There are five main kingdoms: plants, animals, fungi, protists, and monerans. There are seven levels to classify organisms. As you move down the levels, the number of organisms decreases. The levels are: kingdom, phylum, class, order, family, genus, and species.

32. Use the diagram below to answer the question that follows.

MITOSIS

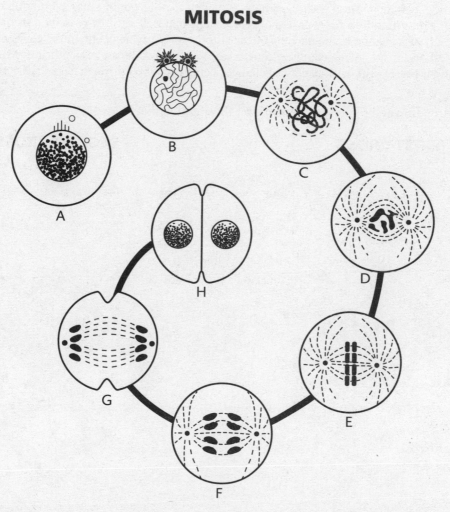

In the diagram of mitosis above, which letter or letters correctly identify the metaphase process in cell division?

A. A and B
B. C and D
C. E
D. H

The correct answer is C. Mitosis is the process of cell division in which the nuclear material of the original cell is divided equally between newer cells. Such multiplication of cells permits the growth of an organism. Letter A represents the resting cell. Mitosis begins as the chromosomes thicken and the centrosome (a part of the cytoplasm) divides during the prophase process, letters B, C, and D. The nuclear membrane disappears and a spindle develops between the two parts of the centrosome. Letter E represents the metaphase when the chromosomes line up in the middle of a cell and gather on the spindle. Letter F is the anaphase, where the chromosomes split. Finally, in the telophase (letters G and H), the nuclear membrane forms and two new cells result.

---

33. When a mutation in a gene occurs in an individual, it does *not* have an effect on the group unless the:

    A. environment changes.

    B. threat of predators is reduced.

    C. individual lives long enough to breed.

    D. mutation increases the variability of the group.

The correct answer is C. In analyzing the question, mark the terms *mutation, gene,* and *effect.* If the wording of a question is confusing, restate it—in this case, perhaps as "What factors would cause a mutation *not* to have an effect on a group?" For a mutation to be passed on, the genetic material must be passed on through breeding. A mutation is the result of a change in the makeup of the chromosomes, which contain the genes that determine the characteristics of an organism. When changes occur in sex cells, the result can be significant. Mutations can be both successful and unsuccessful, with beneficial changes being preserved through natural selection.

---

34. Use the information and figures below to answer the question that follows.

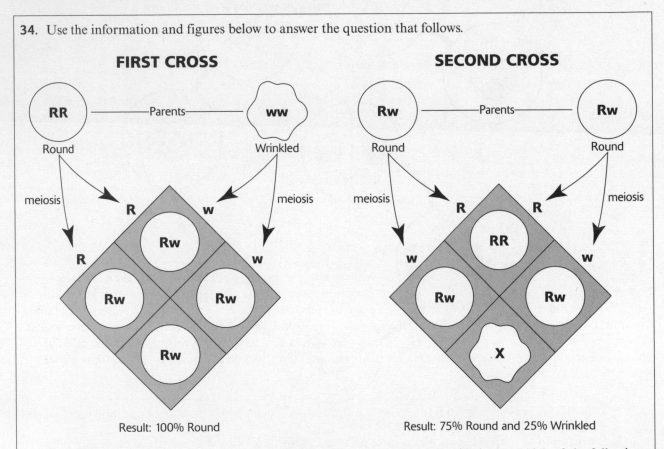

According to the information above about the crossing of round and wrinkled peas, which of the following are the correct letter combinations for the square marked X in the second cross?

    A. RR

    B. Rw

    C. Wr

    D. ww

The correct answer is D. Gregor Mendel studied pairs of genetic traits in generations of garden peas, the seeds of which were either round or wrinkled. Mendel discovered that when he crossed purebred round peas with wrinkled peas, the first hybrid generation was all round peas. Mendel determined that the round characteristic was dominant over the wrinkled characteristic. He assigned an uppercase letter to the dominant characteristic and a lowercase letter to the recessive characteristic—in this case, RR for round and ww for wrinkled. In the diagram on the left, each adult pea plant has two genetic characteristics. However, all the progeny will appear round but will carry a recessive gene for wrinkled. In the second generation, each parent plant carries a recessive gene for wrinkled. The X would be symbolized by ww; this pea type (ww) would be a purebred wrinkled pea without a recessive characteristic for roundness.

Domain 3: Earth and Space Science

3.1 The Solar System and the Universe (Astronomy)

35. Which of the following best explains why the length of a day on the planet Venus is longer than the length of an earth year?

    A. It takes more time for Venus to rotate on its axis than to revolve around the sun.
    B. It takes more time for Venus to revolve around the sun than to rotate on its axis.
    C. The gravitational pull of the sun on Venus is less than on other small planets.
    D. Venus has fewer moons than similar planets.

The correct answer is A. Venus is a unique planet. It takes approximately seven and one-half "earth" months for Venus to revolve around the sun; it takes approximately eight "earth" months to rotate on its axis. Therefore, a day on Venus is longer than a year. Venus is similar in size to Earth. Venus is one of the few planets that rotate from east to west. Venus's atmosphere is primarily composed of carbon dioxide. This thick atmosphere traps heat due to the greenhouse effect. The *Magellan* probe reached Venus in 1990 and provided detailed images of the planet.

36. What two factors keep the planets in their orbits?

    A. Gravity and magnetism
    B. Inertia and gravity
    C. Centrifugal force and inertia
    D. Alpha particles and chemical bonds

The correct answer is B. Both gravity and inertia work together to keep the planets in orbit around the sun. Inertia makes a planet travel in a straight line. By definition, inertia is the tendency of a moving object to stay in a straight line or a stationary object to remain in place. However, the power of the sun's gravity pulls the planets toward the sun. The sun's gravity pulls the planets while their inertia keeps them moving forward in an elliptical orbit around the sun. The strength of gravity in our solar system depends on both the masses of the celestial objects and the distance between them. Gravity helps to explain the tides on Earth. Without inertia, a planet would be pulled into the sun.

37. If an individual weighs 200 pounds on Earth, in theory, on which planet would the same individual weigh the most?

    A. Mercury
    B. Earth
    C. Jupiter
    D. Mars

The correct answer is C. To answer this question, you would need to know which of the listed planets is larger than Earth. The gas giants, Jupiter, Saturn, Uranus, and Neptune, have diameters far larger than Earth's and have far greater masses. Jupiter's mass (C) is more than 300 times Earth's mass (B). For comparison, the mass of the moon is approximately one-sixth that of Earth. Weight is a function of gravity.

38. Which of the following statements is true about the giant star Betelgeuse based on the red color of the star?

   A. The star is relatively large.
   B. The star is millions of light years away.
   C. The star is relatively cool.
   D. The star is extremely hot.

The correct answer is C. Stars with the highest surface temperature appear blue, while stars with the lowest surface temperature appear red. Knowing that red indicates a cooler surface temperature would provide the correct answer. The other choices could not be determined simply by the star's color.

3.2 The Structure and Composition of the Earth (Geology)

39. Igneous rocks are found throughout the world. Which of the following processes yields an igneous rock?

   A. Accumulations on a coral reef
   B. Tremendous pressure over an extended period of time
   C. The laying down of deposits, one on top of the other
   D. The eruption of a volcano

The correct answer is D. Answering this question requires recognizing the geologic process that results in the formation of igneous rocks. Attempt to eliminate incorrect answers based on your general understanding of rock types. For example, the information in Choice B relates to metamorphic rocks, and that in Choice C to sedimentary rocks. A coral reef (A) is the result of the buildup of once-living things. Lava from an erupting volcano (D) is molten rock, which can reach a temperature of approximately 1,200 degrees Celsius. An igneous rock is produced by the solidification of molten rock, which cools and becomes solid either deep within the earth or at the earth's surface.

40. If you were conducting an experiment to identify the hardness of five unknown mineral samples, which of the following would *not* be a reliable indicator in identifying the hardness?

   A. Color
   B. Cleavage
   C. Density
   D. Scratch test

The correct answer is A. A method one could use to determine the hardness of unknown mineral samples would be to test the item against materials of known hardness. For example, use your fingernail or the graphite in a pencil to attempt to scratch the items. This process should result in assigning a relative hardness to the unknown items. In a lab setting, a student would use the Mohs' scale of hardness. This scale assigns a fixed number to ten reference minerals. Talc (one) is softest and diamond (ten) is hardest. Cleavage (breaking along flat surfaces) and density (how much matter is in the object) can aid in determining the hardness of unknown minerals. Color is not a reliable method to identify a mineral's hardness. Factors such as weathering and impurities can affect a mineral's color.

41. Earthquakes vary in intensity, depending on many factors. However, the strongest earthquakes usually occur near the edges of:

   A. divergent boundaries.
   B. convergent boundaries.
   C. transform boundaries.
   D. strike-slip faults.

The correct answer is B. Earthquakes differ in the strength and depth at which they occur. The intensity of earthquakes depends on the type of tectonic motion that caused the initial earthquake. Most earthquakes occur near the edges of tectonic plates. Tectonic plates move in different directions and at different speeds. The three major plate movements are divergent, convergent, and transform. A transform plate motion occurs when two plates slip past each other—for example, the San Andreas Fault. Such faults are generally moderate and are relatively shallow. Divergent plate motion occurs when two plates pull away from each other—for example, the Mid-Atlantic Range in the Atlantic Ocean. Such faults are generally weak and shallow. Convergent plate motion occurs when two plates push together—for example, during mountain building in the Himalayas and the Andes. Such faults are strong and relatively deep.

---

42. In which of the following locations would soft tissue most likely avoid decomposition and survive as a fossil?

    A. In desert soil
    B. In beach sand
    C. In river silt
    D. In lake-bottom mud

The correct answer is D. Soft plant and animal tissues decompose quickly in the presence of decay bacteria, which exist wherever oxygen exists. Therefore, the correct answer will be the most oxygen-free environment listed. Lake-bottom mud prevents oxygen-rich air from reaching the tissues. Choice A is not the best answer because even in the driest desert environment, some decay takes place—even in natural mummification, there is desiccation.

---

43. During exploration for petroleum, varying amounts of oil, water, and natural gas are found in a porous rock reservoir. The substances occur as separate, horizontal layers. In what order would a continuous drill find these three substances?

    A. gas, water, oil
    B. water, gas, oil
    C. gas, oil, water
    D. water, oil, gas

The correct answer is C. The three substances occur in their order of density, with the lightest substance on top and the heaviest on the bottom. Gas is lighter than the two liquids, and so it is at the top. Oil floats on water, and so it is second. On the bottom is the most dense substance, water. Always try to use information you already know to eliminate wrong answers. Here, you might recall seeing oil slicks floating on top of a body of water.

3.3 The Earth's Atmosphere (Meteorology)

44. Taking all things into consideration and on a global scale, which of the following is the primary factor in determining climate?

    A. The atmospheric conditions in the area
    B. The latitude of the area
    C. The meeting of warm and cold air masses
    D. The rain shadow caused by mountains

The correct answer is B. The question calls for identifying a climate determiner that has global significance. The term *climate* refers to the long-term weather patterns of a large geographical area and takes into account temperature, humidity, and precipitation. Of the choices given, latitude is the best determiner of climate (B), as it is consistently and directly correlated with temperature. The equator, at zero degrees latitude, generally has a tropical climate (warm and wet); at the extreme northern and southern latitudes (polar regions), the climate is very cold and dry. Choice A is a possible answer, but atmospheric conditions are generally influenced by latitude. Rain shadows (D), as well as water currents, elevation, and so forth, obviously affect climate, but for this question, latitude is the best, most comprehensive answer.

45. Using the following table, which is the correct association between an air mass and its characteristics?

Line	Air Mass	Characteristics
1	maritime tropical (mT)	warm, wet air
2	maritime polar (mP)	cold, dry air
3	continental tropical (cT)	cold, dry air
4	continental polar (cP)	cold, wet air

    A. Line 1
    B. Line 2
    C. Line 3
    D. Line 4

The correct answer is A. An air mass is characterized by similar temperatures and moisture levels. On maps, the characteristics of an air mass are represented by two letters. The lowercase letter represents moisture, and the uppercase letter represents temperature. Maritime air forms over water and is associated with wet air. Continental air forms over land and is associated with dry air. Polar air forms south of the Arctic and is cold. Tropical air forms over the Tropics and is warm. Maritime tropical (mT) is characterized by warm and wet air—for example, the air mass over the Gulf of Mexico.

46. The earth's climate is influenced by natural events such as volcanic eruptions. Which of the following statements is the most logical global climatic consequence of cataclysmic volcanic eruptions?

    A. A change in the earth's orbit, resulting in increased earthquake activity
    B. A decline in the sun's energy that reaches the earth, resulting in lower global temperatures
    C. An increase in the sun's energy that reaches the earth, resulting in higher global temperatures
    D. An increase in the density of the lithosphere, resulting in increased plate tectonic activity

The correct answer is B. Global climate is affected by many natural factors. Cataclysmic volcanic eruptions can influence climate by sending tremendous volumes of dust, ash, and smoke into the atmosphere. The resulting dust layer would act as a shield, blocking out much of the sun's rays. This would result in lower global temperatures and a general cooling of the earth. Scientists theorize that massive volcanic eruptions on a global scale contributed to the earth's cooling, resulting in the onset of the Ice Age.

47. Almost all weather and cloud formations occur in the troposphere. Which type of cloud indicates an upcoming thunderstorm?

    A. Cirrus
    B. Stratus
    C. Cumulonimbus
    D. Altostratus

The correct answer is C. Cirrus clouds are featherlike clouds that indicate fair weather. Stratus clouds are smooth layers of low clouds that indicate a chance of drizzle or snow. Altostratus clouds are piled in waves and indicate rain or snow. Cumulonimbus clouds are large, dark clouds that indicate thunderstorms.

3.4 **The Earth's Water (Oceanography)**

48. Which of the following diagrams correctly shows the relationship of the sun, moon, and earth during a neap tide?

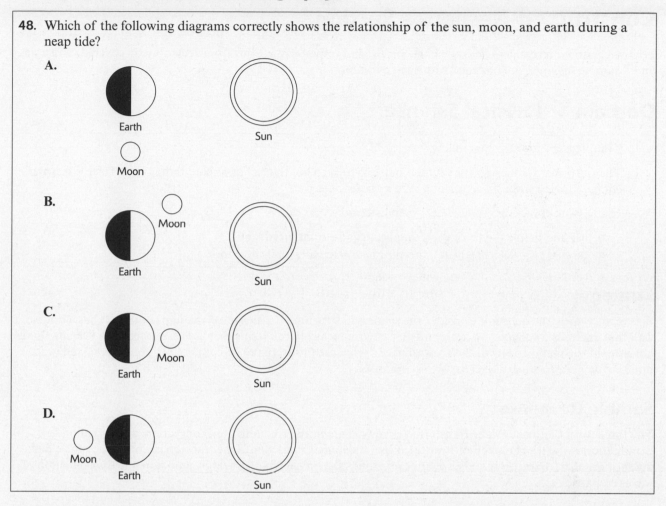

A.

Earth

Sun

Moon

B.

Moon

Earth

Sun

C.

Moon

Earth

Sun

D.

Moon

Earth

Sun

The correct answer is A. During a neap tide, the sun, earth, and moon form a 90-degree (right) angle, with the earth at the vertex. The combined effect of this alignment of the sun, earth, and moon results in tidal ranges on the earth. (A tidal range is the difference between levels of ocean water at high and low tides.) When a neap tide occurs, the gravitational forces on the earth from both the sun and moon are minimized. Tidal range is lowest during neap tide. Choice C is a solar eclipse. Choice D is a lunar eclipse.

49. Why is the climate on the west coast of California relatively cool during the summer compared to temperatures on the east coast of New York?

    A.   The Gulf Stream carries cold water from the Tropics to the North Atlantic Ocean.
    B.   The cold-water California current creates cooler climates in coastal areas.
    C.   The El Niño effect prevents cold water from upwelling and causes higher ocean temperatures.
    D.   Water off the coast of California is warm enough to generate low-pressure cells.

The correct answer is B. Surface ocean currents are classified as warm-water or cold-water currents. Surface ocean temperature is a major determiner of coastal climate. The Gulf Stream is a warm-water current that carries warm water from the Tropics to the Arctic regions of the North Atlantic Ocean. This accounts for the higher temperatures and higher humidity on the Eastern Seaboard during the summer. The cold-water current that flows north to south off the California coast keeps the West Coast fairly cool during the summer. Cold-water currents create cooler temperatures in areas that would otherwise be much warmer.

Sample Questions and Strategies for the Short Constructed-Response Section

Following are representative Science short constructed-response questions from each domain covered. Strategies and a sample response are included with each question.

Domain 1: Physical Science

1. Complete the exercise that follows.

   The purpose of a thermos or vacuum bottle is to keep hot things hot or cold things cold. Heat is thermal energy moving from a warmer object to a cooler object.

   Using your knowledge of how heat is transferred:

   - list and define the three ways that heat can be transferred; and
   - discuss two ways in which a thermos bottle actually limits heat loss.

Strategy

Before answering the question, consider the shape and structure of a thermos (vacuum) bottle. (It has a double wall that encloses a vacuum—a nearly air-free environment.) Recall terms that are associated with keeping things hot or cold (insulation). How is heat transferred? What are the processes of conduction, convection, and radiation? Remember the question calls for *two* examples.

Sample Response

The three ways that heat can be transferred or moved are through conduction, convection, and radiation. Conduction is the transmission of heat through a medium. Convection is the transferring of heat by the circulating motion of particles (in liquid or gas). Radiation is the transferring of heat by emission and dissemination of waves or particles.

A thermos or vacuum bottle blocks the processes through which heat is transferred. Limiting conduction is one example of why a thermos works efficiently. A thermos bottle is double walled, with a vacuum between the walls. Heat cannot be conducted easily because there are few air molecules to move around in a vacuum. The inside of the bottle has a shiny surface that acts like a mirror and reflects the heat (either inside or outside the container) back to its source. This limits heat loss or gain by radiation.

2. Use the diagram below to complete the exercise that follows.

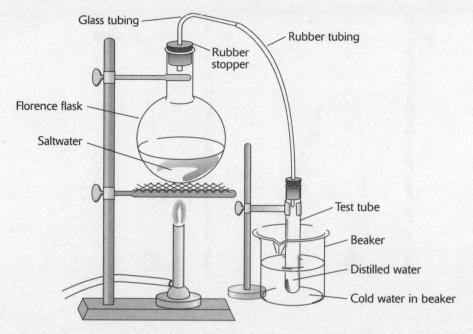

Glass tubing
Rubber tubing
Rubber stopper
Florence flask
Saltwater
Test tube
Beaker
Distilled water
Cold water in beaker

Design an experiment based on distillation that would take a gallon of ocean water and purify it. The materials necessary for the experiment are listed in the diagram.

Using your knowledge of chemistry and physics:

- describe the process that is taking place in the diagram above; and
- identify the product left after the process is completed.

Strategy

Consider these questions. How could you purify ocean water? What is its composition? How could you get salt and other impurities out of the water? What does heat have to do with it? When you distill something, what actually is taking place?

Sample Response

A distillation experiment is designed to separate substances in a liquid through vaporization. Ocean water is composed of a substantial amount of salt. Distillation is usually carried out in an apparatus called a still, which requires a boiler, a condenser, and a receiver.

Heat the ocean water until it reaches its boiling point. As the ocean water boils, it begins to evaporate and change from a liquid into a gas, in the form of water vapor. The gas goes through tubing to a collector container. The container sits in ice, which accelerates the condensation from water vapor back to liquid (or from a gas to a liquid).

The condensed water is pure water. Salt and other impurities remain as a residue in the original pan. Salt has a higher boiling point than water and therefore doesn't evaporate with the water.

3. Use the diagrams below to complete the exercise that follows.

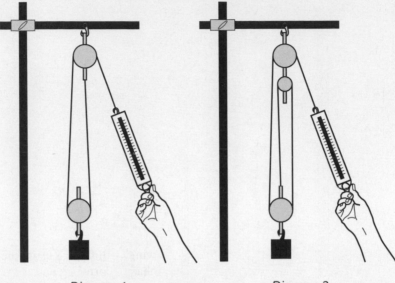

Diagram 1   *Diagram 2*

The diagrams above show two pulley systems. A pulley is one of the six simple machines.

Using your knowledge of simple machines:

- identify which diagram shows a situation that would require more force; and
- explain the lifting principles involved in each diagram.

Strategy

The candidate should be familiar with the six simple machines—the inclined plane, lever, wedge, screw, wheel and axle, and pulley. Why would machines be classified as simple? How do simple machines make work easier and more efficient? Think of common examples of simple machines that make it easier to lift objects—for example, levers and wheel barrows. Can a simple machine make work easier by changing the amount of force a person exerts? Look at the picture of the pulley systems in the question. Think of everyday examples of pulley systems, such as window blinds and flag pole rigging. When you pull down on the rope, what happens? Are you changing the amount and direction of the force you applied?

Sample Response

Diagram one would require more force.

The pulley device will either change the direction of the force, or give the person using the device a mechanical advantage. The change of direction allows an individual to pull downward. The load (item lifted) can be raised only as high as the support holding the pulley.

Diagram one represents a double pulley. As effort is applied (pulling power), the load (weight) is raised. In this system, the load moves only half the distance that the rope is pulled. However, the force raising the load is double the effort pulling the rope. In this system, the pulleys provide a 2-to-1 mechanical advantage.

Diagram two represents a multiple-pulley system. In this system, less strength is used to accomplish the same lifting height as in diagram one. The workload does not change; however, less force, and consequently less effort, is needed. In this system, the load moves one-third the distance that the rope is pulled, and the pulleys provide a 3-to-1 mechanical advantage.

In both diagrams, the top pulley is only a change of direction and does not provide any type of mechanical advantage.

Domain 2: Life Science

> **4.** Use the drawings below to complete the exercise that follows.
>
> Simplified view of the cell cycle
>
>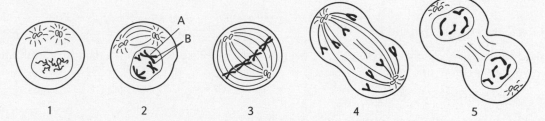
>
> 1   2   3   4   5
>
> Refer to the drawings above that show the five stages of a cell cycle.
>
> Using your knowledge of life cycles and reproduction:
>
> - identify the stages of the cell cycle represented in drawings 1 through 5 using the following terms—telophase, metaphase, prophase, interphase, and anaphase—correctly; and
> - explain what is happening in any one of the drawings.

Strategy

Carefully look at the drawings of the cell cycle before attempting to answer the question. The drawings show the correct order of the cell cycle. What do you remember about cell division? Is there a regular sequence of cell growth and division? Do you recall the terms mitosis and meiosis? What do the structures in the drawings contain? (They contain chromosomes, chromatin, DNA, membrane, and so on.) How many drawings need to be explained? (One drawing needs to be explained.)

Sample Response

The correct order is:

1. interphase
2. prophase
3. metaphase
4. anaphase
5. telophase

Drawing 1 represents the interphase. During this phase, the cell grows to its mature size. The cell is preparing to divide into two cells and make a copy of its DNA.

Drawing 2 represents the prophase stage of cell division during mitosis. In this stage, the chromatin in the nucleus condenses to form chromosomes. The centromere holds the two chromatids of a chromosome together. Spindle fibers form a bridge between the ends of the cell.

Drawing 3 represents the metaphase. The chromosomes are lined up along the center of the cell. The chromosomes attach to the spindle fibers developed during prophase. The centromere holds the chromatids together.

Drawing 4 represents the anaphase. The centromeres split and the two chromatids separate. The chromatids move to opposite ends of the spindle fiber. The cell is preparing for cell division and becomes stretched as the opposite ends pull apart.

Drawing 5 represents the telophase. The chromosomes begin to stretch out in both regions at the end of the cell. A new nuclear membrane forms around each area of the chromosome. The cell is now ready for division into two daughter cells with identical chromosomes.

---

5. Complete the exercise that follows.

   Almost all the energy in an ecosystem starts with the sun. All ecosystems involve the transfer of energy from one organism to another.

   Using your knowledge of ecology:

   - identify the energy flow through an ecosystem; and
   - explain an example of a food chain represented by a prairie.

Strategy

The question provides useful information. Ecosystems involve the transfer of energy from the sun to living organisms. You might recall that solar energy is transformed into chemical energy that is stored as food. How do different types of organisms interact in an ecosystem? How does energy flow through an ecosystem from sunlight to food chains? What makes up a food chain? Would terms such as producer, primary and secondary consumers, and decomposers be helpful in answering the question? Remember that the question also calls for a food chain in a specific ecosystem (*prairie*).

Sample Response

The energy flow through an ecosystem starts with the sun. Energy moves through an ecosystem from one organism to another in the form of food. The first link in an ecosystem is the producer, or a green plant. Photosynthesis enables green plants to manufacture their own food. The next link is the primary consumers, or herbivores (plant eaters). Primary consumers (deer, rabbits, cattle, and so on) are directly dependent upon the producers (grass, lettuce, cabbage, and so on). The next link in the ecosystem involves the flesh eaters. Secondary consumers, or carnivores (snakes, hawks, cougars, and so on), directly eat the primary consumers. Higher carnivores in the ecosystem eat the first carnivores. After an organism dies, the decomposers (bacteria, fungi, and insects) break down dead organic matter and return organic minerals and compounds to the soil.

The food chain in a prairie can be represented by grass (producer), which manufactures its own food through photosynthesis. A rabbit (primary consumer/herbivore) eats the grass. A secondary consumer/carnivore (snake) eats the herbivore. A higher carnivore (hawk) eats the snake. Each stage in the food chain represents a decreasing transfer of energy.

Domain 3: Earth and Space Science

6. Use the map below to complete the exercise that follows.

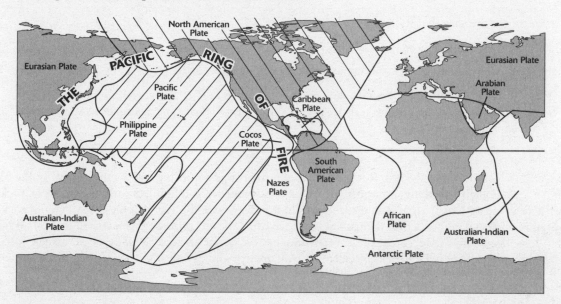

Earthquakes can occur in any area of the world. Refer to the map of plate tectonics in answering the following questions.

Using your knowledge of geology and plate tectonics:

- describe the Ring of Fire; and
- explain why there are fewer earthquakes on the East Coast of the United States than on the West Coast.

Strategy

The map identifies significant plates. Do they move in different directions? What is a fault? (It is a break in the earth's crust.) Where would it be likely for the largest and most active earthquakes to occur? (It would be most likely for them to occur around plate boundaries.) Can you associate fire with geology? (Fire is associated with geology in volcanoes.) Where geologically might a ring of volcanoes occur? (A ring of volcanoes might occur where many plate boundaries meet.) Study the map before answering the questions.

Sample Response

The Ring of Fire is associated with the plate boundaries surrounding the Pacific Ocean. Tectonic plates are giant masses of solid rock that float upon the earth's mantle. The boundaries between plates are likely areas for volcanoes to form. The Pacific Plate collides with, separates from, or scrapes against a number of significant plates, including the North American, Cocos, Eurasian, Philippine, and Australian-Indian Plates. In these boundaries are zones of weakness that allow magma to travel upward through the crust. Volcanoes are generally found along subduction zones. In subduction zones, the denser oceanic plates are forced under continental plates. This adds massive volumes of water to the mantle, allowing magma to melt more readily and rise to the surface to form volcanoes. The narrow band of land along the Pacific Plate accounts for the majority of earthquakes and volcanoes worldwide.

There are fewer earthquakes on the East Coast because most earthquakes occur near the edges of tectonic plates. On the East Coast, the tectonic boundaries do not border the coastline. On the West Coast, the plate boundaries converge on the coastline—for example, the San Andreas Fault on the southern border of California.

---

7. Complete the exercise that follows.

The rock cycle involves three types of rocks.

Using your knowledge of the structure and composition of the earth:

- identify the three types of rocks; and
- explain the origin and characteristics of one type of rock, providing examples to support your answer.

Strategy

A cycle refers to a continuous process. Rocks are placed into groups according to how they form. In the rock cycle, rocks change their shape and composition. What rock types are you familiar with (for example, rocks associated with volcanic activity)? How would such rocks look? (They would possibly look glassy.) Could rocks with bits of organic material embedded in them show evidence from ancient geological time (as in fossils)? What about rocks that have been subjected to great pressure? Would marble be such a rock? What type of surface forces (such as weathering and erosion) act on rocks? Remember, you are explaining only *one* type of rock in the rock cycle.

Sample Response

The rock cycle is the process in which one type of rock changes into another. The three main types of rocks are sedimentary, igneous, and metamorphic.

Sedimentary rocks are composed of the fragments of other types of rocks. Sedimentary rocks are often deposited in distinct parallel layers. Weathering and erosion break down other rock types into sediments. Over time, the sediments become cemented and compacted and form into sedimentary rocks. Conglomerates are sedimentary rocks containing large fragments of other rock material. Sandstone is another example. Texture is important in classifying clastic sedimentary rocks. Chemical sedimentary rocks form when dissolved mineral solutions crystallize out of lakes and oceans. Rock salt (formed from sodium chloride) and limestone (formed from calcium carbonate) are examples of chemical sedimentary rocks. Limestone can contain organic or once-living matter and can record the history of that matter's formation in features such as strata, fossil evidence, and ripple marks.

For purposes of clarification (not required in the question), the other rock types will be briefly explained.

Igneous rocks are classified according to composition and texture. Igneous rocks form when magma or lava cools and solidifies. Depending on the rate of cooling, some igneous rocks can contain visible crystals, while others can appear glassy. Temperature, pressure, and composition explain the three ways magma can form since they affect the melting point of rock. Igneous rock that cools beneath the earth's surface is called *intrusive*. Examples of intrusive rock formations include plutons, dikes, and batholiths. Igneous rock that forms on the earth's surface is called *extrusive*. Examples of extrusive rocks include obsidian, basalt, and pumice.

Metamorphic rocks have undergone tremendous change from intense pressure and temperature. All examples of the rock cycle can change into metamorphic rock. Metamorphic rock generally forms deep in the mantle as one type of rock changes into another. The mineral composition of the rock changes when the minerals in the rock recrystallize. Due to intense pressure, metamorphic rocks can show signs of bending and distortion. Examples of metamorphic rocks include schist, marble, gneiss, and slate. Metamorphic rocks are usually classified according to texture.

8. Complete the exercise that follows.

Over millions of years in the earth's geological history, the continents have changed position to their current locations. In the early 1900s, Alfred Wegener established the theory of continental drift—the theory that the earth's continents were originally united as a supercontinent, Pangaea.

Using your knowledge of geology and the theory of continental drift:

- list three examples that Wegener could have cited as evidence to support the theory of continental drift; and
- explain one example of a force of nature that supports the theory of continental drift.

Strategy

The question calls for providing examples to substantiate the theory of continental drift. Can you explain what the term means? Have the continents drifted in geologic history? How would you determine this? The question statement provides necessary information by stating that the continents were once united as a supercontinent. Would a world map indicate that the continents of Africa and South America were once connected? Would this help in providing support for your answer? If the continents have drifted over geologic time, would fossil evidence help support the theory? What forces in geologic time separated the continents, such as tectonic plate movement?

Sample Response

Three examples to explain the theory of continental drift are:

1. Paleontology: Fossil evidence indicates the similarity of fossils in many continents on both sides of the Atlantic Ocean.
2. Continental "jigsaw puzzle": The outlines of the continents seem to fit together—for example, the eastern coast of South America and the western coast of Africa.
3. Paleoclimatology (study of ancient climates): Ancient coral reefs (associated with warm water) are found in areas that could not currently support such growth.

The above examples indicate that these situations existed because the continents were once joined together in a giant land mass.

The discovery of tectonic plate movement and sea-floor spreading provided proof for Wegener's theory. The oceanic floor is not stationary. The plates move because of incredible amounts of released energy. During sea-floor spreading, new oceanic crust forms. The Mid-Atlantic Ridge is an example. In response to ocean-floor movement, the ocean floor expands in opposite directions. Continents spread apart and away from the Mid-Atlantic Ridge.

Scientific Method and Sample Experiments

Steps in Conducting a Scientific Investigation

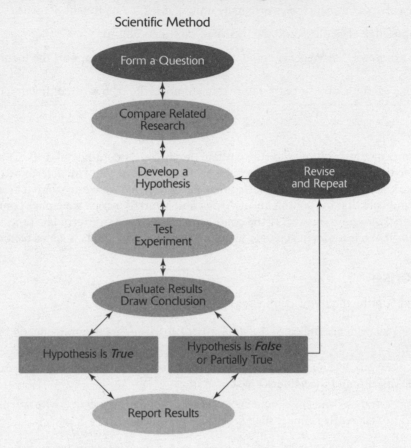

Scientific Method

1. Form a question (state the problem).

    a. A scientific question is one that can be answered on the basis of evidence and that can be measured.

    b. The question often asks, "What effect will something have — what if — and how …?"

    c. Examples: Why is the sky blue? What effect does salt have on the freezing temperature of water? Why does water stay in a straw when a finger is pressed over one end of the straw?

2. Develop a hypothesis.

    a. A hypothesis is an attempt to answer the question or predict the outcome.

    b. A hypothesis is a possible explanation for a set of observations.

    c. Examples: Does air pressure affect how fast fluids move? Does the length of a pendulum's swing influence its frequency?

3. Test experiment

    a. Select the materials.

    1. List the specific materials to be used in the experiment.

    2. This allows for replication of the experiment.

b. Set up the procedure.

    1. State the specific plan on how to test the hypothesis.

    2. Create a written, step-by-step procedure.

c. Determine the variables (any factor that can change in an experiment).

    1. Independent variable (manipulated variable)

    This is the one factor that will be intentionally changed during the experiment. Examples include changing the amount of salt that is added to water to determine its freezing point; introducing different soil types in germinating seeds; and changing the pendulum length to determine frequency.

    2. Dependent variable (responding variable)

    This is the variable that changes as a result of the manipulated variable. The dependent variable is observed and measured. Examples include determining how long various saltwater solutions take to freeze, and determining the number of cycles a pendulum swings if the weight of the bob changes.

    3. Variables that are controlled

    These are the factors that are kept exactly the same in an experiment. In an experiment on plant growth, the variables could include amount of sunlight, type of soil, amount of water, and type of plant. Only one factor at a time is changed, while all other factors are kept constant.

d. Collect data (results).

    1. Analyze the data to look for patterns or trends.

    2. Record measurements and observations during the experiment.

    3. Present data in a graph, table, or another form.

4. Draw Conclusion.

a. A conclusion is a summary and an explanation of the results of an experiment.

b. Does the data support the hypothesis? If not, a new hypothesis can be formulated.

c. For example, the addition of salt lowers the freezing temperature of water, and the weight on the end of a pendulum has no effect on the time required to complete a cycle.

Sample Experiments

The CSET Science Test can include multiple choice or short constructed-response questions based on a science experiment. The following experiments demonstrate various science concepts. Can you predict the outcome of each experiment? Carefully read each explanation to understand the physics behind the experiment.

Experiment 1

Problem: Can atmospheric pressure crush an aluminum can?

Materials:

- Aluminum soft drink can
- Tongs
- Large plastic tub
- Cold water
- Stove or gas burner
- Safety goggles

Procedure:

1. Put on the safety goggles.
2. Pour approximately $\frac{1}{4}$ inch of water into the empty aluminum soft drink can.
3. Heat the can over a gas stove or burner until it comes to a boil and you can see steam coming from the can.
4. Immediately pick up the can with the tongs and turn it upside down.
5. Place the upside-down can in the bucket of water to the point that water covers the opening of the can.

Result: The aluminum can is instantly crushed.

Explanation: At the start of the experiment and throughout the boiling process, atmospheric pressure inside and outside of the aluminum can was equal. Under normal conditions, air is always pushing equally in all directions. The result is that we do not notice the combined weight of atmospheric pressure. However, when the water in the can boiled, it expanded and turned into steam. The steam forced most of the air out of the can. When the can was immediately placed upside down in cold water, the water prevented air from entering the can. The sudden temperature change caused the steam to condense back into water. Since liquid takes up less space than gas, the liquid water took up less space than the steam. Since air couldn't enter the can to replace the extra space created by the change of steam to water, the combined pressure inside the can was less than the pressure pushing on the can from the outside. The can collapsed because atmospheric pressure—pushing from the outside—was greater than the pressure of the gas pushing on the can from the inside. Pressure was reduced inside the can, and the much greater outside pressure crushed the can.

Experiment 2

Problem: Does the weight on the end of a pendulum determine the length of the pendulum swing?

Materials:

- String
- Fishing weights (one 4-oz. weight; one 8-oz. weight)
- Hooks to attach to the string
- A stopwatch or a watch that can measure seconds

Procedure:

1. Cut two lengths of string about 3 feet long.
2. Tie the 4-ounce weight to one string and the 8-ounce weight to the other string.
3. Tie each pendulum (string and weight) to a hook where the string and weight can swing freely.
4. Set the first pendulum swinging (string and 4-ounce weight) and measure how long it takes to complete 10 swings or cycles.
5. Set the second pendulum swinging (string and 8-ounce weight) and measure how long it takes to complete 10 swings or cycles.

Result: Both pendulums take the same amount of time to complete 10 swings or cycles.

Explanation: A pendulum is a rod or string with a weight (bob) attached to the end and suspended from a fixed point so it can swing freely back and forth. The regular motion of a pendulum (moving from one side and returning to the same side) was recognized by Galileo in the sixteenth century. The amount of weight at the end of the pendulum had no effect on the amount of time required to complete the swings. The length of the string determined the frequency at which the pendulum went back and forth per second. The strings were of equal length and therefore had the same frequency. The time of the swing is dependent on the length of the pendulum, not the weight. Regardless of the weight, a bob that is suspended on a set length of string takes the same amount of time to complete a set number of cycles. The weight on the end of the pendulum makes no difference. *Note: Pendulum experiments can be used to demonstrate kinetic and potential energy, inertia, Newton's laws of motion, and even the rotation of the earth.*

Extension: Does the length of the string have an effect on the movement of a pendulum?

Result: If a bob of the same weight is attached to two pendulums, the pendulum with the shorter string swings faster than the one with the longer string.

Explanation: Changing the length of the pendulum will affect how fast it moves back and forth. Note that in a pendulum clock or a cuckoo clock, the speed in the pendulum can be adjusted by moving the bob higher or lower.

Experiment 3

Problem: Why is it easier to swim in salt water than in fresh water?

Materials:

- Two drinking glasses of equal size
- Two chicken eggs
- 5 tbsp. salt
- Water

Procedure:

1. Slowly dissolve the salt into one glass of water.
2. Fill the other glass to the same height with fresh water.
3. Carefully place one egg in the glass of fresh water and one egg in the glass of salt water.

Result: The egg placed in the fresh water sinks, and the egg placed in the salt-water solution floats.

Explanation: It is easier to swim in salt water because the water is denser. In the experiment, when salt was added to the water, it made the solution denser. The denser the water, the greater the buoyancy. Density is how heavy an object is compared to its volume. Water has a density of 1 g/ml. If an object has a density greater than 1 g/ml, it sinks. If an object has a density less than 1 g/ml, it floats. When an object is submerged, its weight pushes down. The water pushes back upward with a force equal to that of the water pushed out of the way (displaced). In the experiment, the increased amount of salt in the glass of water also increased the upward thrust of the water, allowing the egg to float. The weight of the water was increased without increasing its volume. The density of the egg was now less dense than the salt-water solution. *Note: You can tell a fresh egg from a rotten egg by immersing each egg in water. The fresh egg is denser than the water and will sink. The rotten egg will float in a glass of water because the gases in the rotten egg reduce its density, allowing it to float.*

Subject Matter Skills and Abilities Applicable to the Content Domains in Science

Candidates for Multiple Subject Teaching Credentials know how to plan and conduct a scientific investigation to test a hypothesis. They apply principles of experimental design, including formulation of testable questions and hypotheses, and evaluation of the accuracy and reproducibility of data. They distinguish between dependent and independent variables and controlled parameters, and between linear and nonlinear relationships on a graph of data. They use scientific vocabulary appropriately (e.g., observation, organization, experimentation, inference, prediction, evidence, opinion, hypothesis, theory, and law). They can select and use a variety of scientific tools (e.g., microscopes) and know how to record length, mass, and volume measurements using the metric system. They interpret results of experiments and interpret events by sequence and time (e.g., relative age of rocks and phases of the moon) from evidence of natural phenomena. They can communicate the steps in an investigation, record data, and interpret and analyze numerical and non-numerical results using charts, maps, tables, models, graphs, and labeled diagrams. They make appropriate use of print and electronic resources, including the World Wide Web, in preparing for an investigative activity. Candidates communicate the steps and results of a scientific investigation in both verbal and written formats.

Review of Domains

This section is designed to give you an intensive summary of some of the material covered by the Science section of the CSET: Multiple Subjects. This section tests your ability to understand primary scientific concepts, principles, and the relationships that are important to teaching science in the elementary classroom. The material included in this chapter is organized by domains—physical science, life science, and earth/space science—and includes definitions of important terms and concepts within each domain.

The reviews of each domain provide explanations of the major ideas in those fields. Read them slowly and carefully, underlining key words and phrases. The main purpose of your study should be to understand the central concepts (like evolution and energy), not to memorize the technical vocabulary. Don't spend excessive time on any one section. If you have difficulty with a concept, write a question mark in the margin and return later. Further reading frequently clarifies a difficulty.

This chapter includes scientific terms of the five natural sciences. When studying, it is helpful to mentally compare terms that are related (like atom and molecule). Write your own comments after some of the definitions. If you don't understand a term, write a question mark and return later.

DOMAIN 1: PHYSICAL SCIENCE OVERVIEW	
1.1 Structure and Properties of Matter	❏ Physical properties of solids, liquids, and gases, such as color, mass, density, hardness, and electrical and thermal conductivity. ❏ Matter that undergoes physical changes (e.g., changes in state such as the evaporation and freezing of water) and chemical changes (i.e., atoms in reactants rearrange to form products with new physical and chemical properties). ❏ Matter that consists of atoms and molecules in various arrangements; you can also give the location and motions of the parts of an atom (protons, neutrons, and electrons). ❏ Constituents of molecules and compounds, naming common elements (e.g., hydrogen, oxygen, and iron), and explaining how elements are organized on the periodic table on the basis of their atomic and chemical properties. ❏ Solutions (such as acidic, basic, and neutral solutions); you also need to know examples of solutions with different pH levels, such as soft drinks, liquid detergents, and water. ❏ Mixtures that are separated based on physical or chemical properties.

1.2 Principles of Motion and Energy	❏ Motion based on position, displacement, speed, velocity, and acceleration. ❏ Forces (pushes and pulls) such as gravity, magnetism, and friction act on objects and may change their motion if these forces are not in balance. ❏ Electrical charges or magnetic poles that are "like" produce repulsive forces, and charges or poles that are "unlike" produce attractive forces. ❏ Simple machines in which small forces are exerted over long distances to accomplish difficult tasks (e.g., using levers or pulleys to move or lift heavy objects). ❏ Forms of energy including solar, chemical, electrical, magnetic, nuclear, sound, light, and electromagnetic. ❏ Energy in a system is conserved but may be changed from one form to another, as in an electrical motor or generator. ❏ Heat (thermal energy) and temperature; you also need to understand temperature measurement systems. ❏ Transfer of heat by conduction, convection, and radiation (e.g., involving a stove, the earth's mantle, or the sun). ❏ Sources of light including the sun, light bulbs, or excited atoms (e.g., neon in neon lights) and interactions of light with matter (e.g., vision and photosynthesis). ❏ Optical properties of waves, especially light and sound, including reflection (e.g., by a mirror) or refraction (e.g., bending light through a prism). ❏ Conservation of energy resources in terms of renewable and nonrenewable natural resources and their use in society.

Domain 1: Physical Science

Physical sciences are the branches of natural sciences that study the nature and properties of energy and non-living matter.

1.1 <u>Structure and Properties of Matter</u>

Matter is anything that has mass and occupies space. Everything you touch and see is composed of matter. The three states of matter are solids, liquids, and gases.

States of Matter		
States	**Definition**	**Examples**
Solids	Solids are characterized by their ability to retain their shape. They are relatively incompressible. Solids melt when heated and vaporize only slightly. All substances become solid if cooled sufficiently.	Rocks, crystals, wood, feather, ice
Liquids	Liquids take on the shape of their containers, yet cannot be compressed to any significant extent. The volume of a liquid is constant unless evaporation is occurring. Liquids crystallize when chilled sufficiently, while heat causes liquids to vaporize. The liquid state is intermediate between the solid and gaseous states with regard to molecular motion and attractive forces between molecules.	Water, oil, milk, honey
Gases	Gases expand to fill any available space. A gas is a compressible fluid, with its volume determined by the pressure and temperature of the environment. The volume varies inversely with the pressure, a relationship known as Boyle's Law. If the pressure increases, the volume decreases. The reverse is true as well.	Air, helium, steam

Sublimation makes it possible for some elements and compounds to transition from a solid to a gas phase without becoming a liquid. A common example is a block of dry ice (CO_2) which will turn into a gas at room temperature. Some gases can transition directly to a solid, such as the formation of frost. This is called *deposition*.

Mass is the amount of matter in a chemical substance. In everyday usage, mass is commonly confused with weight. But, in physics and engineering, weight means the strength of the gravitational pull on the object—that is, how heavy it is, measured in newtons. In everyday situations, the weight of an object is proportional to its mass, which usually makes it acceptable to use the same word for both concepts.

Density for a homogeneous object is determined by dividing the mass by the volume. The mass is normally measured with an appropriate scale or balance; the volume may be measured directly (from the geometry of the object) or by the displacement of a fluid. For example, if steel and wood have equal dimensions, the steel would have a greater mass as it is more dense.

$$D = \frac{M}{V} \quad \text{or} \quad \text{Density} = \frac{\text{Mass}}{\text{Volume}}$$

Hardness refers to various properties of matter in the solid phase that give it a high resistance to its shape changing when force is applied. Hard matter is contrasted with soft matter. However, the behavior of solid materials under force is complex, resulting in several different scientific definitions of what might be called hardness in everyday usage.

In materials science, there are three principal operational definitions of hardness:

- Scratch hardness: Resistance to fracture or plastic (permanent) deformation due to friction from a sharp object.
- Indentation hardness: Resistance to plastic (permanent) deformation due to a constant load from a sharp object.
- Rebound hardness: Height of the bounce of an object dropped on the material, related to elasticity.

Mohs' scale of hardness rates minerals and puts them on a scale from 1 to 10 (1 is the softest and 10 is the hardest) determined by the ability of a harder mineral to scratch a softer mineral. For example, talc is at 1 and a diamond is at 10.

Physical properties are the characteristics that make up the physical composition of a substance. Physical properties include color, form, electrical conductivity, and density.

Physical changes do not involve one substance changing into another. Water, for example, can change from a gas (water vapor) to liquid (water) to a solid (ice), but the water molecules do not change. The particular state of water is determined by pressure and temperature. (See the figure that follows.) The dashed lines show the behavior of water at one atmosphere (sea level), freezing at 0°C (32°F), and boiling at 100°C (212°F). At other pressures, the freezing and boiling temperatures for water differ from the familiar values.

STATES OF H$_2$O

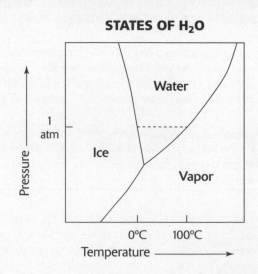

Chemical changes occur when a substance is changed into something else. A chemical change occurs whenever compounds are formed or decomposed. During this reaction, there is a rearrangement of atoms that makes or breaks chemical bonds. This change is usually not reversible, unlike physical changes, which typically are reversible. An example of a chemical change is the formation of rust. Iron chemically reacts with air and water to form rust (ferrous oxide) and is unable to change back to iron. In short, a chemical change is a change of one substance into a different substance.

Chemical reactions show the number of molecules or formula units of the reactants and products. For example, nitrous oxide is a colorless, odorless gas that causes mild hysteria when inhaled, hence the name *laughing gas*; it is prepared by heating ammonium nitrate crystals:

$$\underset{\substack{\text{ammonium} \\ \text{nitrate}}}{\overset{\text{reactant}}{NH_4NO_3}} \overset{\text{heat}}{\rightarrow} \overset{\text{products}}{\underset{\substack{\text{nitrous} \\ \text{oxide}}}{N_2O}} + \underset{\substack{\text{water} \\ \text{vapor}}}{2H_2O\uparrow}$$

Atoms are made up of several tiny parts. At the center of an atom is a core called the nucleus. The nucleus is made up of particles called protons and neutrons. Protons have a positive electrical charge, and neutrons have no charge. Electrons move around the nucleus in electron clouds. Electrons have a negative charge, and they are attracted to the positively charged protons in the nucleus. This attraction keeps the electrons in orbit around the nucleus.

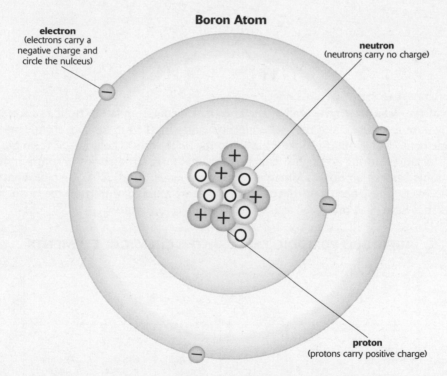

Boron Atom

electron
(electrons carry a
negative charge and
circle the nulceus)

neutron
(neutrons carry no charge)

proton
(protons carry positive charge)

Chemical elements are composed of only one atom and cannot be separated into different substances except in some instances by radioactive decay or by nuclear reactions. Elements are assigned atomic numbers equal to the number of protons in the nucleus of their atoms. Each element has a different number of protons. The sum of the protons and neutrons gives an average atomic mass for the element.

Some Elements and Their Subatomic Makeup				
Element	Symbol	Protons	Neutrons	Mass
Hydrogen	H	1	0	1
Helium	He	2	2	4
Carbon	C	6	6	12
Oxygen	O	8	8	16
Iron	Fe	26	30	56
Uranium	U	92	146	238

Compounds are formed by the chemical combination of two or more elements in a fixed ratio. Water, for example, is made up of molecules with the composition H_2O and the structure (arrangement) shown in the figure that follows. The straight lines denote bonds. One water molecule is built from two atoms of hydrogen and one atom of oxygen. Ordinary table salt is a compound composed of one atom of sodium and one atom of chlorine (NaCl, sodium chloride).

WATER MOLECULE

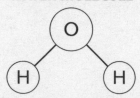

The periodic table of the elements arranges all of the known elements from left to right and top to bottom in order of increasing atomic number, and they generally coincide with their increasing atomic mass. Rows are arranged so that elements with similar properties fall into the same vertical columns to form *groups* or *families*. For example, fluorine and chlorine are highly reactive gases that form strong acids in solution. Helium, neon, and argon are inert, "noble" gases that do not form chemical compounds. As of 2006, the table contains 117 chemical elements whose discoveries have been confirmed. Ninety-four are found naturally on the earth, and the rest are synthetic elements that have been produced artificially in particle accelerators.

ABRIDGED PERIODIC TABLE OF THE CHEMICAL ELEMENTS

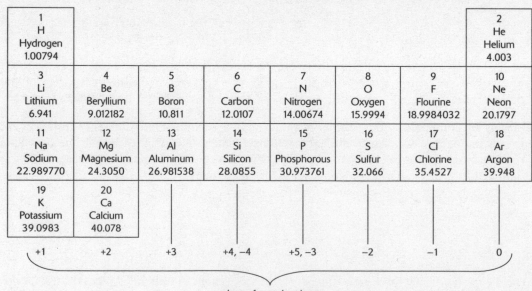

valence for each column

pH is a measure of the acidity or basicity of a solution. The pH scale is not an absolute scale; it is relative to a set of standard solutions whose pH is established by international agreement.

Pure water is said to be neutral. The pH for pure water at 25°C is close to 7.0. When foreign substances are dissolved in water it creates a solution. Solutions with a pH of less than 7.0 are said to be acidic, and solutions with a pH greater than 7.0 are said to be basic or alkaline. pH measurements are important for medicine, biology, chemistry, food science, environmental science, oceanography, and many other applications.

Litmus is a water-soluble mixture of different dyes extracted from lichens. It is often absorbed onto filter paper. The resulting piece of paper or solution with water becomes a pH indicator (one of the oldest), used to test materials for acidity. *Blue* litmus paper turns red under acidic conditions, and *red* litmus paper turns blue under basic (i.e., alkaline) conditions. Another indicator of the presence of an acid is that when acids react with metals, hydrogen gas is released, causing bases to feel soapy when touched.

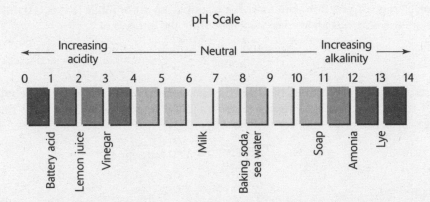

A **mixture** is a substance made by combining two or more different materials without a chemical reaction occurring (the objects do not bond together). They are the product of a mechanical blending or mixing of chemical substances. Each ingredient substance retains its own chemical properties and makeup. For example, a mixture of salt and pepper would still be identifiable as salt and pepper. While there are no physical changes in a mixture, the chemical properties of a mixture, such as its melting point, may differ from those of its components. Mixtures can usually be separated into their original components by mechanical means and are either homogeneous or heterogeneous.

1.2 Principles of Motion and Energy

The scientific method requires observation, conjecture, calculation, prediction, and testing. Successive scientific revelations have taught us that today's laws are not certain, only more accurate than yesterday's laws.

Measurement is the beginning of scientific wisdom. The physicist's first reaction to a new idea is to ask: Can it be measured? Can I describe it with numbers? Numerical data can be manipulated with many powerful mathematical tools, from arithmetic and geometry to statistics and differential equations. Physical quantities range from subatomic smallness to astronomic hugeness, and so the numbers are conveniently expressed in scientific notation, in which any number is written in the form:

$$N \times 10^P$$

where N is a number between 1 and 10, and P is a power of 10. The population of Brazil is about 130,000,000, and that number could be written as:

$$1.3 \times 10^8$$

You should also be aware of the three basic units of the metric system. A unit 1,000 times the basic unit has the prefix *kilo-*, and so a kilometer equals 1000 meters. The prefix *milli-* (as in millimeter) denotes a unit 1/1,000 of the basic unit.

Basic Units of the Metric System			
Quantity	**Unit**	**Symbol**	**Approximation**
Length	Meter	m	1.1 yard
Volume	Liter	l	1.1 quart
Mass	Gram	g	1/30 ounce

Motion

Motion means that there is a constant change in the location of a body, and is described by stating an object's position, velocity, and acceleration.

Velocity is the rate of change of position with time. For example, an automobile that is 100 miles farther along a highway at 3 p.m. than at 1 p.m. has an average velocity during the interval of:

$$v = \frac{\Delta d}{\Delta t} = \frac{100 \text{ miles}}{2 \text{ hours}} = 50 \text{ miles/hour}$$

where the Δd represents change of distance and Δt is the change of time. *Acceleration* is the rate of change of velocity with time. If the automobile in our example had an initial velocity of 40 mph and a final velocity of 60 mph, then its average acceleration would be:

$$a = \frac{\Delta v}{\Delta t} = \frac{20 \text{ miles/hour}}{2 \text{ hours}} = 10 \text{ miles/hour}^2$$

This is sometimes expressed as:

$$a = \frac{\Delta v}{\Delta t} = \frac{20 \text{ miles/hour}}{2 \text{ hours}} = 10 \text{ miles/hour/hour}$$

According to Isaac Newton, three physical laws applied to the effect of force on the motion of an object (see the table that follows):

Newton's Laws of Motion		
Newton's First Law of Motion	The first law is also referred to as the law of inertia. In the absence of the application of an outside force (such as gravity or friction), a body at rest will remain at rest, while a body moving in a straight line will continue to move in a straight line with uniform speed. Simplified, without outside forces, a stationary object will never move, and without outside forces, an object in motion will never stop or deviate from its course.	Friction between the air and the cyclist's body Friction between the tires and the road Friction can cause resistance, slowing forward movement. Friction can also be a useful force to grip the ground when we walk, thus preventing falling.

Newton's Second Law of Motion	The second law relies on the first law and proposes that the acceleration of an object is proportional to the force applied. Simplified, the more force, the more acceleration.	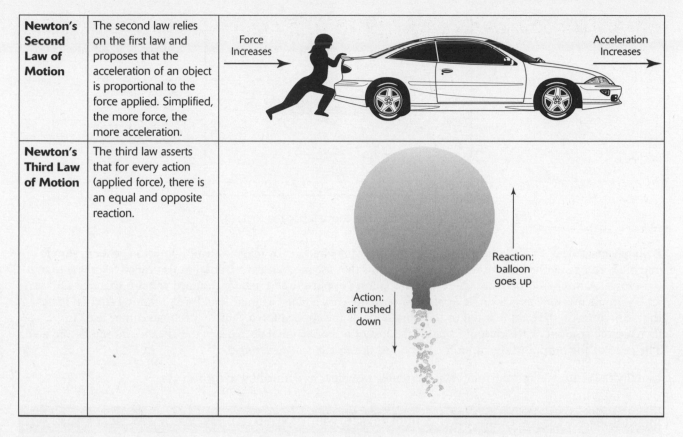	
Newton's Third Law of Motion	The third law asserts that for every action (applied force), there is an equal and opposite reaction.		

Gravitation is a natural phenomenon by which objects with mass attract one another. Gravitation compels dispersed matter to coalesce, and thus it accounts for the very existence of the earth, the sun, and most of the macroscopic objects in the universe. It is responsible for keeping the earth and the other planets in their orbits around the sun; for keeping the moon in its orbit around the earth; for the formation of tides; for convection (by which hot fluids rise); for heating the interiors of forming stars and planets to very high temperatures; and for various other phenomena that we observe.

The terms *gravitation* and *gravity* are mostly interchangeable in everyday use. Gravity refers specifically to the gravitational force exerted by the earth on objects in its vicinity.

Magnetism is displayed by permanent magnets and around electric currents. All of us have had the opportunity to study the interesting properties of permanent magnets, small iron bars, or iron horseshoes which have aligned internal structures induced by other magnets. The north pole of one magnet attracts the south pole of another, but like poles repel each other. Either pole can attract unmagnetized iron objects. Iron filings spread on a piece of paper above a bar magnet become arranged in a pattern that maps a magnetic field in the space around the magnet. (See the following figure.) The earth's magnetic field orients the iron needles of navigational compasses. An electric current also generates a magnetic field, demonstrating an intimate connection between electricity and magnetism. Recent work has united these phenomena, as well as light, into electromagnetic radiation.

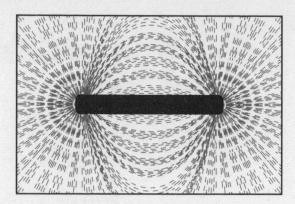

Magnetic field above a bar magnet.

A **simple machine** is a mechanical device that changes the direction or magnitude of a force. In general, simple machines can be defined as the simplest mechanisms that use mechanical advantage (also called leverage) to multiply force. A mechanical advantage results in less force applied over a greater distance. It helps to make work easier. A simple machine uses a single applied force to do work against a single load force. Ignoring friction losses, the work done on the load is equal to the work done by the applied force. Simple machines can be used to increase the amount of the output force, at the cost of a proportional decrease in the distance moved by the load. The ratio of the output to the input force is called the *mechanical advantage*.

Usually the term refers to the four classical simple machines as defined by scientists:

The Four Classical Simple Machines	
Lever	A rigid object that is used with an appropriate fulcrum or pivot point to multiply the mechanical force that can be applied to another object. This leverage is also termed *mechanical advantage*, and is one example of the principle of movements. A wheelbarrow is a type of lever; the wheel works as the fulcrum. Scissors are also levers; the fulcrum is where the blades cross.
Pulley (also called a block)	A mechanism composed of a wheel (called a sheave) with a groove between two flanges around the wheel's circumference. A rope, cable, or belt usually runs inside the groove. Pulleys are used to change the direction of an applied force, transmit rotational motion, or realize a mechanical advantage in either a linear or a rotational system of motion. A pulley helps an individual lift an object by spreading the weight of the object over the length of the rope. This example depicts a two to one mechanical advantage. It requires 150 lbs. of force to lift 300 lbs. For every two feet of rope the person pulls, the weight lifts one foot.

Inclined plane	One of the original four simple machines; as the name suggests, it is a flat surface whose endpoints are at different heights, resulting in a slope. By moving an object up an inclined plane rather than completely vertically, the amount of force required is reduced, at the expense of increasing the distance the object must travel. The mechanical advantage of an inclined plane is the ratio of the length of the sloped surface to the height it spans. The inclined plane allows the same work to be done with a smaller force exerted over a greater distance.	Inclined Plane
Screw	All screws are inclined planes. A screw can convert a rotational force (torque) to a linear force, and vice versa. The ratio of threading determines the mechanical advantage of the machine. More threading increases the mechanical advantage. It is easier to turn a screw than to push a screw directly into a wall. As the screw rotates outward, the weight rises. As the screw rotates inward, the weight lowers.	Force Screw

Energy

Forms of energy include solar, chemical, electrical, magnetic, nuclear, sound, light, and electromagnetic. *Energy* is the ability to perform work, to move objects. That ability can take several forms. The energy possessed by a moving object is called kinetic energy. An object in an unstable position has potential energy, for the position could be converted into movement. Consider a baseball thrown vertically upward. Its speed decreases upward because the acceleration of gravity is acting downward. The rising ball loses kinetic energy (slows down) as it gains potential energy (rises high). At the peak of the ball's flight, the ball is instantaneously at rest, with no kinetic energy but maximum stored potential energy. As the ball falls, the potential energy is transformed into kinetic energy and the ball accelerates. Thermal energy also exists, for it has been shown that heat can be converted to motion, and motion can produce heat. Electricity and magnetism are still other forms of energy, for they can be converted into heat and motion. Notice that this key concept of energy is the abstract idea that there is something identical in motion, heat, and electricity, which appear so different to our senses. It is possible to define the various forms of energy so that their mathematical sum is constant. The law of conservation of energy states that energy can be neither created nor destroyed.

Electricity is a form of energy that can be used to produce sound, light, heat, and power. Electricity exists where the number of negative electrons does not precisely equal the number of positive protons. Electrons are held in the atom by an electrical force and have an electrical charge. When the electrons are not held tightly in their atoms, the electrons can move freely and can carry electricity from one place to another. When the electrons flow in one direction, the flowing electricity is referred to as current. An electric current is simply a flow of electrons through a wire. Electricity can flow easily through materials that conduct electricity. Materials that have high conductivity include metals such as aluminum (Al), iron (Fe), nickel (Ni), silver (Ag), and gold (Au). In materials that act as insulators (poor conductors of electricity) the electrons are held tightly inside their atoms and the electrons cannot move freely. Some examples of good insulators include plastic, rubber, glass, air, and wood.

An **electric circuit** is simply the path or circuit an electric current flows. Electricity requires a complete path for the electrons to flow. If the path is broken and there are not alternative paths for the electrons to follow, the electrons will not move. Electric circuits make it possible for electric energy to operate a vast range of technology.

Static electricity results when electrical charges buildup or increase on the surface of a material. In static electricity, there is no current flowing as would be found in electrical outlets. When certain materials are rubbed together, electrons can move from one object to the other. A material can become negatively or positively charged if electrons in the material are gained or lost—an example would be the spark a person might get by walking across a wool rug and then touching a metal doorknob. Static electricity can also result by rubbing a balloon against your hair or against a wool sweater. Rubbing the objects together can result in the balloon becoming negatively charged and your hair becomes positively charged. Since opposite charges attract, the balloon will cling to your hair. Lightening is another example of static electricity.

Light seems to travel in perfectly straight lines as rays. The direction of a ray changes at the interface between two transparent materials, like air and water. Some of the light is reflected, the angle of reflection being equal to the angle of incidence. The portion of the light that crosses the boundary is, however, deflected in another direction, and the angle of refraction does not equal the angle of incidence. Other optical experiments are inconsistent with a simple ray theory and require that light travel as waves of electromagnetic energy. When white light (including sunlight) is refracted by a glass prism, it is separated into its component colors as a beautiful spectrum. Experiments have shown that the various colors travel at the uniform speed c:

$$c = 186,000 \text{ miles/second} = 3 \times 10^8 \text{ meters/second}$$

The colors differ in wavelength, and the following figure displays the relative wavelengths for all forms of electromagnetic energy.

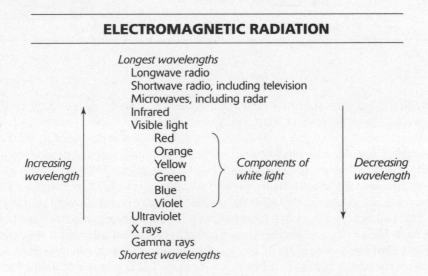

Relative wavelengths for all electromagnetic energy forms.

Nuclear energy has been obtained by two different means, fission and fusion. Nuclear fission releases energy when a heavy nucleus splits into smaller fragments. (See the figure that follows. Black balls show neutrons, and white balls show protons.) Bombarding uranium with a neutron produces an unstable intermediate, which disintegrates to lighter nuclei with the conversion of .1 percent of the mass into energy. Nuclear fission is used in power plants and atomic bombs.

FISSION

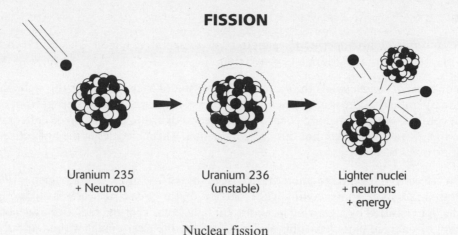

Uranium 235	Uranium 236	Lighter nuclei
+ Neutron	(unstable)	+ neutrons
		+ energy

Nuclear fission

The opposite process of nuclear fusion yields energy when very light nuclei unite to a heavier nucleus. (See the figure that follows.) A hydrogen bomb contains the two heavy isotopes of hydrogen, deuterium (H^2) and tritium (H^3), which unite to form helium nuclei and neutrons, with a conversion of .4 percent of the initial mass into energy. Stars (including the sun) derive their energy from nuclear fusion.

FUSION

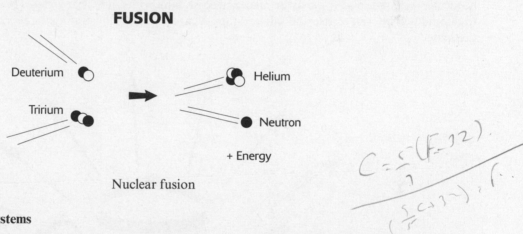

Deuterium

Helium

Tririum

Neutron

+ Energy

Nuclear fusion

Temperature Measurement Systems

Degrees Celsius (°C) can refer to a specific temperature on the Celsius scale, as well as serve as a unit increment to indicate a temperature *interval* (a difference between two temperatures or an uncertainty). Zero degrees on the Celsius scale is defined as the freezing point of water, and 100°C is defined as the boiling point of water under a pressure of one standard atmosphere.

Fahrenheit is a temperature scale that is named after the German physicist Daniel Gabriel Fahrenheit (1686–1736), who proposed it in 1724. On this scale, the freezing point of water is 32 *degrees Fahrenheit (°F)* and the boiling point is 212 °F (at standard atmospheric pressure), placing the boiling and freezing points of water exactly 180 degrees apart. A degree on the Fahrenheit scale is 1/180th of the interval between the freezing point and the boiling point. On the Celsius scale, the freezing and boiling points of water are 100 degrees apart—hence the unit of this scale. A temperature interval of one degree Fahrenheit is an interval of five-ninths of a degree Celsius. The Fahrenheit and Celsius scales coincide at −40 degrees (i.e., −40°F and −40°C describe the same temperature).

$$C = \frac{5}{9}(F - 32) \qquad\qquad F = \frac{9}{5}C + 32$$

Temperature conversions.

Transfer of Heat

Heat tends to move from a high-temperature region to a low-temperature region. This heat transfer may occur by the mechanisms of conduction, radiation, and convection.

Heat conduction or *thermal conduction* is the spontaneous transfer of thermal energy through matter, from a region of higher temperature to a region of lower temperature. Heat energy is transferred from one material to another by direct contact. Metals are good conductors of heat. For example, if a cup of coffee is stirred with a metal spoon, the spoon will quickly get hot through conduction. The molecules in the hot coffee make the atoms in the spoon vibrate quickly.

Thermal radiation is electromagnetic radiation emitted from the surface of an object, which is due to the object's temperature. Infrared radiation from a common household radiator or electric heater is an example of thermal radiation, as is the light emitted by a glowing incandescent light bulb. Thermal radiation is generated when heat from the movement of charged particles within atoms is converted to electromagnetic radiation. When infrared radiation is absorbed by an object, it is changed to heat.

Convection occurs when hot air is less dense than cool air and therefore rises. When the heat moves in a circular pattern, convection currents are formed. Heat can be transferred by the circulation of fluids due to buoyancy from changes in density. Familiar examples are the upward flow of air due to a fire or hot object, and the circulation of water in a pot that is heated from below. For a visual experience of natural convection, a glass full of hot water with red food dye may be placed in a fish tank with cold, clear water. The convection currents of the red liquid will be seen to rise and fall and then eventually settle, illustrating the process as heat gradients are dissipated.

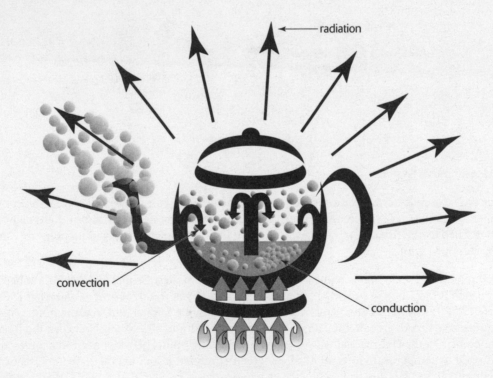

Sources of Light

The **incandescent light bulb** is a source of electric light that works by incandescence. An electric current passes through a thin filament, heating it until it produces light. The enclosing glass bulb prevents the oxygen in the air from reaching the hot filament, which otherwise would be destroyed rapidly by oxidation. Incandescent bulbs are also sometimes called *electric lamps*, a term also applied to the original arc lamps.

A **fluorescent lamp** or *fluorescent tube* is a gas-discharge lamp that uses electricity to excite mercury vapor. The excited mercury atoms produce short-wave ultraviolet light that then causes a phosphor to fluoresce, producing visible light. Unlike incandescent lamps, fluorescent lamps always require a ballast to regulate the flow of power through the lamp. However, a fluorescent lamp converts electrical power into useful light more efficiently than an incandescent lamp; lower energy costs offset the higher initial cost of the lamp. Compared with incandescent lamps, fluorescent lamps use less power for the same amount of light, generally last longer, but are bulkier, more complex, and more expensive than a comparable incandescent lamp.

Refraction of light explains why objects appear bent as light passes from one transparent object into another. Light travels faster through air than through water or glass. For example, an object such as a straw in a glass of water appears bent at the surface of the water due to the refraction of light. Light travels at different speeds through different objects. Refraction is also responsible for rainbows and for the splitting of white light into a rainbow-spectrum as it passes through a glass prism. Glass has a higher refractive index than air, and the different frequencies of light have different wavelengths (dispersion), causing them to be refracted at different angles, so that you can see them. The different frequencies correspond to different colors being observed.

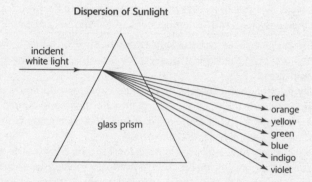

Dispersion of Sunlight

In **optics**, refraction occurs when light waves travel from a medium with a given refractive index to a medium with another index. For example, a ray of light will refract as it enters and leaves glass, assuming there is a change in the refractive index. Understanding this concept led to the invention of lenses and the refracting telescope.

Reflection occurs when light travels only in straight lines. An object is visible because light is reflected from the object into our eyes. Reflection is the change in direction of a wave front at an interface between two different media so that the wave front returns to the medium from which it originated. Common examples include the reflection of light, sound, and water waves. The *law of reflection* says that for smooth surfaces, the angle at which light is incident on the surface equals the angle at which it is reflected. A mirror is an excellent tool for reflecting light.

Renewable and Nonrenewable Energy Sources

Renewable energy is energy generated from natural resources—such as sunlight, wind, rain, tides, and geothermal heat—which are renewable (naturally replenished). In 2006, about 18 percent of global energy consumption came from renewable sources, with 13 percent coming from traditional biomass materials, such as wood burning. Hydroelectricity was the next largest renewable source, providing 3 percent, followed by solar hot water/heating, which contributed 1.3 percent. Modern technologies, such as geothermal energy, wind power, solar power, and ocean energy, together provided some 0.8 percent of final energy consumption.

Nonrenewable energy is energy taken from finite resources that will eventually dwindle, becoming too expensive or too environmentally damaging to retrieve. Fossil fuels include coal, petroleum, and natural gas. Fossil fuels are limited and nonrenewable and contribute to global warming. When fossil fuels are burned, they release trapped energy in the form of carbon dioxide into the atmosphere. Carbon dioxide and methane are major greenhouse gases. The burning of coal also contributes to the formation of acid rain.

DOMAIN 2: LIFE SCIENCE OVERVIEW	
2.1 The Structure of Living Organisms and Their Function (Physiology and Cell Biology)	❑ Plants and animals, including organ systems (e.g., the digestive system), organs, tissues (e.g., ovules in plants and heart chambers in humans), cells, and subcellular organelles (e.g., nucleus, chloroplast, and mitochondrion). ❑ Structures and related functions of systems in plants and animals, such as reproductive, respiratory, circulatory, and digestive. ❑ Principles of chemistry underlying the functioning of biological systems (e.g., carbon's central role in living organisms; water and salt; DNA; and the energetics of photosynthesis).
2.2 Living and Nonliving Components in Environments (Ecology)	❑ The characteristics of many living organisms (e.g., growth, reproduction, and stimulus response). ❑ Basic needs of all living organisms (e.g., food, water, and space), and the ability to distinguish between environmental adaptations and accommodations. ❑ The relationship between the number and types of organisms an ecosystem can support, and relationships among members of a species and across species. ❑ The flow of energy and matter through an ecosystem from sunlight to food chains and food webs (including primary producers, consumers, and decomposers). ❑ The resources available in an ecosystem, and the ability to describe the environmental factors that support the ecosystem, such as temperature, water, and soil composition.
2.3 Life Cycle, Reproduction, and Evolution (Genetics and Evolution)	❑ The ability to diagram life cycles of familiar organisms (e.g., butterfly, frog, and mouse). ❑ The ability to explain the factors that affect the growth and development of plants, such as light, gravity, and stress. ❑ The ability to distinguish between sexual and asexual reproduction, and to understand the process of cell division (mitosis), the types of cells and their functions, and the replication of plants and animals. ❑ The ability to distinguish between environmental and genetic sources of variation, and to understand the principles of natural and artificial selection. ❑ The ability to know how evidence from the fossil record, comparative anatomy, and DNA sequences can be used to support the theory that life gradually evolved on earth over billions of years. ❑ The ability to understand the basis of Darwin's theory, that species evolved by a process of natural selection.

Domain 2: Life Science

2.1 <u>The Structure of Living Organisms and Their Function (Physiology and Cell Biology)</u>

Biology is the science of life. Life has astonishing variety, embracing bacteria and baboons, whales and walnuts, algae and alligators—yet all those life forms share some similar materials and processes. The complexity of life compels biologists to specialize in certain levels of life: organic molecules, cells, organs, individuals, species, and communities. Here are some important characteristics of most life forms: A living organism has a very complicated organization in which a series of processes takes place. Life responds to its environment, often with movement. An organism must maintain itself and grow. Finally, a plant or animal will produce new organisms much like itself; reproduction is the most universal process of life, explaining its survival and variety.

Plants

Plants may be divided into five broad groups. (See the following table.) The more primitive groups are *algae* and *fungi*; these plants lack true roots, stems, and leaves. Algae range from a single cell to huge seaweed; mostly they inhabit lakes and oceans. The fungi include molds, yeasts, and mushrooms. Fungi lack chlorophyll and thus are incapable of manufacturing food, so they are either parasites, preying on other living organisms, or saprophytes, existing on waste products and decaying organisms. Lichens are actually two organisms, a fungus and an alga, living together symbiotically. The more advanced plants possess roots, stems, and leaves. The *ferns* lack seeds and reproduce by means of spores, each of which may develop into a new plant without fertilization. Unlike the ferns, the seed plants require fertilization, and male pollen grains are carried to the female ovule by vectors like the wind and insects. The *gymnosperms* are cone-bearing plants (including pines) with seeds exposed on cone scales. The *angiosperms* are flowering plants that bear their seeds within fruits.

Ovule literally means *small egg*. In seed plants, the ovule is the structure that gives rise to and contains the female reproductive cells. After fertilization, the ovule develops into a seed.

In flowering plants, the ovule is located within the actual flower, the part of the carpel known as the ovary, which ultimately becomes the fruit. Depending on the plant, flowers may have one or multiple ovules per ovary. The ovule is attached to the placental wall of the ovary through a structure known as the funiculus, the plant equivalent of an umbilical cord.

The Plants				
Plant Group	**Chlorophyll**	**Leaves**	**Seeds**	**Flowers**
Fungi	No	No	No	No
Algae	Yes	No	No	No
Ferns	Yes	Yes	No	No
Gymnosperms	Yes	Yes	Yes	No
Angiosperms	Yes	Yes	Yes	Yes

Photosynthesis

Photosynthesis is a metabolic pathway that converts light energy into chemical energy. Plants use the energy in sunlight to convert carbon dioxide from the atmosphere, plus water, into simple sugars. These sugars are then used as building blocks and form the main structural component of the plant. Chlorophyll, a green-colored, magnesium-containing pigment, is essential to this process; it is generally present in plant leaves and often in other plant parts as well.

A commonly used, slightly simplified equation for photosynthesis is:

$$\underset{\substack{\text{carbon} \\ \text{dioxide}}}{6CO_2} + \underset{\text{water}}{6H_2O} + \underset{\text{energy}}{\text{Light}} \xrightarrow{\text{chlorophyll}} \underset{\text{sugar}}{C_6H_{12}O_6} + \underset{\text{oxygen}}{6O_2}$$

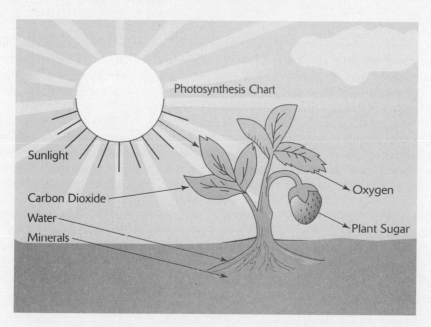

Photosynthesis Chart

Sunlight

Carbon Dioxide

Water

Minerals

Oxygen

Plant Sugar

Thus, plants absorb carbon dioxide and give off oxygen. The sugar made by plants can be oxidized later in a process that releases energy. The oxidation can be in the plant itself or in an animal that eats the plant. The release of energy by oxidation of sugar is respiration.

$$C_6H_{12}O_6 + 6O_2 \underset{}{\overset{\text{Krebs cycle}}{\longrightarrow}} 6CO_2 + 6H_2O + \text{Energy}$$
$$\underset{\text{sugar}}{} \quad \underset{\text{oxygen}}{} \qquad \underset{\substack{\text{carbon} \\ \text{dioxide}}}{} \quad \underset{\text{water}}{}$$

Cell

The *cell* is the smallest amount of living matter, a bit of organic material that is the unit of structure and function for all organisms. Cells range in size from the smallest speck visible through an electron microscope to the yolk of the largest egg. Some tiny organisms like bacteria are one celled, but all larger organisms are composed of many cells arrayed in tissues. Although an isolated cell may be spherical, the cells packed together in plant or animal tissues have flattened walls. The essential subdivisions of a cell are the cell membrane, the cytoplasm, and the cell nucleus. (See the figure that follows.) The cell membrane is semi-permeable, allowing some substances to pass while excluding others. The main material within a cell, the cytoplasm, varies in consistency from a fluid to a semisolid. Embedded in the cytoplasm are functional bodies: the centrosome that participates in cell division, ribosomes for constructing proteins, mitochondria that conduct metabolism, Golgi bodies involved in secretion, and vacuoles used in digestion. The cytoplasm of plant cells also contains plastids, bodies with chlorophyll that carry out photosynthesis. The cell nucleus is a separate mass containing nucleoli and chromosomes, the genetic material.

THE CELL

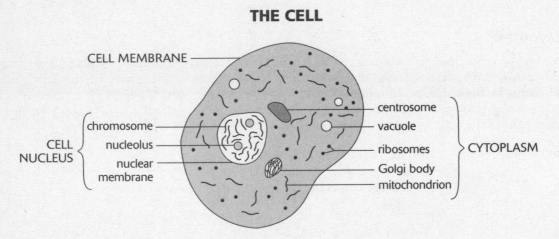

The **nucleus** is a membrane-enclosed organelle found in all eukaryotic cells. It contains most of a cell's genetic material, organized as multiple long and linear DNA molecules in complex with a large variety of proteins, such as *histones*, to form chromosomes. The genes within these chromosomes are the cell's nuclear genome. The function of the nucleus is to maintain the integrity of these genes and to control the activities of the cell by regulating gene expression.

Chloroplasts are organelles found in plant cells and eukaryotic algae that conduct photosynthesis. Chloroplasts absorb light and use it in conjunction with water and carbon dioxide to produce sugars, the raw material for energy and biomass production in all green plants and the animals that depend on them, directly or indirectly, for food. Chloroplasts capture light, and are members of a class of organelles known as *plastids*.

A **mitochondrion** (plural *mitochondria*) is a membrane-enclosed organelle found in most eukaryotic cells. Mitochondria are sometimes described as cellular power plants because they generate most of the cell's supply of adenosine triphosphate (ATP), used as a source of chemical energy. In addition to supplying cellular energy, mitochondria are involved in a range of other processes, such as signaling, cellular differentiation, and cell death, as well as the control of the cell cycle and cell growth.

Animals cannot perform photosynthesis and, therefore, derive their food from other organisms. Herbivores eat plants directly. Carnivores prey on other animals, but this food chain, too, ends in plants. Plants and animals are classified into phyla on the basis of their cells, tissues, organs, and overall organization. Each phylum is a major group of organisms.

Organ Systems

Digestion is the breaking down of chemicals in the body into a form that can be absorbed. It is also the process by which the body breaks down chemicals into smaller components that can be absorbed by the blood stream. Carbohydrates are converted to various sugars by the action of several enzymes, including ptyalin from saliva. Fats are transformed to glycerol and fatty acids by the combined action of bile from the liver and the enzyme lipase from the pancreas. Proteins are broken apart to their constituent amino acids. The final products of digestion—sugars, glycerol, fatty acids, and amino acids—are absorbed into the bloodstream through the millions of projections (villi) lining the small intestine. Once in the blood, these molecules are metabolized in the various body tissues. In mammals, preparation for digestion begins when saliva is produced in the mouth and digestive enzymes are produced in the stomach. Mechanical and chemical digestion begins in the mouth where food is chewed and mixed with saliva to break down starches. The stomach continues to break down food mechanically and chemically by churning and mixing the food with enzymes.

After being processed in the stomach, food is passed to the small intestine. The majority of digestion and absorption occurs in the small intestine. Absorption occurs in the stomach and gastrointestinal tract, and the process finishes with defecation.

THE DIGESTIVE SYSTEM

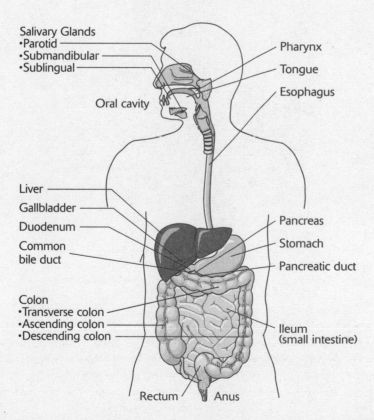

The **circulatory system** is an organ system that moves nutrients, gases, and wastes to and from cells, helps fight diseases, and stabilizes body temperature and pH to maintain homeostasis. This system may be seen strictly as a blood distribution network, but some consider the circulatory system to be composed of the cardiovascular system, which distributes blood, and the lymphatic system, which distributes lymph. Humans, as well as other vertebrates, have a closed cardiovascular system, meaning that the blood never leaves the network of arteries, veins, and capillaries. The main components of the human circulatory system are the heart, blood, and blood vessels.

The circulatory system includes pulmonary circulation, a loop through the lungs where blood is oxygenated, and the systemic circulation, a loop through the rest of the body to provide oxygenated blood. An average adult contains 5 to 6 quarts (roughly 4.7 to 5.7 liters) of blood, which is composed of plasma, red blood cells, white blood cells, and platelets. Also, the digestive system works with the circulatory system to provide the nutrients the system needs to keep the heart pumping.

Red cells transport oxygen in combination with the iron pigment, hemoglobin. The function of white blood cells is to fight infection, while platelets initiate the clotting necessary to stop bleeding after a wound. Nutrients, wastes, hormones, antibodies, and enzymes are dissolved in the plasma.

Two types of fluids move through the circulatory system: blood and lymph. The blood, heart, and blood vessels form the cardiovascular system. The lymph, lymph nodes, and lymph vessels form the lymphatic system. The cardiovascular system and the lymphatic system collectively make up the circulatory system.

The heart pumps oxygenated blood to the body and deoxygenated blood to the lungs. In the human heart, there is one atrium and one ventricle for each circulation, and with both a systemic and a pulmonary circulation, there are four chambers in total: left atrium, left ventricle, right atrium, and right ventricle. The right atrium, which is the upper chamber of the right side of the heart, receives blood from the upper body through the superior vena cava, and from the lower body through the inferior vena cava.

THE CIRCULATORY SYSTEM

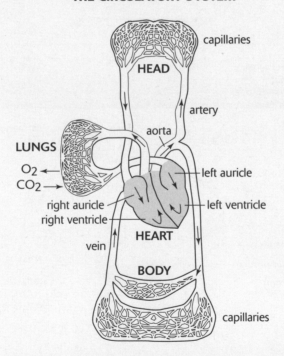

In living organisms, the function of the *respiratory system* is to allow for gas exchange. The space between the alveoli and the capillaries, the anatomy or structure of the exchange system, and the precise physiological uses of the exchanged gases vary, depending on the organism. In humans and other mammals, for example, the anatomical features of the respiratory system include airways, lungs, and the respiratory muscles. Molecules of oxygen and carbon dioxide are passively exchanged, by diffusion, between the gaseous external environment and the blood. This exchange process occurs in the alveolar region of the lungs.

Other animals, such as insects, have respiratory systems with very simple anatomical features, and in amphibians, even the skin plays a vital role in gas exchange. Plants also have respiratory systems but the directionality of gas exchange can be opposite to that in animals. The respiratory system in plants also includes anatomical features such as holes on the undersides of leaves known as stomata.

The **sensory system** includes those specialized structures that initiate a nerve impulse after being affected by the environment. The eyes are the organs of vision. Light rays are refracted as they pass through the cornea, lens, and vitreous body to focus on the retina, where an image is formed. The optic nerve then carries impulses from the light-sensitive cells of the retina to the brain.

THE EYE

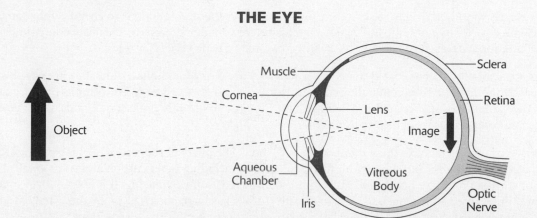

The **nervous system** is composed of the brain, spinal cord, and peripheral nerves that extend throughout the body. The functional unit of the nervous system is the neuron, a nerve cell with short dendrites that carry electrical impulses to the cell body, and a long axon, the outgoing fiber along which the impulse is transmitted further. (See the figure that follows.) Sensory neurons conduct signals from the sense organs to the central nervous system, the spinal cord, and brain. Motor neurons transmit signals from the central nervous system to muscles.

NEURON

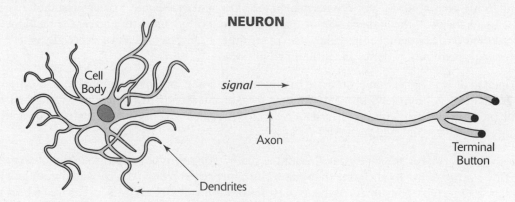

The following figure shows several major parts of the human brain. The hindbrain (cerebellum and medulla oblongata) operates unconsciously and automatically to regulate vital functions like circulation, respiration, excretion, and muscle tension. The cerebrum is the largest part of the brain; it receives information from the senses and makes conscious decisions.

THE BRAIN

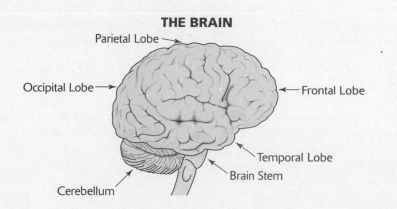

Chemistry: Carbon's Role in Living Organisms

Organisms are complex chemical systems, organized in ways that promote reproduction and some measure of sustainability or survival. It is generally the phenomena of entire organisms that determine their fitness to an environment and therefore the survivability of their DNA-based genes.

Organisms clearly owe their origin, metabolism, and many other internal functions to chemical phenomena, especially the chemistry of large organic molecules. Organisms are complex systems of chemical compounds which, through interaction with each other and the environment, play a wide variety of roles.

Organisms are semi-closed chemical systems. Although they are individual units of life, they are not closed to the environment around them. To operate, they constantly take in and release energy. Autotrophs produce usable energy (in the form of organic compounds), using light from the sun or inorganic compounds, while heterotrophs take in organic compounds from the environment.

The primary chemical element in these compounds is carbon. The physical properties of this element are such that it has a great affinity for bonding with other small atoms, including other carbon atoms. Its small size makes it capable of forming multiple bonds and makes it ideal as the basis of organic life. It is able to form small compounds containing three atoms (such as carbon dioxide), as well as large chains of many thousands of atoms that are able to store data (nucleic acids), hold cells together, and transmit information (protein).

2.2 <u>Living and Non-living Components in Environments (Ecology)</u>

Ecology is usually considered as a branch of biology, the general science that studies living organisms. Organisms can be studied at many different levels, from proteins and nucleic acids (in biochemistry and molecular biology), to cells (in cellular biology), to individuals (in botany, zoology, and other similar disciplines), and finally at the level of populations, communities, and ecosystems, to the biosphere as a whole. Ecology is a multidisciplinary science. Because of its focus on the higher levels of the organization of life on earth and on the relationship between organisms and their environment, ecology draws on many other branches of science, especially geology and geography, meteorology, pedology, genetics, chemistry, and physics.

A central principle of ecology is that each living organism has an ongoing and continual relationship with every other element that makes up its environment. The sum total of interacting living organisms and their non-living environment (the biotope) in an area is termed an *ecosystem*. Studies of ecosystems usually focus on the movement of energy and matter through the system.

Almost all ecosystems run on energy captured from the sun by primary producers through photosynthesis. This energy then flows through the food chains to primary consumers (herbivores who eat and digest the plants), and on to secondary and tertiary consumers (either carnivores or omnivores). Energy is lost as waste heat to living organisms when they use it to do work.

Matter is incorporated into living organisms by the primary producers. Photosynthetic plants fix carbon from carbon dioxide, and nitrogen from atmospheric nitrogen or nitrates present in the soil, to produce amino acids. Much of the carbon and nitrogen contained in ecosystems is created by such plants and is then consumed by and incorporated into secondary and tertiary consumers. Nutrients are usually returned to the ecosystem through decomposition. The entire movement of chemicals in an ecosystem is termed a biogeochemical cycle, and includes the carbon and nitrogen cycle.

Ecosystems of any size can be studied. In fact, the entire terrestrial surface of the earth, all the matter that composes it, the air that is directly above it, and all the living organisms within it can be considered as one large ecosystem. Ecosystems can be roughly divided into terrestrial ecosystems (e.g., forest ecosystems, steppes, savannas, and so on), freshwater ecosystems (e.g., lakes, ponds, and rivers), and marine ecosystems, depending on the dominant biotope. A population includes all the members of a given species that live in a defined geographic area.

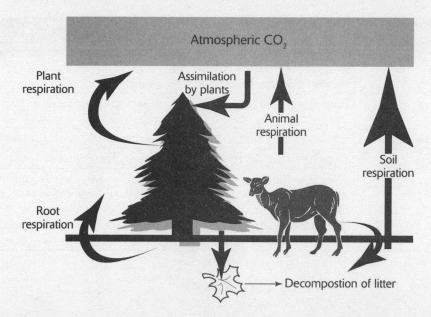

Atmospheric CO$_2$

Plant respiration

Assimilation by plants

Animal respiration

Soil respiration

Root respiration

Decompostion of litter

Adaptation is a characteristic of an organism that has been favored by natural selection and increases the fitness of its possessor. This concept is central to biology, particularly in evolutionary biology. Adaptation is the change in living organisms that allows them to live successfully in an environment. Adaptations enable living organisms to cope with environmental stresses and pressures. Adaptations can be structural, behavioral, or physiological.

Structural adaptations are special body parts of an organism that help it to survive in its natural habitat (e.g., skin color, shape, and body covering). Behavioral adaptations are special ways a particular organism behaves to survive in its natural habitat (e.g., phototropism). Physiological adaptations are systems present in an organism that allow it to perform certain biochemical reactions (e.g., making venom, secreting slime, and homeostasis).

Ecosystem relationships are primarily governed by stochastic (chance) events, the reactions these events provoke on non-living material, and the responses by organisms to the conditions surrounding them. Thus, an ecosystem results from the sum of individual responses of organisms to stimuli from elements in the environment. The presence or absence of populations merely depends on reproductive and dispersal success, and population levels fluctuate in response to stochastic events. If the number of species in an ecosystem is higher, then the number of stimuli is also higher. Since the beginning of life, organisms have survived continuous change through natural selection of successful feeding, reproductive, and dispersal behavior. Through natural selection, the planet's species have continuously adapted to change through variation in their biological composition and distribution. Given the great diversity among organisms on Earth, most ecosystems only changed very gradually, as some species would disappear while others would move in. Locally, sub-populations continuously go extinct, to be replaced later through dispersal of other sub-populations.

Food chains, also called *food networks* and/or *trophic social networks*, describe the eating relationships between species within an ecosystem. Organisms are connected to the organisms they consume by lines representing the direction of organism or energy transfer. Food chains also show how the energy from the producer is given to the consumer. Typically, a food chain or food web refers to a graph where only connections are recorded, and a food network or ecosystem network refers to a network where the connections are given weights representing the quantity of nutrients or energy being transferred.

A food chain is the flow of energy from one organism to the next and to the next, and so on. Organisms in a food chain are grouped into trophic levels, based on how many links they are removed from the primary producers. Trophic levels may contain either a single species or a group of species that are presumed to share both predators and prey. They usually start with a plant and end with a carnivore.

Food Chain	
Producers	Organisms in an ecosystem that produce biomass from inorganic compounds (autotrophs). Producers are the green plants in an ecosystem that can manufacture their own food through the process of photosynthesis.
Primary Consumers (Herbivores)	Plant eaters. Primary consumers can range in size from insects to elephants.
Secondary Consumers	Carnivores. They feed on the primary consumers and are meat eaters.
Tertiary Consumers	Organisms that feed on smaller primary and secondary consumers.
Decomposers	Organisms that consume dead organisms and in doing so, carry out the natural process of decomposition. Like herbivores and predators, decomposers are heterotrophic. This means that they use organic substrates to get their energy, carbon, and nutrients for growth and development. Decomposers use deceased organisms and non-living organic compounds as their food source. The primary decomposers are bacteria and fungi.

FOOD CHAIN

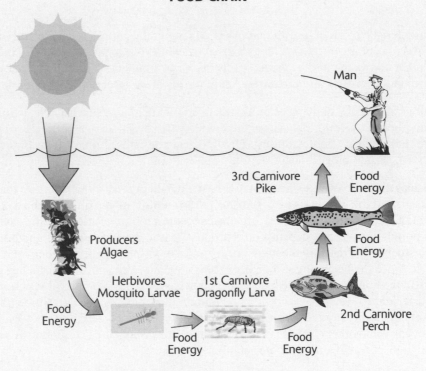

Food webs (see next page) are interconnected energy systems. A food web demonstrates the alternate energy links available to an organism. Food webs help explain predator/prey relationships in an ecosystem and include networks of food chains.

FOOD WEB

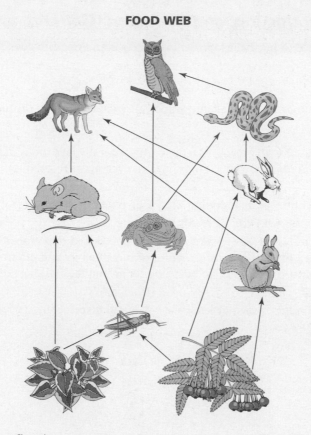

Food pyramids illustrate energy flow in an ecosystem. The base of the pyramid (producers) supports all of the other levels of the pyramid. At each succeeding level of the food pyramid, there is a decrease in available energy.

FOOD PYRAMID

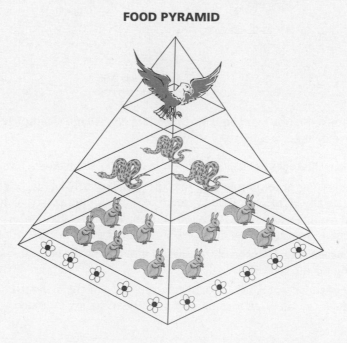

2.3 Life Cycle, Reproduction, and Evolution (Genetics and Evolution)

All living things have a life cycle. A life cycle represents the stages an organism goes through from birth to death.

Metamorphosis

Metamorphosis is a distinct change in physical appearance an organism can go through between birth and adulthood.

1. The **life cycle of a frog** starts with an egg. A female frog generally lays thousands of eggs in water. The eggs are highly vulnerable to predators, and so frogs have evolved many techniques to ensure the survival of their next generation.

2. The eggs hatch and life continues as tadpoles. They lack lungs, eyelids, and front and hind legs. Tadpoles are typically herbivorous, feeding mostly on algae.

3. At the end of the tadpole stage, frogs undergo metamorphosis and they transition into adult form. Metamorphosis involves a dramatic transformation of morphology and physiology, as tadpoles develop hind legs, then front legs, lose their gills, and develop lungs. In the final stage of development, the froglet evolves into an adult frog.

4. After metamorphosis, young adults may leave the water and disperse into terrestrial habitats, or continue to live in the aquatic habitat as adults.

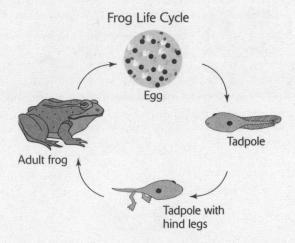

The **butterfly life cycle** is unlike that of many insects. Butterflies go through a complete metamorphosis. The life cycle consists of the following stages:

1. **Egg or embryonic stage:** The eggs are usually laid on plants; this stage lasts a few weeks for most butterflies.

2. **Larva, known as a caterpillar or feeding stage:** From the eggs, butterfly larvae, or caterpillars, consume plant leaves and spend practically all of their time in search of food. Although most caterpillars are herbivorous, a few species are insect eating. When the larva is fully grown, hormones are produced. At this point, the larva stops feeding and begins "wandering" in the quest of a suitable pupation site, often the underside of a leaf.

3. **Pupa (chrysalis) or cocoon stage:** The larva transforms into a pupa (or chrysalis) by anchoring itself to a substrate and molting for the last time.

4. **Adult butterfly (imago) stage:** The adult, sexually mature, stage of the insect is known as the imago. After it emerges from its pupa stage, a butterfly cannot fly until the wings are unfolded.

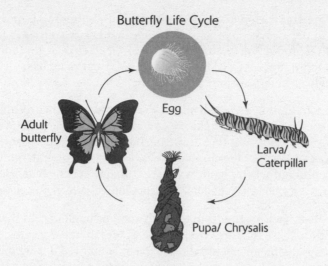

Butterfly Life Cycle

Egg

Adult butterfly

Larva/ Caterpillar

Pupa/ Chrysalis

Reproduction

Flowering plants *reproduce by sexual and asexual means* and are the dominant plant form on land. Often their most distinguishing feature is their reproductive organs, commonly called flowers. The anther produces male gametophytes, and the sperm is produced in pollen grains, which attach to the stigma on top of a carpel, in which the female gametophytes (inside ovules) are located. After the pollen tube grows through the carpel's style, the sex cell nuclei from the pollen grain migrate into the ovule to fertilize the egg cell. The resulting zygote develops into an embryo. The ovary, which produced the female gametophyte(s), then grows into a fruit, which surrounds the seed(s). Plants may either self-pollinate or cross-pollinate. Nonflowering plants like ferns, moss, and liverworts use other means of sexual reproduction.

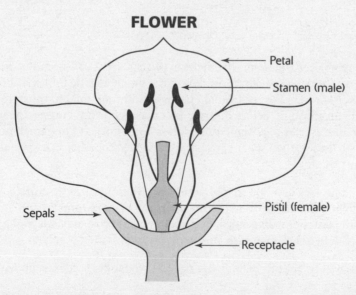

FLOWER

Petal

Stamen (male)

Pistil (female)

Sepals

Receptacle

Asexual reproduction is a form of reproduction which does not involve meiosis, or fertilization. Only one parent is involved in asexual reproduction. Asexual reproduction is the primary form of reproduction for single-celled organisms such as the archaea, bacteria, and protists. Many plants and fungi reproduce asexually as well.

Meiosis is a process of reductional division in which the number of chromosomes per cell is cut in half. In animals, meiosis always results in the formation of gametes, while in other organisms it can give rise to spores. Meiosis is essential for sexual reproduction and therefore occurs in all eukaryotes (animals, plants, fungi, and protists are eukaryotes) that reproduce sexually. Meiosis does not occur in archaea or bacteria, which reproduce through asexual processes such as binary fission.

During meiosis, the genome of a diploid germ cell undergoes DNA replication, resulting in four haploid cells. Each of these cells contains one complete set of chromosomes, or half of the genetic content of the original cell. If meiosis produces gametes, these cells must fuse during fertilization to create a new diploid cell, or zygote, before any new growth can occur. Because the chromosomes of each parent undergo genetic recombination during meiosis, each gamete, and thus each zygote, will have a unique genetic blueprint encoded in its DNA. Together, meiosis and fertilization generate genetically distinct individuals in populations.

In all plants and in many protists, meiosis results in the formation of haploid cells that can divide vegetatively without undergoing fertilization; these cells are referred to as spores. In these groups, gametes are produced by mitosis. Meiosis uses many of the same biochemical mechanisms employed during mitosis to accomplish the redistribution of chromosomes. There are several features unique to meiosis, most importantly the pairing and genetic recombination between homologous chromosomes.

MEIOSIS

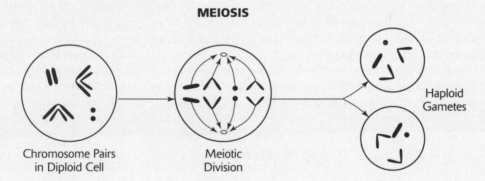

Chromosome Pairs
in Diploid Cell

Meiotic
Division

Haploid
Gametes

The primary result of **mitosis** *or cell division* is the division of the parent cell's genome into two daughter cells. The genome is composed of a number of chromosomes that contain genetic information vital for proper cell function. Because each resultant daughter cell should be genetically identical to the parent cell, the parent cell must make a copy of each chromosome before mitosis. This occurs during S phase, the interphase period that precedes the mitotic phase in the cell cycle where preparation for mitosis occurs. Each new chromosome now contains two identical copies of itself, called sister chromatids, attached together in a specialized region of the chromosome known as the centromere.

The chromosomes align themselves in a line spanning the cell. Microtubules, essentially miniature strings, splay out from opposite ends of the cell and shorten, pulling apart the sister chromatids of each chromosome. As the cell elongates, corresponding sister chromosomes are pulled toward opposite ends and a new nuclear envelope forms around the separated sister chromosomes.

Eventually, the mother cell will be split in half, giving rise to two daughter cells, each with an equivalent and complete copy of the original genome.

MITOSIS
Simplified view of the cell cycle

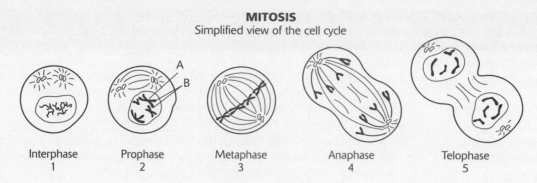

Interphase   Prophase   Metaphase   Anaphase   Telophase
1   2   3   4   5

Stages of mitosis.

Evolution

Natural selection is the process by which favorable heritable traits become more common in successive generations of a population of reproducing organisms, and unfavorable heritable traits become less common. Natural selection acts on the phenotype, or the observable characteristics of an organism, such that individuals with favorable phenotypes are more likely to survive and reproduce than those with less favorable phenotypes. The phenotype's genetic basis will increase in frequency over the following generations. Over time, this process may result in adaptations that specialize organisms for particular ecological niches and may eventually result in the emergence of new species. Natural selection is the mechanism by which evolution may take place within a given population of organisms.

Natural selection is one of the cornerstones of modern biology. The term was introduced by Charles Darwin in his groundbreaking 1859 book, *The Origin of Species*, in which natural selection was described. The concept of natural selection was originally developed in the absence of a valid theory of inheritance. At the time of Darwin's writing, nothing was known of modern genetics. Although Gregor Mendel, the father of modern genetics, was a contemporary of Darwin's, his work would lie in obscurity until the early twentieth century. Natural selection remains the single primary explanation for adaptive evolution.

In *The Origin of Species,* Darwin formulated his theory of evolution, which included the following key points:

- Survival of the fittest
- Natural selection
- Evolution of species over time
- Genetic variation through geographic isolation

The modern view of evolution has unfolded over four billion years. The fossil record is life's evolutionary epic that has borne witness as environmental conditions and genetic potential interacted in accordance with natural selection. The earth's climate, tectonics, atmosphere, oceans, and periodic disasters have invoked the primary selective pressures on all organisms. Organisms that failed to adapt often perished with or without leaving descendants. Modern paleontology has joined with evolutionary biology to share the interdisciplinary task of unfolding the tree of life.

Molecular biologists, using phylogenetics, can compare protein amino acid or nucleotide sequence homology (i.e., similarity) to infer taxonomy and evolutionary distances among organisms. The study of fossils, on the other hand, can more specifically pinpoint when and in what organism branching occurred in the tree of life.

DOMAIN 3: EARTH AND SPACE SCIENCE	
3.1 The Solar System and the Universe (Astronomy)	❑ The planets, their motion, and that of other planetary bodies (e.g., comets and asteroids) around the sun. ❑ Time zones in terms of longitude and the rotation of the earth, and an understanding of the reasons for changes in the observed position of the sun and moon in the sky during the course of the day and from season to season. ❑ Bodies in the universe, including the sun, stars, and galaxies.
3.2 The Structure and Composition of the Earth (Geology)	❑ The formation and observable physical characteristics of minerals (e.g., quartz, calcite, hornblende, mica, and common ore minerals) and different types of rocks (e.g., sedimentary, igneous, and metamorphic). ❑ Characteristics of landforms, such as mountains, rivers, deserts, and oceans. ❑ Chemical and physical weathering, erosion, deposition, and other rock-forming and soil-changing processes and the formation and properties of different types of soils and rocks. ❑ Layers of the earth (crust, lithosphere, mantle, and core) and plate tectonics, including its convective source. ❑ The ability to explain how mountains are created and why volcanoes and earthquakes occur, and to describe their mechanisms and effects. You should also know the commonly cited evidence supporting the theory of plate tectonics. ❑ Factors influencing the location and intensity of earthquakes. ❑ Effects of plate tectonic motion over time on climate, geography, and distribution of organisms, as well as more general changes on the earth over geologic time as evidenced in landforms and the rock and fossil records, including plant and animal extinction.
3.3 The Earth's Atmosphere (Meteorology)	❑ The influence and role of the sun and oceans in weather and climate, and the role of the water cycle. ❑ Causes and effects of air movements and ocean currents (based on convection of air and water) on daily and seasonal weather and on climate.
3.4 The Earth's Water (Oceanography)	❑ Characteristics of bodies of water, such as rivers, lakes, oceans, and estuaries. ❑ The ability to describe tides and explain the mechanisms causing and modifying them, such as the gravitational attraction of the moon, sun, and coastal topography.

Domain 3: Earth and Space Science

3.1 <u>The Solar System and the Universe (Astronomy)</u>

Planets are generally divided into two main types: large, low-density gas giants, and smaller, rocky terrestrials. There are eight planets in the Solar System. In order from the Sun, they are the four terrestrials, Mercury, Venus, Earth, and Mars, and then the four gas giants, Jupiter, Saturn, Uranus, and Neptune. Many of these planets are orbited by one or more moons, which can be larger than small planets. As of December 2008, there are 333 known extrasolar planets, ranging from the size of gas giants to that of terrestrial planets. This brings the total number of identified planets to at least 341. The Solar System also contains at least five dwarf planets: Ceres, Pluto (formerly considered to be the Solar System's ninth planet), Makemake, Haumea, and Eris. No extrasolar dwarf planets have yet been detected.

The Solar System					
Planet	Distance from Sun*	Sidereal Period*	Radius*	Mass*	Satellites*
Mercury	0.39	0.24	0.38	0.05	0
Venus	0.72	0.62	0.96	0.82	0
Earth	1.00	1.00	1.00	1.00	1
Mars	1.52	1.88	0.53	0.11	2
Asteroids	2.8	(Thousands of small bodies)			
Jupiter	5.2	11.9	11.0	317.8	16
Saturn	9.5	29.5	9.2	95.1	17
Uranus	19.2	84.0	3.7	14.5	5
Neptune	30.1	164.8	3.5	17.2	2

*Relative to Earth = 1

A **comet** is a small Solar System body that orbits the Sun and, when close enough to the Sun, exhibits a visible coma (atmosphere) or a tail—both primarily from the effects of solar radiation upon the comet's nucleus. Comet nuclei are themselves loose collections of ice, dust, and small rocky particles, measuring a few kilometers or tens of kilometers across.

Comets have a variety of different orbital periods, ranging from a few years, to hundreds of thousands of years, while some are believed to pass through the inner Solar System only once before being thrown out into interstellar space. *Short-period comets* are thought to originate in the Kuiper Belt, or associated scattered discs, which lie beyond the orbit of Neptune. *Long-period comets* are believed to originate at a much greater distance from the Sun, in a cloud (the Oort cloud) consisting of debris left over from the condensation of the solar nebula. Comets are thrown from these outer reaches of the Solar System inwards towards the Sun by gravitational perturbations from the outer planets or nearby stars, or as a result of collisions.

THE SOLAR SYSTEM

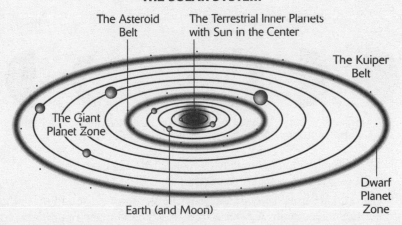

Asteroids, sometimes called *minor planets* or *planetoids*, are bodies—primarily of the inner Solar System—that are smaller than planets but larger than meteoroids, excluding comets. The distinction between asteroids and comets is made by visual appearance; when discovered, comets show a perceptible coma while asteroids do not.

The **earth** travels in an orbit that is slightly elliptical (oval), and so the distance from the sun ranges from 91.5 to 94.5 million miles. Its daily rotation deforms the earth to a flattened spheroid, with a polar radius slightly less than the equatorial radius. Locations of the surface are described by a grid of latitude and longitude lines. *Latitude* is the degrees north or south of the equator, while *longitude* is the degrees east or west of the prime meridian through Greenwich, England. For example, the location of New York City is 41°N, 74°W. The seasons of the year are the consequence of the earth's equatorial plane being tilted about 23° from the orbital plane (see the figure that follows). In each hemisphere at noontime, the sun is near the zenith during summer, and low in the sky during winter.

THE SEASONS OF THE YEAR

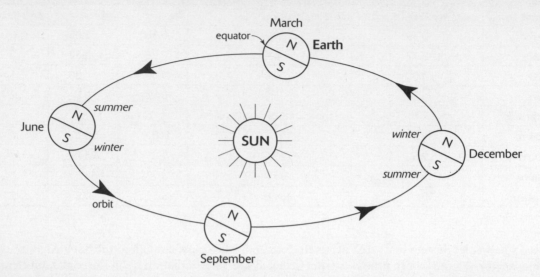

The **moon** travels around the earth each month. Its distance from the earth averages 237,000 miles. The phases of illumination through which the moon passes each month (see the figure that follows) can be understood by contemplating its position relative to those of the earth and the sun. A new moon occurs when the moon sets at sunset; then the moon is between the earth and the sun, and so we see only the dark half of the moon. Each night, the moon sets a few minutes later and we perceive more of its illuminated half. After the moon has waxed through crescent, quarter, and gibbous phases, a full moon appears. At that time, the moon rises at sunset, and so we see all of its illuminated side. Then the phase wanes gradually to another new moon. There are approximately 29.5 days between each cycle. The moon itself has rugged topography formed billions of years ago by volcanic eruptions and meteorite impacts.

PHASES OF THE MOON

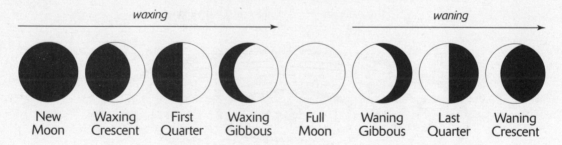

There are approximately 29.5 days between each cycle.

Eclipses of the moon and the sun are quite spectacular. Ancient astronomers found that eclipses occurred periodically and learned to predict them accurately. A *lunar eclipse* (see the following figure) darkens the moon as the earth passes between it and the sun, casting a shadow on the moon. An eclipse of the moon may be seen from anywhere the moon is visible, about half of the earth.

LUNAR ECLIPSE

In contrast, a **solar eclipse** (see the figure that follows) takes place when the moon passes between the earth and the sun, with the moon blocking the sunlight for about two minutes. A total eclipse of the sun may be seen only from a small zone on the earth.

SOLAR ECLIPSE

The **sun** is a huge ball of incandescent gases. Its mass is more than 300,000 times that of the earth, and its volume could engulf a million earths. Analysis of absorption lines in the solar spectrum allows identification of the chemical elements present and measurement of the surface temperature. The principal constituents of the sun are the lightest elements, hydrogen and helium. Under solar conditions, those gases are undergoing nuclear fusion to heavier elements with the release of prodigious quantities of energy. The center of the sun may have a temperature of millions of degrees; the visible surface, the photosphere, is about 6,000°C. Sunspots are somewhat cooler disturbances in the photosphere. The sun's atmosphere is divided into the inner chromosphere with explosive prominences and the outer corona, a glowing halo visible only during a total eclipse. The sun is constantly emitting particles as a solar wind.

Stars are bodies similar to the sun but immensely distant. Astronomers have calculated the distance to many of the closest stars by measuring the parallax, a slight shift in apparent position against the background of more distant stars as the earth travels around the sun. Interstellar distances are described in light-years, one light-year being the distance light travels in one year. Remember, the velocity of light is 186,000 miles *per second!* The nearest stars are 4 light-years away.

Galaxies are huge systems of stars. Our own Milky Way galaxy is estimated to have 100 billion stars arranged in a great disk. The sun is not at the center of the disk, but out toward the perimeter, and is revolving around the galactic center. Some of the faint nebulae beyond the Milky Way have been resolved into myriads of individual stars—galaxies like our own. From studies of Cepheids, stars of variable luminosity that serve as distance indicators, the neighboring Andromeda galaxy is about 20 million light-years away. Galaxies of spiral, elliptical, and irregular form are speckled throughout the visible universe. The largest telescope has detected galaxies to its limit of several billion light-years. The spectra of distant objects display a red shift, which is interpreted as meaning that they are rapidly receding from us. This apparent expansion of the universe has given rise to the big bang theory of cosmology, in which one primeval mass exploded about 12 billion years ago.

Time Zones (Longitude and Rotation of the Earth)

A **time zone** is a region of the earth that has uniform standard time, usually referred to as the local time. Time zones are divided into standard and daylight saving (or summer). Daylight saving time zones (or summer time zones) include an offset (typically +1 hour) for daylight saving time. Standard time zones can be defined by geometrically subdividing the earth's spheroid into 24 *lunes* (wedge-shaped sections), bordered by meridians, each 15° of longitude apart. The local time in neighboring zones would differ by one hour. *Fifteen degrees of longitude equals one hour of time.*

Reasons for Seasons

The **seasons** result from the earth's axis being tilted to its orbital plane; it deviates by an angle of approximately 23.5 degrees. Thus, at any given time during summer or winter, one part of the planet is more directly exposed to the rays of the sun. This exposure alternates as the earth revolves in its orbit. At any given time, regardless of season, the Northern and Southern Hemispheres experience opposite seasons.

Seasonal weather differences between hemispheres are further caused by the elliptical orbit of the earth. Earth reaches *perihelion* (the point in its orbit closest to the sun) in January, and it reaches *aphelion* (farthest point from the sun) in July.

Seasonal weather fluctuations (changes) also depend on factors such as proximity to oceans or other large bodies of water, currents in those oceans, El Niño and other oceanic cycles, and prevailing winds.

In the temperate and polar regions, seasons are marked by changes in the amount of sunlight, which in turn often cause cycles of dormancy in plants and hibernation in animals. These effects vary with latitude and with proximity to bodies of water. For example, the South Pole is in the middle of the continent of Antarctica and is therefore a considerable distance from the moderating influence of the southern oceans. The North Pole is in the Arctic Ocean, and thus its temperature extremes are buffered by the water. The result is that the South Pole is consistently colder during the southern winter than the North Pole during the northern winter.

The cycle of seasons in the polar and temperate zones of one hemisphere is opposite to that in the other. When it is summer in the Northern Hemisphere, it is winter in the Southern Hemisphere, and vice versa.

In meteorological terms, the summer solstice and winter solstice do not fall in the middle of summer or winter. The heights of these seasons occur up to a month later because of seasonal lag. Seasons, though, are not always defined in meteorological terms.

Compared to axial tilt, other factors contribute little to seasonal temperature changes. The seasons are not the result of the variation in the earth's distance to the sun; because of its elliptical orbit, the earth as a whole is actually slightly warmer when farther from the sun. This is because the Northern Hemisphere has more land than the Southern Hemisphere, and land warms more readily than sea.

Equinoxes occur twice a year, when the tilt of the earth's axis is oriented neither from nor to the sun, causing the sun to be located vertically above a point on the equator. The name is derived from the Latin *aequus* (equal) and *nox* (night), because at the equinox, the night and day are equally long.

An equinox happens each year at two specific moments in time (not a whole day) when the center of the sun can be observed to be vertically above the earth's equator, occurring around March 20 and September 22 each year.

The **winter solstice** occurs at the instant when the sun's position in the sky is at its greatest angular distance on the other side of the equatorial plane from the observer's hemisphere. Depending on the shift of the calendar, the winter solstice occurs some time between December 20 and December 23 each year in the Northern Hemisphere, and between June 20 and June 23 in the Southern Hemisphere, during either the shortest day or the longest night of the year.

SEASONAL DATES IN THE NORTHERN HEMISHPERE

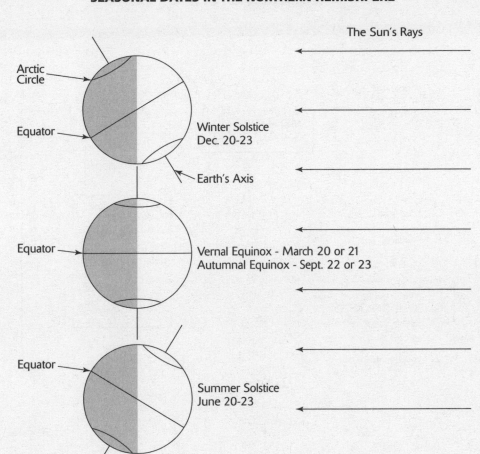

The Sun's Rays

Arctic Circle

Equator

Winter Solstice
Dec. 20-23

Earth's Axis

Equator

Vernal Equinox - March 20 or 21
Autumnal Equinox - Sept. 22 or 23

Equator

Summer Solstice
June 20-23

3.2 Structure and Composition of the Earth (Geology)

Geology is the science that describes and interprets the earth. It classifies the materials that make up the earth, observes their shapes and distribution, and tries to discover the processes that caused the materials to be formed in that manner. Some major geological fields are *geomorphology* (landforms), *petrology* (rocks), *stratigraphy* (layered rocks), and *paleontology* (fossils). All fields contribute to historical geology, an ambitious attempt to list the specific events that have produced the present earth. Processes occurring today are observed carefully and their effects are measured. Then, geologists assume that similar effects in ancient rocks were caused by processes similar to those of the present. This method of using the present to interpret the past is called *uniformitarianism*. For example, glaciation in early eras is indicated by ancient deposits with features very similar to those produced by present-day glaciers.

THE ROCK CYCLE

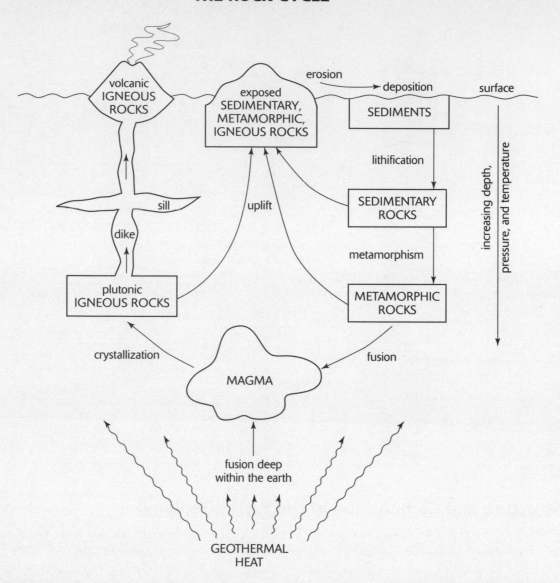

Sedimentary rock is one of the three main rock types (the others being igneous and metamorphic rock). Sedimentary rock is formed by deposition and consolidation of mineral and organic material and from precipitation of minerals from solution. The processes that form sedimentary rock occur at the surface of the earth and within bodies of water. Rock formed from sediments covers 75 to 80 percent of the earth's land area, and includes common types such as limestone, chalk, dolostone, sandstone, conglomerate, some types of breccia, and shale. Sedimentary rocks are classified by the source of their sediments, and are produced by one or more of the following: rock formed from fragments broken off from parent rock—by weathering (erosion by water, ice, or wind)—followed by transportation of sediments, to the place of deposition.

Common Sedimentary Rocks			
Process	Rock Name	Description	Minerals
Clastic	Conglomerate	Cemented pebbles	Rock fragments
	Sandstone	Cemented sand	Quartz and orthoclase
	Shale	Hardened mud	Clays, like kaolin
Chemical	Salt	Crystalline	Halite
Organic	Limestone	Shelly	Calcite

Igneous rocks are formed by solidification of cooled *magma* (molten rock). They may form with or without crystallization, either below the surface as intrusive (plutonic) rocks or on the surface as extrusive (volcanic) rocks. This magma can be derived from partial melts of pre-existing rocks in either the earth's mantle or crust. Typically, the melting is caused by one or more of the following processes: an increase in temperature, a decrease in pressure, or a change in composition. Over 700 types of igneous rocks have been described, most of them formed beneath the surface of the earth's crust. These have diverse properties, depending on their composition and how they were formed.

Common Igneous Rocks			
Occurrence	Rock Name	Grain Size	Minerals
Plutonic	Gabbro	Coarse	Plagioclase, augite, olivine
	Granite	Coarse	Quartz, orthoclase, plagioclase
Volcanic	Basalt	Fine	Plagioclase, augite, olivine
	Rhyolite	Fine	Quartz, orthoclase, plagioclase

Metamorphic rock is the result of the transformation of an existing rock type, the *protolith*, in a process called metamorphism, which means "change in form." The protolith is subjected to heat and pressure (temperatures greater than 150 to 200°C and pressures of 1500 bars), causing profound physical and/or chemical change. The protolith may be sedimentary rock, igneous rock, or another older metamorphic rock. Metamorphic rocks make up a large part of the earth's crust and are classified by texture and by chemical and mineral assemblage. They may be formed simply by being deep beneath the earth's surface, subjected to high temperatures and the great pressure of the rock layers above it. They can be formed by tectonic processes such as continental collisions, which cause horizontal pressure, friction, and distortion. Some examples of metamorphic rocks are gneiss, slate, marble, schist, and quartzite.

Common Metamorphic Rocks			
Rock Name	Texture	Minerals	Parent Rock
Gneiss	Coarse oriented	Quartz, orthoclase	Shale, sandstone
Schist	Medium oriented	Quartz, micas	Shale, sandstone
Slate	Fine oriented	Micas	Shale
Marble	Coarse granular	Calcite	Limestone
Quartzite	Medium granular	Quartz	Sandstone

Minerals are natural chemical compounds that are the crystals that make up rocks. Each mineral has a specific composition or narrow range of composition. In the table that follows, which shows common rock-forming minerals, two chemical elements that may substitute for each other are enclosed by parentheses; thus the mineral olivine—$(Mg, Fe)_2SiO_4$—varies in composition, from Mg_2SiO_4 to Fe_2SiO_4. The most abundant minerals in the crust are the two feldspars (orthoclase and plagioclase), quartz, olivine, and augite. Note that these five minerals are silicates, built from interlocking silicon and oxygen atoms.

Minerals		
Mineral	**Composition**	**Occurrence**
Quartz	SiO_2	Igneous, sedimentary, metamorphic
Orthoclase	$KAlSi_3O_8$	Igneous, sedimentary, metamorphic
Plagioclase	$(Ca, Na)Al_2Si_2O_8$	Igneous
Olivine	$(Mg, Fe)_2SiO_4$	Igneous
Augite	$Ca(Mg, Fe)Si_2O_6$	Igneous, metamorphic
Kaolin	$Al_2Si_2O_9H_4$	Sedimentary; a clay mineral
Calcite	$CaCO_3$	Sedimentary, metamorphic
Halite	$NaCl$	Sedimentary; common salt
Hematite	Fe_2O_3	Iron ore deposit
Chalcopyrite	$CuFeS_2$	Copper ore deposit

Characteristics of Land Forms (Mountains, Rivers, Deserts)

A **mountain** is a landform that stretches above the surrounding land in a limited area, with a peak. A mountain is generally steeper than a hill, but there is no universally accepted standard definition for the height of a mountain or a hill, although a mountain usually has an identifiable summit.

A **river** is a natural flow of water, usually freshwater, traveling toward an ocean, a lake, or another stream. In some cases, a river flows into the ground or dries up completely before reaching another body of water. Usually, larger streams are called rivers, while smaller streams are called creeks, brooks, rivulets, rills, and many other terms. A river is a component of the water cycle.

Deserts take up about one-third of the earth's land surface. They usually have a large diurnal (day) and seasonal temperature range, with high daytime temperatures, and low nighttime temperatures (due to extremely low humidity). The temperature in the daytime can reach 45°C/113°F or higher in the summer, and dip to 0°C/32°F or lower in the winter. Water acts to trap infrared radiation from both the sun and the ground, and dry desert air is incapable of blocking sunlight during the day or trapping heat during the night. Thus, during daylight, most of the sun's heat reaches the ground and as soon as the sun sets, the desert cools quickly by radiating its heat into space.

Many deserts are formed by rain shadows; mountains blocking the path of precipitation to the desert.

RAIN SHADOW

Rising Air Cools and Condenses

Dry Air Advances

Warm Moist Air

Rain Shadow

Prevailing Winds

Weathering and Erosion

Weathering is the decomposition of earth rocks, soils, and their minerals through direct contact with the planet's atmosphere. Weathering occurs *in situ*, or "with no movement," and thus should not to be confused with erosion, which involves the movement of rocks and minerals by agents such as water, ice, wind, and gravity.

Two important classifications of weathering processes exist: physical and chemical weathering. *Mechanical or physical weathering* involves the breakdown of rocks and soils through direct contact with atmospheric conditions, such as heat, water, ice, and pressure. The second classification, *chemical weathering,* involves the direct effect of atmospheric chemicals or biologically produced chemicals (also known as *biological weathering*) in the breakdown of rocks, soils, and minerals.

The materials left over after the rock breaks down combine with organic material to create soil. The mineral content of the soil is determined by the parent material; thus, a soil derived from a single rock type can often be deficient in one or more minerals for good fertility, while a soil weathered from a mix of rock types often makes more fertile soil.

SOIL PROFILE

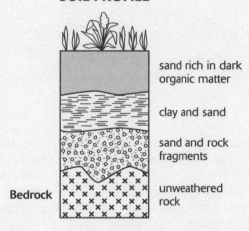

sand rich in dark organic matter

clay and sand

sand and rock fragments

Bedrock

unweathered rock

Erosion is the carrying away or displacement of solids (sediment, soil, rock, and other particles), usually by the agents of currents such as wind, water, or ice by downward or down-slope movement in response to gravity. Erosion is distinguished from weathering, which is the process of chemical or physical breakdown of the minerals in the rocks, although the two processes may be concurrent.

Erosion in many places is increased by human land use. Poor land-use practices include deforestation, overgrazing, unmanaged construction activity, and road-building. Land that is used for the production of agricultural crops generally experiences a significantly greater rate of erosion than that of land under natural vegetation. This is particularly true if tillage is used, which reduces vegetation cover on the surface of the soil and disturbs both soil structure and plant roots that would otherwise hold the soil in place. However, improved land-use practices can limit erosion by using techniques such as terrace building, conservation tillage practices, and tree planting. A certain amount of erosion is natural, and in fact, healthy for the ecosystem, but excessive erosion can cause damage by excessive loss of soil.

Strata and the Geological Time Scale

Strata are the layers of sediment deposited in a quiet environment. Common sites of deposition are lakes, deltas at the mouths of rivers, beaches and sandbars along the coast, and (most important) the marine environment. Strata are commonly very extensive laterally and relatively thin vertically, like a blanket. An important geological rule is the law of original horizontality, which states that most sediments are deposited in beds that were originally horizontal, and any tilting is due to later earth movements. A second stratigraphic principle is the law of superposition: Younger beds were originally deposited above older beds.

Fossils are traces of ancient life preserved in the strata as shells, footprints, and the like. Because life has evolved (changed) continually through geological history, the fossils in older strata differ from those found in more recent deposits. In fact, strata deposited during one geological period contain characteristic life forms different from those of any other period. For example, the earliest fossil-rich beds have many trilobites, early crab-like creatures that have been extinct for hundreds of millions of years; discovery of fossil trilobites in a formation permits assignment of that bed to an early period.

The geological time scale was a major achievement of stratigraphers, who used fossils to arrange strata in a standard order. More recently, geochemists have measured the amount of radioactive decay in minerals and calculated the time at which the rock formed. So the geological time scale in the following table represents interpretations from fossils and radioactivity. The earth is believed to be about 5.6 billion years old. The fossiliferous strata record only the last 11 percent of the earth's history. And human civilization has lasted only 10,000 years, a brief moment on the geological time scale. The immensity of geological time is the major discovery of geology. There has been ample time for very slow processes to produce large consequences.

Geological Time Scale			
Geological Era	**Beginning (Years before Present)**	**Duration (Years)**	**Characteristic Life Forms**
Cenozoic	70,000,000	70,000,000	Mammals
Mesozoic	225,000,000	155,000,000	Reptiles
Paleozoic	600,000,000	375,000,000	Invertebrates
Precambrian	5,600,000,000	5,000,000,000	No life except algae

Layers of the Earth

The earth's structure (see the following figure) has been inferred from its astronomical properties and seismic records of earthquake waves that have traveled through the interior of the earth. Temperature rises from the surface (20°C) to the center (3,000°C) of the earth; this fact is essential to understanding geological processes. About 31 percent of the earth's mass is a dense core of iron and nickel metals, melted by the extremely high temperature of the center of the earth. Around that liquid core is the largest zone of the planet (68 percent), the mantle of crystalline silicates, rich in magnesium, calcium, and iron. The very hot mantle is mainly solid, but local melting to magma (molten rock) is the source of volcanic eruptions. Above the mantle is the crust, which makes up less than 1 percent of the earth. This relatively thin zone (5 to 25 miles) contains the only rocks we can study, even in the deepest mines or drill holes. The table that follows shows the average chemical composition of crustal rocks.

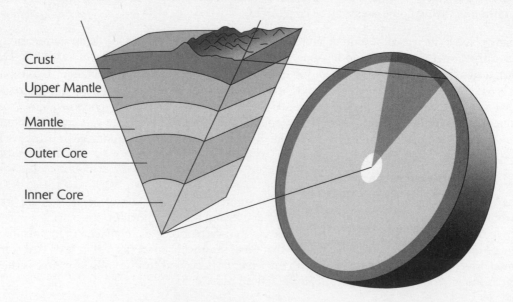

Crust
Upper Mantle
Mantle
Outer Core
Inner Core

Average Composition of Crustal Rocks		
Element	**Abbreviation**	**Percent**
Oxygen	O	62.6
Silicon	Si	21.2
Aluminum	Al	6.5
Sodium	Na	2.6
Calcium	Ca	1.9
Iron	Fe	1.9
Magnesium	Mg	1.8
Potassium	K	1.4

Earth movements are the result of forces within the earth, where temperature and pressure differences lead to instability. The stress is particularly severe in orogenic zones, which are characterized by volcanism, metamorphism, deformation, and uplift. Two styles of rock deformation are faulting and folding. Today, many geologists attribute edge-of-continent deformation to plate tectonics, a modern theory that suggests that oceanic crust emerges from the mantle along the oceanic ridges. Broad plates of oceanic crust may spread outward from the ridges until they crush against the margins of continental crust, the oceanic plate being forced under the continental plate and back into the mantle.

Plate tectonics describes the large-scale motions of the earth's lithosphere. The theory encompasses the older concepts of continental drift, developed during the first half of the twentieth century, and seafloor spreading, understood during the 1960s.

The outermost part of the earth's interior is made up of two layers: above is the lithosphere, comprising the crust and the rigid uppermost part of the mantle. Below the lithosphere lies the asthenosphere. Although solid, the asthenosphere has relatively low viscosity and shear strength and can flow like a liquid on geological time scales. The deeper mantle below the asthenosphere is more rigid again due to the higher pressure.

The lithosphere is broken up into what are called *tectonic plates*— in the case of the earth, there are seven major and many minor plates. The lithospheric plates ride on the asthenosphere. These plates move in relation to one another at one of three types of plate boundaries: convergent or collision boundaries, divergent or spreading boundaries, and transform boundaries. Earthquakes, volcanic activity, mountain-building, and oceanic trench formation occur along plate boundaries. The lateral movement of the plates is typically at speeds of 50 to 100 mm annually.

The **Pacific Ring of Fire** (see p. 255) is an area of frequent earthquakes and volcanic eruptions encircling the basin of the Pacific Ocean. In a 40,000 km horseshoe shape, it is associated with a nearly continuous series of oceanic trenches, volcanic arcs, and volcanic belts and/or plate movements. The Ring of Fire has 452 volcanoes and is home to over 75 percent of the world's active and dormant volcanoes.

Ninety percent of the world's earthquakes and 80 percent of the world's largest earthquakes occur along the Ring of Fire. The Ring of Fire is a direct result and consequence of plate tectonics and the movement and collisions of crustal plates.

A **mountain** is usually produced by the movement of lithospheric plates. The compressional forces, isostatic uplift, and intrusion of igneous matter forces surface rock upward, creating a landform higher than the surrounding features. The height of the feature makes it either a hill or, if higher and steeper, a mountain. The major mountains tend to occur in long linear arcs, indicating tectonic plate boundaries and activity. Two types of mountains are formed, depending on how the rock reacts to the tectonic forces: block mountains or fold mountains.

Some isolated mountains were produced by volcanoes, including many apparently small islands that reach a great height above the ocean floor.

A **volcano** is an opening, or rupture, in a planet's surface or crust, which allows hot, molten rock, ash, and gases to escape from below the surface. Volcanic activity involving the extrusion of rock tends to form mountains or features like mountains over a period of time.

Volcanoes are generally found where tectonic plates are diverging or converging. A mid-oceanic ridge, such as the Mid-Atlantic Ridge, has examples of volcanoes caused by divergent tectonic plates pulling apart. The Pacific Ring of Fire has examples of volcanoes caused by convergent tectonic plates coming together. By contrast, volcanoes are usually not created where two tectonic plates slide past one another. Volcanoes can also form where there is stretching and thinning of the earth's crust. Volcanoes can be caused by "mantle plumes." These so-called hotspots, as in Hawaii, can occur far from plate boundaries. Hotspot volcanoes are also found elsewhere in the Solar System, especially on rocky planets and moons.

3.3 <u>Earth's Atmosphere (Meteorology)</u>

Meteorology is the science of the atmosphere and weather. The composition of air is shown in the following table. The amount of water vapor in the air depends on the prevailing temperature and the availability of water. The hydrologic cycle links the processes.

The Composition of Air		
Gas	Abbreviation	Percent
Nitrogen	N_2	78.08
Oxygen	O_2	20.95
Argon	Ar	0.93
Carbon dioxide	CO_2	0.03
Water vapor	H_2O	Varies

Hydrologic Cycle

The sun, which drives the *water cycle,* heats water in the oceans. Water evaporates as vapor into the air. Ice and snow can sublimate directly into water vapor. *Evapotranspiration* is water transpired from plants and evaporated from the soil. Rising air currents take the vapor up into the atmosphere where cooler temperatures cause it to condense into clouds. Air currents move clouds around the globe and cloud particles collide, grow, and fall out of the sky as precipitation. Some precipitation falls as snow and can accumulate as ice caps and glaciers, which can store frozen water for thousands of years. Snow packs can thaw and melt, and the ensuing water flows overland as snowmelt. Most precipitation falls back into the oceans or onto land, where the precipitation flows over the ground as surface runoff. A portion of runoff enters rivers, with stream flow moving water towards the oceans. Runoff and groundwater are stored as freshwater in lakes. Not all runoff flows into rivers. Much of it infiltrates into the ground through percolation. Some water infiltrates deep into the ground and replenishes aquifers, which store huge amounts of freshwater for long periods of time. Some infiltration stays close to the land surface and can seep back into surface-water bodies (and the ocean) as groundwater discharge. Some groundwater finds openings in the land surface and emerges as freshwater springs. Over time, the water reenters the ocean, where the water cycle started.

THE HYDROLOGIC CYCLE

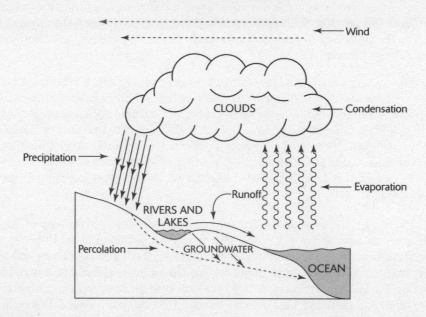

Hydrologic Concepts:

- **Precipitation:** Condensed water vapor that falls to the earth's surface. Most precipitation occurs as rain, but also includes snow, hail, fog drip, graupel, and sleet.

- **Canopy interception:** The precipitation that is intercepted by plant foliage and eventually evaporates back to the atmosphere rather than falling to the ground.

- **Snowmelt:** The runoff produced by melting snow.

- **Runoff:** The variety of ways by which water moves across the land. This includes both surface runoff and channel runoff. As it flows, the water may percolate into the ground, evaporate into the air, become stored in lakes or reservoirs, or be extracted for agricultural or other human uses.

- **Percolation:** The movement of rainwater as it filters through soil and rocks into the ground, becoming groundwater.

- **Subsurface Flow:** The flow of water underground, in the vadose zone and aquifers. Subsurface water may return to the surface (as a spring or by being pumped) or eventually seep into the oceans. Water returns to the land surface at lower elevation than where it entered, under the force of gravity or gravity-induced pressures. Groundwater tends to move slowly and is replenished slowly, and so it can remain in aquifers for thousands of years.

- **Evaporation:** The transformation of water from liquid to gas phases as it moves from the ground or bodies of water into the overlying atmosphere. The source of energy for evaporation is primarily solar radiation. Evaporation often implicitly includes *transpiration* from plants, although together they are specifically referred to as *evapotranspiration*.

- **Sublimation:** The state change where a solid (ice or snow) changes directly to a gas (water vapor).

- **Condensation:** The transformation of water vapor to liquid water droplets in the air, producing clouds and fog.

Weather

On the earth, common weather phenomena include wind, clouds, rain, snow, fog, and dust storms. Less common events include natural disasters such as tornadoes, hurricanes, and ice storms. Almost all familiar weather phenomena occur in the troposphere (the lower part of the atmosphere). Weather does occur in the stratosphere and can affect weather lower down in the troposphere, but the exact mechanisms are poorly understood.

Weather occurs primarily due to density (temperature and moisture) differences between one location and another. These differences can occur due to the angle of the sun at any particular spot, which varies by latitude from the tropics. In other words, the farther from the tropics you are positioned, the lower is the angle of the sun. This causes those locations to be cooler due to the indirect sunlight. The strong temperature contrast between polar and tropical air gives rise to the jet stream.

Surface temperature differences in turn cause pressure differences. A hot surface heats the air above it and the air expands, lowering the air pressure and its density. The resulting horizontal pressure gradient accelerates the air from high to low pressure, creating wind, and the earth's rotation then causes curvature of the flow through the Coriolis effect. The atmosphere is a chaotic system, and so small changes to one part of the system can grow to have large effects on the system as a whole. This makes it difficult to accurately predict weather more than a few days in advance. The sun and oceans can also affect the weather of land. If the sun heats ocean waters for a period of time, water can evaporate. Once evaporated into the air, the moisture can spread over nearby land, thus making it cooler.

Differential heating is the motive force behind *land breezes* and *sea breezes* (or, in the case of larger lakes, lake breezes), also known as on- or off-shore winds. Land absorbs and radiates heat faster than water, but water releases heat over a longer period of time. The result is that, in locations where sea and land meet, heat absorbed over the day will be radiated more quickly by the land at night, cooling the air. Over the sea, heat is still being released into the air at night, and rises. This convective motion draws the cool land air in to replace the rising air, resulting in a land breeze in the late night and early morning. During the day, the roles are reversed. Warm air over the land rises, pulling cool air in from the sea to replace it, giving a sea breeze during the afternoon and evening.

Mountain breezes and *valley breezes* are due to a combination of differential heating and geometry. When the sun rises, it is the tops of the mountain peaks which receive first light, and as the day progresses, the mountain slopes take on a greater heat load than the valleys. This results in a temperature inequality between the two, and as warm air rises off the slopes, cool air moves up out of the valleys to replace it. This upslope wind is called a *valley breeze*. The opposite effect takes place in the afternoon, as the valley radiates heat. The peaks, long since cooled, transport air into the valley in a process that is partly gravitational and partly convective and is called a *mountain breeze*.

El Niño and La Niña are officially defined as sustained *sea surface temperature* anomalies of magnitude greater than 0.5°C across the central tropical Pacific Ocean.

El Niño's warm current of nutrient-poor tropical water, heated by its eastward passage in the Equatorial Current, replaces the cold, nutrient-rich surface water of the Humboldt Current, also known as the Peru Current, which supports great populations of food fish.

La Niña is characterized by unusually cold ocean temperatures in the eastern equatorial Pacific, compared to El Niño, which is characterized by unusually warm ocean temperatures in the same area. Atlantic tropical cyclone activity is generally enhanced during La Niña. The La Niña condition often follows the El Niño, especially when the latter is strong.

3.4 <u>Earth's Water (Oceanography)</u>

An **estuary** is a semi-enclosed coastal body of water with one or more rivers or streams flowing into it, and with a free connection to the open sea. Estuaries are often associated with high levels of biological diversity.

Estuaries are typically the tidal mouths of rivers and they are often characterized by sedimentation or silt carried in from terrestrial runoff, frequently from offshore. They are made up of brackish water. Estuaries are often given names like bay, sound, fjord, etc. The terms are not mutually exclusive.

As ecosystems, estuaries are under threat from human activities such as pollution and overfishing.

Though generally recognized as several separate *oceans,* the oceanic water mass comprises one global, interconnected body of salt water often referred to as the world ocean or global ocean. This concept of a global ocean as a continuous body of water with relatively free interchange among its parts is of fundamental importance to oceanography. The major oceanic divisions are defined in part by the continents, various archipelagos, and other criteria: these divisions are (in descending order of size) the *Pacific Ocean*, the *Atlantic Ocean*, the *Indian Ocean*, the *Southern Ocean* (which is sometimes subsumed as the southern portions of the Pacific, Atlantic, and Indian oceans), and the *Arctic Ocean* (which is sometimes considered a sea of the Atlantic). The Pacific and Atlantic may be further subdivided by the equator into northerly and southerly portions. Smaller regions of the oceans are called *seas, gulfs, bays*, and other names.

The oceans cover three-quarters of the earth's surface and have a great impact on the biosphere. The evaporation of these oceans is how we get most of our rainfall, and their temperature determines our climate and wind patterns. Life within the ocean had already evolved 3 billion years prior to the movement of animal and plant life on land.

CROSS SECTION OF THE ATLANTIC OCEAN

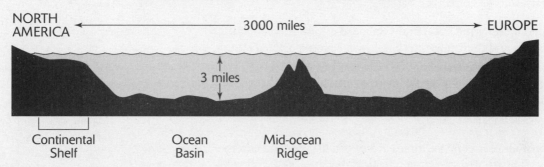

Tides are the rising of the earth's ocean surface caused by the tidal forces of the moon and the sun acting on the oceans. Tides cause changes in the depth of the marine and estuarine water bodies and produce oscillating currents known as tidal streams, making prediction of tides important for coastal navigation.

The changing tide produced at a given location is the result of the changing positions of the moon and sun relative to the earth, coupled with the effects of the earth's rotation and the bathymetry of oceans, seas, and estuaries. Sea level measured by coastal tide gauges may also be strongly affected by wind.

Tides may be *semidiurnal* (two high waters and two low waters each day), or *diurnal* (one tidal cycle per day). In most locations, tides are semidiurnal.

Around a *new* or *full* moon, when the *sun, moon*, and *the earth* form a line, the tidal forces due to the sun reinforce those of the moon. The tide's range is at a maximum and is called a *spring tide*. It is derived not from the season of spring but rather from the verb meaning "to jump" or "to leap up." When the moon is at first quarter or third quarter, the sun and moon are separated by 90° when viewed from the earth. The forces induced by the sun partially cancel those of the moon. At these points in the lunar cycle, the tide's range is at a minimum and is called a *neap tide*, or *neaps*.

The tidal force produced by the sun is therefore only 46 percent as large as that produced by the moon. The gravitational attraction between the moon and the earth (and to a lesser degree, the sun) causes the tides. The gravitational attraction of the moon causes the oceans to bulge out on the side of the earth facing the moon. Another bulge also occurs on the opposite side of the earth as the earth is being pulled toward the moon. Due to the rotation of the earth, two tides occur each day.

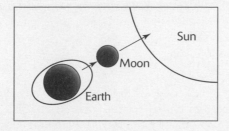

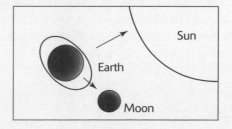

Chapter 5

Subtest III: Physical Education

Content

The Physical Education section focuses on knowing and understanding the three major categories included in a comprehensive physical education program. This section measures your ability to evaluate movement education and to recognize the physical, biological, and social sciences in the context of:

1. Understanding the nature and purpose of physical education activities and their place in the physical education curriculum.
2. Evaluating and interpreting the performance level and physical characteristics of physical education students.
3. Making decisions regarding the conduct and needs of students in physical education classes.

The multiple-choice section contains 13 questions grouped together and 1 short constructed-response question that covers the following three major content areas and focuses on the topics listed under each.

Analysis of Exam Areas: Content Specifications* in Physical Education

*These are the actual California state content specification standards, available online.

Domain 1: Movement Skills and Movement Knowledge

1.1 Basic Movement Skills

❑ Candidates for Multiple Subject Teaching Credentials can identify movement concepts, including body awareness, space awareness, and movement exploration.

❑ They can list locomotor skills such as skipping, nonlocomotor skills such as static balancing, and object manipulation such as catching.

❑ They can recognize basic concepts of biomechanics that affect movement, such as how the body moves and how such movement is influenced by gravity, friction, and the laws of motion.

❑ They can describe critical elements of basic movement skills, such as stepping in opposition when throwing and/or following through when kicking a ball.

1.2 <u>Exercise Physiology: Health and Physical Fitness</u>

- ❑ Candidates for Multiple Subject Teaching Credentials can identify health and fitness benefits and associated risks that support a physically active lifestyle, related to safety and medical factors (e.g., asthma and diabetes).
- ❑ They can recognize exercise principles, such as frequency, intensity, and time, to select activities that promote physical fitness.
- ❑ They can describe physical fitness components, such as flexibility, muscular strength and endurance, cardio-respiratory endurance, and body composition, which are included in comprehensive personal fitness development programs.

1.3 <u>Movement Forms: Content Areas</u>

- ❑ Candidates for Multiple Subject Teaching Credentials know a variety of traditional and nontraditional games, sports, dances, and other physical activities.
- ❑ They are able to cite basic rules and social etiquette for physical activities.
- ❑ They can select activities for their potential to include all students, regardless of gender, race, culture, religion, abilities, or disabilities.
- ❑ They can integrate activities with other content areas, such as math and science.

Domain 2: Self-Image and Personal Development

2.1 <u>Physical Growth and Development</u>

- ❑ Candidates for Multiple Subject Teaching Credentials can identify the sequential development of fine and gross motor skills in children and young adolescents.
- ❑ They can describe the influence of growth spurts (changes in height and weight) and body type on movement and coordination.
- ❑ They recognize the impact of factors such as exercise, relaxation, nutrition, stress, and substance abuse on physical health and general well-being.

2.2 <u>Self-Image</u>

- ❑ Candidates for Multiple Subject Teaching Credentials can describe the role of physical activity in the development of a positive self-image, and how psychological skills such as goal setting are selected to promote lifelong participation in physical activity.

Domain 3: Social Development

3.1 <u>Social Aspects of Physical Education</u>

- ❑ Candidates for Multiple Subject Teaching Credentials recognize individual differences such as gender, race, culture, ability, or disability.
- ❑ They can describe the developmental appropriateness of cooperation, competition, and responsible social behavior for children of different ages.
- ❑ They can list activities to provide opportunities for enjoyment, self-expression, and communication.

3.2 <u>Cultural and Historical Aspects of Movement Forms</u>

- ❑ Candidates for Multiple Subject Teaching Credentials understand the significance of cultural and historical influences on games, sports, dances, and other physical activities.

Sample Questions and Explanations for the Multiple-Choice Section

Each of the following examples represents an area tested on the Physical Education multiple-choice segment. An analysis follows each question.

Domain 1: Movement Skills and Movement Knowledge

1.1 Basic Movement Skills

1. Which locomotor transport skill is described in the following example?

   The balance is on one foot; the body is then thrust forward into space, with the individual landing on the same foot as the take-off foot.

   A. Hop
   B. Skip
   C. Gallop
   D. Jump

The correct answer is A. Visualize the locomotor movement being described. The hop is the only choice listed that uses only one foot. Hopping is a basic structured locomotor movement. In hopping, both the body lean and the position of the hands help balance the movement of landing on one foot. Skipping (B) is a series of step-hops done with alternate feet.

2. A second-grade physical education activity involves throwing a beanbag through a target placed 15 feet from the student. The performance objective of this activity most likely emphasizes:

   A. gross-motor coordination.
   B. object-handling skills.
   C. cross-lateral throwing movement.
   D. static balance.

The correct answer is C. Visualize a student performing this skill. You should eliminate static balance (D) because the term implies a stationary activity. While object-handling skills (B) are necessary for this activity, they would not be emphasized. (Juggling is a good example of object-handling skills.) The emphasis in this activity is on throwing. One of the performance objectives involved in practicing with a beanbag is to develop cross-lateral coordination and throwing for accuracy. In cross-lateral throwing, the student steps forward with the foot opposite the throwing hand, transferring weight and increasing strength and distance. Gross-motor activities (A) involve the whole body (running, jumping, etc.).

3. Which of the following examples best describes a structured movement activity?

   A. Rolling a ball around a room, alternating the pace you choose to traverse the room
   B. Crawling over and under a series of poles supported by cones
   C. Throwing a ball with your right hand while stepping forward with your left foot
   D. Demonstrating how many different ways you can imitate flight

The correct answer is C. A structured movement incorporates specific, quantifiable skills. Therefore, structured skills impose limitations on the activity being performed. Since the activity can be quantified, it can be judged as to its "correctness." Examples of unstructured activities—choices A, B, and D—allow the individual to make fundamental decisions that determine the outcome of the activity.

4. Which of the following is the correct order from simplest to most complex in an elementary tumbling program?

   A. Balance stunts, individual stunts, animal movements, inverted balance
   B. Animal movements, balance stunts, inverted balance, individual stunts
   C. Animal movements, inverted balance, balance stunts, individual stunts
   D. Inverted balance, animal movements, individual stunts, balance stunts

The correct answer is B. Animal movements are the most simplistic and easiest to accomplish in an elementary tumbling program. Knowing this will help you to narrow your answer to choice B or C. The next step is to look at the next item in the sequence. Balance stunts (B) require slightly more technical accomplishments, followed by inverted balance. Individual stunts are the most difficult activity.

5. Which of the following physical activities does *not* utilize the locomotor walking pattern as a requirement of the activity?

   A. The approach step in bowling
   B. Race walking
   C. Basic square dance step
   D. Slide step

The correct answer is D. After reading the question, you should have focused on key phrases, "does not utilize" and "locomotor walking." Since locomotor skills are used to move the body from one place to another, you are looking for an answer that *does not* accomplish this task. Locomotor skills could include walking, running, galloping, skipping, and leaping. An excellent example of a simple locomotor skill is walking. When walking, the feet move alternately, with one foot always in contact with the ground. The approach step in bowling (A) is a walking motion. In race walking (B), your heel must always be in contact with the ground. The basic square dance step is a walking motion (C). However, the slide step (D), is always done to the side. The leading foot steps to the side and the other foot follows quickly. In slide stepping, the same foot always leads, whereas in locomotor, feet alternate positions.

6. Which of the following most accurately describes the proper follow-through body motion when a third-grader throws a ball?

   A. The feet must remain stationary in preparation for the throw.
   B. As the trunk rotates, weight is completely shifted to the foot opposite the throwing side of the body.
   C. In the initial throwing motion, the person throwing steps forward with the foot that is on the same side as the throwing arm.
   D. Weight is shifted from the front to the back foot.

The correct answer is B. The concept of applied force is fundamental in developing the efficient body mechanics used when throwing. In the mature stage of throwing a ball (usually developed by the age of seven), weight is shifted from the back foot to the front foot as the ball is being released. Weight transfer is essential in throwing, batting, and striking skills. A child who throws primarily with the arm (A) will not be able to generate the maximum force for power or distance. Shifting the weight from the front to the back foot (D) is associated with a pitcher's rocking motion as he or she prepares to throw a ball.

7. A kindergarten introductory physical education lesson includes the following activity: The teacher instructs students to walk forward for eight counts using high steps, and walk backwards for eight counts using low steps.

   The primary purpose of this activity is to reinforce:

   A. body imaging.
   B. balance.
   C. rhythmic movement.
   D. hand-eye coordination.

The correct answer is C. An important goal of a primary physical education program is to develop skill progressions that involve rhythmic activities. Rhythmic activities in kindergarten should include fundamental rhythms, creative rhythms, folk dance, and musical games. Fundamental rhythms are associated with movement activities that children are already familiar with (walking, running, and jumping). Practicing a walking movement pattern allows for the introduction of rhythmic activities (walking forward with high steps). A child walking on a balance beam is an example of a balance activity, Choice B. A child making animal shapes is an example of body imaging, Choice A. A child hitting a balloon with his or her hand while the balloon is still in the air is an example of a hand-eye coordination activity, Choice D.

1.2 <u>Exercise Physiology: Health and Physical Fitness</u>

8. Which of the following is *not* a measurable element of health-related fitness?

    A. Cardio-respiratory endurance
    B. Body composition
    C. Coordination
    D. Musculoskeletal fitness

The correct answer is C. The question can be answered through the process of elimination. Before looking at the answer choices, you could have focused on key words "not," "measurable," and "health-related" in the question. This helps you to eliminate any answer choice that is health related. Health-related fitness is associated with disease and illness prevention by the maintenance of a healthy lifestyle. As a physical education term, health-related fitness is not directly related to sports skills or fitness abilities such as dribbling a basketball or catching a football. Notice that sports-related (not health-related) fitness emphasizes skills such as coordination (C). The elements of health-related fitness can be evaluated and measured—(A) by calculating your target heart rate; (B) by measuring the proportion of body fat to lean body mass; and (D) by calculating the amount of time a muscle or muscle group can exert force prior to fatigue.

9. Which of the following is the correct formula to calculate your target heart rate for aerobic activity?

    A. The number 220 minus your age multiplied by 0.70 equals the target heart rate.
    B. The number 200 plus your age multiplied by 0.50 equals the target heart rate.
    C. Your weight minus your age multiplied by 1.0 equals the target heart rate.
    D. Your pulse rate added to your weight divided by 2 equals the target heart rate.

The correct answer is A. When considering health-related fitness, the target heart rate is generally set at 70 percent of an individual's maximum heart capacity. The purpose of reaching and maintaining a target heart rate is to reach a level at which the aerobic training will most benefit the cardiovascular system. The formula is derived at by taking the number 220 (which represents the maximum heart rate for an excellently trained, young individual), subtracting your age, and taking seventy percent of the figure as your target heart rate for aerobic activities. Maintaining the target heart rate (in health-related fitness) is achieved through long-duration and low-intensity activities.

10. Which of the following is *not* a true statement regarding isometric exercises?

    A. Isometric exercises are useful for building strength.
    B. Isometric exercises involve a held contraction against an immovable base.
    C. Isometric exercises can be performed in virtually any location and with little, if any, danger of injury.
    D. Isometric exercises are considered comprehensive because several muscle groups can be strengthened simultaneously.

The correct answer is D. The value of isometric exercises is in producing strength in a relatively short period of time (A). Isometric exercises "isolate" specific muscle groups, and are *not* considered comprehensive because they are designed to work only one muscle group at a time. During isometric exercises, it is common not to see visible movement since it is a static, strength movement. In isometrics, a muscle group often contracts against an immovable object (B). *Isotonic* exercises usually involve the use of weights or heavy calisthenics.

310

11. Improper posture can be the result of a weakness in the abdominal wall as well as in the musculature of the upper back and neck. Identifying and correcting improper posture is a goal of all elementary physical education programs. Of the following, what is the best evidence that a lateral deviation in posture exists?

    A. The back curves slightly.
    B. The pelvis is noticeably tilted forward.
    C. One shoulder is higher than the other.
    D. The body is symmetrical in relation to the spinal column.

The correct answer is C. A lateral deviation in posture indicates that the spinal column is asymmetrical. The spinal column often appears to resemble an S-curve, with one shoulder higher than the other. Choice B is an indicator of poor posture but does not signify a lateral deviation. The degree of the forward/backward plane of the body can also indicate improper posture.

12. A Fitnessgram is a complete exercise and fitness program for elementary students. The assessment portion of the Fitnessgram tests aerobic capacity, body composition, and muscular fitness. The benefits of utilizing a Fitnessgram report card in an elementary physical education program would include all of the following *except:*

    A. providing group exercise recommendations based on assessment results.
    B. indicating current and past test performance.
    C. calculating body fat by using a body mass index.
    D. evaluating performance based on criterion-referenced health standards.

The correct answer is A. A Fitnessgram assessment measures aerobic capacity, body composition, and muscle fitness (strength, endurance, and flexibility). These three components of physical fitness are identified with general health and fitness. In a Fitnessgram, aerobic capacity is measured by the one-mile run/walk; body composition is measured both by percent fat (calculated from triceps and calf skin-folds) and body mass index (calculated from height and weight); and muscular fitness is measured by using curl-ups to measure abdominal strength, push-ups to measure upper-body strength, trunk lifts to measure trunk extensor strength, and shoulder stretches to measure flexibility. The Fitnessgram report card is highly personalized and is designed to provide students, teachers, and parents with a report of an individual child's fitness test results. Criterion-referenced standards do not compare one student to another. Student scores are reported based on standards that are based on levels of fitness.

13. Many exercises are considered reasonably safe, but can be potentially harmful when executed incorrectly. Which one of the following exercises is considered the safest to perform?

    A. Neck-circling exercises for relaxation of the neck muscles
    B. Hands-behind-the-head sit-ups to improve abdominal strength
    C. Deep-knee-bend exercises to strengthen the knee and hip extensors
    D. Curl-ups to develop the upper abdominal muscles

The correct answer is D. The primary reasons why individuals exercise are for health and physical fitness. Major benefits of exercise include improved cardiovascular health, greater lean body mass, improved strength and muscular endurance, and reduced risk of disease. However, many exercises are potentially dangerous. Neck-circling exercises can hyperextend the neck and should be avoided; hands-behind-the-head sit-ups can pull the head and neck into hyperextension; deep-knee-bend exercises can stretch ligaments and damage cartilage. Curl-ups or crunches are reasonably safe exercises used to develop abdominal strength and prevent pulling on the neck.

14. If a third-grade student cannot sustain the locomotor movement of skipping for a distance of fifty feet, one of the best methods to improve this skill is to:

    A. require the student to practice the skill until it is mastered.
    B. isolate the student from the class so that, when practicing skipping, the child's self-esteem will not suffer.
    C. offer a reward to the student for any attempts to improve on skipping skills.
    D. individualize the instruction by breaking down the pattern and reinforcing the components.

The correct answer is D. Breaking down an activity into its component parts facilitates learning. Individualized instruction provides the maximum opportunity to improve on the locomotor skill of skipping. Choice B could actually reinforce negative self-image by isolating the student from the class.

1.3 Movement Forms: Content Areas

15. Which of the following is a nontraditional game that can be safely taught in an elementary physical education program?

    A. Roller skating
    B. Dodge ball
    C. Frisbee golf
    D. Skateboarding

The correct answer is C. Nontraditional sports are those that are *not* generally considered to be in the mainstream of activities played by students. However, nontraditional sports can be incorporated into a comprehensive physical education program. Examples of nontraditional sports include inline skating, roller hockey, ping pong, biking, and fishing. Traditional sports include swimming, football, volleyball, soccer, and baseball. The key to this question is recognizing a safe nontraditional sports activity. Dodge ball, roller skating, and skateboarding are frowned on by physical educators because of the inherent safety issues (A, B, D). Frisbee golf is a safe, nontraditional sport that encourages cooperation and teamwork.

16. In planning a physical education activity for an elementary school, which of the following activities might present the most probable religious objection to the activity?

    A. Teaching a folk dance as part of a comprehensive dance and fitness activity
    B. Mandating stretching exercises before starting a vigorous activity
    C. Allowing boys and girls to participate in co-educational tennis
    D. Introducing co-educational aerobic and anaerobic fitness activities in grade 5

The correct answer is A. Of the choices given, teaching dance involves the greatest potential for cultural or religious objections to the activity. Most primary grade dance activities involve touching the dance partner (holding hands, swing steps, etc.). Although dance is a required component of most comprehensive physical education programs and can be introduced at the kindergarten level with folk dancing, dance participation could raise potential religious objections. The physical education teacher must be cognizant of cultural, religious, gender, ability, or disability issues when planning activities.

17. What would be the primary purpose for a physical education teacher to instruct her third-grade students to point to the scapula, patella, and Achilles tendon while performing a stretching exercise?

    A. To conceptualize the fitness aspects of exercise
    B. To connect physical skills with interdisciplinary knowledge
    C. To make the activity fun and challenging
    D. To meet the requirements of Title IX of the Educational Amendments Act passed by Congress

The correct answer is B. The California Physical Education State Framework emphasizes an integrated, multidisciplinary curriculum. An effective physical education program is interdisciplinary. For example, physical and biological sciences provide information on the biomechanics of body movement. Stretching exercises provide an excellent opportunity to incorporate an interdisciplinary approach to physical education. Students can quickly learn the proper location and name for the bone and muscle groups by pointing to them while performing exercises. Since stretching is done on a regular basis, science concepts can be reinforced regularly.

Domain 2: Self-Image and Personal Development

2.1 Physical Growth and Development

18. All children grow and develop at different rates. Which of the following would have the *least* impact on a child's physical body type?

    A. Nutrition
    B. Heredity
    C. Environment
    D. Exercise

The correct answer is C. Heredity, nutrition, and exercise have a direct correlation in a person's physical development. Heredity involves the traits inherited from one's parents (B). Body composition is a measure of nutritional health (A); body composition measures bone and muscle in relation to the amount of fat in the body. Lack of physical exercise can be a severe health risk (D). Although environment is important to growth and development, compared to the other contributing influences environment would have the least impact on body type.

19. Which of the following is the best example of a fine motor skill that would be taught in a comprehensive upper-primary physical education program?

    A. Underhand volleyball serve
    B. Goal kicking in soccer
    C. Catching a fly ball
    D. Putting a spin on a football throw

The correct answer is D. Fine motor skills are defined as small muscle movements that are generally associated with the fingers in coordination with the eyes. Putting a spin or a spiral on a football involves fine motor coordination. The proper way to grip a football is as follows: The laces on the football face upward or skyward; the ball is gripped lightly behind the middle of the ball with the fingers on the laces; the thumb is underneath the ball. Throwing a spiral also involves using the proper mechanics and follow-through.

20. Teachers need to reinforce the reasons why basic nutritional guidelines are important in maintaining a healthy lifestyle. Which of the following is an *incorrect* statement regarding nutritional health for adolescents?

    A. Basic metabolic rate (BMR) determines caloric intake.
    B. Protein should be the principal source of calories in the diet.
    C. Excessive vitamin intake is not beneficial and can be harmful to one's health.
    D. Total fat in the diet should not exceed 30 percent of the total calories consumed.

The correct answer is B. The California State Standards support the value of reinforcing proper nutrition as part of a comprehensive physical education program. Suggested nutritional health goals in a wellness diet include reducing dietary fat intake, increasing complex carbohydrates intake, increasing calcium intake, and decreasing sodium intake. The food pyramid should serve as a guide in determining dietary recommendations. The three sources of calories in the diet are fat, protein, and carbohydrates. For optimal health, carbohydrates, including complex carbohydrates, should make up 55 to 60 percent of a diet. Protein consumption should be approximately 15 to 20 percent of a diet.

21. What is the physical-fitness rationale for testing middle school students with timed, one-minute, bent-knee sit-ups?

    A. To evaluate upper-body muscle strength and endurance
    B. To evaluate static strength through repetitive flexion exercises
    C. To evaluate abdominal-muscle strength and endurance
    D. To evaluate arm and shoulder-girdle muscle strength and endurance

The correct answer is C. The purpose of timed tests is to measure endurance and strength. Bent-knee sit-ups allow instructors to evaluate abdominal strength and lower-back strength. The traditional push-up is used to measure upper-body strength, (A). An example of Choice B might involve a "donkey kick" exercise. Such a hyperextension exercise (repetitive flexion) often causes lower-back problems.

22. A female teenager is considered obese when her body fat (body-mass index) is higher than what percentile of other teens in her same age group and same gender?

    A. 75th percentile
    B. 95th percentile
    C. 85th percentile
    D. 65th percentile

The correct answer is B. Obesity is a widespread nutritional eating disorder in the United States. Statistics show that obesity among children and teens has doubled since the 1980s. According to the Center for Disease Control (CDC), teens are considered obese when their BMI (body-mass index) is higher than 95 percent of the other teens in the same age group and same gender. BMI is the ratio of weight to height squared. Most California schools participate in BMI testing. Remember that "overweight" and "obese" are different concepts. To be diagnosed as overweight means that the BMI is in the 85th to 95th percentile, and to be diagnosed as obese means that the BMI is in the 95th percentile. This means that obese teens are at greater risk for developing serious health problems such as elevated blood pressure, elevated levels of cholesterol, and increased risk of diabetes and cardiovascular disease.

2.2 <u>Self-Image</u>

23. Which of the following best describes an appropriate guideline for planning a physical education activity?

    A. The activities should be nonvigorous to encourage active participation by all students.
    B. Proportional emphasis should be placed on basic movement, rhythmics, stunts and tumbling, and selected sports.
    C. Program goals should emphasize the affective and cognitive domains but de-emphasize the psychomotor domain.
    D. The program should be geared to exposure rather than mastery of a skill.

The correct answer is B. In planning a successful physical education activity, balanced and varied progression is essential. Such a program would incorporate proportional emphasis on basic movement and encourage a broad range of activities. Choice A is incorrect because an effective program should consider a vigorous physical activity in order to promote physical fitness and competency. Choice D is not the best answer choice because mastery of a skill is the expected outcome in any sound educational program (including physical education).

24. Physical education teachers must understand the impact of substance abuse on the physical and emotional well-being of their students. Which of the following is true regarding one of the underlying causes of substance abuse in middle school?

    A. Substance abuse is often an attempt to compensate for being physically inactive.
    B. Substance abuse is a greater risk for students who live in a higher socio-economic community.
    C. The use of tabacco in early grades is the leading cause of teen substance abuse.
    D. Substance abuse is often an attempt by teens to cope with stress-related problems.

The correct answer is D. Substance abuse is an ongoing problem in today's middle grades and high schools. In addressing substance abuse at the middle school level, educators should address the root cause of the abuse, and not just focus on the results of substance abuse. Telling students only the reasons why not to do something can often result in the opposite of the intended direction. Substance abuse is often associated with low self-esteem and an inability to deal effectively with stress-related pressures. By emphasizing exercise and relaxation as productive alternatives to stress, the physical education teacher is in a unique position to promote emotional and physical wellness.

---

25. Which statement best describes why a physical education teacher should *not* use the popular expression "thin is in" in her middle school physical fitness program?

    A.   Thin people are generally physically fit and look good.

    B.   Ideal, thin body images are not realistic for many teens.

    C.   Physical exercise is an important component of healthy lifestyle choices.

    D.   Physically fit people can do daily activities with high energy and reduced stress.

The correct answer is B. The media often influence modern lifestyles and attitudes. The overemphasis on a thin, model-like body image is a strong motivator for young adolescents to attempt to achieve such a body type. Exercising and decreasing body fat are important in maintaining a healthy lifestyle. However, being physically fit must be addressed in relation to one's specific body type. Heredity is a prime determiner of body type. "Thin is in" is a potentially dangerous slogan.

Domain 3: Social Development

3.1 Social Aspects of Physical Education

---

26. Which of the following examples is *least* likely to promote a student's ability to explore, succeed, and communicate in the context of physical activity?

    A.   A child decreases a two-lap running time by just two seconds and the student receives a high-five from the teacher.

    B.   A child is given a variety of locomotor and nonlocomotor options to use in a rhythmic activity but only incorporates locomotor activities in his/her routine.

    C.   A child misses a free throw but is applauded for proper form.

    D.   A child uses the game "rock-paper-scissors" as an emergency plan to determine who goes first in a sports activity.

The correct answer is B. A component of the social aspects of physical education is to promote risk-taking in a supportive and safe environment. Experimenting and exploring will enable students to try different solutions, evaluate them, and make appropriate choices. A positive self-image is best developed when activities are designed to nurture progressive successes. In a physical education environment, it is essential not to allow put-downs, putting people on the spot, or stereotyping individuals. In a safe, risk-taking environment, given a variety of options, a student could explore by incorporating both locomotor and nonlocomotor (twisting, bending, and stretching) activities in the routine.

---

27. Based on the California State Framework, at what grade level are competitive games appropriately introduced?

    A.   Grade 2

    B.   Grade 4

    C.   Grade 6

    D.   Grade 8

The correct answer is D. The question deals with competitive games and not the concept of competition. According to the California State Standards, competitive games should not be initiated before the eighth grade. In earlier grades, the emphasis should be on personal growth, lead-up games, heath and sports-related fitness, and healthy lifestyle choices, without introducing an organized level of competitive game activities.

---

28. An important goal of elementary physical education programs is to demonstrate cooperative skills during structured group physical activity. Which of the following strategies is likely to be most effective in forming fifth-grade groups or teams?

    A. Student "captains" select team members, one student at a time.
    B. Teams are chosen based on a system of alternating gender selection.
    C. Poorly skilled students act as team captains in choosing team members.
    D. Teams are chosen by the instructor based on a child's abilities.

The correct answer is D. Physical education teachers develop instructional strategies to promote acceptance of individual strengths and differences. When students are empowered to choose teams, team members are often chosen based on superior athletic ability. Choice A, publicly selecting team members, often exposes lower-skilled students to ridicule. Choice B, forming teams on the basis of gender, can pit boys against girls. Choice C, allowing a poorly skilled individual to act as team captain, only provides a short-term self-esteem benefit. The most appropriate strategy in choosing equitable teams is for the teacher to choose teams based on the teacher's knowledge of student skills. Forming teams in such a manner preserves the self-respect of every child.

3.2 Cultural and Historical Aspects of Movement Forms

---

29. Which of the following is a sport that developed in the United States?

    A. Tennis
    B. Marathon running
    C. Volleyball
    D. Lawn bowling

The correct answer is C. Tennis, marathon running, and lawn bowling (A, B, D) are all sports activities that developed in Western Europe and were later incorporated into the American physical education and recreational field. Volleyball, basketball, American-style football, and snowboarding are sports that developed in the United States and spread to other countries.

---

30. Sports are a part of the American social-historical perspective and reflect the social needs of a culture. In the early twentieth century, physical education in the United States moved away from which of the following programs?

    A. Gymnastics and calisthenics
    B. Baseball and basketball
    C. Stretching and exercising
    D. Tennis and swimming

The correct answer is A. In the nineteenth century, gymnastics and calisthenics dominated physical education programs. Formal programs were brought over from Europe and were first introduced in colleges and then in public elementary and high schools. The focus was on the development of the body and not on recreational activities. In the early twentieth century, a shift in perspective began. The influence of John Dewey on the development of modern physical education programs was significant. Dewey stressed the promotion of health and the acquiring of lifetime recreational skills. Therefore, sports and games became a focus of the new physical educational curriculum. A strong focus on cooperative team sports and sportsmanship was stressed.

31. In a well-designed elementary physical education program, at what grade level should rhythmic activities be introduced?

    A. Kindergarten
    B. First grade
    C. Second grade
    D. Third grade

The correct answer is A. Rhythmic activities should be introduced in kindergarten and should represent approximately forty percent of all physical education activities. Rhythmic activities develop gross-motor movements and locomotor patterns and also aid in the development of social interaction. Movement expression through rhythmics and dance affords the primary-level child greater expression in interpreting his or her environment. A drum is a typical primary-grade object used to reinforce movement-in-time and rhythmics.

Sample Questions and Explanations for the Short Constructed-Response Questions

Following are representative Physical Education short constructed-response questions. Strategies and a sample response are included with each question.

Domain 1: Movement Skills and Movement Knowledge

> **1.** Complete the exercise that follows.
>
> A beanbag is a fundamental manipulative tool incorporated into many early-primary physical education activities.
>
> Using your knowledge of physical education activities:
>
> - discuss two ways beanbag activities reinforce perceptual-motor abilities at the early-primary grades; and
> - discuss one example of a beanbag activity designed for this grade span.

Strategy

Visualize a beanbag activity (such as throwing and catching). Consider the advantages of using a beanbag and the perceptual-motor abilities involved (such as balance and hand-eye coordination). Consider why manipulatives are used in a physical education program and what the performance-based objectives are likely to be (student demonstration of a skill).

Sample Response

Beanbag activities advance perceptual-motor skills in facilitating improved hand-eye coordination, balance, laterality, sensory perceptions, and proper body imaging. They also promote kinesthetic awareness and sensory functioning in vision, hearing, and touch.

The manipulative aspects of the beanbag are conducive to early primary exploration. Beanbags are flexible and soft and greatly reduce the fear factor in catching objects.

An example of a beanbag activity would be throwing the beanbag over one's head while clapping one's hands before catching the bag. This would improve hand-eye coordination and laterality. In locomotor and nonlocomotor activities, the beanbag could be used for balance—for example, balancing the beanbag on various body parts while the body is in motion.

> **2.** Complete the exercise that follows.
>
> Health-related fitness and skill-related fitness are both essential components of a comprehensive physical education program.
>
> Using your knowledge of physical education health components:
>
> - list two examples of health-related fitness and two examples of skill-related fitness; and
> - discuss how aerobic fitness is related to overall health fitness.

Strategy

Health-related fitness is a priority in physical education programs. It helps ensure that an individual will be able to function effectively in daily tasks. Physical activity is the key to developing health-related fitness. What aspects are essential to good health? Health-related fitness includes cardiovascular fitness, body composition, flexibility, and muscular strength and endurance. Skill-related fitness is associated with performance in sports. What aspects would benefit an athlete? Skill-related fitness includes agility, balance, coordination, power, and speed. Recall what you already know about this topic. For example, aerobic activities involve continuous motion and are related to cardiovascular fitness. Consider what the term *aerobic* means (related to the presence of oxygen). Recall some aerobic activities.

Sample Response

Two examples of health-related fitness are cardiovascular fitness and body composition. Two examples of skill-related fitness are agility and balance.

Health fitness is directly related to preventing and remediating the degenerative aspects of disease. Instituting an aerobic-fitness program of the proper duration, intensity, and frequency can improve overall health fitness. Oxygen-based aerobic activities, such as jogging, cycling, swimming, and low-impact aerobic dancing, are designed to be continuous so as to reach and maintain a target heart rate. Aerobic activities should be performed at least three times a week for 30 minutes or more at a time. The key result of aerobics is improved cardiovascular fitness and increased oxygen intake; other results include a stronger heart muscle, lower heart rate, and reduced blood pressure. Such exercise also improves strength and endurance and decreases body fat.

---

3. Complete the exercise that follows.

A fourth-grade student is preparing to play a co-educational soccer game. Before starting the activity, the instructor decides to review skill-based soccer activities.

Using your knowledge of sequential sports activities:

- discuss why pre-game drills are important; and
- describe three skill-based soccer warm-up drills and the skills being practiced.

Strategy

It is important to differentiate between skill-based warm-up activities and exercise activities (stretching specific muscle groups). What would be the purpose of introducing skill-based warm-up activities? The purpose would be to improve skills, to demonstrate knowledge of game-like situations, to develop cooperative teamwork, and to improve personal skills. Can other sports help in determining the answer? For example, what types of skill-based warm-up drills are used prior to a basketball game? Would you see basketball players practicing free-throw shooting, two-on-one drills, and rebounding drills?

Sample Response

The purpose of introducing skill-based drills would be to simulate game-like conditions during warm-up. For example, drills would be designed to reinforce basic mechanics used in soccer (shooting, kicking, passing, and trapping). The drills would also reinforce team concepts and cooperation. Three skill-based warm-up activities would include one-on-one shooting drills at the goalie, two-on-two parallel-passing drills, and heading-the-ball drills with a partner.

1. In one-on-one shooting drills at the goalie, the player dribbles the ball toward the goal and attempts to score against the goalie. This drill reinforces dribbling with the in-step and outside foot, body control, and shooting off the dribble.
2. In two-on-two parallel-passing drills, two players run forward parallel to each other. The soccer ball is progressively passed from one player to the next. This drill reinforces passing off the dribble and receiving/trapping skills.
3. In heading the ball with a partner or partners, players practice heading the ball at each other. This drill reinforces directional accuracy and heading and passing skills.

> **4.** Complete the exercise that follows.
>
> An upper-primary physical educator shows a fitness video to her class. In a sequence of activities, the following fitness components are demonstrated. A female child completes one traditional pull-up by swinging her body upward with her palms facing toward the body; a male child completes a sit-up by locking his hands around his neck and in a straight-leg fashion, hooking his legs under an object; a female student completes a cool-down stretching activity by progressively bouncing in a toe-touching exercise.
>
> Using your knowledge of physical fitness exercises, what corrections, if any, would you make in technique before students practiced the activities demonstrated in the video?

Strategy

For safety reasons, physical educators need to instruct students in the proper techniques involved in performing various exercises. Since exercise is a fundamental aspect of physical education programs, the candidate should be familiar with concepts associated with safety and exercise. Use personal experience to formulate possible answers to the question. The candidate should recognize that exercises that put additional stress on the back or neck could be potentially dangerous. People who exercise would also understand that a bouncing motion could injure or strain muscles and joints and should be eliminated from any stretching activity. One might recall that stretching involves slowly applying a stretch to a muscle and holding the position for at least twenty-five to thirty seconds.

Sample Response

The physical education instructor should recognize that the three exercises are being done in a potentially harmful manner.

1. The correct pull-up technique always has the palms facing away from the body and a swaying motion is avoided. An inward-facing hand position and a swaying motion aid the person in completing the pull-up and, therefore, do not give a true measure of muscular strength and endurance.

2. To avoid undue stress on the back and the possibility of lower back complications, hooking one's feet under an object or locking one's hands behind the neck should never be incorporated in practicing sit-ups. The correct sit-up technique for upper-primary students would have the hands placed on opposite shoulders with the elbows in contact with the chest and the knees flexed, feet on the floor. Sit-ups performed in a straight-leg fashion can cause the hip flexor muscle to be strained and place undue force on the lumbar vertebrae. Placing one's hands behind the head or neck may result in hyperflexion of the neck and cause damage to the disc.

3. In stretching exercises, the student should never bounce. Stretching exercises are always performed gradually. Ballistic stretching (or strong bouncing) is thought to increase muscle soreness and is more likely to cause injury.

Domain 2: Self-Image and Personal Development

> **5.** Complete the exercise that follows.
>
> A female middle-school student frequently refuses to dress for her physical education class. The teacher is not making much headway in convincing the student that her behavior is inappropriate. The teacher recognizes that this student is overweight and withdrawn.
>
> Using your knowledge of the social aspects of physical education:
>
> - identify three causes that could be linked to the student's failure to dress for physical education; and
> - discuss two strategies that the instructor can use to effect a positive change in the girl's attitude toward dressing for physical education.

Strategy

Physical education programs should provide an environment for effective social living. Students at the middle-school level often are going through rapid physical changes associated with hormones and growth spurts. This tends to make children clumsy and self-conscious. Overweight children often suffer ridicule, taunting, and bullying. The result is often a student who refuses to dress for physical education. What are the underlying factors associated with being overweight? Are the factors related to poor nutrition? Stress? It is important for children to understand that they are not alone in addressing emotional issues.

Sample Response

Three causes associated with repeated refusal to dress for middle-school physical education are fear of embarrassment, ridicule by one's peers, and low self-esteem.

A student who is withdrawn and overweight is potentially at risk both physically and emotionally. A primary goal for physical education is to improve self-esteem. Not dressing for physical education can underline serious emotional and esteem issues. Strategies to encourage overweight individuals to dress for the class would include such things as conferencing with the student to determine the cause of the problem; once determined, the instructor should involve the student directly in the activity. Another strategy would be suggesting weight-loss programs, and showing the student how physical education can promote healthy lifestyle choices.

Domain 3: Social Development

> 6. Complete the exercise that follows.
>
> A child in your class has mild cerebral palsy. You are teaching a dance unit and the majority of students can participate effectively in this cooperative sports environment.
>
> Using your knowledge of integrating students with physical disabilities into your program:
>
> - discuss two ways to include the child with mild cerebral palsy in a line dance activity; and
> - discuss how you would realistically grade this student so that his/her self esteem is not diminished.

Strategy

It is important to recognize that federal and state law mandates that all students shall be mainstreamed into the least restrictive environment, regardless of one's disability. This can be quite challenging when designing a physical education activity. In this question, knowledge of physical disabilities would determine that a person with mild cerebral palsy would have limited movement and coordination skills. However, one should always look at the total person in providing effective instruction for all students. How would you modify the program and accommodate the student? You might change the length of the activity or provide alternative dance steps. How do you assess a student with disabilities? What criteria should be used?

Sample Response

There are two ways to include this child in line dance activities. The first way would be to determine the limits of the student's abilities so that a realistic program can be developed. By doing this, the child can participate in line dancing rather than be singled out by performing a separate dance routine. A second method would be to modify the line dance to include his/her disabilities. This can be accomplished by using a side-to-side step instead of a more difficult cross-over step. This student can more easily accomplish step-together movements. Also, a jump in place could be incorporated rather than a step-back and turn movement.

Assessing a student with disabilities must be realistic. The assessment tools should recognize the student's effort in performing agreed-on tasks and completing the social behaviors expected of the group. The student should be responsible to the level of the modifications and accommodations agreed upon. Assessment could also include cooperation in the class activities and on-task behavior.

Review of Domains

The healthy, physically active child is more likely to be academically motivated, alert, and successful.

Government Web Sites on Physical Education, Fitness, and Nutrition

- ❏ **Physical Education Model Content Standards for California Public Schools**
  - ❏ www.cde.ca.gov (Click "Curriculum & Instruction" and "Physical Education")
- ❏ **President's Council on Physical Fitness and Sports**
  - ❏ www.fitness.gov
  - ❏ www.presidentschallenge.org
- ❏ **CDC Division of Adolescent and School Health**
  - ❏ www.cdc.gov/HealthyYouth/

Helping children develop healthy, active lifestyles can help cultivate and reinforce a lifetime of health and fitness. The Physical Education section of the CSET: Multiple Subjects understands the importance of helping children create healthy lifestyles and tests your knowledge, ability, and understanding of movement concepts, physiology of movement, and the social components of age-related, appropriate physical education activities, while meeting the diverse needs of a variety of abilities and interests in children. In order for students to achieve competency, most of the physical education activities presented in this section are divided by grade-level ability.

1. Grades kindergarten through two
2. Grades three through five
3. Grades six through nine

CSET candidates understand the key factors in the development, analysis, and assessment of basic motor skills. They understand how to structure lessons to promote maximum participation, inclusion, and engagement in a variety of traditional and nontraditional games, sports, dances, and other physical activities. Candidates select lessons and activities based on factors such as the developmental levels of students and individual differences. They can design appropriate exercise programs and activities based on physical fitness concepts and applications that encourage physically active lifestyles. They analyze the impact of factors such as exercise, relaxation, nutrition, stress, and substance abuse on physical health and well-being and can design activities to provide opportunities for enjoyment, self-expression, and communication. Candidates create cooperative and competitive movement activities that require personal and social responsibility. They understand the significance of cultural and historical influences on games, sports, dances, and other physical activities.

DOMAIN 1: MOVEMENT SKILLS AND MOVEMENT KNOWLEDGE

1.1 Basic Movement Skills	❏ Identify movement concepts including body awareness, space awareness, and movement exploration. ❏ List locomotor skills such as skipping, nonlocomotor skills such as static balancing, and object manipulation such as catching. ❏ Recognize basic concepts of biomechanics that affect movement, such as how the body moves and how such movement is influenced by gravity, friction, and the laws of motion. ❏ Describe critical elements of basic movement skills, such as stepping in opposition when throwing and/or following through when kicking a ball.

1.2 Exercise Physiology: Health and Fitness	❏ Identify health and fitness benefits and associated risks that support a physically active lifestyle, related to safety and medical factors (e.g., asthma and diabetes). ❏ Recognize exercise principles, such as frequency, intensity, and time, to select activities that promote physical fitness. ❏ Describe physical fitness components, such as flexibility, muscular strength and endurance, cardio-respiratory endurance, and body composition, which are included in comprehensive personal fitness development programs.
1.3 Movement Forms: Content Areas	❏ Know a variety of traditional and nontraditional games, sports, dances, and other physical activities. ❏ Cite basic rules and social etiquette for physical activities. ❏ Select activities because of their potential to include all students, regardless of gender, race, culture, religion, abilities, or disabilities.

Domain 1: Movement Skills and Movement Knowledge

1.1 Basic Movement Skills

Body Awareness

The sense of being aware of movement in different parts of the body is an important aspect in the cognitive, social, and physical development of children. Body awareness is called *proprioception,* which is how the body senses the parts of itself (e.g., hands, feet, legs, and arms). Since awareness involves an autonomous sense of the body in relation to personal space, shifting weight, and changing body movements, it is important for teachers to include motor activities that help strengthen perceptual body awareness. The patterns and themes of body awareness help children maintain a sense of personal boundaries, develop patterns of movement through space, understand the concept of shape, and sustain a sense of balance. Exercises that help encourage children to become aware of their physical body include:

Shape	Instruction in concepts of how the body can form different shapes (e.g., "allow your body to form different shapes, wide or tall"; "stand like a pole"; etc.).
Balance	Instruction in concepts of balance in the body (e.g., "balance on one foot; balance on your hands while stretching your body"; "form a tripod with your body," etc.).
Quality	Instruction in the concepts of speed, contrast, force, and relaxation (e.g., "how fast or how slow can you move?"; "tense one part of your body and then relax another part of your body"; etc.).
Space	Instruction in concepts of sharing space with others (e.g., "run in a zigzag fashion without bumping into others"; "point to a spot and see if you can run straight toward it, touch it, and run back without touching someone else"; "do warm-up exercises one arm's length apart"; etc.).
Exploring	Instruction in the concepts of moving over, under, around, and through, and leading with certain body parts (e.g., "make a bridge with a partner and then have a third person go under the bridge"; "lead with your head when walking"; etc.).

Basic movement skills are fundamental to physical education activities in elementary school. The concepts of body awareness as students perform locomotor, nonlocomotor, and manipulative skills (discussed next) help create safe and enjoyable activities in the classroom. In the early grades, K–2, teachers help students become aware of space, basic movement, effort, and cooperative activities. In the upper-elementary and middle grades, 3–9, the fundamental movement skills developed earlier are applied as activity-specific motor skills in a wide variety of settings. The classroom objectives are to increase competency in building motor control, motor skills, and movement patterns already established and refined in earlier grades.

Locomotor Skills

Locomotor skills are basic movement skills that are performed in different directions and at different speeds. They are dynamic movements that propel the body upward, forward, or backward. These movements are the foundation of gross motor coordination, involving large and small muscle movements. By the end of the second grade, students are expected to make smooth transitions between sequential locomotor skills; in the upper grades, they are expected to demonstrate more complex skills combining locomotor and manipulation skills (e.g., dribbling a basketball). There are many different combinations of movement patterns that can describe the type of locomotor skills: walking, running, jumping, skipping, leaping, galloping, and sliding. The CSET short constructed-response questions may ask you to describe and give examples of how to perform basic locomotor movements. The following table provides a brief description of some locomotor skills along with basic instructional techniques.

LOCOMOTOR SKILLS	
Jumping	❑ Jumping creates activity-specific muscle strength and agility. ❑ Jumping requires the body to leap with both feet and to land with both feet. Arms can be used to create an upward momentum and then to create a downward motion that helps balance the landing. Knees bend at the landing to act as shock absorbers. The order of impact is usually the balls of the feet followed by the heels. Ask children to "jump and touch the ceiling." ❑ Jumping incorporated into primary-grade activities helps children create patterns (e.g., jumping like a kangaroo, a frog, and a rabbit). Jumping incorporated into upper-level grades can be used in combination with sports and athletic activities (e.g., warm-up activities, gymnastics, basketball, etc.).
Skipping	❑ Skipping is a series of step-hops completed with alternate feet. ❑ Primary school children love to skip. To help them learn to skip, have them take a step and a small hop on the same foot and then ask them to shift to the other foot. Set a goal of smoothness and rhythm, rather than speed and distance.
Galloping	❑ Galloping is a forward directional movement. As the lead foot steps forward, the back foot steps up to meet the lead foot. ❑ Galloping movements can be taught by having the class hold hands and slide in a circle to a rhythmic beat. Shift this movement into having the children face the direction of the movement while continuing to slide. Alternate between large and small gallops.
Sliding	❑ Sliding is accomplished by movement on one side of the body. It is a one-count movement; as the leading foot steps to the side, the other foot quickly follows. ❑ Sliding is done on the balls of the feet while shifting weight from the leading foot to the trailing foot. ❑ Teachers should have the children change direction so both sides of the body can practice. ❑ Sliding should be performed in a smooth and controlled manner, without bouncing.

Nonlocomotor Skills

Nonlocomotor skills are often referred to as static movements because they are passive movements performed while standing in place. Movements are executed by twisting, turning in place, bending, swaying while moving toward or away from the body center, raising or lowering parts of the body, or stretching in place. These movements are important skills that lead to effective body management such as body control, flexibility, and balance. The range of movement is around the body's joints and surrounding muscles, and these movements are often used in activity warm-up exercises. The CSET short constructed-response questions may ask you to describe and give examples of how to perform basic nonlocomotor movements. The table that follows provides a brief description of some nonlocomotor skills along with basic instructional suggestions.

NONLOCOMOTOR SKILLS	
Stretching	❑ Stretching is perhaps the most valuable of all nonlocomotor movements. Its movement carries body parts away from the body's center core and moves joints and muscles through a range of movements. ❑ All physical education activities should begin with a stretching warm-up exercise. ❑ Teachers should understand that some discomfort is normal, but stretching is necessary for maintaining and increasing flexibility. ❑ Ask children to stretch as far as is comfortably possible while keeping their movement smooth.
Twisting	❑ Twisting is the rotation of a body part around its own long axis, such as turning the head on its neck or wrapping the arms around the body. ❑ Twisting is different from turning in that twisting involves movement around a body part, and the focal point of turning is on the space in which the body is moving. ❑ Twisting instruction should include asking children to twist as fully as is comfortably possible, and then to twist in the opposite direction while holding the supporting body parts steady.
Pushing	❑ Pushing is a controlled, forceful action performed against an object. It moves the body away from the object while applying force. ❑ Pushing should exert force with steady, even, and controlled effort. The student accomplishes this action by broadening and supporting the base of the body while placing the body in a forward stride position. ❑ The line of force is directed toward a specific target. ❑ Teachers should instruct students to maintain a reasonable alignment in their back as the body builds up force for the push.

Object Manipulation Skills

Object manipulation skills are complex motor patterns that are basic to specialized sports and are performed with some kind of object (e.g., a ball or bat). Object manipulation requires hand-eye or foot-eye coordination, and thus requires developmentally appropriate gross and fine motor abilities. If children do not learn manipulation skills, they sometimes have difficulty developing mature patterns of movement (e.g., throwing or catching). Object manipulation is particularly valuable in hand-eye coordination as children learn to track objects in space. Early manipulative skills help form the foundation for many later sports activities. Primary-grade children can begin with throwing beanbags or large rubber balls, preparing them for upper-grade activities such as baseball or water polo. When preparing activities using object manipulation, it's important to identify the appropriate age-related physical development of the child before developing physical activities. Object manipulation skills include throwing, catching, kicking, and striking. The CSET short constructed-response questions may ask you to describe and give examples of how to perform basic object manipulation movements. The following table provides a brief description of some object manipulation movements along with basic instructional suggestions.

OBJECT MANIPULATION SKILLS	
Throwing	❑ Throwing requires an object to be propelled into space. Movement force originates from flexing the hip and moving the shoulder forward while extending the elbow. With the coordinated body movement, the object accelerates into space with greater speed and velocity. ❑ Primary school children need to proceed through preliminary stages of tossing (e.g., beanbags, etc.) before entering the stages of throwing a ball with accuracy. In time and with practice, most children will develop a throwing skill pattern during grades three to five. ❑ Teachers should allow children to practice throwing a variety of objects that have varying weight and size. This helps the child to understand how different objects can travel at different velocities.
Catching	❑ Catching involves using the hands to stop and control a moving object. During the early stages of learning, it is more difficult for children to learn to catch than to throw because tracking the object requires mature hand-eye coordination. ❑ Children often fear being hit by the object, so early instruction can begin with beach balls, balloons, and fleece balls. ❑ As children develop gross and fine motor abilities, instruction should include reducing the size of the object to catch. This helps children develop perceptual abilities. ❑ Instruction should include practice in catching balls that bounce up from the floor to teach rebound angles.

continued

Kicking	❑ Kicking is a striking action performed by the feet.
	❑ Teachers should know several types of kicking: (1) Punt kicking is described as the ball being dropped from the hands and kicked before it touches the ground; (2) place kicking is described as placing the ball on the ground and kicking it from the stationary position; and (3) soccer kicking is a form of kicking that requires an extension of the hip to increase the range of motion.
	❑ Instruction should include reducing the size of the projectile object as skill levels develop.
Striking	❑ Striking takes place when an object is hit with an implement such as a bat, a racket, or the hand.
	❑ Striking involves movement of the body to create the force necessary for the maximum speed of the object.
	❑ Instruction should include practice on stationary objects in primary grades before children can progress to moving objects. A good example of a stationary object is "T-ball," in which the ball is placed on a "T" stand and is struck.

Basic Concepts of Biomechanics

Understanding the physiological responses in the human body helps teachers to apply the laws of biomechanics and physics to athletic performance. CSET candidates should be able to apply the principles of physics to physical fitness as they relate to motion, gravity, and friction. Biomechanics contributes to the explanation and prediction of the mechanical characteristics of movement, exercise, play, and sports activities.

Motion: Newton's laws of motion apply to all movement. In biomechanics, the awareness of body movements can be associated with force, acceleration, and velocity as they relate to maximum effort. The force of the energy in the body causes change in physical motion.

Newton's first law states that when an object is in motion, it will remain in motion until there is an outside force that acts upon it. For example, when a basketball is thrown toward a basket, there can be a few outcomes. If the ball is thrown using very little strength, the effects of gravity (an outside force) will overcome the velocity of the ball and it will fall short of the basket. If the ball is thrown with too much strength, the ball will overcome the effects of gravity and hit the back board (another outside source) and change its direction.

Newton's second law states the relationship between an object's mass, acceleration, and applied force. Continuity of movement is responsible for producing the maximum force and velocity. To illustrate this concept of force, teachers can have upper-grade students sit in a chair while trying to throw a basketball into a hoop. Students should recognize their inability to follow through with motion. They should then ask the students to throw the basketball when standing up. The force of the entire body in motion should produce an accelerated velocity that results in a force-producing movement to achieve the desired result of the ball reaching the basketball hoop.

Newton's third law states that if one object exerts a force on a second object, the second object exerts an equal force on the first object but in the opposite direction. For every action, there is an equal and opposite reaction. For example, when a baseball player uses a bat to hit a pitched ball, the force with which the bat hits the ball (and angle) causes the ball to move in an equal and opposite force and direction.

Gravity: The center of the human body can be associated with the "center of gravity." It is the point around which the mass of the body is equally distributed. The body has a balanced base of support and is affected by height, position, and changing movements. During movement and exercise activities, the body adjusts to maintain its stability.

Friction: Friction can be defined as the resistance of motion of two moving objects. For example, when children play kick ball on grass, the ball may move more slowly than when they play kick ball on asphalt. There is more resistance because of the friction of the coarse, grassy surface.

Elements of Movement

The elements of movement help teachers create dynamic and interesting fitness activities. A few examples of the movement elements of space, shape, time, force, flow, and rhythm are provided in the dance section of the Visual and Performing Arts review. When planning an activity, remember to include a logical progression of motor skills based on the increasing or decreasing degree of difficulty, give feedback and reinforcement to provide a sound basis for future activities, and include the ability to transfer previous learning of movement techniques to new skill areas.

1.2 Exercise Physiology: Health and Physical Fitness

Physical fitness is the ability to carry out tasks with vigor and alertness. It is a form of body conditioning that is part of a child's normal growth and development. Purposeful exercise programs and a sound diet counteract heart disease and related circulatory problems. Establishing health and physical fitness programs in elementary schools is a well-recognized discipline for improving the ability to complete tasks that require endurance, strength, and flexibility.

When assessing the guidelines for fitness activities, teachers should be aware that the natural patterns of movement in children and adolescents are different from those of adults. For example, during recess, children use basic aerobic and bone-strengthening activities, such as running, hopping, skipping, and jumping, to develop movement patterns and skills. They alternate brief periods of moderate and vigorous physical activity with brief periods of rest. Any episode of moderate or vigorous physical activity, however brief, counts toward the daily recommendation of 60 minutes per day. Children also commonly increase muscle strength through unstructured activities that involve lifting or moving their body weight or working against resistance. Children don't usually follow or need formal muscle-strengthening programs, such as lifting weights.

SKELETAL AND MUSCULAR PHYSIOLOGY: BASIC TERMS	
Skeletal Basic Terms	**cranium:** bones of the head **clavicle:** collar bone **femur:** upper leg bone **humerus:** upper arm bone **patella:** knee cap **scapula:** shoulder blade **sternum:** breast bone **tibia:** inner bone of the lower leg **ulna** and **radius:** lower arm bones
Muscular Basic Terms	**abdominals:** stomach muscles **biceps:** top muscles of the upper arm **deltoids:** shoulder muscles **gastronomies:** calf muscles **gluteus maximus:** buttock muscles **hamstrings:** back thigh muscles **quadriceps:** front muscles of the thigh **triceps:** underneath muscles of the upper arm

Components of Physical Fitness

Fitness objectives in elementary school activity programs should include an understanding of the health-related components of physical fitness. A healthy lifestyle is a priority, and the recognition of fitness components can help teachers design activities that will benefit the physically diverse populations of students. Fitness activities should be individualized and uniquely designed to meet the needs of each child to help ensure that the fitness experience is positive and enjoyable. Aspects of the physiological function of fitness activities are included in the components of fitness listed in the following table:

Muscular Strength	Muscular strength is the amount of force exerted with muscles. Although many activities do not build muscle strength, upper-grade activities will often require muscular strength for certain sports (e.g., baseball, basketball, and tennis). Muscular movements can be isometric with no visible movement (static), or isotonic with signs of movement (dynamic).
Endurance	Endurance is the ability to sustain physical effort for long periods of time. Endurance helps children perform fitness activities without excessive fatigue.
Flexibility	Flexibility is the movement which joints and muscles move through a full range of motion. Being flexible helps the student to retain a full range of movement, prevent injury from fitness activities, and improve posture. These are the reasons that stretching should be an integral part of daily warm-up activities.
Body Composition	Body composition is the proportion of body fat to lean body mass. It is the amount of fat in relation to the percentage of non-fat in the total body mass. It is measured by the thickness of selected skin folds.
Cardio-Respiratory (Aerobic)	An efficient cardio-respiratory system may be the most important component of fitness. Cardio-respiratory endurance is the ability of the heart, blood vessels, and respiratory system to sustain work by delivering oxygen and nutrients to the tissues of the body over a period of time. To develop this endurance, activities must be aerobic. During aerobic activity, there is an integrated functional capacity of the heart and lungs, the vascular system, and the muscles to expend energy as the oxygen in the body is given maximum oxygen uptake. If a child is having difficulty during an aerobic fitness activity, the teacher should stop the activity when the child is out of breath. This is a sign that the aerobic activity is causing the cardio-respiratory system to reach maximum oxygen uptake. To check your heart rate, see the following formulas.

Heart Rate Formulas

Aerobic activity should include a 20-minute activity at your target heart rate.

Calculate your Target Heart Rate (THR)

THR = 220 minus your age multiplied by 70% to 85% (0.70 to 0.85)

Maximum Heart Rate (MHR) = 220 – age

Lower Limit Threshold   70% of your MHR

Upper Limit Threshold   85% of your MHR

Target Heart Rate (THR)   70% to 85% of your MHR (lower and upper threshold)

Resting Heart Rate (RHR)   Heart rate taken while standing still (average of three heart rates taken before getting out of bed in the morning)

To check your heart rate, count the beats for ten seconds (use your index finger, not your thumb). Multiply the number of beats by six to equal your heart rate per minute.

Guidelines for Fitness Development Programs

Physical fitness programs are designed with age- and grade-related abilities in mind. This means that teachers should be sensitive to students' grade level, age, fitness level, and abilities. Since part of an instructional fitness activity is to challenge students to perform at higher levels of progressive skills, teachers should use systematic guidelines before implementing fitness programs. Many different fitness guidelines are available to help in creating fitness activities. The table that follows is an example of a guideline that emphasizes the principles of FITT. This is an acronym for "frequency, intensity, time, and type of activity."

FITT Guidelines		
Frequency	How often does the activity occur?	Frequency is the number of sessions that the activity might take to achieve the desired results.
Intensity	How difficult is the activity level (mild to moderate)?	Intensity gives an indication of how difficult the activity might be. This principle is important to monitor so that instruction can be increased or deceased, depending on the intensity of the activity. Remember to always monitor cardio-respiratory exertion.
Time	How long does it take to perform the activity?	The duration of the activity is dependent on the intensity and type of activity. The minimum of aerobic activity should be 8 to 10 minutes, but the ideal aerobic time should be at least 20 minutes during a 1-hour activity.
Type	What kind of activity is it?	The type of activity describes the mode of activity. Most activities can be adapted to comply with the FITT model, so teachers should focus on activities that will help them achieve their desired instructional goals. All activities should include a warm-up, strength development, aerobic activity, and a cool-down.

Physical fitness includes any activity with bodily movements that produce a contraction of skeletal muscles and increase energy through exercise, sports, dance, and other movement forms. Physical education programs, recesses, intramural sports programs, and athletic programs involve physical activity, but each serves a different purpose. Recess, intramural sports, and athletic programs provide opportunities for student learning but do not constitute standards-based physical education instruction. They are not a substitute for a high-quality physical education program. According to the *Physical Education Framework for California Public Schools*, all physical education instruction should do the following:

- **Establish a Safe Environment.** A safe environment has two components. The first refers to the actual physical environment. This includes equipment safety and that the class size is conducive to providing a safe activity; that communication systems are in place in case of an emergency (located in the main office or health office); that proper instruction exists for students to use equipment; and that there is sufficient supervision at all times. The second component refers to the psychological subjective environment of the students. All activities should ensure that students feel physically, emotionally, and socially safe during the instructional process.

- **Include Class Management.** An effective classroom management system sets the stage for high-quality physical education instruction by providing the time and opportunity for learning to occur. It promotes student engagement and maximizes instructional effectiveness. Effective class management does not just happen; it is carefully and systematically planned.

- **Employ Effective Teaching Behaviors.** "When all is said and done, what matters most for students' learning are the commitments and capabilities of their teachers" (Darling–Hammond, 1997). Successful teachers have high expectations for every student and use effective teaching behaviors to ensure that every student achieves the grade-level or course-level standards. "Effective teaching behaviors" refers to the decisions that teachers make regarding the use of time and their interaction with students. Physical education teachers use research-based, effective teaching behaviors to support student learning. These include the following: planning for every lesson; using time effectively; providing effective practice; providing positive specific or corrective feedback; keeping students engaged in moderate-to-vigorous physical activity at least fifty percent of the instructional time; keeping students engaged in academic learning; improving speed and accuracy; and applying motor learning concepts to instructional practices.

- **Transfer Learning.** The learning of one skill can have a positive or negative effect on the learning of another skill. When the impact is positive, it is called a "positive transfer of learning." When the impact is negative, it is called a "negative transfer of learning." Providing students with information about the ways in which skills are similar helps them positively transfer the appropriate learning from the first learned skill to the second. For example, the overhand movement pattern is used in the overhand volleyball serve, tennis serve, and badminton smash. When learning the tennis serve, after having learned the volleyball serve, students should be alerted to the similarities between the two serves. Differences between skills are brought to the attention of the students to minimize the potential interference of the first skill in the learning of the second skill. For example, at the elementary level, students are alerted to the differences between galloping and skipping at the time when the second skill is taught.

- **Encourage Practice.** Practice can be spaced out over time (distributed practice) or completed in one instructional period (mass practice). Distributed practice generally leads to more effective learning, especially in the early stages. Therefore, students practice a number of different skills during each class period. Practice can involve the entire skill (whole practice), or the skill can be broken down into small units (part practice). For example, the triple jump involves a hop, a skip, and a jump. Whole practice would involve performing the hop, skip, and jump together. Part practice would involve practicing the hop, then practicing the skip, and then practicing the jump.

Sample Classroom Fitness Activity

CSET candidates should be prepared to create and develop an appropriate grade-related physical fitness activity for constructed-response questions. Although there are several approaches to developing a successful classroom activity, it is important to first consider the suggested guidelines mentioned in the previous section. The following example is an illustration of a classroom activity for kindergarten through third grade.

Warm-up exercises involve muscles to be used during the physical activity. Try to isolate muscle groups and be sure to ask students not to overextend or bounce. A fitness activity always begins with a sufficient warm-up activity (e.g., light aerobics, calisthenics, walking, slow jogging, etc.).

Instructional Components provide students with step-by-step instruction as stated in the components of fitness, the FITT model, and the guidelines for developing a lesson.

Physical Activity provides students with a targeted activity (e.g., dribbling a basketball) along with modeling of the activity and verbal cues. In grades K–3 (see the Basic Station Activity example that follows), activities should be noncompetitive, and in grades 4–9, activities should be related to sports. All activities should be:

- Safe
- Enjoyable (promoting self-image)
- Inclusive (active for all students)
- Developmentally appropriate

K–3 Basic Station Activity

Set up stations to provide varied activities (e.g., **station 1:** nonlocomotor; **station 2:** locomotor; and **station 3:** object manipulation). Rotate after ten minutes.

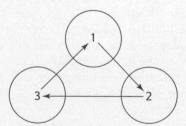

Cool-down exercises are just as important as warm-up exercises. Current research indicates that cool-down activities (e.g., simple calisthenics, breathing exercises, and light walking) are as essential to preventing injuries as warm-up activities.

Discussion and Evaluation provides students with the needed feedback on activities that include proper body mechanics, sportsmanship, learning objectives, and social aspects of the activity.

DOMAIN 2: SELF-IMAGE AND PERSONAL DEVELOPMENT	
2.1 Personal Growth and Development	❏ Identify the sequential development of fine and gross motor skills in children and young adolescents. ❏ Describe the influence of growth spurts (changes in height and weight) and body type on movement and coordination. ❏ Recognize the impact of factors such as exercise, relaxation, nutrition, stress, and substance abuse on physical health and general well-being.
2.2 Self-Image	❏ Describe the role of physical activity in the development of a positive self-image and how psychological skills such as goal setting are selected to promote lifelong participation in physical activity.

Domain 2: Self-Image and Personal Development

2.1 Personal Growth and Development

The growth patterns of children are significantly impacted by genetic inheritance. With this in mind, however, there are average periods of maturation common to the physical development of children. When considering average growth and development and its influence on the ability to perform physical fitness activities, it's important to keep in mind chronological age, gender, environmental influences and dietary practices. A list of some of these normal developmental changes is listed in the Human Development review section of this book on page 363 for your reference. As children change in size and proportion, they begin to perform higher-level skills and activities. The average physical changes that occur in children are represented by periods of:

1. rapid growth from infancy to early childhood.
2. slow, steady growth in middle childhood.
3. rapid growth spurts during puberty.
4. gradual, measured, slow growth during adolescence.

Changes in body proportions have an important influence on how movement skills and fitness activities are performed. For example, the rapid changes in the length of a child's legs can affect movement activities that require running.

Gender Differences

Boys and girls do not grow at the same rate. The peak growth spurt for boys usually spans the ages of 13 through 15 and can be as much as 3 ½ inches per year. The peak growth spurt for girls usually spans the ages of 11 through 13 and can be as much as 3 inches per year. Coinciding with these growth spurt years, the young adolescents experience puberty and additional physical changes. The boys will develop broader shoulders than girls and the girls will develop broader hips than boys. These and other changes affect body mechanics. It can be both frustrating and difficult for boys and girls as their bodies learn to adapt to their new size and shape.

2.2 Self-Image

Physical fitness activities help to formulate lifelong psychological wellness among children. CSET candidates should know that effective classroom fitness activities not only provide an opportunity for physical expression, but also provide children with the necessary psychological and emotional structures to create their self-image. The confidence and competency gained through physical self-expression construct *personal internalized meaning* for children. As children acquire positive experiences, their view of self and their surrounding world is strengthened. The mastery of physical skills is an opportunity for children to modify and improve upon cognitive and emotional internalized processes. Instructional programs that are effective in promoting a positive self-image include:

- **Self-responsibility:** promoting responsibility for one's self, including self-appraisal.
- **Goal-setting:** setting and achieving realistic, personal fitness goals; including goals that are progressively more varied at different skill levels
- **Social Interaction:** developing social interaction among students including communication, cooperation, encouraging and praising others, practicing respectful criticism, and accepting individual differences.
- **Group Interaction:** fostering social concepts of supportive learning as a group or team; working together to form group decisions, respecting the sport rules, and exhibiting good sportsmanship.

DOMAIN 3: SOCIAL DEVELOPMENT	
3.1 Social Aspects of Physical Education	❑ Recognize individual differences such as gender, race, culture, ability, or disability. ❑ Describe the developmental appropriateness of cooperation, competition, and responsible social behavior for children of different ages. ❑ List activities to provide opportunities for enjoyment, self-expression, and communication.
3.2 Cultural and Historical Aspects of Movement Form	❑ Understand the significance of cultural and historical influences on games, sports, dances, and other physical activities.

Domain 3: Social Development

3.1 Social Aspects of Physical Education

Social and emotional development appears in every aspect of a child's educational experience. The social aspects of physical education demonstrate knowledge of psychological and sociological concepts, principles, and strategies that apply to the learning and performance of physical activity. Throughout instruction, teachers should provide an atmosphere that has clear expectations of behavior and achievement. During elementary school, the influences of social development appear in the following:

1. **Team activities:** Students interact in group social dynamics that encourage interpersonal strategies for teamwork, including motivating others, taking turns, working together cooperatively, and accepting the physical strengths and limitations of others.
2. **Self-responsibility:** Students learn to accept personal responsibility for health-related fitness and their own fitness performance without blaming others. This includes responding respectfully to winning or losing.
3. **Social interaction:** Students learn to be empathetic toward others as they respect individual differences. This respect involves including others in activities and motivating others to achieve success.

3.2 Cultural and Historical Aspects of Movement Form

Physical Education Expectations by Specific Grade Level

The *Physical Education Framework for California Public Schools* affirms the standing of physical education as an academic content area. The standards highlight the fact that participation in physical activity is not the same as learning the content in physical education. Every grade- and course-level standard should be taught and assessed for student learning. Elementary physical education programs should emphasize the importance of physical activity and personal fitness. Fitness is developed through the activities in the daily lessons that emphasize high amounts of physical activity, continuous movement, and challenges that involve overloading the major muscle groups. Students are provided with opportunities to understand the fitness components, fitness assessment, and the need for a lifetime of physical activity. Fifth-grade students have their first required experience with the California statewide Physical Fitness Test. To obtain a full description of grade-specific California physical education standards visit the California Department of Education website at www.cde.ca.gov/be/st/ss/documents/pestandards.pdf

Chapter 6

Subtest III: Human Development

Content

The Human Development section measures the understanding of basic skills and knowledge that elementary school teachers must have in order to recognize and effectively respond to a variety of teaching situations. The test stresses the developmental needs of students rather than the academic information taught to them. Teachers are expected to be knowledgeable in birth through adolescent development and to interpret and make assessments regarding age-appropriate student behavior. In addition, teachers are expected to plan appropriate teaching strategies in cognitive, social, and physical development domains in order to facilitate a child-centered and nurturing instructional environment. This section also measures the ability to define, identify, and understand influences concerning human diversity.

The multiple-choice section contains 13 questions, which are grouped together, and 1 short constructed-response question. The essay question is chosen from one of the three domain areas. The question covers the following major content areas and focuses on the topics listed under each.

Analysis of Exam Areas: Content Specifications* in Human Development

*These are the actual California state content specification standards, available online.

Domain 1: Cognitive Development from Birth through Adolescence

1.1 Cognitive Development

❑ Candidates define basic concepts of cognitive and moral development (e.g., reasoning, symbol manipulation, and problem solving).

❑ They identify stages in cognitive and language development and use them to describe the development of individuals, including persons with special needs.

❑ They identify characteristics of play and their influence on cognitive development.

❑ They recognize different perspectives on intelligence (i.e., concepts of multiple intelligences) and their implications for identifying and describing individual differences in cognitive development.

Domain 2: Social and Physical Development from Birth through Adolescence

2.1 Social Development

❏ Candidates define concepts related to the development of personality and temperament (e.g., attachment, self-concept, autonomy, and identity).

❏ They describe the social development of children and young adolescents, including persons with special needs.

❏ They identify characteristics of play and their impact on social development.

❏ They describe influences on the development of prosocial behavior.

2.2 Physical Development

❏ Candidates describe the scope of physical development at different ages.

❏ They identify individual differences in physical development, including persons with special needs.

Domain 3: Influences on Development from Birth through Adolescence

3.1 Influences on Development

❏ Candidates identify potential impacts on the development of children and young adolescents from genetic or organic causes.

❏ They identify potential impacts on the development of children and young adolescents from sociocultural factors (e.g., family, race, and cultural perspective).

❏ They identify potential impacts on the development of children and young adolescents from socioeconomic factors (e.g., poverty and class) and sex or gender.

❏ They identify sources of possible abuse and neglect (e.g., physical, emotional, and substance abuse, and neglect), and describe their impact on development.

Sample Questions and Explanations for the Multiple-Choice Section

Each of the following examples represents an area tested on the Human Development multiple-choice segment. An analysis follows each question.

Domain 1: Cognitive Development from Birth through Adolescence

1.1 Cognitive Development

1. According to preoperational cognitive development theory, egocentrism would most likely:

   A. characterize a child's ability to organize by seriation.
   B. limit a child's perspective of other people.
   C. encourage a global view of familiar surroundings.
   D. explain why children are able to use abstract thinking to deal with problems.

The correct answer is B. Egocentrism, according to Piaget, indicates that children view the world from the reference point of their own perspective. As a result, egocentrism would limit a child's perspective of other people since it inhibits a child from using knowledge objectively. Egocentrism is characteristic of children in the preoperational stage of development (ages 2–7).

---

2. A ten-year-old child of average development is learning to play chess. During this concrete operational stage of development, the child would *not* be able to:

    A. choose a response in reaction to an opponent's move.

    B. think four moves ahead and imagine potential combinations.

    C. complete an end game by checkmating an opponent.

    D. understand the basic instructions and follow the rules of the game.

The correct answer is B. Piaget's stages of cognitive development are ordered into four periods. They are *sensorimotor* (0–2 years), *preoperational* (2–7 years), *concrete operations* (7–11 years), and *formal operations* (11+ years). During the period of concrete operations, logical operations can be applied to real problems. The rules of a variety of games can be learned and applied; however, complex deductions and abstract thinking are not possible until a child enters the period of formal operations. Choice C is not the *best* answer because there is insufficient information regarding the end game (number of pieces left on the board, position on the board, number of moves to checkmate the opponent, and so on) to determine the level of complex reasoning needed to complete the game. Even if you don't know Piaget's theory, you can answer this question correctly. Since there can be only one right answer, the answer must logically be the most difficult task listed, thinking far ahead and identifying complex possibilities.

---

3. A second-grade immigrant child who has no formal schooling in his primary native language:

    A. takes longer to reach the average grade level ability in English than students who have some schooling in their native language.

    B. will never reach the average grade level ability.

    C. takes the same amount of time to reach the average grade level ability as those who have some schooling in their native language.

    D. learns English faster than those students who have formal schooling in their primary language.

The correct answer is A. Children must have a competency in their primary native language before they can understand new concepts of another language. Primary language is necessary so that children can "think about" another new language. Lev Vygotsky theorized that thought development is determined by language and that thought and language each provide a resource for the other.

---

4. Justin is a sixth-grade student who loves to skateboard. Skateboarding is prohibited on school grounds, but Justin's best friend pleads with him to skate after school in order to practice their new skateboarding skills. The school is the only place in town to practice since it has a steep, concrete hill. Based upon Justin's age and his average development in moral reasoning, he will be most concerned with:

    A. the consequences from school authorities.

    B. being injured.

    C. pleasing his best friend.

    D. being grounded by his parents, if caught.

The correct answer is C. During this second level of Kohlberg's stages of moral development, most children in middle childhood or adolescence reason at the *conventional level of morality,* ages 10–13. They are concerned about the opinions of their peers and have a desire to win their acceptance. Children at this stage want to please and help others, and develop their own internal idea of what a good person is. Justin may also justify that "it's the only place in town." Choices A and D suggest Kohlberg's first level of moral reasoning. At this *preconventional level of morality,* ages 4–10, children obey because adults tell them to obey. At this age, Justin would have based this moral decision upon fear of punishment or to win approval from his parents and teachers.

Domain 2: Social and Physical Development from Birth through Adolescence

2.1 Social Development

5. In a school district reading program, middle-school students meet with first-grade students to help the younger children read a book until the children are able to read on their own. All of the following are important educational implications of this reading program, except:

   A. this reading program facilitates a cognitive change in both elementary and middle-school students.
   B. this reading program advocates a phonics approach to reading.
   C. this reading program provides a temporary support to help younger children become more competent readers.
   D. this reading program emphasizes cognitive and social learning experiences.

The correct choice is B. Although a phonics approach to reading is an excellent choice to support a good reading program, it is unknown whether this school district program will use this method of teaching reading. Effective cooperative instruction provides opportunities for younger children to achieve higher-level abilities in both cognitive and social learning, Choice D. Vygotsky's concept of *scaffolding* is defined as a temporary support system for children until they are able to perform on their own. Older children provide instruction to help younger children become more competent readers, Choice C. Since this is a shared learning experience, both students benefit from this reading program, Choice A.

6. What is the best explanation for a four-year-old child who shows signs of aggressive behavior shortly after watching a series of violent cartoons?

   A. Children are innately aggressive, and this behavior has nothing to do with TV viewing.
   B. Children must find a way to release energy after passively watching television.
   C. Rapid eye movements associated with watching cartoons increase aggressiveness.
   D. Children imitate the behavior of characters in the cartoons.

The correct answer is D. Although there is no single cause for a child's aggressive behavior, social learning theories provide evidence to support the idea that violent cartoon characters often become models of aggression that children attempt to emulate. The research of Albert Bandura and others has concluded that children who observe aggressive acts are more likely to imitate aggression. Although television provides us with a "window to the world" through education and information, the excessive use of television can lead to negative reactions such as behavioral problems and stereotypical views of the world. Television also takes time away from social interactions with the family and cognitive development activities, such as reading books.

7. A group of second graders are playing marbles during lunchtime. According to cognitive development theorists, these children are engaging in which of the following forms of play?

   A. Constructive play
   B. Functional play
   C. Pretend play
   D. Games with rules play

The correct answer is D. To answer this question, you must recognize the four types of play as outlined by developmental theorists. Choice B, *functional play,* is described as repeating simple muscular movements and is most commonly observed during the ages of birth through two years, the *sensorimotor* stage of development. Choice A, *constructive play,* involves the use of making objects into something (e.g., building blocks) and is usually observed in toddlers and preschool children during the *preoperational* stage. Another answer common during the preoperational stage is Choice C, pretend play. *Pretend play* is also known as fantasy, dramatic, or imaginative play, substituting imaginary situations or people for real ones. Since marbles has a given set of rules, it is considered a game with rules. It is most common during the *concrete operational* stage, ages 7–11. Games with rules play is the best possible answer for this question.

---

8. A preschool teacher invites parents to observe their child during a typical day in the classroom. While most of the children wanted to stay with their mothers, Samantha consistently ignored her mother and played in an area separate from her. During circle time when all of the mothers were called to join the children, Samantha refused to have her mother sit next to her. This attachment disorder is known as:

    A. anxious-resistant.

    B. disorganized-disoriented.

    C. secure.

    D. anxious-avoidant.

The correct answer is D. Samantha is exhibiting *anxious-avoidant* attachment behavior, a pattern whereby the preschool child rarely cries when separated from her caretaker. She might also avoid contact upon the caretaker's return. Choice C, *secure* attachment, is the type of attachment most children experience with their caretaker. A securely attached preschool child uses the caregiver as the secure base to safely explore the environment. It is important to recognize because attachment is a predictor for all future relationships. Choices A, B and D are forms of insecure attachments. *Anxious-resistant* attachment, Choice A, suggests a pattern in which the child becomes anxious before the caregiver leaves and is upset during the absence. *Disorganized-disoriented* attachment, Choice B, suggests a pattern in which after the child is separated, the child shows behavioral signs of being contradictory or dazed upon the caregiver's return. If you were unfamiliar with this question, and carefully scanned the answer choices, you would realize that Samantha appeared to demonstrate apathetic behavior toward her mother and avoided contact with her.

---

9. Deena is a popular fourth grader who is highly regarded by her peers at school. Which of the following best demonstrates the effects of positive social and emotional support for children, such as Deena, ages 8 to 11?

    A. Children develop intimate friendships.

    B. Children gain higher self-esteem.

    C. Children understand the importance of socializing.

    D. Children gain a sense of gender identity.

The correct answer is B. Positive peer relationships provide children with an opportunity to have a sense of belongingness, overcome egocentrism, share interests, practice conflict resolution, and provide emotional and social support. Emotional and social approval from peers is a powerful influence in the development of the emotional well being of children, enhancing their self-esteem.

---

10. Every child has a uniquely different temperament. Temperament is determined by _____, moods, and the environment, and influences the development of _____.

    Which of the following terms are the best fill-ins?

    A. inborn traits; independence

    B. thought; independence

    C. thought; personality

    D. inborn traits; personality

The correct answer is D. Since the words moods and environment are listed as part of the definition of temperament, and temperament is a component of social development, Choices B and C can immediately be eliminated. "Thought" is a component of cognitive development, not social development. Temperament and personality influence the way a child shows emotional responses.

2.2 Physical Development

11. Daniel is a five-year-old kindergartener. Given the normal progression of physical development for his age, which of the following gross motor skills should he be able to perform easily?

    A. Ride a two-wheel bike.
    B. Accurately pitch a baseball.
    C. Bounce and catch a ball.
    D. Balance with one foot on a balance beam.

The correct answer is C. Five-year-olds develop a noticeable increase in large muscle activity from their previously acquired developments. Although Daniel's muscles and bones are more developed and stronger than when he was a toddler, he is not yet coordinated enough to accomplish more advanced perceptual-motor skills that are observed in middle childhood, ages 7 to 11. Choice C is a skill that he can achieve with ease, since he can now perform locomotor skills such as hopping, jumping, running, and riding a tricycle. Choices A, B, and D require skills that will occur during the next stage of physical development. The gross motor skills he is practicing during early childhood will help prepare him for more coordinated movements required to play sports and other activities in middle childhood and adolescence.

12. Which of the following statements is true about the physical strength and coordination of average seventh-grade students?

    A. Boys have more leg strength and girls have more arm strength.
    B. Boys have greater muscle strength than girls.
    C. Boys tend to retain their baby fat longer and weigh more than girls.
    D. Boys and girls have equal muscle strength.

The correct answer is B. There are significant differences in the physical development of boys and girls during this period of development. In order to answer this question, you must know that this is a period of rapid growth spurts, and that boys tend to develop stronger muscles and bones. Since boys have increased gross motor physical strength in both arms and legs, answers A and D are incorrect.

13. Which of the following statements is *not* true about eating disorders among adolescents?

    A. Eating disorders, such as anorexia, are most commonly diagnosed in teenagers from middle and upper-class backgrounds.
    B. Adolescents who binge-eat do not purge.
    C. Adolescents who have bulimia nervosa tend to have perfectionist traits, while those who have anorexia nervosa tend to be impulsive.
    D. Many eating disorders are often linked to sociocultural and psychological factors.

The correct answer is C. Eating disorders are often characterized by an adolescent's preoccupation with body weight and image. Choice A is a true statement since many incidences of *anorexia* and *bulimia* are higher among adolescent girls from higher socioeconomic backgrounds. Many adolescent girls equate attractiveness with a slim body. Underlying contributing factors can include emotional, social, cultural, and behavioral influences, eliminating Choice D. There are three common forms of eating disorders: *anorexia nervosa*, *bulimia nervosa*, and a *binge eating disorder*. Anorexia is a form of "self-starvation" with intense fear of gaining weight. Bulimia nervosa is uncontrollable eating followed by self-induced purging. A newly recognized eating disorder is called binge eating disorder. Binge eaters often eat large amounts of food, often in secrecy, even when they're not hungry. Binge eaters do not purge their food, and so Choice B is a true statement. Since adolescents with anorexia tend to demonstrate perfectionist traits, and those with bulimia are described as impulsive, Choice C is not a true statement.

Domain 3: Influences on Development from Birth through Adolescence

3.1 Influences on Development

---

14. Which of the following classroom behaviors is the best indicator that a child may have a learning disability?

    A. The child's below-average intelligence matches his classroom performance.
    B. The child appears confused about an assignment, but can stay on task.
    C. The child sometimes has difficulty paying attention, but can stay on task.
    D. The child shows above-average intelligence and below-average classroom performance.

The correct answer is D. Children with learning disabilities exhibit a discrepancy between their measured intelligence and classroom performance. The learning disability interferes with the overall academic performance and daily living, and stress can further magnify the disability. There is not adequate information in Choices A, B, and C to describe a learning disability.

---

15. The second leading cause of death in infancy is low birth weight. All of the following factors can negatively affect the growth and weight of the fetus, *except:*

    A. poor prenatal nutrition.
    B. drinking alcohol during pregnancy.
    C. smoking during pregnancy.
    D. trauma to the newborn during childbirth.

The correct answer is D. Although there are many variables determining the birth weight of an infant, trauma to the newborn during childbirth would not be a contributing factor, since weight has already been established at the time of childbirth. Some reasons why infants have low birth weights may include poor prenatal nutrition, Choice A, and the abuse of drugs and alcohol among expectant mothers, Choice B. Negative environmental influences, such as choices B and C, can produce prenatal abnormal agents known as *teratogens,* which can cause birth defects in the unborn child. Teratogens are known to generate a high incidence of prematurity and low birth weight in infants. Babies born to women who have nutritional deficiencies, as in Choice A, can also adversely affect their development.

---

16. A third-grade student is sent home from a low socioeconomic school. He has symptoms of a headache, fatigue, and a mid-grade fever. His parents most likely will:

    A. keep him home for the day and then send him to school the next day, even with many of the same symptoms.
    B. stay at home with him, with at least one parent, until the fever has disappeared.
    C. take him to an urgent care facility.
    D. take him to see their family doctor.

The correct answer is A. Due to the lack of affordable health care in low socioeconomic families, visits to the doctor occur only when there is a serious illness. His parents will most likely treat him at home. In addition, due to lack of money, both parents probably work and cannot afford to take time off to care for their sick child. B is a possible choice, but many low-income families are forced to keep a sick child home alone while the parents are obligated to work.

17. Teachers have influential roles as sociocultural mediators in the classroom. Teachers can help to reduce cultural prejudice by teaching students to think critically and encourage:

    A. anger management.

    B. cultural segregation.

    C. academic achievement.

    D. emotional intelligence.

The correct answer is D. Cultural prejudice is a narrow-minded view of a targeted group. Anger management, Choice A, will help to temporarily solve individual disputes, but Choice D, emotional intelligence, provides children with a much broader inter-ethnic understanding of the world. Emotionally intelligent children are more able to understand different perspectives, are better listeners, express mature cognitive-emotional feelings, and are more motivated to share and cooperate with other children.

Sample Questions and Strategies for the Short Constructed-Response Section

There is only one short constructed-response question in the Human Development section; however, following are several representative questions from each of the three domains for your review. Strategies and a sample response are included with each question.

Domain 1: Cognitive Development from Birth through Adolescence

---

1. Complete the exercise that follows.

   Using your knowledge of cognitive development, discuss why a child would have difficulty organizing a series of log sticks from shortest to longest. In addition,

   - determine the child's age according to the child's cognitive development; and
   - discuss another example of a similar cognitive development task the child might have difficulty performing.

Strategy

This may be a difficult question, since it requires specific information. You will need to understand a key concept in Piaget's Stages of Cognitive Development called *seriation*. Let's say that you don't remember the concept, but know the stages of cognitive development. You would then be able to visualize young children completing this task. The two polar age extremes in Piaget's stages are *sensorimotor* (infancy) and *formal operations* (adolescence). You could immediately rule out these two stages, since an infant can only perform simple tasks and an adolescent can perform very difficult abstract reasoning tasks. The only two stages left are *preoperational* (preschool) and *concrete operations* (middle childhood). If you can narrow your age group down, the chances are that you'll be able to guess that this child is in Piaget's preoperational period. Knowing this, you'll at least be able to discuss some of the characteristics of a preoperational child so that you will not have to leave the answer blank.

Sample Response

The skill that is required for a child to arrange objects in logical progression from shortest to longest is known as *seriation*. According to Jean Piaget and his Stages of Cognitive Development, this skill is not mastered until a child is about seven years old, during the period of concrete operations. A child who has not yet acquired this skill is operating during Piaget's preoperational stage of development, ages two to six years old. During the preoperational stage of development, Piaget discovered that children name the largest or the smallest stick in a group, but have difficulty arranging sticks in an ordered series due to appearance and reality. Young children cannot conceive of the reality without seeing an example visually before them. Piaget found that children select sticks at random by trial-and-error, rather than picking the smallest stick first and progressing. Children at this age are also limited by centration and cannot focus on two things at one time. *Centration* is the inability to focus on more than one thing at a time.

---

2. Complete the exercise that follows.

   Discuss the cognitive, social, and emotional benefits of imaginary play, including:

   - the definition of imaginary play; and
   - one example of imaginary play.

Strategy

If you're uncertain how child development theorists define *imaginary play*, it is best to approach your answer by appealing to your mind's eye to remember what it was like to be a child. There are two preliminary concepts to consider. The first is to recall what you already know about children and play. You may recall being in elementary school and playing ball or hopscotch on the school playground. Just remember what it was like to play in elementary school. Then, think about what it means to imagine. When you were a child, you may have pretended to be a professional baseball player and made a stick into a bat, or maybe you pretended to be a teacher grading papers for students. It doesn't matter what you've imagined; just continue to visualize being that child with an active imagination. You will then be able to define imaginary play in your own words and be able to provide at least one example. The definition may not be accurate, but there is a good chance you will include some of the main ideas necessary to score a couple of points on this essay question.

Sample Response

During early childhood, as children are forming representational symbols of the world, imaginary play emerges to provide children with a theatre to practice pleasurable activities that are critical to cognitive and social growth and development. *Imaginary play* is defined as play that transforms the natural world into symbols; it is most active during early childhood and gradually declines in middle childhood when children shift to playing with games. Jean Piaget believed that play advances a child's cognitive development, and Lev Vygotsky was especially fascinated with make-believe play. Vygotsky believed that for young children, imaginary play provides an excellent opportunity to play out real-life situations. Imaginary play makes it possible to help children practice new skills, resolve conflicts, and try out new social roles. Children engage in play for no reason, except for its own sake. An example of imaginary play is a preschool child who has a make-believe tea party with her stuffed animals, and pours each animal a cup of tea from an "empty" teapot.

Domain 2: Social and Physical Development from Birth through Adolescence

3. Complete the exercise that follows.

   Using your knowledge of social and cognitive development, discuss the important aspects of prosocial behavior while:

   - citing two types of prosocial behavior; and
   - including the age and/or stage of development at which a child can first master this behavior.

Strategy

This question relates specifically to *prosocial* behavior, a psychological developmental concept. Even if you don't know the developmental definition of the word *prosocial,* you can make an educated guess by analyzing the word. The word *pro* is a prefix meaning "supporting or moving forward." Knowing this, you might guess the child's behavior is positive. The next part of the word is *social.* The definition for social is "having to do with relationships with a person or a group of people." If you put the two together, a good guess would be that the child's behavior is supportive of other people. With this information, you should be able to cite at least two types of a child's positive behavior, even if you don't know when the child will first acquire this behavior. Remember, adequately answering at least part of the question will give you partial credit.

Sample Response

Prosocial behavior involves the act of volunteering efforts to help someone, or to share with someone else. Prosocial behavior has been demonstrated in children as young as preschool. They have exhibited this positive behavior by comforting, helping, and protecting other children. However, just because children can experience the distress of others, it does not mean they will always offer comfort. This is probably because preschool children tend to have an egocentric motivation. This means that prosocial behavior is not clearly selfless until children are much older. Empathy and altruism are two important types of prosocial behavior. Empathy is the ability to experience another person's emotions—that is, to feel what the other person is feeling. Altruism is acting unselfishly out of concern for another person, with no expectation in return. Since children imitate the behavior of teachers, it is important for teachers to model prosocial behavior, especially in the structure of empathy and altruism.

---

4. Use the information below to complete the exercise that follows.

A teacher observes that a few of the boys in a fifth-grade classroom do not do well on paper-and-pencil activities. Using your knowledge of cognitive and physical development for children between the ages of 6 and 12:

- discuss two possible explanations for this behavior; and
- select one of your explanations and discuss possible educational intervention strategies to help remedy this problem.

Strategy

Before answering this question, it's important to determine the main points of the teacher's observation. You should have centered your focus on four main points (i.e., <u>few of the boys</u>, <u>fifth-grade</u>, and <u>paper-and-pencil activities</u>). The phrase, "a few of the boys in a fifth-grade classroom . . ." indicates that this group is out of the normal range for this grade level. A good answer might therefore include suggesting that the boys might have a learning disability such as a *visual-perceptual disability*, *perceptual-motor disability*, or *ADD*. Observing this behavior in boys only indicates that the answer may be gender related, narrowing down the population. And finally, by indicating the activity as paper-and-pencil, this example points out that the behavior is a fine motor activity in physical development. Since boys are typically slower at fine motor skills than girls at this age, this may also be included in your essay. Remember that the question does not give a definitive psychological assessment of the children, only that it was an observation made by the teacher, and so your essay can be exploratory.

Sample Response

According to cognitive theorists, fifth-graders are experiencing the cognitive period of *concrete operations*. During this stage of development, most children can reason logically and their fine motor ability has progressed to handwriting. Based upon average skills, most fifth-graders should have the intellectual and fine motor abilities to perform these tasks. It is worth mentioning, however, that boys at this age are better at gross motor skills and girls are better at fine motor skills. This problem may be gender related, but the inability to perform fine motor tasks may also signal a serious learning problem. If the teacher has consistently observed this problem, these boys may be showing signs of an undiagnosed learning disability such as a visual-perceptual disability or possibly attention-deficit disorder. To help remedy this problem, the teacher can employ alternative learning modalities such as using manipulatives, allowing students to explain orally how a problem could be solved (instead of writing a solution), encouraging students to utilize technology resources to problem solve (e.g., computers and calculators), and designing student worksheets that are magnified, organized, and clearly marked.

Domain 3: Influences on Development from Birth through Adolescence

---

5. Use the information below to complete the exercise that follows.

Ethan is a very active third grader who frequently speaks out loud, interrupts often, and has difficulty paying attention in class. Using your knowledge of human development and children with special needs:

- discuss a possible intervention from the teacher; and
- discuss two possible explanations for his behavior.

Strategy

Notice that this question refers directly to a child's impulsive, overactive behavior. Although many children demonstrate enthusiastic behavioral responses, this question points out that Ethan "has difficulty paying attention in class." For this reason Ethan's classroom performance may be negatively affected by his inability to control his behavior. Even if you're unfamiliar with intervention strategies and the evaluation criteria for attention difficulties, your first response could have been to seek professional advice to explore a possible explanation for his overactive behavior before contacting his parents. Remember that teacher's should always be responsive to varying individual needs of children. Teacher's are never responsible for diagnosis and treatment, but is important to recognize that your observations of extreme inattention usually indicate that further steps must be taken in order to provide an optimal classroom learning experience for the child.

Sample Response

Although it is difficult to explain Ethan's behavior without a professional clinical or medical diagnosis, teachers who observe students consistently struggling to pay attention have a responsibility to take appropriate action to improve the student's ability to learn. Ethan's behavior can be a result of a variety of explanations such as problems at home, defiance, or developmental immaturity; but teachers who are knowledgeable about the symptoms of attention deficit should notify his parents about their concern. Since Attention-Deficit Disorder (ADD) is one of the most prevalent learning disabilities in school-age children, ADD would probably be one of the best explanations for Ethan's behavior, but before a diagnosis can be made, the student must show symptoms of attention deficit at home as well as school. The other possible explanation for Ethan's behavioral symptoms could be Attention-Deficit Hyperactivity Disorder (ADHD). The symptoms of attention deficit include difficulty paying attention, difficulty controlling motor activity, and difficulty staying on task, as well as the child being easily distracted and easily frustrated. Since Ethan is demonstrating many of these symptoms, including hyperactivity, a good explanation for his behavior might be ADHD.

---

6. Use the information below to complete the exercise that follows:

   Most research indicates that children from divorced families experience a difficult time adjusting emotionally, socially, and academically. Using your knowledge of human development:

   - discuss the impact divorce has on a child's school performance between the ages of 7 and 11; and
   - explain the emotional difference between a boy's reaction and a girl's reaction to divorce.

Strategy

You can receive a reasonable score for this question even if you don't completely understand the psychological impact that divorce has on children. Recall the information that you may already know about friends, colleagues, or family members who have experienced divorce and the effects on their children. You will probably come up with a handful of ideas to present in your response, including children feeling grief, anger, and guilt. You might also make an educated guess in stating that boys tend to externalize their feelings (anger and acting out), and girls tend to internalize their feelings (sadness and depression).

Sample Response

Research has indicated that children from divorced homes are likely to exhibit maladaptive behavior in the school environment. The traumatic impact of divorce on children between the ages of 7 and 11 can result in emotional and social deprivation, including feelings of sadness, anger, self-blame, and denial. It is normal for children to experience academic problems at school in this case, as during any other traumatic event. Children often show an inability to concentrate, have frequent absences and behavior problems, and exhibit lack of motivation. Divorce may be the first painful event in a child's life and the child may have difficulty adjusting to the parents' ongoing conflicts, have feelings of intense loss and abandonment, and feel as though he must choose sides against the other parent. The way in which a child might respond to divorce depends upon the child's maturity, temperament, and gender. In general, boys and girls exhibit different reactions to divorce. Boys typically show increased aggression and impulse-control problems in the classroom, and girls exhibit more anxiety, withdrawal, and sadness.

Review of Domains

The nature of human beings is observed through the dynamic lifespan progression of cognitive, social, and physical development from birth through adulthood. The Human Development section of the CSET: Multiple Subjects examines this progression of child development beginning at conception and continuing through adolescence. The exam consists of three domains, including *cognitive development*, *social development*, and *physical development*, while considering the influences on a child's ability to learn. Through the study and interpretation of these domains, educators can better understand the important theoretical perspectives of developmental psychology as they relate to a child's growth and development. It is within this framework that these conceptualized models can be better realized and applied to the classroom experience. In order to successfully pass the Human Development section of the exam, you will be required to recognize, identify, and describe how these conceptual systems interrelate with the developmental milestones of children. These important models can also be used as instructional tools to better recognize how children learn in the classroom.

HUMAN DEVELOPMENT TIMETABLE

Age	Cognitive Development (Piaget)	Social Development (Erikson)	Physical Development
Birth to 2 Years INFANCY - TODDLER	**Sensorimotor** *Egocentric* Understands the world through physical actions. Stage begins with reflexes and ends with starting to understand symbolic thought. Organizes thought by *schemes*. Speaks first word by 1 year old, first sentence (two-words) by 18-24 months. *Object permanence* by 18-24 months (object exists even when not visible.)	**Trust vs. Mistrust (1-1½ years)** **Virtue: HOPE** The infant sees the world as safe and secure. The absence of trust leaves the infant feeling guarded and suspicious. **Functional Play** - repetition of behavior (muscular movements).	Reflexes control newborns behavior (automatic movements). **Gross Motor** Crawls at 6-8 mos. Walks at 11-12 mos. Jumps with both feet at age 2 **Fine Motor** At 2 years can scribble, zip a zipper, turns doorknob (in reach)
2 to 7 YEARS (Preschool and Kindergarten) EARLY CHILDHOOD	**Preoperational (2-4 years)** *Egocentric* *Causal reasoning* (toddler believes his thoughts can cause an action) *Centration* (can only focus on one piece of information at a time). Sees the world as symbolic images & objects. Mastery of symbols (pretending and play). Declarative language "I'm hungry." Vocabulary about 1,000 words **Preoperational (5-7 years)** Understands others can have a different perspective. No longer egocentric. Intuitive reasoning & representational thought. Period of *fast mapping* (using context to determine the meaning of words). Rapid advances in conversation (speaks about 2,500 words), and vocabulary (knows about 20,000 words). Many "why" questions. Can classify by two criteria (shape and color). Can count to 20 using fingers. Understands *conservation* (recognizes that an object does not change if the appearance changes) except liquid.	**Autonomy vs. Shame & Doubt (1½-3½ years)** **Virtue: WILL** Period of exploration and experimentation. Begins with "terrible twos," and period of "self-will." Toddler learns to balance external control with self-control. If enabled or harshly punished, toddler becomes inhibited or unwilling to try new activities. **Constructive Play** - using objects to make something. **Initiative vs. Guilt (3½-6 years)** **Virtue: PURPOSE** Willingness to take risks. Sometimes conflicted because part is enthusiastic about new abilities and at the same time feels more self-conscious about examining his or her actions. **Imaginative Play** - transforms symbols into make-believe play. **Gender Differences:** Girls start school testing higher than boys, but boys graduate high school testing higher on SAT's.	**Gross Motor Skills** Noticeable increase in large muscle activity. Appearance more slender, less *baby fat*. Hopping, jumping, running. Can pedal tricycle. Age 5-6 can skip, roller skate, & skip rope. Bounce & catch a ball **Fine Motor Skills** Right/Left Handed Preference Age 3-4, draws with crayons. Can draw O and + Can dress self. Age 4-5 can string shoelaces, cut on a line with scissors, and prints first name. Age 5-6 can draw square, and triangle Copies most alphabet letters. Sleep problems are common.
7 to 11 YEARS (Elementary) MIDDLE CHILDHOOD	**Concrete Operations** *Classification* skills allows child to classify and divide objects in sets. Fully understands *conservation*. Solves problems by thinking about multiple perspectives to any *real (concrete)* situation. Reasons logically (*inductive reasoning*) instead of intuitively. Can perform *seriation* (can arrange objects in logical progression). An older middle child has practiced enough to perform *transitive inference* (drawing conclusions about two objects, knowing the third object). Understands distinction between appearance and reality. *Metacognition* ability (thinking about thinking).	**Industry vs. inferiority (6-11 years)** **Virtue: COMPETENCE** Development of *social self* and mastering self-assurance. Child learns to work with others. Socializing important, helping to enhance self-esteem. Unsuccessful resolution at this stage may leave the child not feeling valued and feeling inferior to others. **Rough-and-Tumble Play** - tag, chasing, and wrestling, and *Games with Rules Play*.	Slow, constant growth with smoother and more coordinated movements to enable athletic skills. Girls taller, boys stronger. Must stay active. Difficult to sit for long periods. **Gross Motor Skills** Period of engaging in *active* sports such as running, swimming, ball playing and bike riding. **Fine Motor Skills** Handwriting with small print. Can hammer. Girls better at fine motor, boys better at gross motor.
12 to 18 YEARS ADOLESCENCE	**Formal Operations** Teen is now capable of *abstract reasoning*. Capable of *hypothetical-deductive reasoning*. Education focuses on preparing for college. Higher level of moral reasoning, no longer following external rules imposed by others. Logic is now applied to what *might exist*, not just to what is *real*.	**Identity vs. role confusion (12-18 years)** **Virtue: FIDELITY** Adolescent builds upon previous experiences to seek the foundation for a sense of self identity in adult life. Difficulties during this stage will result in confusion and delay mature adult life. **Gender Differences:** Girls concerned with future intimacy; boys tend to be concerned with autonomy and achievement.	Physical changes are dramatic and profound. Growth spurts for both boys and girls. Boys physical strength greater. Reproductive maturity begins with puberty. Health risks from behavioral issues such as drug abuse and eating disorders.

Candidates for Multiple Subject Teaching Credentials apply knowledge of cognitive, social, and physical development to understanding differences between individual children. They interpret similarities and differences in children's behavior with reference to concepts of human development. They use developmental concepts and principles to explain children's behavior (as described anecdotally or viewed in naturalistic settings, on videotape, etc.).

Domain 1: Cognitive Development from Birth through Adolescence

1.1 Cognitive Development

DOMAIN 1: EXAM SPECIFICATIONS	
Birth through Adolescence	1. Define basic concepts of cognitive and moral development (e.g., reasoning, symbol manipulation, and problem solving).
	2. Identify stages in cognitive and language development and use them to describe the development of individuals, including persons with special needs.
	3. Identify characteristics of play and their influence on cognitive development.
	4. Recognize different perspectives on intelligence (i.e., concepts of multiple intelligences) and their implications for identifying and describing individual differences in cognitive development.

Cognitive development includes transformations in a child's thought, language, and intelligence. The theories influencing a child's cognitive development from birth through adolescence are: Piaget's Stages of Cognitive Development, Kohlberg's Stages of Moral Development, and multi-theoretical perspectives of language, intelligence, and children with special needs.

Swiss psychologist, Jean Piaget (Jahn pea-ah-ZHAY), was devoted to observing behavior patterns in children. His contributions to cognitive development are central to how educators understand how children think, feel, and respond to the world. His theory proposes that cognitive development begins with a child's innate ability to adapt to the environment, and that development is a result of the child's interface with the physical world, social experiences, and physical maturation. Children actively move through new life experiences and form new ways to modify and adapt to the world. The child's mind seeks to find a state of equilibrium while moving through each stage of operation.

Piaget named four stages of cognitive development to exemplify his theory:

1. sensorimotor
2. preoperational
3. concrete operations
4. formal operations

Conservation

The idea of *conservation* is a conceptual tool that allows a child to recognize that when altering the appearance of an object, the basic properties do not change. A young child fails to master this task because the way things look influences how the child thinks. This concept is based upon Einstein's famous formula, $E = mc^2$, which states that mass and energy can be transformed from one to the other, but their total amount is fixed (conserved) so that it neither increases nor decreases. Piaget used this concept when referring to numbers, volumes, weights, and matter (concrete operations).

Examples of Lack of Conservation Skills

Task	Manipulation	Preoperational Child's Response
Concept of Numbers		"The row on top has more buttons."
Concept of Length		"The one on the bottom is longer."
Concept of Liquid		(the same amounts of juice are poured into two different glasses) "The taller glass has more juice."
Concept of Matter		(rolling one ball of clay into a log) "The log has more clay."

Adapting to the Environment

The process of adaptation is fundamental to Piaget's stages of development. Children adjust to new information about their environment in order to function more effectively. This process involves two fundamental cognitive concepts as children move from stage to stage. These two concepts are *assimilation* and *accommodation*.

- **Assimilation:** Assimilation refers to the way children incorporate new information with existing schemes in order to form a new cognitive structure. Children fit this new knowledge into a template of existing schemes. Example: A preschool child calls a lion "doggie" because the child only knows one type of four-legged animal.

- **Accommodation:** Accommodation occurs when children take existing schemes and adjust them to fit their experience. Example: A preschool child plays with the keys on a piano to hear the different sounds of musical notes. When he tries this with an electric keyboard, he quickly learns that the keyboard must be turned on before it can be played. He must accommodate this new information to fit the experience.

Piaget's Cognitive Learning Process

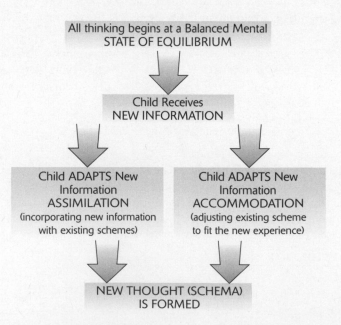

All thinking begins at a Balanced Mental STATE OF EQUILIBRIUM

Child Receives NEW INFORMATION

Child ADAPTS New Information ASSIMILATION (incorporating new information with existing schemes)

Child ADAPTS New Information ACCOMMODATION (adjusting existing scheme to fit the new experience)

NEW THOUGHT (SCHEMA) IS FORMED

Piaget's Cognitive Stages

Four Assumptions of Piaget's Stages of Cognitive Development

1. Children are organically inspired to think, learn, and comprehend.
2. Children see the world differently than adults.
3. Children's knowledge is ordered into mental structures called *schemas*.
4. All learning consists of *assimilation* and *accommodation*.

Piaget's Stages of Cognitive Development		
Stage	**Age**	**Characteristics**
Stage 1 Sensorimotor Period: Infancy	Birth through 2 years	Infant's physical response to immediate surroundings.
Stage 2 Preoperational Period: Early Childhood	2 through 7 years	Egocentric—Focus on symbolic thought and imagination.
Stage 3 Concrete Operations Period: Middle Childhood	7 through 11 years	Mastery of conservation—Child begins to think logically.
Stage 4 Formal Operations Period: Adolescence	12 years through adult	Thinking based on abstract principles.

Stage 1: Sensorimotor Period: Infancy (birth through 2 years)

The first stage of Piaget's cognitive development model is the sensorimotor period. Throughout this stage, we learn that behavior is based upon the infant's physical responses to immediate surroundings. Infants mentally organize and perceive their world through their sensory systems (i.e., what they touch, see, feel, hear, smell, etc.). It is almost by mishap that the infant discovers that his physical reflexes have an impact on the world around him as the infant moves from reflexive actions to representational (symbolic) thought. This transition follows a series of increasingly progressive skills. During this period, infants are at the center of their universe (egocentrism).

Stage 2: Preoperational Period: Early Childhood (2 through 7 years)

Piaget's preoperational period suggests that development of symbolic thought and imagination is boundless. In striving to understand their world, around age five, children begin to ask a multitude of "why" questions. Children can reason intuitively, and representational thought has emerged. Children continue to make errors in spoken language. There is a dramatic difference in the child's development as each year passes. Children love to hear stories, sing songs, and recite nursery rhymes. Independent and cooperative play becomes important during this stage. By the time a child is about six years old, his language development (particularly the child's ability to be a better conversationalist) is dramatically different from that of a two-year-old. Language increases rapidly as children learn many new words each day.

Stage 3: Concrete Operations Period: Middle Childhood (7 through 11 years)

The stage of concrete operations is marked by the child's ability to solve simple problems while thinking about multiple dimensions of information. Children can now "think about thinking" (metacognition). Children understand the world through trial-and-error. Children cannot yet think abstractly, but they do understand the distinction between appearance and reality if presented in terms of tangible objects. This elementary-age child now has a clear sense of seriation, transitivity, reversibility, and conservation. The child also has the ability to set his own values as he becomes more subjective in moral judgments.

Stage 4: Formal Operations Period: Adolescence (12 years through adult)

The mental transformations experienced during adolescence are logical and continue to progress beyond the skills developed during childhood. This period is marked by the adolescent's ability to reason abstractly and solve complex problems, thus expanding possibilities for understanding the world. Adolescents now have the ability to perform hypothetical-deductive reasoning and can integrate what they have learned in the past to consider the many future possibilities.

Understanding Piaget's Stage Theory in the Twenty-First Century

Jean Piaget has had the greatest impact on understanding developmental psychology in the classroom today, but some learning theorists are concerned that Piaget's observations of infants and children must be updated to include the influences of culture and the increased mental learning abilities of infants. One example is found in Renée Baillargeon's (1999, 2001, 2004) studies where infants as young as three months old appeared to know that objects did not disappear when out of sight. Piaget believed *object permanence* could not be mastered until about eight months old. It appears that in recent studies, infants have the ability to form early concepts of their surrounding world prior to eight months old. These new studies bring into question whether Piaget misunderstood an infant's limited physical abilities and lack of mental competency during the sensorimotor stage of development. As educators, it is important to use Piaget's theory to better understand developmental milestones, and to develop a framework in the classroom that recognizes the unique differences of individual students.

The Educational Implications of Piaget's Stages of Cognitive Development

1. Piaget's theory of cognitive development provides an alternative to behavior theorists' belief that children are merely passive learners. Children actively move through *operational stages.*

2. Piaget quantified the conceptual-learning process, suggesting that there are predictable and orderly developmental accomplishments. Children can be tested at each stage to verify their level of cognitive understanding.

3. Piaget suggested that a child's mind seeks a state of equilibrium. At each stage, children form a new way to operate and adapt to the world.

4. By understanding Piaget's stages of cognitive development, teachers can avoid presenting material in the classroom that is beyond the child's cognitive ability.

Piaget's Key Terms and Concepts	
Animism	Refers to children believing that non-living objects have lifelike qualities. It can be demonstrated in imaginary friends, etc. (preoperational, ages 2–4). *Example: When it begins to rain, a child might exclaim, "The sky is pouring water on me."*
Causal Reasoning "Causality"	During preschool, children cannot yet think logically about cause and effect. Children believe that their thoughts can cause actions, whether or not the experiences have a causal relationship. Children reason by transductive reasoning (preoperational). *Example: A child is unkind toward her baby cousin, and shortly thereafter, the baby is accidentally hurt. The child believes that somehow she caused the accident for having "bad thoughts" about the baby.* **Causal Reasoning Changes Over Time** Level 1 (Age 3): Reality is defined by appearance. *"When I move along, the clouds move along too."* Level 2 (Age 5): Child appeals to an all-powerful force. *"God moves the clouds."* Level 3 (Age 7): Child appeals to causes in nature. *"The sun moves the clouds."* Level 4 (Age 10): Child now approaches an adult explanation. *"Clouds move because of wind currents."*
Centration	The tendency for a child to focus on only one piece of information at a time while disregarding all others (preoperational). *Example: A child is playing outside on a swing when his mother decides to bring him in for a nap. The child becomes upset because all he can focus on is riding the swing.*
Egocentrism	Until about age five, young children cannot differentiate between their own perspectives and feelings, and someone else's (preoperational). *Example: While speaking on the phone with her father, a child says, "See my new shoes."*

Equilibrium	Development is motivated by the search for a stable balance toward effective adaptations. This balanced state is called *equilibrium* and has three phases: (1) Children begin in a state of balance, (2) thought changes and conflict emerges, and finally, (3) through the process of assimilation and accommodation, a more sophisticated mode of thought surfaces.
Irreversibility	Children make errors in their thinking because they cannot understand that an operation moves in more than one direction. They cannot understand that the original state can be recovered (preoperational). *Example: If Emma plays with a ball of clay, she believes that the clay must always be in this same form to remain the same amount. When a classmate plays with the clay and gives it back as a long, narrow piece, Emma thinks she's getting back less.* The opposite of irreversibility is reversibility, which is the ability of children to mentally return to a situation or operation just like it was in the beginning.
Metacognition	A child's awareness of knowing about one's own knowledge. Metacognition helps children plan their own problem-solving strategies (concrete operations). *Example: A child who is thinking about thinking.* Another important term is metamemory, which is knowing about memory.
Object Permanence	Recognition that objects and events continue to exist even when they are not visible. This recognition ability begins when the child is about 8 months old (sensorimotor). *Example: In the absence of object permanence, an infant will not search for the object when the object is hidden—"out-of-sight, out-of-mind."*
Reasoning	**Hypothetical-Deductive Reasoning:** Formulating a specific hypothesis from any given general theory (formal operations). This is the ability to form ideas about "what might be." This is done by mentally forming a logical and systematic plan to work out the right solution after considering all the possible consequences. *Example: Tommy makes a general observation that short students are not selected for the school basketball team. Since Tommy is short, he deduces that he will not be selected.* **Inductive Reasoning:** Drawing conclusions from specific examples to make a general conclusion, even when the conclusion is not accurate (concrete operations). *Example: All of the balls on the school playground are round. By developing a mental schema, a child may reason inductively that all balls are round. This would be an inaccurate conclusion since a football is not round.* **Transductive Reasoning:** Children mentally connect specific experiences, whether or not there is a logical causal relationship (preoperational). *Example: Bill was mean to his little sister. His sister got sick. Bill reasoned that he made his sister sick.* A child believes his thoughts will cause something to happen (see also Causal Reasoning).
Schemes "Schemas"	Schemes are the way children mentally represent and organize the world. Children form mental representations of perceptions, ideas, or actions to help them understand experiences. Schemes can be very specific, or they can be elaborate. *Example: While sitting in a highchair, an infant repeatedly drops a plastic cup onto the floor while thinking, "If I drop my cup, someone will pick it up."* This action helps the infant understand that this schema has a cause-and-effect relationship.
Seriation	This is a child's ability to arrange objects in logical progression (concrete operations). *Example: A child arranges sticks in order from smallest to largest.*
Symbolic Function Substage	The child uses words and images (symbols) to form mental representations to remember objects without the objects being physically present. *Example: A child's dog is lost, so the child scribbles a picture of the dog; or the child pretends that a stuffed animal is the missing dog.*
Transitive Inference	The ability to draw conclusions about a relationship between two objects by knowing the relationship to a third object (concrete operations). If A equals B and B equals C, then A and C are equal. *Example: If you know that Danielle is taller than Ghazaleh, and Ghazaleh is taller than Maria, then Danielle must be taller than Maria.*

Moral Development

Morality is defined as an internalized set of subjective rules influencing the feelings, thoughts, and behavior of an individual in deciding what is right and wrong. Although Piaget explored the process of moral development, it was Lawrence Kohlberg who emerged with significant contributions in the way children process moral dilemmas. Although both theories provide us with a basic understanding of a *sequence* of developmental stages, it is more important for CSET candidates to understand that the *level* of moral reasoning is dependent upon how the child responds to challenges and experiences.

Piaget and Moral Development

According to Piaget, morality is coupled with cognitive development in two noticeably different stages, *morality of constraint* (heteronomous) and *morality of cooperation* (autonomous). He believed that young children, ages four to seven years, are distinguished by morality of constraint. This means that children see their moral world through the eyes of justice and rules, which are unchangeable. As children develop, they become more sophisticated and understand that rules are made up by people. Children understand that there are many variables when deciding what is right and wrong. This new thinking moves them to the next stage of morality, age ten years, when children view each dilemma and consider the consequences before making a moral decision. Piaget calls this stage morality of cooperation.

Lawrence Kohlberg and Moral Development

Kohlberg's theory of moral development is perhaps the most widely recognized model for moral decision-making. He describes moral development as sequential stages that individuals pass through while gradually becoming mature in their moral reasoning. These stages progress from concrete to abstract. Children begin to believe that good actions are rewarded and bad actions are punished. As children mature, they begin to look internally for a mature choice based on moral standards of good and bad.

Kohlberg's Developmental Stages of Moral Judgment	
Level I: Preconventional (Ages 4–10 Years)	Children obey because adults tell them to obey. At this level of morality, children judge morality strictly on the basis of consequences (fear of being punished for bad actions, or expecting to be rewarded for good actions).
Level II: Conventional (Ages 10–13 Years)	Most children in middle childhood or adolescence reason at the conventional level of morality. They are most concerned about the opinions of their peers. Children at this stage want to please and help others, while developing their own internal idea of what it means to be a good person.
Level III: Postconventional (Ages 13 Years–Adult)	This level of morality begins with adolescence and continues through adult life. Morality is judged in terms of abstract principles and not by existing rules that govern society. Moral and ethical choices rise above the laws of society, and individuals look within themselves for the answers rather than basing moral decisions on external sources of authority. Many people never enter into this level of moral development.

The Educational Implications of Moral Development

1. Teachers must recognize that children internalize what is right and wrong based upon their basic values and sense of self.

2. Teachers must recognize the sequential foundation upon which higher moral principles are based.

3. Teachers must recognize that children respond differently to various moral dilemmas depending upon age, education, and socioeconomic influences.

Language Development

Psychologists view language as an instinctive mental ability that emerges as the brain develops and matures. The CSET requires that potential teachers understand that language is a communication system of words that are symbolic representations of objects, actions, and feelings, and that language is a key component of cognitive development. It is through native rules and symbols (grammar and words) that a child constructs cognitive and emotional *meaning*. Language development is a complex process that interfaces with every aspect of a child's development. Children use physical structures to produce sounds, cognitive structures to produce a thought process, and social structures to experience language through learning and practicing. Parents play an active role in the development of their child's language.

Vygotsky: Language Shapes Thought

Lev Vygotsky theorized that thought development is determined by language. This theory provides a rich foundation for understanding contemporary concepts of language development. Language is not just an expression of one's knowledge; it is a powerful tool in shaping thought. To acquire knowledge, thought is a fundamental necessity. It must be "thought about" before any new ideas can be formulated (e.g., a student who is learning English as a second language must be competent in his primary native language before he can "think" or understand new concepts in another language). Therefore, intellectual expression cannot take place until thought and knowledge exist, and this internal intellectual process cannot progress without the interrelation of thought and language. Each one provides a resource for the other. Children transform mental thoughts to organize, guide, and control their behavior through the use of language.

According to Vygotsky, the initial emergence of language and thought are separate from each other, until about the age of three when a transition takes place in the child from the external to the internal. During this stage of development, children practice *private speech* (self-talk) to become more competent. The use of private speech helps children to self-regulate through organizing, guiding, and controlling their behavior. According to Vygotsky, private speech is responsible for all higher levels of mental functioning. Vygotsky's sociocultural theory will be discussed further in Domain 2: Social Development.

Noam Chomsky and Language Acquisition

Language acquisition is a theory based upon the work of Noam Chomsky which states that language learning is innate. Chomsky believes that children are prewired to learn language and that infants have a language acquisition device (LAD) built-in neurologically so that they can intuitively understand grammar. Chomsky also suggests that there is a critical period when children find it easy to acquire language.

Language Development Milestones		
	Age	**Developmental Expectation**
Infant	(0–12 months)	Early vocalizations are spontaneous sounds of cooing (vowels) or crying. Then babbling sounds (phonemes) begin with sounds more like *patterned speech* with consonant-vowel strings ("da-da-da-da").
Toddler	1 year old (12–18 months)	First words are spoken, usually familiar objects or people. Simple monosyllabic words are used, such as "momma" or "bye-bye."
	18–24 months old	First sentences (two-words) are spoken. The toddler can understand grammatical relationships, but cannot yet express them. The toddler uses articles (the, a), prepositions (on, in), conjunctions (and, but), and the verb "to be" (am, are, is). Word errors include *underextending* word meanings.
Early Childhood	3–4 years old	Learns about 8 to 9 words each day. The average vocabulary consists of 1,000 words. The child can talk about things not present, and uses plural and possessive forms of nouns (e.g., cats and cat's). The child adds "-ing" to verbs, and knows that more than one adjective can apply to the same noun (Rusty is black and fluffy). The child also starts *private speech*.
	5–7 years old	Asks many *why* questions (How many stars are in the sky?). The child can understand metaphor (Don't be a quacking duck), and can use 4- to 5-word declarative sentences (I am not sleepy), or interrogative sentences (Why can't I go?) and imperative sentences (Turn off the TV!). The child uses conjunctions, prepositions, and articles regularly, and understands syntax. The child makes errors in *over-regularizations* of transitive or intransitive verbs ("She singed a song"). At six years old, the average vocabulary is 2,500 words, but the child speaks about 8,000 to 14,000 words. Speech is more adult-like.

The Educational Implications of Language Development

1. Teachers must be aware that the process of language development is multifaceted, including physical sounds, cognitive thought, and social interactions.

2. Teachers should recognize that language cognitively, linguistically, and emotionally begins at home. Parents play an active role in teaching language to children. Adults teach language to children through infant-directed speech, recasting, echoing, expanding, and labeling.

3. Teachers should recognize that children will acquire the use of English even when their native language is the only language spoken at home.

4. Since the work of Vygotsky supports the notion that language is essential to the development of thinking, teachers should support appropriate private speech in order to help children self-regulate and access a higher level of functioning.

Intelligence and IQ

Educators and psychologists today face controversy over the fairness of intelligence testing to determine mental abilities, performance ranking, and academic potential. Although most educators and psychologists have different definitions for intelligence, most would agree that intelligence is a trait that is inferred on the basis of observable behavior. Another acceptable definition is that intelligence is an individual's general mental abilities ("g" factor), including: reasoning, problem solving, knowledge, memory, and successful adaptation to the environment.

When CSET candidates are thinking about intelligence, there are two perspectives to consider. The first is the traditional IQ (intelligence quotient) tests, which identify variables to test and measure (such as the *Wechsler Intelligence Scale for Children* and the *Stanford-Binet Intelligence Scales*). Although IQ is often equated with intelligence, it is not the same as intelligence. Intelligence is a collection of abilities that allow the child to learn, think, experience, and adapt to new situations in the world. IQ is a score on an intelligence test. If intelligence is equated with academic achievement, then IQ tests are a good way to measure intelligence. However, if intelligence is viewed as equal to socioeconomic success or carrying out goals of social value, then IQ does not reflect intelligence. This is why contemporary psychologists suggest a different view in intelligence testing which includes a measure of a child's cognitive future potential. Theories such as Howard Gardner's multiple intelligence and Robert Sternberg's triarchic theory of intelligence emphasize multiple dimensions of a child's mind.

130+ = very superior   97th percentile

90–109 = average   50th percentile

69 and below = extremely low   2.275 percentile

$$IQ = \frac{\text{mental age}}{\text{chronological age}} \times 100$$

Intelligence Testing Perspectives		
Traditional IQ Tests	**Stanford-Binet Intelligence Scales (SB-5)** for ages 2 to 85	The *Stanford-Binet Intelligence Scales* test is one of the most widely used tests to assess a student's intelligence. It is used to measure patterns and levels of cognitive development, including verbal, nonverbal, quantitative, and memory. It is a useful assessment to help diagnose childhood developmental disabilities and provides information for special education interventions (i.e., IEP or IFSP).
	Wechsler Intelligence Scale for Children (WISC-IV) for ages 6 to 16	The *Wechsler Intelligence Scale for Children* is used to measure verbal and performance abilities, including verbal comprehension, perceptual organization, working memory, and processing speed. Each subtest is scored separately to help pinpoint strengths and weaknesses. For example, if a child does well on performance subtests, but is weak on the verbal subtests, this may indicate a language disability. The *Wechsler Adult Intelligence Scale* is frequently administered to adults.

| Multiple Intelligence Tests | Gardner's Multiple Intelligence | Howard Gardner created a theory known as multiple intelligences, which proposes a pluralistic view of a child's mind. He states that children possess different intelligences with multiple dimensions. His theory recognizes that children have many different cognitive strengths, as well as contrasting cognitive styles. Gardner believes that intelligence has roots in evolutionary history, and that we are much like our ancestors who had a variety of intellectual strengths to cope with environmental challenges. While most other tests emphasize math and linguistics, Gardner's theory outlines eight types of intelligences that are not typically considered when examining competencies. 1. **Linguistic-Verbal Ability:** The ability to think in words and to use language to express meaning (poets, authors, journalists, and speakers). 2. **Logical-Mathematical Ability:** The ability to carry out mathematical operations (scientists, engineers, and accountants). 3. **Spatial Ability:** The ability to think three-dimensionally (architects, artists, and engineers). 4. **Bodily-Kinesthetic Ability:** The ability to solve problems using the body and physical skill (surgeons, craftspeople, dancers, and athletes). 5. **Musical Ability:** Having a sensitivity to pitch, melody, rhythm, and tone (composers, musicians, and sensitive listeners). 6. **Interpersonal Ability:** The ability to understand others, a people person who has good conversation skills and knows how to interact with others (teachers, mental health professionals, salespeople, and politicians). 7. **Intrapersonal Ability:** The ability to understand oneself and effectively direct one's life (theologians and psychologists). 8. **Naturalist Ability:** The ability to observe patterns in nature and understand natural and human-made systems (farmers, botanists, ecologists, and landscapers). |
| | Sternberg's Triarchic Theory of Intelligence | Robert Sternberg's theory states that people who are intelligent possess a high level of common sense and have the ability to succeed according to their personal definition of success, within the limits of their culture and society. They adapt their weaknesses and get the most out of their strengths. The Sternberg Triarchic Abilities Test (STAT) addresses three components of intelligence: analytical, creative, and practical. 1. **Analytical (componental):** Essentially measures the same elements that are measured by traditional intelligence tests, such as memory, critical thinking, and problem solving. 2. **Creative (experiential):** Consists of the ability to create, design, imagine, or invent. A child who scores high in this area is insightful and creative. This child usually does not relate well to the academic demands of school. 3. **Practical (contextual):** A component that focuses on the ability to use, apply, implement, and put something into practice. A child who scores high in this area is typically "street smart." This child does not usually work well with the demands from school. |

The Educational Implications of Intelligence

1. Teachers should appeal to a balanced combination of all intelligences.

2. Teachers can develop programs to instruct students using multiple domains to help students feel socially valued.

3. Teachers should develop a student's learning portfolio based upon the individual intellectual strengths of each student, including assessments that take into account the diversity of intelligences.

4. Teachers should offer a variety of assessment types to allow students to show their strengths and evaluate their weaknesses.

Children with Special Needs

Learning Disabilities

Children with learning disabilities (LDs) are often children with average to above-average intelligence who exhibit emotional and/or physical maladaptive behavior. In observing children with learning disabilities, teachers frequently view a discrepancy between a child's measured intelligence and the child's performance in the classroom. Typically, LD children have a neurological impairment and the brain has difficulty processing information when it receives stimuli. Many children may not receive adequate diagnosis and treatment for LD because their behavior is often misunderstood or misdiagnosed. Children do not outgrow LD; rather, they develop a variety of coping strategies to better help them deal with their disability. Stress can result in further distress for the child and can magnify his or her symptoms. Learning disabilities in school-age children can be visual, auditory, language learning, perceptual-motor, attention deficit, impulsive, or hyperactive. These are a few examples of learning disabilities.

Learning Disabilities	
Visual-Perceptual Disability (Dyslexia)	Children with a visual-perceptual disability see letters and numbers in different positions. When reading, they may confuse right or left, and they may skip or reverse words. They are sometimes observed as having difficulty with physical coordination due to their difficulty with eye-hand coordination. The most recognized visual-perceptual disability is *dyslexia,* whereby a student perceives letters in the reverse.
Auditory-Perceptual Disability (Hearing Difficulty)	Children who have an auditory-perceptual disability may find it difficult to distinguish between the differences in sounds. Teachers will often observe these children as appearing to be "lost" or "confused," when called upon in the classroom. Teachers frequently comment that these children are not paying attention in the classroom, when in reality, they may be struggling to hear what is being said. Sometimes even subtle disabilities in hearing may prevent the child from understanding the full content of classroom material.
Attention and Hyperactivity Disorders	Most children with Attention Deficit Hyperactivity Disorder (ADHD) show symptoms of both inattention and hyperactivity, but there are some children who are inattentive and do not show signs of hyperactivity; these children have Attention Deficit Disorder (ADD). With this in mind, children with a hyperactivity or attention disability may consistently show one or more of the following behaviors: (1) have a difficult time paying attention, (2) are distracted easily, (3) show hyperactivity, (4) become frustrated easily, (5) have difficulty controlling muscle or motor activity (constantly moving), (6) have difficulty staying on task, succumbing to whatever attracts their attention, and (7) show inappropriate over-activity. Teachers will often observe these children speaking out loud, forgetting responsibilities, and giving up easily when they don't see a resolution to a problem. More boys than girls are diagnosed with this disability. Severe ADHD or ADD is treated by a physician who may prescribe a psychotropic drug such as Ritalin, Concerta, or Adderall.
Perceptual-Motor Disability	Children with a perceptual-motor disability have difficulty with coordination and may often appear clumsy or disoriented. Sometimes their hands are in constant motion and may get in the way of their activity.
Mental Retardation (Educationally Delayed)	Children who are educationally delayed are defined as having subnormal cognitive functioning at an IQ level of 70 or below. This impairment may range anywhere from mild (IQ at 55–70) to severe (IQ below 25). Mentally retarded children show maladaptive behavior in learning, social adjustment, and maturation. Some of the causes of mental retardation may be organic in nature, including genetic abnormalities, the mother's abuse of alcohol or drugs during pregnancy (teratogens), environmental deprivation (lack of nutrition to the fetus), or trauma to the fetus during childbirth. Mental retardation affects about one to two percent of the population, and most fall into the mild range of retardation. With the help of intervention programs, children who are educationally delayed can function fairly well in society. Children show significant improvement with early diagnosis and guidance from a supportive educational environment.

The Educational Implications for Children with Learning Disabilities

1. Teachers must be responsive to the varying individual differences among uniquely different children.

2. According to the Individuals with Disabilities Education Act (IDEA), all children with disabilities are guaranteed a free, appropriate public education. An individualized education plan (IEP) can be designed for children with LD. According to the IDEA, children should be educated in the least restrictive environment. Many children integrate in a regular-classroom setting, inclusion program, but there are some children with LD who meet part time in a regular classroom and part time in a special education classroom, mainstream program.

3. Since many children with LD have difficulty processing information, teachers should consider using methods of instruction that communicate to all parts of the child's senses. This helps the brain make mental pictures (e.g., physical movement, visualization tools, music, dance, etc.).

4. Guidelines for teachers to help children with learning disabilities are:

   a. Be consistent and write down predictable outlines, schedules, and deadlines.

   b. Demonstrate and model appropriate behavior, giving positive reinforcement.

   c. Talk slowly, making eye contact when possible, and keep conversations brief.

   d. Keep peripheral distractions in the classroom to a minimum.

   e. Demonstrate with hands-on instruction whenever possible.

   f. Utilize technology whenever possible (videos, computers, CDs).

   g. Allow students to take untimed tests, and read tests aloud.

   h. Stay with one project at a time, rather than skipping around.

   i. Record presentations on audio-cassettes or give notes to children for use at home later.

   j. For hyperactive children, allow the student to sit behind others so that the student won't disturb others, and teach the student to tap his pencil on a sleeve or leg instead of the table.

   k. Divide classroom assignments into "smaller tasks" to help students feel a sense of smaller accomplishments.

Domain 2: Social and Physical Development from Birth through Adolescence

2.1: Social Development

DOMAIN 2.1: EXAM SPECIFICATIONS	
Birth through Adolescence	❏ Define concepts related to the development of personality and temperament (e.g., attachment, self-concept, autonomy, and identity). ❏ Describe the social development of children and young adolescents, including persons with special needs. ❏ Identify characteristics of play and their impact on social development. ❏ Describe influences on the development of prosocial behavior.

The Influences of Behavioral Theory on Social Development

Social development is based on what can be observed and learned through experience in the child's environment. CSET candidates should be familiar with theories of learning, personality, and behavior, as well as their influences on social development, in order to better understand how these theoretical concepts interface with the development of children. There are two important learning behavior theories to first consider: John Watson's *classical conditioning* and B. F. Skinner's *operant conditioning*. Social theories to consider in understanding child development are: Erik Erikson's *psychosocial theory,* Lev Vygotsky's *sociocultural cognitive theory,* and Albert Bandura's *social learning theory.* These three multi-theoretical framework models are important to the understanding of a child's social and emotional development and help us to further understand the concepts of attachment, temperament, and play.

Conditioning

Ivan Pavlov and John Watson's Classical Conditioning

Ivan Pavlov (1927) and John Watson (1913) were pioneers in classical conditioning, stating that behavior is learned based upon repetition, association, and anticipation. Pavlov conducted *stimulus-response* experiments in which dogs learned to involuntarily respond, by salivating, each time a bell rang at feeding time. The dogs were conditioned to respond to the bell, not to seeing or smelling the food. Watson applied this stimulus-response manipulation to children and claimed that based upon his observations, the behavior of children is easily conditioned.

The Educational Implications of Classical Conditioning

1. Teachers can be assured that through repetition (and based upon the child's experience), learning is predictable.
2. Teachers can help children be successful by making their world more orderly and predictable.
3. Teachers will recognize that a child's learned experiences can account for later behavior patterns.

B. F. Skinner's Operant Conditioning

In *classical conditioning,* children respond automatically, since they have formed an association between a stimulus and the response. Remember in Pavlov's experiment, the dog was conditioned to automatically salivate upon hearing the bell. In *operant conditioning,* however (a theory developed by B. F. Skinner in 1938), children learn from operating in the environment. When children operate in the environment, their behavior response produces a consequence of either a reinforced reward or a punishment. To understand the difference between the two theories, ask yourself, "Is the learned response due to an automatic response, or is it due to the learned associations of anticipated consequences?" In simplistic terms, this associative learning process helps children to associate their actions with a positive or negative consequence. Behavior that is reinforced (rewarded) will tend to be strengthened. Conversely, behavior that is not reinforced will tend to be eliminated or extinguished.

The Educational Implications of Operant Conditioning

1. Teachers can use *behavior modification* in the classroom as a learning tool (altering the environment or situation to produce a more favorable outcome).
2. Teachers can reinforce positive behavior to produce subsequent desirable behaviors (e.g., positive feedback, praise, or gold stars) and not reinforce undesirable behaviors.

Personality

Personality consists of the unique characteristic patterns of a person's thoughts, emotions, and behavior. The traditional examination of personality proposed that personality was based upon an individual's traits. Today there is a continued debate about an individual's traits being inherited versus adapted influences from one's environment. Strong evidence supports both positions. In learning about child development, CSET candidates should understand the importance of considering two combined theories of personality—that is, the psychodynamic theoretical approach and the social-learning theoretical approach to developmental psychology. The best illustration combining both of these concepts was developed by Erik Erikson and his psychosocial stages of development.

Erikson's Psychosocial Stages of Development

Theorist Erik Erikson (1902–1994) helped to transform Sigmund Freud's (1953) traditional psychosexual perspectives on human development. Freud proposed that people are biologically influenced by unconscious drives and defenses, whereas Erikson theorized that early childhood experiences helped to permanently shape personality. According to Erikson (1950), personality develops through a series of conflicts that are influenced by society during age-related time periods. It is a lifelong process. Erikson stated that there are eight stages of age-specific crises that we pass through in order to create equilibrium between society and ourselves. Each stage centers on a unique developmental task that must be confronted and negotiated. Children move to the next developmental crisis, no matter what the outcome, even when the outcome is not favorable and may lead to later adjustment problems. The crisis is considered a turning point in the child's life when successfully mastered. Since the CSET Multiple Subjects test examines a child's development from birth through adolescence, only the first five stages of development are listed.

Erikson's Psychosocial Stages: Stages 1 through 5	
Stage 1 Basic trust versus mistrust (1½ years old)	Gaining a sense of trust during infancy helps to set the stage for a lifelong expectation of feeling safe and secure in the world. The infant can count on others to satisfy his or her needs, while feeling loved and cared for. This basic experience of interacting with an attentive caregiver, gives the infant a lifelong feeling of security and predictability. The absence of trust can result in leaving the infant feeling suspicious, guarded, and withdrawn from relationships.
Stage 2 Autonomy versus shame and doubt (1½ – 3½ years old)	The toddler learns how to explore, experiment, make mistakes, and test limits in order to gain a sense of independence and self-reliance. Toddlers are into everything at this age, and many people refer to this period as "terrible twos." It is difficult to keep the toddler under control. If autonomy is inhibited or punishment is harshly inflicted, the toddler may feel a sense of shame. Shame leaves the toddler feeling a sense of dislike for himself. He may also be reticent to try new activities.
Stage 3 Initiative versus guilt (3½ – 6 years old)	Building upon the successes from the previous stages, children at this age feel free to try out new activities and assume greater responsibility for their bodies and their behavior. This new balance of responsibility helps the preschooler have a positive view of self, gives confidence to his decision-making ability, and imparts a willingness to take risks. Unique aspirations surface, and children begin to show definite signs of emerging personalities. The absence of initiative may leave the child feeling a sense of guilt, sometimes about almost anything. The child may feel like anything he does may disappoint people around him.
Stage 4 Industry versus inferiority (6 – 12 years old)	Industry refers to children learning to work with others while developing skills and feeling a sense of achievement. Children who have successfully completed this stage feel a greater sense of competence in adult life. If successful at accomplishing a sense of industry, the children demonstrate the ability to organize and meet goals. If inferiority outweighs industry, low self-esteem may result. Sometimes these children may appear lazy or lack goals and motivation.
Stage 5 Identity versus role confusion (12 – 18 years old)	The physical changes in adolescents awaken the search for self-identity, breaking dependent ties and providing a framework for adult life. Teens push to figure out who they really are, which helps them to cement a solid sense of self. This sense of self is interpreted as unique from others and instills an identity that is communicated as an inner confidence and sense of one's place in the world. Experimenting with identities is common during this age. Failing to make this transition may result in confusion over life goals and self-identity.

The Educational Implications of Psychosocial Stages of Development

1. Teachers can better recognize developmental themes as they appear in the classroom with a greater appreciation of the child's limited strengths and weakness (i.e., children who demonstrate an inability to express feelings, inability to trust others, or lack feelings of autonomy).

2. In understanding age-specific psychosocial tasks, the teacher can better develop curriculum related to specific grade levels.

3. Teachers can recognize developmental deprivations in order to provide instruction that might better fit the child's mental capability.

4. Teachers can use social and emotional development models to identify age-appropriate behaviors, activities, and materials.

Vygotsky's Sociocultural Theory

Theorist Lev Vygotsky (1896–1934) proposed that at the center of a child's cognitive development is shared system of surrounding social, cultural and historical influences. The premise of Vygotsky's theory (1978) is that children actively construct their knowledge through society. Vygotsky stated that every function in the child's cultural development appears twice—first between people and then internally within the child. Vygotsky believed that language is an essential aspect of this development and that cognitive growth and language are socially based. He also stated that a child's cognitive growth is a shared process. Adults (or older peers) help provide children with learning tools in order to master difficult tasks. Two complementary tenets of his theory include the *zone of proximal development* and *scaffolding*.

- **Zone of Proximal Development (ZPD):** The zone of proximal development is the distance between a child's actual performance and a child's potential performance. The ZPD represents the amount of learning possible by a student given the proper instructional conditions. If provided with guidance by someone more skilled, such as an adult or older peer, the child may exhibit a higher level of competency and move beyond what he or she was capable of doing unassisted.

- **Scaffolding:** Scaffolding is the temporary support system from a teacher (or older peer) to support the child until the task can be mastered alone. The essential elements of scaffolding are (1) the use of mediators for learning, (2) the emphasis of language and shared activity for learning, and (3) shared activity, which strongly improves the child's problem-solving abilities (e.g., a fifth grader helping a first grader read a book).

The Educational Implications of Vygotsky's Sociocultural Theory

1. The importance of social and multicultural education should be emphasized in the classroom.

2. Classroom teaching should emphasize inclusion, providing an environment for all students to think and learn. Isolating a child inhibits his ability to develop.

3. When assessing a child, teachers should understand the difference between what a child can do on his own and what the child can do with help (*zone of proximal development*).

4. Teachers should recognize that children can often perform, with an adult's (or older peer's) help, a task that they may have otherwise been incapable of completing on their own (*scaffolding*).

5. Teachers should be organizing, not dictating, a child's development using "guided practice." Teachers initially assume responsibility for problem solving, but gradually allow the responsibility to transfer back to the child.

6. Parents play a key role as significant contributors in the child's intellectual development.

Bandura's Social Learning Theory

Albert Bandura's (b. 1925) *social learning theory* (1977) has had a significant impact in the development of classroom learning experiences. Whereas the behavioral model of development emphasizes environmental influences on learning and conditioning, Bandura's theory emphasizes the value of learning through observation. This theory stresses the importance of observing and modeling the behaviors, attitudes, and emotional reactions of others to advance in learning. Children imitate behavior through socialization by learning gender roles, self-reinforcement, self-efficacy (belief in the ability to do things on their own), and other aspects of personality. Imitation and rehearsing are powerful tools for learning. In Bandura's "Bobo doll experiment," quiet, well-behaved preschool children observed an adult who repeatedly punched and knocked down an inflated doll. Later, children imitated this aggressive behavior in the classroom. According to Bandura, aggressive models encourage aggressiveness in children.

The Educational Implications of Bandura's Social Learning Theory

1. Teachers are important role models for children. Children will imitate teachers they have formed an emotional bond with or teachers they idealize.

2. Teachers must be aware of inappropriate media influences which can have a negative impact on behavior. Viewing violence can increase the probability that violent behavior will be imitated.

3. Childhood learning is acquired through direct experience and by observing the behavior of teachers, peers, and others in the school environment.

Attachment

Mary Ainsworth's (1913–1999) observations of early mother-infant bonding have had a profound influence in the understanding of child development and *attachment theory*. Through her scientific studies called *Strange Situation*, she developed a well-recognized laboratory-based technique to assess attachment. These patterns of attachment stress the importance of early infant-parent bonding in the development of personality. It is observed as being the core to social development and of all future relationships. It is important for CSET candidates to understand that secure attachment is fundamental to a child's ability to emotionally and biologically self-regulate. On this basis, it is reasonable to expect some degree of continuity from the early years to middle childhood, adolescence, and even adulthood. Strong evidence suggests attachment, whether secure or insecure, can predict future development. The infant, in his earliest stages, forges a working emotional model from a close emotional and reciprocal connection between himself and his caregiver.

Patterns of Attachment	
Secure Attachment	The infant uses the caregiver (parent) as the secure base to explore the environment (e.g., child freely separates from parent to play). Children who are securely attached are relatively comfortable with others, believe that most others are trustworthy, and don't worry about abandonment.
Anxious-Resistant Attachment	The infant becomes anxious before the caregiver leaves, and is upset during the caregiver's absence (e.g., child cannot separate to explore or play. The child may hit, cry, or kick [resisting] upon the parent's return). Children who are anxious-resistant might feel skeptical about trying new things, feel that others can't be trusted, feel angry much of the time, and push away those who try to get close.
Anxious-Avoidant Attachment	The infant readily separates from the parent and actively avoids the parent upon reunion (e.g., child moves away, looks away, or ignores the parent upon the parent's return). Children who are anxious-avoidant tend to have difficulty trusting, avoid playing with other children, and become anxious if someone tries to get too close.
Disorganized-Disoriented Attachment	The infant shows insecurity and shows signs of being disoriented (e.g., child looks dazed, confused, and sometimes fearful upon the parent's return). Children who experience disorganized-disoriented attachment often feel confused or misunderstood, feel that others are unreliable, and are often fearful about new situations.

The Educational Implications of Attachment

1. Although infant attachment is not the only path to social competence in children, teachers should recognize the importance of secure attachment as a key role in observable secure relationships.

2. Teachers should be aware that cultural diversity is an important variable in the effects of social competency among children. Children raised in a socially diverse household may respond differently to secure relationships than children raised in Western society.

3. Teachers should recognize that the emotional bond between the child's primary caregiver and his parent may be unconsciously transferred to the relationship between the teacher and the child.

4. Children who can securely self-regulate and who believe they can achieve have a greater ability to successfully face difficulties and master academic learning material.

Temperament

Temperament is a collective set of inborn traits that help to construct a child's approach to the world. These traits are influential in the development of personality and the way a child shows emotional responses. Temperament is based upon the child's mood, environment, activity, and threshold for reacting to stimulation. Most children show some of the same behaviors that fall into three basic groups of temperament:

1. The "easy" child is generally in a positive mood and adapts easily to new situations.
2. The "difficult" child tends to cry frequently and is slow to accept change to new situations. This child has irregular daily routines.
3. The "slow-to-warm-up child" shows slow adaptations to new situations, but slowly accepts new situations when repeatedly exposed.

Goodness-of-fit refers to the match between a child's temperament and environmental demands the child must deal with (e.g., a four-year-old "difficult" child who is expected to sit still for a five-hour plane ride).

The Educational Implications of Temperament

1. Teachers can better manage the classroom by knowing different temperaments (the introverted child, the conversationalist, the class clown, etc.).
2. By understanding that temperament is different for each child, teachers can plan individualized teaching approaches specific to each child.
3. Teachers can help children feel validated by affirming their temperament attributes. This helps children to look at themselves positively.
4. Teachers should be aware that environmental manipulations, such as culture, influence temperament.

Play

Social development refers to behaviors children engage in during interactions with others. Play is a social activity children engage in just for its own sake; it is critical to cognitive advancement in children. All child development theorists agree that play activities are a valuable function in the contribution of important social and emotional skills in children. Play can help children release physical energy, gain mastery over their bodies, acquire new motor skills, form better relationships among peers, try out new social rules, advance cognitive development, and practice and explore new competencies.

Play therapy is a very successful form of childhood counseling treatment, since it allows children to feel less threatened while working out conflicts and expressing their unresolved feelings. Vygotsky believed that play provides an excellent environment for advancing a child's cognition. He was especially fascinated with make-believe and symbolic expressions of play. Vygotsky believed that for young children, imaginary play was real. For the purpose of this exam, we will examine play as outlined by contemporary theorists who emphasize both social and cognitive benefits of play. Note that the following types of play are listed by popular age periods; however, most forms of play can continue throughout life and into adulthood.

- **Functional Play:** This type of play begins during infancy with sensorimotor movements manipulating objects in order to receive pleasure. It involves repeating muscular movements and can be engaged in throughout life. It involves a repetition of behavior (practicing).
- **Constructive Play:** Toddlers and preschoolers use objects to make something (e.g., building blocks), combining sensorimotor movements and the creation (construction) of something.
- **Pretend or Imaginative Play (Fantasy):** Imagination begins at about 18 months old and is boundless during the preschool years. This is a period when children transform symbols into make-believe play. Pretending helps to build a child's imagination.
- **Rough-and-Tumble Play:** Rough-and-tumble play begins about the end of early childhood, but is most popular during middle childhood. Rough-and-tumble play can be in the form of tag, chasing, wrestling, etc.

- **Games with Rules Play:** Children often play games during elementary school. These games often include rules and are competitive and pleasurable. Preschool children play games, but their games are more in terms of taking turns. Games Play or Games with Rules Play involves a given set of rules and declines around age twelve, but can be engaged in throughout life. It is usually replaced by practice play and organized sports as children approach adolescence.

The Educational Implications of Play

1. Teachers must encourage play since much of the child's cognitive advances in learning take place during play.
2. Teachers must be aware of age-appropriate forms of play for classroom activities and encourage imaginative play whenever appropriate.
3. Teachers can use play to help children release physical energy.
4. Teachers should be aware that play helps children to build social interactions among peers.

2.2: Physical Development

Growth and Development (Including Gender Differences)

Infancy (Birth–2 years old)

Infants grow faster during this period than at any other time. Boys and girls have about the same weight and height, with girls growing only slightly slower than boys.

Early Childhood (2–6 years old)

It is during this period that much of the child's "baby fat" disappears as arms and legs grow longer. Children no longer have a protruding "potbelly" look around their abdomen and begin to develop a new slender look. During the previous stage of development, infants and toddlers had a protruding abdomen because their internal organs grew faster than the body cavity. This is no longer true during early childhood. The decrease in weight during early childhood is attributed to the child's ability to walk, coupled with the fact that fatty tissues start growing at a slower rate. Girls tend to have more fatty tissue than boys, but because boys have more muscle tissue, boys and girls measure in weight and height somewhat equal. If there is any gender difference in growth, boys tend to be slightly taller and heavier.

Middle Childhood (7–11 years old)

Many children grow about 2 inches per year until age eleven. Significant changes take place during this period in the difference in growth between boys and girls. Around six years old, girls are typically shorter and weigh less than boys, but from ages ten to twelve, both boys and girls are about the same size. During this period, there are also vast differences between boys and girls regarding their ability to use fine and gross motor skills. Boys' leg and arm muscle coordination is stronger, helping them to jump farther, run faster, catch, throw, and kick balls farther. This is a period that children begin handwriting instead of printing. Girls tend to have an edge in fine motor abilities, being able to have more coordinated hand-manipulated skills.

Adolescence (12–18 years old)

The start of this period begins with puberty. It is a time of "growth spurts" for both boys and girls. Around twelve years old, girls tend to be taller than boys and weigh almost three pounds more. However, around 13–14 years old, girls lose their edge on growth, and boys exceed girls in height and weight. By the age of 18 years old, boys are about 4 inches taller and 20 pounds heavier. Perhaps the greatest difference in physical development is the acceleration of large motor physical strength in boys. Boys tend to be clumsy at first due to the fast growth of their arms and legs, but quickly acquire an ease of movement. Participation in athletics improves physical strength and coordination. If the adolescent is successful at athletics, his self-esteem can be highly boosted since this brings him approval from his peers. This is a period where teens show a considerable interest in body image. Since body image is so important to teens, some teens may struggle with eating disorders such as anorexia nervosa (intense fear of gaining weight) or bulimia nervosa (binge-and-purge eating pattern).

The Educational Implications of Physical Development

1. Teachers can prepare daily age-appropriate opportunities for children to freely express themselves through gross and fine motor activities.

2. Teachers should understand individual physical differences and design activities accordingly.

3. Teachers can identify physical differences in gender development.

Domain 3: Influences on Development from Birth through Adolescence

3.1 Influences on Development

DOMAIN 3: EXAM SPECIFICATIONS	
Birth through Adolescence	❏ Identify potential impacts on the development of children and young adolescents from genetic or organic causes.
	❏ Identify potential impacts on the development of children and young adolescents from sociocultural factors (e.g., family, race, and cultural perspective).
	❏ Identify potential impacts on the development of children and young adolescents from socioeconomic factors (e.g., poverty and class) and sex or gender.
	❏ Identify sources of possible abuse and neglect (e.g., physical, emotional, and substance abuse, and neglect), and describe their impact on development.

Prenatal Influences

The mother's womb is a child's first environment. Even during the earliest stages of prenatal development, the unborn infant is significantly affected by environmental influences. The growth and development of the unborn fetus is largely dependent upon the mother. The fetus is vulnerable to environmental agents that can cause abnormalities known as teratogens. Teratogens prevent or modify normal cell division so the potential danger to the embryo is greatest during the embryonic stage (two to eight weeks) when the infant's body parts and major organs are forming. Common teratogens to avoid are: (1) alcohol, which can cause mental retardation from fetal alcohol syndrome (FAS), low birth weight, and unusual facial characteristics; (2) nicotine, which can cause miscarriage, low birth weight, and poor respiratory functioning; and (3) drugs, which can cause birth defects, premature births, low birth weight, neurological disturbances, high startle rate, learning disabilities, and slowed motor development. Two other considerations in the development of the fetus are the mother's age (older women and adolescent women are at risk for birth complications), and the mother's nutritional care during pregnancy.

Nutrition and Obesity

It is estimated that only one percent of the population of children and adolescents follow all of the recommended dietary guidelines. Children in the United States consume excess amounts of fat and sugar. A child's home environment influences much of what he or she eats, and nutritional diets are especially deprived among minority or socioeconomically deprived children. A good method to evaluate body fat is to review a child's BMI (body mass index) weight in comparison with his or her height. Obesity and cardiac-respiratory problems are at an all-time high. Overweight children often become overweight adults and risk health problems. The causes of obesity range from genetics and environment to lack of exercise and emotional eating.

Child Abuse and Neglect

Children are fundamentally naive and vulnerable. Unfortunately, caretakers sometimes mistreat children and take advantage of their vulnerability while attempting to minimize and hide in secrecy the extent of the problem. Some of the causes of child maltreatment include lack of parenting skills, economic stressors, lack of education, or adults repeating generational family abuse.

Warning Signs of Abuse

According to the U.S. Advisory Board on Child Abuse and Neglect, child abuse can be classified in four categories: physical abuse, physical neglect, sexual abuse, and emotional maltreatment. A child's reaction to abuse varies greatly depending upon the child, the experience, its frequency, and what is done about it. Children must be allowed to work through whatever range of feelings they have surrounding the abuse, but the two most common feelings are anger and sadness. Because children are simply not equipped physically, emotionally, and socially compared to adult caregivers, it is necessary for professionals, such as teachers, to be familiar with the signs and symptoms of child abuse to aid in its prevention and treatment. One or two symptoms do not necessarily mean the child is being abused. Some of the common signs teachers should recognize are:

1. physical abuse—bruises, sores, burns with a child's vague or reluctant response about where they originated;
2. neglect—poor hygiene (soiled clothes, dirty hair, or body odor), or poor nutrition (excessive hunger or weight loss);
3. sexual abuse—age-inappropriate sexual behavior or knowledge, difficulty walking or sitting, sudden onset of wetting, or inflicted self-harm.

Mandatory Child Abuse Reporting Law

Child abuse is a state crime (not a federal crime). In 1963, California became the first state to require by law the reporting of child abuse. Under California law, abuse includes:

1. if a child is physically injured by other than accidental means.
2. if a child is subjected to willful cruelty or unjustifiable punishment.
3. if a child is abused or exploited sexually.
4. if a child is neglected by a parent or caretaker who fails to provide adequate food, clothing, shelter, medical care, or supervision.

According to the California Child Abuse and Neglect Reporting Law (Penal Code 11165.7), teachers are mandated reporters of child abuse. California does not require that the teacher be absolutely certain of the abuse, only that the teacher has sufficient suspicions that there is cause to believe or suspect abuse. Such suspicions must be orally reported within 24–72 hours, followed by a detailed written report. Information on child abuse and its prevention can be obtained from the California Attorney General's office at www.safestate.org (look in "resources").

The Educational Implications of Child Abuse

1. Teachers should know that children of abuse frequently have difficulty adapting in school, but professional intervention and treatment can provide children with hope and stability.
2. Teachers should be aware that children of abuse can show signs of developmental learning difficulties such as poor concentration, anti-social behavior, and lack of trust.
3. Teachers should recognize warning signs of abuse and report to authorities as necessary.

Chapter 7

Subtest III: Visual and Performing Arts

Content

The genesis of all expression begins with creative thought, and the value of cultivating enrichment programs for visual and performing arts education is vital to a child's success in interrelated disciplines. School-based teaching experiences provide children with a life-long conceptual framework for understanding, appreciating, and developing skills for self-expression of their creative potential. The CSET: Multiple Subjects exam is a multidisciplinary exam that recognizes the importance of teaching integrated learning experiences in dance, music, theatre (drama), and visual art while emphasizing:

- artistic perception
- creative expression
- aesthetic valuing
- historic and cultural heritage
- making connections, relationships, and applications

The questions in this section include visual stimuli (such as pictures and diagrams) when appropriate and relevant. Some items test your understanding of the multicultural and multiethnic nature of the arts. You must also be familiar with basic terminology, concepts, and issues of the art world.

The multiple-choice section contains 13 questions grouped together and 1 short constructed-response question; it covers the following four major domains: dance, music, theatre, and visual art.

Analysis of Exam Areas: Content Specifications* in Visual and Performing Arts

* These are the actual California state content specification standards, available online.

In the visual and performing arts, candidates for the Multiple Subject Teaching Credential identify the components of the *Visual and Performing Arts Framework* and the strands of the California *Student Academic Content Standards* in the Visual and Performing Arts.

Domain 1: Dance

❑ Candidates for Multiple Subject Teaching Credential identify the components and strands of dance education found in the *Visual and Performing Arts Framework* and *Student Academic Content Standards*.

❏ They demonstrate a basic fluency with the elements of dance, such as space, time, levels, and force/energy.

❏ They use basic techniques to create dance and movement with children.

❏ Candidates, while grounded in the elements of dance, are able to identify and explain styles of dance from a variety of times, places, and cultures.

❏ They are able to make judgments about dance works based on the elements of dance.

Domain 2: Music

❏ Candidates for Multiple Subject Teaching Credentials understand the components and strands of music education found in the *Visual and Performing Arts Framework* and *Student Academic Content Standards*.

❏ They demonstrate a basic fluency with the elements of music such as pitch, rhythm, and timbre, as well as music concepts, including music notation.

❏ They use basic techniques to create vocal and instrumental music with children.

❏ They are able to identify and explain styles and types of music and instruments from a variety of times, places, and cultures.

❏ They are able to make judgments about musical works based on the elements and concepts of music.

Domain 3: Theatre

❏ Candidates for Multiple Subject Teaching Credentials identify the components and strands of theatre education found in the *Visual and Performing Arts Framework* and *Student Academic Content Standards*.

❏ They demonstrate a basic fluency in acting, directing, design, and scriptwriting (plot and action).

❏ They can apply these elements and principles in order to create dramatic activities with children, including improvisation and character development.

❏ They are able to identify and explain styles of theatre from a variety of times, places, and cultures.

❏ They are able to make judgments about dramatic works based on the elements of theatre.

Domain 4: Visual Art

❏ Candidates for Multiple Subject Teaching Credentials identify the components and strands of visual arts education found in the *Visual and Performing Arts Framework* and *Student Academic Content Standards*.

❏ They demonstrate a basic fluency with the principles of art, such as balance, repetition, contrast, emphasis, and unity, and are able to explain how works of art are organized in terms of line, color, value, space, texture, shape, and form.

❏ They are able to identify and explain styles of visual arts from a variety of times, places, and cultures.

❏ They interpret works of art to derive meaning and are able to make judgments based on the principles of art as they are used to organize line, color, value, space, texture, shape, and form in works of art.

Sample Questions and Explanations for the Multiple-Choice Section

Each of the following examples represents an area tested in the Visual and Performing Arts multiple-choice section. An analysis follows each question.

Domain 1: Dance

1. Historically, the traditional shape of a folk dance was based upon the:

   A. triangle.
   B. square.
   C. circle.
   D. figure eight.

The correct answer is C. Folk dances pass on important historical and cultural importance from ancient civilizations. All folk dance is a form of cultural dance, and the circle is a universal symbol for ancient sacred cultural dances from around the world. Folk dances, from a historical context, employed a circle design because it fostered community spirit and increased dancer interaction.

2. The dance term *choreography* most commonly refers to:

   A. the act of movement without previous planning.
   B. the steps of a dance as put together for performance.
   C. the duration of a dance.
   D. the creation of movement outside traditional modern dance.

The correct answer is B. The act of movement without previous planning (Choice A) is called improvisation. The steps of a dance as put together for performance or the art of composing dances (Choice B) is called choreography. The duration of a dance (Choice C) is the length of time a dance lasts. Postmodern dance is the creation of movement outside traditional modern dance, Choice D.

3. Ballet can be either dramatic or nondramatic. In comparison to a dramatic ballet, a nondramatic ballet emphasizes:

   A. dancing that is based on classical Greek models.
   B. dancing without telling a story.
   C. poetic and lyrical styles.
   D. fewer technical conventions than traditional ballet.

The correct answer is B. Nondramatic ballet emphasizes dance that does not tell a story. Instead, the dance movement, including its expressive qualities, is the central focus. Dramatic (theatrical) ballet often follows classical models, "classical ballet," based on common themes, precise choreography, and a narrative. Both dramatic and nondramatic ballet allow for different styles that may emphasize musical lyrical qualities.

4. A third-grade teacher decides to prepare a dance lesson. Of the following, which is the most probable reason that she decides to teach a square dance?

   A. It is a very simple dance requiring few movements, is easy to learn, and doesn't require partners.
   B. Students can improvise in this unstructured environment.
   C. This dance is structured, requiring concentration and teamwork.
   D. Most students are already familiar with this type of dancing.

The correct answer is C. The square dance can be simple and easy to learn, but it does require a partner, so Choice A can be eliminated. Students can't improvise in a square dance because it is very structured, so Choice B can be eliminated. In the third grade, the teacher cannot be assured that most students are familiar with square dancing, so eliminate Choice D. Square dancing is directed by a caller but does require concentration to follow the caller's directions. Since at least eight people are involved, it also requires teamwork.

5. The flamenco dance originated in:

  A. Ireland.
  B. Russia.
  C. Brazil.
  D. Spain.

The correct answer is D. The flamenco dance originates from the Andalusian Gypsies of Spain. This style of dance is characterized by forceful rhythms, hand clapping, rapid foot movements, the use of castanets, and colorful costumes. Another popular form of the flamenco dance is called the rumba flamenco with its origins in Cuba and Latin America.

6. Maypole dances were originally associated with:

  A. recreation and pleasure.
  B. winter and hunting magic.
  C. courtship and romance.
  D. fertility and rebirth.

The correct answer is D. Maypole dances were originally associated with fertility rituals. In primitive cultures, a pole was placed in the ground and consecrated during a religious ceremony. The maypole symbolizes spring and the rebirth associated with the changing seasons. Maypole dancing is a recurring theme in most Western cultures. Individuals dance around the maypole, often holding long ribbons that are tied to the pole. The dances are also a link between folk dances and Stone Age dance rituals.

Domain 2: Music

7. Rhythm is the flow of music in:

  A. time.
  B. space.
  C. form.
  D. harmony.

The correct answer is A. All music moves in time (A), not space (B). Music must be internalized "as it goes by." After a composition has been played, one must evaluate it in retrospect, necessitating the development of a musical memory. In other art forms, the viewer has the luxury of analyzing the piece in detail, since it exists in space. Each musical composition has a rhythm, a beat, and a pulse, which exist in time. Form (C) is the overall structure of a piece. Harmony (D) is the combination of tones that accompany the main theme (melody).

8. Which of the following sections includes the largest number of instruments in a traditional orchestra?

  A. Brass
  B. String
  C. Percussion
  D. Woodwind

The correct answer is B. Try to visualize orchestras you have seen. Without the string section, it would be a band, not an orchestra. The string section of a standard orchestra usually has a minimum of ten first violins, eight second violins, six violas, four cellos, and two basses. In the brass section (A) there are usually four French horns, two trumpets, three trombones, and one tuba. In the percussion section (C) there are usually timpani (kettledrums) and two or three other percussion instruments (such as xylophone, chimes, and glockenspiel). In the woodwind section (D) are usually two flutes, two oboes, two clarinets, and two bassoons.

Use the diagram that follows to answer the next two questions.

9. In the musical notation above, what is the note labeled as *x*?

   A. A
   B. B
   C. C
   D. D

The correct answer is C. Remember that in a treble clef staff, the lines are identified from bottom to top as EGBDF (mnemonic device—**E**very **G**ood **B**oy **D**oes **F**ine). The spaces are FACE (mnemonic device—**face**).

10. The vertical lines on the staff in the diagram above are called the bar lines. The bar lines are used to:

   A. mark off the grouping of beats.
   B. show the relative duration of the notes.
   C. show the distance between the notes.
   D. indicate the pitch of the notes.

The correct answer is A. Bar lines are the vertical lines on the staff used to mark off the grouping of beats. The relative duration of the notes, Choice B, refers to the rhythm. Choice C, the distance between the notes, is the interval. And Choice D refers to the clef that indicates the pitch of the notes.

11. Use the scale below to answer the question that follows.

   The above scale is a:

   A. diatonic scale.
   B. pentatonic scale.
   C. heptatonic scale.
   D. whole-tone scale.

The correct answer is B. A pentatonic scale has five different notes in an octave. Notice that no half-step intervals are used. Much African music (and music from other parts of the world except Europe) and many of the spirituals known by early jazz musicians were based on the pentatonic scale. The familiar song "Auld Lang Syne" is an example of a pentatonic melody. The whole-tone scale, Choice D, involves only whole-step intervals, but has no true starting or ending point.

12. Blues music is a kind of jazz that evolved from the music of:

    A. European immigrants working in lumber yards.

    B. Asian immigrants working on the railroad lines.

    C. South Americans working in the fields.

    D. African-American work songs and spirituals.

The correct answer is D. Blues emerged in the early twentieth century as it evolved from African-American work songs and spirituals. Blues music was a form of communicating melancholic feelings. Prior to that time, songs consisted of slave work songs known as "field hollers." The first known recording of a blues song was in 1895 when George W. Johnson recorded "Laughing Song," and by 1920 blues had emerged as an important genre of music.

13. Which of the following would *not* be considered an American *functional* folk instrument?

    A. Spoons

    B. Harmonica

    C. Jug

    D. Washboard

The correct answer is B. A *functional* folk instrument is a familiar household item that is used to make music. Although the harmonica is a well-traveled instrument often used in folk music, it would not be classified as functional because its primary purpose is to make music. Folk music often relies on informal, homemade instruments, which have roots in the music traditions of the British Isles and Africa. The spoons are often used to accompany American fiddle and folk tunes (A). The washboard (D) and jug (C) are popular in African-American jazz, blues, and "jug" bands.

Domain 3: Theatre

14. The movie industry flourished in its early years simply because movies were a novelty. But after a short time, audiences became bored and attendance declined. One development that saved movies from extinction in those early years was that the movies began to tell stories. In the late 1920s, what dramatically changed the film industry?

    A. Films became longer and more detailed.

    B. Films changed from black and white to color.

    C. Movie theatres became more elaborate.

    D. The talking film was invented.

The correct answer is D. In 1927, with the invention of talking films (talkies), the movie industry changed dramatically. Vaudeville and Broadway stage performer Al Jolson produced and starred in the first talking picture, *The Jazz Singer,* which was based on his life. This "new" type of movie revitalized and changed the industry forever.

15. The first known European theatres were in which of the following countries?

    A. Greece

    B. England

    C. France

    D. Spain

The correct answer is A. European theatre was first known in ancient Greece. Early Greek tragedies were performed before 500 B.C. in Athens, starting as performing competitions on hills and evolving into performances in outdoor amphitheatres.

16. Which of the following would be the *least* appropriate play for which to use a thrust stage?

    A. A production that calls for elaborate setting and scene changes
    B. A modern drama that deals with an internal problem/solution
    C. A script that requires audience-actor interaction
    D. A play that includes a dramatic soliloquy

The correct answer is A. A thrust stage extends into the audience's seating area, allowing the audience to surround it on three sides. Such an arrangement does not lend itself to elaborate setting or scene changes. In fact, it was the need for more elaborate staging that prompted the development of the proscenium stage. Audience-actor interaction (C) is a primary advantage of a thrust stage. A dramatic soliloquy (D) is a monologue performed by an actor alone on the stage, which would work well on the thrust stage.

17. A fifth-grade teacher decides to double-cast the lead roles in an upcoming theatre performance. Those that are double-cast will perform on alternate nights. Which of the following is the best reason for the teacher's decision to double-cast the lead roles?

    A. To allow the more talented students to try a variety of different leading roles and to have a backup in case of emergency
    B. To give less popular students an opportunity to have study partners
    C. To allow more students to participate in major parts of the play and to have a backup in case of emergency
    D. To give the less talented students a chance to have a lead role without the fear of being embarrassed in front of the audience

The correct answer is C. Double-casting is often used in school plays to allow more students a chance to have a major role. It also gives the teacher a backup (not actually an understudy) to step in, so that the play can continue in the event of an emergency. Choice A is really not the normal purpose of double-casting. Also, this would not provide an emergency backup, because the backup would be in another key role on the same night, possibly causing a number of last-minute cast changes. Choice B gives no guarantee that the students with the same roles will study together. Choice D doesn't really guarantee that the less talented student will not be embarrassed in front of the audience. The student would still have to perform in front of the audience.

18. In drama, the playwright can take the major ingredients of human experience and give them clarity. The audience sees these elements of real life presented:

    A. in an unusual setting that gives meaning to the less significant elements.
    B. in a meaningful form with the significant elements emphasized and the unimportant omitted.
    C. as an endless stream of thoughts and feelings without direction.
    D. as though the playwright was trying to manipulate reality and mystify the audience.

The correct answer is B. The key to answering this question is noting that the playwright is giving *clarity* to the major ingredients or elements. To give clarity would mean to put them into a meaningful form emphasizing the important elements. Choice A focuses on giving meaning to *the less significant elements*. Choice C emphasizes *no direction*. Choice D mentions that the playwright is trying to *mystify the audience,* not give clarity.

19. While rehearsing a play, a third-grade teacher decides to have her class act out the scenes silently. She is probably using this technique to:

    A. get students more involved in the movements and feelings she wants them to express.
    B. give them the experience of working together as a team.
    C. allow them time to learn their lines better without slowing down the rest of the cast.
    D. create a calm and quiet atmosphere as she directs each of their movements.

The correct answer is A. The teacher could use a number of verbal or oral techniques to give them the experience of working together as a team, so Choice B is probably not what she is trying to accomplish. There are also many better ways to allow students to learn their lines without slowing down the rest of the cast, so eliminate Choice C. An outstanding technique for getting her class more involved in the movements and feelings is to have them pantomime their parts.

20. In the early 1900s, before filmmakers began to utilize the climate and variety of natural scenery available in Los Angeles, most movies were made in:

    A. New York City, New York.
    B. Miami, Florida.
    C. Philadelphia, Pennsylvania.
    D. San Diego, California.

The correct answer is A. In the early 1900s, most movies were made in New York City and New Jersey.

Domain 4: Visual Art

21. The Cubists viewed objects from different angles. Which of the following is *not* characteristic of the Cubist movement of the early twentieth century?

    A. Making use of linear perspective rather than reassembled space
    B. Incorporating sharp edges and straight lines, depicting nature in geometric terms
    C. Using themes from the dimensional art of primitive peoples
    D. Depicting subjects with solid shapes and detailed textures

The correct answer is A. To answer this question, you should focus on the words "Cubists," "angles," and "*not* characteristic." This would lead you to any answer that appears to *not* include dimensions, geometric shapes, or solids. The Cubists, greatly influenced by Pablo Picasso (1881-1973) and George Braque (1882-1963), used geometric planes and allowed objects to be depicted from several vantage points at the same time. In cubist art, the work is disassembled into geometric shapes, interpreted, and reassembled in an abstract form. This form of art helps to depict "movement through time." Choices B, C, and D are characteristics of the Cubists.

22. The axis line in a painting is:

    A. an imaginary line connecting only the strongest and weakest figures.
    B. the median line within a figure.
    C. used only when dealing with circular objects.
    D. an imaginary line that controls the path of eye movement through a composition.

The correct answer is D. The axis line is the imaginary line resulting from the subtle unity achieved in a painting by placing objects in such a way that the eye follows a path through the composition (D). The starting point is also the focal point. The eye, in viewing a logically sequenced painting, begins at the focal point, follows the path, and then, once again, focuses on the starting point.

23. Use the drawing below to answer the question that follows.

In the drawing above, which area of shading best represents a halftone?

A. A
B. B
C. C
D. D

The correct answer is B. The position of the light source determines the direction of the shadow. The shadows are always on the side opposite the light. A halftone is a middle value. The highlight (A) is the lightest value. The core shadow (C) is the darkest value. Choice D represents the cast shadow, which takes the shape of the surface on which it falls.

24. Use the reproduction of the painting below, *Carriages at the Races* (1875) by Edgar Degas, to answer the question that follows.

The nineteenth-century painting above depicts a family departing from a day at the horse races in the countryside. Which of the following statements best describes the main artistic technique Degas uses to portray a realistic landscape?

A. The use of a natural setting with trees and houses
B. The use of atmospheric perspective with cropped margins
C. The use of a subtle color value in the sky, which occupies most of the space in the painting
D. The use of line form

The correct answer is B. In this famous painting, Degas paints an outing with the Valpinçon family at the horse races. He combines the effects of asymmetrical balance, atmospheric perspective, contrast, radical cropping, and color value to create a realistic portrayal of this family in the countryside. To answer this question, you need to look for the "best artistic technique," and although Choice A describes the objects in the painting, it does not refer to a particular artistic technique. Choice C refers to the artistic technique of color value, but does not address the color value and contrast in the dark carriage and sun-bleached landscape, which adds to the realism of the landscape. The artist did not emphasize Choice D, line form, since this does not help to convey realism. When portraying a realistic landscape, artists frequently use a combination of perspective, value, and cropping. Perspective helps to create depth, value helps to create the illusion of a closer object, and cropping helps to provide the effect of a casual scene. Notice the placement of the carriage and horses at the bottom and right margins. At first glance, it seems almost like a candid snapshot of the countryside rather than a carefully planned painting.

---

25. The vanishing point in a drawing or painting is:

   A.   the point where things disappear.
   B.   the point at which parallel lines appear to converge in the distance.
   C.   the place where objects in the drawing or painting overlap.
   D.   the place where some objects in the foreground of a painting seem to lose their color quality.

The correct answer is B. The vanishing point in a drawing or painting is the point at which parallel lines appear to converge in the distance. They give the drawing or painting perspective.

---

26. Use the reproduction below of John Mecray's *Courageous* (1977) to answer the question that follows.

The painting above shows two sail boats at sea. Which of the following artistic techniques best describes the artist's attempt to suggest the force of nature in relationship to the boats?

   A.   The use of *texture* to depict the size and shape of the waves
   B.   The use of *space* to depict the sea's vastness
   C.   The use of *emphasis* and *line* as depicted in the tilt of the ship
   D.   The use of *color value* to depict dark, foreboding clouds

---

The correct answer is C. This nautical art reproduction replicates the vessel *Courageous* that twice won America's Cup. Even if you're not familiar with this painting or the definitions of art techniques, you should have identified the text, "which of the following artistic techniques best describes," in order to be able to narrow your choices down to two possibilities, choices C or D. Choice A is irrelevant since the waves do not appear to be immense or forceful, and the technique of the use of *texture* does not apply here. Choice B is not the correct answer since vastness does not necessarily imply force, nor does the use of the technique *space*. Although space influences how an object might appear, there is no force associated with space in this composition. This leaves you with two choices, C or D. Remember, when interpreting art, always ask yourself, "What is my first impression, what mood does this composition suggest, and what grabs my attention?" In Choice D, the *color value* of the dark clouds in the upper-left quadrant suggests an impending storm. This might imply a force of nature, but Choice C is the best answer since the artist's use of *emphasis* should lead your eyes directly to the tilted vessel. Notice the fullness of the sails as they touch the sea's dark waters. The artist creatively uses *lines* on the slanted sails to indicate a fast movement forward. This suggests a force of nature influencing the movement of the sails.

27. Use the reproduction of the painting below, *The Banjo Lesson* (1893), by Henry O. Tanner, to answer the question that follows.

The artist uses different techniques to direct your attention to a specific center of interest. Which of the following statements best describes the artist's use of color value in order to communicate the emotional mood in this painting?

A. The intensity of the bright glow of light behind the banjo players' heads
B. The dark shadows on the floor in the front of the painting
C. The contour shapes of the banjo players
D. The diagonal slant of the banjo in contrast to the wall

The correct answer is A. This formal painting is an excellent example of creating mood through the artistic element of color value. Trained in France, Henry O. Tanner was influenced by impressionists and was the first distinguished African-American artist of the nineteenth century to achieve international acclaim. This painting keenly captures an emotional mood of the love between a grandfather and his admiring grandson. This enduring portrait depicts the reverence and dignity of strong cultural home-life values, rather than a portrait of stereotypical struggles of slaves. Tanner's use of color value in the bright glow of light behind the heads of the banjo players helps us to focus our attention on the sentimental mood of these two family members. "My effort has been to give the human touch which makes the whole world kin, and which ever remains the same." (Tanner, 1893).

Sample Questions and Strategies for the Short Constructed-Response Section

Following are representative Visual and Performing Arts short constructed-response questions from each area covered. Strategies and a sample response are included with each question.

Domain 1: Dance

> **1.** Complete the exercise that follows.
>
> All cultures incorporate dance as a form of expression.
>
> Using your knowledge of visual and performing arts:
>
> - briefly describe the development of ritual dance as practiced by ancient Native American Indian tribes; and
> - include in your answer the function of ritual dance and the characteristics of fertility and hunting.

Strategy

Write out key terms in the question—in this case, ritual dance, Native American, fertility, and hunting. Before beginning your response, think about why cultures use rituals of all kinds. Recall modern rituals and consider possible similarities with ancient rituals (such as purpose or setting). Simply defining the terms *ritual dance, fertility,* and *hunting* in a primitive context would give you partial credit.

Sample Response

Ancient Native American dance is rich in symbolism and continues to influence traditional Native American culture. All ritual Native American dances are sacred in nature and have a ceremonial meaning. Native Americans continue to honor their ancestors through dance as a physical manifestation of the sacred mysteries of life. The function of traditional ritual dance among Native Americans is important for celebrating, healing, preparing for events (battle, harvest, rainfall), and honoring the deceased. These wonderful rhythmic dances are accompanied by chants, costumes, prayer, and ceremony. They are often performed at a powwow.

The ceremonial dance of fertility was symbolic of the mystery of the giving of life and a celebration of the joy of living. Fertility dances were performed by many Native American tribes throughout the ages. Although ritual dances varied by region, these dances represented the most basic of human concerns and recognized human dependence on the natural world while honoring nature's elements: earth, air, water, and sun. Ritual dance represented the natural rhythm of the seasons (dances were most common before the planting and harvest seasons) and was an attempt to assure prosperity for present and future generations.

Some dances were intended to create hunting magic. Male dancers, dressed in animal skins and adorned with body paint, would dance and chant to create the proper magic for good hunting. The animal dance was the link between the natural and the supernatural worlds. Their gods were called upon to protect the hunters and provide game for a successful hunt. Although some of the reasons for ritual Native American dance have changed through the years, the shared cultural experience of dance continues to be celebrated throughout North America today.

Domain 2: Music

---

2. Use the musical notation below to complete the exercise that follows.

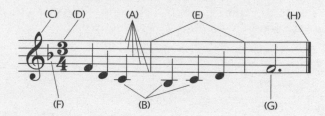

Using your knowledge of music:

- identify the elements and symbols noted in the musical notation; and
- describe the function of these symbols.

Strategy

First determine key terms. Notice in this exercise that you are to identify the elements and symbols that are noted in the musical notation. So pay careful attention to each item noted by the letters (A), (B), (C), etc. Even if you don't know what they all represent, address the ones you know. You are also being asked to describe the function of these symbols. Since there appears to be a lot to do, keep your description of the function short and simple. You don't have time for a long, drawn-out explanation of the function of each.

Sample Response

(A) refers to the staff that is the series of five parallel lines. Musical notes are written on and between these lines. Notes can also be written above and below the staff using ledger lines that are indicated here by (B). The pitch of the notes written on the staff is designated by a clef sign, marked here as (C). In this example, a treble clef (G clef) sign is used, which denotes higher pitches than that of the bass clef (F clef) sign. (D) refers to the meter signature or time signature—3/4. The lower number, 4, indicates the unit of measure (the note that receives the beat), while the upper number, 3, indicates how many of these units comprise a measure. The measure (also called a bar) is noted by vertical bars that break the musical notation into pieces. The measure or bars are noted here by (E). The 3/4 time is commonly associated with the rhythm pattern used for a waltz. (F) refers to a key signature, which in this case shows that there is one flat on the note B, indicating the key of F. (G) refers to the note F, which in this case is a dotted half note. And finally, the double bar at the end marked as (H) indicates the end of the music.

---

3. Complete the exercise that follows.

Symphony orchestra instruments are usually categorized into four different musical families. Using your knowledge of music:

- identify at least three of the categories;
- discuss the uniqueness of each category you identify; and
- give two examples of instruments in each category.

Strategy

Start by concentrating on the key words. Notice that you have to identify at least three and discuss the uniqueness of each, and give two examples. Start by making a simple list of types of instruments and then note how they are different.

Notice that each sample response discusses four possible categories, but you are only required to identify and discuss three.

Sample Response

1. The string category is composed of instruments that produce their tones by the vibrations of one or more strings. These vibrations are caused by plucking, scraping, or bowing the strings. Two instruments of the string family include the violin and cello.

2. The woodwind category got its name because its instruments were originally made of wood. Now some also are made of metal or other materials. Woodwind players produce sounds by blowing through a reed or reeds, or over a hole. Two woodwind instruments are the clarinet and oboe.

3. Brasses are another category of instruments. The player places his/her lips against the mouthpiece in such a way that they vibrate when the player blows, thus producing sound. Sounds are changed by tension of the lips, opening or closing a valve, or sliding a piece of tubing. Two examples of brasses are the trumpet and trombone.

4. Percussion instruments produce sound by being shaken or struck. Two examples are the snare drum and the tambourine. In an orchestra, the piano is usually included in the percussion section.

Domain 3: Theatre

> 4. Using your knowledge of theatre education, answer the question that follows. How can stage lighting create mood and atmosphere in a modern theatre production? Include specific examples to support your answer.

Strategy

Pay attention to the key words in the question—in this case, stage lighting, mood, atmosphere, and specific examples. Before beginning your response, consider how stage lighting is generally used in a theatre production. Recall any recent theatre productions you've seen. Next, use the space provided for prewriting to list some of these uses and their effects on the production.

Sample Response

Stage lighting dramatically enhances the artistic effect of any dramatic presentation. Modern theatres are generally designed to be "light tight." The lighting director or designer can fully illuminate, partially illuminate, or withhold light to focus attention on a specific actor and control the visual focus of the audience.

Front lights, sidelights, and top lights in back are interconnected in order to provide a coordinated visual and sensory effect for a scene. Front lights illuminate the actors' faces. Sidelights give the action dimension, and top lights in back pull the actors away from the set. Theatre lighting has the capacity to transform white light into a mood-altering array of colors. The proper use of the "mixing of light" can manipulate emotions and allow the audience to more fully experience the depth of a character and the mood of a place.

> 5. Write a response to the following statement. Other than in musical style, briefly compare and contrast an opera and a musical.

Strategy

Before you answer the question, try to recall both general and specific information about performances you have seen. What operas are you familiar with? (Perhaps you are familiar with *Madame Butterfly, The Magic Flute,* or *William Tell.*) What is the subject matter of most operas? (The subject matter of most operas is dramatic themes; the drama is set to music.) What about staging? What can you recall about musicals? (Musicals use both songs and spoken dialogue.) Notice that the question asks you *not* to talk about musical style.

Sample Response

Both operas and musicals are staged stories. Both employ costumes, scenery, soloists, dancers, and chorus. Certainly music is the medium that connects all elements in both. However, there are major differences between the two theatrical forms.

In an opera, there may be spoken dialogue, but usually the music is continuous. The emphasis in an operatic stage performance is less upon dialogue; instead, the vocal skills of the singers are displayed.

In comparison, a musical is a form in which there is much spoken dialogue, highlighted with songs. The focus in a musical is upon the acting and story line, rather than the singer. Since its beginnings, musical theatre has integrated drama, music, chorus dancing, and soloists.

Domain 4: Visual Art

6. Use the reproduction of the painting below to complete the exercise that follows.

Using the painting reproduction above and your knowledge of visual art:

- identify the probable historical period from the subject matter and style; and
- briefly discuss the design techniques (such as texture, background, brush strokes, and balance).

Strategy

Although you should always analyze a picture carefully, it is easy to over-answer a visual prompt question, so, as always, be mindful of time. Here, consider whether the subject matter gives clues to the time period or artist. Look at the composition (the arrangement of physical elements in the painting). Is it symmetrical or asymmetrical? Look at the background. Decide if techniques are evident and what they are. Does the picture have a theme? Why might the figure be gazing in a particular direction?

Sample Response

The subject matter and style are representative of the Renaissance period.

In this painting, the main figure is placed flatly against the background. The picture is balanced on each side by an equal amount of space. The illusion of depth is weak in spite of the distant trees. The figure is placed strongly in the foreground, and there is no indication of a middle ground. The background serves merely as a decorative drop to create balance and to fill space.

The eye of the viewer follows the figure in a continuous cycle, starting and ending on the figure's face. The repetitive linear texture of the velvety dress complements and aligns with the flowing structure of the robe. The figure is modeled in light and dark values so that it appears solid, round, and lifelike.

---

7. Use the photos of the sculptures below to complete the exercise that follows.

I.   II.

Using the photos above and your knowledge of visual art:

- compare the two sculptures; and
- contrast them.

Strategy

Notice that this exercise is asking you to compare and contrast. As a result, you need to be careful to find similarities and differences. In your prewriting, make a simple list of each. Then write from your list.

Sample Response

Both sculptures are similar in that they are missing parts: The first sculpture is missing arms, while the second is missing its head. They are obviously different in the parts they are missing. By their appearance, these missing body parts do not seem intentional, which indicates that the creators did not anticipate their sculptures losing those parts. Therefore, both sculptures are similar in that they are now quite different in appearance than they were when originally created. Both sculptures are standing upright, although one is posed balancing on one foot (possibly dancing), while the other seems more stable on both feet. Each figure appears to be based on a female body, although they differ in that one portrays a human, with the other only part human. The wings on the second sculpture clearly indicate that the sculpture's creator was designing a character that was more than human—part angel. Notice the difference in attire. The first sculpture appears either barely clothed or unclothed, while the second one is wearing some sort of toga or dress.

Review of Domains

The Visual and Performing Arts section of the CSET: Multiple Subjects includes four domains: dance, music, theatre, and visual arts. CSET candidates should be able to make informed judgments about the quality of works in the arts based on the elements, principles, and/or concepts of the art form. They develop criteria for their judgments and justify their interpretations with plausible reasoning. Candidates are asked to analyze the components and strands of the *Visual and Performing Arts Framework* and *Student Academic Content Standards,* and examine the connections among them. They are also asked to explore the origins, meaning, and significance of works in the visual and performing arts; raise questions that have been asked by people, past and present; and determine how their responses have varied in significant ways over the years. As candidates explore these meanings, they are better prepared to analyze, weigh, and express ideas about aesthetic issues in the visual and performing arts.

Domain 1: Dance

Dance is the art of movement and expression. As children transform images, thought, and feelings into a series of sequential moves, these movements reveal personal, social, and cultural significance. Dance helps children organize physiological energy within space and time to communicate an artistic form of expression from internalized structures of their surrounding world. The language of dance provides children with a unique opportunity to appreciate movement from the vibrant cultures around the world that interface with music, literature, theatre, and visual arts.

The foundation of the elements of dance begins prior to entering school as children first express movement through their experiences of play. Play helps children to engage their imagination and use their physical and mental abilities. During adolescence, dance provides students with opportunities to express their creative, physiological, and technical abilities as they practice and refine their skills in arranging, performing, and interpreting movement skills.

Elements of Dance

The elements of dance movements are space, time, levels (dynamics), and force (energy). These elements are fundamental to the art of dance, and CSET candidates will be required to know these conceptual tools. These elements should be integrated throughout dance instruction, from warm-up and skill building to expression through classroom dance activities. All dance performances engage, in some aspect, one of these movement elements. The dynamic complexity of these elements can be combined to create dozens of combinations of dance movements. The emphasis of these elements is based upon the student's experience, performance level, and creative expression. Dance activities begin with body awareness and warm-up exercises, including posture, balance, flexibility, strength, and coordination.

Elements of Dance	
Space	**Locomotor** (travelling through space) The Eight Basic Steps – walking, running, leaping, jumping, hopping, galloping, skipping, and sliding (Chasse). **Nonlocomotor** (staying in one place "on spot") – stretching, pushing, twisting, bending, kicking, sinking, or curling. **Combined Locomotor** (often traditional folk steps) – two-step, paddle, grapevine, step-hop, chug, and spinning. When thinking about space, teachers should also be aware of the space between the dancers. ❏ Individual, group, or class (solo, duet, or ensemble) ❏ Space between dancers (side-by-side, supported, far, or near) ❏ Interactions between dancers (leader, follower, mirror, unison, or parting)
Time	**Rhythm** – countable patterns. **Tempo** – fast or slow speed. **Beat** – even or uneven. **Meter** – 2/4 time, 3/4 time, etc. **Syncopation** – a rhythmic pattern produced when a deliberate pattern is upset. **Rhapsodic Rhythms** – non-metric (e.g. breath, water, or wind).

Levels	**Direction** – forward, backward, up, down, sideways (horizontal or vertical), diagonal, straight, circle, out, in, zigzag, or spiral. **Form and Shape** – angular, rounded, twisted, bent, crooked, symmetrical, or asymmetrical. **Level** – high, medium, or low. **Range** – wide, narrow, big, or little. **Pathway** – floor, elevated, or air patterns. **Focus** – gaze, floor, or away.
Force	**Quality of Energy** – sustained (smooth), suspended (light), swing (under-curve), sway (over-curve), collapsed (loose), percussive (sharp), or vibrate (shudder). **Degree of Energy** – strong, weak, heavy, light, dynamic, static, flowing, or tense.

Framework for Dance Activity Instruction

- Determine appropriate age-related expectations for a safe, enjoyable classroom activity.

- Determine the physical abilities, as well as gender-specific and special needs of students.

- Provide students with research and learning opportunities for cross-disciplines.

- Begin with a warm-up and end with a cool-down. Exercises should include steps to be used in the dance activity.

- Separate the dance into the steps. Begin by teaching the steps, describing and demonstrating each separately. Steps are done slowly at first, using counts, and then at the proper tempo.

- Teach one part of the basic step pattern at a time. When two parts have been learned, combine them to establish continuity of the dance.

- Explain the floor pattern. Have the dancers walk through the floor pattern. Then combine the steps with the floor pattern, first without music, and then with music. (Remember that not all dances have a set floor pattern.)

- Use key words and counts to cue the steps and directional changes, and to alert students (e.g., "ready"). This helps students keep the main rhythmic pattern and encourages them to gain a sense of the whole.

- Encourage vigorous activity so that students become involved in the experience and have little time to worry about things such as who their partner is.

- Encourage opportunities for different dance experiences such as solo, line, circle, scatter, or group formations of three and four. This dispels the idea that one must have a partner to dance. Restrict choice when partners are needed (e.g., ask students to dance with the person standing opposite, or the person closest). Encourage frequent and rapid change of partner.

- Provide an opportunity for students to refine their skill level. Once the whole dance has been learned, repeat several times to increase fluency and enjoyment.

- If the dance is to be performed in a formal or public setting, allow opportunities for all students to perform, and not just the most able dancers.

- Provide opportunities for interpretation of dance.

- Provide a classroom dance program that includes different styles of dance from a cultural and historical context.

Adapted from *Arts Education: A Curriculum Guide for Grade 8* (Saskatchewan Education, Training and Employment, September 1994).

Styles of Dance and Movement

Styles of Dance and Movement	
Ethnic and Cultural Dance	**Cultural dances** often carry important historical significance from ancient civilizations. Classic cultural dances from around the world include the Chinese ribbon dance, the Polish polonaise, and India's Kathakali or Bharatanatyam dance. Another cultural dance is "clogging," traditionally from Wales, which involves double taps on both the heel and ball of the foot. Popular performances of the production *Riverdance* demonstrate Irish dancing. Some popular historical dances that are often used today include the pavane or galliard (from the Renaissance period), the minuet, Charleston, twist, disco, hip-hop, and Lambada. **Religious** or **Ceremonial Dance:** Choreography played a significant role in many cultural events throughout history. The origins of dance show that dance was created and performed in celebrations, rituals, and rites of passage. Native Indians, for example, have expressed mourning the spirit in dance movement. They have also used dance as a ritual to prepare for battles and to celebrate joyful occasions. Many cultures consider dance a universal spiritual language.
Folk Dance	All **folk dance** is a form of cultural dance. Folk dance originated from medieval times when townspeople danced to celebrate. Medieval "carolers" were the first folk dancers and could be found throughout England and other parts of Europe. Although there are many dances that originated in Europe, authentic folk dancing in its purest form must include these four factors: 1. Dance movements must predate the nineteenth century. 2. Dance is performed by peasants or royalty. 3. The choreography is derived from tradition. 4. There is no teacher. Variations of the original folk dances are found in dance forms of today, including square dancing and barn dancing. **Play and sing with movement:** Primary school children love to play and sing with movement in the simple sing-along dances of London Bridge, Hokey Pokey, Ring Around the Rosie, The Farmer in the Dell, B.I.N.G.O, Pop Goes the Weasel, and Skip to My Lou. **Maypole dance:** Often danced on May Day in various European nations such as Germany and Sweden, the Maypole dance is taught in American schools today. The maypole itself is a tall pole decorated with floral garlands, flags, and streamers. Ribbons are attached to a pole, so that children can hold a ribbon as they dance.
Modern Dance	**Modern dance** was born in the twentieth century as a result of dancers resisting the rigid structure of classical ballet dance. Modern dance choreography is based upon the subjective interpretation of internalized feelings, emotions, and moods. Unlike formal ballet, modern dance is often unstructured and makes deliberate use of gravity and body weight to enhance movement. Since modern dance encourages free-style dance, teachers should utilize this style of dance in an effort to provide dance opportunities for all ability levels in the classroom. It also encourages students to express feelings and emotions through movement.
Theatrical Dance	**Theatrical dance** is based on music, songs, dialogue, and dance. Audiences often experience it in the form of musical theatre productions. Well-known musical productions are ballet, jazz, and tap. Other productions include ethno-cultural, kabuki, Russian, and Celtic dance.
Social Dance	**Social dance** refers to dances in which socializing is the main focus; therefore, a dance partner is essential. The popularity of competitive social dancing has helped many of these dance styles become household names. Social dance styles include hip-hop, line dance, ballroom, waltz, foxtrot, tango, rumba, jive, and swing.

Dance Interpretation

CSET candidates are expected to assist students in developing interpretation guidelines for analyzing dance from various societies and cultures around the world. Guidelines should include:

- the origin and purpose of the dance (i.e., ceremonial, social, ritual, etc.).
- the geographic location and climate of the country.
- the rituals, customs, and beliefs of the culture.

- historical influences of the dance.
- symbolism, analogies, or metaphors used in the dance.

Dance Historical Timeline	
Prehistory to Beginning of Middle Ages (A.D. 400)	❏ **Characteristics:** Circle form (rhythmic motion within a circle); use of imagery. ❏ **Gender roles:** war and hunting for men, seasons and planting for women. Early accompaniment came from drums, harps, flutes, and chants. ❏ **Forms:** Social dance, which celebrated births, special events, and rights of passage; ritual dance, which maintained tradition, religious rituals (temple dances), and hunting magic; and fertility dance, which marked the changing seasons (especially for planting and harvesting) and sought favor with gods. ❏ **Historic evolution (use of dance movement): Egypt:** movement associated with gods/funerals; **Greece:** in theatre-chorus; also the festival of Dionysus; **Rome:** pantomime/dance expression; **India:** formalized hand movements (e.g., Hindu dance, the oldest world dance); **Java:** elaborate costumes, balance and moderation, and traditional dance; **China:** ceremonial dance with each character having specific hand movement, and martial (war) dancing; **Japan:** Kabuki (traced to primitive rituals; it involves stomping, elaborate costumes, is male only, and is still current).
Middle Ages (500–1400)	❏ **The Church attempted to restrict pagan dance,** often associated with fertility, but folk dances evolved from earlier ritual dance (e.g., Maypole dance; origins in primitive fertility rituals [dancing around a pole]; associated with spring). ❏ **Characteristics of folk dance:** there are many regional differences; all had recreational aspects and basic steps such as running, walking, hopping, and skipping; all are linked to culture, music, and the history of a group; they take the form of a circle. ❏ **Current examples in the twentieth century:** polka; square dances; historic dances—Cossack dance of Russia, polonaise of Poland, Czardas Hungarian tavern dance, and Mexican El Jarabe Tapatio ("hat dance").
Renaissance (1400–1600)	❏ Dancing evolved from pageants and processions of the period. ❏ Ballet developed in France (1500s), and moved to Italy; this led to the development of court dancing in Europe (nobility in a palace setting); patronage of the Medicis; "dancing masters"; steps were slow (adagio) and fast (allegro); lack of spontaneity (defined steps). ❏ Music to accompany specific, technical ballet steps; a theatrical art form developed—music, costumes, setting, plot, and themes such as Greek and Roman mythology and history (Julius Caesar); Shakespeare's *Romeo and Juliet*. ❏ Minuet: a formal aristocratic court dance developed at the end of the period.
Eighteenth and Nineteenth Centuries	❏ Formal dancing spread to the Continent; expansion of professional dancing masters; professional choreography at the Paris Opera (opera and dance); costuming; introduction of the waltz (1-2-3) rhythm; court dance. ❏ Ballet developed throughout Europe; this led to virtuoso dancing; expressive capacity of the body; pointe footwork and the heel-less shoe. ❏ Era of Romanticism (early 1800s): the continued evolution of ballet; emphasis on emotions and fantasy; true pointe work; evolution of "lightness in flight"; this differed from other dance forms in placement and alignment of the body, as well as in training. ❏ Focus on the ballerina; the male dancer was secondary.
Early Twentieth Century	❏ Revolutionary aspects of Ballets Russes (Russia); stretched the boundaries of classical ballet; new movements ("turnout"). ❏ Revolutionary aspects of early modern dance; appreciated the qualities of the individual; primitive expression and emotion; "new freedom" of movement; choreography of Isadora Duncan and Martha Graham and their harsh break from restrictive classical ballet and tutu; broadening the minds of the public; explosion of modern dance in the early twentieth century. It was during this period that ragtime jazz emerged, and the "flapper" era influenced fast-moving dances like the Charleston.

continued

385

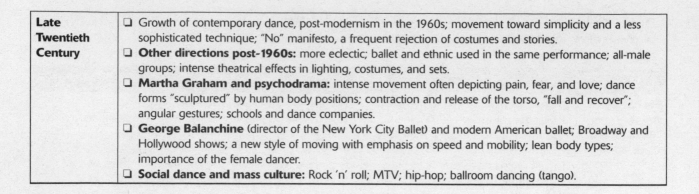

Late Twentieth Century	❑ Growth of contemporary dance, post-modernism in the 1960s; movement toward simplicity and a less sophisticated technique; "No" manifesto, a frequent rejection of costumes and stories. ❑ **Other directions post-1960s:** more eclectic; ballet and ethnic used in the same performance; all-male groups; intense theatrical effects in lighting, costumes, and sets. ❑ **Martha Graham and psychodrama:** intense movement often depicting pain, fear, and love; dance forms "sculptured" by human body positions; contraction and release of the torso, "fall and recover"; angular gestures; schools and dance companies. ❑ **George Balanchine** (director of the New York City Ballet) and modern American ballet; Broadway and Hollywood shows; a new style of moving with emphasis on speed and mobility; lean body types; importance of the female dancer. ❑ **Social dance and mass culture:** Rock 'n' roll; MTV; hip-hop; ballroom dancing (tango).

Dance Glossary

The following glossary suggests terms with which you should be familiar for the CSET: Multiple Subjects.

Abstraction: The essence of an idea applied to the art of movement.

Adagio: As in music, the opposite of *allegro,* or a slower tempo. *Adagio* is also a set of practice exercises in class consisting of extensions and balances.

Alignment: The way in which various parts of the dancer's body are in line with one another while the dancer is moving.

Allegro: From the musical term, this refers to quick or lively movements.

Arabesque: A pose in which the working leg is extended with a straight knee directly behind the body. (Both the height of the leg and the position of the arms are variable.)

Attitude: A pose modeled after the statue of the winged Mercury by Giovanni Bologna in which the working leg is extended behind the body with the knee bent; it can also be held in front of the body.

Barre: A round rail attached to the wall horizontally, about three and a half feet above the floor, for dancers to hold during the first half of technique class; it is also used for stretching the legs by placing the feet or legs on it.

Body movement: Includes locomotor (moving from one place to another) and axial (contained movement around an axis of the body).

Choreography: The steps of a dance as put together for performance or the art of composing dances.

Classical: Refers to the lexicon of dance as taught in the original academies; this is also used in reference to ballets as created during the Imperial Russian days, such as *The Sleeping Beauty, The Nutcracker,* and *Swan Lake;* this also refers to a style of performing that was developed over the years in France, Italy, Denmark, and Russia or the kind of dancing that comes from that style.

Creative movement: Dance movement that is primary and nonfunctional, with emphasis on body mastery for expressive and communicative purposes.

Dance: All-inclusive term meaning the aesthetics of movement. A dance is the organization of moves with a beginning, middle, and end in sequential form.

Dance-pointe: On the ball of the foot, or half toe.

Elevation: The ability to get up into the air and remain there long enough to perform various movements or poses.

Extension: Raising the leg to a straightened position with the foot very high above the ground; the ability to lift and hold the leg in position off the ground.

Force: Release of potential energy into kinetic energy.

Grand jeté: A leap from one leg to the other in which the working leg is kicked or thrown away from the body and into the air; the pose achieved in the air differs, as does the direction the leap takes.

Grand jeté en tournan (tour jeté): In this leap, the dancer turns halfway in midair to land facing the direction in which the movement started.

Improvisation: Movement without previous planning.

Kinesthetic awareness: Feeling the dance movements of others in one's own muscles.

Lifts: A part of *pas de deux* in which one dancer is lifted off the ground by another.

Line: The arrangement of head, shoulders, arms, torso, and legs while dancing.

Modern dance: Type of creative dance involving specialized movement techniques; emphasis is on expression and communication.

Movement materials: Sequences, motifs, and phrases developed as the choreographed dance.

Pas de deux: Literally, "a step for two"; this refers to a specific codified form that is choreographed in many classical ballets; this is also used to refer to any section of a dance performed by two dancers together.

Passé: A "passing" position in which the foot passes by the knee of the supporting leg. When this position is held, as in pirouettes, with the foot of the working leg resting against the knee of the supporting leg, it is known as *retiré*.

Pirouette: "To twirl or spin"; a turn on one foot that can be executed outward, away from the body, or inward, toward the body.

Pointe: Dancing on the toes.

Postmodern dance: A term coined in the 1960s by those who wanted to create movement outside the influences of any of the then-traditional modern dance pioneers, such as Cunningham, Graham, Humphrey, Limón, and Taylor.

Promenade: An *adagio* movement in which the dancer pivots completely around on one foot while maintaining a pose with the working leg.

Romantic Era: A period from about 1820 to 1870 in which ballet was characterized primarily by supernatural subject matter, long white tutus, dancing on the toes, and theatrical innovations that permitted the dimming of the house lights for theatrical illusion.

Space: Immediate area surrounding the body; the area in which bodies can move at all levels.

Spotting: Focusing the eyes on one point in the distance in order to keep balance while turning.

Domain 2: Music

The participation in a primary school music education program has the potential to enhance and improve all other classroom disciplines. Music is a universal language that can motivate, inspire, and stir emotional responses. An effective music program helps students gain an appreciation for music awareness while heightening critical listening skills. CSET candidates are required to understand basic concepts of music in singing, listening, playing classroom instruments, basic music theory, and note reading. This includes understanding the components of music, elements of music, styles of music, and the techniques to create music.

The Elements of Music

Music is an ingredient of the world of sound, and all sound begins with the vibration of an object (e.g., musical instrument or voice). The art of music is the organization of sound in time. There are basic properties and elements that distinguish music from other sounds: dynamics, harmony, pitch, rhythm, tempo, tone, and timbre.

Elements of Music: Key Terms and Concepts	
Dynamics	**Dynamics** is the volume or intensity of a tone. Music can be played loudly (forte) or softly (piano).
Harmony	**Harmony** is two or more tones played simultaneously that support the melody and give music texture or mood. Harmony is a group of notes that are played behind the melody. For example, when you play several different notes at the same time on a piano, you are using harmony. You can change how music sounds by changing the harmony.
Pitch	**Pitch** refers to hearing a note and being able to reproduce it either vocally or with an instrument. Vocal cords and musical instruments produce vibrations in the air; as the frequency of these vibrations change, the pitch changes. The faster the vibration, the higher the note. The slower the vibration, the lower the pitch. Intonation refers to whether the pitch of a particular note is played in tune, sharp (higher) or flat (lower).
Rhythm	**Rhythm** is the pattern of musical movement through time. It's what makes music move and flow. It is measured in units of time and organized by sets or patterns that can be repeated. Rhythm is the way sounds beat within different lengths and accents that combine into patterns. Rhythm is a steady pulse (beat), but it can also have different kinds of beats (i.e., some stronger or longer). The first beat of a bar is typically a strong beat. It is typified by a waltz in 3/4 time.
Tempo	**Tempo** is the pace of the beat. It is the speed at which a composer desires his musical composition to be performed. It is measured by the number of beats per minute. A metronome is a machine that helps musicians adjust rates of speed (tempi) for faster or slower beats. The faster the tempo, the more beats per minute. Tempo is an important component to change the expressiveness of character and mood of the musical composition. For example, if the tempo is fast, the mood of the music changes to reflect more energy, aggression, or vitality. Most marches are performed at a rate of 120 beats per minute. Italian terms that define tempo are: presto – very fast adagio – slow allegro – fast largo – very slow moderato – moderate
Tone	**Tone** refers to the sound produced by an individual instrument or singer. Each family of instruments and type of instrument is distinct from all others. For example, the tone of a brass instrument is easily distinguished from the tone of a string instrument, a woodwind instrument, etc.
Timbre	**Timbre** (pronounced "tam-ber") is the unique tonal quality of a musical sound. It is the tone "color." It could be described as bright, shrill, brittle, or light; or it could be dull, harsh, forceful, or dark. Not only does each type of instrument have a distinct tone, but each instrument can also have a different tone from other similar instruments. Timbre makes one instrument sound different from another. For this reason, timbre has a great effect upon the mood of the music. For example, all violins have the same tone qualities, as do all clarinets and all trumpets, yet each instrument, due mainly to its manufacturer, has a different timbre or tone quality.

Glossary: Further Basic Music Key Terms and Concepts

The following glossary suggests additional terms with which you should be familiar for the CSET: Multiple Subjects.

Chamber music: Music played by one to twenty performers.

Chord: Several notes sounded together.

Consonance: The combination of tones that produces a quality of relaxation.

Dissonance: The combination of tones that produces a quality of tension.

Fugue: A fugue is based upon a short theme called a *subject*. The fugue subject contains both rhythmic and melodic motifs. The opening of the fugue is announced by one voice alone. A second voice then restates the subject, usually on a different scale. A third and then a fourth voice enter, each carrying the subject.

Lied: A type of German song.

Lyre: An ancient harp.

Motif: A recurring group of notes, such as the four notes played at the beginning of (and restated throughout) Beethoven's *Fifth Symphony*.

Movement: A large section of a lengthy composition.

Opera: A drama, either tragic or comic, that is sung to an orchestral accompaniment. An opera is often based in biblical stories. Opera is typically a large-scale composition with vocal soloists, a chorus, and orchestra.

Opus: A work, usually identified by a number.

Oratorio: A major orchestral piece with solo voices and chorus.

Orchestra: An instrumental ensemble composed of strings, woodwinds, brass, and percussion.

Rondo: A musical form whose main feature is the return of the main theme, which alternates with secondary themes. For example:

> simple rondo: ABABA
>
> second rondo: ABACA
>
> third rondo: ABACABA

Sonata: Typically, a multi-movement instrumental work for solo keyboard, or keyboard and another instrument, or small chamber ensemble.

Song form: The structure of a song in which the first section of a simple ternary form is repeated—for example, AABA. (A simple ternary form is music in three sections, with the third generally an exact repetition of the first, ABA.)

Symphony: A symphony is an elaborate musical composition, many of which are between 20 and 45 minutes in length. A classical symphony usually consists of four movements that are intended to stir up a wide range of emotions through contrasts in tempo and mood.

Syncopation: A rhythmic effect produced when the expected rhythmic pattern is deliberately upset.

Music Notation

Music notation is the language system of writing music so that the reader can see what is being communicated. It is similar to using written words to communicate thoughts and ideas.

Name	Description	Illustration
Staff	Staff (staves) is a set of five horizontal lines and four spaces. This is where notes are positioned. The higher the note on a staff, the higher the pitch.	
Clef	Clef is the symbol at the beginning of each staff indicating the pitch or the range of sounds that should be played. There are two main clefs: the treble clef for the higher range of notes, and the bass clef for the lower range of notes.	Treble clef Bass clef

continued

Name	Description	Illustration
Measure and Bar lines	A measure is formed by barlines (vertical lines on the staff) and contains a set number of beats as determined by the time signature.	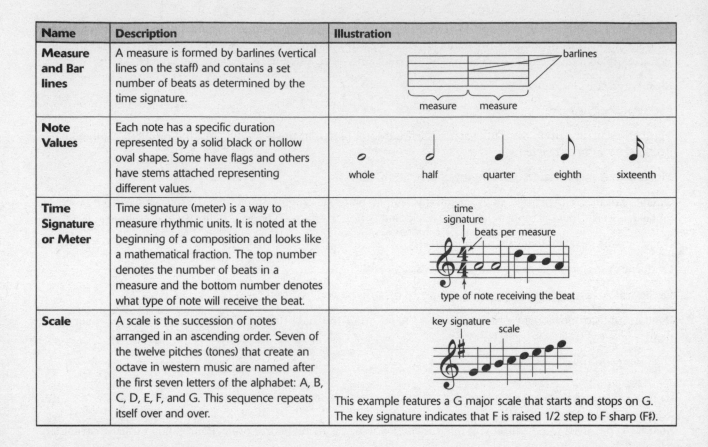
Note Values	Each note has a specific duration represented by a solid black or hollow oval shape. Some have flags and others have stems attached representing different values.	
Time Signature or Meter	Time signature (meter) is a way to measure rhythmic units. It is noted at the beginning of a composition and looks like a mathematical fraction. The top number denotes the number of beats in a measure and the bottom number denotes what type of note will receive the beat.	
Scale	A scale is the succession of notes arranged in an ascending order. Seven of the twelve pitches (tones) that create an octave in western music are named after the first seven letters of the alphabet: A, B, C, D, E, F, and G. This sequence repeats itself over and over.	This example features a G major scale that starts and stops on G. The key signature indicates that F is raised 1/2 step to F sharp (F♯).

Musical Instruments

When referring to musical instruments, they are often associated with being part of a family. As in human families, the instruments in a particular family are related to each other. Instruments within a family are often manufactured from the same types of materials. They also usually have a similar appearance and comparable sound qualities. Instruments are usually classified into six broad categories: string, woodwind, brass, percussion, keyboard, and electronic. Of these, symphony orchestras traditionally have four categories (families): string, woodwind, brass, and percussion.

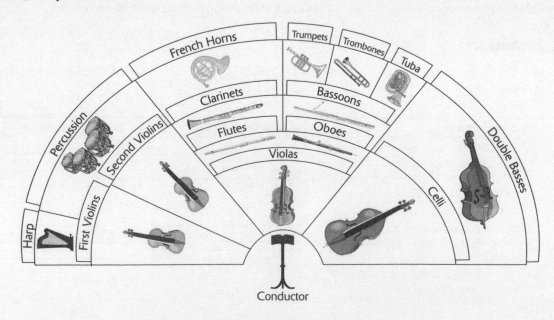

Strings

These curvy, wooden-shaped bodies are the largest family of the orchestra. Strings stretch over the body and neck of the instrument and attach to small ornamental heads where they are tuned by turning pegs.

The violin, viola, cello, and double bass (pronounced "base") form a symphony orchestra's string section. The smaller instruments (violin and viola) make higher-pitched sounds, and the larger instruments (cello and double bass) produce low, rich sounds. They are usually played with a bow, but they may also be plucked. There are two other string instruments that are not considered part of the string section of the orchestra. They are the harp and guitar, which are often plucked, rather than bowed.

Viola

Violin

Guitar

Bass

Cello

Harp

Woodwinds

As the name implies, traditional woodwind instruments are made of wood. Today, they are made of wood, metal, plastic, or some combination thereof. These instruments consist of narrow pipes, with an opening at the bottom end and a mouthpiece at the top (and holes throughout the pipe). As air blows through from the mouthpiece (that's the "wind" in "woodwind"), sound is produced. Metal caps called *keys* cover the holes.

Some of the mouthpieces are made up of a thin piece of wood, called a *reed*. The reed is used on the clarinet, oboe, and bassoon. The clarinet uses a single reed made of one piece of wood, while the oboe and bassoon use a double reed made of two pieces joined together. The smaller woodwinds play higher pitches, while the longer and larger instruments play the lower notes.

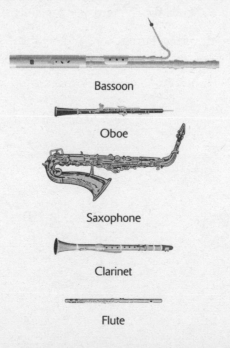

Bassoon

Oboe

Saxophone

Clarinet

Flute

Brass

Brass instruments produce sound through breath as the vibrations from the players' lips buzz against a metal, cup-shaped mouthpiece. The brass section of an orchestra can play louder than any other instrumental section. Most brass instruments have valves attached to their long pipes, which look like buttons that open and close and produce higher or lower sounds of pitch.

Some of the earliest forms of brass instruments were made from tusks, horns, shells, or wood. Today, all brass instruments are made entirely of brass. These instruments are designed like long pipes that widen at their ends into a bell-shaped opening. Their curves make them easier to hold and play.

French Horn   Trombone

Trumpet   Tuba

Percussion

Percussion instruments include any instrument that produces a sound when it is being hit, shaken, rubbed, or scraped. Some instruments require tuning (e.g., timpani), while others are untuned (e.g., cymbals and castanets).

During a symphony, a percussionist often plays many different instruments during one composition. The following illustration shows some popular instruments in the orchestra, but there are many more percussion instruments, including the following: tambourine, maracas, castanets, claves, xylophone, timpani, cymbals, gong, triangle, bass drum, chimes, celesta, bells, wood block, guiro, bongos, conga, cowbells, and snare drum.

When utilized as part of an orchestra, the piano, harpsichord and organ are sometimes included in the percussion family. Often, when used as a solo·instrument, they are referred to as the keyboard family.

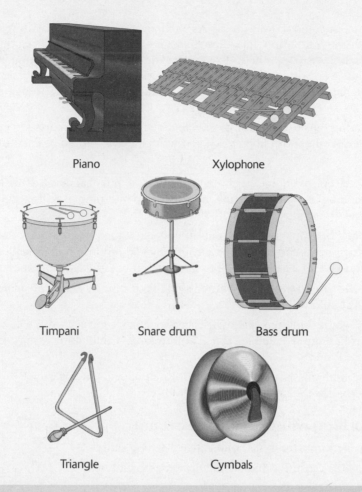

Piano   Xylophone

Timpani   Snare drum   Bass drum

Triangle   Cymbals

There's nothing remarkable about it. All one has to do is hit the right keys at the right time and the instrument plays itself. — Johann Sebastian Bach

Classroom Expectations for Music Education

There is an intrinsic value to music education programs. The instruction, practical application, and expression of musical skills help to shape the development of mental processes in children. Music also offers a modality of creative self-expression and enjoyment. The types of cognitive, social, and physical skills that children can cultivate through the appreciation of music include:

1. **Auditory skills**—hearing the sounds of music. Children engage in attentive listening and further develop aural acuity. This means that children must be able to hear and reproduce the tones of music in their minds when no sound is actually being produced.

2. **Translative skills**—reading and writing music. As children become familiar with reading and writing the language of music through notation, they develop cognitive associations of meaning. Their experience with sound helps children link visual symbols of music notation with sound. Learning is enhanced when teachers use learning in conjunction with singing and playing music. For example, using memorization to understand meter signatures would not produce the same benefits as if the students participated in playing or singing.

3. **Creative skills**—creating music. Composing and creating music should be used in conjunction with other musical activities. Performing both improvised and written music should be encouraged.

4. **Performance skills**

   a. **Singing.** Musical selections should be chosen based on the physical development of students' voices. Listening while singing should be encouraged to develop interpretive skills and understanding of the structure and elements of music.

   b. **Playing instruments.** Instrument-playing aids in understanding the concepts of sound, pitch, rhythm, and so on. Playing instruments can be used to accompany and produce harmony. Students should have access to class instruction and, at a certain level, to playing in orchestras and ensembles.

   c. **Body movement.** Moving to music is a learned skill that promotes acuity of perceptions. A wide range of music and modes should be used.

   d. **Conducting.** Even young children can experience elements of music through conducting speech chants, involving changes in tempo, dynamics, pitch, and so forth. Conducting fosters sensitivity to musical expression.

   e. **Musical analysis.** Students should compare their listening and playing exercises. Students should be encouraged to verbalize their musical analysis.

Implications for Teaching Music in the Classroom

- Music offers a valuable opportunity to build active listening skills.
- Music helps to shape the cognitive and mental processes in children.
- Music has its own forms, time periods, and cultural characteristics.
- Music can be used to enhance other subject areas, particularly visual art.
- Music extends beyond knowledge and skills.
- Music can be a form of therapy that offers a unique medium for self-expression.
- Musical instruments can be created from material from the environment, and children can create instruments in the classroom.

Styles of Music

The style of music refers to the unique sound and style of a composer, culture, country, or period in history. It is by understanding historical/cultural contexts of music that children foster a relationship between themselves and their multicultural heritage. Compositions created around the same time period often have similar styles based upon the historical influences from that era. Western music is divided into the following periods based upon the style of the historical era.

Music History Timeline	
Middle Ages/ Medieval (500–1400)	**Historical themes:** spread of Christianity; development in Europe; the Crusades; the rise of universities; the influence of Islam; this was the longest period. **Music styles/elements:** the Church dominated society for most of the era (900 years); sacred music was the most prevalent (liturgical); *Gregorian chant*, named after Pope Gregory I (590–640) was a melody set to sacred Latin texts. This monophonic style music (meaning one melodic line and no accompaniment) was the official music of the Roman Catholic church. Musical notation originally consisted of just the pitch of the notes; notated rhythm was added at the end of the twelfth century. *Polyphonic style* (two or more melodic lines) appeared at the end of the twelfth century, as did notation (system of writing music) and the *chromatic scale* (octaves of twelve notes). Most composers were anonymous. Secular song developed by the end of the twelfth century; popular songs were not bound by the traditions of the Church, and were performed by troubadours.
Renaissance Era (1400–1600)	**Historical themes:** the end of feudalism; a new concept of humanism; rediscovery of ancient Greek and Roman culture and ideals; art and music for their own sake; scientific advances; the age of patronage. **Instrumental dance music developed:** music and dance were connected; new instruments included the keyboard (clavichord); the lute was a favored instrument through the sixteenth century. The printing press preserved and extended music. **Music styles/elements:** polyphonic emphasis on *harmony* (in which two or more notes are sounded simultaneously as in a chord); sacred (liturgical, such as masses); secular (madrigals/songs).
Baroque Era (1600–1750)	**Historical themes:** importance of scientific investigation; New World exploration and empire; ornate and extravagant; painters included Rubens, Rembrandt, and El Greco; composers included Monteverdi, Handel, and Bach. **Music styles/elements:** heavily ornate style; counterpoint (technique of combining several melodic lines into a meaningful whole); melodic line; emphasis on contrast and volume; imitative polyphony (many-sounding melodic lines are presented by one voice or instrument and then restated immediately by another); homophonic style (chords under a melodic line), also theme and variation (recurring patterns). Secular music advances; "court" composers; keyboard music for the harpsichord and organ. **Developments:** opera (staged dramatic vocal music and entertainment), orchestra, ballet, and sonata (solo instrument with accompaniment).
Classical Era (1750–1820)	**Historical themes:** Industrial Revolution, Age of Reason and Enlightenment, Age of Revolution, revolutionary music (such as the French "Marseillaise"). Orchestra gained in importance; increasing use of flutes and oboes; string and wind sections developed; by the 1800s, trombones were introduced; refinement of sonata (instrumental music with a soloist and standard structure for the opening movement); development of the piano; Rococo style (highly ornamented). Elegance and courtly grace (e.g., minuet developed as a dance style). **Classical style:** homophony (a single melodic line and an accompaniment); simpler textures and melodies; expansion of textures, melodies, and variation. String quartet (two violins, viola, and cello); Haydn the "father" of the string quartet; orchestral symphony (origins in opera overture, four movements); opera, concerto (composition for solo instrument). Creative impulses of giants Haydn, Mozart, and Beethoven.
Romantic Period (1820–1900)	**Historical themes:** Rise of European nationalism; new social orders; intense emotion in arts (paintings of Delacroix and Goya); Poe in literature; "Romanticism" derived from concepts of heroes, love, and chivalry associated with the Middle Ages; visual arts, poetry, drama, and nature as themes. Artistic experimentation by composers Chopin, Liszt, Berlioz, Mendelssohn, and Schumann; style was expressive, melody prominent, and folk music was used to express cultural identity. **Opera:** Verdi (Italy), Wagner (Germany); themes from literature and folk tales; very popular. **Genres:** symphonic poem (orchestral work that portrayed a story) and concert overture (e.g., Rossini's *William Tell*). Emphasis was on the sonata and symphony, and included the introduction of dissonance to create emotion; featuring virtuoso performers.

continued

Modern Era (1900s)	Evolution in the musical world, rebellion; unique sounds; difficult to quantify; nationalism; folk idiom was prevalent (e.g., in Liszt's *Hungarian Rhapsody*, Copland's *Appalachian Spring*); widening gap between "art" and popular music (Beatles). Technology allowed for mass appeal and a new direction in music making (sound recordings, electronically created sounds, computer music, and composing). Polytonality (playing two keys at once). Puccini (Italian) and his operas *Madama Butterfly* and *La Bohème*; Debussy and Impressionism; Stravinsky, post-Romanticism, and his ballet *The Rite of Spring*; Rachmaninoff, Prokofiev, and Shostakovich (Russian). Influence of blues (sorrowful black folk music) and jazz (roots in African rhythms and harmonies with modern instrumentation, improvisation, and syncopation). Rock 'n' roll, R&B (rhythm and blues), country, folk (cultural link, passed on by word of mouth), and hip-hop.

Domain 3: Theatre

The imagination is enacted through the artistic expression of theatre.

Theatre arts programs help to engage intellectual, emotional, and physical responses in children. Children have an innate sense of acting as they create stories, characters, a plot, and action. In primary grades, "make-believe" becomes part of their imaginary theatre of play. The evolutionary development of theatre was born from our natural human tendency to tell stories and to socialize. The art of performing stories started with Greek theatre productions over 2,000 years ago, and has adapted through time to reveal the cultural and collective thoughts, feelings, and perspectives of our society today. The combined elements of stage design, dialogue, and imaginative scripts have helped to create enthusiasm about this very established art form. CSET candidates will be required to understand the basic elements of theatre, including acting, drama, speech, gesture, music, and dance, as they are combined to express a single artistic form. The creative process of theatre instruction includes the contextual understanding of theatre, communicating that understanding to students, and engaging students in theatrical activities. Theatre is an excellent discipline to integrate with other classroom curriculum (e.g., literature, music, history, etc.) since it crosses over many subjects.

Theatre utilizes both language and body movement in stage activities. Theatre helps students develop poise, confidence, ease, and versatility both verbally and physically. Drama develops creative, critical, and communication skills and should be a regular offering at all grade levels.

The following table provides an overview of the elements of drama with which students can be involved.

Elements of Theatre	
Acting	Acting is defined as the development and communication of characters in formal or informal productions or improvisations. Acting techniques include physical and vocal warm-ups, pantomime and mime, improvisations, voice and diction exercises, theatre games, performance, monologues, and script reading. Sensory elements are movement, sound, and spectacle. Expressive qualities are mood, emotion, ideas, and dynamics.
Theatre	Theatre is the formal presentation of a scripted play. It incorporates elements such as acting, directing, designing, and managing. The organizational principles are: ■ Plot and conflict ■ Setting ■ Character ■ Language ■ Rhythm and unity
Drama	Drama involves the reenactment of life situations for entertainment and human understanding. Dramatic expression does not necessarily require a live-formal audience.
Improvisation	Improvisation is a creative, cooperative, spontaneous, and flexible response to changing and unexpected dramatic stimuli. It embraces problem solving without preconception of how to perform, and allows anything within the environment to be used during the experience.

Scriptwriting	Scriptwriting is based on culture, imagination, literature, and personal life experiences. Scriptwriting can apply to theatre, film, television, or electronic media. Classroom activities can include reading and analyzing scripts, outlining dramatic structure, and working together in groups to plan scenarios.
Technical Support Tools	Technical support tools are costumes, sets, lights, props, makeup, and sound.
Stage	The structure where all drama and theatre takes place is known as a stage. Many structures have similar components. For example, proscenium theatres, arena theatres, and amphitheatres are a permanent part of the structure. In a black box theatre, the acting area is undefined so that each theatre may adapt specifically to a particular production. There may also be offstage spaces that are adaptable.

Interpreting Theatre

Teaching theatre arts in elementary schools offers teachers an opportunity to help children demonstrate meaningful experiences while helping them make aesthetic connections to the arts, history, literature and other academic disciplines. Theatre arts programs help children find value in dramatic elements such as communication, gesture, music, dance, and creativity. The objective in interpreting or evaluating elementary school theatre arts programs is to emphasize the appreciation for a supportive, creative environment of practical and experiential expression. This can be accomplished by considering aesthetic perception, creative expression, historical context, theatrical applications, and intended audience. When analyzing dramatic work it is important to keep in mind:

A. **Intent.** Involves the objective, purpose, theme, or basic idea of a work of drama.

B. **Structure.**

1. Involves the interaction of all elements.

2. Includes, but is not limited to, design, rhythm, climax, conflict, balance, and sequence.

C. **Effectiveness.**

1. Involves the degree to which a dramatic work succeeds.

2. Includes the evaluation of the work's success in such things as entertaining, informing, illuminating, persuading, inspiring, amusing, engaging, shocking, and instilling awe.

D. **Worth.**

1. Involves a value judgment.

2. Includes assessment of the knowledge, insight, wisdom, or feeling imparted by a work.

Theatre Historical Timeline	
Ancient Greek Theatre (600–400 B.C.)	■ Amphitheatres (open air; on the sides of mountains; semicircular; orchestra [area in front of the stage]; chorus/dance and music; auditorium; simple scenery). ■ Playwrights: Sophocles (tragedy: heroes glorified but with a tragic flaw, influence of gods) and Euripides. ■ Violence took place off stage (true through to the Elizabethan age). ■ Thespis was the first actor (source of "thespians"). ■ Dionysus Festivals (tragedies/comedies/satire); plots came from legends. ■ Influence of central actors and dialogue; masks were used to show age and emotion. ■ Women were barred from acting but could be spectators. ■ Greek tragedy was not associated with theatre staging today (it was part of a trilogy).
Roman Theatre (300 B.C.–A.D. 500)	■ Latin versions of Greek plays; less influenced by religion. ■ Introduction of subplot. ■ Women were allowed minor parts. ■ Spectacles of the Coliseum. ■ Mass appeal/impressive theatres. ■ Raised stage replaced the Greek semicircular amphitheatre; the stage was built at ground level with a raised seating area. ■ By the later Roman period, Christians disapproved of low comedy and pagan rituals.

continued

Medieval Theatre (500–1300)	■ Theatre buildings were not permitted; minstrels, traveling groups, and jugglers from Greek-Roman period; open stage areas. ■ Church/liturgical dramas: written in Latin/Bible stories; intended to educate regarding religious events, not to entertain. ■ Dramatic form to illustrate religious holidays to an illiterate populace; "Everyman"; allegory. ■ Genres: Passion play, miracle play, and morality play with themes of religious loyalty. ■ Theatre groups evolved into town guilds.
Renaissance and Reformation Theatre (1400–1600)	■ Rebirth of classical Greek and Roman art, culture, and literature. ■ Theatre reemerged with professional actors and set design. ■ Open stages, "apron stages," to proscenium arch (framed and divided stage from the audience; painted sets and scenery). ■ Emphasis was on the performer. ■ Protestant Reformation (moving away from Catholic teachings) led to secular works; Commedia dell'arte (improvisation; acting groups; situational comedy). ■ State licensed official theatre companies.
Elizabethan Theatre	■ Playwrights included Christopher Marlowe and Ben Johnson. ■ Theatre was supported by Queen Elizabeth; patronage; raucous, open-air theatre; language of the educated; satire. ■ William Shakespeare (late 1500s and early 1600s) wrote comedies, histories, and tragedies; Globe Theatre (open-air).
Restoration England: 1660s	■ In 1642, Parliament closed theatres in England; these closings allowed French ascendancy in theatre mechanics. ■ Theatre architecture: France introduced new technology for scenery and set changes; artificial lighting; theatres began to be roofed in; drama moved indoors, and the stage was raised above the audience. ■ Proscenium stage architecture/royal theatre (enclosed/arches); scene changes slid by on panels. ■ Baroque period: French playwrights Racine and Molière influenced theatre. ■ Women began to appear onstage in the roles of boys and young men.
Eighteenth Century	■ Changes in economics, society, ruling powers, determined direction of playwrights. ■ Acting began to more closely mimic life. ■ Art of acting became prominent. ■ Plays more often dealt with ordinary people. ■ Commercial theatre evolved.
Nineteenth Century	■ Industrial Revolution changed the way people lived. ■ Technology changed the theatre (gas lighting was changed to electrical; mechanisms were created for changing scenery). ■ Growth of melodrama. ■ Actor predominated over the author, but playwrights Shaw, Ibsen, and Chekhov stood out; serious drama. ■ Nineteenth century in the United States (playhouses in major cities, resident companies, touring actors, influence of melodrama, minstrels). ■ Late 1880s to 1920s in the United States: Golden Age of American theatre (420 touring companies); mass appeal; more sophisticated plots and staging; moving away from hero character; vaudeville.
Twentieth Century	■ Social upheaval from World Wars I and II. ■ Early twentieth century: new movements such as realism, naturalism, symbolism, and impressionism (meaning of the average man; actors portrayed likeness to life; ordinary life on stage). ■ Commercial theatres (Ziegfeld Follies to musical Oklahoma!, opera Porgy and Bess, and musical The Phantom of the Opera). ■ Serious drama (playwrights Eugene O'Neill, Arthur Miller, and Tennessee Williams). ■ Comedy (playwright and screenwriter Neil Simon). ■ Actor's Studio (Elia Kazan and Lee Strasberg). ■ Experimental theatre (against naturalism). ■ Community theatre and ensemble theatre (group).

Theatre Glossary

The following glossary suggests terms with which you should be familiar for the CSET: Multiple Subjects.

Action: In a character-character interaction, the total array of purposeful activity, both external (physical) and internal (psychological), by which characters attempt to achieve their objectives.

Antagonist: In traditional dramatic theory, an element, usually a character, that resists the protagonist. Conflict results from the efforts of the protagonist to achieve his or her objectives in spite of the obstacles introduced by the antagonist.

Arena staging: The physical configuration of audience and actor in which the audience essentially surrounds the playing area. It is also known as "threatre in the round."

Aristotelian theatre: In general, the traditional theatre thought to be espoused by Aristotle. It includes clear, simple plotting; strong (but not necessarily complicated) characters; high levels of intellectual content; and a minimum of spectacle. In the Renaissance, other criteria were added to these, some native to Aristotle, some imposed through fancied symmetry: Plays should include the three unities, (unity of one main *action,* unity of one physical *space*, and unity of *time*), be written in five acts, avoid violence, and not mix comedy and tragedy.

Block (verb): To decide upon the gross movements of actors upon the stage; assign the physical relationship of actors and the locations of entrances and exits; create stage "pictures." Frequently, early rehearsals (blocking rehearsals) are devoted to this task.

Broadway theatre: The commercial model that dominated the American theatre from the end of the nineteenth century until shortly after World War II. Named for the New York boulevard that runs through the Manhattan theatre district, this kind of theatre is essentially a profit-making enterprise in which shares of a production are sold to investors with the expectation that, after meeting the initial expenses of production, they will receive a substantial return on their investment. To enhance these profits, Broadway theatre aspires to very long runs of a single play, frequently using star performers appearing in vehicles with the widest possible audience appeal.

Center stage: The exact center of the floor of the stage.

Character: A figure portrayed in the play; the sum total of the actions that define a person so portrayed.

Chorus: In Greek and Roman drama of the classical period, a group of characters in a play who comment on the action, frequently speaking directly to the audience. The function of the chorus is usually that of an intermediary between the audience and the major characters in the play. Because they are often given a collective role, the individual members of the chorus seldom have separate names or characters. Instead, the group as a whole serves as a surrogate "audience" to the degree that it is detached from the dramatic action and can view with horror or amusement the action of the major characters; at the same time, the chorus can participate directly in the action, advising the protagonist, arguing with the antagonist, and praying to the gods for guidance.

Chronological time: Time as a linear experience related to cause and effect. Most history is written in chronological order, but much theatre chooses to take liberties with the chronological presentation of facts. The earliest modification was to leave out long and unimportant passages of time in order to present scenes that capture the essence of the story in an episodic plot. Later developments include the flashback and the flash-forward.

Climax: In traditional dramatic structure, the point of the play that completes the rising action. The contending forces, having raised the conflict to the highest point possible, face one another in a confrontation so inescapable that only one can emerge victorious. At this point, frequently a new piece of information is made public that tips the balance one way or another. The climax is followed by the dénouement.

Comedy: Historically, comedy is any play that ends happily. More specifically, it is the genre of dramatic literature that is lighter in tone than drama but more serious than farce. Comedy differs from drama in that the characters are less developed, the theme is less weighty, the language is usually wittier, and the ending is invariably happy. Comedy is often difficult to distinguish from farce; in the latter, the humor is more physical, the characters are more broadly drawn, and the plots are more contrived.

Company: In the broadest sense, all of the people associated with producing a play, including the designers, technicians, directors, stage managers, and actors. In the narrowest sense, the concept of "the company" is confined to the actors alone.

Conflict: The central feature of a dramatic action; the arrangement of the objectives of two or more strong characters in such a way that those objectives are competing and mutually exclusive.

Connotative meaning: The meaning conveyed by connotative symbols, symbols that are vague in terms of strict definition, but rich in poetic meaning. Much connotative meaning evokes an emotional rather than intellectual response.

Content: What is portrayed in theatre; namely, the interaction of at least one character with some aspect of his or her environment. Since the portrayed interaction is normally with another person (or an aspect of the natural environment endowed with human qualities), the content of theatre is character-character interaction.

Conventions: The temporary "rules" of the performance. The conventions of the theatre are specific to particular cultures, styles of theatre, and even individual productions.

Creative drama: A form of entertainment in which students improvise scenes for their own growth and edification, not that of an audience. In some cases, the aim of creative drama is to learn subjects other than theatre (history, psychology, literature, and so on); in others, it is to learn about theatre itself.

Dénouement: In traditional dramatic theory, the portion of action that immediately follows the climax of a play. In the dénouement, the last remaining loose ends are "tied up," including the disposition of any unresolved conflicts and the reestablishment of stasis (a condition of balance and harmony).

Director: In the modern theatre, the major interpretive figure, whose job it is to bring to life the vision of the playwright or otherwise provide artistic meaning to the theatre experience.

Downstage: The portion of the proscenium stage that is closest to the audience.

Drama: The category of literature intended for the stage. Also, in general usage, the perception that a series of real-life events have the kind of meaning commonly experienced in the theatre or films, as in "a dramatic rescue" or the "drama of a summit meeting."

Dramatic criticism: The work of a drama critic. It consists of commentary on a play or script intended to enrich the experience of seeing the play or reading the script by others. Dramatic criticism can appear in written form in periodicals, as media presentations, or in public talks.

Dramatic question: The first and most important element in rising action. As soon as conflict has been established, the next question must be, "How will this turn out?" The dramatic question then raises the issue of which of the conflicting parties will prevail and, in doing so, begins to develop suspense.

Environmental staging: The form of physical relationship between audience and performers in which there is little or no clear definition between the space dedicated to each. The conventions of environmental staging dictate that audience and performers use the same space during the course of the experience.

Exposition: The playwriting device of providing information to the audience. Retrospective exposition usually occurs early in the action and gives the audience important information about what has occurred before the play begins; current exposition provides information about events offstage happening during the play.

Flashback: A manipulation of time in the plot in which a scene from earlier in the story is shown after those that occur later. Rather rare in traditional playwriting, flashbacks are common in films.

Form: The relationship of all the parts of plays of a certain type considered apart from any single example of that type, as in the form of farce and the form of the well-made play. What emerges is a model or ideal of a theatrical experience that can be used to describe specific examples.

Full-length play: A single play that typically fulfills the expectation for a complete theatrical experience. In the Western tradition, this means one play of three to five acts, usually filling two to four hours.

Gallery: In the Elizabethan theatre, one of a tier of alcoves surrounding the interior of the "yard" where, in enclosed boxes and on benches, those who could afford the greatest comfort could sit. Comparable galleries are found in most Renaissance theatres; they continue today in tiers of balconies and boxes found in most opera houses.

Illumination: The act of casting light upon an otherwise darkened stage.

Improvisation: Acting without a script or prepared text.

Inciting incident: In traditional dramatic structure, the first incident in the chain of events called rising action. It is the inciting incident that throws the world of the play into disequilibrium (destroying stasis); the remainder of the play is an attempt to reestablish that balance. The inciting incident may be deceptively simple: the arrival of a new person in the community, the delivery of a letter, a piece of news emerging in casual conversation, and the like.

Kabuki: A classical Japanese theatre form that combines colorful song and dance, flamboyant characters, and extravagant plots in a popular art that has retained its wide popularity since the early seventeenth century.

Lighting plot: A plan of the stage showing the location of each lighting instrument, its size and characters, and the area of the stage where its light will fall.

Melodrama: The genre of theatre that is normally placed between tragedy and drama and which shares some characteristics with each. It is largely serious in tone, placing its major figures in great jeopardy, but unlike tragedy, saves them from destruction at the end. The moral stance of melodrama is always clear: the good characters are very good, the bad ones very bad.

Mood: In lighting, the use of elements of stage lighting to evoke or support particular emotional states in the audience of a play. As an element of theatre, this is the place on the humorous-serious scale that a play is expected to occupy.

Multiple plots: The traditional element of theatre plotting in which more than one story line is presented, usually simultaneously. Frequently, the plots are kept separate until late in the play, at which point they intersect in some ingenious way. Multiple plots work best when each separate plot is somehow a treatment of the same theme or in some way shares an important theatrical element with the others.

Neoclassic drama: Plays of the neoclassic period, or plays modeled after them, in which Renaissance writers attempted to recapture the glory of theatre in ancient Greece and Rome. Particularly in seventeenth- and eighteenth-century France, this effort was aided by the application of certain rules of playwriting, such as the unities (action, place, time), the enforced use of rigid verse forms, and the general concern for "decorum" on the stage.

One-act play: A play of short duration (usually less than an hour) that can be presented without an intermission and without major changes in scenery.

Orchestra: In an ancient Greek theatre, the open dancing area in front of the stagehouse. In modern usage, the orchestra is the lowest and usually most expensive array of seats directly in front of the stage. This should not be confused with the "orchestra pit."

Pastoral play: An extinct genre of play, popular during the Italian Renaissance, which is set in a countryside populated by nymphs, satyrs, shepherds, shepherdesses, and wandering knights. Persistently upbeat in tone, the pastoral play existed chiefly to give courtiers a chance to indulge a taste for dressing up as peasants, singing, and dancing. The pastoral play may have been the Renaissance's attempt to recapture the Greek *satyr play*.

Pit: In the Elizabethan theatre, the portion of the theatre immediately in front of the stage. This area was occupied by patrons who had paid the lowest admission fee and were willing to stand for the duration of the production. Over time, this area was filled, first with benches and later with chairs. Today it is called the *orchestra*.

Playscript: "Script" for short. A detailed, written description of a play intended to give the reader as clear a sense of the produced work as possible. When it is first written by a playwright, the playscript refers to an imagined production; later, the playscript may describe an actual production. In either case, the aim is to provide enough information so that a group of performers can mount a production of the play in question.

Plot: The series of incidents that make up the action of a play. These incidents are selected from a series of events which, when described chronologically, make up a story.

Proscenium arch: The major architectural feature of Western theatres since the Renaissance, the proscenium arch is essentially an opening in the wall between two rooms. In one room (the stagehouse), the actors perform; in the other room (the auditorium), the audience is located. The arch itself can range from extremely elaborate and intrusive to nearly undetectable.

Proscenium staging: The form of physical configuration between actor and audience encouraged by (some would say demanded by) the proscenium arch. It consists of a fairly narrow array of audience members gathered on one side of the stage only. There is a clear distinction between the areas occupied by the actors and the audience; in traditional proscenium theatres, there is also an effort to keep the audience directly in front of the center of the proscenium arch.

Protagonist: Literally, the "first person to enter a contest." This is the major figure in traditional theatre, and the person around whom the action of the play turns. The antagonist is the person or force that resists the protagonist, thus forming the conflict of a play.

Restoration comedy: Characteristic comedy of the period known as the English Restoration (1660–1700). Restoration comedy is known for its glittering language, salacious plots, and frequently debauched characters.

Revolving stage: A portion of the stage constructed so that it rotates around a pivot. Such a stage can be used in a number of ways, the most frequent being to change settings; the downstage scenery rotates out of sight, revealing scenery that had previously been set upstage.

Rising action: In traditional dramatic structure, the portion of the plot that begins with the inciting incident and continues until the climax. The incidents that make up rising action are expected to build in intensity and frequency, often alternating good and bad news, in such a way as to increase suspense.

Satyr play: A form of Greek drama that coexisted with tragedy in the classical period. Little is known of the satyr play except that it seems to have been a burlesque of the same ideas presented in tragedies, ridiculing the gods and heroic legends, using the bawdiest language, dance, and song to do it.

Stage left: In a proscenium arch configuration, the side of the stage to the left of an actor facing the audience; sometimes called "audience right."

Stage right: In a proscenium arch configuration, the side of the stage to the right of an actor facing the audience; sometimes called "audience left."

Stereotyped character: One based on the assumption that all members of a given group possess certain simple behavioral traits. Hence, a few swift strokes of character development (a dialect, a distinctive walk, a costume, and so on) suffice to communicate the stereotype to the audience. Contrasted with the "unique character," who shares nothing of consequence with any other person and whose life experiences have created a character that is, taken as a whole, entirely distinct from all others.

Stock company: In the eighteenth, nineteenth, and early twentieth centuries, a form of resident company in which actors were hired according to lines of work and large numbers of plays were prepared, usually with very short rehearsal periods and for relatively short runs. The practice and the term continue to live in the experience of "summer stock" (theatre presented during the summertime).

Storyboard: A visual display of the plot of a play or film in which each scene (or shot) is represented by a single picture or short description. The pictures or notecards are then arranged on a wall or bulletin board in such a way as to depict the flow of the plot.

Tempo: The speed with which incidents that make up the action take place.

Thrust staging: The physical configuration of audience and performers in which at least some part of the stage extends into, and is surrounded by, the audience. In thrust staging, the audience surrounds the acting area to no more than 270 degrees; beyond that, the configuration is called *arena staging*.

402

Upstage: In proscenium staging, the portion of an acting area that is farthest from the audience.

Vomitoria: In Roman theatre, the vomitoria were the tunnels that allowed the audience to enter and exit the large theatres with ease. In contemporary theatres, the vomitoria ("voms" for short) are the tunnels that allow the actors to reach the downstage portions of a thrust stage by passing through the audience.

Domain 4: Visual Art

Art is the process of purposefully arranged elements that appeal to aesthetic and emotional senses. It is through the cognitive processes of creating images and thought that the conception of all tangible expression takes place. Teachers are instrumental in stimulating visual art appreciation and expression. In an elementary school program, teachers can help students discover the evolutionary history of artistic design while providing an opportunity for students to discover a medium for self-expression. CSET candidates will set a foundation for learning and appreciating the value of visual arts around the world. Candidates are asked to understand the principles and elements of art and to be able to explain styles of visual arts from a variety of times, places, and cultures.

The Principles of Art

CSET candidates are asked to be fluent in the principles of visual art. Visual art can generate powerful symbolic representations of the imagination, but the principles of art help us to understand underlying patterns and concepts of the visual world. The expression of these fundamental principles can be found in balance, contrast, emphasis, pattern, unity, perspective, space, and color.

Principles of Art	
Balance: symmetrical and asymmetrical	Balance is a sense of visual stability in a composition. It is the harmonious arrangement of elements in order to create a feeling of equilibrium. When a composition is symmetrical, it gives the feeling that the weight is equally distributed. This is called **formal balance** since this is a classical appearance of formality. When a composition is asymmetrical, there is a visual emphasis, or pull, to one side of the composition. This is sometimes called **informal balance**. For example, think about a seesaw or scales. When the seesaw is equally weighted, it is symmetrical. When the seesaw is not weighted equally, it is asymmetrical.
Contrast	Contrast represents two things that are opposite. Artists use contrast to help a composition depict two dramatic differences. This helps to make objects become apparent to the viewer. For example, contrasts can be heavy and light, curved or straight, or positive and negative.
Emphasis	Emphasis draws your eye to a visual focal point. Artists use emphasis to help an object stand out and grab your attention. It is the center of interest.
Pattern	Patterns are objects in a composition that are repeated. Regular patterns appear as predicted designs with easily identifiable features so that the viewer can visually recognize what may appear next. When there's no exact predicted design, but the viewer can generally predict what may appear next, the artist is using random patterns. Artists create patterns by repeating shapes, colors, or lines. In the example below, French impressionist Claude Monet uses patterns of water lilies floating on a pond in *Water Lilies* (1914).
Unity	Unity is the sense that all components of a composition belong together. The intention of every successful artist is to master unity. The elements of art such as shape, line, and color appear to fit together as the viewer gazes upon the piece of art, with nothing left to complete, delete, or change. Unity creates a sense that the artwork is self-contained and has life of its own, whole and complete.

continued

Perspective: Linear	Linear perspective is a technique for representing three-dimensional objects on a flat surface. During the Renaissance, artists invented this technique based upon math principles in order to give paintings a realistic appearance. The technique shows that when converging lines meet at a single vanishing point, the human eye perceives objects at a distance. When our eyes focus on the vanishing point, all shapes and objects become smaller, giving us the illusion of depth and distance. Larger objects appear closer, and smaller objects appear more distant. The lines of buildings and objects are slanted to make them appear at a distance. In the example below of the Basilica di San Lorenzo (San Lorenzo Church) in Florence, Italy, you will notice that the design of this church was influenced by perspective. Notice the vanishing point at the end of the altar.
Perspective: Atmospheric or Aerial	Atmospheric perspective is used to create depth and dimension. Artists use overlapping, color, size, and contrast to reproduce the effects of distant objects. For example, darker objects appear to be closer when using lighter and duller colors for distant objects. In a landscape, lighter objects lose focus and clarity as they appear farther away.

The Elements of Art

Color

Color is visible light reflected off objects. Artists use color to imitate the colors of reflected and refracted light. Color can be used in a composition to create a symbolic representation of mood and emotion. *For example, the colors red, orange, and yellow are warm colors. When gazing at a composition with warm colors, people often feel their body temperature rise since these warm colors are symbolic of the sun, heat, and fire. The opposite is true for the colors green, blue, and purple, which suggest cooler colors. People tend to have relaxed, calm, and peaceful feelings with cool colors.*

Hue: Color has three main qualities: hue, value, and intensity. Hue is the characteristic feature by which we distinguish one color from another, but it does not distinguish the color's value (dark from light) or intensity (bright from dull). The hue of a color simply refers to a particular point on the color spectrum. Hue colors, like the rainbow, are in a sequenced order. The colors on a rainbow are primary and secondary colors: yellow, orange, red, purple, blue, and green.

Hue Order	
Primary Colors	Primary colors are red, yellow, and blue. These colors are the foundation for the color wheel (hue) and are the only colors that can be mixed to create secondary colors.
Secondary Colors	Secondary colors are orange, green, and violet (purple). These colors are created when mixing two primary colors. For example, if you mix red with blue, you get violet, and if you mix yellow with red, you get orange.
Tertiary Colors	Tertiary colors are created by mixing secondary colors. When mixing these colors, the secondary color tends to be muted or grayish to provide a variation of the secondary color.

Complementary Colors	Complementary colors are pairs of colors that sit opposite one another on the color wheel and do not share any common characteristics. For example, purple is directly opposite from yellow, making them complementary colors. If mixed together, they produce a neutral color such as gray. Artists use complementary colors to create **contrast** that can be interpreted as vibrant and stimulating.

Value: Value describes the lightness or darkness of color. Its range is from white to black, and the value of a color is changed by adding either white or black. Artists use value to create mood. *For example, dark colors in a composition can suggest melancholy, gloom, mystery, or foreboding.*

Intensity: Intensity describes the brilliance or dullness of color. *For example, brighter colors in a composition are often associated with stronger emotions and heightened energy, while subtler, dull colors are associated with a weaker, anesthetized state of energy.*

Line

Line is a continuous mark that can change direction, length, and width. Lines joined together form a *shape*. Line can also create an outline, silhouette, or *contour*. Artists often use line to define the edges of a form to lead your eye in a certain direction. Lines can be real or implied, and their possibilities are endless (e.g., straight, curved, jagged, diagonal, horizontal, vertical, wavy, parallel, perpendicular, zigzag, or dashed). Horizontal lines can suggest a state of rest, continuity, and stability since objects that are parallel to the earth are often at rest. Horizontal lines can also give a sense of *space*. Vertical lines communicate a sense of strength, rigidity, or height, and artists often use vertical lines to suggest spirituality, or reaching toward the sky. Diagonal lines often communicate an opposition or movement, while curved lines communicate a sensual or softening quality.

The vertical lines in the reproduction of *American Gothic* (1930), by Grant Wood, extend upward toward the sky or toward the heavens. Notice the vertical lines in the pitch fork. This painting was a chronicle of history of midwestern moral values during the Great Depression. These rigid, upright characters were a symbol of the bond between God and hard work. Notice the horizontal church roof, "a house of God," and the farmer holding a pitch fork. The horizontal lines on the roof are symbolic of the inseparable stability that the church and God can provide during difficult socioeconomic times.

Shape (form and contour)

Shape and form help to define objects on a piece of art. Shapes are often defined by a continuous *line* that meets to create a closed shape. Artists use *contour* line to create dimension. Shapes have two dimensions, height and width; and *form* has three dimensions, height, weight, and depth. Geometric shapes (e.g., circles, squares, etc.) have uniform measures, but natural, organic shapes are related to things that appear in the natural world (e.g., plants and animals). Repeated shapes and forms create *patterns*.

This painting of a woman bathing a child by Mary Cassett (1893), *The Bath*, is a good example of the use of *form*. Inspired by the work of Edgar Degas and Japanese prints, this artist uses bold circular contour shapes of figures, a basin, and a pitcher. Notice the rounded, natural forms created to illustrate clear, crisp lively patterns.

Texture

The element of *texture* is used to describe the way a composition might actually feel, or the way it might appear to feel with our eyes. Texture depicted in three-dimensional art has a tactile quality that can be physically touched (e.g., sculpture and architecture). Texture depicted in two-dimensional art gives you a "sense" of how an object might feel when touched, but you cannot physically touch the object. Some examples are collage or other works of art where artists creatively use color, line, and shape to simulate the object.

Space

Although space can refer to real three-dimensional space, artists refer to space within the boundaries of the composition. Space helps the composition look like it has *form* and gives the artwork a feeling of depth. Artists use both positive and negative space to influence how an object might appear. Negative space is the space between or around the object.

Original

Positive
Space

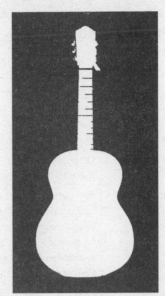

Negative
Space

Interpreting Works of Art

Here are some questions to ask when analyzing art:

- What dominant object stands out as you first look at the composition?
- What is your first emotional response to the composition? What is the mood?
- What do you believe the artist is trying to convey?
- What is the historical, cultural, or social context? What is the time, style, and place of composition.

Apply your responses from the first four questions to the elements and principles of art (color value, contrast, balance, perspective, emphasis, etc.), and notice if there are similarities to these principles. Now answer some of the questions below that apply to this composition.

- How are the lines in the composition arranged (horizontally, vertically, or diagonally)?
- How is color used to show contrast, highlight an area, or create a mood?
- What are the spatial relationships? Are objects far or near?
- Where are the light and dark areas in the composition? How does light enhance directionality? Does it "lead" the viewer?
- What types of shapes are used? Geometric? How do the various shapes affect the composition as a whole?
- What textures are used in the pictures? What feelings do the textures convey?
- Does the composition include depth, linear perspective, or atmospheric perspective?
- Is the composition balanced (symmetrical or asymmetrical)? How is the balance achieved?
- What elements are repeated? Do the various elements contrast with or complement each other?

Art History Timeline	
Classical (400 B.C.– A.D. 400)	**Ancient Greece and Rome** Art encompassed: **architecture** (e.g., Parthenon, Coliseum, aqueducts, vaults, and domes); **sculpture** (ideal form, beauty); **pottery** (black on white, Greek and Roman life); **painting** (murals, portraiture); **frescoes** (pigments with water). **Key characteristics:** physical beauty; mathematical; definite proportion; celebrated great events.
Byzantine (400 – 1400)	**Eastern Roman Empire** **Key characteristics:** religious imagery; **mosaics** (flat, two-dimensional); icons; elongated bodies; stylized background; gold leaf; mosaics decorated churches; **triptych** (three panels).
Early Middle Ages (500–1000)	**Greco-Roman influence;** influence of religion; sacred art; spatially flat; illustrated Book of Kells. **Romanesque architectural style:** heavy walls; round, ribbed arches; transept and nave; grand.
Later Middle Ages (1000–1400)	**Gothic art:** religious—the Church was almost the sole patron of the arts; spatially flat; shape of human body was used to communicate emotions; manuscript illumination. **Gothic architectural style (1200);** influenced by Christianity; Age of Chivalry; rapid growth of commerce; led to the proliferation of **majestic cathedrals** (Chartres; Notre Dame; Cologne); **gothic window** (stained glass); flying buttress (higher, lighter)—towering monuments to God. **Frescoes;** tempera painting (1400s), with egg tempera as binder; illuminated manuscripts; vegetable oils.
Renaissance (1400–1600)	**Rebirth of Greco-Roman classical forms**; development of cities (Florence, Venice, etc.); **art patronage:** church or court/private collectors (Medicis); **Humanism** (individuality and self-worth); **sculpture** ("David"—life from marble); art and architecture (Sistine Chapel—perspective; anatomy; emotion; oil painting techniques). **Art influenced by religion** (pyramidal structure); Raphael—unity of subject, style, and technique ("Madonna and Child"); **Humanism;** depictions of the natural world; study of light and perspective; complex and crowded space. **New technology:** printing press; use of oils—lasting (egg tempera used previously); landscapes. **Drawings:** Michelangelo's studies. **Influence of Northern Europe/Flemish:** surface details; realistic light; religious; portraits.
Baroque (1600–1750)	**Foundations in Italy and Germany** but with regional differences (e.g., Rembrandt); influenced by **Scientific Revolution** (Newton, Galileo); Age of Enlightenment; **Counter-Reformation** (against Protestantism—paintings of faith/martyrdom); Age of Absolute Monarchs (Louis XIV). **Characteristics** (diversified stylistically but often very grand): complex style; appeal to senses/ spectator involvement/drama; strong emotion; emphasis on depth/space; genre scenes (landscapes without people); movement with grandeur. **Rococo (1750s–1800s):** Influenced by the French Revolution and the Industrial Revolution (drastic societal changes); Salons; carefree lifestyle/high fashion; moved away from Baroque heroic subjects and dark color; moved to more delicate/pale colors; theme of romantic love. **Revolt against Rococo:** movement toward **naturalism** and **Romanticism** (1850s) (beauty of nature—senses over intellect); love of ruins and exotic cultures; new sense of nationalism; uniqueness, not conformity (e.g., Goya).
Impressionism (1860s–1900): Origin of Modern Art	Influenced by science (principles of harmony; contrast of colors; reaction of eye in viewing composition); **concern for light and color on object.** Experience of the fleeting moment: new techniques allowed for painting outside; rejected themes of the French Salon (not grand subjects but daily life); **emphasis on primary colors and small brush strokes;** side-by-side placement of primary colors (optimal mixing); little white or black. Manet; Monet; Renoir; Cassatt; Degas. **Sculpture:** Rodin—rebel against the perfect body type ("David"); rough-hewn. **Neo-Impressionism (Pointillism);** tiny dots of primary colors to produce secondary colors; colors placed in scientifically measured dots (e.g., Georges Seurat).

Post-Impressionism (1880s–1900s)	**Characteristics:** paint indoors or outside; emotions through the use of color/swirling color/thick applications; complementary colors; new subject matter: away from the narrow spectrum of viewing (e.g., "Starry Night"; primitive art of the South Pacific). **Examples:** van Gogh; Gauguin; Cézanne. **Watercolor (transparent);** overpainting; Turner.
Twentieth Century	**Fauvism (early twentieth century—"Wild Animals"):** Influenced by technology of the early twentieth century; expansion of color—right from the tube in assertive brush strokes; discord of color; non-Western themes (e.g., Matisse). **Cubism (early twentieth century):** traditional subject matter portrayed by **overlapping geometric forms** (reduced to cubes); fragmentation of form; influenced by African tribal arts: masks and sculpture; move toward abstract art (exploration of space and color); **multiple images of one subject on a two-dimensional surface**. Examples: Picasso; Braque; development of collages; "found" sculpture. **Surrealism (1920s): metaphysical painting;** evolved from Dada art (reaction against commonplace and WWI); workings of the **subconscious mind** (Freud) through fantastic imagery. Examples: Salvador Dali; Chagall—distorted everyday objects. **Abstract Impressionism (1950s): "dribbles, splatters, splashes";** everyday objects to apply art (e.g., brooms); influenced by Navajo sand paintings; examples: Jackson Pollock, de Kooning, and Kandinsky. **"Pop" Art/Popular Art:** "Why is it art?"; reaction against abstract painting (soup cans; comics); Warhol; Lichtenstein (iconic art); acrylics. **American Regional Art** (from 1930s/rural art): everyday life; expanded on landscape painting of the 1870s; example: Grant Wood ("American Gothic").

PART II

TWO FULL-LENGTH PRACTICE TESTS

Practice-Review-Analyze-Practice

This section contains two full-length simulation CSET: Multiple Subjects exams. The practice tests are followed by complete answers, explanations, and analysis techniques. The format, levels of difficulty, question structures, and number of questions are similar to those on the actual CSET: Multiple Subjects. The actual CSET: Multiple Subjects is copyrighted and may not be duplicated, and these questions are not taken directly from the actual tests.

When taking these exams, try to simulate the test conditions. Remember the total testing time for each practice test is 5 hours. Although you may divide your time among the three subtests in any way you wish, in order to be sure that you have enough time to finish all sections, budget your time effectively. Try to spend about 1 minute on each multiple-choice question and about 10 minutes on each short constructed-response question.

Chapter 8

Practice Test I

Answer Sheet for Practice Test I

(Remove this sheet and use it to mark your answers)

Multiple-Choice Questions

Subtest I

1 Ⓐ Ⓑ Ⓒ Ⓓ	21 Ⓐ Ⓑ Ⓒ Ⓓ	41 Ⓐ Ⓑ Ⓒ Ⓓ
2 Ⓐ Ⓑ Ⓒ Ⓓ	22 Ⓐ Ⓑ Ⓒ Ⓓ	42 Ⓐ Ⓑ Ⓒ Ⓓ
3 Ⓐ Ⓑ Ⓒ Ⓓ	23 Ⓐ Ⓑ Ⓒ Ⓓ	43 Ⓐ Ⓑ Ⓒ Ⓓ
4 Ⓐ Ⓑ Ⓒ Ⓓ	24 Ⓐ Ⓑ Ⓒ Ⓓ	44 Ⓐ Ⓑ Ⓒ Ⓓ
5 Ⓐ Ⓑ Ⓒ Ⓓ	25 Ⓐ Ⓑ Ⓒ Ⓓ	45 Ⓐ Ⓑ Ⓒ Ⓓ
6 Ⓐ Ⓑ Ⓒ Ⓓ	26 Ⓐ Ⓑ Ⓒ Ⓓ	46 Ⓐ Ⓑ Ⓒ Ⓓ
7 Ⓐ Ⓑ Ⓒ Ⓓ	27 Ⓐ Ⓑ Ⓒ Ⓓ	47 Ⓐ Ⓑ Ⓒ Ⓓ
8 Ⓐ Ⓑ Ⓒ Ⓓ	28 Ⓐ Ⓑ Ⓒ Ⓓ	48 Ⓐ Ⓑ Ⓒ Ⓓ
9 Ⓐ Ⓑ Ⓒ Ⓓ	29 Ⓐ Ⓑ Ⓒ Ⓓ	49 Ⓐ Ⓑ Ⓒ Ⓓ
10 Ⓐ Ⓑ Ⓒ Ⓓ	30 Ⓐ Ⓑ Ⓒ Ⓓ	50 Ⓐ Ⓑ Ⓒ Ⓓ
11 Ⓐ Ⓑ Ⓒ Ⓓ	31 Ⓐ Ⓑ Ⓒ Ⓓ	51 Ⓐ Ⓑ Ⓒ Ⓓ
12 Ⓐ Ⓑ Ⓒ Ⓓ	32 Ⓐ Ⓑ Ⓒ Ⓓ	52 Ⓐ Ⓑ Ⓒ Ⓓ
13 Ⓐ Ⓑ Ⓒ Ⓓ	33 Ⓐ Ⓑ Ⓒ Ⓓ	
14 Ⓐ Ⓑ Ⓒ Ⓓ	34 Ⓐ Ⓑ Ⓒ Ⓓ	
15 Ⓐ Ⓑ Ⓒ Ⓓ	35 Ⓐ Ⓑ Ⓒ Ⓓ	
16 Ⓐ Ⓑ Ⓒ Ⓓ	36 Ⓐ Ⓑ Ⓒ Ⓓ	
17 Ⓐ Ⓑ Ⓒ Ⓓ	37 Ⓐ Ⓑ Ⓒ Ⓓ	
18 Ⓐ Ⓑ Ⓒ Ⓓ	38 Ⓐ Ⓑ Ⓒ Ⓓ	
19 Ⓐ Ⓑ Ⓒ Ⓓ	39 Ⓐ Ⓑ Ⓒ Ⓓ	
20 Ⓐ Ⓑ Ⓒ Ⓓ	40 Ⓐ Ⓑ Ⓒ Ⓓ	

Subtest II

1 Ⓐ Ⓑ Ⓒ Ⓓ	21 Ⓐ Ⓑ Ⓒ Ⓓ	41 Ⓐ Ⓑ Ⓒ Ⓓ
2 Ⓐ Ⓑ Ⓒ Ⓓ	22 Ⓐ Ⓑ Ⓒ Ⓓ	42 Ⓐ Ⓑ Ⓒ Ⓓ
3 Ⓐ Ⓑ Ⓒ Ⓓ	23 Ⓐ Ⓑ Ⓒ Ⓓ	43 Ⓐ Ⓑ Ⓒ Ⓓ
4 Ⓐ Ⓑ Ⓒ Ⓓ	24 Ⓐ Ⓑ Ⓒ Ⓓ	44 Ⓐ Ⓑ Ⓒ Ⓓ
5 Ⓐ Ⓑ Ⓒ Ⓓ	25 Ⓐ Ⓑ Ⓒ Ⓓ	45 Ⓐ Ⓑ Ⓒ Ⓓ
6 Ⓐ Ⓑ Ⓒ Ⓓ	26 Ⓐ Ⓑ Ⓒ Ⓓ	46 Ⓐ Ⓑ Ⓒ Ⓓ
7 Ⓐ Ⓑ Ⓒ Ⓓ	27 Ⓐ Ⓑ Ⓒ Ⓓ	47 Ⓐ Ⓑ Ⓒ Ⓓ
8 Ⓐ Ⓑ Ⓒ Ⓓ	28 Ⓐ Ⓑ Ⓒ Ⓓ	48 Ⓐ Ⓑ Ⓒ Ⓓ
9 Ⓐ Ⓑ Ⓒ Ⓓ	29 Ⓐ Ⓑ Ⓒ Ⓓ	49 Ⓐ Ⓑ Ⓒ Ⓓ
10 Ⓐ Ⓑ Ⓒ Ⓓ	30 Ⓐ Ⓑ Ⓒ Ⓓ	50 Ⓐ Ⓑ Ⓒ Ⓓ
11 Ⓐ Ⓑ Ⓒ Ⓓ	31 Ⓐ Ⓑ Ⓒ Ⓓ	51 Ⓐ Ⓑ Ⓒ Ⓓ
12 Ⓐ Ⓑ Ⓒ Ⓓ	32 Ⓐ Ⓑ Ⓒ Ⓓ	52 Ⓐ Ⓑ Ⓒ Ⓓ
13 Ⓐ Ⓑ Ⓒ Ⓓ	33 Ⓐ Ⓑ Ⓒ Ⓓ	
14 Ⓐ Ⓑ Ⓒ Ⓓ	34 Ⓐ Ⓑ Ⓒ Ⓓ	
15 Ⓐ Ⓑ Ⓒ Ⓓ	35 Ⓐ Ⓑ Ⓒ Ⓓ	
16 Ⓐ Ⓑ Ⓒ Ⓓ	36 Ⓐ Ⓑ Ⓒ Ⓓ	
17 Ⓐ Ⓑ Ⓒ Ⓓ	37 Ⓐ Ⓑ Ⓒ Ⓓ	
18 Ⓐ Ⓑ Ⓒ Ⓓ	38 Ⓐ Ⓑ Ⓒ Ⓓ	
19 Ⓐ Ⓑ Ⓒ Ⓓ	39 Ⓐ Ⓑ Ⓒ Ⓓ	
20 Ⓐ Ⓑ Ⓒ Ⓓ	40 Ⓐ Ⓑ Ⓒ Ⓓ	

CUT HERE

(continued)

Subtest III

1 Ⓐ Ⓑ Ⓒ Ⓓ	21 Ⓐ Ⓑ Ⓒ Ⓓ
2 Ⓐ Ⓑ Ⓒ Ⓓ	22 Ⓐ Ⓑ Ⓒ Ⓓ
3 Ⓐ Ⓑ Ⓒ Ⓓ	23 Ⓐ Ⓑ Ⓒ Ⓓ
4 Ⓐ Ⓑ Ⓒ Ⓓ	24 Ⓐ Ⓑ Ⓒ Ⓓ
5 Ⓐ Ⓑ Ⓒ Ⓓ	25 Ⓐ Ⓑ Ⓒ Ⓓ
6 Ⓐ Ⓑ Ⓒ Ⓓ	26 Ⓐ Ⓑ Ⓒ Ⓓ
7 Ⓐ Ⓑ Ⓒ Ⓓ	27 Ⓐ Ⓑ Ⓒ Ⓓ
8 Ⓐ Ⓑ Ⓒ Ⓓ	28 Ⓐ Ⓑ Ⓒ Ⓓ
9 Ⓐ Ⓑ Ⓒ Ⓓ	29 Ⓐ Ⓑ Ⓒ Ⓓ
10 Ⓐ Ⓑ Ⓒ Ⓓ	30 Ⓐ Ⓑ Ⓒ Ⓓ
11 Ⓐ Ⓑ Ⓒ Ⓓ	31 Ⓐ Ⓑ Ⓒ Ⓓ
12 Ⓐ Ⓑ Ⓒ Ⓓ	32 Ⓐ Ⓑ Ⓒ Ⓓ
13 Ⓐ Ⓑ Ⓒ Ⓓ	33 Ⓐ Ⓑ Ⓒ Ⓓ
14 Ⓐ Ⓑ Ⓒ Ⓓ	34 Ⓐ Ⓑ Ⓒ Ⓓ
15 Ⓐ Ⓑ Ⓒ Ⓓ	35 Ⓐ Ⓑ Ⓒ Ⓓ
16 Ⓐ Ⓑ Ⓒ Ⓓ	36 Ⓐ Ⓑ Ⓒ Ⓓ
17 Ⓐ Ⓑ Ⓒ Ⓓ	37 Ⓐ Ⓑ Ⓒ Ⓓ
18 Ⓐ Ⓑ Ⓒ Ⓓ	38 Ⓐ Ⓑ Ⓒ Ⓓ
19 Ⓐ Ⓑ Ⓒ Ⓓ	39 Ⓐ Ⓑ Ⓒ Ⓓ
20 Ⓐ Ⓑ Ⓒ Ⓓ	

CUT HERE

Directions: Choose the best answer to each question and fill in the appropriate circle on your answer sheet (5 hours).

Subtest I: Reading, Language, and Literature
Multiple Choice

1. The best instructional reason for a teacher to encourage independent reading at home is:

   A. parents need to be included in the learning process.

   B. the more a student reads, the better he/she becomes at reading.

   C. students need to be assigned more homework in early grades.

   D. reading at home helps the student to develop reading more smoothly.

2. A first-grade teacher decides to reread a story to her class instead of selecting a new story. Which of the following is the greatest benefit of this technique?

   A. Rereading a story promotes good listening skills.

   B. Rereading is a valuable technique that leads to more enjoyment of literature for the students.

   C. Reading a story over again engages the student in a familiar text, enhancing their comprehension and building confidence.

   D. Rereading a story is a delightful technique to use with young children.

3. In the following conversation, a kindergarten teacher is preparing a student for a phonemic awareness test. Read the following dialog and answer the question that follows.

   Teacher: "I'm going to say the sounds in a word. The sounds are /k/../i/../t/. When I put those sounds together, they say *kit*. Now I'm going to say some more sounds, and I want you to put them together to make a word. This time, the sounds are /f/../i/../t/. Can you put those sounds together to make a word?"

   Student: "/f/../i/../t/. That says *fit*!"

   Teacher: "That's right, *fit*. Now, I'd like you to do this for some more words."

   This assessment would be an appropriate way to measure which of the following phonemic awareness tasks?

   A. Identifying phonemes and their letters

   B. Blending the phonemes in a given word

   C. Matching phonemes in rhyming words

   D. Segmenting the phonemes in a given word

4. A first-grade student is capable of reading stories at her grade-level. However, when asked by the teacher to recall details about the story, she is unable to recall specific details and responds by saying, "I liked the story." What does this suggest to the teacher for reading instruction?

   A. The student needs direct instruction in reading comprehension skills, followed with guided and independent practice.

   B. The student needs to be given more structured situations for writing about stories so that she can better express herself.

   C. Instructional suggestions would include cooperative groups and paired learning.

   D. The teacher needs to structure her day to include opportunities for student interaction.

5. A first-grade teacher is working with her class during morning circle time. She is teaching a mini-lesson on onsets and rimes. The teacher uses the word "hair" as an example. Which of the following best represents an understanding of onsets and rimes?

   A. Hare and hair

   B. Hair and care

   C. /h/ and /air/

   D. Hair and chair

GO ON TO THE NEXT PAGE

6. A fourth-grade teacher is teaching a class with 30 students, many of whom are English Language Learners from different cultural backgrounds. When the teacher is selecting reading material for her classroom, she should:

   A. be sure to select reading material that is sensitive to each culture in her class.
   B. include reading material that covers many different reading levels in order to reach all students' abilities.
   C. continue to use the same material that she used with her previous fourth-grade class and use the materials used in other fourth-grade classes.
   D. use the same reading material that the other fourth-grade classes are using and include culturally sensitive material.

7. A second-grade teacher listens to his students read orally in a small, guided reading group. He notices that one of his students is continually struggling with fluency and is often unable to recognize grade-level words. What intervention strategies would best provide for the needs of this student?

   A. The teacher should teach word identification strategies such as phonics and high-frequency sight vocabulary. In addition, the teacher should provide very simple text for this student to become an independent reader.
   B. The teacher needs to concentrate on using related workbook pages in word recognition skills for this student to become an automatic reader.
   C. The teacher should increase time for read-alouds, which would provide this reader with more exposure to good literature. This would also result in the added benefit of increasing the student's vocabulary.
   D. The teacher should provide the student with time for sustained, silent reading, which increases fluency when the student is reading books that are at his reading level.

8. Mr. Farley reads aloud the book *The Three Little Pigs*, a story in which a wolf tries to destroy the home of three pigs. The next day, Mr. Farley reads aloud *The True Story of the*

Three Little Pigs, in which the wolf explains how he was framed by the pigs. The teacher leads a discussion comparing the two stories. This discussion is most likely to promote students' reading proficiency by:

   A. guiding students to compare stories and determine a character's perspective and/or bias.
   B. helping students self-monitor and identify common themes in related stories.
   C. guiding students to distinguish fact versus opinion in similar stories.
   D. helping students to use evaluative comprehension skills to determine the mood and theme of the stories.

9. Which of the following strategies is most effective in teaching spelling to children?

   A. Memorizing lists of words that are related to reading material
   B. Looking at spelling patterns and vocabulary items
   C. Taking a spelling test every week
   D. Spelling words aloud

10. Which of the following sentences contains an adjective clause?

   A. Although I saw the storm with my own eyes, I could not believe its intensity.
   B. The program that I bought at the opera simplified the confusing plot.
   C. We swam in the ocean, but we never saw any fish.
   D. As the man came closer, we saw a scar on his cheek.

11. In which of the following sentences is the underlined word used correctly?

   A. Your complaints have finally had the desired <u>affect</u>.
   B. The soldiers were negatively <u>affected</u> by the long and gruesome battle.
   C. After a long day's hike in the desert, we were <u>effected</u> by the heat.
   D. <u>Effecting</u> a desire for simplicity, we bought a small car with no extra options.

12. **Read the passage below; then answer the two questions that follow.**

¹One of the dominant philosophical theories during the Renaissance came initially from the Ancient Greeks, the concept of the "Great Chain of Being." ²According to the chain-of-being concept, all existing things have their precise place and function in the universe, and to depart from one's proper place was to betray one's nature. ³An object was placed in the hierarchy, depending on its relative proportion of "spirit" and "matter." ⁴Its major premise was that every existing thing in the universe had its "place" in a divinely planned hierarchical order. ⁵The items with the most spirit and least amount of matter were placed higher on the scale, and vice versa. ⁶Therefore, God was placed at the very top, followed by angels, and then man and other mammals. ⁷Trees and flowers, members of the vegetative class, were below man, and at the very bottom, one found various types of inanimate objects, such as metals and stones. ⁸Playwrights and poets of the Renaissance, such as Shakespeare, demonstrated the consequences of disrupting this logical order, notably in their tragedies.

Which of the following changes would most improve the logical organization of the passage?

A. Move Sentence 3 so that it follows Sentence 6.

B. Move Sentence 3 so that it follows Sentence 4.

C. Move Sentence 8 so that it follows Sentence 1.

D. Move Sentence 5 so that it follows Sentence 2.

13. In order to further develop the passage, the idea(s) in which of the following sentences would most benefit from additional detail and explanation?

A. Sentence 1

B. Sentence 3

C. Sentence 6

D. Sentence 8

14. **Read the passage below and then answer the question that follows.**

¹On December 17, 1903, Orville Wright lay prone in what would come to be known as the *Wright Flyer.* ²His left hand held the control for the front elevator. ³He used his right hand to control the engine by moving a small, horizontal lever on the wing. ⁴Wilbur Wright, behind him, swung one of the propellers, and the engine coughed to life. ⁵The *Flyer* began moving down the launching rail as Wilbur ran along beside it, steadying the right wing tip. ⁶Orville adjusted the elevator, and the *Flyer* lifted off the launch track. ⁷Man's eternal quest for flight had finally been fulfilled.

Which of the following identifies the topic sentence of the paragraph?

A. Sentence 1

B. Sentence 5

C. Sentence 6

D. Sentence 7

15. Which of the following is *not* a common strategy of persuasive writing?

A. Devoting equal discussion to the positive and negative aspects of the writer's stand

B. Appealing to the reader's sense of ethics

C. Using concrete details to convince the reader of the plausibility of the writer's stand

D. Ending with a positive reaffirmation of the writer's stand

16. Which of the following purposes is the goal of a speaker who adjusts his or her volume and tone of voice during a speech or an oral presentation?

A. Distracting the audience from any slurred or mispronounced words

B. Giving the audience a visual cue to follow important points

C. Engaging the audience's attention at appropriate places in the presentation's content

D. Reminding the audience of the presentation's organization

17. Which of the following is *least* important to include in a research paper?

A. A summary in the conclusion that reminds the reader of the main points

B. A thesis statement that presents what the paper will address

C. Clear transitions between major points

D. An anecdote in the introduction to which the reader can relate

GO ON TO THE NEXT PAGE

The following excerpt is from a speech entitled "What to the Slave Is the 4th of July?" which was delivered by Frederick Douglass (1818–1895) on Independence Day in Rochester, New York, in 1852. In his speech, Douglass advocated voting rights for African-Americans. Read the excerpt and answer the two questions that follow.

¹We may be asked, I say, why we want it [the right to vote]. I will tell you why we want it. ²We want it because it is our right, first of all. ³No class of men can, without insulting their own nature, be content with any deprivation of their rights. ⁴We want it again, as a means for educating our race. ⁵Men are so constituted that they derive their conviction of their own possibilities largely by the estimate formed of them by others. ⁶If nothing is expected of a people, that people will find it difficult to contradict that expectation. ⁷By depriving us of suffrage, you affirm our incapacity to form an intelligent judgment respecting public men and public measures; you declare before the world that we are unfit to exercise the elective franchise, and by this means lead us to undervalue ourselves, to put a low estimate upon ourselves, and to feel that we have no possibilities like other men.

18. Which of the following rhetorical devices does Douglass *not* utilize in his speech?

    A. An appeal to logic
    B. An appeal to ethics
    C. An appeal to pathos
    D. An appeal to common decency

19. What is the intended effect of the repetition of *we want it* in the speech?

    A. It reminds the listener of just how many people Douglass refers to.
    B. It shows the intensity of the collective desire of African-Americans for voting rights.
    C. It lulls the listener before presenting more important ideas.
    D. It clarifies whom Douglass means by *we*.

20. Which of the following is *least* likely to be included in the mythology of ancient cultures?

    A. The foundation of political hierarchies
    B. A description of Earth Mother
    C. The sly actions of a trickster
    D. A requisite trip to the underworld

21. **Read the excerpt below from the Native American folk tale, "The Snake With the Big Feet," and then answer the two questions that follow.**

Long ago, there was a snake who had feet—big feet. The other snakes, because he was different, drove him away saying, "A good long way from here live other ugly creatures with feet like yours. Go and live with them!" And the poor, unhappy snake had to go away.

For days and days, he traveled. The weather grew cold, and food became hard to find. At last, exhausted, his feet cut and frostbitten, he lay down on the bank of a river to die.

A deer looked out of a willow thicket and saw the snake. Pitying him, the deer took the snake into his own lodge and gave him food and medicine for his bleeding feet.

The deer told the snake that there were indeed creatures with feet like his who would befriend him. He showed the snake how to make a shelter for protection from the cold and taught him how to make moccasins of deerskin to protect his feet. And at dawn the snake continued his journey.

It was bitter cold when the snake made camp the next night. As he gathered boughs for a shelter, a porcupine appeared. Shivering, the porcupine asked him, "Will you give me shelter in your lodge for the night?"

The snake said, "It's very little that I have, but you are welcome to share it."

"I am grateful," said the porcupine, "and perhaps I can do something for you. Those are beautiful moccasins, brother, but they do not match your skin. Take some of my quills, and make a pattern on them, for good luck." So they worked a pattern on the moccasins with the porcupine quills, and the snake went on his way again.

At last he met an Indian who greeted him in a friendly manner. The snake had no gifts for this kindly chief, so he gave him the moccasins. And that, so the old ones say, was how our people first learned to make moccasins of deerskin and to ornament them with porcupine quills in patterns, like those on the back of a snake. And from that day on, the snake lived in the lodge of the chief for a long time, and he was happy.

The preceding passage shares which of the following traditions of folk tales?

    A. The inclusion of a sinister foil
    B. The inclusion of animals to represent essential human traits
    C. The reliance on a trick of fate to bring a favorable outcome
    D. The retelling of the story of the origins of a tribe

22. Which of the following aspects of traditional folk tales does the passage *not* employ?

    A. An inclusion of humanity in the world of animals

    B. A series of travel adventures that teach a lesson

    C. The use of supernatural power to solve a problem

    D. The use of simplistic narration and dialogue

Read the poem below, "Fable for When There's No Way Out," and then answer the two questions that follow.

Grown too big for his skin,
and it grown hard,
without a sea and atmosphere—
he's drunk it all up—
his strength's inside him now,
but there's no room to stretch.
He pecks at the top
but his beak's too soft;
though instinct and ambition shoves,
he can't get through.
Barely old enough to bleed
and already bruised!
In a case this tough
What's the use
if you break your head
instead of the lid?
Despair tempts him
to just go limp;
Maybe the cell's
already a tomb,
and the beginning end
in this round room.
Still, stupidly he pecks
and pecks, as if from under
his own skull—
yet makes no crack . . .
No crack until
he finally cracks,
and kicks and stomps.
What a thrill
and shock to feel
his little gaff poke
through the floor!
A way he hadn't known or meant.
Rage works when reason won't.
When locked up, bear down.

23. The word *fable* in the poem's title is most fitting of common fables because the poem:

    A. has a moral that is woven in and explicitly stated at the end.

    B. utilizes animals to prove a point about nature.

    C. explores creation myths.

    D. mirrors the structure of hero stories.

24. The most important aspect of the analogy the poet makes between the baby chick and humanity is best clarified as follows:

    A. Babies need to slowly feel their way into the world.

    B. All beings must face the world alone.

    C. Humans and animals face the same hardships.

    D. When faced with adversity, one needs to fight the opposing forces.

Read the poem below, "Persephone, Falling," by Rita Dove, and then answer the two questions that follow.

One narcissus among the ordinary beautiful
flowers, one unlike all the others! She pulled,
stooped to pull harder—
when, sprung out of the earth
on his glittering terrible
carriage, he claims his due.
It is finished. No one heard her.
No one! She had strayed from the herd.

(Remember: go straight to school.
This is important, stop fooling around!
Don't answer to strangers. Stick
with your playmates. Keep your eyes down.)
This is how easily the pit
opens. This is how one foot sinks into the ground.

25. In this poem, the title's allusion, combined with the image of the narcissus, reinforces which of the following themes?

    A. The beauty of nature can blind us to potential dangers.

    B. One can avoid peril if one stays with others.

    C. Temptation is a slippery slope one should avoid.

    D. One never knows what is under the surface.

GO ON TO THE NEXT PAGE

26. The advice in parentheses in the second stanza is most likely spoken by which of the following figures?

    A. A teacher
    B. A constable
    C. A parental figure
    D. A religious figure

Subtest I: History and Social Science Multiple Choice

27. By the early 1500s, Spain had developed a foothold in the New World. In a period of fewer than four decades following Columbus's first voyage of discovery, the Spanish defeated both the Aztec and Inca empires. Which of the following best illustrates the primary factor that led to the collapse of the Aztec and Inca empires?

    A. Mesoamerican geography prevented the Aztecs and the Incas from uniting to face a common enemy.

    B. A religious belief in the immortality of the soul allowed both the Aztecs and the Incas to view the Spaniards as gods and superior beings.

    C. The sophistication of Spanish military technology, as well as the introduction of the horse, rendered the Aztecs and Incas incapable of sustaining military success.

    D. The lack of resistance to European disease disseminated the Aztec and Inca populations.

28. Which of the following factors best describes the impact of geography on the development of early civilizations in Mesopotamia?

    A. The earliest civilizations in Mesopotamia arose in the northern plateaus, which received adequate rainfall for farming and food production.

    B. Central irrigation projects in the barren southern plains resulted in agricultural advances and a surplus of food, which allowed civilizations to develop.

    C. The desert offered protection from both northern and southern nomadic invaders and thus provided a "safety valve" for civilization to develop.

    D. Population growth outstripped food production and forced large population centers to relocate to areas of greater rainfall.

29. **Use the picture below to answer the question that follows.**

Considered one of the great archaeological finds of the twentieth century, the tomb complex of the terra-cotta army pictured above is most closely associated with which of the following Chinese dynasties?

A. The Mogul Dynasty
B. The Qin Dynasty
C. The Ming Dynasty
D. The Qing (Manchu) Dynasty

GO ON TO THE NEXT PAGE

30. The Industrial Revolution of the eighteenth century led to major changes in western countries. Which of the following best describes a primary result of the Industrial Revolution's impact on the economic and social structure of Europe?

 A. New inventions and increased technological advances facilitated a stable rural population.

 B. The development of shipbuilding on a massive scale promoted the Age of Discovery and provided the basis for European imperialism.

 C. The population of Europe gradually declined as a result of an increase in health-related illnesses associated with overcrowded cities and poor working conditions in the factories.

 D. The division of defined classes, including a merchant middle class, was a direct result of changing economic conditions.

31. **Use the list below to answer the question that follows.**

 - Founding of the Society of Jesus
 - Revival of the Inquisition
 - Establishment of the *Index of Prohibited Books*
 - Adherence to the Council of Trent

 The political events listed above are most closely associated with which of the following?

 A. The Counter-Reformation
 B. The Protestant Reformation
 C. The Church of England
 D. The Anabaptist movement

32. **Use the map below to answer the question that follows.**

The Old Silk Routes

The Silk Road was an extensive network of maritime and overland trade routes that connected Asia with the Mediterranean World, North Africa, and Europe. Which of the following religions became established in China as a direct result of the cross-cultural contact associated with the Silk Road?

 A. Buddhism, Taoism, and Confucianism
 B. Christianity, Confucianism, and Taoism
 C. Christianity, Buddhism, and Islam
 D. Judaism, Zoroastrianism, and Hinduism

33. In the Age of Constantine, Rome was divided into the Western and Eastern Roman empires. The Western Roman Empire was destroyed by the end of the fifth century A.D. However, Byzantium survived. What geographical factors accounted for the emergence of Byzantium as a powerful trading empire?

 A. It was located geographically between Europe and Africa and had contact with the Muslim world.

 B. Constantinople controlled both the Mediterranean Sea and the Black Sea trade routes.

 C. Europe was in a protracted economic downturn during the Early Middle Ages and lacked the technology to trade across the Mediterranean.

 D. There were few strong empires in the geographic region that encompassed Byzantium.

34. Which of the following best illustrates the influence of Islamic scholarship on the development of European civilization during the early Middle Ages?

    A. The development of sophisticated metallurgy and the emergence of alchemy

    B. The introduction of competing monotheistic religious beliefs

    C. The development of architectural techniques utilized in cathedral building

    D. The introduction of new mathematical concepts, such as algebra and calculus

35. The United States entered the War of 1812 with military objectives to take Canada from Britain and Florida from Spain. The country failed on both accounts. However, a positive result of the War of 1812 was that

    A. the British gave up control of New Orleans to the United States.

    B. Native American tribes were restricted from settling in the Ohio Valley.

    C. the Federalist Party gained in strength as a result of its support for the War.

    D. American industry prospered when trade was restricted by the British during the War.

36. Following the purchase of the Louisiana Territory in 1803, President Jefferson sent Meriwether Lewis and William Clark on a journey of discovery to the newly acquired lands. Which of the following was the central focus of the Lewis and Clark expedition?

    A. To contact and trade with Indian tribes and bring peace to the new frontier

    B. To identify and collect new species of flora and fauna and to map the new land

    C. To discover an all-water route to the Pacific

    D. To prevent Spain, Russia, and England from reestablishing a presence in the Louisiana Territory

37. "No taxation without representation" became a symbol of American defiance against British taxation. The rallying cry was a direct result of which of the following British policies?

    A. The Stamp Act of 1765, which taxed newspapers and legal documents

    B. The Townshend Acts of 1767, which taxed glass, paper, and paint

    C. The Tea Act of 1773, which allowed a British company to sell tea directly to the colonies

    D. The Coercive Acts of 1774, which closed the Port of Boston

38. The Treaty of Guadalupe Hidalgo was a logical extension of which of the following political philosophies?

    A. The antislavery movement

    B. The proslavery expansionist movement

    C. The Homestead Act

    D. The doctrine of Manifest Destiny

39. Which of the following had the most profound impact on the expansion of slavery in the United States?

    A. The cotton gin

    B. The geography of the South

    C. The annexation of Texas

    D. The election of Lincoln

40. Early North American history was linked to the European fur trade. Which of the following animals became synonymous with the fur trade in the first half of the nineteenth century?

    A. Beaver

    B. Buffalo

    C. Deer

    D. Fox

GO ON TO THE NEXT PAGE

41. Use the print below to answer the question that follows.

Which of the following best describes the impact of conditions depicted in the print above?

A. Poor working conditions in England encouraged individuals to agree to indentured servant contracts in order to immigrate to America.

B. The potato blight in Ireland caused massive immigration to America.

C. Political unrest in Germany encouraged immigration to America.

D. Governments in Europe passed child labor laws to protect children.

42. The Northwest Ordinance of 1787 prohibited slavery north and west of the Ohio River. What was the primary factor that allowed Missouri to become a slave state in 1821?

A. Geographically, Missouri was south of the Ohio River and not subject to the Ordinance of 1787.

B. The South wanted new land for slavery, and Missouri was considered a border state.

C. The admission of Maine as a free state preserved the slave state/free state balance in the Senate.

D. The abolitionist movement had not yet gained strength in the North.

43. Use the statement below to answer the following question.

"We hold these truths to be self-evident: that all men and women are created equal ..."

Which of the following documents expressed the view above?

A. The Declaration of Sentiments, Seneca Falls

B. The Declaration of Independence

C. The Preamble to the Constitution

D. The Gettysburg Address

44. Progressive reforms became part of the California Constitution in 1910. Which progressive reform allows the California electorate to rescind legislation that has already become law?

A. Initiative

B. Referendum

C. Recall

D. Direct primary

45. The Imperial Valley is one of California's important agricultural regions. The California water distribution system that supplies water to the Imperial Valley comes primarily from

A. runoff from the Sierra snowpack.

B. the Colorado River.

C. the Los Angeles Aqueduct.

D. expanding watersheds.

46. During Spanish rule in California, a common characteristic that linked the missions, presidios, and pueblos was that they were

A. built by Spanish explorers.

B. run by the clergy.

C. geographically close to the major California river systems.

D. connected by El Camino Real.

47. Shortly after Mexico defeated the Spanish and gained control of California, the Mexican government

A. expanded the mission system.

B. made Indians citizens of Mexico.

C. restricted international trade.

D. discovered gold in the Sierras.

48. California became a U.S. territory as a result of the Mexican-American War (1846–1848). Prior to the war, the most important industry in California in the period between 1821 and 1848 was

    A. cattle ranching.
    B. manufacturing.
    C. grain farming.
    D. shipping.

49. **Use the poster below to answer the question that follows.**

The famous World War II poster titled "We Can Do It!" best symbolizes

    A. the industrial strength of the United States during World War II.
    B. traditional values associated with women entering the industrial workplace.
    C. government efforts to sell war bonds and promote patriotism.
    D. a propaganda campaign to encourage women to seek work in wartime industrial plants.

50. During the period of 1960–2000, Los Angeles underwent profound cultural changes. Which of the following best supports the view that Los Angeles in that period became the new "Ellis Island"?

    A. The backgrounds of the new immigrants reflected the same identifying factors that were associated with immigration to Ellis Island in the early twentieth century.
    B. A dramatic increase in immigration from Mexico resulted in an increase in nativism and discriminatory legislation against immigrants.
    C. Immigration from Southeast Asia and Central America resulted in a dramatic increase in voter registration and political activism.
    D. The evolving diversity of culture in Los Angeles was associated with the same geographic areas that sent massive numbers of immigrants to America in the early twentieth century.

51. Based on statutes included in the California Constitution, which of the following groups historically experienced the most discrimination?

    A. Women
    B. Chinese
    C. African-Americans
    D. Mexican-Americans

52. Which of the following novels symbolizes the plight of migrant workers who came to California after being displaced by the Dust Bowl?

    A. *Two Years Before the Mast*
    B. *The Octopus*
    C. *The Grapes of Wrath*
    D. *How the Other Half Live*

GO ON TO THE NEXT PAGE

Subtest I: Reading, Language, and Literature Short Constructed Response

Directions: Write your answers legibly on a clean sheet of lined paper.

Assignment 1

1. Use the information below to complete the following exercise.

    In analyzing a fluency assessment, a third-grade teacher notices that one of her students, José, rushes when he is reading. His assessment indicates that he is having difficulty with comprehension, and does not apply his knowledge of prefixes and suffixes when encountering multi-syllabic words.

    Using your knowledge of reading text comprehension, prepare a response in which you identify and discuss:

    - the reading comprehension benefits of understanding prefixes and suffixes; and
    - at least one instructional strategy that will help to improve his reading fluency.

Assignment 2

2. Use the information here to complete the exercise that follows.

    It is important to have an implementation plan when teaching specific skills—for example, phonemic awareness. Study the Curriculum Implementation Plan that follows.

FLUENCY ASSESSMENT

1. ASSESS
Informal/Formal:
- Fluency
- Sight word Check Off
- Decoding Test (BPST)
- Other Assessments

2. PLAN
Data Use:
- Standards & Framework
- Grouping
- Scheduling
- Instructional Strategies
- Student Tasks
- Technology
- Individual Needs

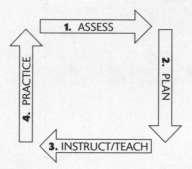

1. ASSESS
2. PLAN
3. INSTRUCT/TEACH
4. PRACTICE

4. MEANINGFUL PRACTICE
Instructional Tasks:
- Highly Structured Practice
- Guided Practice
- Independent Practice
- Decodable Text
- Leveled Readers

3. INSTRUCT/TEACH
Direct & Explicit Instruction:
- Decoding
- Sight Word Mastery
- Comprehension Strategies
- Comprehension Skills
- Writing Skills
- Other Instructional Strategies

Based on the information given and your knowledge of reading, write a response in which you:

- explain how phonemic awareness is related to reading achievement; and
- describe the steps or instructional process a teacher must take to teach phonemic awareness to his/her kindergarten class.

Subtest I: History and Social Science Short Constructed Response

Directions: Write your answers legibly on a clean sheet of lined paper.

Assignment 3

3. Complete the exercise that follows.

   The Transcontinental Railroad, completed in 1869, transformed California.

   Using your knowledge of California history, prepare a response in which you:

   - identify the role of the Big Four in furthering the project and list their members;
   - list one economic and one cultural impact on California as a result of the railroad; and
   - discuss the effect of one factor from above that transformed California.

Assignment 4

4. Following the end of the Civil War in 1865, the American economy began three decades of rapid industrial expansion that changed the face of America.

   Using your knowledge of U.S. history, prepare a response in which you:

   - identify two American inventions of the period;
   - identify two positive and two negative effects of industrialization during this period; and
   - explain how one of the effects impacted the quality of life in America.

Subtest II: Mathematics Multiple Choice

1. When the value 7,500 is written in prime factored form, it becomes $2^x 3^y 5^z$. What is the value of xyz?

   A.   6
   B.   8
   C.   12
   D.   30

2. **Use the diagram below to answer the question that follows.**

   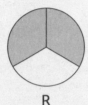 

   R   S

   What is the sum of the shaded area of figure R and the shaded area of figure S if each circle represents a unit circle divided into equal parts?

   A. $\frac{9}{16}$

   B. $1\frac{7}{16}$

   C. $\frac{7}{24}$

   D. $1\frac{1}{24}$

3. **Use the problem below to answer the question that follows.**

   Hot dogs are packaged with h hot dogs in each package. Hot dog buns are packaged with b buns in each package. If you were to buy an equal number of hot dogs and buns in order that each hot dog gets a bun, what would be the *least* number of each you would need to buy?

   Which of the following methods could be used to find the solution to this problem?

   A.   Add h and b.
   B.   Find the greatest common factor of h and b.
   C.   Find the least common multiple of h and b.
   D.   Multiply h and b.

4. Which of the following directions, when followed, would correctly express the value 24.7×10^3 in scientific notation?

   A.   It already is correctly expressed in scientific notation.
   B.   Move the decimal point to the left one position and increase the exponent by 1.
   C.   Move the decimal point to the left one position and decrease the exponent by 1.
   D.   Move the exponent to the right one position and decrease the exponent by 1.

5. **Use the number line below to answer the question that follows.**

   Assuming the spaces are equal in length, which of the following expressions produces a value that lies between C and D on the number line?

   A. $\frac{1}{3} \times \frac{2}{5}$

   B. $\frac{2}{5} - \frac{1}{3}$

   C. $\frac{1}{3} + \frac{2}{5}$

   D. $\frac{1}{3} \div \frac{2}{5}$

6. In a senior citizens' home with a population of 250 people, everyone is from 75 to 90 years old, and 12 percent of this population is aged 80 or younger. If the remaining population is evenly distributed, how many people in this home are age 85?

   A. 22
   B. 25
   C. 28
   D. 30

7. The price of gasoline went from $2.25 per gallon to $2.50 per gallon. What was the percent increase in the cost of gasoline?

   A. 10%

   B. $11\frac{1}{9}$%

   C. $12\frac{1}{2}$%

   D. 25%

8. **Use the information below to answer the question that follows.**

   The annual salaries of three people are listed below:

   Person 1: $45,256

   Person 2: $57,254

   Person 3: $72,978

   Jim estimated the sum of these salaries by first rounding each to the nearest thousand. Bob estimated the sum of these salaries by first rounding each to the nearest ten.

   By how much do these estimates differ?

   A. $110
   B. $490
   C. $600
   D. $3,490

9. The number 24 is x less than half of y. Which of the following expresses this relationship?

   A. $x - 24 = \frac{y}{2}$

   B. $24 = \frac{y}{2} - x$

   C. $24 = \frac{2}{y} - x$

   D. $x - \frac{y}{2} = 24$

10. A snail moves $4\frac{1}{3}$ inches every $\frac{1}{4}$ hour. At this pace, how long will it take the snail to move 26 inches?

    A. $\frac{2}{3}$ hour

    B. $1\frac{1}{2}$ hours

    C. 6 hours

    D. $450\frac{2}{3}$ hours

11. The problem below shows the steps in finding the product of a two-digit number and a three-digit number using the standard multiplication algorithm. The missing digits are represented with the letters x, y, and z.

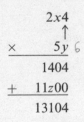

$$
\begin{array}{r}
2x4 \\
\times \quad 5y \\
\hline
1404 \\
+ \quad 11z00 \\
\hline
13104
\end{array}
$$

    What is the result of $x + yz$?

    A. 136
    B. 63
    C. 45
    D. 16

GO ON TO THE NEXT PAGE

12. **Use the table below to answer the question that follows.**

Hours worked	Money earned
0	0
2	15
4	30
6	45
8	60
10	75

The table shows the amount of money earned for different amounts of time worked. Which of the following graphs best represents the data in the table?

A.

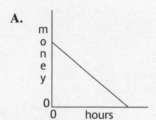

B.

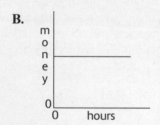

C.

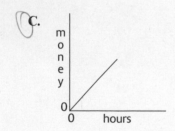

D.

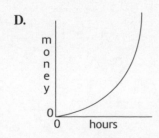

13. A fruit display in a market is in the shape of a pyramid with one piece of fruit at the top. Each layer below the top forms a square shape with one additional piece of fruit per side. If a total of 55 pieces of fruit are used, and a single piece of fruit at the top counts as a layer, how many layers of fruit will there be?

  A. 5
  B. 6
  C. 7
  D. 8

14. The ordered pair (–3, 5) lies on a line with a slope of $-\frac{2}{3}$. Which of the following points will also lie on this line?

  A. (–1, 8)
  B. (–1, 5)
  C. (–6, 7)
  D. (–6, 3)

15. A plumber charges d dollars per minute plus $25.00 for driving time to get to the job. What will be the total amount the plumber charges for a job that takes 3 hours?

  A. $28d$
  B. $3d + 25$
  C. $3(d + 25)$
  D. $180d + 25$

16. **Use the equation below to answer the question that follows.**

$$7x + 3(x + 5) = 2x - 7$$

Which of the following equations could occur as a step in solving the equation for x?

  A. $8x = -22$
  B. $8x = -12$
  C. $12x = 8$
  D. $12x = -22$

17. Use the diagram below to answer the question that follows.

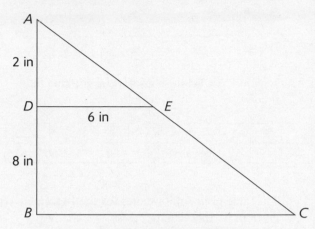

(Figure not drawn to scale.)

$AD = 2$ in $BD = 8$ in $DE = 6$ in $\overline{DE} \parallel \overline{BC}$

What is the length of $\overline{BC}$?

A. 12
B. 18
C. 24
D. 30 ✓

$$\frac{AD}{AB} = \frac{DE}{BC}$$

18. Triangle ABC is obtuse. Angle A has a measure of 45°. Which of the following could be the measure in degrees of one of the other angles?

A. 35
B. 45
C. 55
D. 65

19. A right triangle has legs with lengths of 9 inches and 12 inches. What is the perimeter of this triangle?

A. 15 inches
B. 36 inches
C. 42 inches
D. 54 inches

20. Use the diagram below to answer the question that follows.

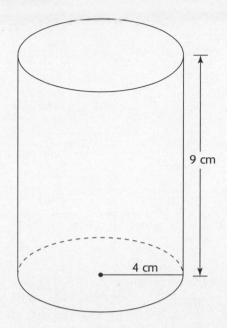

A right cylinder has a base with a radius of 4 centimeters and a height of 9 centimeters. Between the surface area and the volume of this cylinder, which measurement will have the greater numerical value and by how much?

A. Volume, 40π
B. Surface area, 40π
C. Volume, 72π
D. Surface area, 72π

GO ON TO THE NEXT PAGE

21. Use the diagram below to answer the question that follows.

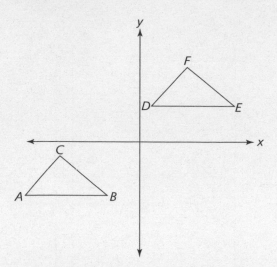

$\triangle ABC$ is congruent to $\triangle DEF$. The coordinates of points A, B, C, and D are $A\,(-7, -5)$, $B\,(-2, -5)$, $C\,(-4, -1)$, and $D\,(1, 6)$. What are the coordinates at point F?

A. (4, 10)
B. (6, 6)
C. (8, 15)
D. (6, 11)

22. If the quadratic expression $x^2 - 13x - 48$ is correctly written in factored form, then what must be one of the factors?

A. $(x + 3)$
B. $(x - 6)$
C. $(x - 8)$
D. $(x + 4)$

23. On a map, the scale is given as 1 centimeter = 25 miles. The map distance between two cities is 15 centimeters. If you plan on driving between these two cities at an average speed of 35 miles per hour, which of the following is the best estimate for how long the trip should take?

A. Between 8 and 9 hours
B. Between 9 and 10 hours
C. Between 10 and 11 hours
D. Between 11 and 12 hours

24. How many square feet are there in 2 square yards?

A. 6
B. 9
C. 18
D. 27

25. Use the table below to answer the question that follows.

1	2	3	4	5	6	7	8	9	10
65	49	32	65	65	82	50	75	60	57

The table gives John's scores for the 10 tests given in his mathematics class.

Find the mean, median, mode, and range for these values. Use them to calculate the following:

$$(\text{mean} - \text{median}) \times (\text{mode} - \text{range}) = ?$$

A. $-37\frac{1}{2}$

B. $37\frac{1}{2}$

C. $-62\frac{1}{2}$

D. $62\frac{1}{2}$

26. Two dice with number representations from 1 to 6 are tossed. What is the probability that the product of the two numbers shown on the dice is less than 20?

A. $\dfrac{7}{36}$

B. $\dfrac{2}{9}$

C. $\dfrac{7}{9}$

D. $\dfrac{29}{36}$

Subtest II: Science
Multiple Choice

27. Which of the following is the best example of a chemical reaction?

    A. An electric current is sent through water, producing hydrogen and oxygen.
    B. Liquid water boils and changes into water vapor.
    C. Carbon dioxide bubbles are produced when a soft drink bottle is opened.
    D. Vegetable coloring is dissolved in water and a color change occurs.

28. **The formula for photosynthesis, below, is used to answer the following question.**

    $$6CO_2 + 6H_2O + X \rightarrow C_6H_{12}O_6 + 6O_2$$

    In the above formula for photosynthesis, the letter X represents

    A. carbon dioxide (CO_2)
    B. glucose
    C. water (H_2O)
    D. light energy

Use the table below to answer the question that follows.

Line	Element	Atomic Number	Protons	Electrons
1	lithium	3	2	5
2	carbon	6	6	12
3	iron	26	26	26
4	copper	29	29	58

29. Which line correctly identifies the element, atomic number, protons, and electrons?

    A. Line 1
    B. Line 2
    C. Line 3
    D. Line 4

30. Your class is studying the colors of objects. The teacher brings a yellow daffodil to class and asks the following question about the plant: "Why are the petals of the daffodil yellow but the leaves green?"

    Which of the following best answers the question?

    A. Objects look different depending on the color of the light in which they are observed.
    B. The color observed depends on the color reflected and how the object absorbs the other colors.
    C. The primary colors of light are red, green, and blue and when combined in equal amounts, they produce any visible color combination.
    D. The petals absorb the yellow color of the electromagnetic spectrum, and the leaves absorb the green color of the electromagnetic spectrum.

GO ON TO THE NEXT PAGE

31. The question below is based on the following picture.

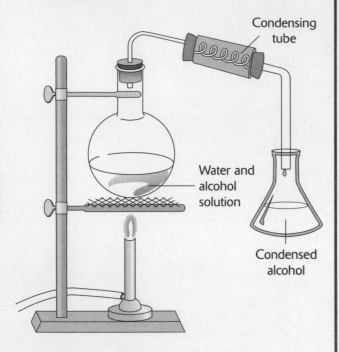

Condensing tube

Water and alcohol solution

Condensed alcohol

What is the best explanation for alcohol being condensed in the beaker?

A. The boiling temperature of alcohol is slightly above the boiling point of water.
B. Alcohol and water are both liquids and evaporate at similar rates.
C. Each liquid becomes a gas at its given boiling temperature.
D. The temperature in the alcohol/water solution is dependent on how long the water boils.

32. Which of the following examples would demonstrate when an individual has maximum potential energy?

A. Sitting at the top of a medium slope
B. Walking up a small slope without stopping
C. Running down a steep hill
D. Sitting at the bottom of a steep hill

33. The following question is based on the illustration below.

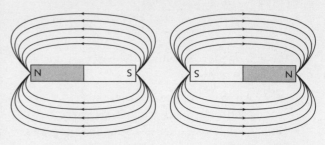

As part of a fourth-grade assignment, a student draws the shape of the magnetic field surrounding two bar magnets that have been brought together. The teacher indicates that the student's drawing of the magnetic field is accurate. Which statement best supports the information presented in the illustration above?

A. The field force of a magnet is weakest at the poles.
B. The north magnetic pole of each bar magnet attracts the other.
C. Magnetic fields spread out from one pole to another and cross at the polar opposites.
D. The space exactly between the two magnets has the weakest magnetic field.

34. Balance the following chemical reaction by determining X.

$$3Fe + 4H_2O \rightarrow X + 4H_2$$

A. FeO_4
B. Fe_3O_4
C. Fe_6O_6
D. Fe_7O_8

35. A tightly fitting metal lid on a glass jar was loosened by holding the metal lid under a stream of very hot water. Which of the following most accurately describes what caused this reaction?

A. Hot water did not make the lid expand but made the glass contract.
B. The thermal energy of the metal lid increased, its particles spread out, and the substance expanded.
C. Metal absorbs thermal energy, contracting the substance and decreasing its size.
D. The very hot water produced enough thermal energy to accelerate a change in the state of the metal.

36. Seatbelts in a car were invented to address which of the following scientific concepts?

    A. Friction
    B. Centrifugal force
    C. Inertia
    D. Thermodynamics

37. Ecology represents the interactions that take place between organisms and their environment. Which of the following is an abiotic feature of the environment?

    A. Soil
    B. Ducks
    C. Algae
    D. Phytoplankton

38. Metamorphosis is an important stage in the life cycle of some animals. In the metamorphosis of both a bullfrog and a monarch butterfly, which of the following accurately identifies a shared characteristic?

    A. Both species remain herbivores throughout their life cycles.
    B. When the animal is an adult, the offspring go through the same cycle stages.
    C. During the chrysalis stage, both species adapt to new environmental conditions.
    D. Both species lay eggs on leaves.

39. The following question is based on the picture below.

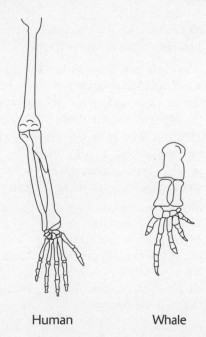

Human   Whale

In the study of evolution, which of the following statements would most accurately assess the significance of the bones shown?

    A. The DNA sequence of the two structures indicates a close genetic relationship.
    B. The structures being compared share a similar evolution but different applications.
    C. There is little evolutionary evidence to suggest that the bones came from a common ancestor.
    D. The structures are analogous, but the organisms do not share a common ancestor.

40. Use the information below to answer the question that follows.

FLOWER

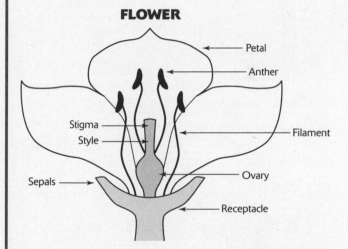

In the picture of the flower details above, which statement demonstrates pollination?

    A. when pollen is transferred from an anther to a stigma
    B. when the sperm cell joins with an egg to form a zygote
    C. when the anthers produce the pollen
    D. when sperm cells move down the pollen tube and into the ovule

GO ON TO THE NEXT PAGE

41. **Use the information presented in the statements below to answer the following question.**

    Line 1. Species produce far more offspring than can normally survive.

    Line 2. A particular environment is not capable of supporting all organisms born into that environment.

    Line 3. Natural selection is the mechanism of evolution.

    Line 4. Favorable variations gradually accumulate in a species, while unfavorable traits disappear over time.

    Which of the following lines correctly identifies Charles Darwin's theory of evolution?

    A. Lines 1 and 3
    B. Lines 1, 3, and 4
    C. Lines 1, 2, and 3
    D. Lines 1, 2, 3, and 4

42. In comparing the organelles found inside a plant and animal cell, a similarity of both cells is that

    A. plant and animal cells contain a cell membrane and a cell wall.
    B. mitochondria are responsible for the oxidation of food.
    C. chloroplasts in the nucleus are the site of energy transfer.
    D. vacuoles contain the genetic material of the cell.

43. In a typical energy pyramid, which level would contain the largest amount of useable energy?

    A. First level—producers
    B. Second level—primary consumers
    C. Third level—secondary consumers
    D. Fourth level—top predators

44. Assume a stable habitat with all normal control mechanisms in place. Population statistics show little change over time in both the predator (fox) and prey (rabbit) populations. Which of the following results would most likely occur if a significant number of foxes were introduced into the habitat?

    A. The prey population would develop camouflage to help avoid detection.
    B. The number of prey offspring would increase as a buffer against the increase in predators.

C. The number of predators would increase and the amount of vegetation would decrease.
D. Both the predator and prey populations would decrease over time.

45. After a person consumes carbohydrates, in what organ of the digestion system do the nutrients enter the bloodstream?

    A. Salivary glands
    B. Stomach
    C. Small intestine
    D. Pancreas

46. During the Jurassic and Cretaceous periods, large reptiles dominated the earth. The vast majority of fossil evidence from these periods is found in which types of rocks?

    A. Obsidian, quartz, and pumice
    B. Limestone, sandstone, and shale
    C. Slate, sandstone, and coal
    D. Limonite, mudstone, and marble

47. **Use the list below to answer the following question.**

    Dew forms on a plant leaf in the morning.

    Windows on a car fog up after a humid night.

    Water forms on the outside of a cold glass of water.

    Droplets collect on frozen peas removed from the freezer.

    Which of the following accurately demonstrates the reaction in the examples above?

    A. Condensation occurs when humid air contacts a cold surface.
    B. Evaporation occurs when liquid water is changed into water vapor.
    C. Molecules break free when energy is added to a liquid.
    D. Surface tension occurs when water molecules form bonds and connect to each other.

48. During the heat of the midday sun, air over land near the shore becomes warmer and absorbs more heat than the air over the water; the warm air from the land rises, and cooler air from the water rushes in to take its place.

    Which of the following air patterns best describes the information above?

    A.   Sea breeze
    B.   Land breeze
    C.   Moderate gale
    D.   Trade winds

49. Which of the following is the most significant environmental disadvantage of obtaining biofuel energy from biomass?

    A.   Biomass in the form of existing fossil fuels is recyclable but nonrenewable.
    B.   Using biofuel waste products for energy production reduces methane accumulation in the atmosphere.
    C.   Biofuel production is not carbon neutral and is a major factor in global climate change.
    D.   Biofuels contribute to deforestation and compete with existing food prices.

50. **Use information in the picture below to answer the following question.**

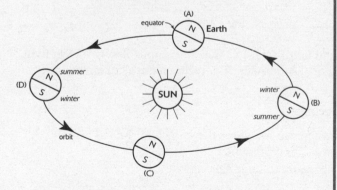

THE SEASONS OF THE YEAR

    Based on the configurations of the seasons in the diagram above, which letter would represent the shortest day of the year in the Northern Hemisphere?

    A.   Letter A
    B.   Letter B
    C.   Letter C
    D.   Letter D

51. Students in a fourth-grade classroom are attempting to classify five unknown minerals placed on their lab table. Which of the following tests would be most reliable for classifying the unknown minerals?

    A.   Collecting data on the streak color left behind after rubbing the unknown minerals on a porcelain streak pad.
    B.   Collecting data on the observed difference in the actual color of the raw samples.
    C.   Collecting data on the luster of the samples, knowing that the luster of metallic and nonmetallic minerals is observable.
    D.   Collecting data on the relative hardness of the mineral samples by scratching the samples against each other.

52. The composition of the earth is made up of an inner core, outer core, lower mantle, upper mantle, and crust. Which of the following would most likely determine whether solid rock in the interior will become magma?

    A.   High pressure and high temperature
    B.   Low pressure and low temperature
    C.   High pressure and low temperature
    D.   Low pressure and high temperature

GO ON TO THE NEXT PAGE

Subtest II: Mathematics
Short Constructed Responses

Directions: Write your answers legibly on a clean sheet of lined paper.

Assignment 1

1. Complete the exercise that follows.

   There are 300 marbles in a collection. The green marbles make up 30 percent of the collection. The yellow marbles make up 10 percent of the collection. The blue marbles make up 20 percent of the collection. The remaining marbles are either red or black.

   Using your knowledge of percentages and probability:

   - Find the percentage of marbles in this collection that are either red or black.
   - If 30 percent of the marbles that are either red or black are red marbles, find how many marbles are black.
   - If a marble in this collection was randomly selected, find the probability that it is black.

Assignment 2

2. Use the diagram and the information below to complete the exercise that follows.

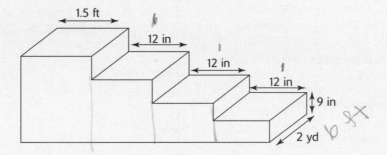

   The staircase pictured above consists of four steps and four risers. The step at the upper left is 1.5 feet long. Each of the other three steps is 12 inches long. Each of the four risers is 9 inches high. The staircase is 2 yards wide.

   Using your knowledge of measure conversions and geometry:

   - Find how many square feet of carpeting would be necessary to cover the stairs and risers. Then determine how many square inches and square yards this represents.
   - Find how many cubic feet of concrete would be necessary to build this staircase.

Subtest II: Science
Short Constructed Responses

Directions: Write your answers legibly on a clean sheet of lined paper.

Assignment 3

3. A teacher is conducting an experiment in her sixth-grade classroom. The teacher presents the following information and asks the students to develop a hypothesis regarding this information.

   Two water samples are shown to the class. Both water samples are in glass beakers.

   One water sample contains a salt-water mixture (sample A); the other water sample contains fresh water (sample B).

   Both samples are placed in the same freezer for the duration of the class.

   Make a prediction on which water sample will freeze faster.

   Using your knowledge of the scientific method, prepare a response in which you:

   - list the steps of the scientific method;
   - list three factors that will invalidate any hypothesis based on the information above; and
   - briefly discuss the science behind why salt is placed on icy roads.

Assignment 4

4. Fossil fuels constitute the vast majority of the world's nonrenewable energy resources. The largest consumers of fossil energy are the industrialized and emerging industrialized countries of the world. However, fossil fuel resources are limited and pose significant environmental and health issues.

   Based on your knowledge of environmental science, prepare a response in which you:

   - list the three main forms of fossil fuels;
   - choose one fossil fuel and briefly discuss how it was formed; and
   - briefly discuss how that energy source increases greenhouse gases and impacts on global warming.

Subtest III: Physical Education Multiple Choice

1. In a comprehensive physical education program, students learn how the laws of motion affect how the body moves. Isaac Newton's third law of motion states: For every action there is an equal and opposite reaction. Which of the following is the best example of applying Newton's third law of motion?

   A. During a game of tug-of-war, both sides pull with the same force, and the rope does not move in either direction.

   B. In hitting a volleyball, the amount of force you apply will determine both the speed and the height of the ball in motion.

   C. A student bounces a ball on the ground, and the ball bounces back up to the student.

   D. A baseball player rounds the base at first on his way to second.

2. In an elementary school physical education program, which of the following is a fact rather than a popular misconception?

   A. A key goal of physical education is to provide students with the skills necessary to be an athlete.

   B. Children in a comprehensive physical education program need to understand the "why" behind the content of the activity being performed.

   C. Once skill levels are determined, it is important to focus on a specific activity or sport to achieve success.

   D. Winning and losing is a fact of life, and a successful physical education program emphasizes competition to prepare children for the real world.

3. Which of the following best describes the instructional resources available to an elementary school physical education program?

   A. Instructional resources should reflect the background skills of the student population.

   B. Instructional resources should first address the key goals and then subordinate the non-key goals to available time in the curriculum.

   C. Instructional resources should reflect grade-level guidelines put forth in the state framework.

   D. Instructional resources should incorporate team sports, tumbling, and gymnastics in a comprehensive physical education program.

4. Specific grade-level skill areas support the goals of physical education. Which of the following is the best example of hand-eye coordination at an upper-primary school grade level?

   A. Kicking a soccer ball after it has been deflected off another player's leg

   B. Bouncing a rubber ball five times but only catching the ball four times

   C. Dribbling a ball around a series of cones placed exactly five feet apart

   D. Punting a football during punting and kicking practice

5. Which of the following is the most appropriate indicator that a third-grade student should be assessed for placement in an adaptive physical education program?

   A. The health record of the student indicates that the child has type 2 diabetes.

   B. The student has difficulty throwing a ball but has satisfactory skills in catching a ball.

   C. A child with low self-esteem has always been unsuccessful in competitive sports, and the parents have formally requested that the child be enrolled in an adaptive physical education program.

   D. The student is unsuccessful at mastering specific motor skills, even when the teacher has regularly adapted and modified activities to accommodate the student.

6. Which line in the table matches the exercise activity with the correct exercise principle as detailed in the concepts of frequency, intensity, and time?

Line	Exercise Activity	Exercise Principle
1	Stretch to the point of slight discomfort	Frequency
2	Add to the number of repetitions in a set	Time
3	Increase the level of activity to reach a target heart rate	Intensity
4	Run at least three to five days a week	Intensity

    A. Line 1
    B. Line 2
    C. Line 3
    D. Line 4

7. Which of the following activities is best defined by the skill cues below?

- Use a forward stride position sideways to the target.
- Bend your trunk slightly forward at the waist.
- Keep your center of gravity within the base of support.
- Square your shoulders toward the target.
- Swing your arms down, out, and up to the ready position.

    A. A fielder preparing to catch a ball at second base
    B. A basketball player completing a lay-up
    C. A pitcher preparing to throw a ball
    D. A batter positioning himself to hit a ball

8. Which of the following is the best example of positive social development in a fourth-grade physical education setting?

    A. A shy student creates an individual movement pattern involving time, space, and flow.
    B. A poorly coordinated student is chosen as team captain for an upcoming volleyball game.
    C. An aggressive student considers participating in a conflict-resolution approach to solving a disputed call.
    D. Students in a small group help one another improve their object manipulation skills.

9. A sixth-grade physical education instructor in a culturally diverse school is preparing to introduce a dance unit that focuses on creative expression. The instructor chooses a West African dance to engage the students in the activity. This activity is best designed to promote students' awareness of how:

    A. an African culture has influenced dance movements in America.
    B. historical aspects of movement have a place in the curriculum.
    C. dance is a key component of understanding people of diverse cultures, especially as it relates to the local community.
    D. locomotor and nonlocomotor skills are necessary components of creative expression and are seen in many cultures.

10. Which of the following is the best rationale for modifying activities to reflect the growth patterns of boys and girls in elementary school physical education?

    A. The rate of growth for boys and girls is rapid in elementary school, and this allows for increased opportunities to improve motor skills.
    B. When height and weight are plotted on a graph, girls between the ages of 8 and 12 grow at a faster rate than boys of the same age.
    C. The center of gravity for children in kindergarten through first grade is higher than it will be in later elementary school years.
    D. A child's physique is the most important criterion in meeting the goals for health-related fitness.

GO ON TO THE NEXT PAGE

11. The Physical Education Framework for California Public Schools recognizes the importance of human growth and development in curriculum planning. Which of the following is most important for understanding the body-type variations of endomorph, mesomorph, and ectomorph?

   A. An understanding of body-type variations can help students accept their individual capabilities and limitations.

   B. Students with a mesomorphic body type generally perform better in activities that require strength, speed, and agility.

   C. Recognizing that a child has an endomorphic body type can enable the teacher to lead the child to more aerobic-type activities.

   D. Skill-related fitness tasks are more easily accomplished by students with an ectomorphic body type.

12. In the evolution of elementary school physical education programs in the United States, the most significant effort to address fitness has been:

   A. to emphasize games and sports as a means to improve overall physical fitness.

   B. to establish a uniform Fitnessgram to assess health-related fitness.

   C. to implement the FITT program to address health-related fitness.

   D. to implement federal mandates to provide the least restrictive environment for children with disabilities.

13. Which of the following would most likely help a right-handed child develop the proper technique for accomplishing an underhand serve in a volleyball activity designed for fifth graders?

   A. The player stands facing the net with both feet together; holding the ball in the left hand, the player hits the ball with the right hand in a pendulum swing and follows through with the lead arm.

   B. The player stands facing the net with the left foot slightly forward and, upon serving the ball, transfers weight to the front foot; the ball is lined up with a straightforward swing of the right hand when hitting the ball.

   C. The player stands with both feet facing the net and tosses the ball straight up; as the ball is tossed, the weight shifts to the back foot, and the forward arm contacts the ball above the shoulder.

   D. The player stands close to the net and practices various underhand serve techniques until he or she can consistently serve the ball over the net; after each successful set, the player moves five steps back and continues the same process until he or she is able to successfully serve the ball from the serving line.

Subtest III: Human Development
Multiple Choice

14. A ten-year old child understands that drinking from a half-pint milk carton is the same as drinking from an eight-ounce glass of milk, even when one looks larger than the other. According to cognitive development theorists, this child understands the concept of

    A. equilibrium.
    B. causal reasoning.
    C. conservation.
    D. object permanence.

15. Language development is a key component in the cognitive mental processes of the growing child. Which of the following is the best answer choice to encourage language development?

    A. Prompt the child with appropriate word choices.
    B. Encourage imaginative play.
    C. Take the lead in conversations so that the child can hear formal adult speech.
    D. Talk with the child about past events.

16. Which of the following statements best describes intelligence?

    A. IQ is innate and cannot be influenced by classroom learning experiences.
    B. IQ and classroom performance are equally matched.
    C. IQ is not determined by socioeconomic status.
    D. IQ is influenced by both environmental experiences and heredity.

17. During the concrete operations stage of development, children are able to understand all of the following cognitive thought processes except:

    A. understanding that a bouquet of a dozen roses has the same number of flowers as twelve roses lined up in a row.
    B. thinking about ways to develop new ideas to organize a baseball card collection.
    C. recognizing that a pound of gold weighs the same as a pound of feathers.
    D. thinking about the contrasting moods of an abstract painting.

18. Angel and his friends go to a local video store to rent a DVD. When Angel pays for the rental, the clerk mistakenly gives him $10 too much in change. Angel's friends notice the mistake and tell him to keep the money, but he tells the clerk about the mistake and returns the money. Based on Angel's age, ten years, and his average development in moral reasoning, Angel would most likely say he gave the money back because:

    A. he wanted to be praised for his good actions and was fearful of being caught.
    B. his friends are bad influences, and he didn't want his friends telling him what to do.
    C. it was morally the right thing to do.
    D. he wanted to please God.

19. According to sociocultural theorists, when a child is struggling with a task, adults can give hints, support, and guidance until the child learns to do the task on his or her own. This process is called:

    A. positive reinforcement.
    B. operant learning.
    C. scaffolding.
    D. classical conditioning.

20. There is strong evidence to suggest that the early emotional bond between a child and his or her caretaker is critical to the emotional development of the child and his or her ability to self-regulate.

    Which of the following developmental terms best explains the statement above?

    A. Assimilation
    B. Autonomous
    C. Maturation
    D. Attachment

21. "Who am I?" is a question most commonly asked during which of the following stages of psychosocial development?

    A. Early childhood
    B. Adolescence
    C. Middle childhood
    D. Infancy

GO ON TO THE NEXT PAGE

441

22. Teachers can improve students' memory recall by using techniques such as rehearsal, recitation, selection, and mnemonics. Memory is a mental processing system that is best described as:

    A. a system that echoes cognitive thought.
    B. a system that stores long-term memories.
    C. a system that encodes, stores, and retrieves thought.
    D. a system that stores short-term memories.

23. Adolescents who identify with a peer group:

    A. create a higher risk of antisocial behavior.
    B. have difficulty forming relationships outside of that group.
    C. generate destructive parent-child conflicts.
    D. are provided with a setting to achieve autonomy and independence from their parents.

24. In cultures around the world, infants share similar physical motor abilities. These similarities appear in the:

    A. sequence and stages in which abilities appear.
    B. age at which the abilities first appear.
    C. methods of childrearing used to encourage development.
    D. correlation between intelligence and motor development.

25. Paul was born premature, weighing only five pounds. By the time he was four years old, he had noticeable facial malformations, difficulty mastering basic tasks, and difficulty focusing his attention on the world around him. He was diagnosed with mild mental retardation. During pregnancy, his mother may have:

    A. smoked a pack of cigarettes daily.
    B. frequently used aspirin for headaches.
    C. drank alcohol excessively.
    D. experienced chronic depression.

26. According to the Individuals with Disabilities Education Act (IDEA), which of the following must be true?

    A. Qualifying students must meet in specialized classes.
    B. Qualifying students must be excluded from regular classrooms.
    C. Qualifying students must be provided with the least restrictive environment.
    D. Qualifying students must have abbreviated schedules.

Subtest III: Visual and Performing Arts
Multiple Choice

27. The dance form in the picture above can best be characterized as:

    A. a series of movements that adhere to the conventions of traditional ballet training.
    B. a visual pattern that tells a specific story.
    C. extemporaneous movements that present abstract subject matter.
    D. intricate shapes that require each dancer to balance and support specialized movements.

28. Many folk dances have inherent symbolism in their dance movements. One of the most popular folk dances of Mexico is *El Jarabe Tapatio* ("the hat dance"). In this dance, the boy flings his sombrero at a girl's feet. The girl then steps on the brim of the sombrero and dances around the hat. The symbolism in this dance is most associated with the importance of

    A. costume in traditional folk dances.
    B. courtship in traditional societies.
    C. social relationships in emergent societies.
    D. intricate footwork in dances of a secular nature.

29. A choreographer must consider incorporating the elements of dance when putting movements together in a dance composition. In dance, the term *force* refers to the

    A. use of energy while moving.
    B. rhythmic pattern and the duration of movement.
    C. shape, level, and pathways of movement.
    D. design of the body as it exists in space.

30. Which of the following is a percussion instrument?

    A. Trombone
    B. Viola
    C. Chimes
    D. Harp

31. What style of jazz music was developed in America in the late nineteenth century that combines the influences of Western European music and African music?

    A. Swing
    B. Bossa Nova
    C. Ragtime
    D. Bebop

32. **Use the following figure to answer the question below.**

    The notes shown on the above staff are

    A. C and G
    B. G and E
    C. G and H
    D. D and G

GO ON TO THE NEXT PAGE

33. Woodwind instruments are so named because:

   A. they all use reeds.
   B. they were all once made of wood.
   C. they can't be made of metal.
   D. they all have the same shape.

34. The proscenium stage was developed during the Renaissance but relied on architectural concepts first developed by the Ancient Greeks. Which of the following would be considered the primary feature of a proscenium stage?

   A. The stage configuration allowed for intimate audience and actor interaction.
   B. The stage configuration facilitated theatre-in-the-round seating.
   C. The sides of the stage or wings could be utilized as an orchestral pit.
   D. The audience viewed the performance through a large arch.

35. In scriptwriting, developing the character of the protagonist involves all of the following except the

   A. ability to evoke empathy.
   B. antagonist must be a formidable opponent.
   C. main character needs to be likeable or heroic.
   D. antagonist can be both internal and external.

36. A fourth-grade teacher provides her students with various improvisational strategies to be used in developing a class play. What would be the primary goal of this assignment?

   A. Developing students' ability to critique a student performance.
   B. Allowing students to portray a variety of characters and emotions.
   C. Encouraging students to become the focus of attention.
   D. Displaying traits that can be seen in real people.

37. Which of the following factors would have been rejected by the Impressionist art movement?

   A. The experience of reality
   B. The freshness of a quick sketch
   C. The prominent use of secondary colors
   D. The influence of light and color

38. Use the reproduction of the painting below, *An Interior with a Woman Drinking* (1658), by Pieter de Hooch (1629–1684), to answer the question that follows.

What is the primary technique used by the artist to achieve a "keyhole" effect in the above painting?

   A. The viewer is pulled into the piece by the use of perspective and light.
   B. The eye of the viewer focuses on the darkened interiors.
   C. The emphasis on everyday life is enhanced by the natural light.
   D. The asymmetrical composition achieves unity through a defined central focus.

39. Use the illlustrations below to answer the question that follows.

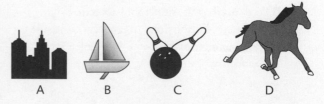

Which of the following pictures most clearly represents an organic shape?

   A. Picture A
   B. Picture B
   C. Picture C
   D. Picture D

Subtest III: Physical Education
Short Constructed Response

Directions: Write your answers legibly on a clean sheet of lined paper.

Assignment 1

1. Complete the exercise that follows.

   Integrating physical education with other content areas is an important goal of physical education.

   Using your knowledge of an integrated curriculum:

   - list two specific examples of integrating math into the physical education curriculum;
   - list two specific examples of integrating science into the physical education curriculum; and
   - discuss one advantage of content integration in a physical education setting.

GO ON TO THE NEXT PAGE

Subtest III: Human Development Short Constructed Response

Directions: Write your answers legibly on a clean sheet of lined paper.

Assignment 2

2. Complete the exercise that follows.

   Using your knowledge of cognitive and social development:

   - discuss the importance of play;
   - identify two types of play that are commonly observed; and
   - select one of the types of play and provide a description.

Subtest III: Visual Arts
Short Constructed Response

Directions: Write your answers legibly on a clean sheet of lined paper.

Assignment 3

3. Use the reproduction below to answer the following question.

The classroom teacher is introducing a fifth-grade art lesson on cubism and Picasso. She shows the class *Girl With a Mandolin* (1910), painted by Picasso (1881–1973).

Using your knowledge of art history:

- briefly discuss two elements that would be evident in the picture that would demonstrate an understanding of cubism; and
- discuss one in-class assignment that would demonstrate the elements discussed above.

Answers and Explanations for Practice Test I

Answer Key for Practice Test I

Reading, Language, Literature	History, Social Science	Math	Science	Physical Education	Human Development	Visual and Performing Arts
1. B	27. D	1. B	27. A	1. C	14. C	27. C
2. C	28. B	2. D	28. D	2. B	15. B	28. B
3. B	29. B	3. C	29. C	3. C	16. D	29. A
4. A	30. D	4. B	30. B	4. B	17. D	30. C
5. C	31. A	5. C	31. C	5. D	18. A	31. C
6. B	32. C	6. A	32. A	6. C	19. C	32. D
7. A	33. B	7. B	33. D	7. C	20. D	33. B
8. A	34. D	8. B	34. B	8. D	21. B	34. D
9. B	35. D	9. B	35. B	9. C	22. C	35. C
10. B	36. C	10. B	36. C	10. C	23. D	36. B
11. B	37. A	11. C	37. A	11. A	24. A	37. C
12. B	38. D	12. C	38. B	12. B	25. C	38. A
13. D	39. A	13. A	39. B	13. B	26. C	39. D
14. D	40. A	14. C	40. A			
15. A	41. B	15. D	41. D			
16. C	42. C	16. A	42. B			
17. D	43. A	17. D	43. A			
18. C	44. B	18. A	44. D			
19. B	45. B	19. B	45. C			
20. A	46. D	20. A	46. B			
21. B	47. B	21. A	47. A			
22. C	48. A	22. A	48. A			
23. A	49. D	23. C	49. D			
24. D	50. A	24. C	50. B			
25. A	51. B	25. A	51. D			
26. C	52. C	26. C	52. D			

Short Constructed-Response Questions

See the Essay Checklist on page 449 and the discussion of essay scoring beginning on page 9 to evaluate your short essays.

Analyzing Your Test Results

Use the following charts to carefully analyze your results and spot your strengths and weaknesses. Complete the process of analyzing each subject area and each individual question for Practice Test I. Examine your results for trends in types of error (repeated errors) or poor results in specific subject areas. This re-examination and analysis is of tremendous importance for effective test preparation.

Practice Test I Analysis Sheets

Multiple-Choice Questions					
		Possible	Completed	Right	Wrong
Subtest I					
	Reading, Language, and Literature	26			
	History and Social Science	26			
	Subtotal for Subtest I	**52**			
Subtest II					
	Mathematics	26			
	Science	26			
	Subtotal for Subtest II	**52**			
Subtest III					
	Physical Education	13			
	Human Development	13			
	Visual and Performing Arts	13			
	Subtotal for Subtest III	**39**			
	Total	**143**			

Essay Checklist

Compare your short constructed-response answers to the answers given. A good short constructed-response answer will do the following:

_____ address the assignment

_____ be well focused

_____ use key words ("buzzwords")

_____ show an understanding of the subject

For each of your responses, check to see if your answer fulfills the criteria above. Fill in the following charts with the number of criteria fulfilled for each essay to get a general idea of the effectiveness of your answer. These numbers do not represent a score but are simply meant to help you evaluate your response.

Short Constructed Response				
		Essays Possible	**Criteria Fulfilled Response I**	**Response II**
Subtest I				
	Reading, Language, and Literature	2		
	History and Social Science	2		
	Subtotal for Subtest I	**4**		
Subtest II				
	Mathematics	2		
	Science	2		
	Subtotal for Subtest II	**4**		
Subtest III				
	Physical Education	1		
	Human Development	1		
	Visual and Performing Arts	1		
	Subtotal for Subtest III	**3**		
	Total	**11**		

Subtest I: Reading, Language, and Literature Multiple Choice

1. **B.** Choices A and D are both benefits to assigning reading for homework. However, the goal of every effective reading program is to provide children with the necessary skills for life-long enjoyable and independent reading (Choice B). Those who can read well will probably read more, and although above-average intelligence is not a predictor for good readers, children with good reading skills tend to have greater possibilities for future learning opportunties.

2. **C.** In this question, you are looking for the "greatest benefit" to rereading a story. Although choices A, B and C are advantages to rereading, only Choice C addresses increased "comprehension." Comprehension is the goal for all reading instruction. When teachers reread a story, students benefit by increased cognitive awareness in forming mental images, increased comprehension, expanded vocabulary, and a greater appreciation for literature. Students are also exposed to literary-level language and different authors' styles. Rereading aloud is one of the most important strategies for increasing aptitude, providing motivation and confidence in reading, while instilling the love of reading.

3. **B.** Blending phonemes (Choice B) is the only choice that matches the phonemic awareness task listed. Phoneme blending is the act of listening to a "sequence of separately spoken phonemes and then combining the phonemes to form a word" (National Institute for Literacy, 2003).

4. **A.** The student needs direct instruction in comprehension skills followed by consistent practice (Choice A). A significant number of struggling readers enter school with poor verbal abilities interfering with their reading comprehension performance. To be successful readers, children must have a command of both phonological and oral language skills. Without these skills, even if adequate reading skills are learned, students may continue to struggle with comprehension.

5. **C.** An onset is the initial consonant or consonant blend in a syllable, such as /sh/ in shook. A rime is a vowel and any consonants of a syllable, such as /ook/ in shook.

6. **B.** In a balanced, comprehensive reading program, the teacher must provide reading materials to meet the diverse population of the classroom and the variety of reading levels of all students in the class.

7. **A.** Marilyn Adams's research suggests that there is a firm base for the position that a balance between systematic word-recognition instruction and reading meaningful text produces superior achievement (Choice A). There is evidence that repeated reading of text develops a young reader's fluency. Repeated reading must be at the independent level, beginning with decodable text. It is important that the text be matched to the reader. When reading text that is too difficult, instruction in word strategies cannot take place. The teacher must also include writing activities that reinforce word recognition. A child's ability to make visual discriminations between words has a positive effect on reading.

8. **A.** Choice B is incomplete since it does not mention perspective or bias. Since the stories are clearly fiction, determining fact versus opinion is not relevant (Choice C), and determining mood and theme (Choice D) has no relevance to reading proficiency.

9. **B.** In addition to many other meaningful activities in which teachers guide children in word study, looking at spelling patterns and vocabulary is probably the most effective method in teaching spelling. As students increase recognition of patterns and build vocabulary, their spelling abilities will improve.

10. **B.** The adjective clause contained in this sentence is *that I bought at the opera* (Choice B), which modifies the noun *program*. The placement of an adjective clause has specific rules; for example, it must immediately follow the noun it modifies. The sentences in choices A and D each contain a clause, but they are adverb clauses, making them incorrect. The sentence in Choice C is incorrect because it is a compound sentence, with no subordinate clause at all.

11. **B.** *Affect* is a verb that means to influence or bring about a change, particularly in regard to one's emotions or physical state. While *affect* can be used as a noun, that usage is rare and most often confined to the field of psychology. Conversely, the word *effect* is most commonly used as a noun (not a verb), and it refers to that which has been changed, as in "Daily exercise has had a positive effect on my overall health."

12. **B.** The passage begins by introducing and defining the "Great Chain of Being" concept (sentences 1 and 2). Sentence 4, beginning with "Its major premise," should immediately follow that definition. Also note that Sentence 4 ends with the idea about an object's "place" in the hierarchical order, which would lead directly to the concept of Sentence 3: an explanation of the logic as to where an object is placed. Thus, the logical development of the passage would improve if Sentence 3 were placed after Sentence 4 rather than before it.

13. **D.** The passage ends just as it introduces a new idea: how Renaissance playwrights and poets infused their conception of the "Great Chain of Being" into their writing. Thus, in order to further develop this passage, the addition of details, explanations, and examples from their plays and poems would be most effective.

14. **D.** In this paragraph, the final sentence is the topic sentence because it summarizes the information found in the passage, namely that the Wright brothers had finally conquered mankind's long quest for human flight. All of the other sentences in the paragraph simply describe and explain the mechanical aspects of the flight.

15. **A.** Giving equal weight to both sides of an issue is not an effective strategy for persuasive writing, which is more successful if the writer devotes extra attention to his or her own stand than that of opposing viewpoints. Alternately, a comparison/contrast essay would be a more appropriate type of writing to devote equal weight to both sides, the "positive and negative aspects" of an issue. All of the other choices present strategies that *are* commonly used in persuasive writing.

16. **C.** When a good speaker modulates his or her voice during a presentation, the volume adjustments and tonal changes help engage the listeners' attention and hold their interest; a monotone delivery misses this important aspect. Choice A is incorrect because adjusting one's volume and tone would hardly distract the audience, regardless of slurred or mispronounced words. Choice B is incorrect because of the word *visual,* which is not relevant to spoken language. Choice D is incorrect because adjusting one's volume or tone would not necessarily affect the audience's understanding of the organization.

17. **D.** While an anecdote may sometimes be an appropriate method of introducing an essay, it is not commonly used as a writing strategy in research papers. All of the other choices describe commonly used strategies in research papers.

18. **C.** Douglass never evokes pathos, which is the strong feeling of pity, sympathy, or sorrow for the misfortune of others; nothing in Douglass's speech is designed to appeal to emotional sympathy. He does use an appeal to logic (Choice A) in sentences 6–7 as he explains the logical progression of depriving people of the right to vote. Douglass also appeals to one's sense of ethics (Choice B) in sentences 2–4, establishing the moral principles of the right to vote. Finally, Douglass presents an appeal to common decency (Choice D), which is established at various points in the excerpt.

19. **B.** Douglass' repetition of the phrase *we want it* adds greater intensity to the heartfelt cry from the class of people to which Douglass refers: African-Americans. It adds strength to his presentation, and it reinforces his message. Choices A and D are incorrect because this intentional repetition is not meant to "remind the listener of just how many people Douglass refers to" or clarify who these people are. Nothing in Douglass's speech is designed to "lull" the listener (Choice C).

20. **A.** Classic myths rarely, if ever, address any political considerations; on the other hand, all other choices are commonly addressed in mythologies of ancient cultures.

21. **B.** Folk tales often use anthropomorphic animals to demonstrate human traits, and this tale displays the basic human desire to be accepted and nurtured. The tale does not contain any sinister characters, let alone a foil (Choice A). It does not depend upon a trick of fate (Choice B), nor does it retell the story of the origins of any tribe (Choice D).

22. **C.** The events of this particular folk tale do not demonstrate the characters' use of any supernatural powers; they depend only upon their natural traits. This tale does, however, employ the inclusion of humanity (Choice A) in the last paragraph when the Indian is introduced. The snake must indeed travel to learn lessons during his adventures (Choice B), and the entire tale uses simplistic dialogue and narration (Choice D). This tale has no elaborate detail, no nonessential description, and no long-winded dialogue.

23. **A.** A common trait of fables is that they embody a moral lesson, whether it is implied in the tale or stated explicitly. This poem resembles a fable in the way that it presents the moral at the end: "Rage works when reason won't/When locked up, bear down." Choice B is incorrect because the poem ultimately presents a point about human nature in the last two lines, not just "nature." The hatching of a chick is not analogous to a creation myth (Choice C) or to the tale of a hero (Choice D).

24. **D.** The baby chick clearly faces adversity; specifically, it must work hard to break through its shell; this is most analogous to the fight people must wage against adversity. The other choices are not reasonable descriptions of the most important analogy the author intended.

25. **A.** The poem's title allusion refers to the ancient Greek myth in which Persephone is abducted by Hades when she plucks an unusual (hundred-blossomed) narcissus from the ground. The allusion is that, while she is distracted by the beauty of the flower, she is unaware of the danger lurking below the surface. The other choices are too simplistic in that they do not address *both* the title allusion and the narcissus.

26. **C.** A parental figure is the one who is most likely to repeat the parenthetical advice in the second stanza. This insight is reinforced by the fact that in the original myth, Persephone's mother, Demeter, deeply mourned the loss of her daughter and pleaded for her return. While the figures in the other choices are perhaps plausible, they are not as likely to repeat this advice.

Subtest I: History and Social Science Multiple Choice

27. **D.** Regardless of vast technological advantages (oceangoing vessels, weaponry, metal armor, and cannons), it was the lack of resistance to European diseases, such as smallpox and measles, that decimated Mesoamerican populations (Choice D). In the 1500s, there were more than 60 million Aztecs. By the 1570s, the population was fewer than 4 million. The Incas faced the same fate. By 1570, the Inca population was reduced by 80 percent. Disease also decimated the ruling classes of both empires, making them politically unstable. Prior to Spanish incursion, civil unrest in both the Aztec and the Inca empires also weakened their ability to rule, collect taxes (tribute), and stop the threat posed by foreign invaders.

28. **B.** Mesopotamia is referred to as the "land between the rivers"—the Tigris and the Euphrates. However, "necessity proved the mother of invention" for civilization to develop in Mesopotamia. Although the northern plateau received more rainfall, the more arid southern plain developed technologically advanced irrigation systems with dams, gates, and canals to bring water to a parched land. With the development of central irrigation projects in lower Mesopotamia (today's Iraq), an agricultural revolution ensued. This allowed for rapid population growth, the rise of city-states, and the development of the complex Sumerian civilization (3500 B.C.).

29. **B.** By 222 B.C., Qin Shi Huangdi conquered China. Qin was the name of the most powerful state. Qin Shi Huangdi united the warring kingdoms and became the first emperor. He created a powerful government bureaucracy and army, standardized government measurements, established the first universal written Chinese language, and built the first true Great Wall. In 1974, the buried army of the first emperor was discovered in Shaanxi province. More than 8,000 life-size terra-cotta warriors in battle formation were excavated. The terra-cotta warriors attest to the grandeur and power of the emperor. The Mogul Dynasty (Choice A), was most associated with Genghis Khan and Kublai Khan. The Mongols were non-Chinese and conquered China in A.D. 1234. The Ming Dynasty (Choice C) ruled China from 1368 to 1644 and was credited with establishing a new capital in Beijing, completing the Great Wall, and building the Imperial City. The Ming Dynasty also promoted the naval voyages of Zheng He to Asia, India, and Africa. The Manchus originated from the northern Mongolian steppes. They defeated the Ming Dynasty in 1644 and established the Qing Dynasty (Choice D). The Qing Dynasty ruled China until 1911.

30. **D.** The Industrial Revolution (1750–1850) resulted in major economic, political, and social changes. The impact of the Industrial Revolution by the early 1800s was profound, especially on the textile industry. New technologies, such as the spinning jenny (cloth), the flying shuttle (spinning and weaving), steam power, and the railroad, allowed for the emergence of the factory system to replace earlier cottage industries. Markets

expanded, as did the need for labor. Workers left rural areas and relocated to towns dependent on the new factories. Working conditions were appalling, and the overcrowded towns quickly evolved into slums. However, a new merchant middle class evolved to bridge the previous two-tier system of the wealthy and the poor (Choice D). Shipbuilding (Choice B) and the Age of Exploration preceded the Industrial Revolution. Population actually increased rapidly (Choice C) as a result of a decline in the death rate, the elimination of the plague, a substantial increase in food production, and an increase in the birth rate.

31. **A.** The Counter-Reformation was a direct response to the Protestant Reformation. Martin Luther, a German Catholic priest, argued against corruption in the Catholic Church, particularly the sale of indulgences (Choice A). Martin Luther's *Ninety-Five Theses* (1517) defined the abuses of the Church and was the catalyst for the actual Reformation. The Reformation spread throughout Europe. The Catholic response was the Counter-Reformation. The Council of Trent (1545) attempted to rid the Church of abuses and to uphold traditional Catholic beliefs. The Inquisition, a Church court to judge heretics, tortured or executed people for refusing to uphold the Catholic Church and renounce Protestantism.

32. **C.** The Silk Road was a vast network of trade and cultural exchange from Asia to Europe that extended for almost 7,000 miles. The road was in existence in some form from ancient times to the sixteenth century. The Silk Road linked traders, merchants, and missionaries with the Far East. Christianity, Buddhism, and Islam did not originate in China. During the seventh and eighth centuries A.D., foreigners settled in China and brought with them new religions: Islam from the Arabian Peninsula and Christianity from Europe. Buddhism entered China from India through cultural and trade contacts as far back as the first century A.D. and became the dominant religion by the sixth century A.D. Confucianism (circa 550 B.C.) was already present in China as a distinct philosophy, as was Taoism. Hinduism remained the major religion of India and had only a slight impact on China. Zoroastrianism was primarily associated with Persia and India.

33. **B.** The emperor Constantine moved the Roman capital to the Greek town of Byzantium (Constantinople) circa A.D. 330. By the late fourth century A.D., political unrest and warring border tribes weakened Rome. The Eastern Roman Empire survived and became the Byzantine Empire, and the capital was renamed after Constantine. The Byzantine Empire was successful for many reasons, including its unifying aspects of Christianity, its wealth, and the strategic location of Constantinople, which controlled both the Black Sea and the Mediterranean Sea entrances to the empire. The city was surrounded by water on three sides, and the Balkan Mountains provided further geographic protection. Constantinople soon controlled trade between Europe and the Far East and lasted for eleven centuries as a political entity.

34. **D.** While Europe languished in the early Middle Ages (Dark Ages), Islamic scholars excelled in the arts, medicine, mathematics, literature, and navigation. Islamic navigators explored the East African coast and Indian Ocean long before Medieval Europe knew of their existence. Islamic scholars were at the forefront of scientific thought and mathematics, introducing algebra and advanced number theory to Europe. Mathematical terms, such as *algebra* and *algorithm*, are Arabic in derivation. Muslim astronomers charted the solar system, and physicians accurately described such diseases as smallpox and measles.

35. **D.** American manufacturing in the North prospered during the War of 1812. U.S. manufacturing dramatically increased during this period. The U.S. trade embargo passed prior to the War, violations of our neutrality, and the British blockade during the War, resulted in a dramatic increase in domestic manufacturing. Other positive results of the War included Britain agreeing to stop Indian raids in the Northwest Territory and the national pride garnered from naval victories by Captain Oliver Perry on the Great Lakes and Andrew Jackson at the Battle of New Orleans. The Federalist Party (Choice C) had opposed the war and subsequently disappeared as a political party.

36. **C.** The Louisiana Purchase (1803) added vast new territory to the United States. The frontier now extended from the Mississippi River west to the Rocky Mountains. President Jefferson's primary goal was to have Lewis and Clark follow the Missouri River to its source and, in so doing, discover a direct water route (Northwest Passage) to the Pacific Ocean. It was hoped that a direct water route would enable the United States to extend its borders quickly and efficiently. The exploration was a tremendous success but failed in its primary mission. When the expedition traversed the Rocky Mountains, Lewis and Clark realized that the Continental Divide separated the rivers that flowed west from those that flowed east, and the dream of a Northwest Passage ended.

37. **A.** All of the acts are considered to be causes of the American Revolution. The rallying cry "No taxation without representation" was expressed following the Stamp Act of 1765. The phrase referred to the fact that colonial assemblies were not represented in Parliament and therefore had no voice in taxes that directly affected them. Besides slogans, the colonists used boycotts, embargoes, intimidation, and violence to protest British tax policies. As colonial resistance increased, so did the British response. Following the Boston Tea Party in 1773, Britain passed the Coercive Acts to punish the colonists. Colonial America referred to the Coercive Acts (Choice D) as the Intolerable Acts—intolerable to their "rights as Englishmen."

38. **D.** The doctrine of Manifest Destiny influenced the Mexican-American War (1846–1848). President Polk used a territorial border issue (the disputed territory between the Rio Grande and the Nueces River) to justify war with Mexico. Manifest Destiny supported the argument that it was the will of God (our destiny) for the United States to expand from the Atlantic to the Pacific. The Treaty of Guadalupe Hidalgo achieved the territorial promise inherent in Manifest Destiny. As a result, the United States doubled in size. New territories were Utah, California, Nevada, and parts of Colorado, Wyoming, and Arizona.

39. **A.** The cotton gin, invented by Eli Whitney in 1793, revolutionized the cotton industry. The cotton gin provided a quick method to clean seeds from the short fibers of the cotton plant. Previously, this process had to be done by hand. Cotton production in the South rapidly expanded, and the need for new lands and more slaves quickly followed. After the cotton gin, the South became a one-crop economy, and the social, political, and economic structure of the South joined to protect its "peculiar institution" of slavery. By 1830, cotton accounted for almost 50 percent of all U.S. exports, primarily to France and England. The new states of Arkansas, Mississippi, Louisiana, Alabama, and Texas quickly became slave/cotton states. The election of Lincoln (Choice D) was a main reason for Southern secession.

40. **A.** In the early to middle 1800s, the beaver was by far the most profitable fur-bearing animal. The main impetus for the beaver trade was the European hat industry. Entire industries and fortunes were developed around the trade of beaver pelts. In the early history of the United States, John Jacob Astor became a millionaire trading in beaver pelts. Many companies established strings of trading posts across North America to control the market. By the 1830s, mountain men, such as Jim Bridger, Jedediah Smith, and William Sublette, explored the Rocky Mountains while trapping beaver. At the height of the trade, beaver pelts sold for $6 a pound. The buffalo (Choice B) did not become commercially important until after the Civil War.

41. **B.** The print depicts the poverty and hopelessness caused by the Irish potato famine in the late 1840s. The potato blight produced widespread starvation and the almost-total destruction of the main Irish food staple. The impact of the blight was devastating and forced millions of Irish to immigrate to America. Unlike earlier European immigrants, the Irish were poor tenant farmers, lacked industrial skills, and had little savings or education. The Irish faced anti-Catholic sentiment and strong nativist resentment. Between the years of 1845 and 1850, more than 220,000 Irish immigrated to the United States.

42. **C.** The Missouri Compromise of 1820 temporarily settled the expansion-of-slavery issue on the national level by allowing for the admission of Missouri and Maine as new states. The Northwest Ordinance of 1787 prohibited slavery in most of the area encompassed by the Missouri Territory. The issue was further complicated by the fact that if Missouri was admitted as a slave state, the South would gain control of the Senate. This was unacceptable to the North. The Missouri Compromise allowed Missouri to be admitted as a slave state and Maine to become a free state, thus preserving the balance in the Senate. Maine was originally part of northern Massachusetts.

43. **A.** These words were part of the Declaration of Sentiments signed at the first women's rights convention held at Seneca Falls, New York, in 1848. The Declaration of Independence (Choice B) only mentioned men when Jefferson wrote of inalienable rights. The aim of the Seneca Falls Convention was to discuss the social and political conditions of women, as well as voice their opposition to slavery. Lucretia Mott, Elizabeth Cady Stanton, and Susan B. Anthony were spokespeople for many of the social reform movements in the 1840s, including the temperance movement.

44. **B.** The referendum was part of the Progressive Movement of the early twentieth century that also included the initiative and recall. These reforms became part of the California Constitution in 1910. The purpose of the reforms was to bring government closer to the people. The referendum is a petition by citizens to seek

an election to place on the ballot legislation that has already become law. As such, the referendum allows citizens to veto legislation. The initiative allows citizens to qualify legislation for the ballot through a petition process. The recall allows citizens to remove an elected official from office. California has utilized the initiative process dramatically, from immigration and property tax legislation to school reform. When an initiative qualifies for the ballot, it is officially called a proposition—for example, Proposition 13 that reformed school funding and placed limits on property taxes.

45. **B.** The Colorado River is the primary source of the water delivered to the Imperial Valley. Water is also supplied by the State Water Project. The Imperial Valley, or Inland Empire, encompasses southeastern California between the Colorado River and the Salton Sea. A series of canals and pipelines distributes the water to the Imperial Valley, enabling such crops as alfalfa, fruits, and vegetables to be commercially profitable. Most of the Imperial Valley is below sea level, creating serious environmental issues associated with pesticide removal and smog.

46. **D.** Since the question calls for a common characteristic of Spanish control over missions, presidios, and pueblos, one can use a process of elimination to arrive at the correct answer. Spain ruled California from the sixteenth century until 1821. The Spanish explorers did not build the missions, and the presidios (forts) and pueblos (towns) were not controlled by the clergy. The presidios were set up to protect the missions and often built near defensible harbors. The pueblos (farming communities) were the first settlements not run by the clergy but were in close proximity to the missions. El Camino Real (the Royal Road) connected all three. Between 1683 and 1834, Spain established missions throughout the state, from Mission San Diego in the south to Mission San Francisco in the north. The missions were approximately 30 miles apart (each one day's journey from the next).

47. **B.** After Mexico gained control of California from Spain in 1821, the new Mexican government changed many former Spanish government practices. The new government abolished the mission system and allowed citizenship for Indians. The Mexican government wanted to reduce the power of the Church and annexed mission land holdings. Many mission areas evolved into pueblos (towns). While the Spanish restricted foreign contact, the new Mexican government encouraged contact with Europe and the United States (Choice C). Gold was discovered in 1848 (Choice D) when California was already a U.S. territory.

48. **A.** Mexico controlled California from 1821 to 1848. This time frame, when large land grants dominated the landscape and cattle ranching was the dominant industry, is often referred to as the Ranchero period. Mexico parceled former mission land into more than 700 new ranchos (large cattle ranches) just in the period between 1834 and 1846. The purpose of the land grants was to establish ranchos and encourage settlement in California.

49. **D.** The famous government-commissioned World War II poster "We Can Do It!" portrays "Rosie the Riveter" as the ideal American industrial worker. The term *Rosie the Riveter* was first popularized in a 1942 song and became the nickname for millions of women working in wartime industries. Posters depicting women wearing overalls and using industrial tools soon appeared as part of a national propaganda campaign to sell the war effort and recruit women workers in shipyards, foundries, steel plants, and other wartime industries. The Rosie the Riveter Memorial, completed in 2006, is located in Richmond, California, and commemorates the wartime contributions of the six million women who were part of the World War II labor force. At the height of the war, Kaiser Shipyards in Richmond employed more than 25,000 women.

50. **A.** During the period of 1960–2000, immigrants from Central America (Honduras, Guatemala, El Salvador, etc.); Southeast Asia (Laos, Cambodia, and Vietnam); Iran; and Armenia embodied many of the same identifying characteristics that represented immigration at the turn of the twentieth century. For example, identifying characteristics included many of the following: non-English speakers with limited educational backgrounds and limited finances, service-sector job skills, victims of political unrest, and escape from poverty. Historically, Ellis Island (1892–1954) in New York Harbor was the main entry point for immigrants entering the United States. The first great waves of immigrants in the early 1890–1910 period were largely from Eastern Europe and Italy. Many of the new immigrants were attempting to escape from political unrest and poverty. Most didn't speak English and had limited funds and few job skills. They often faced some form of legal discrimination. Los Angeles in the period between 1960 and 2000

saw a dramatic demographic shift in its population base. Similar to Ellis Island at the turn of the century, Los Angeles represented a new "melting pot" of cultures and a dramatic demographic shift in its population base. Choice B is too narrow to be the best answer. Choice C is incorrect because voter registration is dependent on U.S. citizenship.

51. **B.** While all groups mentioned have seen legal restrictions placed against them, the Chinese have been by far the most discriminated against by statute—actual laws passed by the California Legislature and included in the California Constitution. While statutory discrimination is illegal today, Jim Crow laws aimed at restricting the rights of Chinese were present from 1850 (California's first constitution) to well into the 1950s. At various times in California history, Chinese were denied citizenship (1879 to 1926), barred from public education, prevented from providing testimony against Caucasians, faced with restrictive covenants (Alien Land laws) to prevent home or land ownership (only declared unconstitutional in 1952), forced to carry certificates of residence, placed in segregated schools, and subjected to racial marriage restrictions. The Chinese were also discriminated against at the national level with the Chinese Exclusion Act of 1882.

52. **C.** *The Grapes of Wrath* (1939), by California author John Steinbeck (1902–1968), earned him a Pulitzer Prize for his gripping tale of a family destroyed by the impact of the Dust Bowl during the Depression. The story took place in the Central Valley. Historically, the derogatory term *Okies* referred to the migration of poor farmers from Oklahoma who came to California in search of work. The hope was that California growers needed migrant work. But there were so many unemployed and desperate Californians during the Depression that the "new arrivals" were met with limited opportunity, discrimination, and collusion by the big growers. *Two Years Before the Mast* (1840) by Richard Henry Dana, Jr. (1815–1882), depicted the life of a common sailor, and chronicled early California under Mexican rule and encouraged migration to California (Choice A), and *The Octopus* (1901) by Frank Norris (1870–1902), exposed the evils of the railroad industry (Choice B).

Subtest I: Reading, Language, and Literature Short Constructed Responses

Assignment 1

1. Use the information below to complete the following exercise.

   In analyzing a fluency assessment, a third-grade teacher notices that one of her students, José, rushes while he's reading. The teacher's assessment indicates that he is having difficulty with comprehension, and does not apply his knowledge of prefixes and suffixes when encountering multi-syllabic words.

   Using your knowledge of reading text comprehension, prepare a response in which you identify and discuss:

   - the reading comprehension benefits of understanding prefixes and suffixes; and
   - at least one instructional strategy that will help to improve his reading fluency.

Sample Response

Reading comprehension is a cognitive skill that develops over time and through practice. Fluent readers achieve competency by starting with easy text and by dividing words into recognizable words. Since José is skipping over words and concepts that he does not understand, he would benefit from a review of decoding strategies that might improve his vocabulary and comprehension abilities. It is also important to check to make sure that the text José is reading is easy to comprehend (no more than 1 in 20 words are difficult). Decoding multi-syllabic words helps students by dividing text into meaningful chunks. In this instructional strategy, the teacher might explain the meaning of prefixes and suffixes and give examples to illustrate this technique. For example, *un-* means not, *-est* means most, and *-less* means without. The teacher would model reading a word with an affix by covering the prefix and or suffix and having José decode the root word first. Guided practice may include repeatedly blending the prefix or suffix before adding it to the root word. This skill will increase in time. The student activity for independent practice would include dividing the prefix or suffix from a given root word by using a slash. The teacher might ask José to create a paper with two columns: one column would contain words with prefixes, and the other column would contain words with suffixes. This direct instructional strategy helps students to be more aware of the reading process. The goal of creating reading comprehension is fluency so that José will eventually be able to comprehend text with accuracy and ease.

Assignment 2

2. Complete the exercise that follows.

   It is important to have an implementation plan when teaching specific skills—for example, phonemic awareness. Study the Curriculum Implementation Plan that follows.

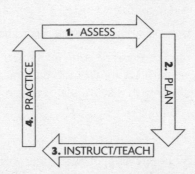

FLUENCY ASSESSMENT

1. ASSESS
Informal/Formal:
• Fluency
• Sight word Check Off
• Decoding Test (BPST)
• Other Assessments

2. PLAN
Data Use:
• Standards & Framework
• Grouping
• Scheduling
• Instructional Strategies
• Student Tasks
• Technology
• Individual Needs

4. MEANINGFUL PRACTICE
Instructional Tasks:
• Highly Structured Practice
• Guided Practice
• Independent Practice
• Decodable Text
• Leveled Readers

3. INSTRUCT/TEACH
Direct & Explicit Instruction:
• Decoding
• Sight Word Mastery
• Comprehension Strategies
• Comprehension Skills
• Writing Skills
• Other Instructional Strategies

Based on the information given and your knowledge of reading, write a response in which you:

- explain how phonemic awareness is related to reading achievement; and
- describe the steps or instructional process a teacher must take to teach phonemic awareness to his/her kindergarten class.

Sample Response

Phonemic awareness, as noted in Marilyn Adams' research, is one of the three predictors of success in early reading. Adams notes that if a student does not attain mastery of phonemic awareness, he/she will probably never be able to read at their grade level. Keith Stanovich's research has shown that phonemic awareness is a core causal factor separating normal from disabled readers.

To teach phonemic awareness, the teacher must first assess the student, using a phonemic awareness (PA) survey, such as the Yopp-Singer Survey, to determine the student's skill needs in phonemic awareness. The teacher would use the results (data) from the assessment to plan and target instruction in such sub-skill areas as identifying phonemes, blending phonemes, or deleting and adding phonemes. Planning for instruction would address teaching one or two sub-skills at a time and would include a variety of variables such as grouping (small groups are best for PA instruction), individual student needs, and resources. Students should have many opportunities to practice phonemic awareness skills, first with the teacher and then independently. The teacher monitors practice and provides intervention as needed. Skill mastery is noted in retesting with the original assessment tool (e.g., Yopp-Singer). Large group and individual practice in phonemic awareness is ongoing throughout the year in songs, games, and other activities.

Subtest I: History and Social Science Short Constructed Responses

Assignment 3

3. Complete the exercise that follows.

The Transcontinental Railroad, completed in 1869, transformed California.

Using your knowledge of California history, prepare a response in which you:

- identify the role of the Big Four in furthering the project and list their members;
- list one economic and one cultural impact on California as a result of the railroad; and
- discuss the effect of one factor from above that transformed California.

Sample Response

The Big Four were the primary economic and political leaders behind the building of the Transcontinental Railroad. They provided the financial backing for the Central Pacific Railroad, which developed the western part of the route through the Sierras connecting Sacramento to Utah. The Big Four soon became the wealthiest and most influential Californians. They were: Leland Stanford, governor of California and president of the Central Pacific; Collis Huntington, financier of the project and vice-president of the railroad; Charles Crocker, director of the railroad; and Mark Hopkins, financier and coordinator of the project.

Linking the east and west by rail had significant economic impact. California farmers and merchants could transport goods to distant markets, resulting in the growth of port cities like San Francisco and Los Angeles. It served as a vital link for commerce and trade, and greatly expanded the economic potential of the country.

One social impact was the tremendous population growth in Southern California. The Southern Pacific Railroad became the largest landholder in the state. They used advertising and cheap rail fares to "encourage" migration to California.

But the hopes for a positive economic effect upon completion of the Transcontinental Railroad did not immediately materialize. An economic depression that began in 1873 ensued. The availability of the railroads themselves created new problems. Factories in the east and Midwest could now ship raw materials and finished goods directly to the west. This led to a surplus of cheap goods competing in the California marketplace. California merchants and businessmen were faced with hard times. The impact on the California economy was dramatic as both land values and commodity prices dropped. The resulting impact on unemployment further decreased wages. It was not until the boom years of the 1880s that the economic promise of the railroad was fulfilled.

Assignment 4

4. Following the end of the Civil War in 1865, the American economy began three decades of rapid industrial expansion that changed the face of America.

Using your knowledge of U.S. history, prepare a response in which you:

- identify two American inventions of the period;
- identify two positive and two negative effects of industrialization during this period; and
- explain how one of the effects impacted the quality of life in America.

Sample Response

Two American inventions of the period were the telephone by Alexander Graham Bell in 1876 and the electric light bulb by Thomas Edison in 1879.

Two positive aspects of industrialization during this period were increased opportunities for non-farm employment and unprecedented expansion in transportation.

Two negative effects of industrialization during this period were the accumulation of wealth in the hands of a small number of industrialists and the impact of unsafe working conditions in the factories.

As industrialization expanded after the Civil War, so did the factory system. There was a rapid expansion of textile, steel, meatpacking, and other types of factories. Demands on labor became more defined and a large pool of unskilled and semi-skilled workers became essential. Factory workers faced many hazards in the whirl of the machines and in the long hours and rapid pace of work. The constant pressure to work faster resulted in numerous accidents and lost limbs. Most workers worked 12-hour days, six days a week. A majority of textile workers were children. There were few safety devices on the machines; there were no unemployment programs for the injured or sick; families received no subsidies for workers killed or injured on the job; low wages kept the average factory worker barely able to provide for a family; labor unions were just emerging and faced opposition from both business and government; and strikes were often violent and seldom achieved measurable goals for workers. During this period of rapid industrialization, the quality of life for many American workers at the lower end of the economic spectrum, many of them immigrants, was very poor.

Subtest II: Mathematics
Multiple Choice

1. **B.** Factor 7,500 into the product of primes. One method looks like this:

$$7,500 = 75 \times 100$$
$$= (3 \times 25) \times (4 \times 25)$$
$$= 3 \times 5 \times 5 \times 2 \times 2 \times 5 \times 5$$
$$= 2^2 \times 3^1 \times 5^4$$

Hence $x = 2$, $y = 1$, and $z = 4$, and therefore $xyz = (2)(1)(4) = 8$.

2. **D.** The first circle has 2 of 3 parts shaded, so it represents the fraction $\frac{2}{3}$. The second circle has 3 of 8 parts shaded, so it represents the fraction $\frac{3}{8}$. Adding $\frac{2}{3}$ to $\frac{3}{8}$ requires a common denominator.

$$\frac{2}{3} + \frac{3}{8} = \frac{16}{24} + \frac{9}{24} = \frac{25}{24} = 1\frac{1}{24}$$

3. **C.** Use an example. Suppose hot dogs come 8 in a package and hot dog buns come 6 in a package. The least amount of each you would need is 24 (the least common multiple of 6 and 8) so that each hot dog has a bun. If you were to multiply 6 and 8, and use 48, that also would make it so that each hot dog had a bun, but it would not be the *least* amount that makes this situation true.

4. **B.** If you were to expand the value 24.7×10^3, it would become 24,700 (move the decimal point to the right 3 positions). Now rewrite 24,700 in scientific notation. It becomes 2.47×10^4. Hence the decimal point in the original expression is moved to the left one position, and the exponent is increased by 1.

5. **C.** Six equal spaces are marked from 0 to 1, which makes each space represent a length of $\frac{1}{6}$. This puts C at $\frac{4}{6}$ and D at $\frac{5}{6}$. One method to determine which of the expressions has a value between $\frac{4}{6}$ and $\frac{5}{6}$ is to use decimal approximations. $\frac{4}{6} \approx 0.6666$ and $\frac{5}{6} \approx 0.8333$. Choice A has the value $\frac{2}{15} \approx 0.1333$, which is not between the C and D values. Choice B has the value $\frac{1}{15} \approx 0.0666$, which is not between the C and D values. Choice C has the value $\frac{11}{15} \approx 0.7333$, which *is* between the C and D values. Choice D has the value $\frac{5}{6}$, which is the D value, but it is not *between* the C and D values.

6. **A.** First find 12% of 250 ($0.12 \times 250 = 30$). This means that 30 people are aged 75 to 80. The remaining people are 81 to 90, a range that includes 10 age groups. Because there are 250 people total at the home, and 30 people are 80 years old and younger, this means that 220 people are 81 to 90 years old. Since the remaining people are evenly distributed in age, divide 220 by the remaining 10 age groups ($220 \div 10 = 22$).

7. **B.** Percent change $= \dfrac{\text{amount of change}}{\text{starting amount}} \times 100\%$

The change from \$2.25 to \$2.50 is \$0.25. The starting amount was \$2.25.

$$\frac{0.25}{2.25} = \frac{25}{225} = \frac{1}{9} \times 100\% = 11\frac{1}{9}\%$$

8. **B.** Jim rounds to the nearest thousand, and then adds up the values.

Jim's estimates and sum become: \$45,000 + \$57,000 + \$73,000 = \$175,000.

Bob rounds to the nearest ten, and then adds up the values.

Bob's estimates and sum become: \$45,260 + \$57,250 + \$72,980 = \$175,490.

The difference between these amounts becomes: \$175,490 − \$175,000 = \$490.

9. B. Make a literal translation of the English.

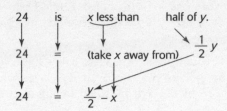

$$24 = \frac{y}{2} - x$$

10. B. Create a proportion.

$$\frac{\text{inches}}{\text{hours}} : \frac{4\frac{1}{3}}{\frac{1}{4}} = \frac{26}{x}$$

Cross multiply to clear the proportion.

$$4\frac{1}{3}x = \frac{1}{4} \times 26$$

$$\frac{13}{3}x = \frac{13}{2}$$

$$x = \frac{3}{2} = 1\frac{1}{2}$$

11. C. 45

$$
\begin{array}{r}
2x4 \\
\uparrow \\
\times \quad 5y \\
\hline
1404 \\
+ \quad 11z00 \\
\hline
13104
\end{array}
$$

Step 1. Start with the y. Since y times 4 ends in a 4, y is either a 1 or a 6.
$(1 \times 4 = 4,\ 6 \times 4 = 24)$

Step 2. If y was a 1, then the first product line would have been the repeat of $2x4$.
Since this was not the case, the y must have been 6.

Step 3. So now the problem looks like this:

$$
\begin{array}{r}
2x4 \\
\nwarrow \\
\times \quad 56 \\
\hline
1404 \\
\downarrow \\
+ \quad 11z00 \\
\hline
13104
\end{array}
$$

Step 4. The x has to be a number that, when it is multiplied by 6 (remember, $y = 6$) and 2 is
added to that $(6 \times 4 = 24$, carry the 2), the result ends in a zero. Only the value 3 or 8 can work.
If $x = 8$, then $254 \times 6 = 1524$, hence $x \neq 8$. Hence $x = 3$. $234 \times 6 = 1404$.

Step 5. Finally, since 4 is added to z to make a number that ends in a 1, z must be 7.

Step 6. Therefore, $x = 3$, $y = 6$, and $z = 7$

Step 7. Therefore, $x + yz = 3 + (6)(7)$
(recall the order of operations)
$= 3 + 42$
$= 45$

12. **C.** According to the table, as the hours increase, so does the money. Only choices C and D show that. The table shows that (0, 0) belongs on the graph. Both choices C and D show this. According to the table, as hours increase by 2, money increases by 15. Since this rate of change is constant, the graph is linear; hence, only C is correct.

13. **A.** The top of the pyramid has 1 piece of fruit. The layer below it is a square with 2 pieces of fruit per side. Hence, the second layer from the top has 4 pieces of fruit. The layer below forms a square with 3 pieces of fruit per side, and would then have 9 pieces of fruit. Keep adding these square numbers together until the total is 55:

$$1 + 4 + 9 + 16 + 25 = 55.$$ Hence, 5 layers of fruit.

14. **C.** A slope of $-\frac{2}{3}$ means either $\frac{-2}{3}$ or $\frac{2}{-3}$. Slope means $\frac{\text{rise}}{\text{run}}$. Therefore, from one point to another point, you can have either a "rise" of -2 and a "run" of $+3$, or a "rise" of $+2$ and a "run" of -3. If you start at $(-3, 5)$ on a graph and plot a "rise" of -2 and a "run" of $+3$, you would be at the point $(0, 3)$. (See the illustration below.)

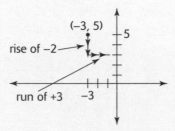

If you start at $(-3, 5)$ and plot a "rise" of $+2$ and a "run" of -3, you would be at $(-6, 7)$, Choice C. (See the illustration below.)

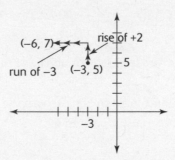

Choice A is the result of plotting a "rise" of $+3$ and a "run" of $+2$. Choice B is the result of plotting a "rise" of 0 and a "run" of $+2$. Choice D is the result of plotting a "rise" of -2 and a "run" of -3.

15. **D.** Notice that the plumber charges by the minute. There are 180 minutes in 3 hours. Since the plumber charges d dollars per minute, he will charge $180d$ dollars for 3 hours. He also charges \$25 for driving time, hence the total charge will be $180d + 25$ dollars.

16. **A.** Notice that all the choices have the "x's" on the left side of the equation and the constants on the right side of the equation. Go through the solving process and stop when you recognize the answer.

$$7x + 3(x + 5) = 2x - 7$$
$$7x + 3x + 15 = 2x - 7 \text{ (distributive property)}$$
$$10x + 15 = 2x - 7 \text{ (combine like terms)}$$
$$8x + 15 = -7 \text{ (subtract } 2x \text{ from each side of the equation)}$$
(At this point, you could eliminate choices C and D)
$$8x = -22 \text{ (subtract 15 from each side of the equation)}$$

17. D. With segment *DE* parallel to segment *BC*, △*ABC* is similar to △*ADE*. This makes corresponding sides (sides in the same relative position) proportional.

That means $\dfrac{AD}{AB} = \dfrac{DE}{BC}$.

$AD = 2$, $AB = 10$, ($AB = AD + DB$), $DE = 6$.

Substitute these values into the proportion and solve.

$\dfrac{2}{10} = \dfrac{6}{BC}$ (cross multiply to clear the proportion)

$2BC = 60$ or

$BC = 30$

$\dfrac{AD}{DE} = \dfrac{AB}{BC}$

$\dfrac{2}{6} = \dfrac{10}{x}$

$2x = 60$

$x = 30$

18. A. Since triangle *ABC* is obtuse, one of its angles is more than 90°. Since the sum of the angles of any triangle is 180° and one angle is already given as 45°, the remaining angle must be less than 45°.

(more than 90) + 45 + (remaining angle) = 180 (but more than 90) + 45 = more than 135

So, (more than 135) + (remaining angle) = 180 (take away more than 135, which leaves less than 45)

Remaining angle < 45

The only answer less than 45° is Choice A.

19. B. To find the perimeter of a triangle, add together the lengths of its sides. The triangle given is a right triangle, which means you can use the Pythagorean theorem to find the missing side because the other two sides are given. The legs of a right triangle refer to the sides that form the right angle; hence, the missing side is the hypotenuse, or the longest side.

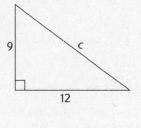

$c^2 = 9^2 + 12^2$

$c^2 = 81 + 144$

$c^2 = 225$

$c = \sqrt{225}$

$c = 15$

Remember, the question asked for the perimeter of the triangle, not how long the hypotenuse is.

The perimeter is 9 + 12 + 15 = 36, Choice B.

20. A. To find the surface area of the right cylinder, picture having the circular top and bottom removed and the shell rolled out to form a rectangle.

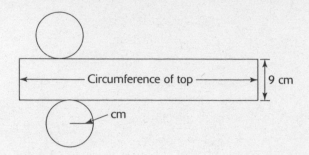

To find the surface area of the right cylinder, add together the areas of the two circles and the area of the rectangular shell. The area of a circle is found by using the formula $A = \pi r^2$. The radius of each circle is 4 cm; therefore, the area of each circle is $(4)^2\pi$ or 16π cm². The rectangular shell has a length the same as the circumference of the top of the cylinder. The formula for the circumference of a circle is $C = \pi d$, where d is the diameter of the circle. Since the circle had a radius of 4 cm, it's diameter will be 8 cm. The rectangle now has an area of $8\pi \times 9 = 72\pi$ cm². The total surface area is $2(16\pi) + 72\pi = 32\pi + 72\pi = 104\pi$ cm².

To find the volume of a right cylinder, you use the formula $V = $ (area of base) $\times$ (height)

The base of the cylinder is a circle of radius 4 cm and the height of this cylinder is 9 cm.

The volume of this cylinder is $(16\pi$ cm²$)(9$ cm$) = 144\pi$ cm³.

Numerically, the volume had the greater value by 40π ($144\pi - 104\pi = 40\pi$), Choice A.

21. A. Since $\triangle ABC$ is congruent to $\triangle DEF$, segment AC has the same length as segment DF. Point A is located at $(-7,-5)$ and point C is located at $(-4,-1)$. In order to get from point A to point C, you can move 3 units to the right and 4 units up. Therefore, in order to get from point D to point F, you would do the same thing. Point D is located at $(1,6)$. Moving 3 units to the right and 4 units up puts you at $(4,10)$, Choice A.

22. A. In order to factor the expression $x^2 - 13x - 48$, you need to find two expressions that would multiply out to become this expression.

$$x^2 - 13x - 48$$
$$(\qquad)(\qquad)$$

The first positions in each set of parentheses must multiply together to make x^2, hence $(x \qquad)(x \qquad)$.

The last positions in each set of parentheses must multiply together to make -48 in such a way that the remaining two multiplications combine to make $-13x$. All possibilities that multiply to make x^2 at the beginning and -48 at the end are listed in the chart below.

First #	Second #	Sum of the other two multiplications	Result when multiplied out
1	−48	−47	$(x + 1)(x - 48) = x^2 - 47x - 48$
−1	48	+47	$(x - 1)(x + 48) = x^2 + 47x - 48$
2	−24	−22	$(x + 2)(x - 24) = x^2 - 22x - 48$
−2	24	+22	$(x + 2)(x - 24) = x^2 + 22x - 48$
3	−16	−13	$(x + 3)(x - 16) = x^2 - 13x - 48$
−3	16	+13	$(x - 3)(x + 16) = x^2 + 13x - 48$
4	−12	−8	$(x + 4)(x - 12) = x^2 - 8x - 48$
−4	12	+8	$(x - 4)(x + 12) = x^2 + 8x - 48$
6	−8	−2	$(x + 6)(x - 8) = x^2 - 2x - 48$
−6	8	+2	$(x - 6)(x + 8) = x^2 + 2x - 48$

Notice that only the factors $(x + 3)$ and $(x - 16)$ produced the desired result.

Only Choice A had one of these factors.

23. C. First use proportions to find the actual distance to be traveled.

$$\frac{\text{map (cm)}}{\text{actual (miles)}} \quad \frac{1}{25} = \frac{15}{x}. \text{ (Cross multiply to clear the proportion.)}$$

$$x = 375. \text{ The distance traveled is 375 miles.}$$

In order to find the amount of time it will take to travel this distance at 35 mi./hr., use the formula that says

$$(\text{rate}) \times (\text{time}) = (\text{distance})$$

$$(35 \text{ mi./hr.}) \times (t \text{ hr.}) = 375 \text{ mi. (divide each side of the equation by 35 mi./hr.)}$$

The time is between 10 and 11 hours.

24. C. A square yard is a square that is 1 yard on each side. See the illustration below.

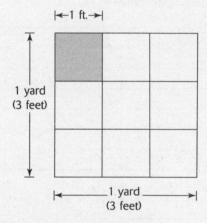

Each small square is 1 foot on an edge, which makes it a square foot. Notice that one square yard contains 9 square feet. Therefore, two square yards have 18 square feet.

25. A. The *mean* of a set of data is the sum of the data values divided by the number of data values.

$$\text{Mean} = \frac{65 + 49 + 32 + 65 + 65 + 82 + 50 + 75 + 60 + 57}{10} = \frac{600}{10} = 60$$

The *median* of a set of data values is the middle value when the data is listed from smallest to largest.

Smallest   Largest

32   49   50   57   60   65   65   65   75   82

Middle values

Because there was an even number of data values, there are two middle values.

The median becomes the mean of these two values.

$$\text{Median} = \frac{60 + 65}{2} = \frac{125}{2} = 62.5$$

The *mode* of a set of data values is the value repeated most often.

$$\text{Mode} = 65$$

The *range* of a set of data values is the difference between the largest and smallest values.

$$\text{Range} = 82 - 32 = 50$$
$$(\text{mean} - \text{median}) \times (\text{mode} - \text{range})$$
$$(60 - 62.5) \times (65 - 50) = (-2.5) \times (15) = -37.5 \text{ or } -37\tfrac{1}{2}, \text{ Choice A.}$$

26. **C.** Probability is the comparison of the number of favorable outcomes in an event versus the total number of outcomes possible in the event.

$$\text{Probability} = \frac{\#\,\text{favorable}}{\#\,\text{total}}$$

The table below shows a setup for viewing all the possibilities. Across the top are the possibilities for one die, and along the side are the possibilities for the other die.

X	1	2	3	4	5	6
1	✓	✓	✓	✓	✓	✓
2	✓	✓	✓	✓	✓	✓
3	✓	✓	✓	✓	✓	✓
4	✓	✓	✓	✓		
5	✓	✓	✓			
6	✓	✓	✓			

Notice that there are 36 total spaces within the table, indicating that there are a total of 36 possible outcomes. In this table, checkmarks are placed where the product of the numbers on the two dice is less than 20. Recall that the product is the answer to multiplication. The locations for 4×5 and 5×4 were left blank because 20 is *not* less than 20. Therefore,

$\text{Probability} = \dfrac{28}{36} = \dfrac{7}{9}$, Choice C.

Subtest II: Science
Multiple Choice

27. **A.** In a chemical reaction, either a new product or substance is formed, or a substance is broken down. In this case, water was broken down by electrolysis to form hydrogen and oxygen gases but not water. The other examples are physical changes. Physical changes can involve changes in state (liquid, solid, gas), volume, and density. In the case of carbon dioxide bubbles (Choice C), the carbon came out of solution (a physical change). In a chemical change, a totally new substance with new properties is formed. Other examples of chemical change include rusting (iron chemically combined with oxygen), wood burning, and digesting.

28. **D.** The reactants in photosynthesis are carbon dioxide + water + chlorophyll + light energy (sun). The products are glucose and oxygen. Photosynthesis can take place only in the presence of light (Choice D). In photosynthesis, the chlorophyll (green pigment) in plant leaves absorbs carbon dioxide from the atmosphere. Chlorophyll captures the sun's light energy and combines with water and carbon dioxide to make sugar (stored food) and oxygen. Respiration is the opposite process of photosynthesis. Carbon dioxide and water are released into the atmosphere.

29. **C.** Iron is the only element that has the same number of protons (26) and electrons (26). The atomic number will always equal the number of protons. The number of protons will always equal the number of electrons surrounding the nucleus of the element. All atoms are made up of protons, neutrons, and electrons. The nucleus is made up of a proton (positive charge) and a neutron (no electrical charge). Surrounding the nucleus is an electron (negative charge). An element is a substance that is made up of only one particular type of atom (gold, silver, carbon, etc.).

30. **B.** The color of an object depends on the colors of light that it reflects (Choice B). An object appears yellow because it reflects yellow light and absorbs all the other colors. The leaves appear green because chlorophyll in the plant leaf reflects green light. Plants need the red and blue wavelengths of light for growth. Green light is not needed by the plant, and so it is reflected toward your eyes. Similarly, a black object appears black because it doesn't reflect any light and absorbs all colors of the visible spectrum. Conversely, a white object appears white because it reflects all the colors of light equally.

31. **C.** Alcohol boils at 78 degrees Celsius (172 degrees Fahrenheit), and water boils at 100 degrees C (212 degrees F). In the experiment, once the liquid was heated to 78 degrees (Choice C), the alcohol in the solution would begin to boil off. The alcohol could then be condensed into pure alcohol and collected in the collection beaker. Water would be left in the original beaker. The key to the experiment is that different substances in mixtures can be separated by taking advantage of their different boiling points. Therefore, comparing boiling points can be used to tell one liquid from another. This information is especially useful in the petroleum industry, in which hydrocarbons (lubricating oil, fuel oil, kerosene, and gasoline) can be separated from crude oil because each liquid becomes a gas at its own given boiling point.

32. **A.** The individual would have maximum potential energy at the top of the slope. The two main types of energy are kinetic and potential. Potential energy is energy that comes from position (a wound spring in a toy car, a book sitting on top of a desk). It has the potential to do work. Kinetic energy is the energy of motion. The amount of potential kinetic energy an object has depends on its mass and speed. As an individual runs up and down the slope, the individual increases in potential energy while ascending the slope, and decreases in kinetic energy while descending the slope. Roller coasters and other amusement park rides make excellent examples for demonstrating potential and kinetic energy.

33. **D.** All magnets have a north (N) and south (S) pole. A magnetic field surrounds a magnet and is strongest at the poles (not weakest), but the field force can be exerted around the entire magnet. When the north poles of two magnets are brought together, the magnetic poles repel each other. Therefore, the space exactly between the two magnets has the weakest magnetic field. Conversely, unlike magnetic poles attract each other and show a strong magnetic field between the two magnets.

34. **B.** A chemical reaction can be written as a chemical equation. In a chemical equation, the reactants are on the left side, and the products are on the right side. In balancing the equation, atoms on one side of the equation (reactants) are equal to atoms on the other side (product). The coefficients need to be added (count the number of atoms on each side of the equation). The $\rightarrow$ symbol means "yields." If a number is in front of the molecule or compound, it tells you the entire number of molecules or compounds present in the equation. In the problem stated, the reactants are 3 atoms of iron + 8 atoms of hydrogen + 4 atoms of oxygen. One part of the product was already given (8 atoms of hydrogen, or $4H_2$). To balance the equation, 3 atoms of iron + 4 atoms of oxygen ($Fe_3 + O_4$) are needed. The equation shows 3 iron atoms + 8 hydrogen atoms + 4 oxygen atoms on each side of the equation.

35. **B.** Heat applied to metals results in expansion of the metal. Heat energy makes molecules move faster and expand (take up more space). Colder molecules move more slowly and cause most objects to contract (water is an exception). The metal lid on the jar was loosened because the particles in the metal spread out (expanded).

36. **C.** Newton's first law of motion, also known as the *law of inertia*, states that an object at rest tends to stay at rest, and an object in motion tends to stay in motion at the same speed and in the same direction, unless acted on by an unbalanced force. If a person is sitting in a moving car, and the car stops suddenly, the person's body has a tendency to keep moving. The seatbelt acts as the unbalanced force to prevent the person's body from continuing to move forward. The unbalanced force brings the person from a state of motion to a state of rest. Centrifugal force (Choice B) is any force that causes an object to move in a circle.

If you spin a bucket full of water around fast enough, centrifugal force keeps the water moving in a circle and prevents it from pouring out. Thermodynamics (Choice D) is the study of the flow of heat. The *first law of thermodynamics* states that energy can be neither created nor destroyed.

37. **A.** The abiotic, or nonliving, factors in the environment include such items as soil, water, gases in the atmosphere, temperature, and light. The biotic, or living, factors in the environment include one-celled organisms (bacteria), protists, fungi, plants, and animals. The abiotic and biotic factors in a particular location interact to form communities, food chains, and food webs. For example, plants need light, water, and carbon dioxide to make food and reproduce. The abiotic and biotic features are also limiting factors that restrict the population density of differing organisms in a particular location.

38. **B.** In both a bullfrog and a butterfly, the animal's *offspring* each go through the same stages of metamorphosis. Metamorphosis is the distinctly different life cycle stages an organism's body undergoes as the organism transforms from egg to adult. A bullfrog is an amphibian. Amphibians start life in the water but spend most of their adulthood on land. Amphibians return to the water to reproduce. The life cycle stages of a bullfrog are: (1) fertilized eggs in water, (2) tadpole without legs, (3) tadpole with hind legs, (4) tadpole with front legs developing as gills are lost and lung breathing starts, and (5) adult frog with both front and hind legs. The life cycle stages, or complete metamorphosis, of a butterfly are: (1) egg, (2) larva (caterpillar), (3) pupa (chrysalis), and (4) adult (butterfly).

39. **B.** Comparative anatomy shows the similarity in structure (bone arrangement) of both the human arm and the whale's flipper. Both structures being compared are homologous and indicate that they both evolved from a common ancestor and use the same bones and muscles. However, homologous features do not have to have the same function and can serve different purposes (arm and flipper). Choice A is incorrect because DNA sequencing would not indicate that the genes of whales and humans are closely related. Choice D is incorrect because the structures are not analogous. Analogous structures share the same function (wings on different types of flying animals, for example, such as bird wings and wasp wings), but the structures are composed of different materials and took different evolutionary paths.

40. **A.** Pollination is the transfer of pollen from an anther to a stigma. The pollen is actually produced in the anthers (small organs at the top of the stamens). The anther and filament form the male parts of the flower. The pistil is the female reproductive part of the flower and contains the stigma, style, and ovary. The stigma is often sticky, which helps hold the pollen. To fertilize the ovules (eggs), sperm cells move down the pollen tube into the ovules. Fertilization is the joining of a sperm cell and an egg (Choice B). Note that fertilization occurs only during sexual reproduction.

41. **D.** All the statements (lines 1–4) summarize Darwin's theory of evolution and help explain variations and differences in species. Darwin theorized that complex organisms evolve from less complex organisms over time. Darwin's book *On the Origin of Species* (1859) detailed his theory of evolution, which included concepts such as survival of the fittest, natural selection, species tendency toward overpopulation, and genetic variation through geographic isolation. Voyages to the Galapagos Islands helped him formulate his ideas that species are constantly changing and that new species can evolve over time. He observed that environmental limitations within a habitat restrict the population growth of a species and that the biological success of an organism is dependent on how that organism adapts to the environment. These observations became the central point in his explaining *natural selection,* which is that organisms that successfully adapt to their environment have a greater chance of survival and are able to pass on genetic characteristics to their offspring. He also theorized that limitations on resources and the competition for those resources determine which organism will survive (survival of the fittest).

42. **B.** Mitochondria are organelles (subcellular structures that have specific functions) present in both plant and animal cells that contain enzymes responsible for the oxidation and release of energy from food. Only plant cells contain cell walls (Choice A) and chloroplasts. Chloroplasts (Choice C) are organelles that contain chlorophyll and are part of the photosynthetic process. The nucleus is the organelle present in both plant and animal cells that contains chromosomes and controls genetic material. Vacuoles (Choice D) are organelles present in both cells that store food and water.

43. **A.** At each step in an energy pyramid, the flow of available energy decreases as it moves through the system. Producers use only a fraction of the sun's energy to manufacture their own food. The first level of an energy pyramid (producers) contains the largest amount of useable energy. Since primary and secondary consumers can't manufacture their own food through photosynthesis, these organisms must rely on energy originally stored by the producer. Only about 10 percent of the useable energy is transferred to the next level; 90 percent is either lost to the environment as heat or used for growth and maintenance by the organism. The pyramid is smaller at the top, showing that the amount of available trapped energy is greatly reduced for organisms at upper levels of the pyramid.

44. **D.** Both predator and prey species are reduced over time. When additional predator species (foxes) are suddenly introduced into a stable habitat, the short-term effect is a sharp increase in the predator population and a sharp decrease in the prey population (rabbits). With an increased food source, more predators survive to breed. However, the additional predator offspring begin to compete for a limited food resource. As a result of this rapid decrease in prey, the predator population comes under enormous stress and the resulting starvation and parasitic disease further reduce the remaining numbers. In the long term, equilibrium returns to the habitat. Adaptations such as camouflage (Choice A) evolve over long periods of time. If the prey population decreases, the plant population increases (Choice C).

45. **C.** Digestion of food into nutrients is completed in the small intestine. The nutrients are absorbed through the walls of the small intestine and enter the bloodstream. Digestion begins in the mouth when food is chewed. Chewing results in both mechanical digestion (teeth physically crush the food) and chemical digestion, but most chemical digestion takes place in the stomach. Gastric juices and enzymes in the stomach aid in the chemical breakdown of food proteins. Carbohydrates are the sugars and starches found mainly in potatoes, cereals, plants, vegetables, grains, and fruits. The breakdown of food in the digestive system takes place in the following series of organs: mouth → esophagus → stomach → small intestine → large intestine → rectum.

46. **B.** The vast majority of fossil remains are found in sedimentary deposits such as limestone, sandstone, and shale (mudstone). Sedimentary rocks are the most common type of rocks on earth and cover approximately 80 percent of the earth's land area. Sedimentary rocks are formed as mud or sand is eroded from the land and in time settles on the bottoms of lakes or oceans. Eventually, the sediments are cemented together and form thick layers of rock. The layering quality of sedimentary deposits helps in the discovery of fossils because over geologic time, the layers can be exposed as outcroppings, revealing what is trapped within. With the exception of trace fossils, fossil deposits in igneous rocks are unlikely because igneous rocks form when magma or lava cools and becomes a solid; examples of igneous rocks include obsidian, basalt, granite, and pumice. Metamorphic rocks, such as marble and slate, form from heat and pressure deep in the earth's mantle. Metamorphic rock was once sedimentary or igneous rock. The rock cycle demonstrates the recycling of igneous, sedimentary, and metamorphic rocks.

47. **A.** All the choices are examples of condensation. Condensation is the process whereby water vapor (gas) becomes a liquid and adheres to the surface of an object. An example is dew forming on the leaf of a plant. Condensation occurs because the capacity of air to hold water decreases as the air surrounding an object is cooled to its dew point. The amount of water vapor that air can hold depends on the temperature of the air. The dew point is the temperature at which condensation begins as the air surrounding the object is saturated and cannot hold additional water. Surface tension (Choice D) is how molecules on the surface of water are held together by mutual attraction. Surface tension allows some insects to walk on water.

48. **A.** The information presented describes a sea breeze. A sea breeze results because of the unequal heating of land and sea surfaces and the resulting convection currents. Land near the shore becomes hotter during the day and absorbs thermal energy. The air above the land becomes warmer than the surrounding air above the water. The warm air over the land surface rises and the cooler air from the water rushes in to take its place. The result is a breeze that comes from the sea toward the land. At night, the opposite situation occurs, and a land breeze results. A land breeze is created when the land surface cools more rapidly than the sea, and warmer air over the sea rises. The now denser and cooler air flows toward the land (Choice B).

49. **D.** Advantages of biofuel production are many (renewable energy source, less dependency on fossil fuels, possible reduction in greenhouse gases), but this question called for a disadvantage. A major criticism of increased biofuel production (especially in the production of ethanol and other biofuels) is the resulting deforestation associated with clearing vast tracts of land for biofuel resources. As more potential food-producing land is converted to energy use, less food becomes available, food costs increase, and underdeveloped countries feel the greatest impact. Critics of increased implementation of biofuels would also argue that non-greenhouse alternative energy sources (solar, geothermal, hydroelectric, and wind) would substantially lower greenhouse gas emissions in the long term.

50. **B.** You can infer from the diagram that letter B (position of the sun in reference to the tilt of the earth) represents winter in the Northern Hemisphere. Note that in this configuration the Northern Hemisphere is tilted farthest away from the sun and receives less solar radiation. The days get shorter. December 21 in the Northern Hemisphere is referred to as the winter solstice (shortest day and longest night). The day length varies because of the tilt of the earth's axis. The Southern Hemisphere has its summer solstice when the Northern Hemisphere has its winter solstice. Letter A would represent the spring equinox in the Northern Hemisphere (March 20 or 21), and Letter C would represent the autumnal equinox (September 21 or 22) when daylight and nighttime hours are equal because neither hemisphere is tilted toward the sun. Letter D would represent the summer solstice in the Northern Hemisphere, or the longest day of the year.

51. **D.** The most reliable classification in the scenario presented would come from a scratch test. A scratch test can determine the relative hardness of unknown minerals by scratching each mineral against the other minerals. By doing so, the unknown minerals could be classified from softest to hardest. Mohs Scale of Hardness rates minerals from softest (#1, talc) to hardest (#10, diamond). While the other examples are useful in identifying unknown minerals, each has a disadvantage when compared to the scratch test in the scenario given. A streak test (Choice A) is useless for clear or white minerals. A color test (Choice B) is the least reliable because many minerals have the same color (white and clear), and often the same mineral can be found in different colors. Luster (Choice C)—the way a mineral shines—would be a good test to determine metallic or nonmetallic minerals. However, the samples could be exposed to weathering and might not display true luster.

52. **D.** The combination of low pressure and high temperatures in the earth's mantle melt rock and form magma (liquid rock). The magma rises to the surface through cracks in the mantle because it is less dense than the surrounding rock. Rock in the mantle remains solid if the weight of rock above the mantle exerts tremendous pressure on the underlying rock. This great pressure prevents the rock from becoming liquid by raising the material's melting point. Therefore, the release of pressure causes solid rock to become magma.

Subtest II: Mathematics
Short Constructed Responses

Assignment 1

1. Complete the exercise that follows.

   There are 300 marbles in a collection. The green marbles make up 30% of the collection. The yellow marbles make up 10% of the collection. The blue marbles make up 20% of the collection. The remaining marbles are either red or black.

   Using your knowledge of percentages and probability:

   - find the percent of the marbles in this collection that are either red or black;
   - if 30% of the marbles that are either red or black are red marbles, find how many marbles are black; and
   - if a marble in this collection is randomly selected, find the probability that it is black.

Sample Response

First, find how many of each color marbles there are.

$$30\% \text{ of } 300 = 90. \text{ There are 90 green marbles.}$$
$$10\% \text{ of } 300 = 30. \text{ There are 30 yellow marbles.}$$
$$20\% \text{ of } 300 = 60. \text{ There are 60 blue marbles.}$$
$$(30\% + 10\% + 20\% = 60\%)$$
$$100\% - 60\% = 40\%$$

This means that 40% of the marbles in the collection are either red or black.

Now find how many marbles are either red or black. This can be done by taking 40% of 300 or by adding together the marbles known and subtracting that from 300.

$$40\% \text{ of } 300 = 120$$
$$300 - (90 + 30 + 60) = 120$$

Therefore, there are 120 marbles that are either red or black.

Since 30% of these 120 marbles are red, and the question is how many are black, you can either find 30% of 120 and subtract this from 120, or find 70% of 120.

$$120 - (30\% \text{ of } 120) = 120 - 36 = 84$$
$$70\% \text{ of } 120 = 84$$

There are 84 marbles that are black.

The probability of an event is a fraction that puts the number of favorable outcomes as the numerator and the total number of outcomes as the denominator.

$$\text{The probability of randomly choosing a black marble} = \frac{84}{300}$$
$$\text{(If necessary, this reduces to } \frac{7}{25} \text{ which can also be expressed as 28\%)}$$

Assignment 2

2. Use the diagram and the information below to complete the exercise that follows.

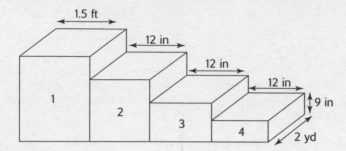

A staircase is pictured above. It consists of four steps and four risers. The step at the upper left is 1.5 feet long. Each of the other three steps is 12 inches long. Each of the four risers is 9 inches high. The staircase is 2 yards wide.

Using your knowledge of measure conversions and geometry:

- Find how many square feet of carpeting would be necessary to cover the steps and risers. Then find how many square inches this would be, as well as how many square yards this would be; and
- Find how many cubic feet of concrete would be necessary in order to build this staircase.

Sample Response

Since the first part of the question asks for an answer in square feet, each of the dimensions given needs to be converted into feet.

$$1.5 \text{ feet is already in feet.}$$
$$12 \text{ inches} = 1 \text{ ft.}$$
$$9 \text{ inches} = \frac{9}{12} = \frac{3}{4} = 0.75 \text{ ft.}$$
$$2 \text{ yards} = 2(3 \text{ feet}) = 6 \text{ ft.}$$

Finding the amount of carpeting necessary to cover the steps and risers involves the concept of area.

There are four steps in the shape of rectangles and four identical risers in the shape of rectangles.

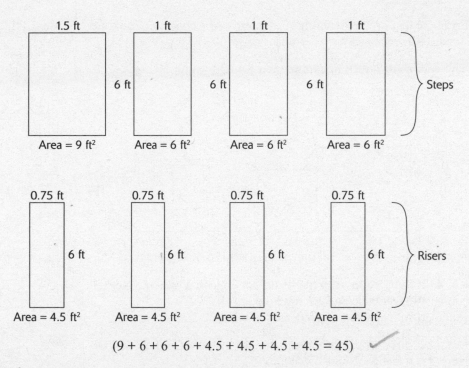

$$(9 + 6 + 6 + 6 + 4.5 + 4.5 + 4.5 + 4.5 = 45)$$

<u>There will be 45 ft.^{2} of carpeting necessary to cover the steps and risers.</u>

This same result could have been found by finding the area of one large rectangle in the following manner:

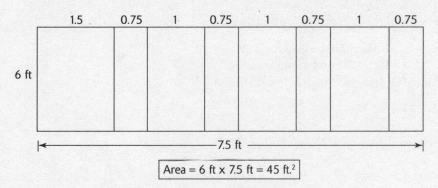

To find how many square inches this would be, you need to know that 1 ft.^{2} = 144 in.^{2}

$$45 \text{ ft.}^2 = 45(144 \text{ in.}^2) = 6{,}480 \text{ in.}^2$$

To go from square feet to square yards, you need to know that 1 yd.^{2} = 9 ft.^{2}

$$45 \text{ ft.}^2 = (45 \div 9) \text{ yd.}^2 = 5 \text{ yd.}^2$$

To find how many cubic feet of concrete is needed involves the concept of volume. In order to find the volume of the staircase, it needs to be seen as four rectangular prisms.

The volume of a rectangular prism is found by multiplying length × width × height.

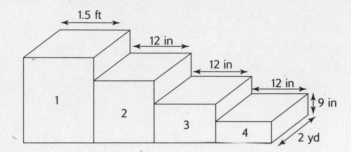

Since the volume is to be in cubic feet, all dimensions need to be in feet.

Rectangular prism #1 is four groups of 9 inches tall, or 36 inches tall, or 3 feet tall.
Rectangular prism #1 is 6 feet wide and 1.5 feet long.
Volume (rectangular prism #1) = (1.5 ft.)(6 ft.)(3 ft.) = 27 ft.^{3}

Rectangular prism #2 is three groups of 9 inches tall, or 27 inches, or 2.25 feet tall.
Rectangular prism #2 is 6 feet wide and 1 foot long.
Volume (rectangular prism #2) = (1 ft.)(6 ft.)(2.25 ft.) = 13.5 ft.^{3}

Rectangular prism #3 is two groups of 9 inches tall, or 18 inches, or 1.5 feet tall.
Rectangular prism #3 is 6 feet wide and 1 foot long.
Volume (rectangular prism #3) = (1 ft.)(6 ft.)(1.5 ft.) = 9 ft.^{3}

Rectangular prism #4 is 9 inches tall, or 0.75 feet tall.
Rectangular prism #4 is 6 feet wide and 1 foot long.
Volume (rectangular prism #4) = (1 ft.)(6 ft.)(0.75 ft.) = 4.5 ft.^{3}

27 + 13.5 + 9 + 4.5 = 54

<u>There will be 54 ft.^{3} of concrete necessary to build this staircase.</u>

Subtest II: Science
Short Constructed Responses

Assignment 3

3. A teacher is conducting an experiment in her sixth-grade classroom. The teacher presents the following information and asks the students to develop a hypothesis using the information.

   ■ Two water samples are shown to the class. Both water samples are in glass beakers.
   ■ One water sample contains a salt-water mixture (sample A); the other water sample contains fresh water (sample B).
   ■ Both samples are placed in the same freezer for 30 minutes.
   ■ Make a prediction on which water sample will freeze faster.

   Using your knowledge of the scientific method, prepare a response in which you:

   ■ list the steps of the scientific method;
   ■ list three factors that will invalidate any hypothesis based on the information above; and
   ■ briefly discuss the science behind why salt is placed on icy roads.

Sample Response

The steps of the scientific method necessary to test a hypothesis include the following:

1. Observe the situation.
2. Turn the question into a testable hypothesis.
3. Predict the outcome of your experiment.
4. Control the variables in the experiment.
5. Perform the experiment.
6. Collect data and analyze the results.
7. Evaluate your hypothesis.

Three factors that will invalidate any hypothesis based on the information above are as follows:

1. The variables in the experiment were not controlled (amount of salt, size of glass beakers, duration/time).
2. The amount of salt in the salt-water solution was not specified and a manipulated (or independent) variable was not present.
3. The amount of time in the freezer was not monitored in regular intervals, and observations/data were not recorded to assess the responding (or dependent) variable.

When salt is placed on icy roads, the salt has the effect of lowering the freezing point of the water solution and dissolving the water molecules. Salt has a different size and shape than water and therefore doesn't freeze into ice at the normal freezing point of water. The crystalline structure of salt prevents the solution from freezing until the temperature drops low enough for freezing to begin again.

Assignment 4

4. Fossil fuels constitute the vast majority of the world's nonrenewable energy resources. The largest consumers of fossil energy are the industrialized and emerging industrialized countries of the world. However, fossil fuel resources are limited and pose significant environmental and health issues.

Based on your knowledge of environmental science, prepare a response in which you:

- list the three main forms of fossil fuels;
- choose one fossil fuel and briefly discuss how it was formed; and
- briefly discuss how that energy source increases greenhouse gases and impacts on global warming.

Sample Response

The three main forms of fossil fuels are oil, coal, and natural gas.

Oil was formed millions of years ago mainly from the organic remains of microscopic sea life and marine organisms that eventually sank to the bottom of seas and oceans. As tremendous pressure and heat acted on accumulated layers of organic fossil sediments, the sediments eventually turned into rock and trapped the carbon in the decayed organisms. Over millions of years, physical and chemical changes and tremendous pressure caused the fossilized rock to turn into oil. The oil eventually migrated through pores in sedimentary rock layers and accumulated in non-porous reservoir layers that trapped the oil.

The original source of energy stored in fossil fuels came from the sun through the process of photosynthesis. When fossil fuels such as oil are burned, stored organic chemical energy is released into the atmosphere in the form of hydrocarbons and carbon dioxide. Carbon dioxide is the most potent greenhouse gas and accumulates in the atmosphere. The CO_2 traps the heat that normally would be re-radiated into space. The rapid increase in CO_2 through industrialization and other energy demands is making the planet warmer, similar to how the sun's energy warms a greenhouse. The impact of global warming can lead to far-reaching climatic changes. An increase of only a few degrees in global ocean temperatures can lead to collapse of food chains, threaten coral reefs, alter weather patterns causing droughts in some areas and increased hurricanes in others, and potentially cause massive population relocation due to coastal flooding.

Subtest III: Physical Education
Multiple Choice

1. **C.** Newton's three laws of motion can be applied to physical education activities and demonstrate how science can be integrated into the biomechanics of physical education. Applying a force often results in movement. When a student bounces a ball on the ground, there is an opposite and equal reaction when the ball bounces back toward him or her. Choices A and D are examples of Newton's first law, often stated as the law of inertia—an object at rest tends to stay at rest, and an object in motion tends to stay in motion, unless acted upon by an outside force. In Choice D, inertia forces the runner to make an arc while rounding second base. Choice B is an example of Newton's second law—objects accelerate in the direction of the force applied to them.

2. **B.** One of the goals of an elementary school physical education program is to dispel common myths associated with physical education. A goal of physical education programs is for students to understand both the "how" and the "why" of physical activities. The Physical Education Framework supports activities that de-emphasize competition and emphasize a program that develops the abilities of all children.

3. **C.** Instructional resources, including instructional guides, should reflect and support the vision, goals, and grade-level guidelines as stated in the Physical Education Framework for California Public Schools. Instructional resources should provide elementary school teachers with lesson-specific directions to support learning in a multitude of content areas, including rhythm, dance, team sports, and fitness. Choice A is not the best choice because a comprehensive physical education program would not be based on the individual skill level of students. Choice B is incorrect since a comprehensive elementary school physical education program must address all stated goals. Choice D is incorrect because it does not reflect an emphasis on grade-level guidelines as stated in the state framework. Also, gymnastics, because of liability and a lack of specific training, is not included in most elementary school programs.

4. **B.** Skill development in such areas as locomotor, nonlocomotor, balance, and hand-eye coordination supports the goals of a comprehensive physical education program. Only Choice B is an example of hand-eye coordination. The other choices are examples of eye-foot coordination.

5. **D.** Assessment and evaluation of motor skills is a prerequisite for determining eligibility for placement in an adaptive physical education program. Having applied modifications without success is a reason to pursue an adaptive physical education assessment. The California Department of Education states that children with disabilities who qualify for adaptive physical education have a legal right to a physical education program that meets their special needs. Section 504 of the Rehabilitation Act of 1973 and the Americans with Disabilities Act of 1990 specify that children with identified disabilities have a right to modification of the regular program.

6. **C.** When an individual reaches a target heart rate, the intensity level of the exercise has increased. The FITT prescription for exercise is based on the following principles: F stands for frequency (how often); I stands for intensity (how hard); T stands for time (how long or for what duration); and T stands for type (what activity). Line 1 is an example of intensity. Line 2 is an example of frequency. Line 4 is an example of time or duration. To improve the cardiovascular health of students, physical educators plan many of their activities around the goals of FITT. An example of implementing the FITT model for aerobic conditioning for elementary school children is as follows: frequency (a minimum of three days a week); intensity (heart rate should be maintained at approximately 170 beats per minute); and time (25 to 30 minutes of continuous activity).

7. **C.** The skill cues describe many of the proper mechanics involved in throwing a baseball. Recognizing and implementing the proper mechanics involved in an activity (e.g., hitting, catching, kicking, or throwing) allows an individual to better utilize the mechanical aspects of technique. Proper technique allows for increased acceleration, distance, and accuracy in sports activities. Understanding proper body mechanics also provides input to both the physical educator and the student in recognizing common biomechanical errors made at various developmental stages.

8. **D.** The Physical Education Framework identifies fourth grade as the appropriate developmental level to emphasize manipulating objects in and through space. Fourth graders are ready to take the initiative and demonstrate leadership in a cooperative setting and are ready for the introduction of more complex games. A primary goal of social development at the fourth-grade level is to emphasize, through play, working together in a cooperative setting. Choice A is an example of self-image and personal development. Choice C is incorrect because the student only considers participating in a conflict-resolution setting. Conflict-resolution strategies should be taught at all elementary school grade levels and is an important component in preparing students to resolve conflicts at their own level.

9. **C.** There are many factors that affect curriculum choices in teaching dance programs at the middle school level. Dance education has become part of an integrated arts approach to a comprehensive physical education program. As such, dance units often include activities that demonstrate movement expression and dances of other cultures, especially as they relate to the local community. The Physical Education Framework for California Public Schools recognizes the role of dance in getting to know and understand people of diverse cultures.

10. **C.** Children in kindergarten through first grade generally have short legs in relation to their upper body and therefore have an unstable center of gravity, which makes it more difficult for them to perform simple curl-up exercises and to maintain balance. Physical educators in these grades introduce basic locomotor, nonlocomotor, rhythmic, and manipulative skills to address balance and stability issues. Continued growth through the elementary school grades gradually lowers the center of gravity and improves balance and stability. Choice A is an incorrect statement. Physical educators understand that when growth is rapid, the ability to learn new motor skills decreases.

11. **A.** Understanding that the body-type variations of endomorph (fat), mesomorph (muscular), and ectomorph (thin) can affect the quality of motor performance is important for both the physical educator and the student. Students who understand that both skill-related fitness and health-related fitness are greatly influenced by body-type variation are better able to accept individual differences and begin behavior modification programs. Choice B is a correct statement but is not the most important consideration of choices given. Choice C describes activities better suited to an ectomorphic body type. Students with endomorphic body types are likely to be obese. Physical educators must be alert to the growing problem of obesity in the United States. The factors that cause obesity in elementary school children include diet, genetics, emotional instability, and hormonal functions. Not only are obese children at risk for cardiovascular disease, but their lack of skill development also sets them up for ridicule and low self-esteem.

12. **B.** Increased social awareness of health-related fitness led to a renewed emphasis on physical fitness testing. The President's Council on Physical Fitness and Sports (1969) was an outgrowth of earlier efforts in the 1950s to address the state of physical fitness in American children. The Presidential Physical Fitness Award for exceptional achievement by girls and boys aged 10 to 17 was established in 1966 to further this goal. As a result of this renewed emphasis on health, California instituted a mandatory Fitnessgram (1982) in grades five, seven, and nine to assess students on components of health-related fitness, which includes cardiovascular health (mile run and walk), body composition (skin fold test, height and weight measurement), flexibility (sit and reach), muscular strength (pull-ups), and muscular endurance (push-ups). After completing the Fitnessgram, each student is given an individualized physical fitness report. In California in 2007, approximately 25 percent of fifth graders, 29 percent of seventh graders, and 27 percent of ninth graders met all standards on the annual fitness test.

13. **B.** The following instructional cues focus on the correct technique for an underhand serve for a right-handed person in the upper-elementary school grades:

1. Use opposition in performing the skill. Place your left leg forward and bend at your knees.
2. Place the volleyball in the palm of your left hand and hold it out in front of your body. Make a fist with your right hand.
3. Bring your right hand back in preparation for hitting the ball underhand.
4. On the serving motion, transfer your weight to the forward foot.
5. Swing your serving hand forward and strike the ball just below center.
6. After making contact with the ball, follow through with your serving hand.

Choice C is a technique associated with an overhand serve, which is rarely mastered at the elementary school level. Choice D is a good strategy to increase strength. Volleyball is an excellent cooperative group activity at the upper-elementary school grade level and can address hand-eye coordination, game strategy, passing skills, body coordination, and team sports concepts.

Subtest III: Human Development Multiple Choice

14. **C.** During this period of *concrete operations*, ages seven to eleven years, children have the ability to solve simple problems while thinking about multiple dimensions. At this age, children have gained the understanding of conservation of liquid, Choice C. Choice A, equilibrium, refers to a child's cognitive search for mental balance. Choices B and D refer to tasks children master at younger stages of cognitive development, preoperational and sensorimotor.

15. **B.** Although creating explicit learning opportunities for children is an important developmental process (Choices A and D), providing children with opportunities for expression through imaginary play (Choice B), is critical to the cognitive development of language. Choice C is incorrect since adults should minimize taking the lead in conversations when trying to promote language development. Imaginary play helps children organize thought while forming symbolic representations in order to create meaningful schemes. When children translate imaginary thought from symbolic representations into an expressive communication system, they are further developing cognitive mental processes.

16. **D.** Intelligence is based on general mental abilities (g-factor), which include the overall capacity to think rationally while dealing effectively with the environment and the influences of heredity, Choice D. Choice A is incorrect since it suggests that learning experiences do not influence intelligence, and Choice B is incorrect since classroom performance does not always reflect intellectual potential. Since environment does affect intelligence, Choice C is incorrect.

17. **D.** During the *concrete operations* stage, children have the ability to solve simple problems while thinking about multiple dimensions. At this age, children have gained an understanding of conservation, choices A and C. They also have achieved the ability to mentally process using *metacognition* ability to "think about thinking," Choice B. However, according to Jean Piaget, children do not have the ability to think abstractly until adolescence, Choice D.

18. **A.** Children have thoughts, feelings, and behaviors about what is morally right and wrong, depending on their level of moral development. Lawrence Kohlberg's cognitive theory of moral development characterizes moral thought in a series of three developmental stages. Angel is experiencing the *preconventional level of morality*, ages four to ten years, Choice A. Choice B would have been an option if he had wanted to please his friends since children move to a *conventional level of morality* at ten to thirteen years of age. During this stage of morality, children are most concerned with the opinions of their peers, but Angel demonstrates no signs of concern. Choice C represents the *postconventional level of morality*, which most children don't achieve until at least age thirteen. Many people never enter into this level of moral development.

19. **C.** *Scaffolding* is a concept developed by sociocultural theorist Lev Vygotsky. Vygotsky proposed that children construct their knowledge through social and cultural interactions. Choice C is correct because *scaffolding* helps children show cognitive improvement in didactic situations while adapting to new concepts and tasks. Choices A, B, and D are all behavioral concepts of conditioning and reinforcement. Choice A, positive reinforcement, is a concept developed by behaviorist B. F. Skinner. Although it is an important behavioral concept to use in the classroom, Choice C better explains problem-solving support.

20. **D.** The core of psychosocial development is found in the emotional bond that infants have with their primary caretakers through *secure attachment,* Choice D. Infancy is considered a *critical period* in the formation of psychosocial and physical development. This is a sensitive period when children need reassurance that their psychological, social, and physical needs will be met. During this period, infants are particularly sensitive to environmental influences, and according to Mary Ainsworth, infants develop patterns of anxiety or security during this early stage of development, depending upon these influences.

Choice A, assimilation, refers to incorporating new information into existing knowledge, a cognitive process, and Choice B, autonomous, refers to independence.

21. **B.** According to Erik Erikson and his theory of psychosocial development, adolescents experience confusion over personal identity, Choice B. During this stage of development, *identity versus role confusion*, adolescents are caught between childhood and adulthood. Adolescents are faced with the task of developing a practical and socially acceptable sense of self as they continue to seek their identity. Those who are successful will establish a solid identity, while those who are not will suffer role confusion.

22. **C.** Memory is an active system that receives, encodes, stores, and recovers information, Choice C. In many ways, memory is like a computer that encodes information into usable form and then stores that information to be retrieved at a later time. Students can improve memory by *rehearsing* and reviewing information; by *reciting* as they summarize aloud; by *selecting*, which, with the help of the teacher, helps the student decide what is important (much like a net will catch the big fish); and by practicing *mnemonics,* which helps students associate mental pictures to create meaning from words. Although choices B and D, short- and long-term memory, are memory storage centers, Choice C consolidates all of the elements within a memory system.

23. **D.** During adolescence, there can be intense pressure from peers to conform to both positive and negative behaviors, Choice A, which may cause conflicts between parents and their teens, Choice C. These behaviors intensify around the ninth grade when adolescents challenge parental views and authority. It is during this stage of psychosocial development that the teens are in search of autonomy and independence, Choice D. This time period is critical and serves as practice for all future adult relationships.

24. **A.** The development of motor skills in infants is a universally consistent and sequential occurrence, Choice A. When children receive proper nutrition and care, and can freely experience their surroundings, normal motor development is expected. What is thought of as normal behavior in some cultures may be considered unusual in others; therefore, Choice B, the age at which developmental milestones appear, is greatly determined by cultural and environmental influences. Choice C is incorrect since the cultural influences of childrearing practices can vary significantly.

25. **C.** Prenatal exposure to high concentrations of alcohol during pregnancy can cause alcohol to enter the bloodstream and disrupt normal cell development, causing permanent and irrevocable brain damage to the fetus. "For the fetus, the hangover may last a lifetime" (Enloe, 1980). Symptoms such as low birth weight, a flattened area between the eyes, a thin upper lip, oddly shaped eyes, and a small head become less observable as the child reaches adolescence. *Fetal alcohol syndrome* continues to be the leading cause of environmentally influenced mental retardation in children.

26. **C.** IDEA mandates that children with disabilities are entitled to a free, appropriate public education in the United States and provides a legal basis on which to offer education to disabled children in the regular classroom; therefore, choices A and B are incorrect. Appropriate public education includes the evaluation and eligibility determination, an individualized educational plan, and a least-restricted environment that is suitable to meet the needs of children with disabilities, Choice C.

Subtest III: Visual and Performing Arts Multiple Choice

27. **C.** The picture best reflects modern dance movements that rely on natural and extemporaneous movements (Choice C). The dancers clearly demonstrate a freedom of movement and an energetic style. Although the scene depicted does show a visual movement pattern, Choice B, there is not enough information to determine a specific subject matter. Modern dance freed choreographers to implement a team dance approach that did not rely on the structure and conventions of traditional ballet. Dancers were freed to incorporate natural shapes in a variety of abstract dance forms.

28. **B.** *El Jarabe Tapatio* is one of the most popular of all Mexican dances. The symbolism involved in the dance steps is reflective of traditional courtship rituals (Choice B). This particular dance was based on an older courtship dance. As the dance evolves, the girl puts the sombrero on her head, signifying acceptance of the young man. The dance concludes with the boy and girl dancing at a faster and faster pace with the

boy's serape thrown around both the dancers. Other themes in traditional folk dances often include fertility and harvest rituals.

29. **A.** Force is the release of potential energy into kinetic energy or the energy of motion. In movement, force can be defined as heavy or light, sharp or smooth, percussive or suspended, and sustained or collapsing. There are four basic elements of dance: force, space, levels and time. Choices C and D are examples of space and levels. To use space and levels effectively, choreographers and dancers also consider direction (forward, backward, and diagonal), form (angular, rounded or bent), pathways (floor, elevated or air), levels (distance from the floor), and shape (design of the body as it exists in space). Time refers to the speed and rhythmic patterns of a dance movement—how fast or slow (tempo), even or uneven (beat), and long or short (duration).

30. **C.** Percussion instruments make sounds by hitting them with a stick or by shaking them. Choice A, the trombone, is a brass instrument. Choice B, the viola, is a string instrument. Choice D, a harp is a string instrument.

31. **C.** The musical heritage of ragtime jazz brought the cultural sounds from Africa and Western Europe to America at the end of the nineteenth century, Choice C. During the 1930s, the focus of jazz was big bands and swing jazz, Choice A. Around 1945, bebop jazz became vogue as saxophonist Charlie Parker and trumpeter Dizzy Gillespie highlighted jazz music, Choice D. Bossa nova, Choice B, was popular in the 1960s when the influences of Brazilian jazz contributed to a new "cool jazz" sound.

32. **D.** These quarter notes on this music notation ledger show two notes, D and G; therefore, Choice D is correct. The notes on the lines are E, G, B, D, and F (every good boy does fine), and the notes in the spaces between the lines are F, A, C, and E (face). A simple mnemonic memory technique helps children remember the sequence of notes on a staff.

33. **B.** Woodwind instruments were once all made of wood. Many of these are now made of metal and other materials. The flute, oboe, clarinet, and bassoon are all types of woodwinds.

34. **D.** The large arch is the most recognizable and primary feature of a proscenium stage. The arch allows audiences to view events as if looking through an opening. The proscenium arch is erected "down stage" and therefore the audience directly faces the stage. An advantage of this type of stage is that sides of the stage (wings) can be hidden from the audience by curtains or stage scenery. The proscenium stage is the dominant form used in theatre today.

35. **C.** The protagonist is the main character in a drama. Understanding the protagonist's motivation, strengths and weaknesses, and ability to resolve conflict are essential factors in developing a story. An effective protagonist should display the ability to evoke empathy in an audience as he or she resolves a central conflict. The audience does not have to view the main character as either likeable or heroic. However, the audience must be able to understand why the protagonist took a particular action. The antagonist is the main character in opposition to the protagonist. The primary conflict caused by the antagonist can be based on external or internal issues.

36. **B.** Improvisation can provide opportunities for elementary students to take risks in a non-judgmental setting and without working on an actual play. Improvisation provides opportunities for students to make up actions and words in a variety of settings and circumstances. Improvisation can take the form of simple actions like showing frustration or more complex scenarios like role-playing during a basketball practice. Student cooperation is essential for good improvisation to flow. Students need to accept what other students do and then build on that concept as the improvisation evolves.

37. **C.** The Impressionist movement started in the late nineteenth century and included such artists as Claude Monet, Edward Manet, Pierre-Auguste Renoir, Edgar Degas, and Mary Cassatt. The Impressionists emphasized the primary colors of red, blue, and yellow. The basic pure and unmixed primary colors intensified the vividness of the composition. The secondary colors (when two primary colors are mixed in equal proportion to create orange, green, and violet) were considered muted and were generally rejected. Impressionists' paintings were characterized by the use of vibrant color; short, quick, and visible brushstrokes; an emphasis on everyday life; natural outdoor settings; and prominently capturing the changing qualities of light.

38. **A.** The Pieter de Hooch painting is characteristic of the Baroque style. De Hooch perfected the classic "keyhole" effect of an interior scene that pulls the eye of the viewer through the room. The use of geometric squares that shrink in size adds to the keyhole effect by creating a sense of perspective. This painting is also characteristic of how Baroque artists used diagonal composition, light, and color to create a unified whole.

39. **D.** Organic shapes (curvilinear) are shapes with a natural look and generally are curvy and irregular. Organic shapes resemble the shapes of living things, for example, the shapes of trees, flowers, leaves, and animals. Geometric shapes (rectilinear) are angular, incorporate straight lines, and have a mathematical form. Geometric shapes generally are composed of circles, rectangles, squares, and triangles. Most man-made objects are geometric in shape.

Subtest III: Physical Education
Short Constructed Response

Assignment 1

1. Complete the exercise that follows.

Integrating physical education with other content areas is an important goal of physical education.

Using your knowledge of an integrated curriculum:

- list two specific examples of integrating math into the physical education curriculum;
- list two specific examples of integrating science into the physical education curriculum; and
- discuss one advantage of content integration in a physical education setting.

Sample Response

The first example of integrating math would be for upper-primary school students to calculate their working heart rate. The first step would be to calculate a maximum heart rate. To do so, students would take the number 220 and subtract their age. The resulting number would be their maximum heart rate. Students could then calculate the upper and lower threshold limits during aerobic exercise. To do so, they would find the lower threshold, or 70 percent of the maximum heart rate, and the upper threshold, or 85 percent of the maximum heart rate.

The second example of integrating math would be for elementary students to learn geometric principles by calculating the layout of ball fields and game areas. The majority of playground space includes rectangles, diamonds, and circles.

The first example of integrating science would be for students to identify the bones of the body while performing warm-up calisthenics—for example, pointing to the cranium, clavicle, patella, and ankle in succession as part of a nonlocomotor activity.

The second example of integrating science would be to have students take their pulse immediately before and after exercise. The physical educator could then have a follow-up discussion on the effect of exercise on the cardiovascular system.

One advantage of integrating other content areas into the physical education curriculum is that an interdisciplinary approach enables students to integrate knowledge and skills across curricular lines and make meaningful connections to real-world situations.

Subtest III: Human Development Short Constructed Response

Assignment 2

2. Complete the exercise that follows.

   Using your knowledge of cognitive and social development:

   - discuss the importance of play;
   - identify two types of play that are commonly observed; and
   - select one of the types of play and provide a description.

Sample Response

Although children typically play because they find it enjoyable, most theories consider play a major contribution to the development of social, cognitive, and emotional skills. It is fundamental to a child's physical and mental health. Play helps children to release physical energy, acquire and experiment with new motor abilities, form relationships among peers, and practice real-life situations. Two types of play are "constructive play" which is usually observed in toddlers, and "rough-and-tumble play" which is usually observed at the end of early childhood. Rough-and-tumble play requires intense physical activity, and helps children gain mastery over their bodies while building social interactions. Forms of rough-and-tumble play are wrestling and tag. Some of the movements of rough-and-tumble play may appear to be aggressive, but the signals that children demonstrate, such as laughter, giggling, and open hands, typically indicate that children are playing.

Subtest III: Visual and Performing Arts
Short Constructed Response

Assignment 3

3. Use the reproduction below to answer the following question.

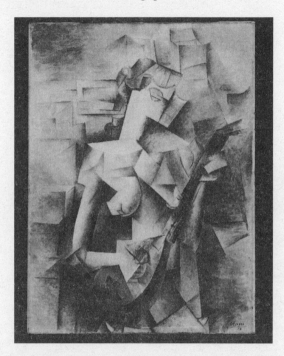

The classroom teacher is introducing a fifth-grade art lesson on cubism and Picasso. She shows the class *Girl with a Mandolin*, painted by Picasso in 1910.

Using your knowledge of art history:

- briefly discuss two elements that would be evident in the painting that would demonstrate an understanding of cubism; and
- discuss one in-class assignment that would demonstrate these two elements.

Sample Response

This portrait clearly demonstrates how Picasso used geometric shapes to create organic images and simplify an object. Firstly, Picasso broke apart and rearranged the woman in angular, geometric shapes, but it is still clear that the woman is playing a mandolin. Secondly, Picasso used squares, rectangles, semi-circles, and triangles to deconstruct objects into simplified components so that different viewpoints could be seen in one plane.

After assessing the students' prior knowledge of cubism, an example of an in-class assignment would be for students to create a self-portrait only using a ruler. Students would be limited to using geometric shapes and straight lines to create an organic shape of their face and body. The self-portrait would be simplified, breaking surfaces into flat planes.

Chapter 9

Practice Test II

Answer Sheet for Practice Test II

(Remove this sheet and use it to mark your answers)

Multiple-Choice Questions

CUT HERE

Subtest I

1 Ⓐ Ⓑ Ⓒ Ⓓ	21 Ⓐ Ⓑ Ⓒ Ⓓ
2 Ⓐ Ⓑ Ⓒ Ⓓ	22 Ⓐ Ⓑ Ⓒ Ⓓ
3 Ⓐ Ⓑ Ⓒ Ⓓ	23 Ⓐ Ⓑ Ⓒ Ⓓ
4 Ⓐ Ⓑ Ⓒ Ⓓ	24 Ⓐ Ⓑ Ⓒ Ⓓ
5 Ⓐ Ⓑ Ⓒ Ⓓ	25 Ⓐ Ⓑ Ⓒ Ⓓ
6 Ⓐ Ⓑ Ⓒ Ⓓ	26 Ⓐ Ⓑ Ⓒ Ⓓ
7 Ⓐ Ⓑ Ⓒ Ⓓ	27 Ⓐ Ⓑ Ⓒ Ⓓ
8 Ⓐ Ⓑ Ⓒ Ⓓ	28 Ⓐ Ⓑ Ⓒ Ⓓ
9 Ⓐ Ⓑ Ⓒ Ⓓ	29 Ⓐ Ⓑ Ⓒ Ⓓ
10 Ⓐ Ⓑ Ⓒ Ⓓ	30 Ⓐ Ⓑ Ⓒ Ⓓ
11 Ⓐ Ⓑ Ⓒ Ⓓ	31 Ⓐ Ⓑ Ⓒ Ⓓ
12 Ⓐ Ⓑ Ⓒ Ⓓ	32 Ⓐ Ⓑ Ⓒ Ⓓ
13 Ⓐ Ⓑ Ⓒ Ⓓ	33 Ⓐ Ⓑ Ⓒ Ⓓ
14 Ⓐ Ⓑ Ⓒ Ⓓ	34 Ⓐ Ⓑ Ⓒ Ⓓ
15 Ⓐ Ⓑ Ⓒ Ⓓ	35 Ⓐ Ⓑ Ⓒ Ⓓ
16 Ⓐ Ⓑ Ⓒ Ⓓ	36 Ⓐ Ⓑ Ⓒ Ⓓ
17 Ⓐ Ⓑ Ⓒ Ⓓ	37 Ⓐ Ⓑ Ⓒ Ⓓ
18 Ⓐ Ⓑ Ⓒ Ⓓ	38 Ⓐ Ⓑ Ⓒ Ⓓ
19 Ⓐ Ⓑ Ⓒ Ⓓ	39 Ⓐ Ⓑ Ⓒ Ⓓ
20 Ⓐ Ⓑ Ⓒ Ⓓ	40 Ⓐ Ⓑ Ⓒ Ⓓ

41 Ⓐ Ⓑ Ⓒ Ⓓ
42 Ⓐ Ⓑ Ⓒ Ⓓ
43 Ⓐ Ⓑ Ⓒ Ⓓ
44 Ⓐ Ⓑ Ⓒ Ⓓ
45 Ⓐ Ⓑ Ⓒ Ⓓ
46 Ⓐ Ⓑ Ⓒ Ⓓ
47 Ⓐ Ⓑ Ⓒ Ⓓ
48 Ⓐ Ⓑ Ⓒ Ⓓ
49 Ⓐ Ⓑ Ⓒ Ⓓ
50 Ⓐ Ⓑ Ⓒ Ⓓ
51 Ⓐ Ⓑ Ⓒ Ⓓ
52 Ⓐ Ⓑ Ⓒ Ⓓ

Subtest II

1 Ⓐ Ⓑ Ⓒ Ⓓ	21 Ⓐ Ⓑ Ⓒ Ⓓ
2 Ⓐ Ⓑ Ⓒ Ⓓ	22 Ⓐ Ⓑ Ⓒ Ⓓ
3 Ⓐ Ⓑ Ⓒ Ⓓ	23 Ⓐ Ⓑ Ⓒ Ⓓ
4 Ⓐ Ⓑ Ⓒ Ⓓ	24 Ⓐ Ⓑ Ⓒ Ⓓ
5 Ⓐ Ⓑ Ⓒ Ⓓ	25 Ⓐ Ⓑ Ⓒ Ⓓ
6 Ⓐ Ⓑ Ⓒ Ⓓ	26 Ⓐ Ⓑ Ⓒ Ⓓ
7 Ⓐ Ⓑ Ⓒ Ⓓ	27 Ⓐ Ⓑ Ⓒ Ⓓ
8 Ⓐ Ⓑ Ⓒ Ⓓ	28 Ⓐ Ⓑ Ⓒ Ⓓ
9 Ⓐ Ⓑ Ⓒ Ⓓ	29 Ⓐ Ⓑ Ⓒ Ⓓ
10 Ⓐ Ⓑ Ⓒ Ⓓ	30 Ⓐ Ⓑ Ⓒ Ⓓ
11 Ⓐ Ⓑ Ⓒ Ⓓ	31 Ⓐ Ⓑ Ⓒ Ⓓ
12 Ⓐ Ⓑ Ⓒ Ⓓ	32 Ⓐ Ⓑ Ⓒ Ⓓ
13 Ⓐ Ⓑ Ⓒ Ⓓ	33 Ⓐ Ⓑ Ⓒ Ⓓ
14 Ⓐ Ⓑ Ⓒ Ⓓ	34 Ⓐ Ⓑ Ⓒ Ⓓ
15 Ⓐ Ⓑ Ⓒ Ⓓ	35 Ⓐ Ⓑ Ⓒ Ⓓ
16 Ⓐ Ⓑ Ⓒ Ⓓ	36 Ⓐ Ⓑ Ⓒ Ⓓ
17 Ⓐ Ⓑ Ⓒ Ⓓ	37 Ⓐ Ⓑ Ⓒ Ⓓ
18 Ⓐ Ⓑ Ⓒ Ⓓ	38 Ⓐ Ⓑ Ⓒ Ⓓ
19 Ⓐ Ⓑ Ⓒ Ⓓ	39 Ⓐ Ⓑ Ⓒ Ⓓ
20 Ⓐ Ⓑ Ⓒ Ⓓ	40 Ⓐ Ⓑ Ⓒ Ⓓ

41 Ⓐ Ⓑ Ⓒ Ⓓ
42 Ⓐ Ⓑ Ⓒ Ⓓ
43 Ⓐ Ⓑ Ⓒ Ⓓ
44 Ⓐ Ⓑ Ⓒ Ⓓ
45 Ⓐ Ⓑ Ⓒ Ⓓ
46 Ⓐ Ⓑ Ⓒ Ⓓ
47 Ⓐ Ⓑ Ⓒ Ⓓ
48 Ⓐ Ⓑ Ⓒ Ⓓ
49 Ⓐ Ⓑ Ⓒ Ⓓ
50 Ⓐ Ⓑ Ⓒ Ⓓ
51 Ⓐ Ⓑ Ⓒ Ⓓ
52 Ⓐ Ⓑ Ⓒ Ⓓ

(continued)

Subtest III

1 Ⓐ Ⓑ Ⓒ Ⓓ	21 Ⓐ Ⓑ Ⓒ Ⓓ
2 Ⓐ Ⓑ Ⓒ Ⓓ	22 Ⓐ Ⓑ Ⓒ Ⓓ
3 Ⓐ Ⓑ Ⓒ Ⓓ	23 Ⓐ Ⓑ Ⓒ Ⓓ
4 Ⓐ Ⓑ Ⓒ Ⓓ	24 Ⓐ Ⓑ Ⓒ Ⓓ
5 Ⓐ Ⓑ Ⓒ Ⓓ	25 Ⓐ Ⓑ Ⓒ Ⓓ
6 Ⓐ Ⓑ Ⓒ Ⓓ	26 Ⓐ Ⓑ Ⓒ Ⓓ
7 Ⓐ Ⓑ Ⓒ Ⓓ	27 Ⓐ Ⓑ Ⓒ Ⓓ
8 Ⓐ Ⓑ Ⓒ Ⓓ	28 Ⓐ Ⓑ Ⓒ Ⓓ
9 Ⓐ Ⓑ Ⓒ Ⓓ	29 Ⓐ Ⓑ Ⓒ Ⓓ
10 Ⓐ Ⓑ Ⓒ Ⓓ	30 Ⓐ Ⓑ Ⓒ Ⓓ
11 Ⓐ Ⓑ Ⓒ Ⓓ	31 Ⓐ Ⓑ Ⓒ Ⓓ
12 Ⓐ Ⓑ Ⓒ Ⓓ	32 Ⓐ Ⓑ Ⓒ Ⓓ
13 Ⓐ Ⓑ Ⓒ Ⓓ	33 Ⓐ Ⓑ Ⓒ Ⓓ
14 Ⓐ Ⓑ Ⓒ Ⓓ	34 Ⓐ Ⓑ Ⓒ Ⓓ
15 Ⓐ Ⓑ Ⓒ Ⓓ	35 Ⓐ Ⓑ Ⓒ Ⓓ
16 Ⓐ Ⓑ Ⓒ Ⓓ	36 Ⓐ Ⓑ Ⓒ Ⓓ
17 Ⓐ Ⓑ Ⓒ Ⓓ	37 Ⓐ Ⓑ Ⓒ Ⓓ
18 Ⓐ Ⓑ Ⓒ Ⓓ	38 Ⓐ Ⓑ Ⓒ Ⓓ
19 Ⓐ Ⓑ Ⓒ Ⓓ	39 Ⓐ Ⓑ Ⓒ Ⓓ
20 Ⓐ Ⓑ Ⓒ Ⓓ	

CUT HERE

Directions: Choose the best answer to each question and fill in the appropriate circle on your answer sheet (5 hours).

Subtest I: Reading, Language, and Literature Multiple Choice

1. Teachers often ask students to predict what will happen in a text they are about to read. Which of the following is the best explanation of why this is a valuable technique?

   A. Students' ability to predict the outcome of a story is often a predictor of reading success.
   B. The teacher's ability to ask thought-provoking questions will lead the students to become more proficient readers.
   C. Prediction questions often stimulate students' interest in the text, encourage thinking, and give opportunities to share background knowledge.
   D. This technique encourages students to take risks.

2. Ruben is seven years old and recently moved to the United States with his Spanish-speaking parents. He is entering a second-grade classroom where English-speaking and foreign-speaking children all learn together. Ruben will learn in his native language and in English simultaneously. This approach to teaching English learners is called:

   A. English-immersion.
   B. English-inclusion.
   C. dual-language immersion.
   D. metalinguistic.

3. The rule system in a language for producing phonemes in words is called:

   A. morphology.
   B. phonology.
   C. topology.
   D. phonics.

4. Which of the following is an example of phoneme manipulation tasks?

   A. Syllable-splitting tasks
   B. Sorting words by categories
   C. Adding or deleting letters to a word
   D. Spelling words on a pretest

5. A second-grade student skips over five or more words per page that he doesn't know while reading. Which of the following would be the best action that the teacher should consider?

   A. The teacher should select simpler material for the child and strategies to decipher unknown words.
   B. The teacher should provide direct instruction in context clues.
   C. The teacher should do more shared reading to help the child with word recognition skills.
   D. The teacher should present the new words before he has the children begin reading.

6. Which of the following are the best predictors of learning to read in first grade?

   A. Mental age, pretending to read, family income, and IQ
   B. Perceptual/motor skills, mental age, and parental education
   C. Letter recognition, knowledge about print, and linguistic awareness
   D. Hours of television watching, preferred modalities, and scribbling

GO ON TO THE NEXT PAGE

7. A first-grade teacher frequently assesses his students' reading to determine their reading levels and to select guided reading books. When listening to one of his students read an unfamiliar text, the teacher notices that the student is able to read all the words in the text without making any errors, but when asked to recall the story, the student is unable to do so with any detail. What does this information tell the teacher about the student's reading ability?

   A. The student cannot decode the text and needs simpler material to read.

   B. The student is able to comprehend text at a very high level, and the teacher needs to select more difficult text for the student to read.

   C. The student is able to decode the text but does not comprehend what he or she is reading.

   D. The student has a reading ability level above other students in the class but a reading comprehension level below that of other students in the class.

8. When assessing a kindergarten student in May, the teacher notes that the student is able to name the letters of the alphabet and has mastered print concepts but is unable to identify rhyming words. What does this tell the teacher about the student?

   A. The student has completed most of the requirements of kindergarten and will be successful in first-grade reading.

   B. The student has not mastered a phonemic awareness skill that should be mastered by the end of kindergarten.

   C. The student will not be able to perform at grade level in first grade.

   D. The student needs direct instruction and practice in phonemic awareness skills such as rhyming and sound substitution.

9. During daily writing, a third-grade student consistently confuses long vowel sounds and writes *hiev* for *hive*, *bote* for *boat*, and *trea* for *tree*. What instructional strategies should the teacher use to meet the student's identified need?

   A. Assign more independent reading and additional homework with long vowel sounds, and perform frequent assessment

   B. Complete crossword puzzles, read independently to encounter more similar vocabulary, and complete word hunts

   C. Add weekly spelling words using the *look, see, say* method, and use picture sorts and vocabulary hunts

   D. Give direct instruction in long vowel patterns, sorting word families, and other activities to practice long-vowel spelling patterns

10. The linguistic system (language forms, structures, and styles) used by an individual as opposed to systems characteristic of communities is called:

    A. dialect.

    B. idiolect.

    C. idiom.

    D. syntax.

11. A third-grade student is confusing consonant pairs when writing. She writes *juncl* for *jungle*, *efryone* for *everyone*, and *carrod* for *carrot*. What instructional strategy would probably be most useful for this student?

    A. The teacher should assign related workbook pages from their reading series to improve this student's errors.

    B. The student would benefit from worthwhile practice in sound-blending to make meaning of words.

    C. The teacher needs to instruct the student in articulating phonemes.

    D. The student needs to add similar words to her spelling lists and study the words.

12. **Read the paragraph below; then answer the question that follows.**

¹According to recent studies, it certainly can. ²Consequently, environmentalists are filing suit against six plumbing manufacturers. ³Tests in Oregon have shown that lead contamination from faucets is a hundred times higher than the state's standard. ⁴Can an old or new faucet be dangerous?

Which of the following is the most logical order of the four sentences in the paragraph above?

    A. 4-3-2-1

    B. 4-1-3-2

    C. 3-4-1-2

    D. 2-3-1-4

13. A sixth-grade physical education teacher asks her class to do a report on a current basketball, baseball, or football superstar. The report is due in two weeks. Which of the following sources would be valuable in helping the student get started?

Line	Source	Information
1	Sports magazine	To get the latest information on top athletes
2	Internet search engine	To get background information and a list of sports
3	Encyclopedia	To find historical information about Hall of Fame athletes
4	Sports record book	To find the record-setting athletes and their records

   A. Line 1
   B. Line 2
   C. Line 3
   D. Line 4

14. **Read the excerpt below; then answer the question that follows.**

The population explosion of coyotes has alarmed sheep ranchers in the western states, and they have responded with a new weapon: a collar worn by sheep that contains the fiercely toxic Compound 1080. Ranchers say the amount of deadly poison is so small that it presents no threat to the environment. _____ the Environmental Protection Agency has approved the use of the collars in several sheep-raising states. _____ there is still opposition from many environmental groups. They point to the cruelty of the coyotes' death, which can last from three to twelve hours. They claim that Compound 1080 can kill innocent animals and poses a special threat to eagles. Because the collars may find their way into streams, they fear the widespread killing of fish and fish-eating birds and animals.

Which of the following words or phrases used respectively to fill in the blanks would make this paragraph clearer?

   A. However; Also
   B. Thus; And
   C. But; On the other hand
   D. Furthermore; But

15. **Read the lines from a poem by John Milton below; then answer the question that follows.**

How soon hath Time, the subtle thief of youth,
Stolen on his wing my three-and-twentieth year!
My hasting days fly on with full career,
But my late spring no bud or blossom show'th.

The phrase "late spring" is a metaphor for:

   A. infertility.
   B. the speaker's hopes.
   C. a season of promise.
   D. the speaker's age.

Read the poem, "The Soldier" (1914) by Rupert Brooke (1887–1915), below; then answer the two questions that follow.

If I should die, think only this of me
That there's some corner of a foreign field
That is forever England. There shall be
In that rich earth a richer dust concealed;
A dust whom England bore, shaped, made aware,
Gave, once, her flowers to love, her ways to roam,
A body of England's breathing English air,
Washed by the rivers, blest by suns of home.

And think, this heart, all evil and shed away,
A pulse in the eternal mind, no less
Gives someone back the thoughts by England given,
Her sights and sounds, dreams happy as her day;
And laughter, learnt of friends, and gentleness,
In hearts at peace, under an English heaven.

16. In the fourth line, "In that rich earth, a richer dust concealed" refers metaphorically to:

   A. the futility of war.
   B. defeating the enemy.
   C. the soldier and his honor.
   D. the sweetness of death.

GO ON TO THE NEXT PAGE

Practice Test II

17. Which of the following best describes the primary technique used to express the main theme of the poem?

    A. Comparing the beauty of flowers to the beauty of English dreams

    B. Using figurative language to represent individual sacrifice

    C. Using sarcasm to define the individual's disdain for war

    D. Discovering universal truths inherent in the human spirit

18. **Read the paragraph below; then answer the question that follows.**

[1]More than half of this time is necessary to allow the rising or the resting of the dough. [2]Or you will have to bake them earlier and freeze them. [3]To make a good croissant takes eleven hours. [4]So if you want fresh croissants for breakfast, you will have to stay up all night.

Which of the following is the best topic sentence in the paragraph above?

    A. Sentence 1

    B. Sentence 2

    C. Sentence 3

    D. Sentence 4

19. **Read the paragraph below; then answer the question that follows.**

To transfer a design to be cross-stitched onto fabric, use graph paper with boxes the size of the stitches you plan to embroider. _____ mark the crosses on the graph paper to correspond to the design. _____ place a piece of carbon paper facedown on the material and adjust the graph paper over it. _____, being careful to avoid smudging, use a fine pencil to mark each cross.

To make the instructions in the paragraph clear, which of the following, in the order given, should replace the three blanks?

    A. First; On the other hand; Then

    B. You should; You can; You should

    C. First; Then; Finally

    D. To begin; Or; As a last step

20. An eighth-grade English teacher assigns topics to her class for oral reports next week. One of the students, Cindy, selects "Shakespeare, his life, and his works" as her topic. Which of the following would be most helpful to start her research?

Line	Source	Information
1	Literary review magazine	To find reviews of his works
2	Online encyclopedia	To find background information on Shakespeare
3	Historical reference	To find information about his contemporaries' books
4	Newspaper	To find interesting articles

    A. Line 1

    B. Line 2

    C. Line 3

    D. Line 4

21. **Read the lines from "Essay on Criticism" (c. 1710) by Alexander Pope (1688–1744) ; then answer the question that follows.**

'Tis with our judgments as our watches, none
Go just alike, yet each believes his own.
In poets as true genius is but rare,
True taste as seldom is the critic's share.

With which of the following would the author of these lines most likely agree?

    A. We should not trust our own conclusions.

    B. Great poets are rarely appreciated.

    C. Most criticism is inadequate.

    D. Most poets are better critics than are professional critics.

22. **Read the excerpt below; then answer the question that follows.**

Creative writing may serve many purposes for the writer. Above all, it is a means of self-expression. It is the individual's way of saying, "These are my thoughts and they are uniquely experienced by me." But creative writing can also serve as a safety valve for hidden tensions. This implies that a period of time has evolved in which the child gave an idea some deep thought and that the message on paper is revealing this deep inner thought. Finally, a worthwhile by-product of creative writing is the stimulus it gives students to do further reading and experimentation in their areas of interest. A child may become an ardent reader of good literature in order to satisfy an appetite whetted by a creative writing endeavor.

The primary purpose of the author of this passage is:

A. to call attention to a widespread lack of self-expression.

B. to stress the value of good literature, both amateur and professional.

C. to encourage the reader to try some creative writing.

D. to discuss some positive purposes and effects of creative writing.

23. **Read the lines below, from "The Eagle" (1851) by Tennyson (1809–1892); then answer the question that follows.**

The wrinkled sea beneath him crawls;
He watches from his mountain walls,
And like a thunderbolt he falls.

The first line uses a(n):

A. metaphor.

B. simile.

C. antithesis.

D. paradox.

Read the excerpt below from Herman Melville's (1819–1891) *Moby-Dick*, then answer the three questions that follow.

Call me Ishmael. Some years ago — never mind how long precisely — having little or no money in my purse, and nothing particular to interest me on shore, I thought I would sail about a little and see the watery part of the world. It is a way I have of driving off the spleen and regulating the circulation. Whenever I find myself growing grim about the mouth; whenever it is a damp, drizzly November in my soul; whenever I find myself involuntarily pausing before coffin warehouses, and bringing up the rear of every funeral I meet; and especially whenever my hypos get such an upper hand of me, that it requires a strong moral principle to prevent me from deliberately stepping into the street, and methodically knocking people's hats off — then, I account it high time to get to sea as soon as I can. This is my substitute for pistol and ball.

24. According to the passage, which of the following is the main reason that Ishmael usually goes off to sea?

A. To carn money when times are hard and he needs food and lodging

B. To explore the oceans of the world whenever possible

C. To calm himself when he gets upset or angry with others

D. To stop himself from committing suicide when he gets depressed

25. The narrator, Ishmael, implies that:

A. he is enamored with funerals.

B. he has strong moral principles.

C. he is prone to violence.

D. his hypos rarely get the best of him.

26. In the excerpt, the author, Herman Melville, is creating the image of Ishmael as:

A. one who is always at sea.

B. an adventurer.

C. a responsible citizen.

D. one who is emotionally unstable.

GO ON TO THE NEXT PAGE

Subtest I: History and Social Science
Multiple Choice

27. The birth of classical civilization was rooted in the remarkable achievements of ancient civilizations. Which of the following ancient civilization is credited with the first implementation of democracy into government?

    A. Hebrews
    B. Greeks
    C. Romans
    D. Chinese

28. Review the picture below; then answer the question that follows.

The symbolic representation of the picture above is most frequently associated with:

    A. Roman worship of animal fertility figures.
    B. Mesopotamian cult figures offering food to a deity.
    C. Egyptian subservience to a deity.
    D. Greek statues of naturalistic design.

29. Which line in the table below correctly identifies the civilization and the original accomplishment?

Line	Civilization	Accomplishment
1	Sumerians	System of writing called hieroglyphics
2	Babylonians	Belief in monotheism
3	Egyptians	Invention of the calendar
4	Phoenicians	Trade throughout the Mediterranean

    A. Line 1
    B. Line 2
    C. Line 3
    D. Line 4

30. Which of the following series of American civilizations is in the correct chronological order, starting with the earliest civilization?

    A. Aztec, Mayan, Olmec, Toltec
    B. Olmec, Toltec, Aztec, Mayan
    C. Mayan, Inca, Aztec, Toltec
    D. Olmec, Mayan, Toltec, Aztec

31. **Review the map below; then answer the question that follows.**

The map above best represents conditions on which of the following dates?

    A. 100 B.C.
    B. A.D. 200
    C. A.D. 500
    D. A.D. 800

32. The "remission of temporal punishment for a sin through the sale of indulgences" was an immediate cause of the:

    A. Protestant Reformation.
    B. Renaissance.
    C. English Reformation initiated by Henry the Eighth.
    D. Age of Exploration.

33. **Use the picture below to answer the question that follows.**

The statue above is associated with a particular religion. A person who follows this religion would accept which of the following statements as true?

A. All religions are equally acceptable to all people.

B. Reincarnation is part of an extended life process.

C. Meditation cannot replace confession in gaining enlightenment.

D. The Koran is the direct word of God.

34. Which line in the table below does not make the correct association?

Line	Explorer	Accomplishment
1	Vasco da Gama	First European explorer to reach India by sea
2	Juan Cabrillo	First European explorer to reach coastal California
3	Francisco de Coronado	First European explorer to explore the U.S. southeast
4	Ferdinand Magellan	First European explorer to circumnavigate the globe

A. Line 1
B. Line 2
C. Line 3
D. Line 4

35. Which of the following religions is most closely associated with the development of a theocracy in America?

A. Roman Catholic
B. Quaker
C. Anglican
D. Puritan

36. **Read the chart below; then answer the question that follows.**

A Comparison of Three State Constitutions, as Originally Written			
	South Carolina	**Pennsylvania**	**Massachusetts**
	President	Council	Governor
Chief Executive	2-year term, legislature elects, has full veto.	3-year term, voters elect.	1-year term, voters elect, 2/3 vote can override veto.
Upper House	Life term, lower house elects.	None.	1-year term, voters elect.
Judges	Life term, legislature elects.	7-year term, appointed by council.	Life term, appointed by governor.
Requirements for Having Voting Rights	Must have 100 acres or £60 or pay 10 shillings in taxes.	Must pay taxes.	Must have £60 or £3 income from real estate yearly.
Eligibility to Hold Office	Must have 500 acres in parish or 500 acres and 10 slaves in county, or £1,000.	Must pay taxes.	Governor: £1,000 real estate; Senator: £300 real estate or £600; Representative: £100 real estate or £200.

Which of the following inferences can be drawn from information presented in the chart above?

A. Land ownership and wealth were prerequisites to direct involvement in government.

B. The framers of the state constitutions limited the term of the executive branch to three years.

C. The legislative branch would dominate the political process.

D. The state constitutions were modeled on the federal Constitution.

GO ON TO THE NEXT PAGE

Practice Test II

37. Which line in the table below correctly identifies both a major advantage of the Articles of Confederation and a major advantage of the Constitution of the United States?

Line	Articles Advantage	Constitution Advantage
1	Bicameral legislature	Two-thirds Congressional vote required to override a veto
2	Declare war and raise military forces	Provisions for a strong central government
3	Establish post office system	Unicameral legislature
4	Independent judiciary	Power to regulate interstate commerce

    A.   Line 1
    B.   Line 2
    C.   Line 3
    D.   Line 4

38. **Use the statement below to answer the question that follows.**

The people's right to know is a cornerstone of the American legal system. However, media accounts of sensational criminal trials often result in prejudicial trial publicity.

    This statement most clearly represents a basic constitutional conflict between which of the following?

    A.   Freedom of speech and the right to privacy
    B.   Freedom of speech and the right to a fair trial
    C.   The right to an impartial jury and the equal protection of the law
    D.   The due process of the law and the legal requirement of being charged with a crime

39. In the United States, if a bill is sent to the president during the last ten days of a legislative session and the president refuses to act on the bill, the bill:

    A.   automatically becomes law.
    B.   may be overridden by a two-thirds vote in both the House and Senate.
    C.   cannot become law during that session of Congress.
    D.   becomes law without the president's signature.

40. The U.S. federal government has used protective tariffs since the early 1800s as part of a comprehensive fiscal program. Which of the following is the best reason to eliminate a protective tariff?

    A.   To strengthen the national government
    B.   To protect the auto industry
    C.   To encourage manufacturing
    D.   To encourage free trade

41. **Use the map and chart below to answer the question that follows.**

Election of 1868

Candidates 1868	Electoral Vote	Popular Vote
Republican Ulysses S. Grant	214	3,013,421
Democratic Horatio Seymour	80	2,706,829
Not Voted	23	
	317	5,720,250

The numbers refer to the number of electoral votes of each state. Those areas without numbers had <u>not</u> become states in 1868.

According to the chart above, which of the following paired states had the largest number of electoral votes in the 1868 election?

    A.   California and Massachusetts
    B.   Illinois and Tennessee
    C.   Pennsylvania and Ohio
    D.   New York and Kentucky

42. The election of 1876 is considered a watershed in American political history. Which of the following was a direct result of the contested presidential election of 1876?

    A.   Federal troops were withdrawn from the South, ending Reconstruction.
    B.   The majority of contested electoral votes went to Rutherford B. Hayes.

C. Congress passed the Fifteenth Amendment, extending citizenship to the freedmen.

D. Radical Republicans maintained control of Congress.

43. Two of the most obvious elements of U.S. industrialization in the late nineteenth century were the increase in the labor force and the effect on the growth of urban areas. Which of the following was not associated with the industrialization of the United States?

A. The trade-union movement

B. Humanizing aspects of technological innovations

C. Government protection of management through the use of court injunctions

D. The growth of the suburbs

44. If a plane left San Francisco and traveled on a direct course to Lake Tahoe, the plane would cross which of the following geographical features?

A. Mt. Shasta, Central Valley, Cascade Range

B. Coast Range, Central Valley, Sierra Nevada

C. Rockies, Mojave Desert, Sierra Nevada

D. Coast Range, Mt. Whitney, Sequoia National Park

45. Shortly after the discovery of gold in California, the issue of water rights became a significant factor in the state's growth. Which of the following mining practices had the greatest impact on both farmers and steamboat companies?

A. Hydraulic mining

B. Intricate irrigation ditches

C. Dams and canals

D. Wooden flumes

46. Which of the following statements best describes how natural resources influenced the culture of the California Chumash Indians?

A. The Chumash made houses of wooden planks from the redwoods and cedars that grew in the area.

B. The Chumash utilized salmon spawning areas to supplement their basic diet.

C. The Chumash developed farming methods to grow food in dry climates.

D. The Chumash used tar to waterproof their canoes.

47. The mission system in California was originally intended to be temporary. However, it lasted for almost a century. Which of the following best describes the primary purpose for establishing the mission system?

A. To teach Indians to speak Spanish and to adopt the values of the Church.

B. To train useful citizens who could practice a trade.

C. To maintain a self-sufficient agricultural economy that produced a food surplus.

D. To relocate the Indian population.

48. Which line in the table below correctly identifies a power provided for in both the California Constitution and the U.S. Constitution?

Line	California Constitution	U.S. Constitution
1	Make treaties among bordering states	Regulate interstate commerce in the 50 states
2	Establish 12-year terms for members of the state Supreme Court	Make life appointments for members of the federal Supreme Court
3	Authorize increases in taxes	Require a 2/3 vote in Congress to increase taxes
4	Establish state post offices	Establish procedures for a national draft

A. Line 1

B. Line 2

C. Line 3

D. Line 4

GO ON TO THE NEXT PAGE

49. In 1942, both Japanese aliens and American citizens of Japanese ancestry were interned in detention camps in California. Historically, which of the following constituted the most serious objection to the relocation program?

   A. The mass hysteria against the Japanese and the threat of violence following the attack on Pearl Harbor necessitated the relocation of Japanese aliens and Americans of Japanese ancestry to detention facilities.

   B. The Japanese in Hawaii, following the attack on Pearl Harbor, were not relocated or removed in an arbitrary or encompassing manner.

   C. The mass internment of the Japanese without evidence of disloyalty demonstrated that constitutional safeguards could be rendered ineffective in wartime.

   D. The Japanese in the agricultural industry were interned at a time when agricultural production for the war effort was most needed.

50. Which of the following is a power that the governor of California possesses but the president of the U.S. does not possess?

   A. Power to override acts of the legislature
   B. Power to veto specific sections of a spending bill
   C. Power to issue economic forecasts
   D. Power to appoint members to educational commissions

51. In 1900, there were 8,000 Mexicans living in California; by 1920, there were 121,000 Mexicans living in California; by 1930, there were 368,000 Mexicans living in California. Which of the following statements best describes the primary reason for this dramatic population increase?

   A. The Mediterranean-type climate encouraged migrants to settle in warm weather areas.

   B. The emerging collective farm movement in California provided economic opportunities for migrant workers.

   C. The need for skilled labor in the industrial sectors of the economy provided new job opportunities.

   D. The Mexicans replaced the Japanese as low-paid agricultural workers.

52. The California state legislature responded to pressure from both the Republican and Democratic parties to change the date of presidential primaries in the state from March to February. What was the primary reason for this change?

   A. To prevent one party from gaining political advantage

   B. To limit the power of national parties in determining state priorities

   C. To provide a greater voice in determining national politics

   D. To increase the electoral advantage of California in the Electoral College

Subtest I: Reading, Language, and Literature
Short Constructed Responses

Directions: Write your answers legibly on a clean sheet of lined paper.

Assignment 1

1. Complete the exercise that follows.

    Using your knowledge of reading, language, and literature:

    - describe the common elements in nursery rhymes and explain why teachers use the genre in primary classrooms;
    - provide examples to support your answer; and
    - discuss one disadvantage of using nursery rhymes.

Assignment 2

2. Complete the exercise that follows.

    Using your knowledge of literature:

    - identify three major elements of the novel; and
    - discuss these elements.

GO ON TO THE NEXT PAGE

501

Subtest I: History and Social Science Short Constructed Responses

Directions: Write your answers legibly on a clean sheet of lined paper.

Assignment 3

3. Complete the exercise that follows.

   During World War II, the population of California increased dramatically. The population grew by more than two and a half million people during the war years.

   Using your knowledge of California history, prepare a response in which you:

   - identify two specific minority groups that migrated to California during this period;
   - select one of the groups; and
   - explain how the group you have selected affected the war effort and changed the face of California society.

Assignment 4

4. Complete the exercise that follows.

   In Egypt, as well as in all early civilizations, the influence of geography was a significant factor in the area's development as a civilization.

   Using your knowledge of world history, prepare a response in which you:

   - list three reasons to demonstrate how geography influenced the historical development of ancient Egypt;
   - select one of the factors you have identified; and
   - explain how the geographical factor you have selected helped shape ancient Egypt's history.

Subtest II: Mathematics Multiple Choice

1. Which of the following is the answer to .062 divided by .000002 in scientific notation?

   A. 3.1×10^{-4}
   B. 3.1×10^{4}
   C. 3.1×10^{8}
   D. 12.4×10^{12}

2. If the ratio of men to women to children at a party is 5:3:2, which of the following is a possible number of adults at the party?

   A. 20
   B. 16
   C. 10
   D. 5

3. The problem below shows the multiplication of two three-digit numbers.

$$
\begin{array}{r}
231 \\
\times\, z2x \\
\hline
231 \\
4y2 \\
y93 \\
\hline
74151
\end{array}
$$

   Each letter represents a digit. If a letter appears more than once, it always represents the same digit. What is the value of $x + y + z$?

   A. 6
   B. 8
   C. 10
   D. 12

4. The fraction $\frac{1}{8}$ lies between which pair of numbers?

   A. $\frac{1}{10}$ and $\frac{2}{17}$
   B. .1 and .12
   C. $\frac{1}{9}$ and $\frac{2}{15}$
   D. 1 and 8

5. Which of the following is the smallest fraction?

   A. $\frac{3}{5}$
   B. $\frac{4}{9}$
   C. $\frac{7}{13}$
   D. $\frac{23}{44}$

6. In a senior class of 800, only 240 decided to attend the senior prom. What percentage of the senior class attended the senior prom?

   A. 8%
   B. 24%
   C. 30%
   D. 33%

7. John is 18 years old. He works for his father for $\frac{3}{4}$ of the year, and he works for his brother for the rest of the year. What is the ratio of the time John spends working for his brother to the time he spends working for his father per year?

   A. $\frac{1}{4}$
   B. $\frac{1}{3}$
   C. $\frac{3}{4}$
   D. $\frac{4}{3}$

8. Arnold purchased one pair of slacks, a dress shirt, a tie, and a sports coat. The shirt and slacks each cost three times what the tie cost. The sports coat cost twice what the shirt cost. If Arnold paid a total of $156 for all four items, what was the price of the pair of slacks?

   A. $12
   B. $36
   C. $48
   D. $78

GO ON TO THE NEXT PAGE

9. How many paintings were displayed at the County Museum of Art if 30 percent of them were by Monet and Monet was represented by 24 paintings?

   A. 80
   B. 76
   C. 60
   D. 50

10. If $3x + 7 = 19$, then $3x + 1 =$

    A. 4
    B. 8
    C. 12
    D. 13

11. Tom is just four years older than Fran. The total of their ages is twenty-four. What is the equation for finding Fran's age?

    A. $x + 4x = 24$
    B. $x + 4 = 24$
    C. $4x + x = 24$
    D. $x + (x + 4) = 24$

12. Use the graph below to answer the question that follows.

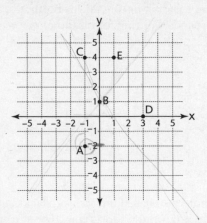

In the x-y plane above, point B is on a line with a slope of -3. Which of the following points is also on the same line?

    A. A
    B. E
    C. C ✓
    D. D

13. Use the table below to answer the question that follows.

x	y
2	8
1	1
−1	−1
−2	−8

Which of the following graphs best represents the data in the table above?

A.

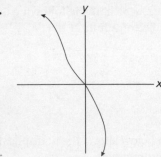

B.

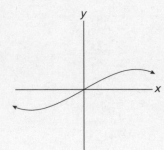

C.

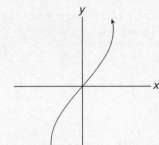

D.

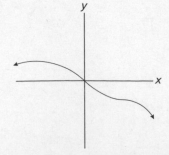

14. What are the possible values of x in the inequality $2x + 7 < 4x - 9$?

    A. $x > 1$
    B. $x < 1$
    C. $x < 8$
    D. $x > 8$

15. Use the graph below to answer the question that follows.

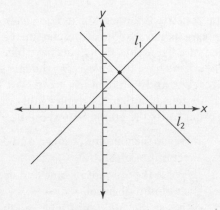

In the graph above, what is the solution of the equations of the two lines l_1 and l_2?

    A. $x = 2$; $y = 4$
    B. $x = 0$; $y = 2$
    C. $x = 2$; $y = 0$
    D. $x = 4$; $y = 2$

16. Which of the following are the possible values for x in the quadratic equation $x^2 + 3x + 2 = 0$?

    A. 1, 2
    B. 2, 3
    C. –1, –3
    D. –1, –2

17. Use the diagram below to answer the question that follows.

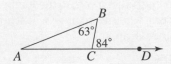

Given triangle ABC above with $\angle BCD = 84°$ and $\angle B = 63°$, what is the measure of $\angle A$ in degrees?

    A. 21
    B. 27
    C. 84
    D. 96

18. Use the diagram below to answer the question that follows.

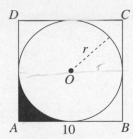

Circle O is inscribed in square $ABCD$ as shown above. The area of the shaded region is closest to which of the following choices?

    A. 10
    B. 25
    C. 30
    D. 50

19. Use the diagram below to answer the question that follows.

The large square above consists of squares and isosceles right triangles. If the large square has sides of 4 cm, the area of the shaded portion in square cm is:

    A. 2
    B. 4
    C. 6
    D. 8

GO ON TO THE NEXT PAGE

20. Use the figure below to answer the question that follows.

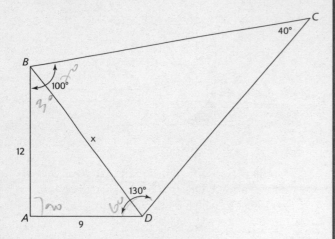

If $\angle ABC = 100°$, $\angle BCD = 40°$, and $\angle CDA = 130°$, what is the length of x?

A. 10
B. 15
C. 18
D. 24

21. Use the diagram below to answer the question that follows.

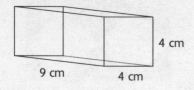

4 cm

9 cm   4 cm

The figure above is a rectangular solid with the longest edges 9 cm each and the shorter edges 4 cm each. Which of the following must be true about the figure above?

A. The volume is 144 cm³.
B. The surface area is 170 cm².
C. The area of each face is equal to 16 cm².
D. The areas of exactly three of the faces are equal.

22. Use the graph below to answer the question that follows.

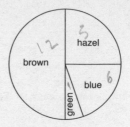

Sam constructs a pie graph as shown above, representing eye colors of his classmates. In his class of 24 students, 6 students have blue eyes, 12 students have brown eyes, 5 students have hazel eyes, and 1 student has green eyes. His teacher tells him that his graph is not correct. In order to fix the graph, Sam should:

A. increase the amount of green and decrease the amount of blue.
B. increase the amount of blue and decrease the amount of hazel.
C. decrease the amount of blue and increase the amount of brown.
D. decrease the amount of hazel and increase the amount of brown.

23. Use the graph below to answer the question that follows.

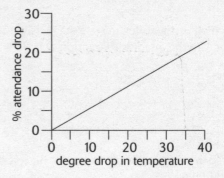

According to the graph, if the temperature falls 35 degrees, what percentage will school attendance drop?

A. 10%
B. 20%
C. 30%
D. 40%

24. If five plumbers each worked five days and six electricians each worked six days, what is the average number of days worked for each person?

A. $4\frac{1}{2}$

B. $5\frac{1}{2}$

C. $5\frac{6}{11}$

D. $6\frac{1}{11}$

25. What is the probability of tossing a penny twice so that both times it lands heads up?

A. $\frac{1}{8}$

B. $\frac{1}{4}$

C. $\frac{1}{3}$

D. $\frac{1}{2}$

26. Use the graph below to answer the question that follows.

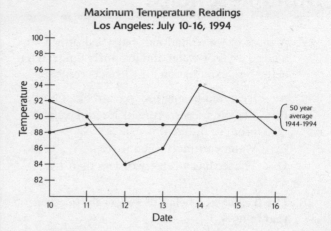

Of the seven days shown in the graph above, on approximately what percent of the days did the maximum temperature exceed the average temperature?

A. 3%

B. 4%

C. 43%

D. 57%

GO ON TO THE NEXT PAGE

Subtest II: Science
Multiple Choice

27. A piece of ice of unusual shape is dropped into a large glass of water and instantly floats. What is the best explanation for this occurrence?

    A. Ice contains microscopic bubbles of air.
    B. The atomic structure of ice and water produce different densities.
    C. Water contracts when frozen.
    D. The ice has a density of less than 1.0.

28. **Use the diagram below to answer the question that follows.**

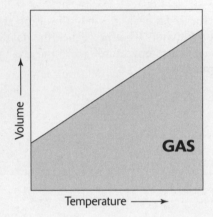

    Which of the following is true based on the information presented in the diagram above?

    A. A higher temperature causes molecules to move more slowly.
    B. As the temperature of the gas increases, the volume of the gas increases.
    C. As the pressure of the gas increases, the volume decreases.
    D. The gas in the container does not expand with increased temperature.

29. Which of the following examples identifies the compound with the correct elements?

Line	Compound	Elements
1	Rust	Iron, oxygen
2	Water	Hydrogen, carbon
3	Carbon dioxide	Carbon, hydrogen
4	Sugar	Oxygen, nitrogen

    A. Line 1
    B. Line 2
    C. Line 3
    D. Line 4

30. Which of the following processes causes the contents of an aerosol can to spray out when the top button is depressed?

    A. The change from a gaseous to a liquid state
    B. The expansion of a gas after being heated
    C. The movement of molecules toward a lower-pressure area
    D. The change in temperature from the can to the atmosphere

31. **Use the diagram below to answer the question that follows.**

    The following diagram shows the decomposition of water by an electric current.

    ELECTROLYSIS

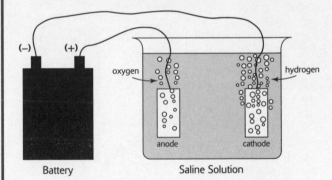

    If you examine the diagram carefully, you will see more bubbles of hydrogen than of oxygen. What is the best explanation for this reaction?

    A. The cathode material is considerably more porous than the anode material.
    B. Hydrogen gas is less dense than oxygen gas, so hydrogen bubbles rise faster.
    C. Some oxygen is dissolved into the solution, while all the insoluble hydrogen escapes.
    D. The water being decomposed has twice as much hydrogen as oxygen.

32. Two items are dropped simultaneously from a ten-story building. The items are shaped similarly and are relatively the same weight. Which of the following statements is correct concerning the rate at which the objects fall?

    A. The weight of the objects has no effect on the falling rate.
    B. The resistance of the air has no effect on the falling rate.
    C. The shape of the objects has no effect on the falling rate.
    D. The distance of the fall has a major effect on the falling rate.

33. An experiment is conducted in which five circular holes of equal size are cut into a large plastic bottle. The holes are arranged from top to bottom, with each hole exactly one inch from the next. The holes are covered with tape, and the bottle is filled with water. The tape is then removed.

    Which of the following is a true statement based on the information above?

    A. Water from each hole will squirt out the same distance from the bottle.
    B. Water from the top hole will squirt out farther than that from the bottom hole.
    C. Water from the bottom hole will squirt out farther than that from any other hole.
    D. Water from all five holes being released simultaneously will cause the bottle to partially collapse.

34. During a moderate windstorm, a bridge collapsed. After studying the structural failure, the Army Corps of Engineers issued an order mandating that soldiers cannot march in step while crossing a bridge.

    What is the principle on which the order discussed above is based?

    A. The cumulative effect of synchronized marching might cause small amplitude variations.
    B. The sustained in-step marching might result in a change in the air pressure.
    C. The sound produced by in-step marching might result in a series of different harmonics.
    D. The marching might make the bridge vibrate at its own natural frequency.

35. A student in a science class drops a permanent magnetic bar and it breaks into two dissimilar pieces. What would happen to the two pieces of magnet?

    A. When brought together, the north pole of one broken piece would repel the south pole of the other broken piece.
    B. When brought together, the north pole of one broken piece would attract the south pole of the other broken piece.
    C. When brought together, both the north and south poles would lose their magnetic polar fields.
    D. When brought together, the atomic structure of the magnets would change.

36. Amoebas can live in soil or water. Which of the following biological processes is most helpful in explaining the metabolism of an amoeba?

    A. Photosynthesis
    B. Reproduction
    C. Respiration
    D. Secretion

37. In what part of the subcellular organelle is genetic material stored?

    A. Vacuoles
    B. Chromosomes
    C. Cytoplasm
    D. Membranes

38. All life forms have common characteristics. Which of the following properties is the best evidence for considering viruses a life form?

    A. They have a crystalline structure.
    B. They are found inside animals, plants, and one-celled organisms.
    C. They produce nucleic acids to reproduce themselves.
    D. They possess the ability to become larger.

39. There are many interactions between two species. All of the following pairs are examples of symbiosis, whether beneficial, neutral, or harmful, except:

    A. fungi and orchids.
    B. egrets and rhinoceroses.
    C. foxes and chickens.
    D. whales and barnacles.

GO ON TO THE NEXT PAGE

40. Within a natural community of many different plant and animal species, which of the following is most likely to be true?

    A. Competition between two species will upset the delicate natural balance.
    B. Each species occupies its own niche in the environment.
    C. The largest carnivore will command the greatest territory.
    D. Owls hunt at night and therefore do not compete with nocturnal animals.

41. Use the chart below to answer the question that follows.

    The following chart summarizes a study of 244 species of insects offered to a monkey as food.

	Eaten by Monkey	Rejected by Monkey
Insects of Bright Colors	23	120
Insects of Dull Colors	83	18

    Which of the following is the most likely interpretation of the results of the study in terms of animals adapting to their environment?

    A. Insects have adapted to have dull colors to avoid being eaten.
    B. Some insects of bright colors have likely adapted to have bitter tastes.
    C. Color as a variable is not sufficient in explaining the monkey's behavior.
    D. Monkeys have adapted to eat most species of insects.

42. What would be the primary reason that a genetic counselor would want to know the karyotype of an individual's chromosomes?

    A. To determine the number and pairs of chromosomes
    B. To predict the sex of an unborn child
    C. To determine if the chromosomes were formed in the nucleus of the cell
    D. To determine if the chromosomes have an XY pattern

43. Use the diagram below to answer the question that follows.

    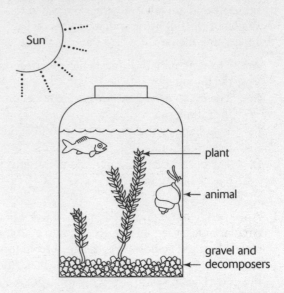

    What is the major contribution of the plants to the welfare of the animals in this system?

    A. They produce carbon dioxide needed by the animals.
    B. They produce oxygen needed by the animals.
    C. They produce carbon dioxide needed by the other plants.
    D. They filter the water to maintain cleanliness.

44. The moon at night appears to be a white object in the night sky. At the same time, the planet Mars appears to be reddish. What is the best explanation for the difference in color between the two objects?

    A. The fact that the Moon revolves around Earth and Mars revolves around the Sun
    B. The radioactive dust on the Moon's surface
    C. The mineral compositions of the cores of the planetary objects
    D. The light that is reflected by each

45. The tilt of the earth's axis relative to the sun is responsible for the seasons of the year. Which of the following corresponds to the tilt of the earth at its maximum and the sun at its highest point on its path through the sky in the Northern Hemisphere?

    A. The Winter Solstice
    B. The Vernal Equinox
    C. The Autumnal Equinox
    D. The Summer Solstice

46. According to the Richter scale, an earthquake with a magnitude 6 is how many times stronger than an earthquake with a magnitude 4?

    A. 10
    B. 100
    C. 1,000
    D. 10,000

47. **Use the diagram below to answer the question that follows.**

    ### SOIL PROFILE

    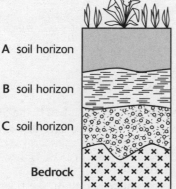

    The diagram above shows a soil profile that might be exposed on the side of a recently dug trench. Notice the different soil zones. At the top of the profile, a long period of weathering has produced fine soil. Deeper into the profile, weathering is just beginning to produce fragments which will eventually become sand.

    What does the profile suggest about the origin of soil?

    A. An accumulation of organic material leads to soil.
    B. The soil forms by the breakdown of bedrock.
    C. Soil results where much clay has been deposited.
    D. Soil requires an underground source of water.

48. Which of the following would provide the best evidence to support the theory of continental drift?

    A. The discovery on two continents of an extinct plant that lived around the time of Pangaea
    B. The similarity in DNA of an extinct species discovered on both the east and west coasts of North America
    C. The east coast of Africa and the west coast of North America showing a puzzle-like fit
    D. The disappearance of the dinosaurs during the Cretaceous period

49. Most deposits of ore that are rich in copper, lead, and zinc are believed to have been formed from hot-water solutions.

    Based on the information above, which of the following would not be considered a significant factor in exploration for these ores?

    A. Exploration based on identifying the magnetic properties of the ores
    B. Exploration based on recognizing the location of fissures and faults
    C. Exploration based on the fact that nearby rocks display intense changes due to the presence of water
    D. Exploration based on the fact that ore crystals contain microscopic bubbles filled with water

GO ON TO THE NEXT PAGE

50. Use the weather map below to answer the question that follows.

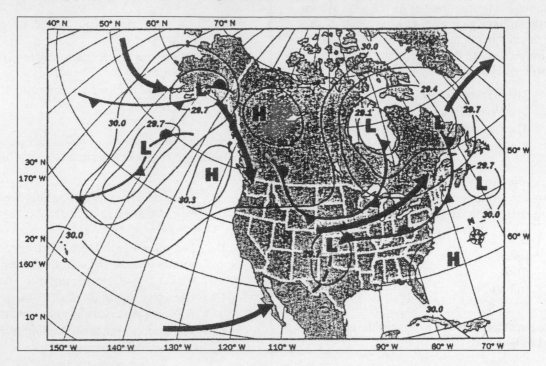

According to information presented in the weather map, the Great Lakes area of the United States is most likely to experience:

A. continued fair weather.
B. partly cloudy but fair weather.
C. stormy and inclement weather.
D. a rise in barometric pressure.

---

51. Which of the following statements correctly identifies the phase of the moon with what an individual would actually see during that particular phase?

Line	Phase	What You See from Earth
1	New moon	Moon is lit
2	First quarter	Half the moon is lit
3	Third quarter	Moon is dark
4	Full moon	Most of the moon is lit

A. Line 1
B. Line 2
C. Line 3
D. Line 4

52. What would be the most likely effect if the Sun, Moon, and Earth, in that order, were directly aligned?

A. Earthquake clusters
B. Increased gravitational pull on the tides
C. A lunar eclipse
D. Slight tectonic plate movement

Subtest II: Mathematics
Short Constructed Responses

Directions: Write your answers legibly on a clean sheet of lined paper.

Assignment 1

1. Use the right circular cylinder below with the dimensions given to complete the exercise that follows.

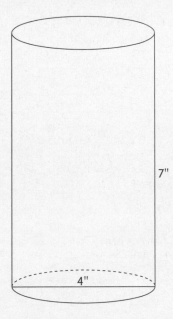

The right circular cylinder above has a base diameter of 4" and a height of 7".

Using your knowledge of geometry and measurement:

■ find the surface area of the figure above and explain the steps used; and
■ find the volume of the figure above and explain the steps used.

Assignment 2

2. Complete the exercise that follows.

$x^2 + 3x + 2 = 0$ is called a quadratic equation.

Using your knowledge of algebra:

■ solve this equation; and
■ explain the steps used to solve the equation.

GO ON TO THE NEXT PAGE

Subtest II: Science
Short Constructed Responses

Directions: Write your answers legibly on a clean sheet of lined paper.

Assignment 3

3. Use the diagram below to complete the exercise that follows.

THE HYDROLOGIC CYCLE

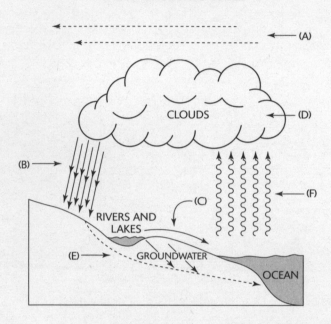

The picture above shows the various interrelationships that take place during the hydrologic (water) cycle. The following terms make up the water cycle: precipitation, evaporation, wind, condensation, percolation, and runoff.

Using your knowledge of meteorology:

- identify each element or process labeled (A)–(F) in the hydrologic cycle; and
- briefly describe the processes that show how water is constantly being recycled through the hydrologic cycle.

Assignment 4

4. Use the information below to complete the exercise that follows.

Gene expression for a particular trait is influenced by dominant and recessive alleles. In the following scenario, a blue-eyed individual marries a brown-eyed individual who carries only the dominant brown eye-color gene and no recessives.

Using your knowledge of genetics:

- identify a Punnett square describing the possible eye colors that can occur in the offspring of the above individuals; and
- explain why a baby with blue eyes can be born to two parents with brown eyes.

Subtest III: Physical Education Multiple Choice

1. To practice catching skills, a child should reach out for an object and then draw the arms toward the body as the catch is made. Which of the following mechanical actions is evident in the sequence of catching a ball described here?

   A. Determine the proper follow-through based on the force-production phase of motion.
   B. Bend the ankles, knees, and hips while visually tracking the object.
   C. Allow the force of the object to be absorbed over a longer period of time.
   D. Balance the center of gravity and the base of support to gain a mechanical advantage.

2. In tracking an object, the visual concentration of a primary-grade level child will dramatically improve if:

   A. the object is circular.
   B. the object is thrown to the child with an arc, or loft.
   C. the child is familiar with the rules of the game being played.
   D. the child has modeled the expected outcome.

3. The following lines identify fundamental locomotor, nonlocomotor, and manipulative motor skills. Which line does not correctly identify a skill associated with the appropriate category?

Line	Locomotor Skills	Nonlocomotor Skills	Manipulative Skills
1	Walking	Bending	Kicking
2	Sliding	Pushing	Twisting
3	Skipping	Stretching	Throwing
4	Hopping	Turning	Trapping

   A. Line 1
   B. Line 2
   C. Line 3
   D. Line 4

4. Before starting a strenuous activity, the instructor's methodology calls for completing a series of introductory warm-up activities. Which of the following would not be considered a beneficial effect of warm-up activities?

   A. Greater delivery of oxygen to working muscles
   B. Decrease in muscle viscosity
   C. Earlier onset of sweating
   D. Decrease in blood flow to the working muscles

5. An upper primary grade-level class is completing a running and aerobics unit. The instructor has used the FITT model (frequency, intensity, time, type) to develop her instructional program. According to the FITT criteria, what would be an accurate application of the principle of frequency in developing an aerobic conditioning program?

   A. Performing the activity a minimum of three days a week
   B. Maintaining a target heart rate during the activity
   C. Running continuously for a minimum of 20 minutes
   D. Increasing the duration of the activity

6. An important goal for young people is to increase the level of physical activity for health and wellness. The principle of overload is the basis for improving physical fitness. Which of the following lines correctly identifies the proper application of the principle of overload?

Line	Application of Principle of Overload
1	In order for a heart muscle to get stronger, the muscle must be worked against a load greater than normal.
2	In order to develop cardiovascular health, strength-building exercises are the key to fitness.
3	In order to increase flexibility, a muscle should never be stretched beyond normal length.
4	In order to develop a particular characteristic of fitness, one should never overload specifically for one particular fitness component.

   A. Line 1
   B. Line 2
   C. Line 3
   D. Line 4

GO ON TO THE NEXT PAGE

7. Which of the following would be considered the most significant obstacle of integrating other content areas into the physical education curriculum?

   A. It requires additional expertise in core areas, and physical educators are generally specialists in single subject area.

   B. It is not feasible to fit every subject into the physical education curriculum.

   C. It requires careful planning to integrate a content area in an appropriate time/context manner.

   D. It breaks down the disciplinary boundaries and provides real-world applications to current problems.

8. The best reason for a "start-and-expand" activity in a physical education program is to:

   A. provide positive reinforcement in presenting a particular skill-based lesson.

   B. introduce an activity at a low skill level and appropriately adjust the complexity of the skill.

   C. individualize a lesson based on the goals of the student.

   D. demonstrate a specific skill as part of an integrated unit.

9. The desire to enhance athletic performance has led to the misuse of diet supplements and the illegal use of controlled substances used to increase one's ability to exercise harder. Which of the following is *not* considered a side effect of a prolonged use of anabolic steroids?

   A. Reproductive abnormalities associated with infertility, including atrophy of the testicles

   B. Increase in the incidence of adult acne

   C. Adverse psychological effects

   D. Increase in HDL (high density lipoproteins)

10. In an upper primary grade-level physical education program, which of the following strategies would be least appropriate in developing effective prosocial skills?

    A. Allowing social expectations to determine group participation

    B. Reinforcing the reasons for rules and valuing success within the framework of rules

    C. Demonstrating activities that stress discovery and problem-solving

    D. Providing opportunities for students to discuss the limiting aspects of stereotyping in sports

11. A primary education teacher uses expressions such as "you guys" and "man-to-man defense" in introducing a unit on basic basketball strategies. The most important reason to avoid such expressions would be that:

    A. value-laden terminology would lead to children identifying themselves as "winners" and "losers."

    B. students would respond to teacher commands more quickly if the directions were given in a teacher-to-student neutral setting.

    C. opportunities to interact equally with both boys and girls would be restricted.

    D. boys and girls would be denied equal access to educational facilities.

12. An important goal of elementary physical education programs is to demonstrate cooperative skills during structured group physical activity. Which of the following strategies is likely to be most effective in forming upper-elementary groups or teams?

    A. Student "captains" select team members one student at a time.

    B. Teams are chosen based on a system of alternating gender selection.

    C. Poorly skilled students act as team captains in choosing team members.

    D. Teams are chosen by the instructor based on a child's skill abilities.

13. Professional physical educators are cognizant of the historical and philosophical developments that helped shape their profession. Which of the following is the most important influence of Greek culture on American physical education programs?

    A. The role of physical education in enhancing the health of women

    B. The introduction of competitive sports based on the Greek Olympic Games model

    C. The development of muscular strength and flexibility in fitness programs

    D. The pursuit of individual excellence in mind and body

Subtest III: Human Development Multiple Choice

14. A child learns to finger paint before he learns to paint with a brush. During preschool, when he tries to put his hands in paint, his teacher explains how to paint using a paintbrush. This process of taking existing cognitive knowledge and modifying it to fit a new experience is called:

    A. information-processing.
    B. equilibration.
    C. schemes.
    D. accommodation.

15. While thinking about an *imaginary audience*, an adolescent with average cognitive development thinks, "Everyone is looking at me!" Which of the following cognitive thought processes best describes this reaction from an adolescent?

    A. Adolescent egocentrism
    B. Adolescent social cognition
    C. Adolescent critical thinking
    D. Adolescent identity confusion

16. Ricardo is eight years old and his father is a culinary master chef. Based upon Ricardo's age, which of the following thought processes might he understand when he observes his father plan a dinner menu and instruct student chefs at the same time?

    A. He understands that his father can perform only one task at a time.
    B. He understands that it is possible for his father to perform two tasks at the same time.
    C. He understands that his father can think about abstract cooking ideas.
    D. He understands that his father must read recipes exactly as they are written.

17. Kindergarten students observe classroom pet chameleons changing their skin color to match a branch with green leaves. Which of the following responses best represents how most of the children will respond to the teacher's question, "Why do the chameleons change colors?"

    A. Because they are protecting themselves from danger.
    B. Because someone painted them green.
    C. Because they are communicating their moods.
    D. Because their moms and dads are green.

18. Which of the following statements best reflects the moral thinking of most children in grades K–2?

    A. Break the rules if you have permission from an authority figure.
    B. Break the rules if it supports a friend.
    C. Follow the rules to avoid punishment.
    D. Follow the rules to support a friend.

19. After studying soil composites, students are given an assignment to form a conclusion about the growth process of planted seeds in five different soil samples. Which of the following forms of reasoning might sixth-grade students use to help form their conclusion?

    A. Inductive reasoning
    B. Hypothetical-deductive reasoning
    C. Transductive reasoning
    D. Moral reasoning

20. A third-grade teacher refers a student to the school psychologist. The student is a gifted musician, but the teacher is concerned with his future academic success, since the student lacks the ability to pay attention and focus in the classroom. Which of the following assessments would most benefit this child and be the best predictor of this student's intelligence?

    A. Stanford-Binet Intelligence Test
    B. Wechsler's Intelligence Scale for Children
    C. Gardner's Theory of Multiple Intelligences
    D. Sternberg's Triarchic Abilities Test (STAT)

GO ON TO THE NEXT PAGE

21. Which of the following behaviors is the *best* example of a child exhibiting *autonomy*?

    A. The child demonstrates the ability to self-govern.

    B. The child demonstrates an easy temperament.

    C. The child demonstrates the ability to regulate feelings.

    D. The child demonstrates the ability to take risks.

22. Sherry is an eleven-year-old girl who is struggling with her science homework. She has difficulty mastering science concepts and has failed her last test. Based upon her psychosocial stage of development, which of the following negative emotions might Sherry be experiencing?

    A. Shame and doubt

    B. Feelings of inferiority

    C. Guilt

    D. Mistrust

23. Self-concept refers to a way of looking at our "self" within a frame of reference. When referring to a child's self-concept, all of the following statements are true *except*:

    A. a child evaluates his competence based upon internal values.

    B. a child unconsciously rates himself (e.g., smart-slow, strong-weak, attractive-unattractive).

    C. a child's self-concept is based primarily on a positive regard for himself.

    D. a child's self-concept sets the stage for the development of moral consciousness.

24. Mike and Alyssa are seven-year-old twins. Which of the following gross motor skills is Alyssa most likely to perform better than Mike?

    A. Balancing

    B. Running

    C. Kicking a ball

    D. Throwing a ball

25. Which of the following statements best illustrates the relationship between delayed language development and intelligence?

    A. Children with delayed language have below-average intelligence.

    B. Children with delayed language have parents with below-average intelligence.

    C. There is no correlation between delayed language and intelligence.

    D. Children with delayed language perform well on IQ tests.

26. Teachers have influential roles as sociocultural mediators in the classroom. Teachers can help to reduce cultural prejudice by teaching students to think critically and encourage:

    A. anger management.

    B. cultural segregation.

    C. academic achievement.

    D. emotional intelligence.

Subtest III: Visual and Performing Arts
Multiple Choice

27. An arabesque is fundamental in ballet. By definition, an arabesque is:

    A. a pose in which one leg is extended with a straight knee and pointed foot directly behind the body.

    B. a pose in which one leg is raised and bent either behind or in front of the dancer.

    C. a movement in which a dancer jumps straight up and rapidly crosses his or her legs before and behind each other.

    D. a movement in which a dancer completes a full turn on one foot.

28. The dances of Native Americans were a form of folk art that also served an important purpose for the tribe. This purpose encouraged dancers to be careful to maintain dignity and precision in their performance. Which of the following was the most important purpose that many dances served for the tribe?

    A. Providing recreation for the tribal leaders

    B. Seeking special favors from the gods

    C. Separating boys from men as warriors

    D. Discouraging enemies from attacking the villages

29. *Use the chart below to answer the question that follows.*

Line	Dance	Place of Origin
1	Flamenco	Spain
2	Rumba	Cuba
3	Samba	South America
4	Waltz	England

    Which one of the dances above is not matched with its place of origin?

    A. Line 1
    B. Line 2
    C. Line 3
    D. Line 4

30. A string quartet most typically consists of which of the following combinations of instruments?

    A. Violins, viola, cello
    B. Clarinet, viola, double bass, violin
    C. Violin, cello, harp, oboe
    D. Viola, cello, bass, double bass

31. The length in time that a note lasts is designated by:

    A. the shape of the note.
    B. the size of the note.
    C. the position of the note.
    D. the pitch of the note.

32. **Use the melody below to answer the question that follows.**

    Which of the following notes is represented by the *x* in the melody above?

    A. A
    B. B
    C. B flat
    D. C sharp

33. Which of the following is *not* a percussion instrument?

    A. Timpani
    B. Harp
    C. Castanets
    D. Xylophone

GO ON TO THE NEXT PAGE

34. Traditional Kabuki theatre developed in Japan in the seventeenth century. It still remains popular in modern Japan. Which of the following is *not* associated with this theatre form?

    A. All roles being played by male actors
    B. Elaborately choreographed struggles in which the hero maintains a "freeze" during the action segments
    C. Plots that often place the hero in an impossible moral dilemma but in which good wins out over evil in the end
    D. Actors not elaborately costumed

35. Blocking is a fundamental technique used by directors in staging a play. Which of the following is least associated with the initial stages of blocking?

    A. The scene-by-scene placement of the characters on the stage
    B. The gross movement of actors in a stage space
    C. The speed in which specific scenes take place
    D. The positioning of actors so that perspective is achieved by both upstage and downstage placement

36. Stage directions are always given from the point of view of an actor standing on stage facing the audience. From this information, which of the following would be considered an atypical stage direction?

    A. Exit stage right and to the audience's left.
    B. Move upstage and away from the audience.
    C. Move up center to a position in the center area of the stage farthest from the audience.
    D. Move downstage right to the area of the stage closest to the audience and to the audience's right.

37. In art, contour lines move across the form of an object to indicate:

    A. distance and space.
    B. mass and volume.
    C. solid and void.
    D. strength and stability.

38. **Use the reproduction of the portrait below to answer the question that follows.**

    Which technique does the artist use to give an illusion of depth?

    A. Natural lighting
    B. Atmospheric perspective
    C. Geometric perspective
    D. Obvious brushstrokes

39. Which of the following is the best example of a technique an artist might use to emphasize the shape of an object?

    A. Contour
    B. Pattern
    C. Unity
    D. Contrast

Subtest III: Physical Education
Short Constructed Response

Directions: Write your answers legibly on a clean sheet of lined paper.

Assignment 1

1. Complete the exercise that follows.

   Baseball is a traditional American sport. Baseball mechanics and skills are introduced in the early primary grades.

   Using your knowledge of basic movement skills:

   - define the proper mechanics involved in catching a ball; and
   - discuss two verbal cues an instructor can use in correcting the avoidance reaction in an early primary child.

GO ON TO THE NEXT PAGE

Subtest III: Human Development
Short Constructed Response

Directions: Write your answers legibly on a clean sheet of lined paper.

Assignment 2

2. Complete the exercise that follows.

   Eleanor Roosevelt said, "No one can make you feel inferior without your consent."

   Using this reference to self-esteem and your knowledge of cognitive and social development:

   ▪ discuss at least three important characteristics of self-esteem; and
   ▪ provide one example of an approach a teacher can take to help increase self-esteem among children in the classroom.

Subtest III: Visual and Performing Arts
Short Constructed Response

Directions: Write your answers legibly on a clean sheet of lined paper.

Assignment 3

3. Use the reproduction below to complete the exercise that follows.

Using your knowledge of visual art:

- briefly discuss the imagery associated with the subject matter of the painting above; and
- identify the specific techniques the artist used to achieve unity, balance, and controlled space.

Answers and Explanations for Practice Test II

Answer Key for Practice Test II

Reading, Language, Literature	History, Social Science	Math	Science	Physical Education	Human Development	Visual and Performing Arts
1. C	27. B	1. B	27. D	1. C	14. D	27. A
2. C	28. C	2. B	28. B	2. B	15. A	28. B
3. B	29. D	3. C	29. A	3. B	16. B	29. D
4. C	30. D	4. C	30. C	4. D	17. D	30. A
5. A	31. C	5. B	31. D	5. A	18. C	31. A
6. C	32. A	6. C	32. A	6. A	19. B	32. C
7. C	33. B	7. B	33. C	7. C	20. C	33. B
8. B	34. C	8. B	34. D	8. B	21. A	34. D
9. D	35. D	9. A	35. B	9. D	22. B	35. C
10. B	36. A	10. D	36. C	10. A	23. C	36. D
11. C	37. B	11. D	37. B	11. C	24. A	37. B
12. B	38. B	12. C	38. C	12. D	25. C	38. C
13. A	39. C	13. C	39. C	13. D	26. D	39. A
14. D	40. D	14. D	40. B			
15. D	41. C	15. A	41. B			
16. C	42. A	16. D	42. A			
17. B	43. B	17. A	43. B			
18. C	44. B	18. A	44. D			
19. C	45. A	19. D	45. D			
20. B	46. D	20. B	46. C			
21. C	47. C	21. A	47. B			
22. D	48. B	22. B	48. A			
23. A	49. C	23. B	49. A			
24. D	50. B	24. C	50. C			
25. B	51. D	25. B	51. B			
26. B	52. C	26. D	52. B			

See the Essay Checklist at the bottom of this page and the discussion of essay scoring beginning on page 9 to evaluate your short essays.

Analyzing Your Test Results

Use the following charts to carefully analyze your results and spot your strengths and weaknesses. Complete the process of analyzing each subject area and each individual question for Practice Test II. Examine your results for trends in types of error (repeated errors) or poor results in specific subject areas. This re-examination and analysis is of tremendous importance for effective test preparation.

Practice Test II Analysis Sheets

Multiple-Choice Questions					
		Possible	Completed	Right	Wrong
Subtest I					
	Reading, Language, and Literature	26			
	History and Social Science	26			
	Subtotal for Subtest I	**52**			
Subtest II					
	Mathematics	26			
	Science	26			
	Subtotal for Subtest II	**52**			
Subtest III					
	Physical Education	13			
	Human Development	13			
	Visual and Performing Arts	13			
	Subtotal for Subtest III	**39**			
	Total	**143**			

Essay Checklist

Compare your short constructed-response answers to the answers given. A good short constructed-response answer will do the following:

_____ address the assignment

_____ be well focused

_____ use key words ("buzzwords")

_____ show an understanding of the subject

For each of your responses, check to see if your answer fulfills the criteria above. Fill in the following charts with the number of criteria fulfilled for each essay to get a general idea of the effectiveness of your answer. These numbers do not represent a score but are simply meant to help you evaluate your response.

Short Constructed Response				
		Essays Possible	Criteria Fulfilled Response I	Response II
Subtest I				
	Reading, Language, and Literature	2		
	History and Social Science	2		
	Subtotal for Subtest I	**4**		
Subtest II				
	Mathematics	2		
	Science	2		
	Subtotal for Subtest II	**4**		
Subtest III				
	Physical Education	1		
	Human Development	1		
	Visual and Performing Arts	1		
	Subtotal for Subtest III	**3**		
	Total	**11**		

Subtest I: Reading, Language, and Literature Multiple Choice

1. **C.** Prediction questions are among the best text comprehension strategies because they actively engage the student in higher-level thinking. The teacher can use this strategy before reading a story or when the students are already involved in the story.

2. **C.** This question refers specifically to teaching English to non-native students. The answer you are looking for should include a "two-way," or "dual," approach to learning, such as in Choice C, *dual-language immersion*. This is an excellent approach to learning English, since it recognizes that children are cognitively, emotionally, and linguistically attached to their primary language spoken at home. Dual-language immersion encourages teachers to value both languages equally. Choice A, *English-immersion*, refers to an approach in which children are immersed in special English classes from the beginning. Choice D, *metalinguistic*, is not an approach to learning English; it is the ability to attend to language as an object of thought rather than only to the content. Another possible choice is *bilingual education*; though not mentioned in the answer choices, it refers to children being taught in two languages; first they learn in their primary language with others who speak it, and then they move on to regular classes in English only.

3. **B.** Phonology is the rule system within a language by which phonemes are sequenced, patterned, and uttered to represent meaning—the rules of producing phonemes in words.

4. **C.** Phoneme manipulative tasks, such as saying *pill* without the *p*, reordering phonemes in a syllable, or adding/deleting extra phonemes to a word or syllable correlate with ability to blend and decode words.

5. **A.** Teachers can help children who are challenged by difficult vocabulary by first providing them with easier reading material. Students should recognize approximately nine out of ten words in a challenging text, and recognize nineteen out of twenty words in an easy text for ninety to ninety-five percent reading success. In addition, teachers can use explicit instruction strategies to increase word recognition such as: using context clues, breaking words into parts, providing repeated exposure to words, and showing students how to use reference guides.

6. **C.** Reading success begins when children can recognize print in the environment and recognize simple letter shapes. These visual clues help prepare children to read. Choice C provides the best prediction of reading success in the first grade. Linguistic awareness includes knowledge of words, syllables, and phonemes.

7. **C.** Reading fluency is the ability to "decode" and "comprehend." The goal of all beginning reading programs should be to have all students comprehend grade-level material. The teacher should be sure that the students are given an opportunity to discuss the meaning of any words they might not understand, use strategies such as "literature circles" that promote discussion of text, support readers by tapping into any prior knowledge that relates to the story, discuss the pictures before reading the story, and give clues to the story line beforehand. Adequate reading comprehension is the ultimate result of effective instruction in reading. If a student is able to decode but not comprehend, the student is not able to enjoy and understand written language. The knowledge and active application of certain reading strategies is necessary for comprehension.

8. **B.** The greatest predictors of a child's success in beginning to read are mastery of the alphabetic principle, phonemic awareness, and understanding concepts of print. The *Reading Program Advisory, Teaching Reading* states that phonemic awareness skills such as rhyming, clapping syllables, substituting sounds, and blending phonemes are end-of-kindergarten skills that virtually every kindergartener must possess.

9. **D.** In this stage of spelling, the student is using confusing long vowel spelling patterns. The student is aware of how long vowels are represented but is using them incorrectly. The most generic activity for children in this stage is sorting word families. A sequence the teacher might follow when working with this skill is to: (1) focus on the spelling patterns of one long vowel; (2) compare and contrast short and long vowels; or (3) collect words that have the long vowel sound.

10. **B.** *Idiolect* refers to a linguistic system used by an individual.

11. **C.** The errors that this student is making show a lack of discrimination between two very similar consonant sounds. There are nine pairs of consonants (in English) that differ only in that one of the pair is quiet (unvoiced), and the other is heard (voiced). The nine pairs of consonants are:

/p/, /b/ pet, bet

/t/, /d/ tip, dip

/k/, /g/ cake, gate

/f/, /v/ fast, vast

/th/, /th/ thin, this

/s/, /z/ cease, seize

/sh/, /zh/ attention, measure

/ch/, /j/ hatch, Madge

/wh/, /w/ when, was

Some activities that would help this child include: (1) articulating phonemes; (2) looking in a mirror, and feeling the throat while articulating the sounds; and (3) reading and spelling contrasting pairs of words to establish the distinctions.

12. **B.** The paragraph must begin with the question in sentence 4, "Can an old or new faucet be dangerous." The sentences that follow attempt to respond and support this question. Knowing this, you can eliminate choices C and D because they do not begin with sentence 4. Sentence 1 immediately responds with an answer by stating "…it certainly can." Choice B is the only answer that follows the sequence of sentence 4, then sentence 1. To check your answer, read the paragraph out loud in this sequence 4-1-3-2. Remember the logical sequence of the passage must have a clear beginning, supporting ideas and a conclusion.

13. **A.** Probably the best way to start research on a current sports superstar would be to review a sports magazine, which would give you the latest information on top athletes. An Internet search engine would be helpful, Choice B, but some internet sources provide inaccurate information and may not be reliable resources for academic reports. An encyclopedia that gives you historical information about Hall of Fame athletes, Choice C, might be interesting, but you are looking for a current superstar, which means that he or she hasn't made the Hall of Fame yet. A sports record book, Choice D, would not typically give you important information about the current superstars; it would focus on listing athletes and records.

14. **D.** This type of question requires that you "fill in the blanks" based upon the context of the passage. Start with making a prediction about possible word choices in the blank spaces. The first blank space requires a conjunctive adverb showing a *continuation* of the author's thought from the preceding sentence. The poison is not a threat and "thus" and "furthermore," as in choices B or D, support that opinion. Next, notice that the second blank space requires a *contrasting* conjunctive adverb which expresses that an opposing opinion will follow. "On the other hand," "But," and "However" are all good choices, C, D, and E. The use of "Furthermore" makes it clear that the sentence about the EPA is part of the argument on one side. The "But" signals the shift to the opposition's point of view.

15. **D.** The phrase "late spring" is a metaphor for the speaker's age. Poets use figurative language, like metaphors, to enhance the meaning of a word or phrase. Metaphors tend to stir up a sensory "feeling" rather than a literal translation for a word. CSET test takers frequently see questions about metaphor on the exam. This poem refers to a man who is now in his twenties but has not yet produced anything noteworthy. Although it is not clear from the lines, the poet may be concerned that he has not yet written notable poetry.

16. **C.** Line 4 uses figurative language to create an image of a soldier's willingness to die in defense of England. The poet is speaking of the possibility of death in a foreign land. The poet answers this question by suggesting that the earth would be richer from an English death. Line 5 further develops this sense of duty.

17. **B.** The two stanzas of the poem metaphorically support England's entry into WWI. Each line develops a sense of duty and responsibility to protect an English way of life. The sensory details of the poem, "England's breathing English air," "pulse in the eternal mind," and "hearts at peace, under an English heaven," further develop the concept of the ultimate sacrifice (death) being honored.

18. **C.** The topic sentence is Line 3. To make a good croissant takes eleven hours. Making a good croissant is the main point, and the other sentences follow with specifics or alternatives.

19. **C.** As you read this passage out loud with the suggested insertions, it should be clear that Choice C is the best reponse. This response shows a beginning, middle, and end to the steps in cross-stitch. The addition of these three adverbs, which specify the order of the steps, makes the instructions clearer.

20. **B.** An online encyclopedia would be a good place to start. Getting background information is necessary before doing additional research.

21. **C.** The lines say that poets of genius and critics with true taste are both rare, so most criticism would be inadequate. Choice A is a tempting answer, since the first two lines say that we all believe our own judgments, but the poem does not explicitly say we should not do so, while Choice C is a logical deduction from lines 3–4.

22. **D.** As you look at all of the answer choices, notice that Choice D is the most comprehensive choice, describing the overall purpose of the passage rather than secondary purposes and implications.

23. **A.** The first line compares the sea to something that has been wrinkled and to someone or something that crawls without using *like* or *as*. These figures of speech are metaphors. A simile would use *like* or *as*; antithesis is a contrast or opposition of ideas; a paradox is an apparent self-contradiction.

24. **D.** Ishmael explains that when he is depressed ("grim about the mouth," "drizzly November in my soul"), he goes off to sea to stop himself from committing suicide ("substitute for pistol and ball").

25. **B.** Ishmael implies that he has strong moral principles; otherwise, he would be "stepping into the street, and methodically knocking people's hats off."

26. **B.** Since Ishmael has little or no money and nothing to interest him on shore, he picks up and goes off to sea. These would be the actions of an adventurer, Choice B. You know that he is not always at sea because at this time, he had nothing to interest him on shore. There is nothing to indicate that he is a responsible citizen except that he refrains from knocking people's hats off. Ishmael may get depressed, but seems to have a method to handle his depression. Melville is creating the image of an adventurer.

Subtest I: History and Social Science Multiple Choice

27. **B.** During the Golden Age of Athens, circa 500 B.C., the Greeks implemented a new government based on the principles of democracy. Citizens were allowed to hold public meetings, discuss political events, choose public officials, and pass laws. Greek democracy was based on the principle of direct democracy through majority rule. However, in actual practice, Greek citizenship was not extended to women, slaves, or foreigners. The Romans, Choice C, were instrumental in developing representative or indirect democracy based on earlier Greek models of government.

28. **C.** The dress and head ornament are representative of ancient Egypt. The falcon is symbolic of Horus, the son of Isis and the avenger of Osiris. The relative size of the two figures also suggests the significance of religious deities in the daily life of ancient Egypt. Horus is often depicted holding an ankh (a symbol of enduring life). Choice B is incorrect because neither object is representative of Mesopotamia, and nothing in the representation suggests a cult figure.

29. **D.** This question calls for recognizing accomplishments of ancient civilizations. The Phoenicians were one of the greatest seafaring nations in the ancient world. Geography explains the development of Phoenician civilization. They were desert nomads who migrated to the eastern Mediterranean in the area of present-day Lebanon.

   With little land to farm, the Phoenicians became sea traders and built the great trading cities of Tyre and Sidon. The accomplishments that would correctly match the other listed civilizations are the Egyptians and hieroglyphics; the Sumerians and the first written language; and the Babylonians, under Hammurabi, the first written code of law.

30. **D.** Knowing that the Aztecs were conquered by the Spanish in the sixteenth century would eliminate all other choices, making it last in chronological order. The Olmecs (circa 1200 B.C.) were the first civilization that developed in Mesoamerica, the area that includes Mexico, Central America, and the Yucatan Peninsula. The Olmecs became a strong influence on the development of other civilizations and were recognized for carving great heads of stone and developing a calendar. The Maya (prominent circa A.D. 250) followed the Olmecs and achieved a complex culture. Their accomplishments included the solar calendar, a great knowledge of astronomy, and an advanced writing system. The Toltecs (circa A.D. 900) preceded the Aztecs and were builders of great pyramids. The Aztecs (circa A.D. 1325) ruled a massive empire that was based on war and religion.

31. **C.** The map represents Europe in A.D. 500, shortly after the fall of the Roman Empire. The year 100 B.C. represents Rome shortly before Julius Caesar; A.D. 200 represents Rome at the end of the two-hundred-year *Pax Romana* (Roman Peace); and A.D. 800 represents the Frankish Empire at the end of the reign of Charlemagne. A key to identifying the time period of this map is recognizing the change in territory once controlled by Rome. Choices A and B indicate the expansion of Rome, not its decline. Note that the Byzantine Empire was not established until the fourth century; recalling this information would limit your response to just two choices, C and D.

32. **A.** The sale of indulgences was an immediate cause of the Protestant Reformation. Martin Luther objected to this policy on both theological and moral grounds, and these objections became the basis of the *Ninety-Five Theses*. After the *Theses* were circulated, Luther was excommunicated.

33. **B.** The statue is representative of a Buddhist priest at peace with himself. Among the beliefs of Buddhism are a belief in reincarnation, a belief that through meditation one can find freedom from suffering and enter Nirvana, and a respect for all living creatures. Choice D refers to the Islamic religion.

34. **C.** It is important to look carefully at all choices in association-type questions. Francisco de Coronado of Spain in 1540 explored the area that was to become the southwest of the United States. Ponce de León explored Florida in 1513 and claimed the area for Spain. Juan Cabrillo of Spain explored the California coast in 1542.

35. **D.** The objective of the Puritan migration to America (1620s) was to set up a Bible commonwealth. In practice, Puritan New England was a theocracy (a government by ecclesiastical authorities), with civil authority residing in members of the clergy. The social order and civil laws were predicated on religious concepts, with the Bible the overall regulator of society. Dissent was severely restricted.

36. **A.** The chart indicates that not all people were allowed to participate in government. Although the new state governments were the beginning of the democratic process, it is clear that only landholders were eligible to vote. There is insufficient evidence to support choices C and D. Note that the information in Choice B (that the executive branch was limited to three years or less) is *stated* in the table and that a stated fact is *not* inference. The executive branch was restricted in this way to keep it from becoming powerful enough to restrict the rights of the people.

37. **B.** Line 2 is the only choice that correctly identifies an advantage of both the Articles and the Constitution. The Articles of Confederation held the new nation together from 1781 to 1789. Recognizing the military's difficulties in raising an army during the American Revolution, the Articles provided for both declaring war and establishing a military. The Constitution provided for a strong central government with powers over taxation, interstate commerce, and eliminating the veto power of a state over legislation. The Articles did not provide for a *unicameral*, or one-house legislature (Line 1). The Constitution provided for a *bicameral* legislature, one with a House and a Senate (Line 3). The Articles did not provide for an independent judiciary (Line 4).

38. **B.** The right to an impartial jury is an essential ingredient of a fair trial and is protected by the Sixth Amendment. In recent history, the public's right to know, protected by the First Amendment (freedom of the press), has come into conflict with the Sixth Amendment. Lawyers have argued successfully that in certain cases, pretrial and/or trial publicity can jeopardize a defendant's right to an impartial jury. The courts are the final arbiters in maintaining a balance between First- and Sixth-Amendment rights.

39. **C.** The president has ten days (not including Sundays) to sign or veto a bill. If the president receives a bill from Congress during the last ten days of a legislative session and does not act on the bill (sign it or veto it), the bill automatically dies—a situation referred to as a pocket veto. If the president receives a bill from Congress and it is *not* during the last ten days of a legislative session, excluding Sundays, and no action is taken on the bill, the bill automatically becomes law without the president's signature.

40. **D.** In free trade, all products (foreign and domestic) can be traded without government regulations that restrict the free flow of goods. A protective tariff, on the other hand, is designed as more than a revenue measure. Its purpose is to restrict foreign products from competing with domestic products and thus encourage the expansion of domestic industries. However, in the interdependence of world economies, protective tariffs often invite retaliation in the form of restrictive tariffs on American goods.

41. **C.** Pennsylvania had 26 electoral votes and Ohio had 21 for a total of 47. The electoral vote of a state is equal to the number of votes the state has in Congress (House and Senate). Thus, the most populous states have greater representation not only in the House (which is based on population) but also in the Electoral College. It should also be apparent that in 1868, the most populous states would be in the northeastern and midwestern sections of the United States.

42. **A.** In the election of 1876, the Republican candidate, Rutherford B. Hayes, ran against the Democratic candidate, Samuel Tilden. Tilden won the popular vote but the electoral vote (which determined the presidency) was in dispute. Hayes was eventually declared the winner after the Republican-controlled Electoral Commission awarded Hayes all 19 of the disputed electoral votes in Florida, South Carolina, and Louisiana. Fearing a Democratic Party backlash, the Republicans reached a "compromise" which, in effect, ended Reconstruction in the South. Federal troops were withdrawn and carpetbaggers and scalawags were swept out of office. The Fifteenth Amendment, passed by the Radical Republicans in 1869, guaranteed voting rights to African-American men. Earlier, the Thirteenth Amendment (1865), which freed the slaves, and the Fourteenth Amendment (1866), which gave citizenship to the former slaves, were cornerstones of Republican Reconstruction legislation.

Practice Test II

43. **B.** The industrialization of the United States was essentially dehumanizing and impersonal. Technological innovations resulted in more efficient, labor-saving machinery, but as machines replaced workers and factories grew larger, the labor-management relationship became increasingly impersonal. The quality of urban life, as evidenced by slums, economic dislocation, alcoholism, and insecurity, was a conspicuous reminder of the dehumanizing aspects of the industrialization of the United States.

44. **B.** A trip from San Francisco to Lake Tahoe (adjacent to Nevada) would cross the following: Coast Range, Central Valley, and Sierra Nevada. The Coast Range extends in a north-south direction from northern to southern California. The Central Valley is the most productive agricultural area in the state and separates the Coast and Sierra Nevada ranges. With the exception of the Rockies, the other choices are part of the physical geography and topography of California.

45. **A.** This question calls for identifying the impact of water rights during a specific period of California history. Following the discovery of gold and the tremendous population increase in the mining towns, the importance of water in mining operations became critical. As gold became scarcer, the mining industry looked for innovative ways to make gold mining productive. The use of hydraulic pumps had a two-fold environmental impact on the Sacramento basin area. Water for farming became limited and the water routes became clogged with silt produced by the hydraulic pumps. River travel became more difficult and the practice of using hydraulic pumps caused economic consequences for both farmers and steamboat companies.

46. **D.** The diverse tribes of California utilized natural resources in adapting to their environment. The Chumash lived along the southern part of the coastal region. Salmon provided a staple diet for the Yurok who lived along the northern Pacific Coast. The warmer and drier climate of the Chumash lands limited the possibility for salmon fishing, and acorns became their main food. Tar was a natural resource available only on Chumash lands; it was used to waterproof canoes and cooking vessels. The dry conditions of the desert provided the impetus for the Mojave (not the Chumash) to develop subsistence farming.

47. **C.** The mission system did not accomplish its primary goal to establish a self-sufficient community capable of producing an agricultural surplus. The first missions were founded in 1769 by the Spanish. However, Mexico secularized all California missions between 1834 and 1836. The virtual land monopoly given to the missions as well as the forced relocation of the Indians ended with secularization. The Indians often found mission life intolerable due to a combination of culture shock, disease, cramped and forced living conditions, and the dictatorial and punitive policies of the Church.

48. **B.** The California Constitution provides for a 12-year term for Supreme Court Justices. Under the U.S. Constitution, Justices of the Supreme Court are appointed for life or while they maintain good behavior. California is prohibited by the U.S. Constitution from making treaties or establishing a post office. Only a majority of 51 percent is necessary to raise U.S. taxes, not two-thirds. In 1990, California passed term limits for members of the state Assembly and Senate. The U.S. Constitution does not provide for term limits in Congress. However, both the governor of California and the president of the United States are limited to two terms in office.

49. **C.** The most serious objection to the Japanese relocation program centered on the fact that race was the sole factor in the decision to intern the Japanese. American citizens of Japanese ancestry were interned without a trial, thus calling into question basic constitutional guarantees. However, at the same time, American citizens of Italian and German ancestry were not interned or held without trials. Choice A was a reason for the relocation program. Choice B indicates the cultural bias that faced people of Japanese ancestry living in California, but it was not the most serious objection to the relocation.

50. **B.** The governor of California has the authority to veto particular items from a spending or appropriation bill while leaving other items intact. This is referred to as the line-item veto. The president of the United States does not have this power. The president must veto an entire bill and does not have authority to reject specific parts of a bill. The line-item veto gives tremendous executive power to the governor.

51. D. The Mexican-American population of California dramatically increased throughout the 1920s due to the need for cheap immigrant labor in the state's vast, fertile agricultural areas. This was especially evident in the expanding beet and cotton fields of the San Joaquin Valley. Ironically, it was prejudice against the Japanese in the early twentieth century and their subsequent forced withdrawal from the agricultural labor market that allowed for the influx of Mexican workers. Unfortunately, the pattern of abuse and mistreatment of the "new" immigrant labor force continued in the decades that followed.

52. C. In March of 2007, Governor Schwarzenegger signed into law a bill that changed the date for presidential primaries in California from March to February. New Hampshire (a small electoral state), by holding its primary in March, has had a far greater impact on the direction of national politics than has California. In recent elections, both the Democratic and Republican candidates were basically determined prior to the California primary, in effect, disenfranchising California, the largest delegate state. Therefore, it was felt that by holding the primary on the first Tuesday in February, California would have a major voice in determining the course of national politics. None of the other choices would have a significant effect on national politics. The Electoral College, Choice D, is based on the congressional representation (House and Senate) of a state and has nothing to do with the date of a state primary. Based upon the 2000 census, in the 2004 Presidential election California has 55 electoral votes, the largest number in the United States. Texas has the second most votes with 34 and New York is third with 31.

Subtest I: Reading, Language, and Literature Short Constructed Responses

Assignment 1

1. Complete the exercise that follows.

   Using your knowledge of reading, language, and literature:

   - describe the common elements in nursery rhymes and explain why teachers use the genre in primary classrooms;
   - provide examples to support your answer; and
   - discuss one disadvantage of using nursery rhymes.

Sample Response

Nursery rhymes are a wonderful way to increase a child's understanding of the mechanics of language. Students hear the rhythmic sounds of words and this supports the teaching of phonemic awareness. Nursery rhymes also provide opportunities to acquire an oral language. Nursery rhymes lend themselves to music, since they have a tempo and rhythm. They reinforce the fundamental relationship between the rhythm of movement and the rhythm of sound. Nursery rhymes, like those featuring Mother Goose, were meant to be read aloud. Children love to chant them. They are also easy to memorize, and reciting them reinforces oral language development.

The experiences of children listening, reciting, and retelling nursery rhymes contribute to the development of language and an appreciation for literature. Nursery rhymes often have drama (for example, "Little Miss Muffet").

One disadvantage of nursery rhymes is the language style and vocabulary. Often, the archaic language limits reinforcement at home. For example, the terms "curds and whey," "sixpence," and "baby bunting" would not be familiar to children.

Assignment 2

2. Complete the exercise that follows.

   Using your knowledge of literature:

   - identify three major elements of the novel; and
   - discuss these elements.

Sample Response

Three major elements of the novel include plot, setting, and characterization.

The plot is the story line, including all the events and their connection to one another. The events may be presented chronologically or by other methods such as the flashback. Plot is often said to move from exposition to rising action to climax to falling action to resolution.

The setting includes the physical location in which the action takes place (for example, New York City), the time it takes place (for example, in December), and the historical era in which it takes place (for example, during World War II).

Characterization involves the depiction of the people of the novel, including both their physical and mental attributes. Characterization can be achieved directly by the author, who tells us about the person, through the eyes of another character, through the eyes of the character himself or herself, and through dialogue.

Subtest I: History and Social Science
Short Constructed Responses

Assignment 3

3. Complete the exercise that follows.

During World War II, the population of California increased dramatically. The population grew by more than two and one-half million people during the war years.

Using your knowledge of California history, prepare a response in which you:

- identify two specific minority groups that migrated to California during this period;
- select one of the groups; and
- explain how the group you have selected affected the war effort and changed the face of California society.

Sample Response

During this period, over 300,000 African-Americans migrated from the South to California in search of jobs. This movement became known as the Great Migration. In addition, over 200,000 workers came from Mexico to help fill farm jobs that were vacated when Californians went to war.

Approximately 750,000 Californians joined the armed forces during WWII. This created an unprecedented need for both skilled and unskilled labor to work in the aviation, manufacturing, and shipbuilding sectors of the economy. The Great Migration resulted in large numbers of African-Americans working in factory jobs during the war. By 1943, shipyards in California employed more than 280,000 workers. This resulted in substantial African-American population growth in cities such as Los Angeles, San Diego, and Richmond. Although racial discrimination was prohibited in defense projects, prejudice and discrimination were commonplace, especially in housing and education. Restrictive covenants were legalized to prevent blacks and other minorities from home ownership in white areas. The Great Migration did provide economic gains for African-Americans by establishing an urban, industrial work force and fostering working-class black communities. These communities would be in the forefront of the Civil Rights movement of the 1960s.

Assignment 4

4. Complete the exercise that follows.

In Egypt, as well as in all early civilizations, the influence of geography was a significant factor in the area's development as a civilization.

Using your knowledge of world history, prepare a response in which you:

- list three factors that demonstrate how geography influenced the historical development of ancient Egypt;
- select one of the factors you have identified; and
- explain how the geographical factor you have selected helped shape ancient Egypt's history.

Sample Response

Egyptian history began along the banks of the Nile River; and Egyptians depended on the river for sustaining their way of life. Egypt's naturally defensible borders of desert and sea generally prevented foreign invasion. Also, inventions and technology, such as the development of papyrus and surveying, were tied to geography.

Egypt is referred to as the "Gift of the Nile" because its history, culture, and religious beliefs are so closely tied to this river. Since Egypt has little rainfall and is mostly desert, without this river, Egypt would not have become an early cradle of civilization. The annual flooding of the Nile each September provided huge amounts of fertile soil for the development of agriculture and abundant water for irrigation along the Nile delta. The Egyptians learned to control the waters of the Nile and built a series of dams to bring water to the fields during the dry season. Because of the predictability of the flood season, Egyptians were able to plan for planting and harvesting. Inventions such as the shadoof (water-lifting machine), papyrus, and the calendar were directly connected to harnessing the Nile. A need for local government developed in response to the irrigation projects associated with the Nile—for example, complicated building projects such as dams.

Subtest II: Mathematics
Multiple Choice

1. **B.** $.062 \div .000002 = (6.2 \times 10^{-2}) \div (2 \times 10^{-6}) = (6.2 \div 2) \times (10^{-2} \div 10^{-6}) = 3.1 \times 10^{4}$. Scientific notation is written as a number from 1 through 9 times 10 to some power. Doing the division problem on a calculator gives a quotient of 31,000. Rewritten in scientific notation, 31,000 is 3.1×10^{4}.

2. **B.** Since the ratio of men to women is 5:3, there must be a total of 8 adults, or any multiple of 8. Choice B, 16, is the only choice that is a multiple of 8. For example, if there were 10 people at the party, there would be 5 men, 3 women, and 2 children. If there were 20 people at the party, there would be 10 men, 6 women, and 4 children. A ratio of 10:6:4 is the same as the ratio 5:3:2.

3. **C.** Since x times 231 is 231, then $x = 1$. Since 2 times $231 = 462$, then $y = 6$. Since z times 231 is 693 (remember, $y = 6$), then $z = 3$. So $x + y + z = 1 + 6 + 3 = 10$.

4. **C.** The fraction $\frac{1}{8}$ equals .125.

   When all the values given are expressed in decimal form, you have the following: $\frac{1}{8} = .125$

   Choice A: $\frac{1}{10} = .1$ and $\frac{2}{17} \approx .118$. The fraction $\frac{1}{8}$ does not lie between these two values since it is larger than each of the values.

   Choice B: .1 and .12. The fraction $\frac{1}{8}$ does not lie between these two values since it is larger than each of the values.

   Choice C: $\frac{1}{9} \approx .111$ and $\frac{2}{15} \approx .133$. The fraction $\frac{1}{8}$ does lie between these two values since its decimal value is larger than the decimal value for $\frac{1}{9}$ and smaller than the decimal value for $\frac{2}{15}$.

   Choice D: 1 and 8. The fraction $\frac{1}{8}$ does not lie between these two values since it is smaller than each of the values.

5. **B.** Note that all choices except B are larger than $\frac{1}{2}$. Choice B, $\frac{4}{9}$, is smaller than $\frac{1}{2}$.

   You could also have converted each value into its equivalent decimal form,

   $$\frac{3}{5} = .6 \qquad \frac{4}{9} \approx .444 \qquad \frac{7}{13} \approx .538 \qquad \frac{23}{44} \approx .523$$

   and then selected the smallest value, $\frac{4}{9}$.

6. **C.** The amount 240 out of 800 can be expressed as $\frac{240}{800}$, which reduces to $\frac{3}{10}$, or 30%.

7. **B.** $1 - \frac{3}{4} = \frac{4}{4} - \frac{3}{4} = \frac{1}{4}$ (the part of the year John works for his brother). The problem becomes that of finding the ratio of $\frac{1}{4}$ to $\frac{3}{4}$, which is expressed as

   $$\frac{\frac{1}{4}}{\frac{3}{4}} = \frac{1}{4} \div \frac{3}{4}$$

   $$\frac{1}{4} \div \frac{3}{4} = \frac{1}{\cancel{4}_1} \times \frac{\cancel{4}^{1}}{3} = \frac{1}{3}$$

8. **B.** If the price of the tie is x, then the price of the shirt is $3x$, the price of the slacks is $3x$, and the price of the coat is twice the shirt, or $6x$. Totaling the x's gives $13x$. Since the total spent was $156, $13x = \$156$. Dividing both sides by 13 gives

   $$\frac{13x}{13} = \frac{\$156}{13}$$

   $$x = \$12$$

   Therefore, the price of the pair of slacks, $3x$, is $3(\$12) = \$36$.

9. **A.** This question gives us information about part of a collection (24 paintings), and asks us to determine the whole collection (x paintings). A percentage is always a part/whole comparison: 30% means "30 compared to 100." Using these part/whole relationships, we can set up a proportion and solve for the unknown quantity:

$$\frac{\text{part}}{\text{whole}} = \frac{\text{part}}{\text{whole}}$$

$$\frac{30}{100} = \frac{24}{x}$$

Cross products:

$$30x = 2400$$

Divide both sides by 30,

$$\frac{30x}{30} = \frac{2400}{30}$$
$$x = 80$$

10. **D.** Since you are solving for $3x + 1$, simply subtract 6 from each side.

$$3x + 7 = 19$$
$$\underline{-6 \quad -6}$$
$$3x + 1 = 13$$

11. **D.** If Tom is four years older than Fran, and Fran's age is x, then Tom's age must be four years more, or $x + 4$. Therefore, since the total of their ages is twenty-four, Fran is 10 and Tom is 14.

$$x + (x + 4) = 24$$

$$x + x + 4 = 24$$

$$2x = 20$$

$$x = 10$$

12. **C.** Since a slope of –3 means that for every 1 to the right you go 3 down, or for every 1 to the left you go 3 up, you can see that point C is on the same line. If you draw a line from point C to point B, you see that you go 3 down and 1 to the right to get to point B. A common mistake is point E, which would be on the same line if the slope were 3, not –3. Remember, a negative slope goes down to the right; as x increases, y decreases or as x decreases, y increases.

13. **C.** By carefully reviewing the chart, you can see that $x^3 = y$, so (0,0) must be plotted. When x is 2, y is 8; when x is 1, y is 1; when x is –1, y is –1; and when x is –2, y is –8. The best plotting of these coordinates is graph C. Another method to recognize the answer is to consider the following:

Since (2,8) belongs with the graph, choices A and D are eliminated. Since (1,1) belongs with the graph, (2,8) needs to be much higher up than (1,1), which helps to eliminate Choice B. Hence, Choice C remains.

14. **D.** Solve the inequality by getting x's on one side of the inequality sign and numbers on the other. First subtract $2x$ from each side.

$$2x + 7 < 4x - 9$$
$$\underline{-2x \quad\quad -2x}$$
$$7 < 2x - 9$$

Next, add 9 to each side.

$$7 < 2x - 9$$
$$\underline{+9 \quad\quad +9}$$
$$16 < 2x$$

Finally, divide each side by 2.

$$\frac{16}{2} < \frac{2x}{2}$$

So, $8 < x$ or, written another way, $x > 8$

You could also have solved this inequality by arranging for all the x's to be on the left side of the inequality.

$$2x + 7 < 4x - 9$$
$$\underline{-4x \qquad -4x}$$
$$-2x + 7 < \qquad -9$$
$$\underline{-7 \qquad -7}$$
$$-2x \qquad < \quad -16$$

Now when you divide each side by –2, remember to switch the direction of the inequality.

$$\frac{-2x}{-2} > \frac{-16}{-2}$$
$$x > 8$$

15. **A.** The solution of two lines can be determined by the coordinates of the point at which the lines intersect. Lines l_1 and l_2 intersect at (2,4). Therefore, $x = 2$ and $y = 4$.

16. **D.** You could solve the quadratic equation by first factoring $x^2 + 3x + 2 = 0$ into $(x + 2)(x + 1) = 0$. Next, set each factor to equal 0 and solve.

$x + 2 = 0$, so $x = -2$

$x + 1 = 0$, so $x = -1$.

So, –1 and –2 are the possible values.

You could also have used a trial-and-error approach.

Notice choices A and B both have the value 2.

Replace x with the value 2 and see if the resulting equation is true.

$$(2)^2 + 3(2) + 2 = 0$$
$$4 + 6 + 2 = 0$$
$$12 \neq 0$$

Therefore, x cannot be 2, which eliminates choices A and B.

Since choices C and D each have –1, replace x with one of the other values. Try –3 from Choice C.

$$(-3)^2 + 3(-3) + 2 = 0$$
$$9 + (-9) + 2 = 0$$
$$2 \neq 0$$

Therefore x cannot be –3, which eliminates Choice C.

Hence, the answer is D.

Another method would be to simply plug in the choices to see which ones worked.

17. **A.** $\angle BCD = \angle A + \angle B$ (the exterior angle of a triangle equals the sum of the opposite two angles). Then $84° = \angle A + 63°$, and $\angle A = 21°$.

18. **A.** There are several approaches to this problem. One solution is to first find the area of the square.

$$10 \times 10 = 100$$

Then subtract the approximate area of the circle.

$$A = \pi\left(r^2\right) \approx 3\left(5^2\right) = 3(25) = 75$$

Therefore, the total area inside the square but outside the circle is approximately 25. One quarter of that area is shaded. Therefore, $\frac{25}{4}$ is approximately the shaded area. The closest answer is 10, Choice A.

A more efficient method is to first find the area of the square.

$$10 \times 10 = 100$$

Then divide the square into four equal sections, as follows.

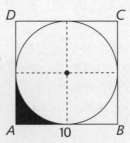

Since a quarter of the square is 25, the only possible choice for the shaded area is 10, Choice A.

19. **D.** Since the large square has sides that are 4 cm, its area must be 16 cm². By careful grouping of areas, you see that there are four unshaded, smaller squares and four shaded, smaller squares (match the shaded parts to four squares). Therefore, half of the area is shaded, or 8 cm².

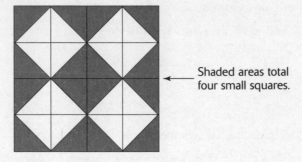

Shaded areas total four small squares.

20. B. Since there are 360° in a quadrilateral shape, $\angle DAB$ must be a right angle.

$$(100 + 40 + 130 = 270; \ 360 - 270 = 90)$$

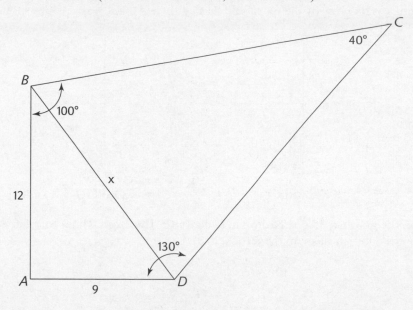

Since you are given two legs of a right triangle, you can simply use the Pythagorean theorem to find the hypotenuse.

$$a^2 + b^2 = c^2$$

Plugging in gives

$$(9)^2 + (12)^2 = c^2$$
$$81 + 144 = c^2$$
$$225 = c^2$$
$$\sqrt{225} = c$$
$$\text{So } 15 = c$$

If you noticed that the two legs were in the ratio of a Pythagorean triple (in this case, multiples of a 3-4-5 triangle), the problem would have been easier to solve. Since one leg was 9, or $\underline{3} \times 3$, and the other leg was 12, or $\underline{4} \times 3$, then the hypotenuse would be $\underline{5} \times 3$, or 15.

21. A. To find the volume of the rectangular solid, multiply all the dimensions together.

$$V = 4 \text{ cm} \times 4 \text{ cm} \times 9 \text{ cm} = 16 \text{ cm}^2 \times 9 \text{ cm} = 144 \text{ cm}^3.$$

This rectangular solid has six surfaces. Two of the surfaces are squares with sides of 4 cm and have an area of 16 cm² each. The other four surfaces are rectangles with dimensions of 4 cm, by 9 cm, and they have an area of 36 cm² each. The areas of all the surfaces are not equal, which eliminates Choice C, and exactly four, not three, of the faces are equal, which eliminates Choice D. This leaves only the evaluating of the surface area and the volume of this figure. The surface area is the sum of all the area's surfaces. Therefore, the surface area becomes

$$2(16 \text{ cm}^2) + 4(36 \text{ cm}^2) = (32 \text{ cm}^2) + (144 \text{ cm}^2) = 176 \text{ cm}^2,$$

which eliminates Choice B.

22. B. In order to have the pie graph represent blue-eyed students as 6 out of 24, the piece of the "pie" representing blue-eyed students should be $\frac{6}{24}$, or $\frac{1}{4}$. So the blue piece needs to be increased. Likewise, for hazel to represent $\frac{5}{24}$, its piece of the pie should be slightly less than $\frac{6}{24}$, so its size should be decreased.

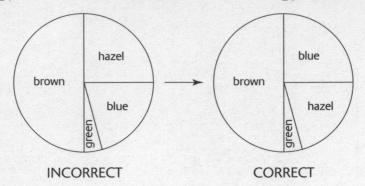

INCORRECT   CORRECT

23. B. Note that on the graph, a 35-degree drop in temperature (horizontal line) correlates with a 20% attendance drop (the fourth slash up the vertical line).

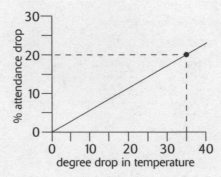

24. C. This is a weighted-average question. First multiply the five plumbers by the five days worked: $5 \times 5 = 25$

Next, multiply the six electricians by the six days worked: $6 \times 6 = 36$

Then add the totals and divide by the number of people, which is 11.

$$25 + 36 = 61$$
$$61 \div 11 = 5\frac{6}{11}$$

Since this is a weighted average problem, and there are more workers at 6 days than at 5 days, we would expect the answer to be between 5 and 6, but closer to 6. Being between 5 and 6 eliminates choices A and D. Being closer to 6 than to 5 eliminates Choice B. Hence, Choice C.

25. B. The probability of throwing a head in one throw is

$$\frac{\text{chance of a head}}{\text{total chances (1 head + 1 tail)}} = \frac{1}{2}$$

Since you are trying to throw a head *twice*, multiply the probability for the first toss ($\frac{1}{2}$) times the probability for the second toss (again, $\frac{1}{2}$). Thus

$$\frac{1}{2} \times \frac{1}{2} = \frac{1}{4}$$

and $\frac{1}{4}$ is the probability of throwing heads twice in two tosses. Another way of approaching this problem is to look at the total number of possible outcomes.

First Toss   Second Toss

H ———————→ H
          ↘ T

T ———————→ H
          ↘ T

The four possibilities are:

     H,H

     H,T

     T,H

     T,T

Thus, there are four different possible outcomes. There is only one way to throw two heads in two tosses. So the probability of tossing two heads in two tosses is one out of four total outcomes, or $\frac{1}{4}$.

26. **D.** There were four days (July 10, 11, 14, and 15) on which the maximum temperature exceeded the average. Thus, $\frac{4}{7}$ is approximately 57%. Notice that $\frac{4}{7}$ is greater than $\frac{1}{2}$, so the answer must be more than 50%. Only Choice D was more than 50%.

Subtest II: Science
Multiple Choice

27. **D.** Any material with a density less than that of the liquid it is in will float. Since water has a density of 1.0, the ice must have a density of less than 1.0 in order to float. The unusual shape of the ice is not relevant. Choice B is incorrect because the atomic structure of water and ice is the same (two hydrogen atoms and one oxygen atom). The formula for density is $D = \dfrac{M}{V}$

28. **B.** The diagram of Charles's law shows a direct relationship between the volume and temperature of a gas. The law states that higher temperatures cause gas molecules to move rapidly. As the temperature of a gas increases, and the pressure remains constant, the volume of the gas also increases. An everyday demonstration of this relationship would be to place a tied-off balloon, half-filled with air, in the sun. The sun's heat warms the air inside the balloon, causing the gas and balloon to expand.

29. **A.** The formation of rust is the result of a chemical reaction. Rust, by definition, is iron oxide. When atoms of oxygen in air come into contact with atoms in iron, a new compound results. Anything made of iron eventually begins to rust if left exposed to air long enough.

30. **C.** Aerosol cans are under high pressure. When the top button is pressed, gas escapes to the lower pressure in the surrounding air, "pushing" the product out of the pressurized can. If an aerosol can is heated, Choice B, the gases inside it expand, and in time, the expansion causes the can to rupture.

31. **D.** The diagram shows the decomposition of water by an electric current (electrolysis). The purpose of an electrolytic experiment is to break down water into its elements, hydrogen and oxygen. Each molecule of water contains two hydrogen atoms and one oxygen atom, so the decomposition of water gives off twice as much hydrogen as oxygen.

32. **A.** The weight of an object does not affect the rate at which the object falls. Two objects of different weights, if they have the same shape, fall at the same rate. This was the basis for Galileo's classic experiment involving the dropping of weights (purportedly from the Leaning Tower of Pisa). However, with objects of different shapes and weights, air resistance (wind and friction) does have an effect on the falling rate, as you could see by dropping a flat piece of paper from a height. (In a vacuum, there is no air resistance, and any two objects would fall equal distances in equal times. In a vacuum, a feather and a piano would both hit the ground at the same time; they would accelerate at a uniform thirty-two feet per second squared.)

33. **C.** Water pressure increases with depth; the deeper the water, the greater the pressure. In the experiment, the water near the bottom of the bottle has the force of all water above it.

34. **D.** Sound travels in sound waves, which consist of different layers of air pressure. When something vibrates, the air surrounding the object also vibrates. A windstorm could cause a bridge to vibrate at its natural frequency, which all objects have. Once the bridge begins to vibrate in this way, it could begin to sway, a motion that over time could lead to structural failure and eventual collapse. Soldiers marching in step or a large group of people dancing in step could potentially cause such collapses. The same principle discussed here also explains why some singers can shatter glass. By singing at the natural frequency of the glass, they create strong enough vibrations to break it.

35. **B.** When a magnet is broken in half, both pieces retain their original magnetic domains. There are many north and south poles that still face each other in the broken pieces. Even the shorter pieces still have strong north-south ends. Two like poles repel each other and two opposite poles attract each other.

36. **C.** Respiration is the central life process during metabolism. Oxygen is taken in, allowing stored chemical energy to be released. Respiration takes place within a cell. Photosynthesis, Choice A, is the process opposite to respiration. In respiration, an individual inhales air rich in oxygen and exhales air rich in carbon dioxide. In photosynthesis, green plants take carbon dioxide and water from the atmosphere and release oxygen, water, and glucose as by-products. Amoebas are protists that have nuclei, cytoplasm, and food vacuoles and can live in soil and water.

37. **B.** Chromosomes contain all genetic material. Inside each chromosome is stored the long DNA molecule that carries the coded messages that control all inherited traits. The chromosomes are in the nucleus of a cell. The cytoplasm, Choice C, makes up the majority of a cell and ranges in consistency from a fluid to a semisolid. There are many organelles in a cell, including the nucleus, chromatin, mitochondria, and ribosome.

38. **C.** Some of the key characteristics suggesting classification as a life form are metabolism, growth, respiration, excretion, motion, and most important, *reproduction.* Viruses can be classified both as living organisms and as chemical compounds. The fact that a virus can produce nucleic acids would argue for including it as a life form. Many nonliving substances can increase in size, Choice D; for example, metals and gases can expand, and rocks can accumulate as conglomerates.

39. **C.** All other choices are examples of symbiosis, a relationship in which dissimilar organisms live in close association. Such relationships may be beneficial to both organisms or just to one. For example, in the symbiotic relationship between whales and barnacles, the barnacle attaches itself to the whale, getting both transportation and protection. The relationship between a fox and a chicken is an example of a predator/prey relationship, not symbiosis, because the two animals do not live in close association. A fungus and an orchid plant are other examples of a symbiotic relationship. The fungus increases the amount of water and nutrients, which the orchid needs, and the orchid supplies the fungus with carbohydrates.

40. **B.** In a natural community, a balance usually develops, allowing organisms to exist and reproduce. Each plant and animal occupies its own niche. Choice A is incorrect because competition is an ongoing natural process. Choice D is incorrect because owls are nocturnal animals.

41. **B.** Adaptations enable organisms to better survive in an environment. It is to the advantage of each insect species to avoid being eaten, and many have adapted by having bright colors for protection. From the information presented, one could logically assume that monkeys have learned that insects with bright colors taste bad. Even insects that don't taste bad would then find that bright colors are helpful protection. In nature, many species mimic a potentially dangerous species in order to protect themselves. For example, the "eye" markings on a butterfly's wings may scare off potential predators.

42. **A.** Chromosomes contain all genetic material. Inside each chromosome is stored the long DNA molecule that carries the coded messages that control all inherited traits. The chromosomes are in the nucleus of a cell. The number and pairs of chromosomes would be an indicator to a genetic counselor if an abnormality occurs. Genetic disorders are caused by mutations, or changes in a person's DNA. In karyotypes, a picture of the chromosomes is analyzed for abnormal chromosomes. A karyotype can reveal if a baby has the correct number of chromosomes. For example, an individual with Down's syndrome has an extra copy of chromosome 21. Humans have 23 pairs of chromosomes. A male's sex chromosomes do not match (XY); a female's chromosomes match (XX). Choice B is correct but is not the primary reason for genetic counseling. *Genotype* is the genetic makeup of an organism, while *phenotype* refers to the physical characteristics exhibited by an organism.

43. **B.** The diagram clearly involves the photosynthetic process, in which green plants (producers) manufacture food. In the example, the major contribution of the plants is to produce the oxygen needed by the other organisms. Sunlight provides continuing energy necessary for plants to produce oxygen.

44. **D.** All planets and moons are visible *only* by the sunlight reflected from them. Only stars (suns) have an independent source of constant light, from the nuclear reactions taking place in their thermonuclear cores. All other planetary objects depend on reflected starlight to be seen. The exterior composition of a planetary object does, in part, determine how light is reflected. Mars is conspicuous for its red light, a result of the fact that the other colors in sunlight tend to be absorbed by the Martian surface. Choice C is incorrect because the statement deals with the core, which would not affect the reflected color.

45. **D.** The Summer Solstice is when the sun reaches its highest point in the sky and the earth is at its maximum tilt. The dates of zero tilt to the earth's axis correspond to the Vernal (Spring) Equinox and Autumnal (Fall) Equinox, which eliminate choices B and C. The Winter Solstice is when the earth is at maximum tilt, but the sun is at its lowest path in the sky, which eliminates Choice A.

46. **C.** The Richter scale is a common tool for measuring the strength of earthquakes. The Richter scale is based on measurements from seismographs. A seismograph traces ground motion during an earthquake. In the Richter scale, each ascending magnitude number (1–10) dramatically increases the potential for damage. For every point increase in the scale, there is an approximate 10 times increase in the amount of energy released. For example, from 4 to 5 would be 10 times as great, and from 4 to 6 would be $10 \times 10 \times 10$ times as great. A magnitude of 6 on the Richter scale would release approximately 1,000 times more energy than a 4 on the scale.

47. **B.** The information presented in the diagram and the statement is enough to answer this question correctly. The statement suggests that each soil zone is the result of a weathering, or breaking down, process in which bedrock is slowly transformed into fine soil material. Weathering may occur through chemical or physical processes and is a primary factor in soil formation.

48. **A.** Continental drift is the theory that all continents were once connected into a super continent. Through tremendous tectonic forces and millions of years, the continents gradually separated. The discovery of two extinct plant species on two continents would support the theory of continental drift. Continental drift explained puzzling evidence such as fossils of ancient plant and animal species found on continents on both sides of the Atlantic Ocean. Choice C should read "the west coast of Africa and the east coast of North America." Glacial evidence and distinct rock formations in separate continents can also be used to support the theory of continental drift.

49. **A.** The question calls for determining the correct answer based on the information presented in the statement. Therefore, only Choice A, which deals with the magnetic properties of ores, can be eliminated. The other choices are consistent with the idea that deposits of ore were formed from hot-water solutions seeping along underground cracks.

50. **C.** The markings over the Great Lakes indicate stormy and inclement weather. Generally, a low-pressure (anticyclone) area is associated with poor weather, and a high-pressure (cyclone) area is associated with improving weather. Temperature has a great effect on air pressure. Cool air is heavier than warm air. Cool air sinks down from areas of high pressure. Air always moves from areas of high pressure to low pressure. Warm air rises and produces low pressure near ground level. As cooler air moves down, it leaves areas of high pressure. When two air masses meet, a front develops and generally poor weather results. Note that a rising barometer (rising pressure) generally indicates improving weather and a falling barometer (lower pressure) generally indicates poor weather.

51. **B.** During the first and third quarters, half the moon is lit. The moon is dark during a new moon, and during a full moon the whole visible side of the moon is lit. The far side of the moon always faces away from the earth because the moon revolves around the earth in the same amount of time it takes the moon to rotate on its axis. The near side always faces the earth.

52. **B.** The gravitational attraction of the moon (and to a much lesser extent, the sun) causes tides. Since the moon is nearer to the earth than is the sun, the moon's mass attracts and distorts the oceans, causing the highest tides when the moon and sun are on the same side and aligned with the earth. A lunar eclipse, Choice C, occurs when the alignment is in the order sun, earth, and moon. An alignment of sun, moon, and earth would cause a solar eclipse.

Subtest II: Mathematics
Short Constructed Responses

Assignment 1

1. Use the right circular cylinder below with the dimensions given to complete the exercise that follows.

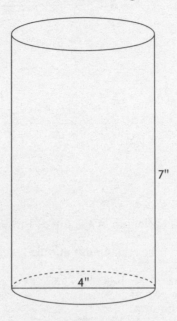

7"

4"

The right circular cylinder above has a base diameter of 4" and a height of 7".

Using your knowledge of geometry and measurement:

■ find the surface area of the figure above and explain the steps used; and
■ find the volume of the figure above and explain the steps used.

Sample Response

First, find the surface area of the top and bottom.

Remember, since the diameter is 4", the radius is 2".

$$A = \pi r^2 = \pi(2)^2 = 4\pi$$

Since the area of the top is 4π, the area of the top and bottom is 8π.

Next, find the circumference of the top.

$$C = 2\pi r \text{ or } \pi d = 4\pi$$

Now unroll the cylinder so it appears as follows:

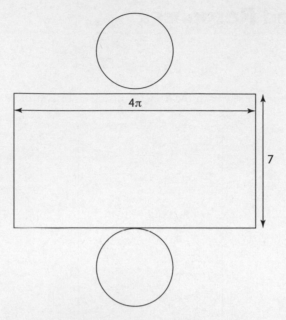

Notice that the circumference of the top is the length of the top of the unrolled side.

Next, multiply the length times the width of the rectangular unrolled section.

$$4\pi \times 7 = 28\pi$$

Now add that to the areas of the top and bottom.

$$28\pi + 8\pi = 36\pi$$

The surface is 36π sq. in.

To find the volume of the right circular cylinder, multiply the area of the top times the height of the cylinder.

Area of top = 4π sq. in.

Height of the cylinder is 7 in.

So the volume is 4π sq. in. $\times$ 7 in. = 28π cu. in.

Assignment 2

2. Complete the exercise that follows.

$x^2 + 3x + 2 = 0$ is called a quadratic equation.

Using your knowledge of algebra:

- solve this equation; and
- explain the steps used to solve the equation.

Sample Response

First, factor the first term, x^2.

This factors into $x \times x$.

Next, place the factors in the front part of each parenthesis:

$$(x \quad)(x \quad)$$

Factor the last term, 2.

This factors into 2×1.

Place the factors in the back part of each parenthesis:

$$(x \quad 2)(x \quad 1)$$

Since all the signs are positive in the originals, all the signs must be positive, so insert positive signs (addition signs):

$$(x + 2)(x + 1)$$

Check to make sure you have factored properly by multiplying the means and extremes together (outer term and inner term) and see that they total the middle term.

$$(x + 2)(x + 1) \rightarrow x \text{ times } 2 \text{ plus } 1 \text{ times } x = 3x$$

and since $3x$ is the middle term, the trinomial is properly factored.

Next, set each factor equal to 0:

$$(x + 2) = 0 \qquad (x + 1) = 0$$

Now solve each equation to get the answer:

$$
\begin{array}{rl}
x + 2 = & 0 \\
\underline{-2} & \underline{-2} \\
x = & -2
\end{array}
$$

$$
\begin{array}{rl}
x + 1 = & 0 \\
\underline{-1} & \underline{-1} \\
x = & -1
\end{array}
$$

So $x = -2$ or -1.

Practice Test II

Subtest II: Science
Short Constructed Responses

Assignment 3

3. Use the diagram below to complete the exercise that follows.

THE HYDROLOGIC CYCLE

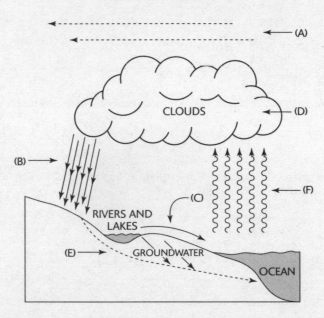

The picture above shows the various interrelationships that take place during the hydrologic (water) cycle. The following terms make up the water cycle: precipitation, evaporation, wind, condensation, percolation, and runoff.

Using your knowledge of meteorology:

- identify each element or process labeled (A)–(F) in the Hydrologic Cycle; and
- briefly describe the processes that show how water is constantly being recycled through the hydrologic cycle.

Sample Response

(A) wind

(B) precipitation

(C) runoff

(D) condensation

(E) percolation

(F) evaporation

The sun initiates the water cycle. The sun's rays warm the oceans, changing water into water vapor through the process of evaporation. Evaporation allows water from rivers, lakes, streams, etc., to escape into the atmosphere.

The moisture-carrying warm air rises to altitudes of lower pressure in the troposphere. The air expands and cools; the cooling results in the condensation of the water vapor, which forms into clouds. The clouds may be blown inland and cool further.

As the clouds become saturated, moisture is returned to the earth as precipitation (rain, snow, sleet, etc.). As the water is returned to the surface, the process begins again in a continuous cycle.

Assignment 4

4. Use the information below to complete the exercise that follows.

   Gene expression for a particular trait is influenced by dominant and recessive alleles. In the following scenario, a blue-eyed individual married a brown-eyed individual who carries only the dominant brown eye-color gene and no recessives.

   Using your knowledge of genetics:

   - identify a Punnett square describing the possible eye colors that can occur in the offspring of the above individuals; and
   - explain why a baby with blue eyes can be born to two parents with brown eyes.

Sample Response

	b	b
B	Bb	Bb
B	Bb	Bb

A dominant gene "masks" a recessive gene. In this example, brown is dominant over blue, and blue is recessive. A Punnett square shows the possible gene combinations in the example. A dominant gene is shown with a capital letter, while a recessive gene is shown with the lowercase of that same letter. Letters representing eye color are placed on the outside of the square. A pure brown dominance is shown as (BB), and a pure recessive blue as (bb). All of the offspring will be brown-eyed, but each will carry a recessive for blue because all offspring must receive one gene from each parent.

Two brown-eyed individuals can have a blue-eyed child only if each individual carries a recessive for blue eyes.

Subtest III: Physical Education
Multiple Choice

1. **C.** A rigid catching motion makes catching any thrown object, such as a ball, difficult to accomplish. When a person attempts to catch a ball, proper catching technique includes the following: the fingers are spread apart in a relaxed manner; the ball is caught with the pads of the fingers; and the ball is visually tracked until the catch is made. By bringing the ball "into" the body after initial contact is made, the force of the object can be absorbed over a longer period of time. This is easily demonstrated during an egg-toss game. A rigid catching technique results in a broken egg.

2. **B.** A young child's visual tracking is greatly improved if the child can easily see the flight of the thrown object. A ball thrown with an arc, or loft, allows additional time to adjust to any directional changes in the path of the ball. Other factors associated with visual tracking include the size and velocity of the object being thrown.

3. **B.** Locomotor skills are used to move the body from one place to another (running, leaping, and galloping); nonlocomotor skills are performed in place/stationary (swaying, rocking, and stretching); manipulative skills are based on handling an object (kicking, catching, and throwing). Twisting is a nonlocomotor skill.

4. **D.** Warm-up activities are designed to do the following: elevate the pulse to an aerobic level; speed up the onset of sweating, which reduces the risk of high body temperature during exercise; increase the breakdown of oxyhemoglobin, allowing greater delivery of oxygen to working muscles; and decrease muscle viscosity, which improves mechanical efficiency and power. Warm-up exercises *increase* blood flow to the working muscles. Injuries often result when connective tissues are cold and have low blood saturation.

5. **A.** For an exercise to be most effective, an exercise prescription must give specific instructions for frequency, intensity, time, and type. The FITT prescription for aerobic exercise is based on the following principles: F stands for frequency (how often); I stands for intensity (how hard); T stands for time (how long); and T stands for type (what activity). In order to improve cardiovascular endurance, research has determined that it is necessary to exercise at least three times per week with no more than two days between workouts.

6. **A.** Only Choice A is a correct statement. The principle of overload states that an individual must perform exercises in a greater-than-normal capacity (overload) in order to improve physical fitness and health. In order to increase muscle strength, the muscle must be worked against a load greater than normal. To increase flexibility, a muscle must be stretched greater than normal. Strength-building exercises may have only a limited effect on cardiovascular fitness. Overload is specific to each component of fitness and is specific to each body part exercised. Associated with the principle of overload is the FITT formula. For exercise to be effective, it must be done with the proper amount of *frequency* (how often), *intensity* (how hard), *time* (how long), and *type* (actual activity performed).

7. **C.** It is clear that an interdisciplinary approach to physical education is a desired outcome; however, the question called for assessing a disadvantage of an interdisciplinary approach to curriculum planning. To effectively integrate subjects across curricular lines, it takes careful planning of not just what material to include but also to determine when that material should be meaningfully introduced. Learning would not necessarily be enhanced simply because additional content from other subjects is included in the lesson. Choice A is not the best answer because in most elementary settings, the classroom teacher is also the physical educator. As such, the classroom teacher should have the expertise to integrate all subjects across curricular lines. Choice D is an advantage of a cross-curricular approach.

8. **B.** Start-and-expand techniques are based on the principle that the initial activity (start) should be so simple that all children can experience a measure of success in performing the skill. Expansion activities can be added to challenge capable students and to increase the complexity of the activity. Start-and-expand activities are most evident in beginning gymnastics programs. For example, an initial activity might simply involve jumping up and touching one's hands together while in the air. An expansion activity might involve jumping up, turning one's body, and clapping one's hands while in the air.

9. **D.** Anabolic steroids are derivatives of the male hormone testosterone. Athletes use steroids as "program enhancers" in that steroid use can increase body mass and muscular strength. The side effects of steroids are largely detrimental, including reproductive abnormalities, liver problems, increased body hair, and increased incidence of adult acne. Also, the potential for prolonged steroid use to induce adverse psychological side effects is well documented. High-density lipoproteins, Choice D, are actually decreased. Anabolic steroids and related compounds have been banned by the United States Olympic Committee and are considered controlled substances in many countries.

10. **A.** A physically educated person demonstrates responsible personal and social behavior in a physical setting. Prosocial skills help an individual get along in a group setting. Prosocial development includes learning to cooperate with team members, appreciating the efforts and abilities of others, stressing the value of competition, and learning not to focus on winning or losing. Differentiating group assignments based on social expectations could lead to reinforcing gender-based (male and female) negative stereotyping. Society often expects males to be better athletes than females. Males and females all have the ability to learn physical skills.

11. **C.** Recognizing and eliminating gender inequities is an important goal for all physical educators. Teachers should be aware that gender-biased language could reinforce negative stereotyping. Research studies indicate that in most physical education programs, male students receive more attention and feedback. Teachers often subconsciously call on males more frequently than females. By substituting gender-neutral language in defining skills or in discussing physical education goals, opportunities to interact equally with males and females would be enhanced.

12. **D.** Physical educators develop instructional strategies to promote acceptance of individual strengths and differences. When students are empowered to choose teams, team members are often chosen based on superior athletic ability. Publicly selecting team members often exposes lower-skilled students to ridicule. Forming teams on the basis of gender can pit boys against girls. Allowing a poorly skilled individual to act as team captain only provides a short-term self-esteem benefit. The most appropriate strategy in choosing equitable teams is for the teacher to choose teams based on the teacher's knowledge of student skills. Forming teams in such a manner preserves the self-respect of every child.

13. **D.** Physical educators need to understand how and why sport has changed over time. The influence of ancient Greek culture on sport is profound. The ancient Greeks believed in the physical development of the body and in the importance of athletics in attaining physical perfection. The health of the mind was considered interconnected to the health of the body. Physical education today stresses this concept (healthy body/healthy mind). Examples include the emphasis on wellness in a comprehensive physical education program and selecting physical activities to attain an active and healthy lifestyle. Choice B is incorrect, since the Olympic Games model was based on athletic competition and religious practice.

Subtest III: Human Development Multiple Choice

14. **D.** According to Jean Piaget, children move through stages of development, adapting existing cognitive structures (schemes) in order to function more effectively. Children incorporate new information with old schemes (assimilation), and adjust old schemes or create new ones to fit the new experience (accommodation).

15. **A.** During adolescence, there is an amplified self-consciousness. Although it is difficult to determine why adolescents become egocentric, a few explanations are: (1) the adolescent's ability to think abstractly (i.e., think about love), although they may lack the broader perspective that is attained only through life experience; (2) the adolescent's development of identity; and (3) the increased social demands that lead adolescents to feel that they are unique and that their feelings are not universal. David Elkind proposes two types of adolescent social thinking—imaginary audience ("everyone is looking at me") and personal fable ("my problems are unique and/or I am invincible").

16. **B.** A third-grade student is no longer egocentric and has the ability to focus on more than one piece of information at a time. This is the beginning of Piaget's period of concrete operational thought; Ricardo is no longer limited to thought by centration and he understands that people can perform two tasks at one time. Choice C is a skill Ricardo will master during the next period of formal operational thought.

17. **D.** Choices A and C can be eliminated immediately since they indicate answers from an older, more mature child. Older children have the ability to reason logically and appeal to natural science to explain this phenomenon. Children do not have the ability to form logical cause-and-effect reasoning until they are about ten years old. Causal reasoning changes over time and preoperational children give reasonable, and sometimes "invented" explanations when they don't understand a plausible cause. A five-year old often responds based upon an "omnipotent or authority" force, such as in Choice D. Choice B is an excellent possible answer for a preschool child, since a preschool child's reality is formed by appearance. Since the chameleons changed in front of the students, however, this answer is not possible.

18. **C.** Moral decision-making evolves through a series of developmental stages. According to Lawrence Kohlberg, moral development progresses in children from concrete (e.g., young children believing that good actions are rewarded and bad actions are punished) to abstract (e.g., individuals looking within themselves

for answers). At this preconventional level of morality, young children, grades K–2, are encouraged to obey for fear of punishment.

19. **B.** Hypothetical-deductive reasoning best describes an adolescent's ability to "figure out" or "reason with known facts." Adolescents create a hypothesis to form a conclusion from a given general theory. Younger children reason with inductive or transductive reasoning, but it is not until adolescence that hypothetical-deductive reasoning is possible.

20. **C.** High intelligence in one area is not necessarily accompanied by high intelligence in other areas. Traditional tests to measure IQ, such as Choice B, Wechsler's Intelligence Scale for Children, are fairly good predictors of school success; however, this IQ test may be unfair to many students in determining multiple intelligences. Most IQ tests measure only three types of intelligences: linguistic, logical-mathematical, and some spatial. Howard Gardner, in his theory of multiple intelligences, investigates the "many kinds of minds." This theory is a better predictor of human potential. It recognizes potential in intelligence types such as language, music, logic, spatial, kinesthetic, interpersonal, and intrapersonal, which encourage multiple domains as defined in terms of culture or society. Choice D is an excellent alternative to traditional IQ testing since it tests analytical, creative, and practical intelligence, but before making any predictions, it is best to consider the multiple intellectual strengths of the child.

21. **A.** As children mature emotionally and cognitively, they naturally seek a level of self-reliance. It is a shift from an external control by the parents to a balance of independence and self-control in the child. According to Erikson, young children strive to gain this independence as early as one to three years old. Another critical period in which children strive to be autonomous is during adolescence.

22. **B.** According to Erikson's Stages of Psychosocial Development, Sherry is confronting an age-related crisis known as *industry versus inferiority,* ages 7–11. At this stage of development, children acquire the competency and skill to build self-esteem. If she is successful at establishing a sense of *industry,* she will gain recognition so that she can continue to do good work. This helps her to develop a sense of accomplishment to successfully tackle future tasks. The contrast is *inferiority,* which will leave Sherry with a sense of inadequacy and incompetence. Choices A, C, and D are negative outcomes of Erikson's other psychosocial stages of development confronted at younger ages.

23. **C.** The concept of "self" consists of impressions and an appraisal of our self-image. Since the impressions are not always positive, Choice C is not true. The development of self begins in young children as they look into the mirror and become more aware of their physical self. As children grow older, in elementary school they begin a process of self-evaluation by learning to describe themselves. As this maturation process continues, children are able to emotionally respond to the world by reflecting what they perceive as the "real" image of themselves. This vision is often viewed as internal values and moral consciousness.

24. **A.** There are significant physical development changes that take place among children during elementary school. At age seven, most girls are typically shorter and weigh less than boys. Most boys have greater leg and arm muscle coordination, making it possible for them to jump, run, and throw farther. Girls have an advantage with coordinated hand-manipulated skills and balance.

25. **C.** Although delayed language may be an indication of a child's learning disability, there is no concrete evidence supporting a correlation between delayed language and intelligence. The best example to support this lack of correlation is perhaps illustrated by Albert Einstein, who did not speak until he was three years old. Boys are more likely than girls to be late talkers. Intelligence expressed in multiple dimensions is best supported by Howard Gardner's theory of multiple intelligences. Most children have multiple cognitive strengths, and high intelligence in one area is not necessarily a predictor of a high IQ.

26. **D.** Cultural prejudice is a narrow-minded view of a targeted group. Anger management, Choice A, will help to temporarily solve individual disputes, but Choice D, emotional intelligence, provides children with a much broader interethnic understanding of the world. Emotionally intelligent children are better at understanding different perspectives, are better listeners, express mature cognitive-emotional feelings, and are more motivated to share and cooperate with other children.

Subtest III: Visual and Performing Arts Multiple Choice

27. **A.** An arabesque is a pose in which one arm is extended in front and the other arm and one leg are extended behind, with the leg straight and the toe pointed. Choice B refers to an attitude pose, Choice C to an entrechat jump, and Choice D to a pirouette.

28. **B.** Probably the most important purpose of Native American dance was to seek special favors from the gods. The dances were of serious religious significance as the dancers addressed the gods. They prayed for rain, sun, crops, etc. The dancers were careful to maintain dignity and precision in their performance in hope that their prayers would be answered.

29. **D.** The waltz, a ballroom dance for couples, originated in Germany. All of the others are properly matched.

30. **A.** A quartet is a musical ensemble consisting of four instruments or singers. The string quartet typically consists of a first violin, a second violin, a viola, and a cello. Music written specifically for the string quartet is quite common, such as that by Mozart, Haydn, and Mendelssohn.

31. **A.** The shape of a note or rest indicates the time value. Whole notes have an open oval shape. Half notes have an open oval shape with a stem. Notes with shorter time values have a solid oval shape with a stem. One or more flags are attached to the stem to make the note last an even shorter time.

32. **C.** The note represented by the x is B flat. At first it appears that the note is B, but you must take the context of the complete work into consideration and notice that a key signature is used to indicate the B is flat throughout the work. Notice the flat symbols next to the treble clef.

33. **B.** Percussion instruments include any instrument that produces a sound when it is being hit, shaken, rubbed, or scraped. Percussion instruments include a piano, timpani, xylophone, cymbals, and castanets. Choice B, harp, is a string instrument since it can be plucked or strummed.

34. **D.** Kabuki is vibrant, energetic, and interactive theatre. A characteristic of Kabuki is its use of elaborate costumes. Actors often wear layers of clothing that can be removed at critical points in the play to reveal changing or "new" characters. Other characteristics of Kabuki include the following: (1) The actors do not use masks but rely on heavy make-up to develop characterization. (2) The plots are generally complex. (3) Virtue is rewarded. (4) The actors strike a mie stance (a stationary pose) to direct the audience's attention to a key point in the play. (5) The plays last all day. (6) All roles are played by men (women being banned from the stage as undesirable elements). (7) Violent action is displayed in picturesque settings.

35. **C.** In the early stages of blocking, a director would be least concerned with the speed of a specific scene. This refinement would be one of the final rehearsal adjustments. In blocking during rehearsals, a director choreographs the position of actors on the stage and is initially concerned with the actors' gross stage movements. As the rehearsals go on, more specific blocking refinements are made. When blocking on one scene is complete, the director continues the process until all scenes have been blocked.

36. **D.** Stage geography can be defined with five basic terms: upstage, downstage, center stage, stage right, and stage left. The description of each area can be further refined—for example, down center ("down" or "up" is used with "center") or upstage right. The information given in the question tells you that all stage directions are from the point of view of an actor standing on stage facing the audience. So the only atypical (not normal) direction is Choice D. Downstage right is the area closest to the audience, but it is to the audience's left (the actor's right).

37. **B.** Mass is shown in art by the use of a line to indicate contour. A contour line separates an area from its surrounding background. Since contour lines follow both the interior and exterior structure, they can indicate shadows and textures.

38. **C.** The straight lines of the window obey the laws of geometric perspective. Parallel lines seem to converge to a point in the distance, the vanishing point. This technique gives a very convincing illusion of depth.

39. **A.** *Shape* is defined as a continuous line that meets to form an object. The use of *contour* line (line drawing) is a technique that helps to create the visual experience of shape and form without using shading or texture. By changing the thickness and darkness of a contour line, an ordinary shape can be transformed into a three-dimensional object.

Subtest III: Physical Education
Short Constructed Response

Assignment 1

1. Complete the exercise that follows.

   Baseball is a traditional American sport. Baseball mechanics and skills are introduced in the early primary grades.

   Using your knowledge of basic movement skills at the early primary grades:

   - define the basic mechanics involved in catching a thrown ball without a glove; and
   - discuss two verbal cues an instructor can use in correcting the avoidance reaction in an early primary child.

Sample Response

In the early primary grades, a child is 6 to 8 years old. There are three components involved in the proper mechanics of catching a ball. The first technique involves proper head action. The child can demonstrate this technique by following the ball from the point of release to the final contact. The second technique involves proper arm action. The child can demonstrate this technique by holding his/her arms bent at the elbows with the arms relaxed at the sides or in front of the body in preparation for the throw. The third technique involves hand action. This technique can be demonstrated as a child cups both his/her hands together in an open and relaxed manner as the ball is received with the pads of the fingers. Drawing the ball inward toward the center of the body reduces the force of the ball.

Many early primary children are fearful of receiving a thrown ball. The avoidance reaction is turning one's face away from the thrown ball or closing one's eyes when contact with the ball is made. Two verbal cues that an instructor can use in correcting the avoidance reaction would be to say "watch the ball until it touches your hands" and "keep your arms and hands in the ready position."

Subtest III: Human Development
Short Constructed Response

Assignment 2

2. Complete the exercise that follows.

   Eleanor Roosevelt said, "No one can make you feel inferior without your consent." Using this reference to self-esteem and your knowledge of cognitive and social development:

   - discuss at least three important characteristics of self-esteem; and
   - provide one example of an approach a teacher can take to help increase self-esteem among children in the classroom.

Sample Response

Children who have high self-esteem are motivated to achieve, express confidence, express a sense of self-worth, feel a sense of belonging, and generally feel a sense of being valued and accepted by others. In general, children with high self-esteem have "good feelings" about themselves. The higher the self-esteem, the more successful a child is in dealing with life so that "no one can make a child with high self-esteem feel inferior." The emotional and social advances children make toward high self-esteem are synergistic. That is, self-esteem is cognitively stimulated through emotional and social rewards to further increase self-esteem. Self-esteem has a direct correlation to behavior among children.

One approach to improving self-esteem is for teachers to listen carefully to each child while focusing on at least one positive attribute within each child. Students' accomplishments should be recognized and encouraged. A teacher's positive regard for children helps children have a high positive regard for themselves. This effective approach helps children feel valued and respected for their individual strengths and opinions.

Subtest III: Visual and Performing Arts Short Constructed Response

Assignment 3

3. Use the reproduction below to complete the exercise that follows.

Using your knowledge of visual art:

- briefly discuss the imagery associated with the subject matter of the painting; and
- identify the specific techniques the artist used to achieve unity, balance, and controlled space.

Sample Response

The imagery associated with this painting is that of a religious setting. The artist is depicting religious symbols, not reality—notice the halos and wings. The angels are placed on each side of the large central figure, the Madonna.

There are a number of different techniques that the artist uses to achieve unity, balance, and controlled space. Since all of the figures are tightly placed around the centered Madonna, there seems to be a unity of purpose. All of the expressions are stoic and the gestures stilted. The repetitive shapes of halos and wings also show a unity. The centering of the Madonna and the three vertical rows gives the painting a balance. The three angels on each side of the Madonna (and child) also show some symmetry in balancing the painting. The artist shows control of the space by making the painting flat, linear, and, as mentioned, balanced. The figures overlap, but there is a lack of depth. The artist has carefully placed all of the elements to convey a formal, spiritual, religious setting.

PART III

APPENDICES

Charts, Graphs, Maps, Cartoons, and Diagrams

Some questions on the CSET: Multiple Subjects require you to understand and use information given in charts, graphs, maps, cartoons, and diagrams. The following section will give you some insight into how to approach these question types.

Charts, Tables, and Graphs

Strategies

A chart, table, or graph is given so that you can refer to it. Look for trends or changing patterns that might appear. Also, look for additional information and key words or headings that are included. In dealing with this type of question, you should do the following:

- Focus on understanding the important information in the chart, table, or graph.
- Don't memorize the information; refer to it when you need to.
- Sometimes, skimming the questions first can be helpful. This will tell you what to look for.
- Quickly, but carefully, examine the whole graph and all additional information before you start to answer questions. Make sure that you understand the information given.
- Read the question or questions and possible choices, and notice the key words. Decide on your answer from the information given.
- Sometimes, the answer to a question is available in extra information given with a graph (headings, scale factors, legends, etc.). Be sure to read and understand this information.
- Look for the obvious large changes, high points, low points, trends, etc. Obvious information often leads to an answer. Unless you are told otherwise, use only the information given in the chart or graph.

Chart and Table Examples

Charts and tables are often used to give an organized picture of information or data. Be sure that you understand *what is given*. Column headings and line items give the important information. These titles give the numbers meaning.

Mathematics

Use the table below to answer the question that follows.

Burger Sales for the Week of August 8–14		
Day	**Hamburgers**	**Cheeseburgers**
Sunday	120	92
Monday	85	80
Tuesday	77	70
Wednesday	74	71
Thursday	75	72
Friday	91	88
Saturday	111	112

1. If the pattern of sales continues:

   A. the weekend days will have the fewest number of burger sales next week.
   B. the cheeseburgers will outsell hamburgers next week.
   C. generally, when hamburger sales go up, cheeseburger sales will go up.
   D. hamburgers will be less expensive than cheeseburgers.

The correct answer is C. To answer this question, you must notice one of the trends. Most days that hamburger sales go up, cheeseburger sales go up (with the exception of Saturday and Sunday). If you cannot recognize the correct answer, see if you can eliminate some choices. Since weekend sales were greater than weekday sales, Choice A would be incorrect. Since cheeseburgers only outsold hamburgers once during the week, Choice B would be incorrect. Since the chart made no indication of how expensive either type of burger is, Choice D would be incorrect.

Science

Use the chart below to answer the question that follows.

Temperature of Objects in °C	
Absolute zero	−273
Oxygen freezes	−218
Oxygen liquefies	−183
Water freezes	0
Human body	37
Water boils	100
Wood fire	830
Iron melts	1,535
Iron boils	3,000

2. As shown in the table above, the difference in temperature between the point at which oxygen freezes and the point at which iron melts is:

   A. 1,317°
   B. 1,535°
   C. 1,718°
   D. 1,753°

The correct answer is D. To answer this question, you must be able to read the chart and do some simple calculations. The freezing temperature of oxygen is −218° Celsius. Iron melts at 1,535° Celsius. To find the difference between the two, you must subtract:

$$1,535 - (-218) = 1,535 + 218 = 1,753$$

Graphs

Information may be displayed in many ways. The three basic types of graphs you should know are bar graphs, line graphs, and circle graphs (or pie charts).

Bar Graph Example

Bar graphs convert the information in a chart into separate bars or columns. Some graphs list numbers along one edge and places, dates, people, or things (individual categories) along another edge. Always try to determine the *relationship* between the columns in a graph or chart.

Science

Use the graph below to answer the question that follows.

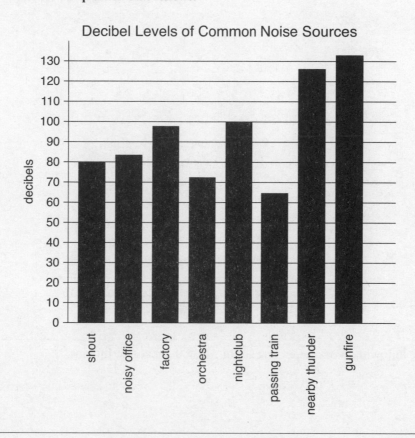

3. The graph above shows the average decibel levels associated with various common sources of noise. Listening to high levels of noise for a long time can damage the eardrum and cause loss of hearing.

   According to the graph, which of the following sources of noise would be most likely to damage the eardrum?

   A. an orchestra
   B. a passing train
   C. nearby thunder
   D. gunfire

The correct answer is D. To answer this question, you must be able to read the graph and understand the information included. Notice that the decibels of noise are listed along the left side in increments of 10. The common sources of noise are listed along the bottom of the graph. Since gunfire has the highest decibel rating, it is usually the loudest of the choices. This would cause it to be the most likely to damage the eardrum.

Line Graph Examples

Line graphs convert data into points on a grid. Notice the slopes of lines connecting the points. These lines show increases and decreases. The <u>steeper</u> the line slants *upward towards the right*, the greater the *increase*. The <u>steeper</u>

561

the line slants *downward towards the right*, the greater the *decrease*. Line graphs can show trends, or changes in data over a period of time.

History/Social Science

Use the graph below to answer the two questions that follow.

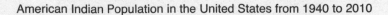
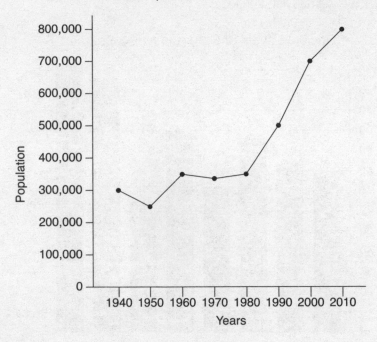

American Indian Population in the United States from 1940 to 2010

---

4. In which of the following years were there about 500,000 American Indians?

    A. 1970
    B. 1980
    C. 1990
    D. 2000

The correct answer is C. To answer this question, you must be able to read the graph. The information along the left side of the graph shows the number of Indians in increases of 100,000. The bottom of the graph shows the years from 1940 to 2010. You will notice that in 1990, there were about 500,000 American Indians in the United States. Using the edge of your answer sheet like a ruler will help you see that the dot in the 1990 column lines up with 500,000 on the left.

---

5. During which of the following time periods did the American Indian population decrease the most?

    A. 1940 to 1950
    B. 1950 to 1960
    C. 1960 to 1970
    D. 1990 to 2000

The correct answer is A. Since what is being asked involves a decrease, you need to find segments joining points that slant down as they go to the right. The segment that joins the points for 1940 to 1950 and that joins 1960 to 1970 slants down as it goes to the right. Since the segment joining 1940 to 1950 is steeper than the one joining 1960 to 1970, as it goes to the right, it shows the greater decrease.

Mathematics

Use the graph below to answer the question that follows.

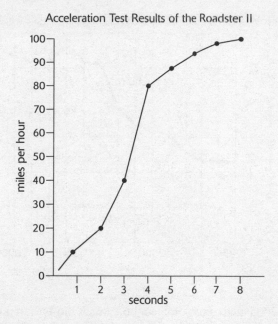

Acceleration Test Results of the Roadster II

6. The Roadster II accelerates the most between:

   A. 1 and 2 seconds.
   B. 2 and 3 seconds.
   C. 3 and 4 seconds.
   D. 4 and 5 seconds.

The correct answer is C. To answer this question, you must understand how the information is presented. The numbers on the left side of the graph show the speed in miles per hour (mph). The information at the bottom of the graph shows the number of seconds. The movement of the line can give important information and show trends. The steeper the line slants upward to the right, the greater the acceleration.

The greatest slope upward is between 3 and 4 seconds. The Roadster II accelerates from about 40 to about 80 mph in that time.

Mathematics and History/Social Science

Use the graph below to answer the two questions that follow.

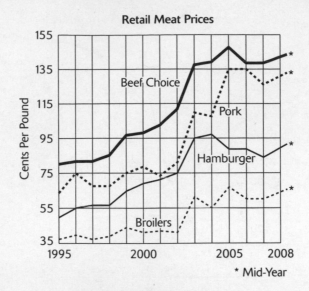

Retail Meat Prices

7. A pound of hamburger in 2005 cost approximately how much more than it did in 2000?

   A.   20 cents
   B.   25 cents
   C.   30 cents
   D.   35 cents

The correct answer is A. A line graph shows the relationship between two or more items. This question calls for comparing the price of hamburger in 2005 with the price of hamburger in 2000. You are asked to determine the *approximate price increase during the given period.* To answer the question, you must be able to see the differences among the four items listed on the chart. Notice that the lower horizontal line indicates the time reference as given in years, 1995–2008. Each line extending from it represents a one-year increment. The vertical line on the far left gives the price, or cents per pound (35 cents to $1.55 per pound). Each line extending from it represents a 20-cent increment (35 cents to 55 cents; 55 cents to 75 cents, etc.). In 2005, hamburger sold for slightly more than 85 cents per pound and in 2000 it sold for slightly more than 65 cents per pound. The price increase from 2000 to 2005 was approximately 20 cents per pound.

8. Which of the following is an accurate statement based on the information provided in the graph?

   A.   The figures for mid-year 2008 indicate a downward trend in retail meat prices.
   B.   Pork prices increased more gradually than broiler prices.
   C.   More Beef Choice was sold than hamburger.
   D.   The figures for mid-year 2008 indicate a continued increase in retail meat prices.

The correct answer is D. To answer this question, you must be able to determine the *one* statement that is consistent with the information provided in the graph. Mid-year 2008 is shown by the continuation of the lines representing meat prices beyond the 2008 line. Notice that all lines represent an *upward* trend. Choice A does not agree with the data in the chart. Choice B asks you to compare two items to see which one showed the most consistent price over the entire period of the study. You should notice that pork prices, especially since 2001, increased more dramatically than broiler prices. Choice C cannot be supported by the information given. What can be determined is that the cost per pound for Beef Choice was always greater than hamburger, but there is no indication of how much of any of the products were sold. The only statement that agrees with the information is D. All meat prices, as shown by mid-year 2008 prices, show a continued increase.

Circle Graph (Pie Chart) Examples

A circle graph, or pie chart, shows the relationship between the whole circle (100 percent) and the various slices that represent portions of that 100 percent. The larger the slice, the higher the percentage.

Mathematics

Use the graph below to answer the question that follows.

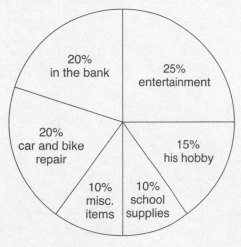

How John Spends His Monthly Paycheck

---

9. If John puts $250 from his monthly paycheck into the bank, what is his monthly paycheck?

    A. $20

    B. $50

    C. $1000

    D. $1250

The correct answer is D. To answer this question, you must read the graph carefully and apply some simple math. John puts 20 percent of his monthly paycheck in the bank. The $250 represents what money went to the bank. First, recognize that his paycheck amount must be greater than what went into the bank. Thus choices A and B are incorrect. To solve the problem, you can either use trial and error or solve using arithmetic. Using trial and error, find 20 percent of $1000 and 20 percent of $1250 and see which produces $250. The correct answer is D. Doing this problem using arithmetic, you could set up an equation like the following:

Let x = amount of paycheck

20% (x) = 250.

Now divide 250 by the decimal name for 20%. This gives $x = 1250$, or Choice D.

You could have solved this problem using proportions:

$$\frac{\text{Bank}}{\text{Total}} = \frac{\overset{\$}{250}}{x} = \frac{\overset{\%}{20}}{100} \text{ (You can reduce } \frac{20}{100} \text{ to } \frac{1}{5}\text{)}$$

Then $1(x) = 5(250)$ Then $20x = 25{,}000$

       $x = 1250$ $x = 1250$

Mathematics and History/Social Science

Use the pie charts below to answer the question that follows.

**Distribution of Earned Degrees
by Field of Study**

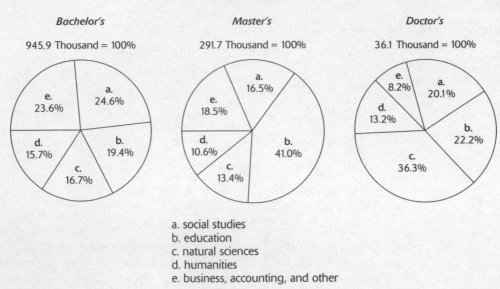

Bachelor's

945.9 Thousand = 100%

Master's

291.7 Thousand = 100%

Doctor's

36.1 Thousand = 100%

a. social studies
b. education
c. natural sciences
d. humanities
e. business, accounting, and other

10. Advancing from a bachelor's degree to a doctor's degree, for which field of study did the percentage numbers increase the most?

   A.   education
   B.   natural sciences
   C.   humanities
   D.   business, accounting, and other

The correct answer is B. To answer this question, first recognize that you are calculating an increase in percentage numbers, not a percent change of the percentage numbers. Choice A, education, showed an approximate increase in percentage values of about 3 percent. Choice B, natural sciences, showed an increase in the percentage values of approximately 20 percent. Choice C, humanities, showed a decrease in the percentage values, hence it is not the answer. Choice D, business, accounting, and other, showed a decrease in the percentage values, hence it is not the answer. Of the two choices showing an increase in the percentage values, choice B showed the most.

Maps

Strategies

A map can represent all or part of the earth's surface. Maps are usually classified into four general types. *Political maps* show government, politics, and political parties. *Physical maps* show the earth's surface, climate, and currents. *Special-purpose maps* show products, vegetation, minerals, population, transportation, and the like. *Relief maps* show the shape of the land. In dealing with this type of question, you should do the following:

Consider the geographic factors:

   - Location of the event
   - Size of the area involved

- Geographic relationship of the area to other concerned places (How far apart are the places? In what direction?)
- Important water areas
- Means of access to the area (How can we get to the area?)
- Physical factors such as mountains and plains
- Natural resources that play a part
- Soil, climate, and rainfall

Consider the human factors:

- Industries of the area
- Trade and other relations with the outside world
- Available means of transportation
- Size and location of the population
- Large cities concerned in the event
- Racial, religious, and other factors involved
- Developments from history

To understand a map, you must first become familiar with the information presented on the map. For instance, the title, legend, scale, direction, longitude, and latitude are all important to interpret a map. The legend is particularly important because it usually explains the symbols used on a map. You should notice the main points of the map first, and then look at the finer details.

Map Examples

Mathematics and History/Social Science

Use the map below to answer the two questions that follow.

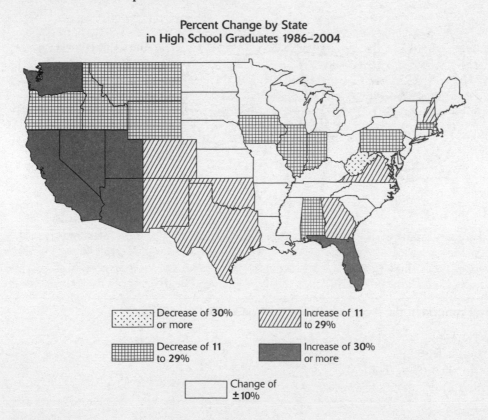

Percent Change by State
in High School Graduates 1986–2004

11. The preceding map uses different shadings to show how the percentage of high school graduates will increase or decrease in each state in an 18-year period.

    According to the map, which of the following will occur in the most states?

    A. a decrease of 30 percent or more
    B. a decrease of 11 percent to 29 percent
    C. a change of about 10 percent
    D. an increase of 11 percent to 29 percent

To answer this question, you must understand the map and the legend given. The legend, or key, at the bottom of the map shows what each type of shading stands for. Read this information carefully. Now, simply count the number of states that have the same type of shading. You may have noticed that most of the states have no shading, so most states have a change of about 10 percent. The correct answer is C.

12. According to the map, generally, the greatest increase is expected in the:

    A. Southeast.
    B. Midwest.
    C. Northwest.
    D. Southwest.

The dark shading reflects the greatest increase. Most of the dark shading occurs in the lower-left corner of the map—the Southwest. If you look for trends, you might immediately notice that most states with large increases are in the Southwest. The correct answer is D.

History/Social Science

Use the map below to answer the two questions that follow.

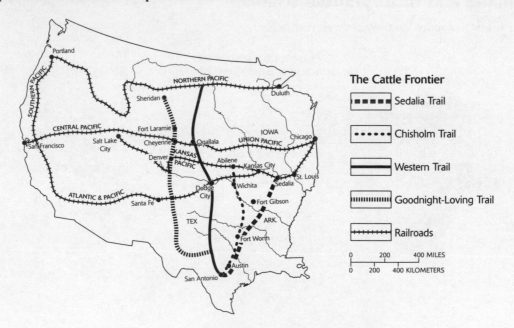

13. Which trail connected the Northern Pacific Railroad with San Antonio?

    A. Sedalia Trail
    B. Chisholm Trail
    C. Goodnight-Loving Trail
    D. Western Trail

The Western Trail is the only trail that connects with the Northern Pacific. Notice that the legend and the title "The Cattle Frontier" are clues to the historical importance of this special-purpose map. You can see that many questions can be made from data included in this map. For instance, what would be the importance of having a western trail cross a major railroad line? Possible answers could include the fact that towns would develop around the connecting point, or that the railroad could be used to bring western cattle to various markets. The correct answer is D.

---

14. If you were to leave St. Louis with a final destination of Portland, the most logical route would be to:

A. go by rail to Santa Fe; connect by rail with the Atlantic & Pacific and Southern Pacific; proceed by rail to Portland.

B. go by rail to Chicago; go by rail to the Central Pacific and Southern Pacific connection; proceed by rail to Portland.

C. go by rail to Denver; go by trail to connect with the Central Pacific; proceed by rail to Portland.

D. go by rail to Sedalia; go by trail to the Atlantic & Pacific connection at Santa Fe; proceed by rail to Portland.

The correct answer is B. You can quickly eliminate choices C and D because they use trails to connect with various railroads. Using a trail with unpredictable road conditions and traveling by wagon would be far slower than traveling by a longer rail route. Choice B is the most *direct* rail route to Portland. Look for the shortest route before you eliminate each possible answer.

Cartoons

A political cartoon represents an amusing or satiric picture of people, places, or things and is used to make a special point about or to deride some subject of popular interest.

Strategies

In considering a political cartoon, identify the event used and look for the point of view of the cartoonist, that is, what the cartoonist is trying to say. Remember that most good political cartoonists are critics who comment on the social issues that face the United States and the world. To deal with questions based on a political cartoon, you should do the following:

- Become familiar with the symbols used in political cartoons. For example, the donkey is a symbol of the Democratic Party; the elephant is a symbol of the Republican Party; the dove is a symbol of peace; the hawk is a symbol of war; and Washington D.C. and Uncle Sam are symbols of the U.S. government.

- Try to understand the meaning of the statement, if any, that goes with the political cartoon. This statement is often a clue to the cartoonist's attitude.

Cartoon Example

History/Social Science

Use the cartoon below to answer the question that follows.

Copyright 1977 by Herblock in the *Washington Post*.

15. How does the cartoonist feel about neutron nuclear weapons?

   A. Nuclear weapons are necessary if the United States is to maintain the current balance of power with Russia.

   B. Neutron nuclear weapons are not as deadly as conventional nuclear weapons.

   C. The military is responsible for developing nuclear weapons.

   D. Advanced nuclear designs cannot change the deadly nature of nuclear weapons.

The correct answer is D. In this political cartoon, a comparison is drawn between neutron nuclear weapons and non-neutron nuclear weapons. The symbols are clues to the cartoonist's point of view. Notice that the refined, or technically advanced, neutron bomb still represents death and destruction. The neutron bomb is dressed in the cloak of death; the refined cigarette holder still produces a mushroom cloud. (A mushroom cloud is a symbol of the destructive nature of the bomb.) The question asked by the military—"Notice how much more refined?"—is an indication that the cartoonist considers refinements in nuclear weapons as nothing but more-sophisticated killing devices. In other words, in the cartoonist's point of view, a refined nuclear weapon is still a nuclear weapon.

Diagrams

Sometimes information will be given in a simple diagram or picture.

Strategies

When a diagram or picture is given, you should look for its main emphasis. Also look for key words, markings, directions of arrows, distances, and so forth. Look for both the obvious and the unusual. In dealing with questions based on diagrams or pictures, you should keep the following in mind:

- You may wish to skim the question or questions before looking at the diagram.
- Examine the diagram carefully. Make sure that you understand the information given.
- Carefully read any additional information given.
- Don't try to memorize the diagram.

Diagram Examples

Science

Use the diagram below to answer the question that follows.

CROSS SECTION OF THE ATLANTIC OCEAN

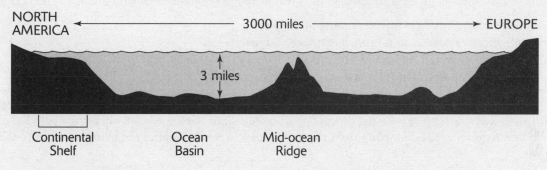

16. According to the diagram, all of the following are true *except:*

    A. Europe does not have a continental shelf.
    B. The mid-ocean ridge is about halfway between the two continents.
    C. The ocean basin is of fairly consistent depth.
    D. The mid-ocean ridge is less than three miles high.

The correct answer is A. To answer this question, you must understand the information given in the diagram. You must also notice that you are looking for what is *not* true. Choice A is *not* true. Europe *does* have a continental shelf, although it appears smaller than that of North America. Notice also that only the continental shelf of North America is marked in the diagram. You must analyze this diagram to see that this marking is showing *one example*. Notice that the ocean basin is also marked on only one side of the mid-ocean ridge, but there is an ocean basin on the other side. By careful inspection, you will see that all the other choices are *true*, and so you can eliminate them.

Use the diagram and information below to answer the question that follows.

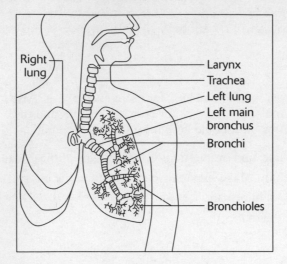

17. Air enters the body through the nose and mouth and passes into the throat. Next, it goes into the larynx, and then to the trachea (windpipe). The trachea branches into two main bronchi. Each main bronchus leads to a lung, which also contains many smaller bronchi and bronchioles. Inside the lungs, oxygen enters the bloodstream while, at the same time, carbon dioxide leaves the blood and enters the lungs to be breathed out.

From the information given above, which of the following is the path of carbon dioxide as it is exhaled?

A. larynx/trachea/main bronchus/bronchi/bronchioles
B. bronchioles/bronchi/main bronchus/trachea/larynx
C. trachea/larynx/main bronchus/bronchioles
D. bronchi/larynx/trachea/main bronchus/bronchioles

The correct answer is B. To answer this question, you must understand not only the diagram, but also the additional information given. By *reversing* the process of air coming into the lungs, you will get the path *out of* the lungs. Carbon dioxide is exhaled starting from the bronchioles to the bronchi to the main bronchus to the trachea to the larynx.

Mathematics

Use the diagram below to answer the question that follows.

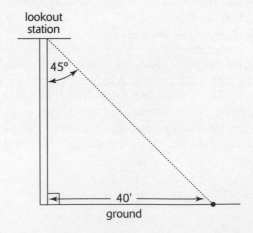

18. As pictured in the diagram above, Felipe has built a lookout station but does not know the height of the station from the ground. Felipe climbs to the top of the station and spots a coin 40 feet from the base of the station. He accurately marks the angle of his sight at 45 degrees (as shown above). From this information, he correctly determines the height of the lookout station as:

  A. 20 feet.
  B. 30 feet.
  C. 40 feet.
  D. 80 feet.

The correct answer is C. To answer this question, you must understand the diagram and apply some basic geometry. Since the lookout station is shown to be vertical—or 90 degrees—to the ground, and the angle of sight is 45 degrees, the third angle must be 45 degrees. This is because there are 180 degrees in a triangle. Now, since two of the angles in a triangle are equal, it is an isosceles triangle and the sides opposite those angles are also equal. So, the sides opposite the 45-degree angles are each 40 feet.

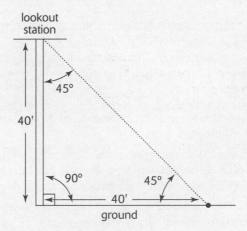

The Final Touches

1. Make sure that you are familiar with the testing center location and nearby parking facilities.

2. Spend the last week of preparation on a general review of key concepts and computer test-taking strategies and techniques.

3. At least one week before the exam, take all three practice tests in this study guide and review your notes. Take the CSET online practice test at www.cset.nesinc.com.

4. Don't cram the night before the exam. It is a waste of time!

5. Arrive at the testing center in plenty of time.

6. Remember to bring the proper materials: identification, admission ticket, and a watch.

7. On each subtest, start off crisply, working the questions you know first, then going back and trying to answer the others.

8. On the multiple-choice questions, try to eliminate one or more choices before you guess, but make sure that you fill in all the answers. There is no penalty for guessing!

9. Write down key words from questions. Write out important information, and draw diagrams, making notations. Take advantage of taking notes on scratch paper.

10. Make sure that you answer what is being asked and that your answer is reasonable.

11. On multiple-choice questions, eliminate incorrect choices immediately; this can keep you from reconsidering a choice that you have already eliminated.

12. On the short constructed-response questions, take a minute to jot down a few notes to organize your thoughts. Remember, you are writing a short response to show how much you know about the exercise or topic given.

13. On the short constructed-response questions, if you don't know the answer, at least try to give a partial response. Always write something; you could get partial credit.

14. Don't get stuck on any one question. Never spend more than $1\frac{1}{2}$ minutes on a multiple-choice question and never spend more than 8 minutes on a short constructed-response question. After this amount of time, take a reasonable guess and return to the problem later (if time permits).

15. The key to getting a good score on the CSET: Multiple Subjects is reviewing properly, practicing, and getting the questions right that you can and should get right. A careful review of parts I and II of this book will help you focus during the final week before the exam.

Sources

The Read Aloud Handbook by Jim Trelease, 2001.

Physical Education Framework. ©2009. Reprinted by permission of the California Department of Education, CDE Press, Sacramento, California 2008.

Framework for Dance Activity Instruction, adapted from *Arts Education: A Curriculum Guide for Grade 8.* Saskatchewan Education, Training and Employment, September 1994.

California Indian Tribal Groups map, California Indian Library Collections. Ethnic Studies Library, CILC, U.C. Berkeley.

California Missions map, courtesy of Daniel Faigin of California Highways.

California Aqueducts map, courtesy of Central Basin Municipal Water District.

The Old Silk Routes map, courtesy of The Silk Road Foundation.

The Making of Eastern Roman Empire map from *History of the World* by J.M. Roberts. Oxford University Press, New York, 1993.

Houghton Mifflin Harcourt
End-User License Agreement

READ THIS. You should carefully read these terms and conditions before opening the software packet(s) included with this book "Book". This is a license agreement "Agreement" between you and Houghton Mifflin Harcourt "HMH". By opening the accompanying software packet(s), you acknowledge that you have read and accept the following terms and conditions. If you do not agree and do not want to be bound by such terms and conditions, promptly return the Book and the unopened software packet(s) to the place you obtained them for a full refund.

1. **License Grant.** HMH grants to you (either an individual or entity) a nonexclusive license to use one copy of the enclosed software program(s) (collectively, the "Software") solely for your own personal or business purposes on a single computer (whether a standard computer or a workstation component of a multi-user network). The Software is in use on a computer when it is loaded into temporary memory (RAM) or installed into permanent memory (hard disk, CD-ROM, or other storage device). HMH reserves all rights not expressly granted herein.

2. **Ownership.** HMH is the owner of all right, title, and interest, including copyright, in and to the compilation of the Software recorded on the physical packet included with this Book "Software Media". Copyright to the individual programs recorded on the Software Media is owned by the author or other authorized copyright owner of each program. Ownership of the Software and all proprietary rights relating thereto remain with HMH and its licensers.

3. **Restrictions on Use and Transfer.**

    (a) You may only (i) make one copy of the Software for backup or archival purposes, or (ii) transfer the Software to a single hard disk, provided that you keep the original for backup or archival purposes. You may not (i) rent or lease the Software, (ii) copy or reproduce the Software through a LAN or other network system or through any computer subscriber system or bulletin-board system, or (iii) modify, adapt, or create derivative works based on the Software.

    (b) You may not reverse engineer, decompile, or disassemble the Software. You may transfer the Software and user documentation on a permanent basis, provided that the transferee agrees to accept the terms and conditions of this Agreement and you retain no copies. If the Software is an update or has been updated, any transfer must include the most recent update and all prior versions.

4. **Restrictions on Use of Individual Programs.** You must follow the individual requirements and restrictions detailed for each individual program on the Software Media. These limitations are also contained in the individual license agreements recorded on the Software Media. These limitations may include a requirement that after using the program for a specified period of time, the user must pay a registration fee or discontinue use. By opening the Software packet(s), you agree to abide by the licenses and restrictions for these individual programs that are detailed on the Software Media. None of the material on this Software Media or listed in this Book may ever be redistributed, in original or modified form, for commercial purposes.

5. **Limited Warranty.**

    (a) HMH warrants that the Software and Software Media are free from defects in materials and workmanship under normal use for a period of sixty (60) days from the date of purchase of this Book. If HMH receives notification within the warranty period of defects in materials or workmanship, HMH will replace the defective Software Media.

    (b) HMH AND THE AUTHOR(S) OF THE BOOK DISCLAIM ALL OTHER WARRANTIES, EXPRESS OR IMPLIED, INCLUDING WITHOUT LIMITATION IMPLIED WARRANTIES OF MERCHANTABILITY AND FITNESS FOR A PARTICULAR PURPOSE, WITH RESPECT TO THE SOFTWARE, THE PROGRAMS, THE SOURCE CODE CONTAINED THEREIN, AND/OR THE TECHNIQUES DESCRIBED IN THIS BOOK. HMH DOES NOT WARRANT THAT THE FUNCTIONS CONTAINED IN THE SOFTWARE WILL MEET YOUR REQUIREMENTS OR THAT THE OPERATION OF THE SOFTWARE WILL BE ERROR FREE.

    (c) This limited warranty gives you specific legal rights, and you may have other rights that vary from jurisdiction to jurisdiction.